D0073815

THE EUROPEAN UNION SERIES
General Editors: Neill Nugent, William E. Paterson

The European Union series provides an authoritative library on the European Union, ranging from general introductory texts to definitive assessments of key institutions and actors, issues, policies and policy processes, and the role of member states.

Books in the series are written by leading scholars in their fields and reflect the most up-to-date research and debate. Particular attention is paid to accessibility and clear presentation for a wide audience of students, practitioners and interested general readers.

The series editors are **Neill Nugent**, Visiting Professor, College of Europe, Bruges, and Honorary Professor, University of Salford, UK, and **William E. Paterson**, Honorary Professor in German and European Studies, University of Aston. Their co-editor until his death in July 1999, **Vincent Wright**, was a Fellow of Nuffield College, Oxford University.

Feedback on the series and book proposals are always welcome and should be sent to Steven Kennedy, Palgrave Macmillan, Houndmills, Basingstoke, Hampshire, RG21 6XS, UK, or by e-mail to **s.kennedy@palgrave.com**.

General textbooks

Published

Laurie Buonanno and Neill Nugent **Policies and Policy Processes of the European Union**

Desmond Dinan **Encyclopedia of the European Union** [Rights: Europe only]

Desmond Dinan **Europe Recast: A History of the European Union** [Rights: Europe only]

Desmond Dinan **Ever Closer Union: An Introduction to European Integration (4th edn)** [Rights: Europe only]

Mette Eilstrup Sangiovanni (ed.) **Debates on European Integration: A Reader**

Simon Hix and Bjørn Høyland **The Political System of the European Union (3rd edn)**

Dirk Leuffen, Berthold Rittberger and Frank Schimmelfennig **Differentiated Integration**

Paul Magnette **What is the European Union? Nature and Prospects**

John McCormick **Understanding the European Union: A Concise Introduction (5th edn)**

Brent F. Nelsen and Alexander Stubb **The European Union: Readings on the Theory and Practice of European Integration (3rd edn)** [Rights: Europe only]

Neill Nugent (ed.) **European Union Enlargement**

Neill Nugent **The Government and Politics of the European Union (7th edn)**

John Peterson and Elizabeth Bomberg **Decision-Making in the European Union**

Ben Rosamond **Theories of European Integration**

Esther Versluis, Mendeltje van Keulen and Paul Stephenson **Analyzing the European Union Policy Process**

Hubert Zimmermann and Andreas Dür (eds) **Key Controversies in European Integration**

Forthcoming

Magnus Ryner and Alan Cafruny **A Critical Introduction to the European Union**

Sabine Saurugger **Theoretical Approaches to European Integration**

Also planned

The Political Economy of European Integration

Series Standing Order (outside North America only)
ISBN 978–0–333–71695–3 hardback
ISBN 978–0–333–69352–0 paperback
Full details from www.palgrave.com

Visit Palgrave Macmillan's EU Resource area at
www.palgrave.com/politics/eu/

Policies and Policy Processes of the European Union

Laurie Buonanno
and
Neill Nugent

First published 2013 by
PALGRAVE MACMILLAN

Palgrave Macmillan in the UK is an imprint of Macmillan Publishers Limited, registered in England, company number 785998, of Houndmills, Basingstoke, Hampshire RG21 6XS.

Palgrave Macmillan in the US is a division of St Martin's Press LLC, 175 Fifth Avenue, New York, NY 10010.

Palgrave Macmillan is the global academic imprint of the above companies and has companies and representatives throughout the world.

Palgrave® and Macmillan® are registered trademarks in the United States, the United Kingdom, Europe and other countries

ISBN 978-1-403-91513-9 hardback
ISBN 978-1-403-91514-6 paperback

This book is printed on paper suitable for recycling and made from fully managed and sustained forest sources. Logging, pulping and manufacturing processes are expected to conform to the environmental regulations of the country of origin.

A catalogue record for this book is available from the British Library.

A catalog record for this book is available from the Library of Congress.

10   9   8   7   6   5   4   3   2   1
22 21 20 19 18 17 16 15 14 13

Printed in China

Summary of Contents

Contents

List of Illustrative Material

Boxes

Figures

Tables

List of Abbreviations

ACER	Agency for the Cooperation of Energy Regulators
ACP	African, Caribbean and Pacific countries
AFSJ	area of freedom, security and justice
ALDE	Alliance of Liberals and Democrats for Europe
AMCHAM-EU	EU Committee of the American Chamber of Commerce
AMR	alert mechanism report
APEC	Asia-Pacific Economic Cooperation
APPE	Association of Petrochemical Producers in Europe
ASEAN	Association of Southeast Asian Nations
BASIC	Brazil, South Africa, India and China
BEPG	Broad Economic Policy Guideline
BEUC	European Consumer Association
BKA	*Bundskartellamt* (German competition authority)
BRICS	Brazil, Russia, India, China and South Africa
BTO	Brussels Treaty Organisation
CAP	Common Agricultural Policy
CBI	Confederation of British Industry
CCP	Common Commercial Policy
CCT	Common Customs Tariff (also known as the Common External Tariff)
CEAS	Common European Asylum System
CEC	European Confederation of the Footwear Industry
CEEC	Central and Eastern European country
CEFIC	European Chemical Industry Council
CEN	European Committee for Standardization
CENELEC	European Committee for Electrotechnical Standardization
CEPOL	European Police College
CET	Common External Tariff
CFI	Court of First Instance
CFP	Common Fisheries Policy
CFSP	Common Foreign and Security Policy
CIAA	Confederation of the Food and Drink Industries of the EU (since 2011 called Food-Drink Europe)
CIVICOM	Committee for Civilian Aspects of Crisis Management
CJEU	Court of Justice of the European Union
COGECA	General Confederation of Agricultural Cooperatives in the EU
COPA	Committee of Professional Agricultural Organisations in the EU
COPS	Political and Security Committee (PSC) (French acronym)
CoR	Committee of the Regions
COREPER	Committee of Permanent Representatives
COSI	Standing Committee on Operational Cooperation on Internal Security
CSCE	Commission on Security and Cooperation in Europe
CSDP	Common Security and Defence Policy
CST	Civil Service Tribunal
DG	Directorate General
DSM	Dispute Settlement Mechanism
EACEA	Education, Audiovisual and Culture Executive Agency
EADS	European Aeronautic Defence and Space Company
EAFRD	European Agricultural Fund for Rural Development
EAGF	European Agricultural Guarantee Fund
EAGGF	European Agricultural Guidance and Guarantee Fund
EAHC	Executive Agency for Health and Consumers

EAP	Environmental Action Programme	EMCDDA	European Monitoring Centre for Drugs and Addiction
EASO	European Asylum Support Office		
EAW	European arrest warrant	EMCF	European Monetary Cooperation Fund
EBA	European Banking Authority; *also* Everything But Arms		
		EMEA	European Medicines Agency
EC	European Community	EMI	European Monetary Institute
ECB	European Central Bank	EMS	European Monetary System
ECHA	European Chemicals Agency	EMU	European Monetary Union
ECHR	European Court of Human Rights	ENA	European NAvigator
ECJ	European Court of Justice	ENP	European Neighbourhood Policy
Ecofin	Council of Economic and Finance Ministers	EP	European Parliament
		EPA	Economic Partnership Agreement
ECRE	European Council on Refugees and Exiles	EPC	European Political Community; *also* European Political Cooperation
ECSC	European Coal and Steel Community	EPP	European People's Party
		ERDF	European Regional Development Fund
ECN	European Competition Network		
ED	European Democratic Group	ERM	Exchange Rate Mechanism
EDA	European Defence Agency	ERRF	European Rapid Reaction Force
EDC	European Defence Community	ERT	European Round Table of Industrialists
EDF	European Development Fund; *also* European Defence Force		
		ESA	European Security Authority
EDP	excessive deficit procedure	ESA	European Space Agency
EEA	European Economic Area	ESBG	European Savings Bank Group
EEA	European Environment Agency	ESC	Economic and Social Committee
EEAS	European External Action Service	ESCB	European System of Central Banks
EEB	European Environmental Bureau	ESDI	European Security and Defence Identity
EEC	European Economic Community		
EEG	European Employment Guideline	ESDP	European Security and Defence Policy
EES	European Employment Strategy		
EESC	European Economic and Social Committee	ESF	European Social Fund
		ESFS	European System of Financial Supervisors
EFPIA	European Federation of Pharmaceutical Industry Associations		
		ESO	European Standards Organization
		ESM	European Stability Mechanism; *also* European Social Model
EFSA	European Food Safety Authority		
EFSM	European Financial Stabilization Mechanism	ESMA	European Securities and Markets Authority
		ESPRIT	European Strategic Programme for Research and Development in Information Technology
EFSF	European Financial Stability Facility		
EFTA	European Free Trade Association		
EIB	European Investment Bank		
EIF	European Investment Fund	ESRB	European Systemic Risk Board
EIGE	European Institute for Gender Equality	ESRO	European Space Research Organization
		ESS	European Security Strategy
EIOPA	European Insurance and Occupational Pensions Authority	ETS	emissions trading system (greenhouse gases)
EIP	excessive imbalance procedure		
ELDO	European Launcher Development Organization	ETSI	European Telecommunications Standards Institute

ETUC	European Trade Union Confederation		G-20	Group of Twenty
			GA	UN General Assembly
ETUF – TCL	European Trade Union Federation – Textiles, Clothing and Leather		GAERC	General Affairs and External Relations Council
EU	European Union		GATT	General Agreement on Tariffs and Trade
EUAFR	European Union Agency for Fundamental Rights		GDA	Guideline Daily Amount (nutrition labelling of foods)
EUBAM	European Union Border Assistance Mission		GDP	gross domestic product
EUISS	European Union Institute for Security Studies		GMES	Global Monitoring for Environment and Security
EUJUST LEX	European Union Integrated Rule of Law Mission for Iraq		GMO	genetically modified organism
			GNI	gross national income
EULEX Kosovo	European Union Rule of Law Mission in Kosovo		GNP	gross national product
			GSP	Generalized System of Preferences
EUMC	European Union Military Committee		HICP	Harmonized Indices of Consumer Prices
EUMS	European Union Military Staff		IA	impact assessment
EU NAVFOR	European Union Naval Force		IAB	Impact Assessment Board
EUPM	European Union Police Mission		IAS	Internal Audit Service
EUPOL Afghanistan	European Union Police Mission to Afghanistan		IGC	Intergovernmental Conference
			IGO	International Governmental Organization; *also* intergovernmental organization
EUPOL COPPS	European Union Coordinating Office for Palestinian Police Support			
EURATOM	European Atomic Energy Community		IMF	International Monetary Fund
			IO	international organization
EUREKA	European Research Coordinating Agency		ISS	Internal Security Strategy
			JHA	Justice and Home Affairs
EUROJUST	European Union's Judicial Cooperation Unit		JRC	Joint Research Centre
			LDC	less developed country
EUROPOL	European Police Office		LGBTQ	lesbian, gay, bisexual, transgendered and questioning
EUROSUR	European border surveillance system			
			LTRO	long-term refinancing operation
EUSEC RD Congo	European Union Security Sector Reform Mission in the Democratic Republic of the Congo		MAD	mutually assured destruction
			MAP	EU's Market Access Partnership
			MEP	Member of the European Parliament
FAO	Food and Agriculture Organization of the United Nations			
			Mercosur	Southern Common Market
FAC	Foreign Affairs Council		MFF	multi-annual financial framework
FDI	foreign direct investment		MFN	Most Favoured Nation
FERM	Federation of European Rice Millers		MiFID	Market in Financial Instruments Directive
FRA	European Union Agency for Fundamental Rights		MIP	macroeconomic imbalance procedure
FRONTEX	European Agency for the Management of Operational Cooperation at External Borders		MLG	multi-level governance
			MNC	multi-national corporation
FTA	free trade area		MTO	medium-term (budgetary) objective
FTT	financial transaction tax		NAAG	National Association of Attorney Generals (of the US)
G-8	Group of Eight			

NAFTA	North American Free Trade Agreement	REACH	Registration, Evaluation, Authorisation and Restriction of Chemicals
NAP	National Action Plan		
NATO	North Atlantic Treaty Organization	RQMV	reverse qualified majority voting
NCA	National Competition Authorities	S&D	Group of the Progressive Alliance of Socialists and Democrats
NCB	national central bank		
NGO	non-governmental organization	SCA	Special Committee on Agriculture
NMG	new mode of governance	SCP	Stability and Convergence Programme
NPAA	national programme for the adoption of the *acquis*		
		SEA	Single European Act
NRP	national reform programme	SEM	Single European Market
NTA	New Transatlantic Agenda	SGP	Stability and Growth Pact
NTB	non-tariff barrier (to trade)	SMEs	small and medium-sized enterprises
NYSE	New York Stock Exchange		
OCA	optimal currency area	SOLVIT	on-line problem-solving network for EU member states
ODI	Overseas Development Institute		
OECD	Organisation for Economic Co-operation and Development	SWIFT	Society for Worldwide Interbank Financial Telecommunication
OEEC	Organisation for European Economic Co-operation	TAC	total allowable catch (fish stocks)
		TBT	technical barrier to trade
OHIM	Office for Harmonization in the Internal Market	TEC	Treaty Establishing the European Community
OJ	*Official Journal of the European Union*	TEN	Trans-European Networks
		TEU	Treaty on European Union
OLAF	European Anti-Fraud Office	TFEU	Treaty on the Functioning of the European Union
OMC	open method of co-ordination		
OSCE	Organization for Security and Co-operation in Europe	TFTP	Terrorist Finance Tracking Program
PDB	preliminary draft budget	TFTS	(European) Terrorist Finance Trading System
PESCO	permanent enhanced structured cooperation		
		TSCG	Treaty on Stability, Coordination and Governance
PJCM	police and judicial co-operation in criminal matters		
		UK	United Kingdom
PKKP	Polish Confederation of Private Employers	UN	United Nations
		UNHCR	United Nations High Commissioner for Refugees
PLO	Palestinian Liberation Organization		
PSC	Political and Security Committee (*also known as* COPS)	UNICE	Union of Industrial and Employers' Confederations of Europe (now renamed BUSINESSEUROPE|)
PTA	preferential trade agreement		
QMV	qualified majority voting	UNSC	UN Security Council
Race	R&D in advanced communications technologies for Europe	USA	United States of America
		VAT	value added tax
R&D	research and development	WEU	Western European Union
R&TD	research and technological development	WMD	weapon of mass destruction
		WTO	World Trade Organization

Preface

This book provides a comprehensive and integrated overview of 'the big picture' of European Union (EU) policies and policy processes. All the key feature of the policies and policy processes are covered and are so, for the most part, in considerable detail.

As is explained in the Introduction, a number of themes run through the book. They include the considerable width and constant evolution of the policy portfolio, the creation of particular policy processes to meet specific policy needs, and the central importance of the internal market to most EU policy activity.

Our intention is to provide not just a description of EU policies and policy processes but also an explanation of them. This has necessitated placing our narrative of the evolution, development and current functioning of policies and policy processes in a conceptual and theoretical framework. It is our view that while established conceptual and theoretical approaches – such as intergovernmentalism, supranationalism, multi-level governance, institutionalism and social constructivism, to name but a few of the more familiar paradigms – certainly contribute significantly towards understanding the nature of EU policies and policy processes, they do not provide a wholly comprehensive explanation. They need, we think, to be supplemented. The supplement we provide draws on economic integration theory and federalist theory to produce an approach we call 'federal integration'.

Since we began writing this book, the global financial and economic crisis, and the related eurozone crisis, have come to dominate much of the attention of EU policy practitioners and observers. Previous challenges to the 'European integration project' – such as the Eurosclerosis of the 1970s–1980s, followed by the end of the Cold War in 1989–91 – which at the time were accompanied by much hand-wringing about the European Community's future, in hindsight seem almost as bumps in the road compared to the all-consuming crises that have shaken European integration to its very core since 2007–8. It has even become fashionable to question whether European integration has reached an irrevocable turning point, possibly involving some of its members moving towards full economic, and perhaps also political, union, while other members are increasingly marginalized and, in effect, are left as members of what amounts to little more than a disaggregated trade association. Naturally, we pay considerable attention to these and other crises-related matters in the book. In so doing, we argue that, despite dire warnings of the EU's imminent demise, there is enough evidence to suggest that the EU's system of governance is sufficiently flexible to enable it to adapt successfully to the major challenges it has been, and still is, facing.

Many people have helped us, both in staying the course and helping to craft this book. Our first thanks must be to our publisher at Palgrave Macmillan, Steven Kennedy, who – always with good humour and armloads of patience – continued to believe in us, prod us and encourage us. Also at Palgrave Macmillan, Helen Caunce and Stephen Wenham provided superb assistance throughout the project. The excellent work of Keith Povey, Elaine Towns and Ian Wileman in the production of the book must also be acknowledged. William Paterson, the co-editor of the European Union Series in which the book is located, encouraged us and challenged us to not to lose sight – as we became mired in policy minutiae – of the big questions we needed to address. Anneliese Dodds and Wyn Grant read our manuscript several times, in each round offering exceptionally insightful and detailed comments. Michele Chang, Roy Ginsberg and Christian Kaunert generously read the relevant policy chapters in their areas of expertise and offered important correctives and insights. We are enormously grateful to all of these people for helping us. Naturally, we take full responsibility for any errors that may be found in the book.

We would also like to thank the many students whom we have had the pleasure of teaching and learning from at Manchester Metropolitan University, the College of Europe at Bruges, and the State University of New York (Buffalo State and Fredonia). Thanks are given also to the Institute for European Union Studies at SUNY, on whose executive board we have had the privilege to serve, and whose activities and programmes have provided us with the opportunity to work on the EU with European and American faculty and students in a variety of interactive settings.

Finally, we would like to thank our families, friends and colleagues who have supported us, usually patiently, in the long process of researching and writing this account of the nature of EU policies and policy processes.

Laurie Buonanno
Neill Nugent

Acknowledgements

Figure 7.1 contains public sector information licensed under the Open Government Licence v1.0. The following figures and tables are European Union copyright: Table 2.1, Box 7.4, Figure 8.2, Figure 8.3, Figure 8.4, Box 10.5, Box 11.5, Table 12.2, Table 12.3, Table 12.4, Figure 14.1, Table 14.1, Figure 14.3.

Introduction

The purpose of this book is to examine what the European Union (EU) does, and how and why it does it. That is to say, it examines the nature of the EU's policy responsibilities and policy processes and seeks to explain why they are as they are.

Naturally, covering such a broad area of EU activities and academic enquiry is a daunting task. In attempting to meet the challenge we have not attempted to examine every policy and policy process in detail, but rather have focused on their overall nature and main features.

A number of themes run through the book, of which three are especially prominent. The first is that EU policies and policy processes are in constant evolution and the nature of their evolution is intertwined. So, a new policy may appear on the EU's policy agenda but it may not be politically possible for it to be developed to any significant degree within the framework of existing policy processes. As a consequence, a new policy process may be devised or an existing policy process may be given a tailored form. This new or tailored policy process may then come to be seen as a suitable way of also dealing with quite different policy areas that hitherto have not featured on the policy agenda because there have been considered – particularly by the governments of the member states – to be no suitable or acceptable policy processes available for them.

Policy and policy process development can thus feed off one another, as, for example, Economic and Monetary Union (EMU) demonstrates. In the 1990s most of the EU member states moved towards full monetary union, but they had much greater difficulty with fiscal union – primarily because of concerns about the restrictions this would impose on national revenue raising and public spending policies. However, the need for some economic policy co-ordination, especially between prospective EMU members, was recognized, so new and, for the most part relatively loose, policy processes were created – most of them built around a system that came to be called the open method of co-ordination (OMC). Once the OMC was created, it quickly came to be seen as a suitable way of initiating and/or extending EU policy involvement in other politically sensitive areas, such as aspects of social welfare, and research and innovation policies. At the same time, the policy limitations of using the OMC for the operation of the fiscal side of EMU were increasingly apparent, with the consequence that as the policy area was increasingly seen to require harder policy instruments – especially from 2007/8 in response to the growing global economic and financial crisis and

1

the ensuing eurozone crisis – then so were new EMU policy processes adopted. Some of these processes were restricted to eurozone members.

The second prominent theme running throughout the book is the crucial importance of the internal market to most policy activity and development. That the internal market looms large in policy terms is not, of course, surprising given that the most important of the EU's founding treaties – the 1957 European Economic Community Treaty – had the creation of a common market as its principal policy aim. So, the very great number of direct market policies – such as those dealing with standards' specifications for traded products and those outlawing unfair competition – is hardly surprising. But, over the years there has been a continuing expansion of what has been seen to be necessary for a fully functioning and fair internal market, which has resulted in market factors and considerations being behind much of the policy development in such non-direct market policy areas as the environment, social policy and the area of freedom, security and justice (AFSJ). Taking the AFSJ, for example, which since the early 2000s has been one of the EU's fastest growing policy areas, its concerns with such matters as asylum, anti-terrorism and human rights may at first sight not appear to be market-related. But, in fact, as is shown in Chapter 11, they and many other AFSJ policies have been driven in large part by the EU's commitment to free movement of people, which – along with free movement of goods, services and capital – is one of the foundations on which the internal market stands.

The third theme is that the EU can reasonably be viewed as a quasi-federal system, albeit one of a special sort. A focus on EU policies and policy processes suggests, we believe, that the EU is perhaps not as unique in the history of federal development as is generally thought, and nor are some of the factors that explain policy development in the EU so different from those that explain federal policy development elsewhere. While the EU is certainly not a fully-developed federal system, it has, we argue, been following a path that in important respects is familiar to that of more established federal systems in respect of the sharing of policy space between a central level and sub-central levels. Certainly, the precise nature of policy development in the EU has not been exactly the same as in classic federal systems – with the most obvious difference being in the foreign and defence policy areas, which were an early policy priority in the classic systems but which have been only relatively weakly developed at EU level. However, a strong case can be made that this difference is a result of the exceptional circumstance of the American defence umbrella, which Europe has enjoyed since the end of the Second World War, and which has enabled the EU to focus its energies on market integration and not be too concerned about border defence.

* * *

In writing the book, we naturally had to decide on its structure. Our initial inclination was to divide it into three parts, with one part focusing on policy actors, a second on policy processes, and a third on policy content. This idea certainly had merits and, as the titles of the chapters show, has been partially retained. However, to enable us to capture the inter-related and overlapping nature of EU policy activity, we have not divided the book into parts as rigidly as had initially been envisaged.

We start, in Chapter 1, with an overview of the EU's policy portfolio. The very considerable breadth of the policy portfolio is a central theme of the chapter. There are virtually no areas of public policy that do not include at least some EU involvement.

Chapter 2 considers explanations for the portfolio. After reviewing traditional explanations, we set out an explanatory approach drawing on economic integration theory and federal theory that we call federal integration.

Chapters 3 and 4 examine the policy actors that are so central to the nature and conduct of EU policy processes. Chapter 3 looks at the principal EU institutions and Chapter 4 at such other important actors as the EU member states and policy interests. These two chapters do not attempt to cover all features of every policy actor, but rather focus on their policy responsibilities, roles and influence.

Chapters 5–7 examine the EU's policy processes. The examination begins, in Chapter 5, with a review of the key features of these processes. These features are seen as including their great number, their complexity, their heavily consensual nature, their variable speeds, and their considerable policy outputs.

Chapters 6 and 7 then make use of conceptual devices that are helpful in enabling the policy processes to be better understood. The device employed in Chapter 6 is the much-used public policy studies device of the policy cycle. While the device has its limitations, it is helpful in bringing out how in the EU – as in the policy processes of the member states, and indeed in all types of political system – policy ideas pass through several stages as they move from conception, to formal adoption by authorized decision-makers, to implementation and evaluation.

Chapter 7 is organized around a classificatory system of EU policy processes. The classification suggests that, notwithstanding the many processes and their seemingly bewildering nature, they can be grouped into four broad categories: the Community method; intensive transgovernmentalism; supranational centralization; and new modes of governance.

Chapters 8–13 examine the EU's main policies, and Chapter 14 examines how they are funded. So, for example, Chapter 8 examines the internal market which, as explained above, has always been at the heart of the EU's policy portfolio and has been crucially important not only in itself but also in helping to advance many other policies. Among these other policies are EMU, which has received so much attention since the onset of the eurozone crisis and which is examined in Chapter 10, and environmental and cohesion policies which are examined in Chapter 9.

The main focus of the examinations in Chapters 8–13 is on policy content. However, we also discuss policy processes in so far as the processes in particular policy areas have distinctive features.

In addition to the three themes of the book outlined above, a number of specific themes run through Chapters 8–13, of which the following are particularly prominent:

- The policy portfolio has been expanding since the European Communities were founded in the 1950s, and it continues to do so. Policy areas that in the early years of the EC were regarded as being exclusively national responsibilities – such as monetary policy and internal security – have entered the portfolio, while most of those that were then part of the portfolio have greatly expanded in scope. A notable development since the early 1990s has been the considerable attention given not only to economic policies but also to policies associated with what may be called 'political union': which means essentially foreign and defence policies and justice and home affairs policies.

- The extent and nature of the EU's involvement varies greatly between policy areas. Regarding the variation in extent, the spectrum runs from policy areas such as external trade and agriculture, where there is considerable involvement, to areas such as health and housing, where the involvement is minimal. Regarding the variation in nature, the differing ways in which law is used as a policy instrument is particularly striking: in some policy areas, such as the internal market, it is used extensively, while in other areas, such as much of employment policy, there is a strong reliance on softer – non-legal – instruments.

- EU policies are heavily regulatory in nature. Indeed, agriculture is the only really prominent distributive policy, while cohesion is the only prominent redistributive policy. A consequence of this regulatory emphasis is that, as Chapter 14 shows, the EU has only limited responsibilities for 'spending' policies.

- It is increasingly the case that not all member states participate in, or fully participate in, all policies. When the European Community was founded it was an assumption that all policies applied to and would be implemented by all of the (then six) member states. However, as the EU has become involved in an increasingly broad range of policy activities and as it has grown in size to approaching thirty members, then so has the 'one size fits all' assumption about EU policies become impossible to sustain.

* * *

The ways in which readers approach this book will doubtless vary. Most, we hope, will be interested in the book as whole, but we recognize that some may be interested only in parts of it – perhaps, for example, just in specific policy areas. Whatever the reasons may be for using the book, we hope that our descriptions, explanations and analyses of EU policies and policy processes help to throw light not only on extremely important, but also sometimes highly perplexing, issues and questions.

Chapter 1

The Policy Portfolio

This chapter examines the EU's policy portfolio. The most distinctive feature of this portfolio is that it has continued to expand since the founding of the European Economic Community (EEC) in 1957. The result of this expansion is that today there are many policies in which the EU is actively involved, or even for which it has prime responsibility, that previously had been under the sole control of the individual member states. A very important example is that of monetary policy, in which even in the 1970s the EU had minimal involvement. Since 2002, for those member states that relinquished their national currencies and adopted the euro, all major monetary decisions have been taken at the EU level.

This chapter is thus presented as a broad sweep of the key features of the nature and character of EU policies. (Policy details are examined in Chapters 8–14.) The first section details the continually expanding portfolio in terms of the nature of the policy expansion and its variable pace. The second section examines the broadening policy portfolio, suggesting that no policy area is now beyond the EU's reach. However, the extent to which the EU is involved in any policy area varies – a subject taken up in the third section. The fourth section explains the various legal statuses of EU policies. The fifth section utilizes classificatory schemes to present the differing purposes of EU policies. The sixth section reviews policy differentiation. Differentiation has become a crucial feature in the expansion of the EU's policy portfolio, because this expansion has increasingly been predicated on acceptance of the notion that there are some circumstances in which some member states cannot, or should not, be full participants of a particular policy. The final section offers some concluding comments.

A Continually Expanding Portfolio

The nature of policy expansion

The treaties that created the European Communities in the 1950s – the European Coal and Steel Community (ECSC) Treaty of 1951, the European Atomic Energy Community (EURATOM) Treaty of 1957, and the European Economic Community (EEC) Treaty of 1957 – focused in policy terms almost exclusively on economic policies, and more specifically on market-related policies. Non-economic policies were barely touched upon in the Founding

Treaties. So, Article 2 of the EEC Treaty, which set out the EEC's goals, was, in its entirety, as follows:

> The Community shall have as its task, by establishing a common market and progressively approximating the economic policies of Member States, to promote throughout the Community a harmonious development of economic activities, a continuous and balanced expansion, an increase in stability, an accelerated raising of the standard of living and closer relations between the States belonging to it.

From this original market-focused base, the breadth of the EU's policy portfolio has expanded so much over the years that the EU now is involved in just about every area of public policy. The nature of the expansion is shown in Box 1.1, which summarizes the EU's evolving responsibilities in major areas of policy since 1970. Aspects of Box 1.1 can doubtless be queried, both in respect of how policies are grouped and what the precise 'balance' between the EU level and the national level at any point in time is deemed to be, but the steadily evolving nature of the EU's policy portfolio over time is not in question.

In the years immediately after the EEC Treaty came into operation in 1958, the main tasks were seen as being the creation of a common market in goods – which was achieved by 1968, when most internal tariffs and quota restrictions had been removed and a common external tariff established – and the construction of the Common Agricultural Policy (CAP). Once these early policy priorities had been dealt with, policy-makers began to broaden their policy horizons. This broadening continues to the present day and, as is shown below in the section on the increasing breadth of the policy portfolio, has mainly involved policies that:

- are intended to open the market further and to improve market performance – by, for example, tackling non-tariff barriers to internal trade, paying more attention to the free movement of capital, services and labour, and outlawing anti-competitive practices;
- are less concerned with creating market efficiency per se and more concerned with managing undesirable market consequences and problems that the market is not seen as being able to handle satisfac-

torily – such as with much of environmental policy and certain aspects of social policy; and
- are largely non-market in character, and that, until recently, have been regarded as being essentially national preserves – as most notably with foreign and external security policies, and justice and home affairs policies.

The variable pace of policy expansion

The former UK Prime Minister, Margaret Thatcher, was broadly correct when she compared EU policy development to being like a ratchet: once a notch is turned on the ratchet it is very difficult to turn it back. And over the years there have been many such turns of the ratchet. However, the turns have not occurred at a uniform rate. Rather, the pace of EU policy development has varied, both with regard to developments in particular policy areas and to general policy development.

With regard to development in particular policy areas, competition provides a good example of variable pace. The EEC Treaty identified various practices that would not normally be permitted in the common market, including anti-competitive cartels and related restrictive practices, the existence of monopolies and the abuse of dominant trading positions, and state aid subject to certain specified exceptions. However, as McGowan (2007, pp. 15–16) has pointed out, until the mid-1980s attention was focused largely on cartels and other restrictive practices, with other anti-competitive practices being given only limited attention. But since the mid-1980s there has been a much broader and more active pursuit of competition policy, with some of the more sensitive corners of protectionism, including the existence of monopolistic public utilities, being the focus of vigorous policy activity. What explains this change? A number of factors have been important, of which the most notable have been the more pro-competitiveness climate that began to emerge among policy-makers from the early 1980s (which itself was largely a reaction to the greater competitiveness of American and Asian rivals), and stronger policy entrepreneurship and leadership from the Commission's Competition Directorate General.

With regard to general policy development, the 1960s saw the rapid creation of the customs union and the CAP, but the next fifteen years or so, while not – as

Box 1.1

The development of EU policy competences

Type of policy	1970	1985	2000	2012
Direct market				
Free movement of goods	4	4	4	4
Free movement of services	2	2	3	3
Free movement of labour	2	2	4	4
Free movement of capital	1	1	5	5
Competition	2	3	4	4
External trade	3	3	3	4
Agriculture	4	4	4	4
Consumer protection	2	2	3	3
Broader economic				
Public spending and taxation	1	1	1	2
Monetary policy	1	1	2	5*
Macroeconomic policy	1	1	3	3**
Regional	1	3	3	3
Transport	1	2	3	3
Energy	1	2	2	3
Research	1	2	2	2
Environment	1	3	3	3
Development	2	3	3	3
Social and social-related				
Working conditions	2	2	3	3
Health	1	1	2	2
Education	1	1	2	2
Housing	1	1	1	1
Justice and home affairs				
Monitoring and controlling movements across internal borders	1	1	3	4***
Movements of peoples into the EU(including visa, immigration, and border control issues)	1	1	2	3
Citizenship issues	1	1	2	2
Police and judicial co-operation	1	1	2	3
Domestic crime	1	1	1	1
External political relations and security				
Foreign policy	1	1	3	3
Defence policy	1	1	2	2

Notes:
5: All major policy decisions taken at EU level.
4: Most major policy decisions taken at EU level.
3: Major policy decisions shared between EU and national levels.
2: Most, but not all, major policy decisions taken at national level.
1: All, or virtually all, major policy decisions taken at national level.

* For eurozone members.   ** Especially for eurozone members.   *** Especially for Schengen members.

is sometimes suggested – completely stagnant in policy development terms, witnessed a slowdown as the Luxembourg Compromise (the 1966 agreement between the member states that resulted in virtually all major decisions requiring unanimous support) took its toll. The launch of the Single European Market (SEM) programme in the mid-1980s led to a flood of policy activity, much of it as part of the programme itself, but some as a consequence of programme over-spill into related policy areas – such as the attention given to what came to be called the social dimension, and with the movement towards EMU. Since the completion of the SEM programme in 1992, policy integration has continued, though perhaps at a marginally slower pace in terms of moving into new policy areas.

Indeed, it might have been expected that EU policy development in recent years would have been slower than it has been in practice. After all, has not most of the EU's *grand projet* – the creation of the internal market – already been achieved? Have not most other 'acceptable' EU-level policies – such as environmental and regional policies – not been developed just about as far as they can? Are not most policy areas lying largely outside of the EU's policy reach – such as education and social welfare – just too naturally 'national' in character and too politically sensitive to warrant being much touched by EU policy-makers? And has the considerable emphasis that has been given since the early 1990s to the principle of subsidiarity – that is, to the notion that policy actions should be taken at the level that is the closest to the citizens as possible – not made EU policy development into new areas very difficult to justify? EU policy practitioners have often answered these and related questions in the affirmative. But they have not always done so. In consequence, as Pollack and Ruhlman (2009) have demonstrated, the overall EU *acquis* has continued to expand steadily year by year. It has not, however, done so on a consistent basis in all policy areas: some areas have slowed down in terms of new policy development as basic policy frameworks have been established, while others have come 'on stream' in response to new or changing preferences and requirements. Among the main policy areas to have come on stream in this way are the area of freedom, security and justice (AFSJ), the Common Foreign and Security Policy (CFSP), the Common Security and Defence Policy (CSDP), energy and transport.

An Increasingly Broad Portfolio

Despite the expansion of the policy portfolio noted above, policies concerned with the internal market are still very much at the heart of the Union's policy portfolio. There are three main – in practice, overlapping and mutually reinforcing – reasons why the market remains at the core of EU policy. First, EU policy-makers are agreed that the internal market brings considerable benefits to member states. While there are often disagreements over specific aspects of internal market policies, it is not disputed that the internal market itself is desirable and beneficial in economic terms. Second, the internal market is not yet complete. The creation of the customs union by 1968 was just the first step in what have been countless ongoing actions to open up the market – and not just the market in goods, but also in services, capital and labour. These actions have involved not only the removal of barriers to internal movement – so-called 'negative integration' – but also many kinds of 'positive integration'. Among the many sorts of actions that have been, and still are, necessary to ensure that the market is truly open are the creation of cross-market standards designed to minimize non-tariff barriers to trade in the form of different national specifications for trading activity, and a highly active competition policy designed to ensure that competition is not weakened by, for example, power within markets being concentrated in the hands of just a few large companies, or by companies arranging anti-competitive cartels. Third, what has been deemed to be necessary for the creation of a truly integrated, and properly competitive, internal market has broadened over the years. While the necessary conditions for a competitive market have been disputed constantly between the member states, it has come to be generally accepted that if, for example, minimum common standards do not apply in respect of much of environmental law and labour law, then countries with the lowest standards have, all else being equal, a competitive advantage.

Economic and Monetary Union (EMU) is also a policy area where much of the rationale for its development is located in the search and drive to enhance the efficiency of the internal market. Certainly, EMU has also been seen by some of its supporters as having a political rationale – in the form of advancing the federalization of the EU – but the main case that has been advanced for it has been that it will help to promote market performance. It is seen as potentially doing this in a number of ways, most notably: by removing uncertainties associated with the possibility of currency fluctuations so that market stability and confidence is increased and, in consequence, there is more encouragement to invest and trade across EU borders; by increasing price transparency, so that business is obliged to be more price sensitive – and therefore competitive; and by removing currency transaction costs, which saves business considerable fees.

Alongside polices that are directly concerned with creating an open and competitive market, are many policies that are market-related but have rather different goals. Four examples may be taken to illustrate this. First, some policies are designed to ensure that the market is not only open and competitive but also provides protection for potentially vulnerable participants. Such policies may be said to have the aim of ensuring that the market is socially just. Examples include policies on working conditions and consumer protection. Second, there are policies that aim to try to ensure that market growth and benefits are not – as they risk being in an open market – over-concentrated at the geographical centre and in already wealthy geographical areas. These policies are at the core of what is called cohesion policy and include regional policy and aspects of social policy, such as the funding of vocational training centres. Third, a range of policies are based on public-sector-led intervention, and some spending, to try to improve specific features of the market that are seen as not working satisfactorily and as contributing to lacklustre market performance. Starting with the launch of Research and Technological Development (R&TD) policy in the late 1970s, which arose from concerns that the EU was not promoting innovation sufficiently, especially in high-tech industries, such policies have increased considerably in importance in recent years as part of the Lisbon/Europe 2020 Strategy. As is shown in Chapters 7 and 9, Europe 2020 has among its core goals making the EU a leading knowledge-based economy, promoting internal economic and social reform, and increasing employment. Fourth, there are a small number of policy areas where policies are designed specifically to ensure that full market principles do not fully apply. The best-known of these areas is agriculture, where the CAP has long given non-market support of vari-

ous kinds to farmers – initially mainly in the form of price support, but since the mid-1990s increasingly in the form of direct income support. The Common Fisheries Policy (CFP) also curtails the full operation of market principles: to protect fish stocks, fishermen are restricted as to when they may fish and what volumes of what species they may catch.

But the EU's policy portfolio is far from being restricted to economic and market-related polices. Or, to be more precise given that most public policies can be said to have at least some economic aspects, it is far from being restricted to policies that are primarily economic and market-related in nature. Important EU policy areas that are driven to a significant degree by other considerations – mainly quality of life and security considerations – include environmental policy, AFSJ policy, and foreign and external security policies.

Taking environmental policy, which first appeared on the EC's policy agenda in the early 1970s, it is true that the very considerable policy attention that is now given to such matters as the emission of toxic substances into the air, onto the land, and into rivers and coastal waters is partly driven by concerns that the market is based on a level playing field. But it is also partly – and for many policy actors is largely – driven by demands for a clean and healthy living environment. Moreover, policies focused on issues such as the protection of natural habitats, the preservation of endangered species and tackling climate change are almost purely environmental in origin: at their base, they are quality of life policies. (Though, that being said, EU policy-makers recognize that green technologies – which involve high growth and leading edge industry – can encourage European entrepreneurship.)

Regarding AFSJ policy, its first real appearance on the policy agenda was in the mid-1980s, largely as a result of the Commission's attempt – as part of its programme to 'complete' the internal market by 1992 – to create freer movement of labour. This was seen to offer not only economic advantages but also to increase the likelihood of cross-border 'people problems', including crime. In the 2000s such 'people problems' – especially with respect to security considerations – have increased greatly in intensity, resulting in AFSJ issues rising to near the top of the EU's policy priorities. The main developments that have brought security considerations to the fore have been the 2004/2007 enlargement (with some of the newer member states being seen as having relatively weak internal security controls and porous external borders), the increased international mobility of people, threats of international terrorism, and the uncertain political climate in many neighbouring countries (as witnessed, for example, by the 2011 'Arab Spring', which led to a mass exodus of illegal migrants seeking entry to the EU). Policy areas that have been overhauled extensively to try to deal with these challenges include immigration policy, visa policy, and police and judicial co-operation.

The most important EU policies areas that do not, at first sight at least, directly have any economic base or rationale at all are the foreign and external security policies. While not being mentioned in the Founding Treaties, foreign policy began to be developed, albeit tentatively and on a strictly intergovernmental basis, from the early 1970s, under the (deliberately) vague title of European Political Cooperation (EPC). The main reason for this interest in foreign policy was a growing dissatisfaction with the fact that, while the voice of the EC was increasingly influential on the world stage in respect of economic issues, and more especially in respect of world trading issues (where the EC spoke with one voice because of the existence since 1968 of the customs union), in respect of international political issues it exercised virtually no influence – in fact, it did not even have a voice. However, over the years, foreign and security policies have been developed greatly, especially since the Maastricht Treaty, which put them on a solid legal foundation by creating the CFSP, which now has a highly-developed institutional apparatus, an extensive range of policy instruments, and oversees a wide range of policy actions. Significantly, in terms of just how wide the EU's policy portfolio has become, in the 2000s a fledgling defence policy – in the form of the CSDP – has been developed alongside the CFSP.

It should be noted, however, that even in the ostensibly non-economic policy areas of the CFSP and CSDP, economics are not completely absent. This is witnessed in concerns not to upset major trading partners where possible, and in the increasing pursuit of reaping economic benefits for European commerce through the pursuit of a more integrated European weapons industry, which could achieve economies of scale similar to those in the US. But, for the most part, the CFSP and CSDP are based on the pursuit of primarily political objectives, as is illustrated, for example, with the EU's leadership in promoting the UN's Millennium Development Goals – which arises from both humanitarian concerns and the EU's long-standing commitment to promoting democratization.

To make a more general comment, policy development in the highly sensitive CFSP and CSDP spheres – the public policy areas that are associated more than any other with national sovereignty – is testimony to how no policy area is now beyond the EU's reach.

The Varying Extents of EU Policy Involvement

The nature of the EU's policy expansion has resulted in great variations between policy areas regarding the extent of EU involvement. As Boxes 1.1 and 1.2 show, in a few policy areas the EU has extensive policy responsibilities, in a few it has virtually no responsibilities, and across a broad spectrum of policy areas it shares responsibility with the individual member states.

Despite the use of the word *common* before a number of the EU's best-known policies – as in Common Agricultural Policy, Common Fisheries Policy, Common Foreign and Security Policy, and Common Security and Defence Policy – there is in fact only one policy that is truly common: the Common Commercial Policy (CCP) (the technical term for the external trade policy), and then only as it applies to goods. The existence of a Common External Tariff (CET) on goods entering the EU market means that the member states are required to act as one (in practice via the Commission) when engaged in trade negotiations with third countries or the CET would break down very quickly. Monetary policy may also be said to be common for eurozone states, but many EU states are not eurozone members. Since the creation of the single currency, all decisions for eurozone states with regard to interest rates, exchange rates and the money supply are taken by the European Central Bank (ECB), acting within a framework laid down in the treaties.

With respect to the CAP and the CFP, virtually all major policy decisions are taken at EU level. In the case of the CAP this covers such matters as the nature of market regimes (which vary among agricultural

---

Box 1.2

The varying extents of EU policy involvement

Extensive EU involvement	Considerable EU involvement	Policy responsibilities shared between the EU and the member states	Limited EU policy involvement	Virtually no EU policy involvement
External trade Agriculture Fishing Monetary (for eurozone members)	Market regulation Competition	Regional/Cohesion Industry Foreign Development Environment Equal opportunities Working conditions Consumer protection Movement across external borders Macroeconomic (especially for euro members) Energy Cross-border crime Civil liberties (especially via the Charter of Fundamental Rights)	Health Higher education Defence Social welfare Transport	Housing Domestic crime Primary and secondary education

---

products), income support measures available to farmers, and measures to dispose of agricultural surpluses. In the case of the CFP, it covers the conditions on which fishermen can leave port to fish, and what and how much they can catch when they are at sea. However, significant 'second-level' CAP and CFP decisions can be taken at the national level, albeit on the basis of usually being subject to Commission authorization. The most important of these decisions cover support measures of various kinds that national governments may wish to make available to their farmers and fishermen.

From the 'extensive' end of the policy spectrum shown in Box 1.2, EU policy involvement moves 'down' through various degrees of shared responsibility with the member states before tapering into virtually no policy involvement at all. Three generalizations can be made about the nature of this distribution of policy responsibilities between the EU and the member states:

- The more that policies are direct-market ones or, at least, market-related, the more likely they are to be towards the 'extensive EU involvement' end of the spectrum.
- The more that policies cover matters with clear cross-border implications, the more likely they too are to be towards the 'extensive EU involvement' end of the spectrum.
- Virtually all policy areas involving heavy public expenditure are at the end of the spectrum where the EU's policy responsibilities are low or virtually non-existent.

Reasons for the nature of this distribution of policy responsibilities are considered later in this chapter and in Chapter 2.

A final point to be made concerning the varying nature of the EU's policy responsibilities is that the sharing involved is not always restricted to a sharing between the EU and the governments of the member states. This is because, below the level of national governments, sub-national and local levels of government often have policy responsibilities. For the most part these are confined to tasks of policy execution, with regional and local levels of government being in the 'front line' and acting in practice as the EU's implementation agents in respect of the implementation of many EU policies. But, in a few policy areas, most notably cohesion policy, sub-national levels of government are involved to at least some degree in policy management as well as in policy administration.

The Varying Legal Statuses of EU Policies

There are three main sources of EU law:

- *The treaties.* The EU's treaty structure and contents have, via a series of amending treaties, evolved considerably over the years. Under the most recent amending treaty – the 2007 Lisbon Treaty, which came into effect in December 2009 – the EU's main treaties are: the Treaty on European Union (TEU), which was initially created by the 1992 Maastricht Treaty; and the Treaty on the Functioning of the European Union (TFEU), which is the successor to the previously named Treaty Establishing the European Community.
- *EU legislation.* This is issued primarily in the form of directives, regulations and decisions.
- *Judicial law.* This takes the form of rulings of the EU's court – the Court of Justice of the European Union (CJEU).

There are considerable variations between EU policy areas regarding the extent to which the policies that exist have legal status. Thinking of the variations in terms of a spectrum, Box 1.3 illustrates that at one end of the spectrum are policy areas making considerable use of EU law, while at the other end are policy areas relying much more on non-legal forms of co-operation and co-ordination between the member states.

While there is considerable overlap in the category placements of policy areas in Boxes 1.2 and 1.3, there are also significant differences. There is no fixed rela-

tionship between the extent of EU policy involvement in a policy area and the propensity of that policy area to use legal or non-legal policy instruments. So, some policy areas where the EU has significant policy responsibilities make little use of EU law, while some areas where the policy responsibilities are light make extensive use of it in respect of that involvement. Foreign policy is an example of a policy area in the former category, while employment rights is an example of a policy area in the latter category.

The variations in the extent to which policies have a legal, as opposed to a political, base are extremely important. This is because policies that are based on law have a significantly different character from those that do not. Most crucially, where laws are involved, those to whom the laws are addressed – be they national governments, business corporations or citizens – must abide by them or risk being subject to legal action. Where, by contrast, policies rely more on voluntary co-operation, there may be strong political pressures on those to whom the policies are directed to fully implement them, but these pressures are not usually as powerful as the threat of legal proceedings.

Given the seemingly much greater attraction of basing EU policies on law, why is there only a limited use of law in some important policy areas? To put this another way, why do some policy areas rely more on such policy instruments as political agreements, joint understandings and common guidelines than they do on law? The answer to this apparent puzzle is considered in later chapters of this book, especially Chapter 7, but is essentially based on whether the use of legal policy instruments is or is not politically acceptable to the governments of the member states.

The Differing Purposes of EU Policies

Every EU policy naturally has its own specific purpose, or purposes. So, for example, the purpose of EU regional policy is to assist in the development of the EU's poorer economic regions. The purpose of the Common Commercial Policy is to ensure that international trading conditions are as favourable as possible to the EU. And the main purposes of the CAP are to ensure that EU farmers are guaranteed a reasonable

Box 1.3				
The varying use of legal regulation in different policy areas				
Heavy reliance on legal regulation	Very considerable reliance on legal regulation	A mixture of legal regulation and interstate co-operation	Some legal regulation but a considerable reliance on interstate co-operation	Largely based on interstate co-operation
Trade Agriculture Fishing Market regulation	Regional Competition Consumer protection Working conditions Equal opportunities Civil liberties	Industry Environment Transport Movement across external borders Macroeconomic Energy Cross-border crime	Social welfare Energy Police and judicial co-operation Europe 2020 policies Education Health	Foreign Defence

income, that the EU produces as much as possible of its required foodstuffs, and that the countryside is protected.

But while all policies are unique in their specific purposes, they invariably share certain broad purposes with a number of other EU policies. The nature of this sharing varies between policies according to both the particular characteristics of individual policies and how general policy purposes are identified and thereby classified.

Of course, given the broad scope of EU policies, various classificatory systems of the purposes of EU policies are possible. In this section we make use of two classificatory systems that we judge to be particularly helpful: one devised in the context of EU policies that emphasizes the importance of the market; and the classic classificatory system initially devised by Theodore Lowi to describe various aspects of the relationships between politics and policies in the US, but which has come to be seen subsequently as having a much wider usage.

A market-focused classificatory system

Box 1.4 sets out a classificatory system that identifies four possible purposes of EU policies. The most striking feature of this system is the appearance of the word 'market' in the title of three of the four categories. This feature highlights the prominence of market-focused and market-related policies in the EU's portfolio. It is a feature that, in one way or another, is inevitably prominent in any classificatory system of EU policies, because the market is at the very centre of so much that the EU does. It is at the centre most obviously in terms of direct market building –involving such activities as removing barriers to free movement and to competition – but it is also very important in terms of correcting and cushioning the consequences of the operation of the market.

A point to be emphasized about Box 1.4, and therefore also about the purposes of EU policies, is that while individual policies have only been entered once in the box, on the basis of their main purpose, in fact many policies have more than one purpose. Environmental and social policies are examples of such multi-purpose policies, with both being concerned not only with improving the quality of life in various ways (market correcting and market cushioning) but also with ensuring that the internal market works fairly by establishing a level competitive playing field (market building).

Related to this point about the multi-purpose nature of some EU policies, it should be noted that the boundaries between the categories of the classificatory system set out in Box 1.4 are porous and overlap. This

---

Box 1.4

Classifying EU policies by purpose

Policy purpose	Explanation of purpose	Examples
Market building	To create a single market by removing barriers, by carrying out regulatory reform, and by stimulating market forces.	Policies concerning the customs union, product standards, competition, indirect taxation, energy, EMU.
Market correcting	To compensate particular groups for market costs, to channel or constrain the market, and to limit inequality.	CAP, CFP, cohesion.
Market cushioning	To minimize the harm economic activities impose on nature and humans.	Environment, occupational health and safety, equal opportunities.
Non-market policies (polity-building)	To develop certain policies that are not related to the market, but which have the effect of making the EU a more powerful political system.	CFSP, CSDP, aspects of AFSJ.

Source: Adapted from Sbragia, 2003, p. 131.

---

is especially so in respect of the market correcting and market cushioning categories – with the consequence that it is, for example, a marginal decision as to whether cohesion policy should be judged to be primarily market correcting or market cushioning.

The classic Lowi classificatory system

A very well-established way of distinguishing between policies is in terms of regulatory, redistributive and distributive policies. This typology was first advanced by Theodore Lowi (1964), who later added a fourth policy type to his classificatory scheme, which he called constituent policies (Lowi, 1972). While much of what Lowi was interested in goes beyond our scope here, many scholars have observed that his typology has a number of possible uses (see, for example, Heckathorn and Maser, 1990; Nicholson, 2002). It is for its usefulness in capturing key features of, and differences between, EU internal policies that it is

employed here. (Lowi's typology was devised to apply to domestic politics in the US, so it does not directly embrace external policies.) We thus now apply Lowi's much-used schema to EU policies. A key point to emerge from the application of the schema is that while all four policy types certainly exist in the EU, regulatory policies are the most important.

Regulatory policies

EU policies as a whole have a strong regulatory emphasis. The word 'regulatory' is very broad and can be used to embrace a wide range of EU policy activities. Most commonly, however, 'regulatory' is used to refer to the adoption of rules by public authorities to control behaviour, especially the behaviour of economic actors. There are a number of possible reasons why public authorities may wish to adopt such rules. One is to deal with and correct market failures, in the form perhaps of negative externalities such as air and water pollution, or the formation of anti-competitive cartels. Another possible reason is to protect consumers by, for example, specifying essential standards that marketed products must meet, or providing compensation measures in the event of the sale of defective products. And a third possible reason is to protect market producers by, for example, laying down laws covering health and safety at work or imposing limits on the number of hours workers can be required to work over a specified period. (A good summary of rationales for regulation is provided in Baldwin and Cave, 1999.)

Such is the focus on regulatory policies in the EU's policy portfolio that one of the most eminent of academic commentators on the EU, Giandomenico Majone (1994, 1996), has gone so far as to suggest that the EU can be thought of as being a regulatory state. The regulatory emphasis of EU policies is seen most obviously with respect to the internal market, where an extensive legislative framework exists for the purpose of governing actors' behaviour in the market. This framework covers not just pure market activities, such as rules governing product specifications and market movements, but also some seemingly non-market policy areas that are regulated in part because they have market implications. An example of such a policy area is the environment, where much of the extensive volume of EU legislation that is in place can be explained, to some extent at least, by a desire to ensure that the internal market is based on level and fair foundations. Such foundations would not be level or fair if, say, the regulatory framework on the disposal of toxic substances into the atmosphere or on the tipping of rubbish on landfill sites was to be less stringent in some member states than in others. Accordingly, the EU requires some commonality.

The reason that EU regulatory policy is so wide-ranging and, as Pollack (2000) and Pollack and Ruhlman (2009) have shown, has displayed little sign of slowing down in its advance, is that there is both a demand and a supply for it. The *demand* comes from various quarters, not least large businesses, which want as integrated a market as possible – which means having a single regulatory system in place rather than numerous different systems with different national standards. Having a single regulatory system benefits large businesses because products do not have to be adapted to meet different regulatory requirements. Further to this, established business enterprises have the additional motivation that a single regulatory system ensures that *all* European companies face the same compliance costs: so, a single regulatory system gives large businesses some protection from 'upstart' competitors trying to gain a foothold in the internal market by taking advantage of lower standards in one part of the market to cut costs at the expense of worker safety, environmental compliance and product standards.

The *supply* comes mainly from the Commission, which, through its policy and legislative proposals, plays a crucial role in setting the regulatory framework. The Commission produces this supply for a number of reasons. One reason is simply that it is much more able to do so than it is with redistributive or distributive policies. This is partly because the technical nature of much regulatory policy tends to make it less contentious than the other two policy types, and is partly because most of the costs of implementing regulatory policies fall not on the EU budget but on the budgets of private firms and public authorities in the member states. Another reason why the Commission produces the supply is, in the view of public choice theorists, because expanding EU regulatory powers also expands the Commission's own powers (see, for example, Hix, 2006).

The intensities of and interactions between demand and supply do, of course, vary between policy areas, with the consequence that there are many differing types of regulatory regimes in the EU. Shawn Donnelly (2010) illustrates this clearly with an analysis of the nature of the regulatory regimes in three areas: corporate governance, which continues to be primarily nationally based in that most company law is national law; the regulation of financial markets, which is more supranational – and has rapidly become much more so in the wake of the post-2008 financial crisis; and accounting standards, which are regulated by two parallel regimes based on EU and national rules. For Donnelly, the key factor in explaining the differing degrees of EU-level development of the regimes is national norms: where member state norms on such key matters as the objectives of public policy and the relationship between the state and the market broadly coincide, then EU regulation is likely; where, by contrast, national norms clash, then proposals for EU-level regulation are likely to be resisted. Donnelly's approach is thus essentially constructivist in nature, but it can easily be re-thought in terms of the extent to which there is a demand for EU-level regulation.

Redistributive policies

Redistributive policies transfer financial resources from groups of individuals (most commonly social classes), regions or countries to others. Redistributive policies loom large in the national policy portfolios of the EU member states. There are variations between the states regarding the nature and extent of their redistributive policies – variations that are accounted for mainly by the extent to which certain services rest on private or social models, and the bases on which they operate – but in broad terms policy areas that are primarily redistributive in character include education (which redistributes to the young), health (which redistributes to those who are unwell), social welfare (which redistributes to the less well-off and to those who are not part of the active workforce), and pensions (which redistributes to retired people). By contrast, the EU's policy portfolio includes only very limited provision for redistribution. Indeed, only one policy area has a significant redistributive capacity – cohesion policy, which redistributes, albeit on a limited basis, to less prosperous regions via the European Regional and Development Fund (ERDF) and to some disadvantaged groups via the European Social Fund (ESF).

There are a number of reasons why EU redistributive policies are not well developed. The first is that governments generally want to retain control over public revenues, and transfers of responsibility for redistributive policies to the EU level would weaken this control. Second, most of the more expensive redistributive policies – including health, education, social welfare and pensions – are generally seen, by policy-makers and citizens alike, as naturally being national policies. Apart from a few specific examples such as supporting educational exchanges between students and promoting some health campaigns and research programmes, no pressing reasons have presented themselves for policies of this type to be transferred to the EU level. Third, since the Maastricht Treaty identified subsidiarity as an essential principle, the practicalities of developing EU spending policies have become more difficult, since Commission proposals for EU legislation have to be justified on the grounds that policy matters covered by proposals will be pursued more effectively at the EU level. Fourth, proposals to advance spending policies tend to be more politicized than regulatory policies, and as such tend to promote stiffer opposition. A key reason for this is that whereas with regulatory policies the likely gainers and losers are not always obvious, since much depends on how quickly and efficiently the targets of regulations adapt to regulatory change, with redistributive policies the core gainers and losers are immediately obvious: the core gainers include those member states that will be beneficiaries of spending increases, and the core losers include those states that will see their contributions to the EU budget increase. This has been brought to the fore particularly during the eurozone debt crisis, where citizens of wealthier states (Germany in particular) have resisted bailing out financially troubled eurozone member states. Fifth, since the early 1990s most member states have adopted increasingly tight attitudes towards EU spending. Key factors accounting for these attitudes are that they conform to the broad ideological shift in most Western capitalist systems in favour of a more restrictive stance towards all forms of public expenditure; the EMU convergence and Stability and Growth Pact criteria (see Chapter 10) and the related EU Broad Economic Guidelines (which apply to non-EMU members) place a strong emphasis on budgetary discipline; the prospect and then the reality of many relatively poor countries joining the EU has not encouraged EU-15 states to expand redistributive policies – from which most of them have little to gain but for which they must pay; and Germany, long the major net contributor to the EU budget, has come to suffer from 'donor fatigue'.

As a result of these pressures in the direction of EU budgetary restraint there has been a virtual standstill in spending on redistributive policies in recent years. It is true that expenditure on the Regional and Social Funds was doubled during the first of the EU's multi-annual financial perspectives, covering the years 1988–92, and was then doubled again during the 1993–9 perspective. However, though these increases were large in absolute terms they were modest in relative terms. In fact, the EU's budget has always been, and still is, tiny when compared with national budgets, hovering over the years at only just over 1 per cent of total EU wealth and around 3 per cent of total public expenditure in the EU (see Chapter 14 for an examination of the EU's budget revenues and expenses).

An important consequence of the EU having only limited responsibilities and capacities with respect to redistributive policies is that, as Moravcsik (2001, pp.

163–4) has noted, the EU plays only a minor role in most of the areas about which European voters care the most. Policies on education, health, welfare, policing, defence and direct taxation are still largely determined and financed at the national level.

Distributive policies

Distributive policies involve allocations of financial resources and benefits, but not from one 'side' to another (as from the better-off to the worse-off, for example) but rather from diffuse contributors (with taxation being the customary collection system) to selected beneficiaries (typically, a small, but always identifiable, group). In many political systems, including in the US, distributive policies are often 'patronage' policies, evoking a 'patron–client relationship' (Nicholson, 2002, p. 167). So, much of distributive policy is meant to be under the radar rather than 'open and public politics' and is obscured in budgets (Lowi, 1972, p. 308). A particular feature of distributive policy is thus that it can be difficult for 'outsiders' to know the extent to which it is taking place at all. A principal reason for this is that in distributive policy-making processes there are so many participants with disparate views as to the best course of action (unlike the two usually identifiable sides in redistributive policy). A second reason why the existence of distributive policy can be difficult to identify is that participants in distributive policy-making processes often engage in unpredictable alliance shifting.

But despite this identification difficulty, it is clear that distributive policies are not developed very much in the EU, and those that do exist are quite different in character from the kinds identified by Lowi in the US. The most important of the EU's distributive policies is agriculture, which is distributive rather than redistributive because it does not consist of 'haves' and 'have nots' and is much closer to patronage politics in its operation. Nicholson (2002, p. 169) notes that distributive policies are characterized by close political ties between the bureaucracy and the clientele, where they 'become entitlement programs and insulated from reform' – which seems to be an apt description of aspects of the CAP, which has spawned powerful agri-interests operating at the EU level.

Another distributive policy is import protection, with its range of tariffs and non-tariff barriers. Like agriculture, it is distributive because while the costs of the policy are widely distributed among the public, the beneficiaries are selected politically – European-based producers in this case. Other examples of EU policy activities that can be classified as distributive include some of those included in the Europe 2020 programme – most notably R&TD (a form of industrial policy because governments make judgements about promising technologies and in the process pick 'winners' and 'losers') and other activities that involve the awarding of subsidies. However, the funds assigned to Europe 2020 comprise a very small proportion of the total EU budget.

An example of a distributive policy area that might have been expected to be developed extensively by the EU, but which has not, is transportation policy. Transportation is a classic distributive policy and was given its own title (Title IV) in the original EEC Treaty, where it was stipulated that 'The objectives of this Treaty shall, in matters governed by this Title, be pursued by Member States within the framework of a common transport policy' (Article 74). But though there is an inherent rationale for a European transportation policy, especially in supporting the internal market, the nuts and bolts of jobs and contracts (the stuff of distributive politics) has impeded the development of the policy area and resulted in it remaining primarily a national level policy.

Developing this point about transport policy further, much of the explanation for why distributive policies are not well developed at EU level is that they are seen as being primarily national responsibilities, so only limited budgetary resources are made available for them. In Pollack's (1995) view, another reason why the EU is not much involved in distributive policies is because they are not as closely linked with the operation of the market as are regulatory and redistributive policies. Regulatory policies are a consequence of the need to ensure standard rules and regulations in the internal market, and redistributive policies are, at least in part, a consequence of countries with specific difficulties adjusting to the internal market being given compensation or side-payments. Distributive policies are not so 'advantaged' and are often highly dependent on Commission entrepreneurship for advancement.

Constituent policies

Unlike the other three policy types, constituent policies are not transaction based but rather are concerned with 'the rules of the game' (Spitzer, 1987, p. 678). They customarily involve elite (top-down) policy-making focused on such matters as how should decisions be made (should, for example, new administrative agencies be created); and what should be the nature of interactions between public authorities and the citizenry (should, for example, governing authorities engage in 'propaganda to change the public's behaviour or opinions)?

The Charter of Fundamental Rights of the European Union, which has been 'solemnly proclaimed' by the European Parliament (EP), the Council and the Commission, and which has legal status (albeit a rather complicated one – see Chapter 11), is an example of a constituent policy. In essence, it involves a comprehensive attempt to define civil liberties and rights in the EU. Other examples of constituent policies are the various involvements of the EU in 'propaganda' to promote societal goals. To take two different examples of this: in the area of promoting public health, the European Food Safety Authority (EFSA) is charged with 'restoring and maintaining confidence in the EU food supply' (European Food Safety Authority, 2012); and in the area of fundamental rights, the European Union Agency for Fundamental Rights is tasked with 'promoting dialogue with civil society in order to raise public awareness of fundamental rights' (European Union Agency for Fundamental Rights, 2012).

With respect to the establishment of administrative agencies, many specialized EU agencies have been created over the years – with both the necessity of their establishment and their headquartering usually having been the source of much wrangling among member states. Regarding headquartering, because hosting an EU agency is so valued, there is an informal understanding that each member state should in principle have the opportunity to host at least one specialized agency.

Increasing Differentiation

A central assumption when the Founding Treaties were signed was that all member states should, and would, participate in all EU policies. There was to be no picking and choosing of which policies to participate in and there were to be no laggards in honouring

policy commitments. In short, all member states were to swim abreast in policy terms.

For the most part, this expectation and accompanying obligation continues. However, it does not do so in pristine form. This is because, since the late 1970s, and more particularly since the early 1990s, there has been an increasing acceptance in EU circles that there are circumstances in which some member states will not, and sometimes even should not, be full participants in particular policies. To use the term that has come to be generally used to describe this phenomenon, the need for some policy *differentiation* has come to be accepted.

An important reason behind the pressures for a degree of differentiation is the increasing breadth of the EU's policy portfolio. As the portfolio has broadened out from its initial internal market core to embrace at least some interest in just about every area of public policy, then so have policies come on to the agenda that have been seen to have little attraction and/or to have posed considerable difficulties for particular member states. Prominent among such policies are EMU, CFSP/CSDP, and aspects of social, environmental and AFSJ policies. The enlargement process, which has been under way almost constantly since the early 1960s, has been another important reason behind increased pressure for differentiation. Naturally, with each new member state having its own policy needs and preferences, and with the 2004–7 enlargement round having brought in a large number of states that are in many respects significantly different in character from the EU-15 states, enlargement has increased the likelihood greatly of there being member states that either have no wish or do not have the capacity to be part of particular policy initiatives.

Differentiation takes both formal and informal forms.

Formal differentiation

There are two main types of formal differentiation: *à la carte* and *multi-speed*.

À la carte differentiation is the more important type in that it involves member states choosing not to participate in a policy. Moreover, no commitment is given that they will ever participate. The European Monetary System, which was developed from the late 1970s without the participation of the UK, was the first example of such differentiation. It was followed in the mid-1980s by the Schengen System, which was designed to enable free movement of people across internal borders. The UK and Ireland opted out of, and continue to opt out, of full Schengen participation: in the UK's case this has been because it wants to maintain its own border controls – which are helped by it being an island; and in Ireland's case it is because of its free travel area with the UK. Denmark can choose whether or not to apply any new measures taken under the Schengen title of the TFEU (the Schengen System is examined in Chapter 11).

À la carte differentiation was given a considerable boost in the early 1990s when the 1992 Maastricht Treaty gave it formal authorization. The authorization was very specific, taking the form of allowing the UK and Denmark not to participate in the third stage of EMU (which was to be mandatory for all other member states that met the EMU convergence criteria) and allowing the UK also to opt out of the Social Charter that was included in the Treaty. Along with the creation of the intergovernmental CFSP and Justice and Home Affairs (JHA) pillars, these opt-out provisions can be seen as laying foundations for a less rigid treaty base for policy development. As Majone (2005, p. 15) has put it: 'It is now clear … that the differentiation or flexibility that appeared in several forms in the TEU was no momentary aberration – a sort of *à la carte* integration – but the clear indication of an emergent strategy for achieving progress in politically sensitive areas, even at the price of a loss of overall coherence of the system.'

The 1997 Amsterdam Treaty generalized the Maastricht 'dispensations' by providing for 'Provisions on Closer Cooperation' in the Community and JHA pillars. This authorized policy development within the treaty framework but with not all of the member states involved, subject to a number of safeguards and conditions – including that such co-operation be open to all member states, 'is only used as a last resort', and 'does not affect the "*acquis communautaire*"' (TEU post-Amsterdam Treaty, Article 43). The Amsterdam Treaty did not extend closer co-operation to the CFSP, but did allow for a different kind of flexibility within this policy area in that it allowed for member states not to apply CFSP decisions under specified circumstances. The 2001 Nice Treaty subsequently extended the remit of closer co-operation – which it renamed *enhanced co-operation* – to the CFSP pillar (but with

military and defence matters excluded), and made it easier to operationalize by replacing the Amsterdam stipulation that a majority of member states must be involved in a closer co-operation initiative by a stipulation that only eight (increased to nine when Bulgaria and Romania joined the EU in 2007) must take part. Post-Nice and after the 2007 enlargement, the proportion of participating member states in an enhanced closer co-operation initiative thus became exactly one third. The Lisbon Treaty largely confirmed the post-Nice position, though it was a little more succinct regarding the boundaries of enhanced co-operation: 'Any enhanced cooperation shall not undermine the internal market or economic, social and territorial cohesion. It shall not constitute a barrier to or discrimination in trade between Member States nor shall it restrict competition between them' (Article 326, TFEU). The Lisbon Treaty also dropped the CSDP exclusion. As of late 2012, the treaty provisions on enhanced co-operation have been used twice: for the establishment of a European patent, from which Italy and Spain initially opted out because of objections to the limited use of languages in the operation of the scheme (see Tait, 2010); and for procedures designed to ease divorce arrangements when the couple involved are from different member states (fourteen member states are participating in this). (For fuller acounts of the treaty creation and development of closer co-operation, see Junge, 2007; Nugent, 2010; Leuffen *et al.*, 2012.)

As for *multi-speed differentiation*, that occurs when a member state or states wish to participate in a policy but judge themselves, or are judged by others in authority, not yet to be sufficiently prepared or able to do so. The first clear example of multi-speed differentiation occurred with the launch of the single currency phase of EMU in 1999, when Greece was excluded (though only until 2001, as it turned out) because the Commission, supported by the Council of Ministers, decided that it did not meet the qualifying convergence criteria. The 2004–7 enlargements then saw multi-speed differentiation on a mass scale, with the new member states being prevented by their terms of accession from becoming EMU or Schengen members until they had established their credentials for membership. In the case of EMU, this involved each new member state having to wait for at least two years to enable its economic performance to be judged post-accession. Since the completion of this two-year period for the 2004 acceding states, the size of the eurozone has grown with, in 2007, Slovenia being the first of the new member states to join, followed by Cyprus and Malta in 2008, Slovakia in 2009, and Estonia in 2011. In Schengen's case, most of the new EU member states have now been admitted to the Schengen Area.

The post-2004/7 EMU and Schengen situations are particularly graphic versions of a special type of multi-speed differentiation that arises from all EU enlargements, wherein acceding states are not full participants in certain EU policies for specified periods. This lack of full engagement can take the form of new member states being granted transitional exemptions from features of the *acquis* (such as environmental standards that involve heavy capital expenditure, or being permitted to limit capital investment from non-citizens) and/or being excluded temporarily from features of the *acquis* (as with the 2004/7 accession states being excluded not only from immediate membership of the single currency and of Schengen, but also being prevented from reaping full funding support from the CAP regime under the 2007–13 financial framework).

Informal differentiation

Though the word 'differentiation' is usually applied only to the formal *à la carte* and *multi-speed* processes described above, there is, as Andersen and Sitter (2006) have argued, a strong case for applying it more widely. The basis of this case is that exclusion from a policy activity or opting-out are not the only ways in which there is variation between member states in their policy engagement. There are also other ways, though these are less formal and at times almost hidden. The nature of these other ways rests on two main foundations: the extent to which policy instruments are intended to produce policy conformity throughout the EU; and the pressures at national level for policy activity to reflect national interests and not to be set too closely within a single EU level model. These two foundations are, of course, interrelated, in that it is precisely where pressures for the recognition of national interests are strongest that EU policy instruments are likely to be the least constraining. Andersen and Sitter (2006, p. 320) suggest that this notion of informal types of differentiation is best

understood if it is set within the framework of what they suggest are four different types of European integration:

- *Homogeneous integration.* This combines: (a) tight coupling between the EU level and national levels with respect to normative and organizational requirements (that is, all member states are expected and required, and expect and require it of themselves, to act in much the same manner); (b) weak pressures at the national level for decoupling. Homogeneous integration may be thought of as the 'standard' top-down form of integration, based on reasonably tight EU laws that are expected to be applied in a uniform way at national levels. As such, informal differentiation does not apply here, except in so far as there are some variations between member states in the diligence and efficiency of their 'front line' policy implementation. Much of the internal market regulatory framework is based on this type of integration.
- *Aligned integration.* This is different from homogeneous integration in that EU policy instruments do not impose strong organizational or behavioural models on the member states, but a reinforcing impact of state and EU-level interests results in alignment occurring in any event. The liberalization of telecoms illustrates this: the Commission pressed for it strongly in the 1990s, but left the ways and the timescale in which it was to be achieved to the member states (thus allowing for abundant differentiation); the common nature of the challenges facing them resulted in a strong coalition of key market actors finding this flexibility unwelcome, and led to them pressing the Commission to provide a strong policy lead in pushing through liberalization. In other words, there were only weak national pressures for decoupling. Andersen and Sitter (2006, p. 323) observe: 'The telecoms sector is perhaps the most striking example of a broader tendency for states and other actors to accept and enact EU regulations for their own motives, particularly when this is linked to market liberalisation.'
- *Autonomous integration.* This occurs when weak central demands for particular organizational and behavioural patterns combine with strong national-level pressures for the maintenance of established national practices. Situations of this sort are common in some of the more sensitive

economic and social policy spheres, including those covering industry, employment and social welfare. In such circumstances, one of two types of policy instrument is likely to be used. On the one hand, EU rules, usually in the form of directives, may be agreed, but they are likely to allow considerable flexibility in national transposition and implementation. The Working Time Directive is an example of such a rule. On the other hand, non-legal mechanisms, or 'soft law' as such mechanisms are often called, may be used via the issuing of the likes of communications, recommendations and resolutions. Member states may be pressurized strongly to abide by the requirements of the contents of such mechanisms, but the mechanisms themselves have no binding force behind them. This is one of the main criticisms made of the OMC, which relies heavily on soft law.

- *Deviant integration.* Whereas the first three types of integration involve no breaches of EU requirements, this type does. It occurs when there are strong EU requirements and expectations in respect of policy implementation, but strong resistance at national level(s) results in circumventions and non-compliance with the rules. Deviant integration is found most commonly in policy areas where strong local customs are in conflict with EU rules (such as in food processes and handling), where administrative and legal capacities are relatively weak, and in new member states (which had little or no capacity to help shape the rules when they were being made).

There are, therefore, different types of informal integration. Much of it is officially sanctioned – such as in the form of autonomous integration, which sees a range of policy mechanisms being used that are designed specifically to permit member states to differ significantly in their policy behaviour and actions. But much of it is not officially approved: it arises from inefficient and poor policy implementation.

* * *

Differentiation thus takes many different forms. It is best seen in a broad perspective, with not only its high-profile formal manifestations being recognized but also its more mundane and informal aspects. In this wider sense, differentiation is, as Andersen and Sitter suggest (2006, p. 326), 'a common and normal phenomenon'.

Differentiation arises from the heterogeneity of the EU's member states, each of which has its own policy interests and preferences. This heterogeneity has increased considerably over the years and seems likely to continue to do so in the future, with the continued movement of the EU into highly sensitive policy areas and the continuation of the enlargement process. As has been the case to date, the policy areas most likely to experience the use of differentiation in the future will be those where there are sharp differences between the member states, and those where policies display certain characteristics. Regarding differences between the member states, distinctive national preferences explain why Denmark, Sweden and the UK are the only EU-15 states not to be members of the single currency, and why the UK and the Czech Republic were the only member states not to associate themselves with the Fiscal Stability Treaty that was signed by all other member states in March 2012 (see Chapter 10). Regarding characteristics of policy areas, policies lend themselves most to the possibility of differentiation when: they are not part of the internal market core (it being generally accepted by policy actors that all member states must participate fully in the internal market – though there are disagreements over precisely what are necessary market policies); they are felt by some, but not all, member states to have significant sovereignty implications – as with foreign and defence policies and taxation policy; and when they are of particular rather than general interest – such as with fishing policy and Baltic or Mediterranean policies.

* * *

The increasing use of differentiation is usually presented by supporters of the European integration process as being regrettable. This is understandable in so far as it heralds a looser EU than integrationists would like. But differentiation is also highly functional in integrationist terms in that it enables vertical and horizontal integration to proceed among some member states when it would not be possible if all member states had to be involved. Furthermore, as in established federal systems – where differentiation is a normal feature – it opens up possibilities for bringing innovations into the EU system.

Conclusions

This chapter has emphasized the broad and complex character of the EU's policy portfolio. It has been shown that the EU has at least some involvement in just about every sphere of public policy, but that the extent and nature of that involvement varies considerably between policy areas.

It has been stressed throughout the chapter that the policy portfolio has never ceased to develop in an ever-expanding direction. A key question that arises from this is whether the expansion will continue. The undeveloped and only partially-developed nature of many policy areas certainly indicates that there is no shortage of areas where further policy development *could* occur. Moreover, the strong pressures from some policy actors for the further development of such areas as macroeconomic policy – which since the onset of the world economic and financial crises followed by the eurozone crisis has been something of a special case (see Chapters 10 and 15) – AFSJ, and CFSP and CSDP, suggest that in some areas it *will* occur, albeit sometimes on a differentiated basis.

However, such development is likely to take the form mainly of incremental advances and to be confined to policy areas where a significant EU presence has already been established. The likely development of stronger fiscal policies, especially among eurozone states, illustrates this. In fact, there is no evident thirst for major advancement into new policy areas. This is because, as was explained in the chapter, the policy areas in which the EU has little involvement are those requiring substantial budget outlays and/or are culturally-sensitive policies that are viewed by most policy actors as being best made at national and sub-national governmental levels.

Chapter 2
Understanding the Policy Portfolio

As seen in Chapter 1, the EU's policy portfolio is extensive, with just about every area of public policy featuring in some way. It is furthermore an evolving policy portfolio, with new policy responsibilities frequently being added and existing policy responsibilities being extended almost constantly. And it is also a highly complex policy portfolio, most particularly in respect of the varying degrees of EU involvement, which range from the extensive – as with agriculture, fishing and external trade – to the marginal – as with education, health and social welfare.

How is the nature of this extensive, evolving and complex policy portfolio to be understood? This chapter examines this question by considering insights provided by theoretically-based approaches. There are, of course, many conceptual and theoretical approaches that have proved useful in understanding EU politics and policies, but it is clearly not possible to review and examine them all here, in one book chapter. What we therefore do here is to explore the two most established explanatory approaches and one new approach.

The established approaches are the two classical and most widely used political science-based theoretical approaches to explaining the nature of European integration, namely neo functionalism/supranationalism and intergovernmentalism. While it is fashionable to say that these approaches have had their day, in fact they continue to have a major impact on European Studies, both in their own right and in spawning all sorts of 'sub' approaches that draw heavily on them. The new approach we explore – which we call 'federal integration' – draws from what is arguably under-used theoretical work in both economics and politics. More specifically, it draws from the classic economic integration model and from federalist theory, and suggests that these might be combined in a way that is helpful in explaining the evolution and nature of the EU's policy portfolio.

The Classical Theories of European Integration

European integration essentially involves a process wherein policies are increasingly framed and determined at the European level and impact more and more on the member states. It would therefore be expected that European integration theories would be helpful in explaining the nature of the EU's policy portfolio.

In this section, the two longest-established and most used political science-based theoretical approaches to explaining European integration are examined: neofunctionalism/supranationalism and inter-governmentalism. We suggest that each of the approaches provides useful insights into the nature of the EU's policy portfolio, but we also suggest that neither of them, whether used singly (mutually competing) or in combination (mutually complementary) provides a fully satisfactory explanation.

Neofunctionalism/supranationalism

In its classic formulation, neofunctionalism (and its close cousin, transactionalism) largely revolves around the concept of spillover, which takes two main forms. The first – functional spillover – arises from the inter-connected nature of modern economies, which makes it difficult to confine integration to particular economic sectors. Rather, integration in one sector produces pressures for integration in adjoining and related sectors. The second form – political spillover – follows economic integration and has a number of dimensions: national elites turn their attention increasingly to supranational levels of activity and decision-making; these elites become favourably disposed towards the integration process and recognize their common interests; supranational institutions and non-governmental actors become more influential in the integration process, while nation states and governmental actors become less influential; and the increasing importance of integration generates pressures and demands for political control and accountability at the supranational level. Two of the founding fathers of neofunctionalism, Ernst Haas and Philippe Schmitter (1964, p. 717), predicted the 'automaticity' of political union when transcendence (spillover into new policy areas) came into play: 'economic at first, but increasingly political as the process continues'.

Early neofunctionalism thus suggested, though it certainly did not regard it as inevitable, the progressive development of European integration. Drawing heavily on the experience of the ECSC, which had played such an important part in paving the way for the EEC, Haas (1958) and Leon Lindberg (1963) saw integration as promoting further integration. The slowing down of the integration process following the 1965–6 crisis in the EC and the world economic recession of the early 1970s was thus something of a jolt for advocates of neofunctionalism. Because, far from policy integration proceeding apace and political behaviour and decision-making becoming increasingly supranational in character, policy integration did not develop in the manner that had been anticipated, while political behaviour and decision-making remained essentially nationally-based and conditioned. As a result, neofunctionalism lost much of its gloss and appeal, not least when Haas and Lindberg themselves retreated from it and suggested that future integration theory would need to give greater recognition to, among other things, nationalism and the role of political leadership.

Since the mid-1980s, however, when the pace of integration again picked up, there has been a reassessment and a partial comeback of neofunctionalism, albeit often in a 'disguised' form. As Schmitter (2004, p. 45) has observed, 'Real-live neofunctionalists may be an endangered species, but neofunctionist thinking [is] very much alive, even if it [is] usually ... re-branded as a different animal.' Prominent among those who have been part of this 're-branding' are Wayne Sandholtz and Alec Stone Sweet (1998). Building from a broadly neofunctionalist base, Sandholtz and Stone Sweet (1998, ch. 1) conceptualize EU policy outputs on a continuum based on three interacting features of policy-making processes:

- The involvement of supranational organizations.
- The use of supranational rules.
- The involvement of transnational (transactionalist) society.

As these features become more central in a policy area, a self-sustaining dynamic is generated and the EU becomes more *supranational*. Where these factors are weak, then *intergovernmental* politics provide the bases of policy-making, and the EU more closely resembles an international organization (IO). Furthermore, Sandholtz and Stone Sweet argue that globalization, by increasing cross-border economic transactions (trade, investment, production, distribution) and communications, has instigated the removal of cross-border barriers and the creation of EU-wide rules and regulations. Integration has then been sustained in a number of ways, including by means of a continued expansion of transnational exchanges, and by the supranational institutions seeking to widen and strengthen their powers with a view to further controlling transnational exchanges. The key constituent elements of Sandholtz and Stone Sweet's approach are thus 'prefigured in neofunctionalism: the development of transnational society, the role of supranational organizations with meaningful autonomous capacity to pursue integrative agendas, and the focus on European rule-making to resolve international policy externalities' (ibid., p. 6). Sandholtz and Stone Sweet build on these elements to develop a theory in which '[t]ransnational exchange provokes supranational organizations to make rules designed to facilitate and to regulate the development of transnational society' (ibid., p. 25). Cross-border interactions explain the need for supranational co-ordination of rules: where there are many and significant interactions among societal actors (as in trade), the more likely it is that supranationalism will come into play; where there are fewer interactions (as in foreign policy), the less there is a need for supranational co-ordination and rules (ibid., p. 14).

Much recent work that is based on a neofunctionalist perspective focuses on particular policy areas and seeks to show that the encroachment of the EU into these areas and/or the increased importance of such areas in the EU's policy portfolio can, to a great extent, be explained in neofunctionalist terms. Among policy areas that have been examined are justice and home affairs policies (Niemann, 2006), health policy (Greer, 2006), competition policy (McGowan, 2007), and enlargement policy (MacMillan, 2009). Themes pursued in these studies include the importance of differing forms of spillover, changing cultural attitudes as non-EU-level actors increasingly expect EU-level policy activity, and the influential role of EU supranational institutions – especially the Commission and the CJEU. McGowan (2007, p. 16) comments 'If neofunctionalist accounts are no longer deemed to possess any adherence in terms of a macro theory of European integration, Haas' interpretation still holds analytical purchase as a mid-range theory that is applicable to the dynamics and development of individual sectors.'

An emphasis on the importance of causal factors identified by neofunctionalists does not necessarily have to be located within a full neofunctionalist theoretical framework. Taking, for example, the role of supranational institutions and transnational actors, many commentators who have been much influenced by neofunctionalism but who work within narrower frameworks have also emphasized the policy-shaping roles of these institutions and actors. So, taking supranational institutions, Giandomenico Majone (1994, 1996) is just one of a number of academic writers who have shown that the Commission has provided crucially important leadership and guidance in a number of policy areas. Majone's focus is primarily on the internal market, in respect of which he argues that the Commission's important policy role has stemmed from demand factors on the one hand and supply factors on the other. Regarding demand, Majone demonstrates rising frustration in the 1980s and 1990s in both business and national governmental quarters with the continuance of obstacles in the way of the completion of the internal market. From the late 1970s/early 1980s, big business and most national governments began to press increasingly for the open market – which had seemingly been provided for in the 1957 EEC Treaty but had not been realized – to be brought into effect. The creation of such a market was seen as being the key to tackling Europe's relative economic decline and ensuring that the continent of Europe could compete in the new and rapidly expanding high-tech, knowledge-based global markets. Regarding supply, the Commission has been, Majone shows, uniquely positioned to be able to provide the necessary policy leadership to advance the opening of the market on many fronts. Moreover, it has done so in ways that have resulted in it not just responding, as intergovernmentalists suggest, in an almost semi-automatic manner, to directions given to it by national governments, but rather in ways that have involved the exercise of considerable political discretion and judgement regarding policy choices.

The Commission has acted, and has been able to act, as a powerful policy actor for a mixture of motivational and resource reasons. At the heart of the motivational reasons, Majone and others have suggested, is that the supply of leadership by the Commission bolsters its own institutional position. This is seen most obviously with respect to the building and consolidation of the internal market, with a more integrated market being in the Commission's institutional interests because most internal market decisions are made via the policy-making process – the Community method – where the Commission's powers are strongest. But, more generally, the Commission has, acting as an 'institutional opportunist' (Cram, 1994) and 'policy entrepreneur', consistently sought to strengthen policy areas where the Community method applies. Indeed, in its 2001 *White Paper on Governance* (European Commission, 2001, p. 23) the Commission explicitly called on the Council and the Parliament to use the Community method wherever possible, but also to confine themselves in primary legislation to 'essential elements' and to leave the details to the Commission by way of 'secondary legislation'.

As for the resource reasons that make it a powerful policy actor, the Commission has, as shown in Chapter 1, an array of powerful policy resources at its disposal, including its almost exclusive right to make proposals where legislation is envisaged and its in-house knowledge of policy matters that are often highly technical and complex in nature. The Commission's resources are especially well supplied in the internal market policy area: an area that, because it is mainly regulatory in character, does not impose such direct and heavy costs on the EU budget as distributive and redistributive policies and which, in consequence, can be – but is not always – less politically sensitive.

Intergovernmentalism

Intergovernmentalism has its origins in international relations theory, and more particularly the realist tradition within that theory. Put simply, realism is centred on the view that nation states are the central actors in international affairs, and that the key political relations between states are channelled primarily via national governments. Realism does not allot much importance to the influence of supranational or transnational actors, and only limited importance to non-governmental actors within states.

As applied to European integration, intergovernmentalism thus explains the direction and pace of the integration process mainly by reference to decisions and actions taken by the governments of European states. It is recognized that other actors, both within and beyond states, can exercise some influence on developments, but not a crucial, and certainly not a controlling, influence.

Intergovernmentalism emerged as a critique of early neofunctionalism and transactionalism. For many years, Stanley Hoffmann (1966) was intergovernmentalism's foremost proponent, critiquing neofunctionalism and transactionalism on grounds

such as they underplayed the importance of the distinction between high and low politics and underestimated the diversity that exists in national interests and policy preferences. Since the early 1990s, Andrew Moravcsik (1991, 1993, 1995, 1998) has established himself as the leading exponent of intergovernmentalism. He has done so by developing a more sophisticated intergovernmental perspective, which he and others who have followed in his wake call 'liberal intergovernmentalism'. There are three main components of liberal intergovernmentalism. First, there is an assumption of rational state behaviour, which means that the actions of states are assumed to be based on using what are judged to be the most appropriate means of achieving their goals. Second, there is a liberal theory of national preference formation. This draws on a domestic politics approach to explain how state goals can be shaped by domestic pressures and interactions, which in turn are often conditioned by constraints imposed by, and opportunities provided by, economic interdependence. Third, there is an intergovernmentalist interpretation of interstate relations, which emphasizes the key role of governments in determining the relations between states and sees the outcome of negotiations between governments as being determined essentially by their relative bargaining powers and the advantages that accrue to them by striking agreements.

In terms of helping to explain the nature of the EU's policy portfolio, liberal intergovernmentalism thus suggests a step-by-step approach in which the shape of EU policies are determined: domestic interests play an important role in shaping what the governments of member states deem to be national interests; in deciding how best to pursue national interests, governments weigh the costs and benefits – which may or may not lead them to conclude that policy activity at the EU level is desirable and/or necessary; and when governments decide to engage in policy deliberations at EU level, those from the larger member states usually exercise the most influence.

Underlying this step-by-step interpretation is a core assumption about the importance of national preferences for policy development at the EU level. In broad terms, it is suggested that:

- *Little convergence of national preferences* is likely to result in EU policy activity being very difficult to achieve. Education and health – where policy activity is limited – are seen to demonstrate this in that these are policy areas where there have been no significant calls, from either elites or citizens, for EU policy activity other than in areas related to issues of the free movement of people.

- *Some, but not total, convergence of national preferences* provides foundations, albeit usually contested and often shaky, for EU policy activities. One sort of such policy activity is seen with the CAP and the Structural Funds, where the policy needs and preferences of member states are far from converging, but where a sufficient number of member states, including some large states, have had a shared interest in driving through policy activity. They have normally been able to do this only following very hard bargaining. Another sort of such policy activity is geographically-based, such as 'the Northern Dimension' and the 'Mediterranean' policies, which are of somewhat marginal interest to many member states but do not engender feelings of stiff opposition. And a third, and increasingly important, policy activity is differentiated: that is, policy activity in which only some of the member states participate fully. As is shown in other chapters of this book, EMU and aspects of AFSJ provide clear examples of differentiated policy activity. Significantly, EMU also shows how the popular and elite wills need not be in accord about what is in the national interest: both the Swedish and Danish governments have sought to join EMU, but have seen their recommendations rejected by the citizenry in referendums.

- *Complete or broadly shared convergence*, at least at the elite level, naturally provides the most fertile ground for fruitful policy development. The most obvious policy area where there has been a consensus for the building of a solid EU policy framework is the internal market. There have been, and continue to be, differences over the particular policies the internal market requires and should have, but there has never been any significant questioning of the fact that the nature and operation of the market should be at the EU's policy core.

Liberal intergovernmentalism has mainly been used to focus on major EU decisions – what Peterson and Bomberg (1999, pp. 10–16) call 'history-making' decisions. Certainly, this has been Moravcsik's focus, with his main case studies being EU treaties and the historic policy breakthroughs of the Single European Market (SEM) and EMU programmes and schedules. But, as the phrase 'history-making' decisions indicates, these types of policy decisions are not typical. Moreover, the way in which they are made is also not typical in that, unlike more routine matters, they are usually channelled via the European Council. As such, to over-focus on 'history-making' decisions is to over-emphasize the importance of the characteristics identified by liberal intergovernmentalists in framing the EU's policy portfolio.

This is not to say that all intergovernmental approaches are restricted to focusing on 'history-making' decisions. For example, a study by Treib *et al.* (2011) of why integration has progressed further in environmental policy than it has in social policy provides an essentially intergovernmental explanation based on three major political differences between the two policy areas: domestic policy legacies are more diverse and institutionally more deeply rooted in social policy than they are in environmental policy; less conflict-prone types of regulation are more frequent in environmental policy than they in EU social policy; and domestic electorates are more favourable towards regulating environmental issues at the European level than they are towards transferring social policy competences to the European level.

But, the intergovernmental explanation provided by the Treib *et al.* study of varying degrees of sectoral policy development is in a minority. Most studies of policy development that is not of a path-breaking kind but is more commonplace and routine in nature draw rather different pictures.

In these different pictures great importance is usually attached to the policy-making roles of supranational actors – notably the Commission and the CJEU – and to transnational actors such as European firms and interest groups. Moravcsik recognizes that these actors do take policy-building roles, but regards these roles as being essentially of a secondary nature. Taking the Commission, for example, he sees it as being largely a facilitator that operates within guiding frameworks laid down by the national governments. As he puts it '*intergovernmental demand* for policy ideas, not the *supranational supply* of these ideas, is the fundamental exogenous factor driving integration. To a very large extent, the demand for co-operative policies creates its own supply' (Moravcsik, 1995, p. 618; emphasis in original). Supranational and transnational actors may be important in working out the detail of policies, but they are mainly seen by intergovernmentalists as being somewhat marginal in determining which policies form part of the EU's policy portfolio, and what is the broad shape of those policies.

A key point for many of those who view intergovernmentalism in its various forms as over-stating the policy-making dominance of national governments, is that intergovernmentalism focuses too much on the formal and final stages of decision-making. If, it is argued, attention is concentrated too much on the final, decision-taking stage, then an intergovernmentalist perspective is almost inevitable because national governments – operating in either the European Council or the Council of Ministers – are bound to be seen as the key actors, because important final policy decisions are always taken by them and in their name (though usually now also with the EP when legislation is being made). But if the horizon is broadened to embrace the whole process of decision-making – which runs from policy agenda-setting through to policy evaluation – then, it is argued, the roles and policy influences of many policy actors, in addition to national governments, must be recognized. Moreover, it is also argued that intergovernmentalism pays too little attention to informal integration and the constraints that such integration imposes on the formal decision-makers. For example, Wincott (1995) suggests that the SEM programme and the accompanying Single European Act (SEA) that gave it legal force, which Moravcsik suggests were the outcome of negotiations between national actors, are in important respects better viewed as the formalization by national governments of what had been happening in practice for some time. Tony Judt (2005, p. 326) also finds evidence that key features of the European integration process have, in effect, formalized relationships that were already in place: 'What distinguished the western European economic boom [of the 1950s and 1960s] ... was the degree of de facto European integration in which it resulted. Even before the Treaty of Rome, the future member states of the European Economic Community were trading primarily with one another.'

Thus intergovernmentalism arguably focuses excessively on high-profile moments in EU history at the expense of ongoing policy processes and policy developments. One of the consequences of this is that it underestimates the policy roles of non-governmental actors. Arguably also, intergovernmentalism underestimates the extent to which the EU's policy portfolio has been developed, and is still developing. So, for example, Moravcsik (2001) suggests that 'The EU plays almost no role – at most a weak sort of international coordination – in most of the issue areas about which European voters care most, such as taxation, social welfare provision, defence, high foreign policy, policing, education, cultural policy, human rights, and small business policy.' There is unquestionably much truth in this, but the fact is that even in the short time since 2001, when Moravcsik offered this analysis, there has been considerable EU-level policy advancement in four of these areas – defence, high foreign policy, policing, and human rights. Furthermore, in another policy area of great concern to citizens – macroeconomic policy – the financial crisis that began to unfurl in 2008 has resulted in EU member states agreeing to a much greater surveillance of their national economic performances and policies than had hitherto existed.

A Federal Integration Approach

Drawing from economic theory and political science

If there are limitations to the usefulness of established mainstream political science-based theoretical work in explaining the nature of the policy portfolio, how then is its extensiveness and complexity to be explained more fully? A useful start to answering this question is to recognize that, despite the fact that the market continues to be central to the European integration project, EU policy analysts often fail to give full measure to the economic logic that drives integration. As long ago as the early 1960s, the economist Bela Balassa (1962) observed that economic integration is both 'a process and a state of affairs': when member states choose the path of economic integration, economic determinism comes into play, carrying the member states towards a 'point of no return' when economic dependence (and interdependence) in one policy area triggers economic co-ordination and interdependence in another. The remedy for the unanticipated side-effects of integration is still more integration and an inextricable web of economic relations.

It is now nearly half a century since Haas and Schmitter (1964, p. 705) famously asked: 'Does the economic integration of a group of nations automatically trigger political unity? Or are these two processes quite distinct, requiring deliberate political steps because purely economic arrangements are generally inadequate for ushering in political unity?' They advanced the thesis that 'under modern conditions, the relationship between economic and political union had best be treated as a continuum', meaning that 'definite political implications can be associated with most movements toward economic integration even when the chief actors themselves do not entertain such notions at the time of adopting their new constitutive charter' (ibid., p. 707). It is hard to quarrel with this observation, but explaining the phenomenon has proven elusive.

Despite the early recognition of the importance of looking at both political and economic factors in integration models, over the years single-discipline-based approaches have tended to prevail. So, for the most part, political scientists have placed great emphasis on the many political factors that constrain political decisions while economists have tended to minimize the significance of political variables. This impermeability of single-discipline-based theoretical work can be explained to some extent by the different instruments that political scientists and economists use in scholarly inquiry, but also by the questions they pose. Economists analysing the integration process tend to be concerned mainly with the optimum conditions for achieving economic efficiency, while political scientists are generally focused on such matters as institutional and policy-making arrangements and the power relations between political actors. In consequence, while these two branches of inquiry have contributed significantly to our understanding of European integration and policy development, there has been an inadequate attempt to develop explanatory models that blend both the economic and political components of European integration.

In this section, we suggest an approach to explaining the evolution and nature of the EU's policy portfolio that draws on both economic and political science-based thinking. More specifically, we draw on economic integration theory and federalist theory. Our approach takes into account both the compelling economic efficiency of integration and the nature of political and policy relationships in federal systems.

The key questions we seek to cover are: in what circumstances and when do economic considerations drive integration; and in what circumstances and when do political factors trump 'economic logic?

Economic integration theory

Bela Balassa's (1962) theory of economic integration has been highly influential in understanding the sequencing of European integration. His model drew and built on the writings of such economists as Jacob Viner (1950) and James Meade (1953), but introduced a dynamic element and a set of logical explanations to a non-economic audience. Balassa articulated a stage-based model (depicted in Box 2.1) in which economic integration would proceed via a predictable path of stages marked by increased integration.

The stages identified in the model are:

- *Free trade area.* A free trade area removes tariffs on goods moving between member countries.
- *Customs union.* A customs union surrounds a free trade area with common customs protections, notably common tariffs.
- *Common market.* A common market extends free movement to capital, labour and services.
- *Economic union.* Economic and social policies are harmonized throughout the member states.
- *Economic federalism.* Characterized by a common currency and common monetary and fiscal policies.
- *Political union.* Essentially, a federal state with an internal and external security apparatus.

Building on the work of Jan Tinbergen (1954), Balassa thought that the first three phases of economic integration would mainly entail member states progressively removing artificial barriers to the four freedoms – what Tinbergen had called 'negative integration', while subsequent stages would be characterized by 'positive integration', requiring interventionist governmental policies and enabling institutional structures.

A key feature of the model is its progressive nature. Successful integrationist development at any stage is contingent on the completion of previous stages. So, for example, an economic union can only be achieved once a free trade area, a customs union and a common market have been established.

Box 2.1

The theoretical evolution of political and economic integration

	Removal of internal tariffs	Common external tariff	Free flow of capital, labour and services	Harmonization of social, economic and sectoral policies	Monetary and fiscal union	Political integration
Free trade area *EEC Treaty (1957)*	X					
Customs union *EEC Treaty (1957)*	X	X				
Common market *Single European Act (1986)*	X	X	X			
Economic union *Single European Act (1986) and all subsequent treaties*	X	X	X	X		
Economic federalism *Treaty on Economic Union (1992)*	X	X	X	X	X	
Political union *Treaty on Economic Union (1992) and all subsequent treaties*	X	X	X	X	X	X

Balassa's model is thus first and foremost a theory of economic integration. It predicts that once member states choose the path of economic integration, economic determinism comes into play, carrying members towards a point of no return, with economic dependence in one area triggering the necessity for economic integration in another. While not a perfect fit, Box 2.1 illustrates how the succession of EU treaties lines up with the consecutive phases of the Balassian Model, with the EEC Treaty addressing particularly the first two stages, and each subsequent treaty focussed on policies associated with subsequent stages of integration.

How does this economic integration model differ from neofunctionalism or its 'rebranding' as 'supranationalism'? In essence, what is the value-added to our understanding of the dynamic of integration by this economic approach? Admittedly, economic integration and neofunctionalist approaches resemble each other in the earlier stages of integration in so far as both suggest that once integration occurs in particular economic sectors it 'spills over' into other sectors, and eventually entails political spillover. But, while the economic integration approach identifies economic factors as catalysts for further integration, Sandholtz and Stone Sweet (1998, p. 25), building from a largely neofunctionalist base (see discussion earlier in this chapter), suggest that 'transnational exchange provokes supranational organizations to make rules designed to facilitate and to regulate the development of transnational society'.

* * *

An obvious weakness of the economic integration model is the uncompleted nature of the EU's internal market (see Chapter 8). A key reason for this lack of completion, and for why other aspects of the Balassian model have not wholly 'worked' in the EU (see, for example, Heller and Pelkmans, 1986, p. 324), can be traced to disagreements among policy actors as to the role of the state in advancing successive economic stages. Rather than an inexorable march once economic integration has been launched, both negative integration and the policies entailing positive integration promulgated in subsequent stages in the Balassian model have proved to be highly difficult to attain and have included protracted and gruelling policy-making. So, the EU has attempted a number of approaches to open up its market – based particularly on harmonization and mutual recognition – but there has been considerable resistance from many quarters to aspects of this attempted opening. The right of establishment has been just one problem area (Schioppa, 2004), with different professional licensure requirements severely limiting free movement.

The economic union stage of the economic integration model clearly marks a very significant advance in the integration process, because it is the point at which member states must promulgate policies affirmatively rather than 'merely' strike down artificial barriers to the free circulation of goods, services, persons and capital. This stage is associated with the harmonization of such key sectoral policies as agriculture, transportation and energy, as well as policies involving the health and well-being of citizens in the form, for example, of consumer protection, environment and health care. Policy-wise, economic union is thus clearly a much more advanced and complex stage of the economic integration model, encompassing as it does all four of Lowi's (1964) policy deliberation types – distributive (as in agricultural and research policies); redistributive (as in cohesion, employment training and education policies); regulatory (as in product standards and food safety policies); and constituent

(as in the establishment of new regulatory agencies). While in the first three stages of the economic integration model, policies are easily linked to the interrelated goals of achieving European-wide efficiencies in production and marketing, the problem familiar to federal arrangements of the level at which policy responsibilities should lie begins to assert itself at the economic union stage.

Regarding this problem, the EU has largely escaped the social welfare debate between the public choice/economic liberal school and social democrat preferences. On social issues, the Social Democratic and Conservative/Confessional Parties in post-war continental Europe agreed to generous safety nets, and since then economically liberal parties in EU member states have usually only been able to govern either as minority coalition partners or – as in the UK – within a context in which public support for social welfare policies has limited how economically liberal mainstream political parties can afford to be. Thus the almost complete absence from the EU portfolio of social welfare policies is likely to be too complex for the elegant simplicity of the Balassian model. This is because, unlike most other integration projects, the EU had the advantage in the early stages of its development of a similarity in the policy approaches of its constituent units. So, in this respect, a union of values and norms existed prior to the establishment of the EU, thus diminishing the need for some EU-level policies and making the EU something of an outlier in this aspect of the Balassa model.

Agricultural and fisheries policies are among other policy areas that appear to create problems for the economic integration model, as they were established before the completion of the internal market. There are a number of possible explanations for this divergence of theory and practice, and it may be that particularistic/policy-specific explanations are the best we can achieve. So, for example, the appearance of the CAP on the policy agenda from the very outset of the EEC seems to be better explained by factors such as political expediency and the highly specific post-war experiences of food shortages than by economic integration logic (see Chapter 9 for a discussion of the rationale behind the CAP). On this basis, the early development of the CAP should not be interpreted as a challenge to the capability of the economic integration model.

The staged economic integration approach thus offers an explanation of EU policy development that is based on economic theory and highlights the underlying direction and policy linkages of much of the development. The approach is especially useful when applied to the early integration stages, but it does not lose all of its explanatory power when applied to later stages, as, for example, cohesion policy illustrates. Cohesion policy provides a useful example of the explanatory power of the economic integration approach because its main foundations were laid, just as the approach would anticipate, in the 1970s and 1980s as the common market was becoming increasingly established and as, in consequence, the policy portfolio was being widened (see Buonanno and Nugent, 2011, for a detailed analysis of the usefulness of economic integration theory, and more broadly federal integration theory, in explaining the development of EU cohesion policy). But, as has been shown, the approach has its limitations. As can be seen in Box 1.1 on page 7, EU policy development has not completely followed the path foreseen by Balassa and his followers. For example, under the economic integration model, monetary union and fiscal union should proceed alongside one another, but in the EU they have not done so. In consequence of this, since the onset of Europe's worst post-war financial and economic crisis in 2008–9, a crescendo of voices has questioned the wisdom of the EU – or at least most of its member states – for having adopted monetary union without fiscal union (Castle, 2011). It is therefore clear that, useful though it might be, economic integration theory cannot be a wholly 'stand alone' theory for explaining the nature of the EU's policy portfolio.

Arguably, the lack of parallelism between monetary and fiscal union has occurred because, despite the seemingly inexorable nature of economic integration, politics has a way of derailing 'rational' economics. So, in spite of the unfinished common market project, member states formed the eurozone – which is a later stage of the economic integration model. Similarly, since the late 1990s there has been considerable EU policy development in the field of AFSJ (political union), which has 'leapfrogged' such key features of economic federalism as the creation of a harmonized base for corporate taxation.

Economic integration theory in itself is thus not sufficiently equipped to be able to explain fully how national and EU policy-makers and societal actors have conditioned and shaped EU policy development. It needs to be supplemented by a political input.

Federal theory

There has long been interest among some European political practitioners in the attractions and merits of building European integration with federalist tools and mechanisms. During the Second World War opponents of fascism looked forward to a United States of Europe with a federalist institutional architecture that would eliminate the possibility of future European 'civil wars'. Indeed, the postwar federal movement can be traced to Altiero Spinelli and Ernesto Rossi who, while interned by Mussolini, co-authored the eponymous *Ventotene Manifesto* – 'Towards a Free and United Europe' – which proposed a federal system united by a federal constitution.

But, though widely accepted in wartime Resistance circles, the federal approach to building European integration encountered a number of obstacles when 'normal politics' re-emerged after the war. Kenneth Wheare (1953) identified experience in governing as being key to the successful establishment of federal states (because they require skilled negotiators at the helm) but, as Tony Judt (2005, p. 81) has reminded us, 'by 1945 many continental European countries had lost two generations of potential leaders: the first to death and injury in the Great War, the second to the temptation of Fascism or else to murder at the hands of Nazis and their friends'. Another problem with Resistance-inspired hopes and beliefs that European statesmen could draft a federal constitution for Europe was that it flew in the face of a basic prerequisite of federal union, namely that 'states must have experience of some political association with the states concerned prior to their federal union either in loose confederation, as with the American states and the Swiss cantons, or as parts of the same Empire, as with the Canadian and Australian colonies' (Wheare, 1953, p. 37). This absence of a past history of political association resulted in attachments to national sovereignty being, in some states more than others, blocks to embarking on an openly European federalist road in the post-war years.

In consequence, Jean Monnet's more conservative and pragmatic approach to integration was adopted. But it was an approach that, almost by stealth, was not wholly divorced from federalism, as a number of commentators have noted. Elazar (2001, pp. 36–7), for example, has observed that the EEC was established as 'in effect, confederal arrangements, based on functionalism' as a 'way out' of the post-war governance crisis. And Pinder (1993, p. 159) has suggested that 'the constitutional federalism of Spinelli and functional federalism of Monnet can be seen to be complementary'. On Pinder's point, it is certainly the case that Monnet's approach to integration was rooted in *policy*, while Spinelli's lifelong ambition was to build federal *institutions* as part of establishing constitutional federalism in Europe – and the founding treaties did create at least quasi-federal institutions.

So, federalism has long had a place in the history of European integration, and has come to do so increasingly as the integration process has resulted in an almost constant expansion of the EU's policy portfolio and of the powers of the EU-level institutions. The word 'federal' may not be much used by EU politicians, but the fact is that though the EU falls short of being a pure federal system (if there is such a thing!) it does display key federal features: power is divided between national and sub-national levels, with each level having responsibility for important and significant policy areas; there is a considerable measure of political and legal independence between the two levels; there is a rejection of majoritarian democracy; and a legal system is established in which the central law is supreme in the event of a clash between it and regional (which means national in the EU's case) law. Federalism is, however, as much a 'political' concept as it is a 'constitutional' one, with a central feature of how federal systems work in practice being the nature of the political relationships between the levels of government. Five main types of such federal relationships can be identified in the world today, All these types, we suggest – both here and at various points throughout the book – can be seen as existing to at least some degree in the EU. The five main forms of federal relations are:

- *Vertical federalism* deals with the hierarchical allocation of power between the central government and the constituent units: hence, between the EU and the member states. Much of the policy-making with which this book is concerned deals with vertical federalism.
- *Horizontal federalism* focuses on the relationship and obligations between member states as co-equals, usually with minimal involvement (if any) from the central government. Thus, horizontal federalism is somewhat analogous to intergovern-

mental relations of sovereign, independent countries. But because EU member states must interact within a system characterized by a great deal of vertical federalism (particularly as members of the internal market), 'comity' (the need for member states to respect each other in terms of law-making and the need to maintain the security of their citizens) is critical to smooth relations.

- *Dual federalism* is often described using the metaphor of a 'layer cake', which captures the notion that each constituent unit (the member state governments in the case of the EU) is 'sovereign' within its own policy sphere and 'co-equal' with the central government. Thus in dual federalism constituent units retain significant powers and delegate only specific powers to the centre – as in the EU's treaties.
- *Co-operative federalism* is often described via the metaphor of the 'marble cake', in which constituent units and the centre share responsibilities in policy formulation, planning and implementation, and their relations are characterized by a high degree of co-operation. In the EU this is precisely what occurs in many policy areas.
- *Fiscal federalism* exists when both levels of government have access to considerable funding sources and when the centre can make key decisions on taxation, transfer payments and grants so as to balance the competing governmental goals of equality and efficiency. In the EU, fiscal federalism previously did not exist – except in a very limited way via 'cohesion policy' – but since the onset of the eurozone crisis there have been persistent calls, and some policy developments, to increase the EU's fiscal powers.

The argument for the application of federal theory to European integration studies – and hence also to EU policy development – is thus persuasive. So persuasive, in fact, that it has produced a burgeoning literature in recent years, with European integration studies informed by federal theory having addressed a wide variety of matters: institutions (Sbragia, 1993; Schütze, 2009); the polity (Burgess, 2004; Koslowski, 1999); power-sharing dynamics (Bolleyer, 2009); policies (Benson and Jordan, 2008); and the virtues of comparison (Bolleyer and Börzel, 2007; Börzel and Hosli, 2003; Fabbrini, 2007; Sbragia, 2006; Scharpf, 1988).

Watts (1997, pp. 36, 42) compares the locus of policy in federations. In most federations, international relations, defence, the functioning of economic and monetary union, major taxing powers, and inter-regional transportation are the responsibility of the federal government, while education, health services, social services and labour (unemployment insurance, income security, pensions), maintenance of law and security, and supervising local governments are usually assigned to the states/provinces. Yet within this general framework, there is wide variation in terms of the distribution of powers and functions. Corporate taxation, for example, is a concurrent power in the USA, but exclusively federal in Switzerland. Taking those (relatively few) policy areas that in Box 1.2 on page 11 are categorized by limited or virtually no EU policy involvement, they are almost invariably the same policies that in recognized federal systems are the responsibility of sub-national levels of government.

Moving to how federal theory can help to explain the evolution and nature of the EU's policy portfolio, it certainly is not the case that federal arrangements invariably produce a particular balance of policy responsibilities between central and sub-central levels. Although there are (as noted in the previous paragraph) broad patterns, the precise location of policy responsibilities varies between federal systems. Moreover, it also fluctuates within them, with a tendency for federal systems to become more 'unitary' over the years, but with particular policy responsibilities sometimes shifting back 'down' to sub-central levels.

Two factors are especially important in accounting for the differences between the policy portfolios of federal systems and for differences within federal systems over time. The first is that the dozen or so of the world's states that can be called federal vary considerably in terms of their sizes, historical experiences, resources and social composition, so inevitably there are very great differences between them regarding the level at which policy responsibilities are best exercised. The second reason is that the nature of policy portfolios, and indeed also of each policy area, in federal systems is the product of a unique coalition of federal policy-makers, constituent governments, sub-regional governments and civil society actors. Unlike the situation in international relations, where alliance structures are relatively stable and thus

predictable, federal systems (if they are to be stable), are characterized by shifting alliances between north/south, east/west, rich/poor, agricultural/industrial and so on. As a consequence, federal policy portfolios can vary considerably in nature, and understanding these entails an in-depth knowledge of the circumstances applying in each case.

But, having emphasized that the policy portfolios of federal systems can vary considerably in nature, four shared features of federal systems can be identified that are helpful in furthering an understanding of the nature of the EU's policy portfolio:

- The locus of social policies in modern political systems depends in no small measure on the degree of heterogeneity of the polity. As Buchanan and Tullock (1969, p. 116) have argued: 'Many activities that may be quite rationally collectivized in Sweden, a country with a relatively homogenous population, should not be provided at the national level in India, Switzerland, or the United States.' Most EU states have relatively homogeneous populations who do not object to central decision-making for the provision of collective social goods, but across the EU as a whole, where, as in most federal systems, there is a highly heterogeneous population, few social goods are perceived as being collective. It would follow that the EU's social policy portfolio would be more like that of (heterogeneous) federal states than those of its (mainly) unitary members. Hence, social welfare, education, health and unemployment policy, and most of taxation policy too, reside with the member state rather than at the EU level. The unpopularity among their citizens of well-off member state governments (led by Germany) lending funds to assist troubled EU member states during the sovereign debt crisis from 2010 lends weight to the Buchanan and Tullock observation.
- Polities have opinions as to where they prefer policy responsibilities to be situated. As Table 2.1 shows, public opinion reveals a federal conception among Europeans in attitudes toward the preferred policy roles of the EU and the member states in key policy areas. So, a majority feel that such policy areas as fighting terrorism and crime, managing immigration, protecting the environment, and foreign affairs and defence, should be joint EU–member state responsibilities. On the other hand, the major-

ity of Europeans feel that education, health and social welfare, taxation and pensions are national responsibilities. Significantly, this shows that, on major governmental policy responsibilities, Europeans tend to think in terms of co-operative federalism.

- When the sub-national governments of a federal system cannot solve a crisis – whether it involves border security, economic management, cross-border pollution, or dealing with natural disasters – the central government usually becomes the major policy-maker and does so at the behest (and, typically, the great relief) of the constituent governments. This pattern has been exhibited in the EU in many policy areas, as Box 2.2 illustrates.

- Horizontal arrangements in federal systems (relations among regional governments that may or may not have some central government participation) arise when policy problems occur because the central government does not have the authority to step in and fix a problem with authoritative measures. There are a number of reasons why the central government may not be perceived as being a legitimate actor in a particular policy area – for example, the situation at hand may have a negative effect on only a minority of regional governments and the others may not wish to support central government's entry into the particular policy area. (Indeed, some regional governments may benefit from the policy lacuna.) Because horizontal arrangements are therefore transacted on a voluntary basis, they often lack a policing authority and are conducted through 'soft' policy measures. They can thus be inherently unstable. As is shown in Chapter 7, soft policy measures are much used in the EU, not least as part of the 'new approach' to some aspects of policy activity. Federal theory would be less than sanguine about the EU's ability to promulgate workable policy by encouraging horizontal arrangements because they are often seen as being essentially experimental, though a possible precursor to federal legislative intervention. Nevertheless, horizontal arrangements can sometimes be effective, as has been shown by Zimmerman (2002) in his study of such arrangements among states in the US system. Horizontal federalism in the EU is seen primarily in respect of AFSJ policies, particularly in police and judicial co-operation. Additionally, the EU's

'enhanced co-operation' procedure is a particularly innovative use of horizontal federalism; but as, at the time of writing, it has only been employed twice, it is not (yet) considered to be a major influence in EU policy-making. Far more common are the myriad compacts/treaties made among member states for managing seaports, rivers (flood control, pollution, fishing) and public transportation. Important examples of horizontal co-operation among member states include the International Commission for Protection of the Danube River (the EU is a member) and the Central Commission for Navigation on the Rhine (the EU has observer status). Finally, the EU is actively involved in promoting horizontal relations through its institutions (such as the Committee of the Regions) and through specific programmes such as its 'Common Strategic Framework Funds' for cross-border partnership projects.

Box 1.2 on page 11 shows several policy areas that in established federal systems are handled mainly by the central level of decision-making, and in the EU are more of a mixed competence between the central and sub-national levels. The most obvious of these areas are foreign affairs, defence, and macroeconomic and monetary policies (though there is, of course, a common monetary policy for the eurozone member states and, increasingly, common fiscal constraints). However, despite these differences, looking at the overall picture it is striking how many points of similarity there are in terms of the allocation of policy responsibilities between the two levels of government in the EU and in traditional federal systems. Taking just a few illustrative examples of this:

- Most key market policies are determined at the central level in the EU and in federal systems. This is an important point in Majone's work which examines the EU as a regulatory state, where he has drawn explicit parallels between the policy outputs of the EU and of the US federal government (Majone, 1994, 1996, 2006b). Building on Majone's work, Kelemen (2004, p. 160) has taken a similar view in his advancement of a theory of regulatory federalism.

- A number of scholars have pointed to the federal characteristics of EU environment policy and also

Table 2.1 Attitudes towards policy co-operation

Policy area	National government only (per cent)	Jointly with the EU (per cent)
Fighting terrorism	19	79
Scientific and technological research	25	72
Protecting the environment	28	69
Energy	32	65
Defence and Foreign affairs	31	65
Fighting crime	37	61
Immigration	37	60
Support for regions facing economic difficulties	37	59
Competition	35	58
Fighting inflation	40	56
Economy	44	53
Transport	44	52
Consumer protection	45	52
Agriculture and fisheries	45	51
Fighting unemployment	57	41
Health	62	36
Educational system	63	34
Social welfare	65	33
Taxation	69	27
Pensions	71	26

Notes: Results from Eurobarometer, 2010.

Eurobarometer questions (two asked):

QA22 For each of the following areas, do you think that decisions should be made by the (NATIONALITY) Government, or made jointly within the European Union: Fighting crime; Taxation; Fighting unemployment; Fighting terrorism; Defence and foreign affairs; Immigration; The educational system; Pensions; Protecting the environment.

QA23 And for each of the following areas, do you think that decisions should be made by the (NATIONALITY) Government, or made jointly within the European Union? Health; Social welfare; Agriculture and fishery; Consumer protection; Scientific and technological research; Support for regions facing economic difficulties; Energy; Competition; Transport; Economy; Fighting inflation.

Source: European Commission, 2010, p. 205.

Box 2.2

Examples of the centralizing effects of crises on EU policy development

- **Food safety**. Following European food crises in the mid-to-late 1990s, the European Food Safety Authority (EFSA) was established as an EU-wide network and information agency. Following outbreaks of the deadly E. -coli bacterial infection breakout in Germany and France in the summer of 2011 there were calls for the position of the EFSA to be upgraded to that of a regulatory agency.
- **The CFSP and CSDP**. These were both considerably strengthened considerably and given a much higher focus profile following the EU's ineffectiveness in the Balkans in the 1990s.
- **AFSJ**. This has been given much greater EU-level attention in the 2000s in the wake of: the terrorist attacks on the World Trade Center in New York in 2001, subsequently termed 9/11: the increased movement of peoples across member state borders; and immigration pressures – especially from North Africa.
- **EMU**. The first steps towards EMU were taken in the 1970s, in the form of the attempted stabilization of exchange rates through 'the Snake' and then the Exchange Rate Mechanism (ERM), both of which were driven by severe problems created by international monetary instability. More recently, the European public debt crises, which began to be seen as constituting a major problem from 2010, have resulted in the European Council, the Ecofin Council, the European Commission, and the European Central Bank all playing leading roles in the attempted development of a stronger EU, and more especially specifically eurozone, fiscal policy. So, for example, the Fiscal Compact, which was agreed by 25 EU member states in 2012, was a direct result of the eurozone sovereign debt crisis.
- **Financial services policy**. This policy area has been overhauled, and in important respects considerably centralized, as a direct result of the economic recession that began in 2007. The EU and its member states have reacted to the crisis by establishing three financial supervisory authorities with regulatory powers to supervise national agencies and the power to write legislation. (This new regime is reviewed in Chapter 8.)

---

to aspects of its energy policy (see, for example; Benson and Jordan, 2008; Kelemen, 2004; McCormick, 2001; Vogel *et al.*, 2010). Buchan (2010, p. 364), for example, has written of EU energy policy: 'By way of comparison with another federal system, the Commission will come closer to getting a standard electricity-market design for the twenty-seven EU member states than the US federal authorities have done with the fifty states.' Energy policy is thus one of a number of areas where it is evident that EU policy is sometimes more federalized than the federal system to which it is most often compared, namely the USA (see Fabbrini, 2007, for a study that draws on federal theory to compare the USA and the EU).

- College tuition is another example of a policy area that is more federalized than in the USA, with the CJEU having prohibited differential tuition rates for EU citizens as a violation of free movement of people. In the USA, public universities typically charge higher tuition fees for out-of-state residents.

Conclusions

There are many approaches to explaining the nature of the EU's policy portfolio. All provide insights into why the EU is involved in some policy areas and has little involvement in others. To the well-established explanatory approaches that were explored at the beginning of this chapter, we added a federal integration approach, which takes into account the economic logic of integration but also includes political, and more especially federal, dimensions of policy development. In setting out our approach we sought to show that, while economic integration theory lays out a (largely) convincing sequencing of policy development in the early stages of integration, it cannot fully account for the fact that some policies in the later economic integration stages have gone forward while other have not. So, for example, according to the theory, transport and energy policy would have been expected to be developed at the economic union stage, and fiscal policy at the economic federalism phase, but this has been only partially the case and they still remain largely the responsibility of individual member states. A key reason for this is that economic integration theory was not devised to explain the relationships that exist between the EU and its member states. Federal theory can help to look for patterns of policy-making and policy development in the EU that are exhibited by federal systems. A key feature of federal processes, and of the political, social and economic forces that shape them, is that they are constantly evolving. Power shifts – sometimes slowly and subtly, but at other times quickly and transparently – between the federal government and constituent units but, especially in the early stages of federalism, the overall direction of the shifts is in a generally centralizing direction (Burgess, 2004; Friedrich, 1968).

Another key feature of federal systems is the horizontal relationship among constituent units in which there is little central government involvement in some policy areas. This 'differentiation' occurs because some states wish to develop shared policies while others either oppose the policy, or the particular problem the policy has been developed to resolve does not affect them. As is shown in Chapter 5, differentiation has become an important defining feature in European integration in several important policy areas.

Our belief therefore is that federalist theory, combined with economic integration theory, can be a helpful tool for conceptualizing the EU's policy portfolio.

Chapter 3

The Principal Policy Institutions

This chapter examines the EU's principal policy institutions. It is assumed that readers have some prior familiarity with the institutions and so the chapter does not, as a general text on the EU might, examine such features of the institutions as their organizational structures and memberships. Some core information on such matters is presented in boxes, but otherwise the chapter directs its attention wholly to how the institutions affect policy matters. (Readers may wish to consult comprehensive texts such as Bache *et al.*, 2011; Nugent, 2010; Peterson and Shackleton, 2012, for in-depth treatments of EU institutions.)

There are five main policy institutions. Four of these – the European Commission, the European Council, the Council of Ministers, and the European Parliament (EP) – are 'political' institutions in that they are composed of and/or are headed by politicians and are charged with specific policy functions. The fifth institution – the Court of Justice of the European Union – is not strictly a political institution, but it is an important policy institution because of the major policy implications of some of its judgments.

Four main themes run through the chapter. The first is that the five institutions examined all exercise important, and in significant respects independent, roles across a broad range of policy areas. This distinguishes the EU's institutions from those of more traditional and conventional international organizations, for the vast majority of the latter are largely confined to service functions, dealing mainly with technical issues, in a very restricted number of policy areas.

The second theme of the chapter is that policy power is both distributed between the institutions and also shared by them. This is seen no more clearly than by comparing the EU's political institutional arrangements with those of member states. Whereas the broad pattern in member states is that the political policy-making responsibilities are, to varying degrees, separated between a readily identifiable political executive (the government) and a legislature (the parliament), in the EU there is no such simple arrangement. There is no clear EU political executive but rather three institutions, each with some political executive claims and powers: the European Commission, the European Council and the Council of Ministers. Similarly, legislative powers are shared between three institutions – with the Commission usually having exclusive legislative proposing powers and the Council of Ministers and the EP usually being the decision-takers.

The third theme of the chapter is that the balance of power between the institutions has changed greatly over the years and continues to change. In the early years of the EC, policy-making responsibilities were based mainly on a Commission–Council tandem. But this simple balance has become increasingly complex as: (i) treaty changes have strengthened the EP progressively, to the point that it now has full co-decision-making budgetary and legislative powers with the Council; and (ii) the European Council has become immersed increasingly in policy goal-setting, and sometimes final decision-making on policy. As Jörg Monar (2010) has observed, the bipolar system of the early EC gave way from the 1970s, as the EP gradually increased its powers, to an institutional triangle, and in recent years, as the European Council has become more institutionalized and more engaged across the policy spectrum, to an institutional quadrangle.

The fourth and final theme of the chapter is that the roles and powers of the institutions vary greatly between both policy areas and policy processes. Since the number of policy areas in which the EU is involved have increased greatly over the years, and since also the EU employs several distinctive policy processes, this means that any generalizations about the policy roles and powers of any of the institutions must be hedged and qualified.

The Commission

The Commission is at the very heart of EU policy processes, with very few EU initiatives or actions not involving it in at least some way. The membership and key organizational features of the Commission are set out in Box 3.1.

Policy roles and functions

The Commission undertakes many policy roles and functions. From the early policy-making phases of agenda-setting and initiation through to the final stages of implementation and evaluation, the Commission is almost invariably present, be it as the main, a supporting, or an overseeing actor.

In exercising its various roles and functions the Commission is charged to be impartial and always to act in the EU-wide interest. This can be a difficult task, since arguably there is no such thing as a collec-

tive EU-wide interest but only the interests of individual policy actors. These interests may often coincide, or at least be proximate to one another, but very frequently – both on points of general orientation and of detail – they do not. The Commission must therefore take great care and undertake a careful balancing act when initiating policies and pursuing actions. If it is to be effective it has to be seen by the member states to be acting in an even-handed manner.

A metaphor that is frequently used to capture the position of the Commission in the EU system of governance is that it is the motor of the integration process. That is to say, it provides much of the power behind the functioning and momentum of the EU. In particular, it ensures that the integration process operates smoothly and keeps advancing by bringing forward new policy proposals when appropriate, and by monitoring and keeping existing policies up to date. The metaphor is useful up to a point, but it needs to be emphasized that the motor does not always work well, with the Commission frequently being frustrated in the exercise of its tasks and in its ambitions. Sources of frustration are internal operational problems arising from such factors as understaffing, the multinational nature of the staffing, and sometimes weak leadership. Another source of frustration is that the Commission is not, except on executive matters, the ultimate policy decision-maker – and during decision-making there are many obstacles in the way of its policy ideas being accepted.

A perhaps more useful metaphor is to think of the Commission as the main day-to-day driver of the European integration process. That is, more than any other policy actor it is involved in seeking to set the directions in which the EU is to move, and identifying the routes by which destinations are to be reached. Of course, many other policy actors – most notably national governments, operating both individually and in the collective settings of the European Council and the Council of Ministers – also have, and advance, ideas as to where the EU should be heading. These other policy actors, however, are not so well placed as the Commission to be able to offer, on an independent basis, ongoing directional leadership. As will be seen below, the European Council is the Commission's main 'directional competitor', but it only has the organizational capacity to focus on

Box 3.1

The Commission: membership and key organizational features

The College

- The College of Commissioners makes up the political wing of the Commission. It consists of one Commissioner from each member state.
- With the exception of the President of the Commission, Commissioners are, in effect, national nominees, though the College as whole must be approved by the EP.
- The nominee for President is selected by the European Council, with EP approval then being necessary.
- Commissioners are charged to look to the EU-wide interest and to be impartial between member states in the exercise of their duties.
- All Commissioners have a specific area of responsibility, called a portfolio. Portfolios are assigned by the President of the Commission.
- All important Commission decisions must be approved by the College. College decisions are almost invariably taken by consensus, though majority voting is possible.

The Services

- The Commission's administrative wing is generally referred to as its services.
- The services are organized into sectoral and functional units, most of which carry the title Directorate General (DG). The numbers of units is not constant, but is usually around 45.
- The services employ just under 30,000 people. Virtually all employees are recruited according to meritocratic criteria, with appointment to 'policy grades' being extremely competitive.

'macro' issues and even then it is usually heavily dependent on the Commission for information and advice.

The Commission's specific policy roles and functions can usefully be grouped under three broad headings: initiator and proposer; mediator and broker; and executive functions.

Initiator and proposer

The Commission has a key responsibility for initiating and proposing policies. The nature of this responsibility does, however, vary considerably according to the policy-making mode that applies.

As shown in Chapter 7, there are four main EU policy-making modes: the Community method; intensive transgovernmentalism; new modes of governance; and supranational centralization. The last of these is concerned essentially with 'high-level' policy implementation (most notably with respect to competition policy and eurozone monetary policy), but the other three include policy development within their ambit. The Commission's differing initiating and proposing roles under the first three modes will now be outlined.

Starting with the Community method, which applies to much of the policy development that takes place under the Treaty on the Functioning of the European Union (TFEU), the Commission is assigned central agenda-setting and policy formulation roles. These roles are not exclusive to the Commission: other policy actors are fully able to issue policy documents if they so choose, and the Council, the EP and ordinary citizens (via the Lisbon Treaty-created Citizens' Initiative) have powers to request the Commission to bring forward legislative proposals. But little policy advance is likely to be made, and certainly little legislation will be forthcoming, without the Commission's active participation – because, in all policy areas apart from aspects of AFSJ policy, the Commission has a treaty-based monopoly on the issuing of legislative proposals.

Where, by contrast, intensive transgovernmental-ism is the policy mode, as it is most notably with respect to the CFSP, the CSDP and enlargement policy, the Commission enjoys no such privileged position. Rather, national governments share its initiating and proposing roles. Moreover, in these policy areas – especially CFSP and CSDP – there is not the natural looking to the Commission for policy leadership that exists in most other policy areas. But though the Commission's position is weaker in policy areas where transgovernmentalism prevails, it is not hopelessly weak because it has available a range of power resources it can use to enable it still to exercise a considerable influence over policy direction. The most important of these resources is an ability to link policy areas based on the transgovernmental mode to policy areas based on modes (especially the Community mode) where the Commission's powers are stronger. Another resource is that, with respect to the CFSP and CSDP, the EU's lead figure – the High Representative – has an important foot in the Commission camp by being both a Commissioner and a Commission Vice President.

The third EU policy process, new modes of governance, is used primarily for policy development where the member states are willing to go further than engaging in intergovernmental co-operation but are reluctant to pass EU legislation. Since the mid- to late 1990s, the open method of co-ordination (OMC) in particular has been used increasingly, especially in socio-economic policy spheres. The Commission's proposing and initiating positions under the open method fall somewhere between its positions in the other two modes. So, it is generally not as strong as when the Community method applies, but is stronger than when intergovernmental co-operation is used.

Mediator and broker

It is not normally necessary in liberal democratic systems for all the actors that are involved in the making of public policy to be satisfied with the content of policy for it to be effective. Indeed, a central characteristic of liberal democracy is that it rests in part on majority decision-making. But if unanimous support for public policy is not necessarily required, and in practice is not normally achievable, it is usually desirable that there is as much consensus as possible behind public policy goals and means. This is partly because it makes policy-making processes easier and partly because it facilitates policy implementation.

This desirability of consensual policy-making is particularly marked in EU policy processes. Indeed, in several policy areas it is a necessity. There are three main reasons for this desirability/necessity. First, the overriding of differences between the member states on policy questions risks alienating dissatisfied members. Such a situation is to be avoided if possible, because the EU is a voluntary organization that rests on give-and-take and on states feeling that while there may be implications from EU membership that are unwanted, on balance there is far more to be gained from being a member than not. Second, EU policy procedures are such that policies cannot be made unless there is very broad support behind them. This is most obviously the case in the Council, where policy decisions require the support of either a qualified majority of national governments or all of them. Third, EU policies are mainly implemented by national governments and agencies, so it is clearly in the interests of successful policy implementation that governments are not opposed to the policies they are being required to implement.

With so many policy actors in the EU, and with so many of them having distinctive needs and preferences on particular issues, achieving a consensus, or anything approaching one, is usually a difficult and drawn-out task, especially on major and contentious matters. Agreements often can be achieved only after extensive brokering and mediating designed to close the gap(s) between policy actors. Who is to undertake this mediation? Much depends on the nature of the policy issue and the circumstances that apply. If the content of a 'first-rank' political decision is being disputed – such as on enlargement or on treaty reform – then it is likely that the European Council President and/or the Council Presidency will need to be heavily involved if effective mediation is to be forthcoming. But most EU policy disagreements are not of this nature. Rather, they are more routine and low key, and when this is so the Commission is often highly suited to be the most effective intermediary. This is because it has available to it resources that give it advantages over other potential power brokers. Among these resources are its unparalleled knowledge of the base positions of other policy actors, its perceived impartiality, and the almost instinctive tendency of most policy actors to look to the Commission to broker compromises among the various constituencies.

Executive functions

Most of the policy executive work of the EU is undertaken not by its own agencies but rather by national agencies acting on its behalf. This delegation of routine policy implementation does not, however, mean that the Commission has no policy executive responsibilities. While it does not undertake much of the direct interaction with citizens that are the nuts and bolts of so much public administration, it does exercise an array of very important policy executive tasks. These tasks, which are of different types, are explained in Chapter 6, so they will merely be outlined here:

- The Commission checks that national law is in conformity with EU law. This involves monitoring that new EU framework legislation – which is usually issued in the form of directives – is incorporated (transposed, to use the technical term) into national law in a timely and appropriate manner, and that new national laws do not conflict with existing EU law.
- Some EU policies require not only framework laws that establish the principles of the law that is to apply but also administrative, or executive, laws – which are usually issued in the form of regulations and decisions. These laws do such things as lay down detailed specifications on aspects of EU policies and update existing laws in response to changing market conditions and/or technical advances. It is largely the responsibility of the Commission to develop and promulgate these administrative laws, acting via a Council of Ministers and EP oversight system that is described on pages 110–11 of this book. About 80 per cent of all EU laws are executive acts adopted by and issued in the name of the Commission.
- The Commission oversees the implementation of EU policies by national agencies. The purpose of this is to ensure that policies are implemented in a fair and consistent pattern throughout the member states.
- There are a small number of policies that the Commission itself implements directly. The most important of these is competition policy, which, as is shown in Chapter 8, involves the Commission taking very important decisions on such matters as whether proposed mergers between companies should be permitted, and whether trading arrangements between companies breach EU competition rules.

In undertaking these different executive tasks, the core responsibility for the Commission is to ensure that EU law is respected and applied. It is a responsibility that has to be undertaken with care and sensitivity, because it is not in the Commission's interests for poor relations to exist between it and other political and economic actors. So while the Commission can initiate legal actions against transgressors of EU law – which can range from national governments to private companies – and can issue or recommend fines on all, its customary initial preference is to act softly and see if disputed matters can be resolved by informal means.

Power resources

All policy actors need power resources if they are to be influential policy players. Without such resources there is no reason why other actors will allow themselves to be persuaded, directed, led or cajoled into adopting a course of action.

The Commission is a key EU policy actor because it is well endowed with power resources. One of these resources is its treaty powers in respect of policy initiation and proposal. Of these powers, the most important is its almost exclusive power to draft and launch legislative proposals. The main reason why the Commission is given this power is inextricably linked with another of its resources: its responsibility to act, and the general perception that it does act, in a neutral manner. Proposals and actions of the Commission may often be questioned and opposed by other policy actors, but they are not usually perceived as being partisan and self-interested in the way they often are when they stem from, say, a Council Presidency or a member state. The Commission is widely believed to be seeking to act in the general interest, and hence its policy actions have better chances than do those of other policy actors of being given a reasonable, though not necessarily uncritical, reception.

This perceived neutrality of the Commission results in smaller states in particular looking to it for leadership, and often for protection. The EU may be a union of states that in important senses are equal, but the reality is that in most policy situations and settings the larger states have the political and economic muscle to exercise greater power than do the smaller states. This looking to the Commission on the part of smaller states which, acting by themselves, are limited in their power potential, has grown in importance as the EU has enlarged over the years: 19 of the EU's 27 member states (20 of 28 when Croatia becomes a member) have populations of less than 10 million people.

Another key Commission power resource is its access to information. This is partly technical information about existing and projected EU policies: information that is gathered both from the Commission's own in-house services and from the numerous agencies, advisory networks, and consultative and technical committees clustered around it. It is partly also political information about what other policy actors want and will accept. This political information is acquired in a number of ways, but is essentially a consequence of the Commission being physically represented throughout the EU's policy-making systems – from Council working parties to EP committees – and of the policy actors in these forums usually being more prepared to impart their bottom-line positions to the Commission than they are to others involved in negotiations.

Is the Commission a policy leader?

The Commission exercises a number of functions that can be thought of as leadership functions. Most notably, it is an agenda-setter, a policy proposer, a policy mobilizer and a policy broker. Whether these functions are exercised independently by the Commission or under on instruction and direction from elsewhere has generated an extensive and vigorous academic debate, much of which is couched in terms of principal/agent theory. Using this theoretical approach, the central question is to what extent, if at all, does the Commission (the agent) exercise significant power that is independent of the European Council, the Council of Ministers and the European Parliament (which, in different ways, are formally the Commission's principals)?

In broad terms, academic answers to this question are spread along a spectrum between two 'polar' views. At one end of the spectrum are those who incline to an intergovernmental perspective of EU policy-making, and at the other end are those who take a more supranational position.

The intergovernmental perspective is advanced by, most notably, Andrew Moravcsik (1993, 1998, 1999). Essentially, he argues that the Commission is both in theory and in practice an agent of the governments of the member states, assisting them in many policy tasks but not actually taking the major policy decisions. The structural arrangements of the EU are such that the main directions of EU policies are the outcome of bargaining between national governments, meeting in the contexts of the European Council and the Council of Ministers. In addition to this structural weakness, the Commission's position has been further weakened, argue some commentators, by a conscious desire since the early 1990s on the part of some principals to temper the Commission's political powers (see Kassim and Menon, 2004; Majone, 2002).

The supranational perspective is seen in the writings of such commentators as Susan Schmidt (2004), Wayne Sandholtz and Alec Stone Sweet (1998), and Mark Pollack (2003). None of these commentators disputes that the governments of the member states are very important policy actors, but they do not see the Commission as being so controlled by them as do intergovernmentalists. The supposed 'agent' may not be able to take policy decisions itself other than of an executive kind, but there are nevertheless many circumstances in which it can be, and is, a leading policy actor. Much of the intergovernmentalists' misperception of the policy role of the Commission is, supranationalists claim, accounted for by an over-narrow view of the nature of policy-making. Certainly, most final decisions are taken by the European Council or the Council of Ministers (with many decisions of the latter being in association with the EP), but decision-taking is only the final stage in what usually is a long decision-making procedure. And in the earlier stages of that procedure the Commission is often to the fore through such activities as issuing discussion documents to float ideas (policy initiation and agenda setting), drafting policy and legislative proposals (policy formulation), and working with and through the decision-taking institutions to build support for action.

The position taken on this debate in later chapters of this book can be described as one of 'tempered supranationalism', with the Commission being seen as a central institutional actor whose autonomous policy influence has varied over time and still does vary between policy areas. Regarding variations over time, it is nigh on indisputable that the Commission was a much more dominant policy actor during the first two Colleges led by Jacques Delors (1985–93), when the single market project advanced considerably and the EMU foundations were laid, than it has been since. Regarding variations between policy areas, there are clearly some areas – most notably the CFSP and the CSDP – where the Commission exercises, at best, only a limited independent influence. Even in policy areas where the Commission has strong powers, if a sufficient number of member states are resolved to oppose it on a policy matter then it has no option than at least to amend its proposal. The Commission's inability in 2003–4 to resist 'dilution' of the terms of the EMU's Stability and Growth Pact (SGP), which was particularly pressed by the governments of France and Germany, is one such example of where a Commission proposal could not withstand member state opposition.

However, despite such qualifications about independent Commission influence, in many policy areas the Commission's position is strong. This is illustrated, for example, by the leading role it has played in recent years in driving forward the enlargement process even though several member states have made it plain that they have had reservations about the pace and extent of the programme. It is illustrated too in the many initiatives the Commission has launched with respect to the continuing opening of the internal market, even though some member states have wished for a less liberal approach to be taken on, for example, energy markets and on transport.

What then are the circumstances that are most favourable to the exercise of Commission leadership? Case studies undertaken by those who incline to a supranational position show that the Commission's potential for influential and independent action is greatest when it has strong and clear treaty-based powers; when qualified majority voting (QMV) rules apply in the Council (because the availability of QMV means that the Commission need not neces-

sarily have to weaken a proposal so that it becomes acceptable to the most reluctant state); when it is at the centre of an important policy network; when control mechanisms impacting on it are weak; when there is uncertainty of information among other policy actors; when there is the possibility of exploiting differences between member states; and when member states have come to believe that national solutions are inadequate to address the problem at hand.

The European Council

The European Council is the most visible of the EU's institutions. When the European Council meets – in what are commonly referred to as EU summits – thousands of media representatives hover in the wings, photographs of the participants appear widely in the media, and summaries of the business conducted and decisions taken are reported extensively.

This high profile position of the European Council stems from a combination of the elevated status of its participants and the important nature of the matters that come before it. The membership and key organizational features of the European Council are set out in Box 3.2.

Policy roles and functions

The treaties do not have much to say about the roles and responsibilities of the European Council. A very general description is given in Article 15 of the Treaty on European Union (TEU), which states 'The European Council shall provide the Union with the necessary impetus for its development and shall define the general political guidelines thereof.' A handful of other treaty provisions cover certain specific European Council policy responsibilities, notably in respect of the CFSP and EMU.

Clearly, Article 15 is very general. This is deliberate, since it authorizes the European Council to become involved in just about anything it wants. It is also deliberate that Article 15 is located in the TEU rather than being an article of the TFEU, as this means that most things the European Council does are beyond the jurisdiction of the EU's Court. So, the European Council operates from a very strong position in treaty terms.

But useful though the treaty base is, it is not the principal power resource of the European Council: this is its membership. The Heads of State or Government are the most senior politicians of the member states: there is no EU-level political body with comparable status. If the European Council decides to initiate an action, who is to tell it that it is exceeding its powers, or is acting unwisely? Certainly not the Commission, which recognizes and accepts the political supremacy of the European Council; certainly not the Council of Ministers, most of whose members have been appointed by and can be dismissed by the Heads of State or Government; and certainly not the EP, whose powers are very restricted in respect of much of the business with which the European Council concerns itself.

All this leaves the European Council as a sort of Board of the Directors of the EU. That is, it determines, or at least approves, the EU's strategic direction and broad policy guidelines, but the detailed working-out of specifics is left to others.

There are few major EU policy matters that – politically, not legally – do not require to be at least passed through the European Council. What the European Council does in respect of them varies considerably, ranging from making broad policy declarations to noting ongoing developments. But whatever actions the European Council takes, they are political rather than legal acts. When an action is intended to take on a legal character and have legal effect – as, for example, when the European Council issues a policy statement asserting that a higher priority needs to be given to improving labour market skills – then the matter is taken over by the EU's legislators.

However, despite the political authority of the European Council, there are circumstances in which an action that it intends to be translated into law can later run into difficulties. This may be because a commitment given by a national leader at a European Council meeting is later re-thought or even rejected by a new government that comes to power after a national election. Or it may be because a government whose leader has agreed to a general European Council policy commitment does not like the detailed follow-up advanced by the Commission

---

Box 3.2

The European Council: membership and key organizational features

- Membership consists of the Heads of State or Government of the member states plus the Presidents of the European Council and of the Commission.
- There are at least two meetings every six months. Special meetings are convened when necessary.
- Meetings are chaired by the President of the European Council.
- There are very tight restrictions on who is allowed access to meetings. (On particular matters Heads of State or Government may be accompanied by a particular minister and the President of the Commission by another Commissioner. The High Representative attends for external policy agenda items.)
- Virtually all decisions are taken by unanimity.
- Meetings are carefully prepared, mainly by the European Council President, the General Affairs Council, and the Council Secretariat.
- The President is elected by members of the European Council, for a term of two and a half years which may be renewed once.
- The powers of the President are defined only vaguely (in Article 15 TEU), but they are enough to give him/her the potential to exercise important policy roles.

---

in legislative proposals. Or it may be because the EP, which is not represented in the European Council, raises objections either to the general tack of a proposed European Council action or to its detailed application.

* * *

Becoming more specific now, the European Council can be seen as undertaking four main policy functions. The extent to which these functions feature varies from one summit to another, with some summits being relatively low key and not involving much beyond noting policy documents while others are focused on trying to take decisions on high-profile and contested issues.

Policy initiator, promoter and driver

The European Council's engagement with all dimensions of EU policy activity is seen in the way it often seeks to provide encouragement or impetus to areas it judges to be in need of advancement. This can take a number of forms, the most frequent of which is to use the Conclusions that summarize European Council deliberations and decisions to send messages to the Commission and the Council. Almost all of the sets of Conclusions are studded with phrases such as [the European Council] 'invites a report on', 'calls for action to be taken in regard to', 'confirms its full support for', 'welcomes the progress made by', 'endorses the steps taken in connection with' and so on.

Areas where the European Council has been particularly active in policy building in recent years have included: promoting measures to increase the efficiency of the internal market (notably by encouraging economic liberalization and the Lisbon Strategy/ Europe 2020); advancing the area of freedom, security and justice; and fostering, in the wake of the global financial crisis and economic recession, better EU-wide macroeconomic policy co-ordination and tougher financial regulations. The European Council's actions in these areas have been focused largely on laying down medium-to-long term policy goals, though it has sometimes taken quite specific decisions – as, for example, since 2010 in respect of loans and other forms of financial assistance to eurozone states with major public deficit and debt difficulties. (Though, as the economic and financial crisis deepened from 2011, the practice increasingly developed of key eurozone issues being discussed, and sometimes being resolved, at Heads of Government level outside of European Council meetings; in bilateral meetings (especially between the German Chancellor and French President); in small group meetings; and in Eurogroup summits of the leaders of the 17 eurozone states.)

The European Council is charged with specific CFSP responsibilities by the TEU. Article 22 is the most relevant Treaty article. It states that the European Council 'shall define the strategic interests and objectives' of the Union with regard to the CFSP.

In accordance with this remit, most summits issue policy statements on important aspects of international political affairs. Many of the external relations statements issued by the European Council include general policy directions for the High Representative (see Chapter 13) and the Foreign Affairs Council – though since most CFSP and CSDP summit statements are prepared by the High Representative and Foreign Ministers, they hardly come as a surprise to them.

Beyond the CFSP and the CSDP there are, of course, other EU external policies. The most obvious of these are trade and development, but such 'internal' policies as agriculture, environment and transport also have very significant external dimensions. These dimensions, which can be global in nature, result in the European Council often looking at them, sometimes for the purpose of considering the EU's strategic interests and preferences in relation to other economic powers, and sometimes for the purpose of co-ordinating the EU's position in crucial multi-lateral negotiating settings such as G-8 and G-20 summits and World Trade Organization talks.

Another area of external policy activity that features prominently on European Council agendas is enlargement. All strategic decisions on enlargement – from whether to accept applications in principle to determining whether negotiations have been successfully concluded – are normally taken at summits. For the most part these decisions take the form of endorsing recommendations from the Commission and/or Council of Ministers, but not always – as several different types of decision on the Turkish application demonstrate.

Contributor to the co-ordination of EU policies

As part of its activities in driving policies forward, the European Council contributes to the co-ordination of EU policy goals and activities. This is an important function because policy coordination is something of a problem in the EU, with both the Commission and the Council of Ministers often being accused of being too segmented in their approach to and treatment of certain core policy issues.

In reality, problems with linking policy areas together do not necessarily stem from a lack of sensitivity to co-ordination issues. Rather, the problem is often strongly-held differences between the member states as to what the priorities should be. When this is the case, the European Council may sometimes be said to fail in achieving adequate policy co-ordination. So, for example, when in October 2002, France and Germany succeeded in persuading the European Council to agree that the amount of spending on the CAP would be virtually frozen for the lifetime of the 2007–13 financial perspective, they were well aware that this would curtail the funds available for other policy activities, including innovation policies, that some member states thought were more deserving. But, for domestic reasons, France and Germany (and especially France), wanted to maintain high levels of agricultural support and were able to push their policy preferences through.

Although national political preferences always play a prominent role in European Council policy processes, they do not mean that the European Council cannot contribute to European policy co-ordination. So, for example, the March 2007 summit was important in bringing energy and climate change policies together by specifying that EU policy should be based on three objectives: increasing security of energy supply; ensuring the competitiveness of European economies and the availability of affordable energy; and promoting environmental sustainability and combating climate change. The latter was to be pursued by an objective of a 30 per cent reduction in EU greenhouse gas emissions as compared to 1990 levels if a global climate change agreement could be negotiated, and an independent commitment to achieve at least a 20 per cent reduction (European Council, 2007).

Final decision-taker

The European Council takes final political decisions on two particular types of matters. First, there are matters that have come to be accepted in EU quarters as being the responsibility of the European Council, or at least as needing to be channelled through it. These include: treaty reform, with all Intergovernmental Conferences (IGCs) concluding at summits; key enlargement questions, especially with respect to applications posing special problems (for example, applications from politically unstable

and/or economically weak countries); the final figures within the multi-annual financial frameworks; and(and this is specified in the treaties) a few high-level appointments, including the Commission President-designate, the High Representative and the President of the European Central Bank. Second, there are matters that, because of their importance or their political complexity and sensitivity, cannot be resolved by the Council of Ministers, or which the Council thinks should be determined by the European Council. Such matters naturally vary in nature over time, but in recent years have included whether member states have qualified for eurozone membership and, during the 2010–12 Greek debt crisis, conditions placed on the Greek government to reduce government spending and raise revenue in order to qualify for an EU rescue package (Hope and Spiegel, 2011).

Generally speaking, the European Council is better at undertaking this final decision-taking role when it focuses on 'big picture' issues than when it concerns itself with detailed policy matters. The spotlight can be too intense for policy-making on technicalities and specifics. Negotiations on the intricacies of policy are usually best left to meetings in the Council of Ministers system.

Forum at the highest political level for building mutual understanding and confidence between the governments of the EU member states

When the European Council was created in the mid-1970s it was intended to operate in a quite different way from the Council of Ministers. It should, above all, not be weighed down with detailed and technical policy issues. Rather, it should be a somewhat informal gathering in which national leaders could get to know one another and discuss broad issues without being subject to institutional rules or constraints.

EU enlargement, the increasing institutionalization of the European Council, and the holding now of most meetings in the Council building in Brussels rather than in grand countryside residences in the Presidency state, have combined to consign much of this intended horizon-gazing role of summit meetings to the past. Even the most strictly minimalist full summit meeting involves 29 participants (and will involve 30 when Croatia joins): the Heads of State or Government, the European Council President and the President of the Commission, plus interpreters and Council Secretariat officials. But the function of acting as a forum for building mutual confidence and understanding has not completely disappeared. It is supplemented more than it was originally by other forums that also perform this function – the most important one being the virtual explosion in bilateral meetings between national leaders – but summits still do offer, especially on their margins rather than in formal sessions, opportunities for national leaders to get to know, and to become more comfortable with, one another. Arguably, this function is even more important now than it used to be given that, with so many member states, the faces around the summit table inevitably are changing constantly.

The Council of Ministers

It is within the framework of the Council of Ministers – or 'the Council', as it is conventionally known – that the continuing and ongoing bargaining and negotiation between the governments of the member states that is such a feature of EU policy processes is mainly conducted.

The responsibility of the Council of Ministers for providing the framework for the routine and day-to-day operation of relations between the governments of the member states results in it being a core EU decision-maker. The decisions it takes, which are many and various, include decisions made in association with the EP, under an instruction from the European Council, and in the Council's own name and on its own initiative.

The membership and key organizational features of the Council of Ministers are set out in Box 3.3.

Policy roles and functions

The business to which the Council attends is highly diverse in nature. Hayes-Renshaw and Wallace (2006, pp. 322–7) suggest that the business can be grouped under four main function headings: the Council as legislator; as executive; as helmsman

('devising the big bargains that orient the future work of the Union' – ibid., p. 325), and as a forum ('providing an arena through which the member governments attempt to develop convergent national approaches to one or other policy challenges in fields where the Union does not have clear collective policy powers' – ibid.). A revised threefold categorization is used here, with the steerage function being assigned to the European Council (an assignment that Hayes-Renshaw and Wallace themselves recognize, but they treat the European Council as the most senior formation of the Council rather than as a separate EU institution).

Legislator

As shown earlier in the chapter, the Commission is the principal originator of EU legislation. The Council can, and does, request that the Commission bring forward legislative proposals on matters, but it cannot insist on this and nor can it participate in legislative drafting.

However, while the Council's role is limited in respect of the initiation of legislation, it is crucial in respect of the making of legislation. For the EU has, in effect, a bicameral legislature, with the Council and the EP being the two 'houses'. All significant and political proposed legislation – that is, non-administrative legislation – is referred by the Commission to the two institutions, with the approval of the Council always being necessary if the proposal is to become law and with the approval of the EP usually being necessary.

Much of the work of the Council in exercising its role as law-maker is thus necessarily focused around two core tasks. First, the task of establishing Council positions on legislative drafts. The ways in which this is done are described below. Second, the task of reaching agreement on the contents of legislative drafts with the EP. The latter task involves extensive liaison and negotiation between representatives of the two institutions, most of which on the Council side is undertaken by COREPER 1 officials (especially from the Presidency) and the Council Secretariat.

Executive

EU policies are implemented in a variety of ways. Generally, however, as described earlier in the chapter,

The Council of Ministers: membership and key organizational features

The work of the Council is undertaken through an internal, three-level hierarchical system consisting of, from the bottom upwards:

Committees and working groups
These are composed of governmental officials from the member states. Committees provide specialist advice while the main job of working groups is to examine in detail Commission proposals for legislation.

The Committee of Permanent Representatives (COREPER)
This body gathers in two formations, each of which normally meets at least weekly. COREPER II, which consists of the member states' Permanent Representatives to the EU, deals with most political, sensitive and intergovernmentally-based policy issues; while COREPER I, which consists of the Deputy Permanent Representatives, deals with most of the more routine policy issues, including legislative proposals.

Ministerial meetings
Ministers meet in ten formations – see Box 3.4.

All Council decisions must be taken formally in ministerial meetings, though agreements are usually reached informally on most agenda items before ministers convene. Precisely what proportion of agenda items are agreed beforehand, and listed as 'A' points, varies between Council meetings according to how controversial are the issues that are tabled. However, if attention is restricted merely to legislative proposals then, on average, between 85–90 per cent of EU acts are adopted by ministers as 'A' points (see Best and Settembri, 2008b; Häge, 2008; Hagemann and De Clerck-Sachsse, 2007).

There are around 100 formal ministerial meetings per year, plus 10 or so informal ones. The formations that meet most frequently are General Affairs, Foreign Affairs, and Economic and Financial Affairs.

Ministerial meetings can be almost chaotic affairs, with as many as 150 people in the room (excluding translators), with the compositions of national delegations often changing in response to agenda items, and with people gathering in huddles to discuss matters while meetings are ongoing.

whatever may be the particular nature of implementation arrangements, the Commission is usually the main policy actor at the EU level.

But despite the Commission's lead position with respect to policy implementation, the Council also undertakes some significant implementation tasks. A few of these duties are in policy areas in which it is not always clear precisely where implementation responsibilities lie. One of these policy areas is EMU, where the Commission, the European Council, Ecofin, the Euro Group and the European Central Bank (ECB) all have implementation responsibilities of some kind, several of which overlap. This uncertainty formed part of the background to why the Commission referred the Council to the Court of Justice in 2004 for allegedly failing in its implementation responsibilities, for not having fined France and Germany for breaching the excessive deficits procedure of the Stability and Growth Pact. The Court's ruling was largely in favour of the Commission, though it did not go so far as to suggest that the fines must be paid (regarding this case, see Dougan, 2005, pp. 93–5). Subsequent to the ECJ's ruling, the terms of the SGP were relaxed by the Ecofin Council in a mixed policy-making/policy implementation decision.

Another area where the Council undertakes implementation tasks, at least to some degree, is with respect to the policies that are part of the Europe 2020 Agenda. Consisting mainly of a mixture of economic efficiency and employment-promoting policies, Europe 2020 – which has succeeded what was previously called the Lisbon Strategy (see Chapters 7 and 9) – is based largely on the OMC. The OMC does not, for the most part, rely on EU laws but rather on voluntary policy instruments in such forms as communications and recommendations. But voluntary though most OMC instruments might be, member states are expected to abide by their provisions. To try to ensure that they do so, relevant configurations of the Council receive reports from the Commission that are used to try to pressurize laggards to fall into line.

The policy area where Council executive action is seen most clearly is the CFSP and accompanying CSDP where, since 2003, the EU has launched almost 30 operations of various kinds. Comprised of mixtures of armed personnel, policemen, special representatives and administrators, these operations have, since the Lisbon Treaty, come under the day-to-day administrative control of the High Representative. Political control is, however, very much exercised by the Foreign Affairs Council.

Policy forum

It has long been the case that discussions at Council meetings, especially at senior levels, have often ranged beyond narrowly-framed agenda items. Sometimes open discussions on general and overarching policy issues are timetabled and on occasion specific discussions are just naturally broadened out. In such wide-ranging discussions, it is possible for policy options to be explored and considered on exploratory and non-committal bases. The outcomes of such discussions can take various forms, ranging from a recognition that there are too many differences around the table to allow policy progress to be made in the foreseeable future, to a request to the Commission to research the policy issue in question and to present a paper, report or set of recommendations at a future meeting.

Hayes-Renshaw and Wallace (2006, p. 327) make the point that in recent years a new element has been added to this role of the Council as policy forum, 'namely the role of the Council as a forum for permanent dialogue in policy fields where there is very little prospect of collective powers being agreed'. An example of this is in respect of Europe 2020, which contains policy issues where some governments are unwilling to accept EU legislation – for example, in areas such as

---

Box 3.4

Formations of the Council of Ministers

General Affairs

Foreign Affairs

Economic and Financial Affairs (Ecofin)

Justice and Home Affairs

Employment, Social Policy, Health and Consumer Affairs

Competitiveness (internal market, industry, research and space)

Transport, Telecommunications and Energy

Agriculture and Fisheries

Environment

Education, Youth, Culture and Sport

---

employment promotion and social protection – but where it is recognized that co-ordinated policy action could be beneficial. Accordingly, Council formations dealing with such issues sometimes have relatively open-ended discussions about options and possibilities.

However, though relatively informal and broad-ranging policy discussions are sometimes possible, enlargement has resulted in Council meetings tending to become more formal in nature over the years. This is especially the case at ministerial level, where the almost cavernous nature of some of the meeting rooms and the large number of people in the rooms during meetings makes informality and spontaneous exchanges difficult to achieve. Accordingly, the venue of the Council's role as a policy forum has partly shifted from formal meetings to other forms. One of these is informal gatherings of ministers, which have greatly increased in number in recent times.

Council decision-making

Council decision-making can be very difficult. The main reason for this is that the officials and politicians who represent the member states in the Council system, and who are the Council's main policy actors, have a potentially very difficult balancing act to perform. On the one hand, they must protect and advance the policy interests and goals of their governments – interests and goals that often greatly diverge. And on the other, they must try and reach EU-wide agreements.

How are these potentially clashing requirements on Council policy actors reconciled? How, in short, does the Council make decisions? It does so in a number of ways. Some of these are specified in the treaties, some in the Council's Rules of Procedure, and some are not documented at all but rather have just evolved as working practices to meet practical needs.

A very important part is played by the Council's Presidency. Prior to the coming into force of the Lisbon Treaty, the Presidency rotated among the member states every six months. This arrangement was modified by the Treaty to become a team Presidency made up of three member states for a period of eighteen months, though with each of the three taking a turn to be the lead Presidency state for six months. The main purposes of the Treaty change were to improve Council medium-term policy planning and actions, and to spread the administrative burden that sole occupation of the Presidency imposed on states – especially small member states. Occupying the Presidency is a considerable burden for the lead state because it convenes and chairs virtually all Council meetings at all levels other than meetings of the foreign ministers, which since the Lisbon Treaty have been chaired by the High Representative of the Union for Foreign Affairs and Security Policy. But while occupying the Presidency imposes burdens, it also provides opportunities, not least in respect of influencing the nature and success of the Council's policy work. Presidencies cannot completely control Council policy development, since much policy business is ongoing and/or shaped by other policy actors and events. But Presidencies can, through sensitive operation, do much to influence the nature of the policy agenda and the progress made with policy issues. (On the influence of Presidencies on policy-making, see Schalk *et al.*, 2007; Thompson, 2008; Warntjen, 2008).

Another area where treaty stipulations are very important is in the formal rules for taking decisions. These rules cover three sets of questions:

- In what circumstances can the Council decide by itself and when must it seek the opinions of other institutions? In general, the Council is most independent when it is taking decisions that do not involve making EU law, for then it normally is not obliged to refer matters to other institutions – though in practice it usually keeps the Commission and the EP fully in the picture. The CFSP and CSDP are the most prominent policy areas where the Council enjoys considerable independence, though even here it is often dependent on EP approval when it wishes to go beyond the issuing of declarations to launching operational missions. The Council is least independent when EU legislation is being made via the ordinary procedure, for then no measure can be adopted unless the Council and the EP are fully agreed on its content.
- When must Council decisions be made unanimously, and when can they be made by voting? CFSP and CSDP decisions must be made unanimously, apart from some policy implementing decisions. In other policy areas, unanimity is required for most non-legislative decisions, and for legislative decisions where the TFEU so stipulates. Important policy areas where the TFEU does make this stipulation include taxation, social security and citizens' rights.
- When voting is permissible, what are the voting provisions? These are set out in Box 3.5.

However, formal rules provide only a partial insight into how the Council operates and makes decisions. They do not bring out the many informal processes and understandings that are a central feature of the Council's work and that are vital in enabling the member states to make policy progress. This informal side of the Council is no more clearly demonstrated than in the constant efforts that are made, at all Council levels, to find consensus on policy questions, even when it is possible for decisions to be taken by a vote. For a number of reasons – including retaining the confidence of member states in the EU system, and not wishing to impose unpopular polices on those who are responsible for implementing them – there is always a preference among Council members for taking decisions by general agreement whenever possible. This preference is very much part of the political culture of the Council, of 'how things are done'. There is, as Heisenberg (2005) has put it, a

Box 3.5

Voting provisions in the Council of Ministers

On a few matters, notably procedural ones, simple majority voting rules apply, with one member per vote and a nominal majority being sufficient. More usually, however, a qualified majority voting (QMV) system applies, which has three component parts.

- Each member state is allocated a fixed number of votes, with a specified total number of votes being needed for a majority to be attained. The four largest states – France, Germany, Italy and the UK – each have 29 votes, with the allocations of the other states being tapered down in very approximate relation to size until the EU's smallest member state, Malta, is reached, with three votes. In the EU-27, 255 of the total number of 345 votes are required for a qualified majority to exist. A blocking minority thus requires 91 votes.
- Where votes are on Commission proposals, a majority of states must give their support; and where they are on Council proposals, two-thirds of the states must do so.
- Any member state can require that the QMV majority comprises votes of states representing at least 62 per cent of the EU's total population.

Under the Lisbon Treaty, from 2014 this voting system is to be replaced by a new QMV system in which a majority is defined as 55 per cent of the member states representing 65 per cent of the EU's total population. However, until 2017, a state dissatisfied with a decision taken according to the new voting rules will be able to insist that the old rules be applied. In addition, under a revised version of a safety mechanism created in the 1990s and known as the Ioannina Compromise, 55 per cent of member states constituting a blocking minority will be able to ask for a delay to and reconsideration of draft legislation before it is adopted.

'culture of consensus', in which negotiations are conducted whenever possible until a consensus can be reached. Accordingly, though over 90 per cent of Council legislative decisions are now adopted on a legal base where QMV is available (Pollack and Ruhlman, 2009), in practice votes are used explicitly in only about 15 per cent of the cases where they could be, and in about another 10 per cent of cases they are used implicitly in the sense that states that are known not to be in favour of a proposal choose not to register a dissenting vote. (There are many studies that present more detailed figures on voting in the Council than can be given here. See, for example, Hayes-Renshaw and Wallace, 2006, pp. 259–97; Naurin and Wallace, 2008, especially chapters 2, 3, and 4.)

When there are formal votes, it is unusual for more than a couple of states to abstain or vote against, and their reasons for withholding support are as likely to be based on technical grounds as they are on political ones. Sometimes votes against are not even 'real' dissenting votes, because it is not unknown for governments to vote against a proposal not because of deep opposition to it but rather to satisfy a domestic audience – 'we did our best, but "Brussels" has imposed this measure on us'. On occasion, a negative vote against a proposal may be said to have been almost stage-managed by a seemingly – but not necessarily truly – dissatisfied government! (See, for example, Charlemagne Column, 2009.)

It might have been expected that the 2004/7 enlargement would have increased the use of voting, bringing in as it did not just many more member states but also member states that in important respects had different policy needs from the EU-15. No such increase has occurred, however. Or, to be more accurate, no such increase in formal voting has occurred. What has occurred, though, are two significant developments that may be said to amount to an increase in *de facto* voting. First, the shadow of the vote has become increasingly important, with the possibility of a vote being used resulting in member states in a minority being increasingly willing to negotiate the best deal they can get rather than be formally outvoted. To put this another way, once a majority threshold has been reached, minority states are more likely to become compliant and less likely to want to register formal opposition. This is especially so in Council configurations where a lot of legislation, including much highly specific legislation, is passed, and less so in configurations where there is less legislation and where much of what there is covers politically sensitive ground (see Deloche-Gaudez and Beaudonnet, 2011). Second, there has been an increased practice of governments that are not supportive of proposals registering their opposition not by means of casting dissenting votes but through the issuing of what amount to dissenting statements attached to the published minutes of Council meetings (see Hagemann and De Clerck-Sachsse, 2007, p. 14). This practice enables governments to signal their concerns to other policy actors and domestic audiences, while at the same time also letting them be seen by the governments of other member states as abiding by the consensual culture of the Council and being helpful in difficult circumstances.

The searching for consensus is therefore perhaps not quite as overwhelming as it was, but it is still very important. This means that there is rather more conflict in the Council than is evident from public voting records. But the searching for consensus comes at a price, because it involves an ongoing process of interaction between the member states that is very labour-intensive and time-consuming. The interactions occur at all Council levels, and range in kind from very preliminary exchanges of ideas in corridors or over coffee to explore what might be possible, to Presidency- and/or Council Secretariat-led 'confessionals', in which governments of member states reveal in confidence their 'base line' positions. As Hayes-Renshaw and Wallace (2006, p. 17) put it:

> The whole system depends on a crucial assumption that there is give and take between the positions of the member states, and that, whatever the starting positions of the members, there is both scope for their positions to evolve and a predisposition to find agreement. Thus atmospherics, mutual confidence and reciprocal trust are important ingredients.

As for how the governments of individual member states relate to one another in the Council, there are no permanent coalitions or groupings. Analyses of voting figures show no fixed groupings between member states along such lines as north/south, rich/poor or large/small. Rather, governments ally themselves, or at least identify with one another, in different ways on different issues.

The European Parliament

The European Parliament used to be more of a special sort of advisory body than a 'proper' parliament. However, treaty reforms over the years have increased its powers greatly, to such an extent that in many respects it is now a much more important policy actor with regard to EU policies than are most of the parliaments of the member states with respect to national policies.

The membership and key organizational features of the EP are set out in Box 3.6.

Policy roles and functions

As the sole directly elected EU institution, the EP is the most obvious, and arguably the only, full 'representative of the people' in the EU's policy-making system. In undertaking this representative role, the EP has three main policy functions: policy and law-maker; budget-setter; and controller and supervisor of the executive. Only the first of these tasks is considered here. The budgetary function is examined in Chapter 14, while the controlling and supervisory function, which is a somewhat indirect policy function, is touched on at various points in the book.

Policy and law-maker

The EP is sometimes portrayed as being too reactive a policy actor. That is, it is seen as spending too much of its time responding to the policy initiatives of others and not enough time on developing and promoting its own policy ideas. This portrayal is too harsh. One reason it is so is that legislatures throughout the democratic world are more reactive than proactive. It is in the nature of modern political systems that political executives are normally expected to provide the main policy leads, and are more equipped than legislatures to do so. Although the EU does not have the same sort of political executive as do national political

Box 3.6

The European Parliament: membership and key organizational features

There are (as of 2012) 754 Members of the European Parliament (MEPs), who are directly elected for a fixed five-year term in the June of years ending in four and nine.

- In EP elections, national rather than European political issues prevail in practice.
- In the EP, virtually all MEPs are members of one of the Parliament's 7–9 (the number varies) transnational political groups. The three largest groups represent Europe's three main ideological currents: centre-right MEPs are located mainly in the Group of the European People's Party (EPP), which since 1999 has been the EP's largest group; social democratic and socialist MEPs are located mainly in the Group of the Progressive Alliance of Socialists and Democrats (S&D), the second-largest group; and liberals are located mainly in the Group of the Alliance of Liberals and Democrats for Europe (ALDE), the third-largest group.
- The work of the EP is mainly undertaken in three organizational settings:
  - *Political groups*. Political groups attempt to agree positions on upcoming EP business. Once a group position is reached, group members are expected to follow the group's line. In practice, internal group discipline is weaker than party discipline in the parliaments of the member states – primarily because there is no party-based EU government – but none the less group membership is by far the single most important general factor shaping the voting patterns of MEPs (see, for example, Hix and Noury, 2009; Hix *et al.*, 2007).
  - *EP committees*. There are different sorts of committees in the Parliament, but the most important are the 20 or so standing committees (the number can vary) that deal with policy business before it is referred to plenary session. The main work of the committees is to prepare reports and recommendations – whether it is in the context of a legislative procedure or on an initiative of the Parliament itself – for an upcoming plenary meeting.
  - *Plenary sessions* (formally called *part-sessions*). Every month (apart from August) there is a week-long plenary session in Strasbourg. There are also four or five mini-sessions each year (each usually lasting for two days) in Brussels. It is in plenaries that official EP decisions are taken, though most of what is done in plenary is prepared, guided and shaped by what comes out of the standing committees.

systems, a not dissimilar situation applies in that the Commission, the European Council and the Council of Ministers all have strong positional and power resources that can be used for policy initiation purposes. While the EP has some policy initiation resources of its own – not least its ability to cite its democratic base – these are not comparable with those of the other institutions.

A second reason why the portrayal of the EP as being too reactive is over-harsh is that it does proactively input into EU policy development. This is done primarily by seeking to influence the thinking of the Commission as to what, in what form, and when, legislative proposals should be brought forward. The Commission does this in a number of ways. One way

is by engaging in general policy and legislative discussions with Commission representatives, most commonly in EP committees. Another way is by advancing legislative ideas formally. The Parliament can do this by adopting an own initiative report on a matter and hoping the Commission acts on it, or it can act under Article 225 of the TFEU which states that 'The European Parliament may, acting by a majority of its component members, request the Commission to submit any appropriate proposal on matters on which it considers that a Union act is required for the purpose of implementing the Treaties.' Political realities make it difficult for the Commission not to act on an Article 225 request, though in practice few such requests are made –

mainly because absolute majorities in the EP can be difficult to obtain. A third way in which the EP can seek to influence the Commission at pre-proposal stage is via the annual budgetary cycle, with it being accepted that, within certain limitations, if the EP puts appropriations into the budget for items for which there is no legal base, then the Commission and the Council will seek to provide the necessary base. And a fourth way is through discussions between MEPs and the Commission in EP committees on the Commission's annual work programme and through the plenary resolution that is subsequently voted on the programme.

The importance of these mechanisms was given potential added bite by a new framework agreement the Commission and the EP signed in 2010 on relations between the two institutions (European Parliament and European Commission, 2010). Running through the agreement was an emphasis on there being a 'special relationship' between the two institutions, on them both being attached to intense and structured inter-institutional co-operation at all levels, and on the Commission committing to taking into account the Parliament's priorities and views on policy and legislative matters as fully as possible.

Once the Commission has issued a legislative proposal, the functions and powers of the EP depend on the legislative procedure that is used. The nature of the EU's three legislative procedures – consultation, ordinary and consent – and of the EP's varying powers within them are described in Chapter 5. It is sufficient to note here, therefore, that its powers have grown greatly over the years, and that in respect of most legislative proposals the EP now shares full co-decision-making powers with the Council.

It is not possible to be precise about the impact of the EP on EU policy and legislation. One reason for this is that a great deal of EP activity that is focused on exercising policy and legislative influence cannot be monitored or measured because it is carried out via informal contacts with Commission and Council representatives. That is, EP influence is exercised not just by the formal acts of amending, approving and rejecting legislative proposals. Second, statistical analyses designed to measure the EP's influence are plagued with methodological difficulties. The difficulties do not so much concern outright rejections by the EP of

legislative proposals, which are obvious and which in any event are not common – about one per year on average. Rather, the difficulties concern estimating the influence of EP amendments on legislative proposals. Among the problems are: identifying amendments that are laid down by the EP for bargaining purposes rather than in any real hope that they will be accepted by the Council; distinguishing between politically important amendments and those that are essentially technical or procedural in nature; and how to calculate when a compromise on an amendment is reached in Council–EP negotiations.

Despite these difficulties, at least some indication of the very considerable influence exercised by the EP can be gauged from the fact that under the ordinary legislative procedure only about 15 per cent of legislative proposals go to the final conciliation stage; that is, some 85 per cent of legislative proposals are in an acceptable form for the EP by the end of second reading. Of the 15 per cent that go to conciliation, the EP claims that about a quarter of its amendments are accepted as proposed, about half are accepted following a compromise with the Council, and about a quarter are withdrawn.

Though these figures indicate a considerable EP influence on the content of EU legislation, it is important to note that the EP's influence is usually not as strong when the ordinary legislative procedure does not apply. So, for example, while the EP has a veto power under the consent procedure – which applies to such important policy matters as EU accessions, many agreements with third countries, and financial frameworks – the EP is usually only marginally involved in the processes leading up to the decisions that are presented for its consent; that is, it is often put in what virtually amounts to 'take it or leave it' situations.

It is important also to note that there are crucial areas of EU policy that do not involve much legislation, and where this is the case the EP is generally in a weak position. So, for example, in spite of some strengthening of its position by the Lisbon Treaty, the EP is largely confined to monitoring and consultative roles in respect of the EU's foreign and defence policies. Much the same applies to EMU, with the EP largely having been a spectator to the essentially intergovernmental processes that have over the years built, and more recently sought to protect, the EMU system. The EP is similarly marginalized and confined to an essentially advisory role regarding most aspects of the Europe 2020 Agenda, which is based much more on intergovernmental co-operation and on the OMC than it is on EU legislation.

* * *

An important point to be emphasized about the EP is that the influence it exercises stems not just from its powers but also from the position it occupies in the EU system of governance. This position is one in which, unlike most national legislatures in Europe – that operate within the framework of parliamentary political systems – the EP is not controlled by an executive. At the national level, governments can usually rely on the support of their parliaments for most of their actions. This is because of strong party loyalty and discipline, which is brought about by a mixture of ideological attachments and organizational pressures. However, in the EU there is no party-based government that can use such attachments or pressures. Rather, political executive functions in the EU are undertaken mainly by the politically 'neutral' Commission and the politically heterogeneous Council of Ministers. Neither is looked on by MEPs as a political body to which loyalty must be either accorded or withheld. In fact there is little natural ideological identification between MEPs and either the Commission or the Council (even though all three institutions have included centre-right political majorities since 2004), while organizational pressures on MEPs to back either the Commission or the Council are virtually non-existent – with, for example, the continuity in office of no government being dependent on EP support, and with neither the Commission nor the Council being able to persuade MEPs to fall into line with tempting offers of future career advancement for those who are loyal. In consequence, the EP as a body is much more independent of the political executive than are national legislatures in the parliamentary and semi-presidential systems of the EU member states. (Cyprus, with a 'purer' presidential system, is the exception.) This independence makes the EP more like the legislatures in the many presidential systems that exist in countries outside the EU (see Siaroff, 2003, pp. 296–302 for classifications of systems under presidential, semi-presidential and parliamentary headings).

The Court of Justice of the European Union

It may appear initially to be somewhat odd to include the EU's Court in a chapter on the main EU institutional policy actors. After all, is the role of courts not to interpret the law rather than to make it? Well, the EU's Court is indeed charged with interpreting the law but, for reasons that will be explained below, the room for manoeuvre available to the Court when it interprets EU law is sometimes so wide as to result in its judgments amounting to new law-making. In a number of respects this judicial law has made important contributions to the nature of the EU's policy portfolio and to EU policy processes.

For the most part, the contributions of the Court have been in the direction of advancing European integration. As Kelemen and Schmidt (2012, p. 1) have put it:

> The European Court of Justice (ECJ) has played an indispensable role as a motor of European integration. In judgments addressing the balance between national and supranational authority, the European Court – not unlike high courts in other federal-type systems.... – has demonstrated a bias in favour of centralization. Again and again, the ECJ has demonstrated the independence and the authority necessary to push the scope and depth of European integration beyond what European Union law-makers had intended.

Under the EU's treaties the Court of Justice of the European Union (CJEU) – which was called the European Court of Justice (ECJ) prior to the Lisbon Treaty (and is still often informally, and sometimes mistakenly, referred to as such) – is a single entity. However, in reality, the CJEU consists of three courts: the most senior is the Court of Justice; then there is the General Court, which prior to the Lisbon Treaty was called the Court of First Instance (CFI); and then there is the European Union Civil Service Tribunal (CST), whose work is confined to internal staff cases. This situation clearly makes for some confusion, especially as the name of the most senior of the three courts, the Court of Justice, is very similar to the name of the institution as a whole.

The membership and key organizational features of the Court of Justice and the General Court – which are the courts that concern us here, since they are the ones whose judgments can have policy and policy process implications – are set out in Box 3.7.

Policy roles and functions

It is not possible to ascribe policy roles and functions to the Court in the way that it is to the other institutions that have been examined in this chapter, because the Court is not assigned, and does not see itself as having, such roles or functions. Its job is to interpret EU law.

But in interpreting the law, the effect of Court judgments can sometimes be to change what was thought to be the law, or to extend the law, in important ways. This important law-making effect of some Court judgments is odd at first sight because case law has traditionally not been a major source of law in most of the EU member states. It is so in the EU itself because the two main sources of EU law – the treaties and EU legislation – are in some policy areas and in some respects imprecise and/or incomplete. This is for two main reasons. First, differences between EU policy actors can result in agreements on aspects of the treaties and of legislation only being possible by compromises that require fudging and include language that is open to more than one interpretation. Second, the speed of change in some spheres of EU activity makes it very difficult for the written law to keep abreast of developments.

In the different types of over 1,000 new cases that come before the Court each year – cases of first and only instance, cases of appeal, and preliminary rulings – the Court is thus often enabled and/or obliged to provide clarifications of, and plug gaps in, EU law. For the most part it is the Court of Justice rather than the General Court that is the most important court because, as the more senior court, it deals with most cases raising major issues – including those of a constitutional and/or political nature. It is the more important court also in that General Court judgments are subject to appeal to the Court of Justice on points of law. When, therefore, reference is made to EU law arising from judicial interpretation, the reference is normally to Court of Justice case law.

Box 3.7

The Court of Justice of the European Union: membership and key organizational features

- The membership of both the Court of Justice and the General Court consists of one judge per member state. Judges are appointed – in practice on the basis of nominations from each national government – for a six-year term of office, which is renewable. The judges must be qualified in the law and have experience in practising the law, but they need not have extensive judicial experience. There is no evidence that ideological orientation has played a significant role in influencing nominations, in the way that it does in the USA in nominations to the Supreme Court.
- Most of the work of the two courts is conducted in chambers – that is, by small groups of judges – rather than in plenary sessions. It is also conducted mainly in private rather than in open court.
- Court decisions can be taken by majority vote if necessary, though with no dissenting opinions permitted.
- The length of time cases take before coming to judgment varies, but on average is around 20 months in direct action cases and a few months longer in preliminary ruling cases (the latter are cases involving rulings on points of EU law that have been referred by national courts).

In what specific ways has the Court influenced the EU's policy portfolio and policy processes?

In terms of the policy portfolio, the Court's influence has, as Wincott (1999, pp. 94–5) has put it, been mainly 'to unsettle an established policy regime or to break up a gridlock … rather than to create a policy itself'. This important, but essentially secondary, role necessarily follows from two constraints imposed on the Court: it cannot initiate cases itself but is dependent on cases being referred to it – some of which stem from the Commission seeking to use Court judgments as a substitute for legislative action (Schmidt, 2000, 2004, 2011); and it normally has to base its judgments on the treaties or on existing statutes. But these constraints have not prevented many Court judgments from resulting in either the nature of the EU's policy portfolio being changed in some significant way and/or in legislative action being stimulated. Regarding the policy portfolio being changed directly, this has been seen most notably, although far from exclusively, in internal market-related policy areas. Many Court judgements in these areas have gone far beyond providing narrow technical clarifications and have had the effect of laying down important new rules concerning, for example, the circumstances in which the internal market's mutual recognition principle does and does not apply, the conditions in which governments can provide subsidies to national companies, and where and to whom corporation tax must be paid, and when it can be offset. Regarding Court judgments stimulating legislative action, perhaps the most famous example of this is the 1986 *Nouvelles Frontières* ruling (joined cases 209-213/84), which helped to promote the deregulation of air transport as a result of the Court ruling that EEC Treaty articles on competition prohibited airline price-fixing. In the same sectoral area, the Court's 2002 'open skies' ruling (case 467/98), which held that some aspects of bilateral agreements between eight member states and the US were invalid, on the grounds that they were a Community competence, has helped to promote EU international aviation policy. Wasserfallen (2010, p. 1129) has identified aspects of social, internal market and education policies as being among other areas where judicial activism has promoted the emergence, and shaped the nature, of EU legislation. In the social co-ordination field, for example, he argues: 'By taking activist decisions, the Court forced reluctant member states to overcome their resistance against co-ordination policies. This way, the judiciary paved the way towards complex social co-ordination legislation.'

In terms of policy processes, the most important Court ruling is still the 1979 *Cassis de Dijon* judgment (case 120/78) which, along with a number of other cases of the 1970s, established the principle of mutual recognition, whereby a product that is legally produced and marketed in one member state must, subject to some exceptions, be accepted on the markets of other member states. As is explained in Chapter 8, the establishment of the mutual recognition principle greatly reduced the need for legislation covering trading standards and opened the way for market integration to be built by much less cumbersome means. Other Court rulings that have had important implications for policy processes have covered a number of matters, two of which have been especially significant. First, many cases have focused on which policy process should be used for proposed legislation. The policy process applying depends on the treaty article(s) on which legislative drafts are based, but sometimes this base is not altogether clear, especially when a proposal crosses the boundaries between policy areas. The choice of the treaty base (which is by the Commission in consultation with the Council and EP) can result in disgruntled policy actors – most commonly the EP or the government of a member state – challenging the base in the Court. The reason for challenges is that the base is crucial for the legislative powers of policy actors (determining, for example, whether the EP can veto a legislative draft), and for how the actors must take decisions (determining, for example, whether the Council may use QMV and whether, therefore, a government that is opposed to a proposal can or cannot exercise a veto). Second, many other cases have been concerned directly with the policy powers and competences of EU institutions. The most famous Court judgment in this regard was made in 1980 when, in the isoglucose case (case 138/79), the Court ruled that the Council could not adopt legislation under the consultation legislative procedure until the EP had issued its opinion. Other cases of this second sort have often been taken up with whether the rights of institutions have been infringed. The EP, and to a lesser extent the Commission, both anxious to maximize their influence in EU decision-making forums, have long been active in the Court in this regard – with, for example, the EP successfully using the Court to limit the Council's ability to change legislation after the Parliament has issued its opinion under the consultation procedure.

* * *

Because of its position as the final interpreter of EU law, the CJEU thus exercises a significant influence on policy content and policy processes. This position gives the Court another key role – in respect of policy implementation. This role is explained in Chapter 6.

Conclusions

This chapter has sought to explain and demonstrate the key, and varying, roles exercised by the EU's five principal policy institutions.

Returning to the four central themes of the chapter that were identified in the Introduction: all five institutions have been shown to exercise very important policy roles and powers; policy responsibilities have been shown to be distributed between the institutions in ways that normally require the exercise of power to be shared between at least some of them if there is to be successful policy advancement; the power balance between the institutions has been shown to be in constant evolution, with the European Council and the EP being the principal institutional 'advancers' over the years; and the particular policy roles and powers of each of the institutions has been shown to depend greatly on the circumstances applying. On this fourth theme, to take the Commission as an example: it is a core policy actor when the Community method is the dominant policy-making mode, as it is with respect to such policy areas as the internal market and the CAP, but its powers are much weaker when the preferred policy-making mode is intergovernmental co-operation, as is the case with respect to foreign and defence policy.

The four themes of this chapter will be returned to in later chapters of the book.

Chapter 4

Other Important Policy Actors

In addition to the principal institutional policy actors that were examined in Chapter 3, there are other actors that also feature prominently in EU policy processes. Three of these are different sorts of institutional actors: representational institutions, European agencies and specialized policy institutions. Representational institutions and European agencies are examined in this chapter, while specialized policy institutions – such as the European Central Bank (ECB), the European Investment Bank (EIB), and the European External Action Service (EEAS) – are examined at appropriate points in relevant policy chapters later in the book.

Beyond institutional actors, two other sets of key policy actors are also examined in this chapter: the member states and policy interests.

Representational Institutions

Two institutions exist that have as their purpose providing representation in EU policy processes to interests that otherwise might not be heard formally. One of these institutions is the European Economic and Social Committee (EESC), established by the 1957 Rome Treaties to provide socio-economic interests with a formal consultative body. The other institution is the Committee of the Regions (CoR), established by the Maastricht Treaty to provide a comparable consultative body for the EU's regions. The memberships of the EESC and the CoR are explained in Box 4.1.

The policy roles of the EESC and the CoR are similar. Both undertake a range of such policy-related tasks as gathering and disseminating relevant policy information, liaising with other policy actors, and issuing own-initiative opinions on policy matters of interest and of direct relevance to their constituencies. But at the core of the tasks of both institutions is the issuing of opinions on draft EU legislation, usually after a treaty-required mandatory referral. Most important draft legislation must be referred to the EESC. The policy areas subject to CoR mandatory referral are more narrowly drawn, but still cover most areas that touch on policies with significance for the EU's sub-national levels of government.

In an average year, the EESC issues around 250 policy-related consultative documents, and the CoR around 60. What is their policy impact? The consensus among academic observers is that the policy influence of both institutions is quite marginal. This marginality is seen as stemming from the fact that both institu-

The memberships of the European Economic and Social Committee and the Committee of the Regions

- Each institution has 344 members, who are nominated by the governments of the member states. The four largest states each have 24 members while Malta, with five members, has the smallest allocation.
- In the EESC, membership is divided into three more or less equal-sized groups: employers, employees, and various interests (the latter include agricultural, professional, small and medium-sized businesses, and consumer interests). National nominations are expected to reflect this broad spectrum of social and economic interests.
- In the CoR, members must be elected members of regional or local levels of government, or be accountable politically to an elected assembly.

tions have major power weaknesses, most particularly that their memberships are part-time; their constituencies have other, and often more effective, channels to use when seeking to exercise policy influence – including relevant organized interest groupings, Commission advisory committees (on which some EESC and CoR members sit), and sometimes direct access to Council and Commission representatives; consultation processes may be rushed, with the EESC and CoR sometimes being subject to tight timetables to issue opinions, and with the Commission, Council and EP having virtually established their positions and come to informal agreements between themselves by the time EESC and CoR opinions are issued; and – crucially –the EESC and CoR only have advisory powers.

Having said all that, however, there is some evidence to indicate that when policy matters impact directly on EESC and CoR constituencies, the EU's main policy-making bodies, and especially the Commission, do give their opinions serious consideration. This is seemingly especially the case in respect of the CoR, with its focused regional and local interests (see Carroll, 2011, on the CoR's influence; and Nugent, 2010, pp. 227–33 for fuller descriptions of the EESC and the CoR).

European Agencies

Since the 1970s, and more particularly since the early 1990s, a variety of quasi-independent EU agencies have been established to carry out policy tasks which otherwise would have been assigned to the Commission. They have been created for a mix of two main reasons: to relieve work pressure on the Commission; and to bring subject specialists together in a less political and less centrally-controlled working environment than exists within the Commission.

Over 40 agencies have been created to the time of writing. Though varying considerably in their responsibilities, powers and organizational structures, they can be seen to be of two broad types: regulatory agencies; and executive agencies. *Regulatory agencies*, of which there are over 30, have a wider range of tasks to perform. Precisely what these tasks are varies considerably between agencies, but normally includes some mix of undertaking research, information gathering and dissemination, providing scientific and technical advice (mainly to the Commission), making policy recommendations, facilitating cross-border policy coordination, and – in the case of a few agencies – carrying out policy implementation (almost invariably limited in scope and under Commission supervision). Examples of regulatory agencies include the European Chemicals Agency (ECHA), the European Body for the Enhancement of Judicial Co-operation (EUROJUST), the European Environment Agency (EEA), the European Food Safety Authority (EFSA), and the European Medicines Agency (EMEA). *Executive agencies* have narrower tasks to perform in that they are created, for a specific time period, to manage EU programmes on behalf of the Commission. This management is undertaken under the tight control of a 'parent' Commission DG. Examples of executive agencies include the Executive Agency for Health and Consumers (EAHC), and the Education, Audiovisual and Culture Executive Agency (EACEA).

An important point about agencies, noted by Mark Thatcher (2010, p. 10), is that there is a relative dearth of them in areas of economic regulation in general, and in areas dominated by network industries in particular. There are EU-level networks of domestic regulators in some economic areas, including utilities and financial services, but few agencies as such. Thatcher attributes this to a combination of three types of reluctance: of national politicians to delegate powers in areas of high political salience; of domestic regulatory bodies to delegate powers in areas where they are strong; and of the Commission to delegate powers in areas where it exercises considerable power itself. These three types of reluctance identified by Thatcher are important component elements of a broader point noted by Kelemen and Tarrant (2011) about the creation and design of EU agencies: they are driven more by political considerations related to distributional conflict and the influence of the Commission than they are by functional imperatives. That said, however, the creation of the Agency for the Cooperation of Energy Regulators (ACER) in 2011 may suggest a new and enhanced role in the future for EU agencies in economic regulation, as it was established just as the EU was seeking to offer institutional support to strengthen cross-border co-operation in energy generation and transmission.

The location of the EU's agencies is interesting in relation to what it says about the independence of the agencies from the Commission and, more broadly, about the EU's system of governance. Reflecting how much they are part of the EU's central administration and under Commission control, all the executive agencies are located in Brussels. But the regulatory agencies, by contrast – unlike comparable agencies in mature federal systems, where the seat of federal decision-making is clear – are not all located in 'the capital' (Brussels in this case) but rather are spread around the member states. The creation of new regulatory agencies has sometimes been the subject of hard inter-state bargaining regarding their location, most notoriously in the early 2000s when the Italian Prime Minister, Silvio Berlusconi, fought an ultimately successful two-year campaign to have the EFSA located in Parma rather than, as had initially been intended, in Finland (Buonanno, 2006). (For more information on EU agencies, see Kelemen and Majone, 2012).

The Member States

The presence and influence of the member states is pervasive throughout the EU's policy-making systems. This is because the EU basically exists for the purpose of advancing the needs, preferences and ambitions of its member states.

The member states and the EU institutions

If member states are to be successful in pursuing their policy goals in the EU, they need to be highly active in advancing their cases and defending their positions in EU policy forums. An important way in which they can seek to do this is via their nationals within the EU institutions. Box 4.2 shows how the memberships of the EU's main policy institutions are drawn from the member states.

Helen Wallace and colleagues have emphasized the significance for EU policy-making of this feature of the composition of the institutions (Wallace *et al.*, 2010, p. 9):

> ... we should be careful not to regard these EU institutions as existing in a vacuum. Most of the policy-makers who devise and operate EU rules and legislation are from the member states themselves. They are people who spend the greater part of their time as national policy-makers, for whom the European dimension is an extended policy arena, not a separate activity. Indeed, much of EU policy is prepared and carried out by national policy-makers and agents who do not spend much, if any, time in Brussels. Instead, what they do is to consider how EU regimes might help or hinder their regular activities, and apply the results of EU agreements on the ground in their normal daily work.

Of course, the extent to which the EU institutions can be used to advance national interests varies. Opportunities are naturally greatest in the openly 'political' institutions that are based in some way on national representations and voting weights. Of these institutions, the most prominent are the European Council, the Council of Ministers, and the EP. In the European Council and the Council of Ministers, national representations at the various levels – both political and administrative – work with each other to try to reach agreed decisions, but the prime responsibility of each representation is to promote and defend its own national governmental interests. MEPs also work collaboratively with colleagues from other member states, but they too are charged to advance specific national interests. While political group

---

Box 4.2

The ways in which the EU institutions are 'staffed' by the member states

Commission
- The College consists of one Commissioner per member state.

- In the Commission services, all member states seek to ensure their nationals occupy as many senior positions as possible.

- Of the hundreds of committees on which the Commission is heavily dependent to be able to do its work: (i) *comitology committees*, which work with the Commission on administrative legislation, are comprised of member state government officials; (ii) *expert committees*, which provide specialist advice, consist of national specialists who are nominated by member state governments; (iii) *consultative committees*, which in the main provide policy input from representatives of sectional interests, contain many members who are highly attuned to national interests.

European Council
- Membership consists of the Heads of State or Government of the member states, plus the European Council President and the President of the Commission.

Council of Ministers
- At all operational levels of the Council, membership consists exclusively of governmental representatives:
  – Ministerial level: ministers or their representatives.
  – COREPER level: Permanent Representatives or their representatives.
  – Committee and working group level: governmental officials from the Permanent Representations or from national ministries.

European Parliament
- MEPs are elected on national lists in what are, in all practical ways, national elections.

Court of Justice of the European Union
- Both the Court of Justice and the General Court consist of one judge per member state, all of whom in practice are nominated by their member states.

EESC and CoR
- All members of both institutions are nominated by national governments.

---

membership (and hence ideological orientation) is the single most important factor determining how MEPs vote, specific national interests – especially on 'spending' policy issues – can result in MEPs voting against their group's position.

By contrast, the Commission and the CJEU, which are both charged to be independent in the exercise of their duties, cannot be used as transmission belts for the direct inputting of national positions into EU policy processes. However, the Commission does offer indirect opportunities for member state inputs. One way is through a member state's Commissioner, who

while certainly not a national representative, may sometimes be used by national policy actors, including his/her government, to provide informal 'assistance' on matters of national concern. Another way is through Commission officials, who are sometimes sought out by fellow national policy actors for advice or attempted soft pressure: the Permanent Representations to the EU often contact compatriot officials for precisely such purposes. And yet another way is via the numerous legislative, expert and consultative committees attached to the Commission, which give national representatives of various kinds a chance to 'have their say' on matters ranging from proposed framework directives, through Commission legislation, to the identification of possible policy options.

Opportunities for national policy actors to exercise EU policy roles

An alternative, and in some respects broader, way of thinking about the pervasiveness of the member states in EU policy forums and processes is to take the main national policy actors and identify the various ways in which they can make direct policy inputs; see Box 4.3.

Since much of what is shown in Box 4.3 was covered in Chapter 3 or is covered below in the section on policy interests, attention will be confined here to two sets of national actors that are not considered directly elsewhere: parliaments and sub-national levels of government.

National parliaments

National parliaments have been institutional losers within the European integration process. This is because they have not been involved directly in the exercise of either EU executive power (which has been shared between the Commission, the Council of Ministers, and in some respects the European Council) or legislative power (which has been shared between the Commission, the Council of Ministers and the EP). For the most part, national parliaments have been restricted to trying to influence what their governments do in the European Council and the Council of Ministers, and keeping a watching brief on important EU developments.

However, these potential influencing and watchdog roles should not be dismissed too easily. Regarding the role of trying to influence national governmental actions, the ways in which this occurs and the extent of the influence exercised varies enormously between the member states. Most national parliaments have an EU committee, or committees, with powers to question relevant ministers on a periodic basis, while a few parliaments, including those of the Scandinavian states, have EU committees that can in some respects exercise a degree of control over what proposed EU decisions ministers çan agree to in Council of Ministers meetings. Regarding the watching brief role, all national parliaments have an EU committee or

committees (which may or may not be different from the above-mentioned committees) that (nominally at least) monitor new EU legislation. The role of these committees was enhanced by the Lisbon Treaty, most notably by the creation of a new treaty provision stipulating that if one-third of the member state parliaments declare that a new legislative proposal may breach the subsidiarity principle, the Commission is required to reconsider the proposal.

Sub-national levels of government

Sub-national levels of government are very significant policy actors in many member states. As a result, some EU policy processes are not restricted to a two-level basis (EU and national) but can extend to a multi-level basis, with sub-national levels of government having significant policy roles, especially in member states with federal (Austria, Belgium, and Germany) or regional (Italy, Spain, and the UK) systems. These roles are primarily in respect of policy implementation, but in a few policy areas – mainly associated with the EU's cohesion policies, but also aspects of policy areas such as environment and fishing – there is some, albeit limited, contribution to policy content. A key point made by observers convinced of the significance of the multi-level nature of the EU is that the relations between the different levels are not always conducted in a strictly hierarchical manner. That is, relations between actors at the EU level – notably the Commission – and at the sub-national levels can be direct rather than necessarily being channelled via governments. This directness is greatly facilitated by there being no less than around 250 regional representation offices in Brussels (Rowe, 2011, p. 7).

Member state influence: the importance of size

Policy actors in all member states thus have opportunities to feed into EU policy processes and play a part in influencing policy outcomes. That they do so is an essential way in which confidence in the EU system is maintained, because, if key national policy actors were to be excluded from EU policy processes dissatisfaction with the EU would quickly grow.

Dissatisfaction would also quickly grow if any member state felt its policy interests and preferences

---

Box 4.3

Ways in which national policy actors input directly into EU policy processes

National actor(s)	Input into EU policy processes
Political executive	• Membership of the European Council. • Membership of the ministerial level of the Council of Ministers.
Central administration	• Membership of COREPER and of Council committees and working groups.
Parliament	• Varying degrees of control and influence over actions of ministers in the Council of Ministers. • Varying arrangements for monitoring and inspecting EU policies and laws.
Sub-national levels of government	• Most of the regions of the member states and many other significant sub-national levels of government have EU offices, many of them based in Brussels. • In those member states that have federal or quasi-federal political systems, representatives from sub-national levels of government are sometimes part of national delegations to Council of Ministers meetings. • Represented in the CoR.
Political parties	• Select MEPs • Internal party dynamics impact on the stances adopted by national governments in the European Council and the Council of Ministers.
Policy interests	• Many are active in Eurogroups. • Larger policy interests usually have EU offices of some kind, often based in Brussels. • Smaller policy interests often engage consultants to assist on particular issues. • Some are represented in the EESC and in the consultative committee network that surrounds the Commission.
Public opinion	• Can impose restraints on national decision-makers in EU forums (for example, public opinion makes it very difficult for the UK Government to be flexible with regard to the UK budgetary rebate). • Elects MEPs. • Occasionally make a very direct impact via referendums (for example, Swedish and Danish non-membership of the eurozone).

were not being recognized and accommodated adequately. Of course, states do sometimes feel this about specific policy matters, but not overall. Two factors in particular account for this. The first factor is the EU's preference for consensual decision-making, which means that important national interests and preferences are normally accommodated, at least to some degree, in policy decisions. The second factor is the nature of the policy cleavages between the member states, which frequently cross-cut. That is, in EU policy-making forums – and in the European Council and the Council of Ministers in particular, where 'national voting' is most obviously on display – states do not always 'line-up' in the same combinations. So, for example, the positions of France and the UK tend to be similar with respect to such policy matters as the overall size of the EU's budget, environmental protection, and the activation of CFSP/CSDP missions, but differ with respect to the proportion of the budget that should be allocated to the CAP, the application of aspects of competition policy, and the Turkish membership application. This illustrative case of France and the UK can be extended to all member states, which means that states align with one another in different ways and in different combinations on different policy issues. In consequence, on policy issues that divide member states, no states are in permanent majority or minority positions.

This does not mean that all states exercise equal policy influence in the EU. But statements about precisely what influence individual states exercise must be treated with considerable caution, not least because influence varies so much between policy areas. However, one generalization that does stand up is that larger states are more influential than smaller ones. There certainly is no exact relationship between size and influence – as a comparison of Italy (a large state that traditionally has not been a leading policy player) and the Netherlands (a relatively small state that has been an influential player) shows – but none the less a broad relationship does apply in most cases. There are three main reasons for this. The first is that larger states have a wider range of policy interests than smaller ones and so are active on more policy fronts. The second reason is that larger states have more national resources – in the form, for example, of greater political, economic and administrative weight and capacity – to bring to negotiating tables. To illustrate this importance of national weight, it is, for example, no coincidence that the three most influential member states in the areas of foreign and defence policy – France, Germany and the UK – are the states with the greatest range of overseas interests, contacts and missions, and the largest military dispositions. And the third reason is that the larger states have greater voting strength in some of the EU's core institutions, most notably the Council of Ministers and the EP.

But, as a number of studies have shown (see, for example, Panke, 2010) the influence of smaller states should not be underestimated. Three factors are particularly important in enabling smaller member states to exercise a policy-making influence that is often greater than their size would seem to warrant. The first factor is that while smaller states have fewer policy resources than do larger ones, they also have fewer policy interests, which means that they are able to concentrate such resources as they do have on the issues that are really important to them. So, for example, the Government of Luxembourg does not focus much attention on the Common Fisheries Policy, but it does pay great attention to financial services policies. Similarly, the Cypriot Government does not devote many resources to the EU's Arctic policy, but it does to its maritime transport policy (Cyprus has the third-largest flagged fleet of all EU states). The second factor is that many smaller states are long-standing EU members, with the consequence that their official and unofficial 'representatives' are usually well-connected in the EU system. This means, for example, that their national governmental representatives can lobby – in the Commission, the Council Presidency, the EP and elsewhere – without having to bear the heavy transaction costs that have to be carried by the representatives of newer member states (Panke, 2012). And the third factor is that the power resources available to smaller states are by no means inconsiderable. A key element of these resources is the inflated policy-making power that all small states are given as a result of their 'over-representation' in EU institutions, the continuity of the national veto in some policy areas, and the EU's consensual norm. Arregui and Thomson (2009) suggest that this inflated policy-making power is crucial to enable smaller states to exercise an influence in EU negotiations that is disproportionate to their size.

As with all EU states, the interests of small states on particular policy issues sometimes converge and are sometimes far apart. An important issue on which the interests of virtually all of them converged, and in consequence resulted in them exercising a significant collective influence on the decisions that were taken, was during the building of the single currency from the late 1980s. Small states were among the strongest supporters of the euro project as well as of the need for fiscal constraints to be part of the euro system. Their support for the creation of the euro largely stemmed from the fact that small states usually reap advantages from joining a larger economic unit – as indeed many small eurozone states have done, not least before the

Examples of policy leadership by larger member states

- France, and more especially Germany, have set the pace and direction of EMU from its first stages: from the creation of the European Monetary System (EMS) in the 1970s, through the laying down of the Maastricht Treaty EMU foundations and the reform of the Stability and Growth Pact in 2005, to the construction of financial packages and reform measures from 2010 to deal with the eurozone crisis.
- France, supported by Germany, has been to the fore in ensuring the CAP continues to occupy a central policy position.
- The UK has been very influential in pressing for the momentum on opening-up the internal market to be maintained.
- France and the UK since the late 1990s, with increasing German involvement since the mid-2000s, have done much to drive advances in foreign and defence policy.
- From 2003, the interior ministers of the five largest member states (France, Germany, Italy, Spain and the UK) – joined since 2004 by Poland – have often met informally before JHA Council meetings to try to reach agreement on such sensitive issues as illegal immigration, crime and terrorism.

leader, and Italy, which has been more of a policy follower, demonstrates. But it certainly is the case that in general terms EU policy leadership is provided more by larger states than by smaller ones. Examples of successful policy leadership provided by larger states are set out in Box 4.4.

Policy differences between member states: the big four and the EMU

The EU's member states differ considerably from one another in all sorts of ways. While Europeanization has produced a greater degree of uniformity, the impact of distinct historical experiences and geographical locations, and the importance of differing social, cultural, economic and political systems and values, is still readily apparent. Naturally, these differences feed directly into EU policy-making processes, with a considerable range of national policy interests and preferences being 'in play' in virtually all policy areas.

These policy differences are explored throughout this book, but they will also be illustrated briefly here by considering the implications for 'the Big Four' states – France, Germany, Italy and the United Kingdom – of aspects of their differing economic situations and systems for the policy positions they have adopted towards Economic and Monetary Union (EMU) membership. (EMU is examined in detail in Chapter 10.)

France

For France, EMU provided a way of escaping 'the Deutschmark shadow': that is, the situation in which Germany exercised monetary policy leadership in Europe prior to the adoption of the euro. The strength of the Deutschmark was such that if its exchange rate value was adjusted or if German interest rates were changed, then central banks in many other European states were obliged, in effect, to follow suit. EMU thus offered the French an institutional voice in monetary policy that was otherwise absent in the unofficial Deutschmark zone.

EMU was also a natural progression in the French quest to build a continental economy and a strong Europe as a counterweight to American political and

eurozone debt crisis by being able to borrow at more advantageous interest rates than otherwise would have been possible. Their support for fiscal constraints was because, as Issing (2004, p. 10) explains, budgetary imbalances in larger countries have a strong effect on monetary system interest rates and can wreak havoc on the economic policies of smaller, vulnerable states.

A useful way of demonstrating how size is an important, but not solely determining, factor in affecting the policy influence states exercise is to consider its relationship to policy leadership. The relationship is by no means direct and it certainly is not the case that larger member states necessarily or consistently take advantage of their leadership potential – as a comparison between France, which has often been a policy economic dominance. Indeed, according to Gordon and Meunier (2001, pp. 98, 102), the French response to the vagaries of globalization was *mondialisation maîtrisée* (managed globalization) in which EMU would play an important role by providing 'protection from the vicissitudes of globalization'.

Germany

Germany's export-driven economy would benefit from a single currency, not least because it would eliminate competitive currency devaluations among those member states adopting the euro. German exporters had long been affected negatively by the practice of other EU member states undercutting German exports through competitive currency devaluations. Italy (whose northern industries – chemicals, machine tools, automobile production, white goods, and information technology – compete head-to-head with German manufacturing), in particular, had an exasperating habit of devaluing the lira. Germany resisted competitive devaluation as an economic strategy because of the collective memory of the debilitating hyperinflation of the Weimar Republic, but a single currency would short-circuit the Italian strategy. It would also close off the possibility of a similar strategy being employed by the new European democracies waiting to join the EU.

Italy

Even with the inevitable imported inflation that accompanies currency devaluations, as an export-driven economy and a nation of savers, Italian policy-makers could afford to enact policies that would provide jobs at the expense of import consumerism. But currency devaluations could not compensate for deep-seated weaknesses in the Italian system that excluded necessary economic reforms. Among these weaknesses were: clientelism (involving government jobs being exchanged for political support); corruption and political scandals; and inefficient state capitalism (involving substantial state participation in profit-making and potentially profit-making enterprises).

EMU provided a way of dealing with this need for fundamental economic reform. As Mario Monti, former Internal Market Commissioner and later Prime Minister in the Italian technocratic unity government appointed in 2011, tellingly commented:

'Italians needed Maastricht because they never had a Margaret Thatcher' (quoted in Graziano, 2010, p. 7). (That is: the EMU provisions of the Maastricht Treaty substituted for the fact that Italian governments were not capable of driving through structural economic reform.)

The United Kingdom

The UK is the only one of the Big Four not to have joined EMU's single currency. Political reasons – including domestic euroscepticism, sovereignty concerns, and a resolve that the importance of transatlanticism should not be undermined – partly explain this, but economic reasons have also been important. Indeed, in the late 1990s, when Prime Minister Tony Blair was clearly interested in taking the UK into EMU, the Chancellor, Gordon Brown, prevented progress being made by insisting that five economic tests of the compatibility of the UK economy with EMU must first be passed (see Baimbridge and Whyman, 2008, pp. 85–7).

A central economic concern has focused on the fact that, in important respects, the UK's economy is structurally distinct from those of the other countries in the Big Four. Among distinctive features are: its strong services sector has a particular concentration in financial services and the media; it relies to a greater degree on high technology exports and a large energy sector (both technology and energy products tend be priced in US dollars); it has a relatively small agricultural sector; it has a tendency to use variable rate interest to finance mortgages (home ownership rates are higher than in continental Europe); and it has low savings rates (British consumers rely on credit to a greater extent than do continental Europeans). Among the general implications of these distinctive features is that the UK is quite vulnerable to exchange rate and interest rate changes, and so has good reason to fear the possible consequences of decisions on these matters no longer being in national hands. Among particular implications is that in the very important area of financial services – where the City of London enjoys a competitive advantage – the UK wishes to retain enough policy freedom to be able to develop new financial investment instruments (Baimbridge and Whyman, 2008, p. 87). So, too, the City of London has enjoyed a lucrative niche in foreign currency transactions: a business a single currency could diminish.

Policy Interests

Beyond 'official' EU policy actors there are a host of others that are associated in some way with EU policy processes. These vary enormously in nature, including as they do among their number multi-national corporations, business firms and business associations, sectoral pressure groups, and civil society organizations. But regardless of their many differences, these actors share one key characteristic: they all make, or seek to make, inputs into EU policy processes. As such, they can be grouped under the general heading of 'policy interests'.

The level of policy interest activity, and its nature

It is not possible to provide precise figures on the number of policy interests that are, or seek to be, involved in EU policy activity. There are three main reasons for this. First, it is very much open to question as to just what constitutes an EU policy interest actor. While many policy interests are readily classifiable as such because of their frequent – almost constant in some cases – involvement in EU policy activities, many others are involved only very occasionally. So, for example, a national organization dealing with the rights of disabled people may only ever turn its attention to the EU if the EU legislation covering employment rights has direct implications for disabled people. Second, policy interests do not usually describe themselves in this way, and actively avoid such descriptive labels as 'lobbyists' or 'pressure groups'. Indeed, much policy interest involvement does not take place via policy interest organizations or associations at all, but rather is channelled via consultancies, public affairs associations and law firms. There is not necessarily anything wrong with this – indeed, many policy interests use such channels because they are not normally involved with EU policy-making and/or do not have the resources to have EU-dedicated offices and staff of their own – but it makes the tracking of policy interest activity very difficult. And third, no wholly credible register of policy interests exists. Since 2011, a joint Commission–EP register, on which around 4,000 entities are listed, has existed, but it is widely recognized as being only a very general

not being comprehensive. Similarly, an often-cited figure of there being around 15,000 people based in Brussels who are wholly or in part engaged in EU lobbying must be regarded as being only a very general approximation.

But whatever the precise figures may be, it is evident from the numerous policy interests that are known to exist, and from the countless policy interest nameplates outside buildings in the 'European quarter' of Brussels, that Brussels almost rivals Washington as the world's lobbying 'capital'.

What is the nature of the policy interests that seek to play some part in EU policy activity? Their most striking characteristic is their sheer diversity. Classificatory systems of EU policy interests are, of course, possible, and these naturally vary enormously according to both how the term is interpreted, and the amount and character of the analytical precision required. However, as this classificatory task has already been undertaken elsewhere (see, for example, Greenwood, 2011, pp. 9–11; Nugent, 2010, pp. 245–9) and as the main purpose of this section is to focus on the roles and influence of policy interests, there will not be a long discussion here of possible classificatory frameworks. Instead, we use the simple classificatory system set out in Box 4.5, where three main types of policy interests are identified: corporations; national interest groups; and Eurogroups. The simplicity of this classification naturally means that all three of the categories could, if desired, be broken down into many sub-categories. So, for example, among the many possible sub-categories that could be listed in both the national interest group and Eurogroup categories are economic and non-economic (most interests are focused on economic matters in some way), corporate and non-corporate, sectoral and ideational, and interests having and not having a physical base in Brussels.

The latter suggested distinction – regarding whether or not policy interests have a physical base in Brussels – is part of a broader difference between all policy interests: their relative sizes and resources. Taking Eurogroups – that is, groups that draw their memberships from several European countries and seek to represent European-wide interests at the EU level – the largest and best resourced are mainly, though not exclusively, federations of national associations. Large Eurogroups, examples of which are given in Box 4.5, have strong representational claims, well-

Box 4.5

The main types of policy interests

Type of policy interest	Examples of major policy interests*
Corporations The most powerful and well-resourced are multi-national corporations (MNCs).Around 350 MNCs have offices in Brussels	Ford Microsoft General Electric Hypo Real Estate Group (German-based banking group)
National interest groups Greenwood (2011, p. 8) estimates that over 40 per cent of organised policy interests active at the EU level are national and sub-national organizations.	General Confederation of Italian Agriculture (Confagricultura) Confederation of British Industry (CBI) Polish Confederation of Private Employers (PKKP)
Eurogroups Like national interest groups, Eurogroups also represent a diverse range of policy interests, with the most powerful and well-resourced again representing 'business'	Association of Petrochemical Producers in Europe (APPE) (95 member companies) BusinessEurope (membership of 41 industry and employer federations in 35 countries) Committee of Professional Agricultural Organisations (COPA)/General Confederation of Agricultural Cooperatives in the European Union (COGECA) (COPA has 60 member organisations in EU countries and 36 partner organizations in non-EU European countries. COGECA has 35 full members and 4 affiliated members in EU countries and 36 partner members in non-EU European countries) The European Consumer Organisation (BEUC) (membership of 42 national consumer organizations in 31 countries) European Federation of Pharmaceutical Industry Associations (EFPIA) (membership of 31 national associations and 38 pharmaceutical companies) European Trade Union Confederation (ETUC) (membership of 83 national trade union confederations in 36 countries, plus 12 European industry federations) European Environmental Bureau (EEB) (membership of 140 environmental citizen's organizations in the member states)

Note: *Only policy interests with permanent offices in Brussels are listed.

developed organizational structures, and well-appointed and well-staffed offices in Brussels.

The reasons for the high level of policy interest involvement in EU policy activities

Four factors in particular account for the high level of lobbying presence and activity in EU policy processes.

The first is the breadth, depth and nature of EU policy activity. Few areas of public policy do not have at least some EU involvement, so therefore many policy interests – from the international to the local – are inevitably affected by EU policies and activities. Moreover, this effect is often of a nature that impacts in a fundamental way on the activities of policy interests. So, for example, EU rules on such matters as product standards, working conditions, consumer protection, corporate taxation and law, and environmental safety can be crucial in determining the competitiveness of markets, and of particular firms within markets. For many policy interests, the EU is thus well worth lobbying.

The fact is that lobbyists go where power goes. So, as the range of the EU's policy responsibilities has grown over the years, then so have policy interests focused attention increasingly on EU policy-makers and sought to play a part themselves within EU policy processes.

The second explanatory factor is that EU policy processes offer many potential access points for policy interests. This arises from the multi-institutional, multi-actor and multi-stage nature of the EU policy process system, which has prompted some observers to conclude that the EU resembles the American separation of powers system more than the parliamentary and semi-presidential systems that characterize most of its member states (see, for example, Fabbrini, 2007). To take the making of legislation to illustrate the multiple access points that exist, the Commission, the Council and the EP are all key legislative actors in what can be (when the ordinary legislative procedure runs its full course) a three-stage process even after the Commission has formally issued a proposal.

The third explanatory factor is that two of the EU's core institutional policy actors – the Commission and the EP – normally have open approaches towards policy interests. So the Commission is not only generally receptive to representations from the outside but often actively seeks and encourages them. It does this by, for example, sustaining the host of Commission advisory committees that exist in just about every EU policy area, by encouraging the formation of and providing financial support for civil society interests in some policy areas, and by creating new participatory processes when it is deemed to be appropriate. An example of the latter are the six (at the time of writing) forums that have been created since the late 1990s to bring together energy stakeholders (including national regulatory authorities, transmission system operators, energy suppliers, traders and consumers) to work with DG Energy on different aspects of energy policy.

The Commission adopts an open approach towards policy interests for two reasons in particular. First, policy interests have access to specialized knowledge that can improve the quality of Commission policy proposals. Second, the Commission's legitimacy with other policy actors is strengthened if it can show it is engaged on policy matters with relevant policy interests. Unlike the Council and the EP, the Commission has no 'constituency' and thus has a motive to use policy interests – especially 'civil society' interests' – as a remedy for its 'representational deficiencies' (Kohler-Koch, 2010, p. 108). Significantly in this context, in its 2001 White Paper on Governance, the Commission included a commitment to reach out to civil society organizations so as to establish a countervailing power to the sectoral organizations that have done so much to give the EU a reputation for catering to elites rather than to 'ordinary' Europeans.

The fourth and final explanatory factor is one that has been noted by Aspinwall (1998, p. 198), who has pointed to the 'advocacy void' that exists in the EU, resulting from the weakness of EU political parties. The absence of strong party-political-based leadership (an inevitable consequence of a separation of powers) creates political space for policy interests and, as Aspinwall and Greenwood (1998, p. 3) put it, creates 'striking similarities' between Brussels and Washington, in which the 'EU lends itself to interest articulation in much the same manner as the federal government does in Washington'.

Box 4.6

Channels of influence potentially available to policy interests

Policy channel	Main possible routes within the channel
Commission	• Submission of briefing papers/reports, perhaps in response to Commission consultation calls. • Informal meetings and telephone conversations with relevant officials (and, occasionally, Commissioners). • Use of Commission advisory committees (especially for Eurogroups, who constitute much of the membership of the committees).
European Council	• Direct institutional access not available, but unofficial access via sympathetic heads of government may be possible.
Council of Ministers	• Direct institutional access not available, but unofficial access is often possible via sympathetic governments and governments in need of specialized and technical advice.
European Parliament	• Can provide information to, and lobby, MEPs – particular lobbying 'targets' are *rapporteurs* of relevant reports, and members of relevant committees. • EP committees and political groups sometimes allow representatives of interests to address them in 'hearings'. • EP intergroups (voluntary groupings of MEPs who are interested in a particular matter) usually encourage good relations with relevant interests.
Other policy institutions	• The *European Economic and Social Committee* exists for the precise purpose of representing economic and social interests, while the *Committee of the Regions* exists to represent regional interests.

The policy activities of policy interests

Policy interests can have many aims. While the one that mainly concerns us here is the inputting of preferences and ideas into EU policy processes, sight should not be lost of the fact that policy interests are also involved in other policy-related activities – such as trying to gather advance information on likely forthcoming policy developments, seeking guidance and assistance from EU officials on matters ranging from grant applications to whether the way a policy is being applied in a member state is acceptable, and explaining EU policies to members.

Restricting our attention here to how policy interests can input into policy processes, the main channels that are potentially available are outlined in

Box 4.6. Of course, not all policy interests have access to all of the channels that are listed in Box 4.6, and not all of the channels are suitable for all policy interests.

The influence exercised by policy interests

Policy interests exercise influence at all stages of EU policy processes. They do so because they have resources to 'trade' with policy practitioners. That is to say, policy interests have control of and access to resources that policy practitioners need or would like to have when they are formulating, making, implementing and evaluating policies.

The resources of policy interests take a number of forms, the most important of which are outlined in Box 4.7. Information is usually the key resource. This is partly because most of the EU's decision-making institutions are under-staffed and so often are reliant on specialized information being provided 'from the outside'. Chalmers (2011) has noted how EU under-staffing accentuates the need for these assisting and supporting tasks, and thus helps policy interests to gain access to decision-makers. A related reason why information is a key resource is that most policy practitioners are generalists by training and often also by work experience. So, for example, few of the Commission officials working in DG Energy, few of the national politicians and officials servicing the Transport, Communication and Energy formation of the Council, and few of the members of the EP's Industry, Research and Energy committee had a specialized knowledge of energy issues before assuming their posts. Once in their posts they do, of course, begin to develop an expertise, but they usually can do so only up to a point, since much of what is happening in the energy sector is highly specialized, technical and in rapid transition. This highlights another reason why information is often the key resource for policy interests: EU policy practitioners are, by the nature of their duties, not in the policy 'front line' in the sense of themselves being, or working directly for or with, farmers, fishermen, chemical manufacturers, energy companies, environmental agencies and the like.

In consequence, policy practitioners need expert information and ideas from 'outside' policy interests on an enormous range of matters. Among numerous legislative measures on which the Commission sought and/or took note of such advice in 2010–11 were proposals on: the restriction of the use of certain hazardous substances in electrical and electronic equipment; the creation of a greater free flow of online services across national borders; the setting of emission performance standards for new light commercial vehicles; the setting of budgetary ceilings for direct financial support for farmers; the reform of the Common Fisheries Policy; the prudential requirements for credit institutions and investment firms; and the sulphur content of marine fuels.

So there is no doubt that policy interests are very important policy actors. Evaluating their specific influence is, however, always a difficult task in political systems. One reason why this is so is that policy prac-

titioners are not usually disposed to reveal that a policy interest has played an important policy role, especially if, as is the case with many corporate interests, the policy interest is heavily financed and able to engage in multi-dimensional lobbying. A second reason why it is difficult to be precise in evaluating the influence of policy interests is that policy decisions are taken formally via the EU's decision-making institutions, and the actions of actors in these institutions are influenced by many considerations. For example, national fisheries organizations always lobby their governments to press in the Council for higher national fisheries quotas, but when higher national quotas are 'won' they may reflect not only pressures from national fisheries organizations but also prior and inbuilt governmental preferences, and perhaps too the impact of pressures on governments from elsewhere, such as from regional lobbies and/or from members of the national parliament with constituencies where fishing is an important local industry.

There is no difficulty in identifying situations where particular policy interests have seemingly exercised a considerable influence over final policy outcomes. For example, the Confederation of the Food and Drink Industries of the EU (CIAA) – which changed its name in 2011 to Food-Drink Europe – unquestionably played a key role in persuading decision-makers to weaken the EU Food Information to Consumers regulation issued by the Commission in June 2008. The Commission's proposal called for a 'traffic light' system, in which food and drink products would be labelled with simple colour-coded guidance according to their 'healthiness'. But, following a protracted and intense CIAA-led oppositional campaign, the EP and the Council agreed at second reading in 2011 on a 'softer' system based on Guideline Daily Amounts (GDAs) – which involves the presentation of nutritional information in a 'less intimidating' way!

However, the CIAA case is far from being illustrative of the norm. Because, as Greenwood (2011) and Chalmers (2011) have noted, while there is high access for all policy interests to EU policy processes, there is usually a relatively low impact by any single policy interest. One reason for this is that policy interests can counter-balance one another in a political system that leans more towards pluralist than majoritarian governance. This is most obviously so when policy interests clearly have different policy choices – as, for example,

> **Box 4.7**
>
> ## Factors determining the influence exercised by policy interests
>
> - *The dependence of policy practitioners on policy interests for information.* The position of an interest is strengthened if it has access to information that policy practitioners need. Such information can take many forms. For example, technical information about product requirements and standards; information about the likely market consequences of changing aspects of health and safety requirements; and information about the volume and quality of sectoral outputs.
> - *The dependence of policy practitioners on policy interests for co-operation.* The influence of a policy interest is enhanced if its co-operation is necessary for a policy to be effective. For example, the Commission and the EP rely on civil society organizations to monitor implementation of EU directives and regulations – with, for example, Eurogroups regularly reporting to the Commission on the intransigence of some member states with regard to consumer safety and environmental issues. The alternative to this Commission dependence is an army of EU regulators – which is not feasible given the small size of the EU budget and member states' sensitivity regarding sovereignty over health and safety issues.
> - *The nature of the working relationship policy interests have, or can forge, with policy practitioners.* As a general rule, EU policy practitioners favour policy interests that share a broadly similar ideological framework to their own, that they know can be trusted, that can provide fresh ideas, that can write short and sharp position papers, that have a clear access point, and that are responsive and timely when a request is made of them.
> - *The extent to which policy interests are well-resourced.* Policy interests with well-financed and well-staffed offices, preferably in Brussels, are more able to be policy-active than policy interests that are poorly resourced.
> - *The extent to which policy interests are representative.* This factor applies particularly to Eurogroups, with those that are seen as being genuinely representative of an area of activity or of opinion being more likely to be listened to by policy practitioners than Eurogroups that have only a few members in a small number of member states.

is often the case with business on the one hand and environmental interests on the other. But it can also be the case with respect to expected allied interests: for example, business is represented by many policy interests in Brussels (Greenwood, 2011, estimates that approaching 70 per cent of active interests represent business in some way), and many of these policy interests have differing specific policy needs and preferences – thus limiting their policy impact. Where there is no balance or a near balance of policy interests, the Commission often tries to create one by funding an interest organization – usually a citizens' group of some kind. A second reason why it is difficult for any individual policy interest to make a determining policy impact is the fragmentation of power in the EU, which makes the wholesale 'capture' of a decision-making process virtually impossible. And a third reason is the culture of compromise that runs through so much of EU policy-making.

Concluding on the influence exercised by policy interests, a general point from the academic literature on lobbying is worth recalling: policy interests tend to be less focused on changing the minds of decision-makers who disagree with them and more focused on assisting and supporting those who agree with them. The extent of their influence is thus not just to be judged on their ability to convert policy-makers to their ways of thinking.

A special type of, but an increasingly important, policy interest: the governments of non-member states

As was noted above, the term 'policy interest' embraces a wide variety of different types of EU policy actor. One set of such actors, albeit of a special sort, is the governments of non-member states. They can be considered to be policy interests because, like other policy interests, they seek to influence EU policy content, and in some circumstances may impose constraints on what the EU can do.

Over 170 non-member states have diplomatic missions that are officially accredited to the EU. With EU external policies extending far beyond the obvious policies of trade, development, and foreign and defence policies to include the external dimension of such policy areas as agriculture, fishing, transport, and environmental policies, there is a continuous and wide range of ongoing dialogues and negotiations between the EU and representatives of non-member states. The nature of these dialogues and negotiations naturally varies considerably, according in particular to the size, policy interests and preferences, and the importance to the EU of the non-member state with which it is dealing. In the case of small states with only a narrow range of policy interests and resources, their policy interactions with the EU are usually limited, and their capacity for bringing influence to bear on EU policy decisions is very restricted. But the situation is significantly different with large states that have a wide range of interests, because here non-member state–EU dialogues and negotiations embrace just about the whole of the EU's policy portfolio. So, for example, few of the EU decisions in the areas of its greatest policy competences do not have potential implications for the US. Accordingly, the US inputs its views into EU policy processes across most of the EU's policy spectrum, and on many of them it is able, thanks to its own strong negotiating position and EU–US interdependence, to influence policy outcomes. Examples of policy issue areas where EU decisions in recent years have been influenced by US pressure include agriculture, where the US has been to the fore in obliging the EU to make the CAP less protectionist, and has also

been instrumental in the EU opening its market to some GMO-based agricultural produce, and financial regulation – particularly since the onset of the global economic crisis in 2008.

Conclusions

This chapter and Chapter 3 have shown the large number and wide array of actors that are involved in EU policy processes. The two chapters have further shown that most of these actors have significant policy involvements of some sort – ranging from that of formal decision-maker to informal policy adviser.

The nature of the actors is such as to ensure that a very wide range of representational claims, and of accompanying policy preferences and views, are heard in EU policy processes. To focus only on the institutional actors, as Majone (2002) has pointed out, the primary organizational principle of the EU's institutional system is the representation of interests. So, regarding the most important institutions: 'Europeanwide' interests are supposedly represented through the European Commission and the CJEU; national governmental interests are represented through the European Council and the Council of Ministers; citizens' interests are (directly) represented through the EP; socio-economic interests are represented through the EESC; and regional interests are represented through the CoR.

The large number and wide array of significant policy actors have many important consequences for the operation of EU policy processes. These consequences – which include having to deal with many different sorts of policy inputs and constantly having to find agreements of varying types between actors – are explored in the chapters that follow.

Chapter 5
Key Features of Policy Processes

The EU's arrangements for making policy – that is, its policy processes – display many distinctive features. This chapter identifies and analyses the most striking and important of these, grouping them under the following sub-headings: the large and increasing number of policy processes; the complexity of policy processes; the varying mixtures of supranationalism and intergovernmentalism; the ways in which policy processes are constructed and operate to ensure that all member states have confidence in the EU system; the dispersal of leadership; the consensual nature of (most) policy processes; the role of ideology; the production of policy outputs; variations in the speed of policy processes; and the impact of differentiation.

The Large and Increasing Number of Policy Processes

The growth in policy processes

Looking at EU policy processes over time, perhaps the most striking feature about them is how they have been subject to continuous evolutionary development, and how much of this development has taken the form of increasing the number of policy processes.

Starting with changes to the formal nature of policy processes – that is, to the provisions that are specified in the treaties and, to some extent, in EU legislation and in inter-institutional agreements – these have been affected most obviously via the rounds of treaty reforms that started with the Single European Act and have continued through the Maastricht, Amsterdam, Nice and Lisbon treaties. Each of these reform rounds has provided for, in some measure, the creation of new procedures and amendments to existing procedures, clarifications of and amendments to the powers of the EU institutions that are such key policy actors within procedures, and alterations to the ways the institutions can act within the procedures. Regarding the creation of new procedures and changes to existing procedures, examples include the creation of the co-operation and assent procedures by the Single European Act (SEA), the creation of the co-decision procedure and of procedures for the CFSP and JHA pillars by the Maastricht Treaty, and simplifications to the co-decision procedure and the creation of a procedure to allow for differentiation (the making of policy without all member states participating) by the Amsterdam

Treaty. Regarding clarifications and changes concerning the powers of EU institutions, the assignment by the Maastricht Treaty to the European Council of the task of determining the 'general political guidelines' of the Union provides one example. The widened policy scope of the co-decision procedure provided for by the Amsterdam, Nice and Lisbon treaties – which had the effect of increasing the EP's legislative powers – provides another. Regarding changes to the ways that institutions can act within procedures, the most obvious example is the extension by every treaty reform round since the SEA of the scope of qualified majority voting (QMV) in the Council.

Turning to the informal nature of policy processes, these consist of features that are neither specified in EU law nor in formal agreements between policy actors. Usually having as their general purpose the promotion of more efficient and effective policy-making, these informal features include mechanisms designed to facilitate inter-institutional co-operation and acknowledgements of circumstances in which the formal policy process rules should not be applied fully. As much as formal features, these informal features have evolved over the years, and continue to do so. So, taking mechanisms designed to promote inter-institutional co-operation, since the creation of the co-decision procedure by the Maastricht Treaty there has been a mushrooming of trilogues – informal meetings between representatives of the Commission, the Council and the EP – which have as their main purpose the identification of ways in which the positions of the three institutions can be brought together so that agreements can be reached on legislative proposals. Since the Amsterdam Treaty revised the co-decision procedure to allow final agreements to be made at first- and second-reading stages, some trilogues have virtually become akin to third-reading conciliation meetings. As for acknowledgements of circumstances in which the formal policy process rules should not be applied fully, changing attitudes to the use of QMV in the Council provides an illustration. Until the early 1980s, QMV was rarely used even when it was permitted by the treaties, apart from in a few non-political areas and cases where timetables were pressing. From the early 1980s, however, the use of QMV slowly came to be recognized as a legitimate way of proceeding in some circumstances, though the preference for first trying to find a consensus continued to prevail. This preference among Council participants

for unanimity continues but, as figures on the use of QMV show (see below, and Chapter 3), the anti-voting culture is not as strong as it once was.

Why has there been a growth in the number of policy processes?

Three developments, which in practice have greatly overlapped and intertwined with one another, have been particularly important in stimulating the growth in the number of policy processes since the EC was founded in the 1950s: increased policy responsibilities, an increased number of types of decisions, and an increased number of member states.

Increased policy responsibilities

In the early years of European integration, the policy responsibilities of the EC were relatively narrowly restricted – largely to policies that were related directly to the operation of the internal market. As such, it was virtually automatic that policy processes were based on the framework set out for such policies in the treaties. This framework was the Community method, which essentially involved the Commission initiating, the Parliament advising, the Council deciding, and the ECJ adjudicating.

However, as the integration process has advanced, so has the EU's policy portfolio broadened far beyond what was originally envisaged in the founding treaties of the 1950s. It has done so both because an increasingly expansive view has been taken regarding what policies are necessary for the free and fair operation of the internal market, and because it has come to be accepted that it is desirable that many non-market-related policies are developed at the European level. But as there has been movement into new policy areas, and as the extent of policy activity in existing policy areas has expanded, so have new, or revised, policy processes had to be devised to accommodate different views taken by national politicians as to the nature of the processes that should apply in these areas. Sometimes, for example, policy areas, or at least aspects of them, have been seen by the governments of some member states as being too sensitive to 'risk' being based on the Community method. In the spheres of foreign and defence policy, for example, governments have recognized the merits of EU states trying to act together, but most governments have not wished this co-operative working to be based on a policy process system in which – as is the case under the Community method – the Commission has exclusive initiating rights, the EP can exert a major influence over decisional outcomes, and the Court can make rulings on decisions taken. Rather, the governments have wanted a looser policy process system; hence the intergovernmental base of EU foreign and defence policy.

Taxation is another policy area where an essentially intergovernmental approach, and hence the preservation of national sovereignty, has been seen as being necessary by many member states. However, since, unlike foreign and defence policies, taxation falls under what used to be called the EU's Community pillar, and post-Lisbon Treaty is the TFEU pillar, other policy process features have had to be used to ensure that a strong element of intergovernmentalism characterizes taxation processes. Accordingly, when it comes to making laws on indirect taxation – which is necessary because sales taxes affect the operation of the internal market – QMV is still unavailable in the Council and the EP is restricted to a consultative role. With direct taxation, however, not even this intergovernmental-inclined version of the Community method has been able to produce much in the way of legislative outputs, except in limited areas that are concerned mainly with eliminating double taxation. But a need to tackle aspects of direct taxation, especially problems concerned with varying national corporate tax systems, was recognized increasingly in the 1990s. The 'solution' adopted was to negotiate a voluntary agreement in the form of the 1997 Tax Code. Because EU law was not involved, the processes that led to agreement on the Code were even more intergovernmental than are the indirect taxation processes, with the Commission not in such a strong position as when legislation is being made, and with the EP being almost wholly marginalized.

Foreign and defence policies and taxation policy are just some of many policy areas that could be given as examples of where the classic Community method has not been seen by national politicians (who determine what EU policy processes should be) as providing a wholly suitable policy process and where other processes have therefore had to be devised. Other chapters of this book provide many further examples of how some of the EU's most important policy areas

have significantly distinctive policy process features. Box 5.1 summarizes some of the key differences between important policy areas.

An increased number of types of decisions

The increased range of policy responsibilities discussed above has not only brought about a direct increase in the number of policy processes but has also done so indirectly in that the EU has had to use a wider range of types of decisions to enable the policy system to operate acceptably and effectively. Different types of decisions usually require their own decision-making processes, though what form these processes should take has been disputed almost constantly by policy practitioners – with the consequence that the number of processes being employed has had to be increased, and those being used have been in almost continuous transition. To give just a few examples of how differing types of decisions have their own decision-making processes: major 'directional' decisions are usually channelled through the European Council; most significant legislative decisions, but not all, require the approval of the EP and the Council of Ministers; non-legislative acts (often called administrative acts) are issued by the Commission, but usually with differing sorts of Council and EP involvement depending on their precise nature; and non-major and non-legislative policy decisions – which can range from the issuing of Commission policy guidelines on an aspect of employment policy to a CFSP statement on the Middle East – use a myriad of policy processes. Box 5.2 summarizes these relationships between types of decision and types of decision-making process.

An increased number of member states

When the EC was established it had just six member states, all of which were roughly similar in terms of the nature of their political and economic systems. It might be thought that, with such a restricted and comparable membership, relatively simple and stable policy processes would be able to prevail. Initially they did, but an example of the sort of differences that have plagued the EC/EU over its policy processes quickly emerged when the French President, Charles de Gaulle, resistant to the notion that an international organization should be able to impose decisions on France, opposed the movement that was planned for

Box 5.1

Distinctive policy process features in major EU policy areas

Policy area	Main processes	Main policy actors within the processes
Internal market rules	Community method	*Commission* *Council* *EP*
Competition	The Commission, operating on the basis of the treaties and EU legislation, exercises significant independent powers	*Commission* *Council* and *EP* (where legislation is being made)
Employment	Mixture of the Community method and OMC	*Commission* *Council* *EP* (where the Community method is employed)
Economic and Monetary	A wide array of processes are used, including the Community method, OMC and centralized decision-making (in respect of monetary policy)	*European Central Bank* *Ecofin Council* *European Council* (mainly in respect of the making of major 'directional' decisions) *Euro Summits* (comprised of heads of government of member states whose currency is the euro) *Eurogroup* (meets at different levels and includes eurozone members only)
Taxation	Mixture of Community method (though with unanimity in the Council) and OMC	*Commission* *Ecofin Council* *EP* (where legislation is being made).

the mid-1960s to allow Council decisions in a few policy areas to be made by a qualified majority rather than unanimity. His resistance led, after several months of wrangling in 1965 during which France withdrew its representatives from key EC bodies, to the January 1966 Luxembourg Compromise. The Compromise had no legal foundation, being purely a political agreement between the governments of the member states, but it was of immense importance because it came to be interpreted as meaning that even where qualified majority voting in the Council was authorized by treaty, no majority vote would be taken if a member state declared the proposal in question to be against its vital national interests. The spirit of the

Luxembourg Compromise subsequently hung heavy in the air, and until the early 1980s had the effect of preventing almost any majority voting apart from on procedural matters and in a few areas where pressing timetables meant decisions could not wait until everyone was agreed.

So there were difficulties over policy processes with just six member states. Naturally, therefore, as more states have acceded to the EC/EU – each with its own political and policy needs, preferences and orientations – there has been an increasing array of views of how policy processes should be constructed and operated. Differing national positions have existed on such key questions as: in what policy areas should

Box 5.1 continued

Policy area	Main processes	Main policy actors within the processes
Budget	Separate budgetary processes for: (i) Multi annual financial frameworks (MFFs); and (ii) Annual budgets	*Commission* *European Council* (in respect of MFFs only) *General Affairs Council* (for MFFs) *Ecofin Council* (for annual budgets). *EP* (power of consent on MFFs and full co-decision powers with the Council on annual budgets)
Foreign and Defence	Intergovernmental co-operation, though some implementing decisions can be taken by QMV	*European Council* and its *President* *High Representative for the CFSP* *Foreign Affairs Council*
External trade	Commission negotiates on behalf of all member states, though on the basis of mandates given to it by the Council and with final agreements being subject to Council and usually also EP approval	*Commission* *Council* *EP*
Enlargement	Commission negotiates on behalf of all member states, though on the basis of instructions given to it by the Council and with final agreements being subject to Council and EP approval	*Commission* *General Affairs Council* *European Council* (involvement varies, mainly in relation to the extent of the enlargement 'challenge') *EP* (power of consent)

QMV be permissible, and when must there be unanimity; in what policy areas should the EP be a joint decision-maker with the Council, and when should it be restricted to an advisory role; in what policy areas is the making of EU law undesirable, and in what areas therefore should legislative decision-making processes not apply; and where legislative processes are not to apply, what processes should be employed? Given that decisions on such questions require the unanimous approval of the member states, it follows that an increased number of member states has naturally resulted in increases in the number of policy processes so as to accommodate differing national positions.

This picture of an increasing number of differing national positions on key policy process questions is further complicated by the fact that states do not adopt consistent positions along an intergovernmental/supranational spectrum with regard to which types of processes are desirable and which are not. National positions on which policy process should apply and in which policy area often vary according to specific national circumstances and choices. Germany, for example, is usually thought of as being towards the supranational end of the spectrum, but in recent years this has not been the case in respect of proposed extensions to QMV in several areas, notably aspects of justice and home affairs.

Box 5.2

Types of decision and associated decision-making processes

Type of decision	Decision-making process	Main decision-making actors
History-making decisions (decisions that have major implications for the overall direction of the European integration process).	There is no fixed process, but final decisions are almost invariably taken at, or at least are approved at, European Council meetings.	*European Council* The involvement of other actors varies according to the policy areas within which decisions are made. For example, the *Commission* is always heavily involved in the preparation of decisions on enlargement, while the *Ecofin Council* and usually also the *European Central Bank* are involved in major policy decisions on macroeconomic policy.
Legislative decisions	There are three legislative processes: (i) Consultation (ii) Ordinary (iii) Consent	*Commission*: drafts virtually all legislative acts. The *Council*: is always the decision-taker or, with the EP, the co-decision-taker. *EP*: consultation rights only under the consultation procedure; full co-decision powers with the Council under the ordinary procedure; approval powers only under the consent procedure.
Non-legislative acts	Different processes apply to the two types of non-legislative acts: (i) Delegated acts (ii) Implementation acts	*Commission* drafts acts and issues most of them in its name. The *Council* and *EP* exercise overseeing powers.
Non-history-making and non-legislative decisions	This category includes a wide variety of decisions and, consequently, also a wide variety of policy processes. For example: • CFSP and CSDP decisions are taken very much on the basis of intergovernmental processes. • Policy co-ordination decisions (common in such areas as social, employment and environment policy) often use the processes associated with the open method of co-ordination (OMC) (see Chapter 7).	Varies greatly. For example: • The *High Representative* and the *Foreign Affairs Council* are always important actors in connection with CFSP/CSDP decisions. • The *Commission* and (varying formations of) the *Council* are always important actors in connection with OMC decisions.

Enlargement has, of course, increased the prospect for any member state that it might find itself being outvoted in the Council when QMV applies, because the more member states there are then the more member states are necessary to constitute a blocking minority. In recent years, and in particular after the 2004 and 2007 enlargements, this has become a major concern for the EU's large member states. This is because, while previously a large member state could be, and sometimes was, outvoted, generally it could use its weight and status to resist anything to which it was opposed particularly strongly. The prospect of being able to resist in this way has become much less certain, because enlargement has resulted in many more allies needing to be found if qualified majorities are to be denied. In consequence, policy processes other than the Community method with QMV have been attractive in some – nationally important and/or sensitive – policy areas.

In addition to the impact arising from an ever-increasing number of differing national positions and concerns, enlargement has also impacted on policy processes in a more general way: by raising questions relating to the appropriateness and efficiency of existing policy processes in a larger Union. Clearly, the more participants there are in any decision-making situation, the more difficult decision-making is likely to be unless the decision-making rules are flexible and designed to prevent minorities from being particularly obstructive. This consideration has promoted new EU policy processes as well as changes to the nature of existing processes. An example of the former is the Amsterdam Treaty provision, which was streamlined in the Nice Treaty, providing for differentiation: that is, for policy development to be able to take place within the Union framework without all member states being partially or fully involved. An example of the latter is the provision in all of the major revising treaties for an expanded remit for QMV in the Council.

How many EU policy processes are there?

All advanced democratic political systems have several differing policy process arrangements. So, for example, in the making of major legislation, political executives customarily take the lead in formulation and then legislatures scrutinize and vote on the proposals.

Political executives and legislatures are usually less actively involved in administrative legislation, with their roles tending to be confined to oversight. And in respect of many non-legislative processes, such as much of foreign policy-making, political executives, or sometimes even just the heads of political executives, tend to dominate.

So, to note that the EU has a number of differing policy processes does not say anything very distinctive about it. But what *is* distinctive about the EU is the very large number of its processes. The precise number of processes that can be identified naturally depends on the criteria used for counting them. A figure of well over 100 formal policy processes can be identified if account is taken of what may be thought of as important but not necessarily 'first-rank' variations, such as whether or not the EESC and the CoR must be consulted on a policy proposal. If attention is narrowed to first-rank variations the figure naturally drops but still remains, by comparison with policy processes in national political systems, very high. An indication of this is seen in the figure given by the Constitutional Convention – the body that in 2003–4 prepared and undertook much of the drafting of the Constitutional Treaty and which as part of its work looked closely at the EU's processes. After controlling for significant varying involvements and powers of the major EU institutions, and whether or not QMV was available in the Council of Ministers, the Convention identified no less than 28 significantly different procedures.

Another indication of the EU's large number of policy processes can be given by narrowing 'the catchment area' to legislation-making procedures alone. Three significantly different procedures exist: ordinary (called 'co-decision' until the Lisbon Treaty); consultation; and consent (called 'assent' until the Lisbon Treaty). (Prior to the Lisbon Treaty there was a fourth legislative procedure: co-operation.) However, if variations within these procedures are counted, the number rises to well into double figures, with the most significant variations being according to the availability or not of QMV in the Council, the powers of the EP, and the consultation rights, if any, of the EESC and the CoR. (The nature of these legislative procedure is described in Chapter 6.)

The large number of EU policy processes is not, it should be emphasized, merely a dry observational point. It is extremely important in practical terms, since each process has different implications for such key matters as the number and nature of policy actors involved, their powers, the relations between them, and the duration of policy-making deliberations and negotiations.

The Complexity of Policy Processes

Many of the EU's policy processes are complex in nature.

The most obvious reason for this is the nature of many of the EU's formal decision-making rules. The formal rules EU policy-makers must follow are laid down in a number of places, of which the treaties are the most important. Some of these rules are reasonably clear and simple. For example, the rule as to whether an EU membership application should be accepted is straightforward, with Article 49 TEU stating that 'the Council … shall act unanimously after consulting the Commission and after receiving the consent of the European Parliament, which shall act by an absolute majority of its component members'. But many rules are by no means so straightforward, therefore the rules for making EU laws under the ordinary procedure (which are mainly, but not wholly, set out in Article 294, TFEU) are highly complicated. At their heart they provide for up to a three-stage procedure in both the Council and the EP, while allowing for agreement at stages one or two. Beyond this core, the ordinary procedure rules include variations on matters such as whether or not QMV can be used in the Council, and whether the EESC and the CoR must be consulted on legislative proposals. The procedure is subject to a timetable in its later, but not its earlier, stages.

As in most policy and decision-making systems, the formally laid-down EU rules do, however, tell only part of the story of what actually happens in practice. A host of less formal factors – most of them arising from a mixture of logistical necessities and political pressures and requirements – also play a part in shaping how policy processes operate. An example of semi-informal dimensions of EU policy processes is the contraction of inter-institutional agreements between the main policy institutions. There are several such agreements between, in varying combinations, the

Commission, the Council of Ministers and the EP. Some of these agreements are designed to clarify insufficiently detailed treaty-based rules, while others have the purpose of strengthening an institution's position (usually that of the EP) compared to its treaty-bestowed powers and responsibilities.

As was briefly shown on page 78, an example of semi-informal procedures is the use of trilogues during the ordinary legislative procedure. Bringing together representatives of the Commission, the Council and the EP, these have as their purpose the contracting of informal agreements between the three bodies before legislative proposals are formally considered at the first or second reading stages, or in a conciliation committee. Because the participants in trilogues are usually key policy players – the Commission's team is normally headed by a relevant director or director general, the Council's team by the deputy permanent representative and the relevant working group chairman of the state holding the Council Presidency, and the EP's team by the chairman and *rapporteur* of the relevant committee – deals can often be made that are then accepted when put into the formal procedures. The use of trilogues to supplement formal procedures can thus serve to speed-up policy processes. They can also do two other things. First, they can offer advantages to the positions of the policy actors who participate in the informal exchanges and negotiations (see Farrell and Héritier, 2004, on this). Second, they can strengthen the negotiating positions of the institutions that are least desirous of holding a trilogue. In this context, Häge and Kaeding (2007) have shown that the Council, because it has more limited resources at its disposal, is generally more desirous than the EP to achieve agreements at an early stage of legislative procedures, and in particular is usually more desirous than the EP of avoiding formal conciliation committee negotiations. In consequence, the EP can extract concessions from the Council by the latter's eagerness to arrive at early agreements in trilogues.

The Varying Mixtures of Supranationalism and Intergovernmentalism

EU policy processes vary enormously – both between and within policy areas – regarding the extent to which they incorporate supranational and intergovernmental characteristics. Essentially, the more policy processes are dominated either by policy actors that are not fully controllable by member state governments – which means primarily the Commission, the EP, and the EU's courts – or by decision-making arrangements in which member state governments are involved but which they cannot fully control – which means where European Council or Council of Ministers decisions can be taken by QMV – then the more the processes are supranational in character. By contrast, the more the policy input of the supranational actors is limited and the more member state governments can control policy processes individually – by having recourse to a veto over proposed decisions if necessary – then the more policy processes are intergovernmental.

The extent to which individual policy processes are more or less supranational or intergovernmental is a consequence of judgements made by the governments of the member states over the years. It is the governments that ultimately determine policy activities that the EU will be involved in, and how decisions relating to those activities will be made. In making such determinations, many factors come into play. Broadly speaking, supranationality is most likely to be seen as being an acceptable, or even desirable, component of a policy process when at least one of the following characteristics applies in a policy area: the policy is not viewed as being overly politically sensitive and may even be regarded as being in large part essentially technical in nature (as with many internal market policy matters – where the Commission is expected to provide policy leads and where EU law, made usually on the basis of QMV availability in the Council, is widespread); the policy is thought to require impartial actions by an independent body (as with competition policy – where the Commission's powers to act without Council authorization are considerable); and where speed can be important (as with much of trade policy – where QMV is available in the Council and the Commission has considerable discretion with respect to implementation decisions). By contrast, intergovernmentalism features strongly in policy processes that are politically sensitive and/or where the governments of at least some member states have particular reasons for wanting to maintain control. These reasons include sovereignty and/or national identity considerations (which are important in respect of foreign and defence policies) and reasons arising from concerns that cessa-

tion of control could result in the imposition of unwelcome policies (especially with regard to revenue-raising and expenditure matters).

Box 5.3 provides an approximation of the extent to which the EU's major areas of policy responsibility are supranational or intergovernmental in nature. (The word 'approximation' is used here because exactness is not possible given that most policy areas contain both supranational and intergovernmental features.)

Policy Processes Ensure that Member States Have Confidence in the EU System

The essential purpose of the EU is to enable member states to pursue policy goals more effectively than if they were left to their own devices. The states seek to achieve this greater effectiveness through various forms of policy co-operation and integration.

But policy co-operation and integration come at a price. They may be necessary in an ever more interdependent Europe (even non-member states such as Norway and Switzerland have to work very closely with the EU), but they mean that the identification, and even more so the pursuit, of national policy preferences are no longer solely a matter for national actors. They have become part of processes in which the national has, in important respects, had to give way to the collective.

This movement towards the collective has resulted in the EU as it is now constituted, which is essentially a quasi-federal arrangement. Like all such arrangements with dispersed centres of power, it is necessary that the EU retains the confidence of its members if it is to be an organization that functions efficiently and without too much internal dissension. Federal and quasi-federal systems can only survive if the constituent units believe the benefits of membership outweigh the costs. If an EU member state were to become very disillusioned with the balance between these benefits and costs, it could become a highly disruptive member and could ultimately begin to question the value of its membership.

It is therefore necessary that policy processes are constructed and operate in such a way as to ensure

Box 5.3

Major EU policy areas grouped according to the extent to which they are supranational or intergovernmental in nature*

Mainly Supranational	Mixed	Mainly Intergovernmental
Agriculture	Cross-border crime	Citizenship issues
Competition	Environment	Defence
Fishing	Internal market	Employment
Monetary (for eurozone members)	Internal security and justice Regional Social Transport	Energy Foreign Health Macroeconomic (especially for non eurozone members) Taxation

Notes: * Policy areas are judged to be more supranational according to:

• the extent to which institutions that are not controlled by the governments of the member states have independent decision-making powers (in practice, this primarily means the extent to which the Commission and the CJEU have such powers); and

• the extent to which institutions that are controlled by the governments of the member states (which, in practice, means the European Council and the Council of Ministers) can take decisions by QMV.

Very few policy areas do not contain some supranational and some intergovernmental features but, as the box is intended to show, the nature of the balance varies considerably.

that all member states – not least the smaller member states, which are at obvious risk of being dominated by larger ones – have confidence in the system. All member states need to be satisfied that their policy preferences and interests are recognized and not easily overridden, and that policies devised at the EU level will advance their national goals.

There are three main ways in which this is achieved, one of which is formalized in EU law and the other two of which stem from non-legal factors.

Legal protections and guarantees

There are many ways in which EU law, not least in the form of the treaties, provides arrangements for member states to be able to input directly into policy

processes. The most obvious such way is, of course, via the EU's institutions which, as was shown in Chapters 3 and 4, are based on various forms of national representation. For some institutions, notably the Commission and the CJEU, these representations (using 'representation' loosely, since the members of these bodies are required to act in a non-partisan manner) are based on a principle of equality of member states. For other institutions, notably the Council (in respect of voting strengths) and the EP (in respect of the number of MEPs) a more proportional principle in terms of member state size applies, but with small member states being over-represented. This over-representation principle is found in some form in all federal and quasi-federal systems.

Another very important legally-based assurance that member states have is the continuance of the unanimity requirement in the Council on certain sensitive policy issues. While most legislative decisions can now be taken by QMV, the veto is still available in several key policy areas, including taxation and aspects of AFSJ.

As well as providing for direct input into EU policy processes, EU law also empowers the EU's member states to be able to exercise a certain amount of direct control over the most supranational of the EU's institutions, the Commission and the Court. Control is admittedly limited over the Court, being confined to the power of initial appointment, but over the Commission it is considerable, covering not just the key role of the national governments in the appointment of the College, but also the fact that most Commission proposals need Council approval if they are to be applied.

Informal aspects of policy processes

The governments of the member states are sensitive to one others' political situations and requirements. If it can be avoided, they do not approve policies to which one or more member state governments are strongly opposed. It is recognized that to impose an unwanted policy on another state or states can be a recipe for dissatisfaction in the state or states concerned, and may also result in problems with policy implementation – which is a common concern in federal systems (on the latter, see Falkner *et al.*, 2004). There is also the fact that, while a member state government may be in a majority on one issue it is likely to find itself in a minority position at a later date on another issue, and then it will want a sympathetic view taken of its predicament.

So, whatever the formal rules may provide for, all EU governmental policy actors usually try to ensure that no member state has a policy imposed on it to which its representatives, especially those in the Council, are firmly opposed. At the least, there are normally attempts to temper the proposed policy to allay some of the national concerns. The clearest way in which this informal operating principle works is in the Council, where there is a strong and persisting preference for decisions to be taken by consensus even when a vote is possible. QMV is available for most Council legislative decisions, but it is used explicitly in only around 15 per cent of the cases where it could be.

Moreover, where it is used, it is only after extensive deliberations designed to assuage the concerns of states that are uneasy or opposed, and it is unusual for more than a couple of states to vote against or to abstain. (See Chapter 3 for an account of voting in the Council.)

The nature of inter-state cleavages

Salient cleavages between the EU member states are, for the most part, cross-cutting rather than cumulative. So, for example, the larger states are not all northern states, do not share the same view as to how liberal (non-interventionist) market-related policies should be, are not all committed to the preservation of the CAP in its existing form, do not all participate in monetary union, differ in their support for a common immigration policy, at times part company on what should be the nature of the Atlantic relationship, and so on.

The fact that cleavages are primarily cross-cutting is crucial in promoting a flexible and ever-changing internal alliance system between the member states. Indeed, federal systems depend for their survival on such shifting alliances, not least because they ensure that no constituent unit (member state in the EU's case) is in a semi-permanent minority. In the EU there are no permanent and fixed alliances or blocs grouped around big/small, rich/poor or north/south. Rather, the cleavage system results in member states coming together in an alliance system in which there are different combinations on different issues. As such, this system is crucial in helping both to integrate states into the EU policy system and to ensure that the system is characterized by relatively harmonious inter-state relations.

The Dispersal of Leadership

Compared with the way in which political leadership exists and operates at national levels, there may be said to be a leadership deficit at the EU level. At national levels the precise nature of political leadership varies, according largely to how constitutional stipulations and electoral outcomes combine, but governments provide the main source of, and usually a reasonably clear focus for, leadership. Other political actors respond to this focus, often in an almost semi-automatic positive or negative way according to their political affiliations.

In the EU, where there is a system of governance but no government, there is no such central focus. A key reason for this is that the EU's system of governance contains no clear separation of powers – either of a horizontal nature (with executive, legislative and judicial powers divided between institutions) or of a vertical nature (with policy responsibilities divided between the EU and its member states). Rather, responsibilities are shared and interwoven in a manner that can at times make it difficult to identify precisely who is responsible for what.

Sources of leadership

An important aspect of this sharing of powers is that there are several potential sources of policy leadership. The most important of these are the Commission, the European Council and its President, the Council Presidency, and groups of member states. Each of these potential sources of policy leadership has resources which can in certain circumstances be used to enable leadership to be exercised. Among the most important of the power resources that are available are treaty provisions, political weight, information and expertise and political skills.

Treaty provisions

The Commission's near-exclusive power to make legislative proposals is an obvious example of treaty provisions granting considerable leadership potential. Another is the assignment to the European Council of the task to 'provide the Union with the necessary impetus for its development and [to] define the general political directions and priorities guidelines thereof' (Article 15, TEU). And a third example is the charging to the High Representative of the task to 'conduct the Union's common foreign and security policy' (Article 18, TEU).

Political weight

The European Council has, as has just been shown, strong treaty powers. But, the principal basis of

its ability to act and pronounce on almost anything it wishes is the status of its members, which gives it a very considerable political weight. Who, for example, is to tell heads of government that they cannot launch a policy initiative? Given that the European Council is largely beyond the reach of the CJEU, the extent to which any authority figures or institutions can rein in the heads of government is very limited.

Another example of political status resulting in political weight that can be used as a leadership resource is the way in which the Commission can use its position as a non-partisan policy actor to advantage. Proposals coming from it – whether new proposals or those designed to find a compromise between differing national positions on an existing matter – are likely to be viewed with much less suspicion than they would if they had come from national actors.

The importance of political weight as a leadership resource is also seen in the sizes of member states. As shown in Chapter 4, there is no simple relationship between the size of a member state and the political leadership it exercises in the EU – as the contrasting cases of France and Italy demonstrates: despite being of comparable size on most counts, they have differed hugely in the leadership they have offered. But, none the less, larger member states do normally have greater political standing than smaller ones, which gives them a greater capacity for providing leadership. Whether, of course, they choose to provide leadership can be a quite different matter, as Germany – which is the EU's largest member state but which has been generally reluctant to play the role of a policy leader (apart from with regard to eurozone policy) – shows.

A final example of political weight is provided by the European Parliament, which, as the only directly-elected EU institution, has a claim to democratic legitimacy that other institutions just cannot match. The EP seeks to use this power resource to boost its political status and its claims to be at least heard, if not to lead, in all policy-making situations. Related to this, the Parliament also makes much of how Council decision-making is usually shrouded and inaccessible to the European polity, while it links directly with the citizenry via such operating practices as holding hearings with policy interests, having open committee meetings, and making its plenary sessions available for viewing on the internet.

Information and expertise

Access to information and expertise that others do not have, or do not fully have, provides leadership opportunities. In most policy areas, the Commission is especially well placed in this regard. It is so by virtue of its 'in-house' knowledge and expertise of the EU's policy activities, and by its ability to marshal the knowledge and expertise it does not itself have – the latter being possible through such devices as making use of advisory and expert groups, contracting for research to be conducted on its behalf, and establishing high-level working bodies to examine particular matters (such as the body that in 2005 produced the important Kok report on the Lisbon Strategy).

Information and expertise can take not only a 'hard' form but also a 'softer' form of knowing what other policy actors *really* want and will accept. Because of its perceived impartiality, the Commission has a particular advantage in this regard, with member states sometimes being willing to 'reveal their hand' to it in a way they are not with other policy actors – including the Council presidency. Another policy actor who can benefit from this sort of resource advantage is the High Representative, who has the potential – not least because hid/her term of office is much longer than that of the Council presidency and of most member state foreign ministers – to build up a highly developed sense of what will and will not work: a sense that can owe much to being given the time to cultivate, both within and outside the EU, a network of advantageous personal relationships.

Political skills

The grasp and exercise of political skills varies considerably among EU policy actors. To take, for example, the Council presidency, there can be considerable variations not only between the skills displayed by member states during their term of office but also between ministers from the same state during a term of office. One minister may have an ambitious agenda but be under-prepared for meetings and too rushed in seeking decisions, while another minister may have a more consolidationist agenda but actually achieve more by displaying a firmer grasp of agenda items and displaying a greater sensitivity to the mood of meetings.

The dispersed and shifting nature of leadership

Leadership resources in the EU are thus dispersed, with the consequence that so also is the exercise of leadership. Indeed, not only is leadership dispersed but it also shifts according to context. This dispersed and shifting nature of EU leadership manifests itself in at least three ways in policy processes.

First, because of the differing resources at their disposal, the potential of policy actors to exercise leadership varies between stages of the policy-making cycle. So, for example, member states that have a strong record of achievement, and therefore considerable status in a policy area, are well placed to be able to play a leading role in framing public discourse and setting policy agendas – as, for example, has been the case with the Scandinavian states and environmental policy. States that also have considerable leadership potential during policy framing and agenda setting include ones that possess material resources that the policy area needs if it is to be successful – as with France and the UK in respect of the CSDP. When it comes to another policy stage – policy proposing – the Commission has a particular advantage.

Second, the leadership exercised by specific policy actors can vary over time. The most obvious illustration of this is the variation in the leadership offered by the Commission, which is commonly agreed to have been highly effective during some periods in its history and much less effective during other periods. The most effective periods were the first few years after the EC came into existence, when Walter Hallstein was Commission President, and the early years of the Jacques Delors Presidency – from 1985 until about 1991. The drive provided by both Hallstein and Delors was clearly crucial in advancing policies, but it should be noted also that both were in office at favourable times: in Hallstein's case, when policy foundations were being laid down and before the Luxembourg Compromise served to slow down decision-making; and in Delors' case, when there was general support from all member states for the consolidation of the internal market – from which much of the policy programme of his term of office derived.

A rather different example of leadership potential and practice varying over time is provided by the so-called Franco-German axis. From the early days of the

EC until well into the 1990s, much of the driving force behind the European integration process was provided by France and Germany working in close co-operation. A number of factors facilitated their working relationship and the considerable influence it was able to exert on EU policy development: the historical legacy of the European integration process, which was in large part initiated as a way of bringing these two traditional enemies together; their position for many years as not just two of the large member states but as the perceived two strongest states; and the close personal relations that were established for much of period between the national leaders – De Gaulle and Adenauer in the 1960s, D'Estaing and Schmidt in the 1970s, and Mitterrand and Kohl in the second half of the 1980s and first half of the 1990s. In recent years their leadership influence has not been quite what it was, but it remains important in policy areas where they carry particular weight and where they have actively sought to work together to achieve a policy aim. The most important such policy area has been the EMU, where:

- In 2004–5 the two governments were highly active in the processes that led to the reform – or, more precisely, the loosening – of the conditions of EMU's Stability and Growth Pact.
- From 2010, as the euro came under intense strain in the wake of government debt problems in some eurozone states, Chancellor Merkel and President Sarkozy collaborated closely on plans to resolve the situation. Their collaboration resulted in them being to the fore in devising during 2011 the Fiscal Compact that was accepted by all eurozone states and was (eventually) supported by all non-eurozone states apart from the Czech Republic and the UK (see Chapter 10).

However, EMU apart, France and Germany have not been able to provide and sustain the broad policy drive that once characterized their relationship. A number of factors account for this, of which the most important are: the effects of enlargement – increasing numbers of member states have naturally made it more difficult for just two states, albeit large and traditionally core states, to retain the position they had when the EU was much smaller; the emergence of some significant policy differences between the two – on, for example, the nature of the Atlantic relation-

ship; and less close personal relationships between the occupants of the posts of French President and German Chancellor.

Third, leadership can and does vary between policy areas. This is largely because of variations in motivations to provide leadership, as well as the availability of leadership resources to would-be leaders. So, for example, France is strongly motivated to take a lead in respect of CAP matters and is highly influential in this policy area – because of both its position as a large member state and the importance of agriculture to the French economy. But France is not so motivated to attempt to provide leadership and not so much in command of key leadership resources in policy areas such as environment or transport, and accordingly has not sought to assert a leadership role for itself in these areas.

An example of a policy area where the Commission – working in this case in close collaboration with the European Council – has been the main driving force is enlargement. EU enlargement policy processes place the Commission in a central position, most particularly by charging it with drawing up the reports that provide the guidelines for key European Council decisions on whether negotiations should be opened with an applicant, whether they are proceeding satisfactorily, whether they have been concluded successfully, and when applicants with which negotiations have been concluded should be permitted to accede. In the 2004/7 enlargement round, the Commission was ahead of the field in that it moved enlargement processes along much more quickly than the governments of many member states would ideally have preferred. An important factor in explaining why the Commission was able to do this was that there was no consensus between the national governments on the key enlargement questions, with those in the slow stream risking considerable awkwardness if they were seen to be resisting Commission 'conscience calls' to be open and welcoming to new democracies and liberal economies.

A need for stronger leadership?

Looking at the leadership issue as whole, the dispersal of policy leadership, both between EU institutions and between member states, is functional in helping to promote confidence in the EU system. The fact that policy leadership is not over-concentrated – an integral feature of federal systems – but rather is spread around promotes inclusion, with many policy actors having either the duty or the opportunity to offer leadership, and no policy actors needing to feel that they are consistently being led by actors advancing unwanted or unacceptable policy positions.

That said, however, there is a view that if the EU is to operate effectively and efficiently, it needs stronger leadership structures and arrangements. As the EU has grown in size and come to embrace not just more member states but also a much greater variety of these, each with its own national policy needs and preferences, then so has it become necessary, in the eyes of many EU practitioners and observers, for EU leadership to be more focused and streamlined. This line of thinking provided much of the rationale behind the designing of the Constitutional Treaty and, when this Treaty could not be ratified, the successor Lisbon Treaty. The most important new provisions on leadership provided for in both treaties were the creation of a semi-permanent President of the European Council (to replace the existing rotating presidency) and the merging of the posts of EU High Representative for the Foreign and Security Policy and of Commissioner for External Relations into one post: this post was named EU Foreign Minister under the Constitutional Treaty but was downgraded in the Lisbon Treaty to the seemingly less prestigious, but more accurate, 'High Representative of the Union for the Common Foreign and Security Policy'. Whether these Treaty changes will result in stronger EU policy leadership in the long term remains to be seen, but early indications suggest that only very modest changes will occur. Indeed, there appears to be, if anything, greater leadership dispersal than ever before.

This problem of dispersal of leadership is exacerbated by most of the EU's many potential leaders becoming agitated when leadership initiatives are launched that do not include them. So, concerns about attempts to exercise leadership without including everyone have been expressed almost constantly since the onset of the global financial crisis and economic recession. From the early stages of the crisis there was great uncertainty and no little disagreement in EU elite circles concerning which policy responsibilities lay at the EU level and which at the national level, and also concerning who should be taking the policy lead at the EU level. At varying times, policy leads have

been offered by the Council Presidency (especially when the French were in the chair in the last six months of 2008), the Commission, the European Council, the Heads of Government of the larger member states meeting in different combinations (with, as noted above, Merkel–Sarkozy meetings being the most frequent), and the Eurogroup – with the Eurogroup meeting for the first time at Heads of Government level in December 2008. (The 2012 Treaty on Stability, Coordination and Governance – see Chapter 10 – provides for Eurogroup Heads of Government meetings to be held regularly, and for there to be a President of eurozone summits.)

The lack of inclusiveness of selective meetings of Heads of Government has produced annoyance on the part of many of those who have not been invited. So, for example, when the Heads of Government of six member states (Germany, France, Italy, the UK, Spain and the Netherlands) met in February 2009 to prepare for a G-20 meeting to be held in April, representatives of several other EU governments did not hide their dissatisfaction. It was a dissatisfaction that was driven partly by beliefs that the priority should be to broker an agreed EU position and partly by concerns about the possibly changing nature of leadership in the EU – with the seeming increasing attempts by larger member states to concentrate leadership in their own hands a matter of particular concern.

The Consensual Nature of (Most) Policy Processes

Despite, as has just been shown, there being little shortage of leadership in the EU, albeit of a dispersed kind, EU policy processes are highly consensual in nature. Indeed, consensuality is a central feature of the policy-making culture of the EU. With the exception of those policy areas where differentiation applies, it is all but impossible for policy initiatives to be carried through all policy-making stages unless they command wide initial support and are adapted in their transition to bring doubters on board. As Hix (2006, p. 145) observes, EU policy-making is 'at the extreme end of the majoritarian-consensus spectrum, and is perhaps more consensus orientated in its design than any polity in the history of democratic government'. Hix (2008, pp. 31–49) has also observed that a number of treaty reforms since the SEA – such as the greater provision for QMV in the Council, the possibility of the Commission President-designate being nominated by QMV, and the need for the Commission-designate to be approved by the EP – have all served to edge the EU in a more majoritarian direction. But, it has only been an edging, for while formal and informal voting has increased in the Council, the preference is still for consensual decision-making, QMV has not yet been used to appoint a Commission President (even though the Belgian prime minister, Guy Verhofstadt, almost certainly would have gained qualified majority support in the European Council in 2004 if the vote had been put), and it remains the case that finding majorities in the Council and the EP invariably requires bringing together a wide range of political actors and views. It is true that the existence since the autumn of 2004 of a centre-right majority in the main political institutions – the European Council and Council of Ministers, the Commission, and the EP – has brought the EU closer to majoritarianism than ever before, but, as will be shown below, it has not in practice been majoritarianism as that word is commonly understood. A slightly more liberal economic agenda has been pursued, but it has still not been possible to take decisions on key issues without bringing the most important political actors 'on board'.

The consensual nature of policy-making stems from a number of factors. One of these is the large number of policy actors with significant power resources at their disposal – for example, the Commission's monopoly of legislative initiation, the Council's veto power over virtually all policy and legislative proposals, and the EP's veto power over most legislative proposals. A second factor is the wide spread of political views in the policy-making institutions. On economic orientations, for example, they range from clear economic liberals to firm social democrats. A third factor is the high voting thresholds within the Commission and the Council. In the Commission the threshold is informal because it can take decisions by simple majority vote. It rarely does so, however, and always prefers to try to find an agreed view – not least because the Commission's position on a policy issue would be weakened if it was known to be divided. As for the Council, there are still important policy areas where unanimous agreement is formally required. Where QMV is permissible, the threshold is high (over 70 per cent of weighted votes), and in any event it is not usually used to push through significant policy matters where there is strong opposition from a member state. A fourth factor is that EU policy processes, mirroring a familiar pattern in federal systems, provide an enormous number of access points for non-institutional actors both to have their say and to wield influence. Most of these actors – be they business, environmental, consumer, regional or any other type of policy interest – lobby vigorously at both national and EU levels. They do so at national levels primarily as a way of trying to have their voice heard in the Council and the EP. They do so directly at the EU level, with both the Commission and the EP being generally open to representations from interests. Beyond the Commission and the EP, the EESC and the CoR have the representation of interests as their specific brief.

Of course, the existence of many different views on most policies means that compromise is usually crucial for consensuality to be achieved, and for the way to be opened for decisions to be made. This importance of compromise is seen both within the main policy process actors and between them. Within them, both the College of Commissioners and the Council of Ministers are reluctant to take decisions by voting (though the latter less so than it used to be). Each tries to operate on the basis of consensus whenever possible, which means that Commissioners and ministers often have to shift from preferred positions. There were only about twenty votes in the whole of the Prodi College, and these were mainly of an indicative nature, and voting has all but disappeared under Barroso (interview with former Commissioner; see also Kurpas et al., 2008, pp. 23–4). Voting – of both a formal and informal nature – is certainly used in the Council but, as we have seen, it is not preferred. As Jonathan Aus (2008, p. 100) observes: 'Avoiding isolation, accommodating differences, and reaching agreements along the lines proposed by the permanently involved Commission and rotating Council presidency are dominant features of the Council's political culture.' Box 5.4 sets out the key reasons why there is such a strong preference for consensuality in the Council. In the EP, the existence of several political groups, the absence of a majority political group, and the requirement in some important votes for majorities to consist not just of nominal majorities but a

Reasons why there is a strong preference in the Council for consensual decision-making

- It is important for the smooth running of the EU that no member states become disaffected as a result of their national needs and preferences being overridden.
- States that are in a majority on some issues know that they may find themselves in a minority – and therefore need friends – on other issues.
- Policies and laws imposed on unwilling member states may be badly implemented.
- Some types of decisions – including most of those when the intergovernmental and open method policy process modes apply (see Chapter 7) – are subject to unanimity voting rules.

majority of the EU's membership, combine to mean that the negotiation of deals between the political groups is an ongoing and everyday part of how the EP operates.

Between the institutions, institutional interdependency means that the main policy-making institutions have no option but to be sensitive and accommodating to the others. So, for example, it is not in the interests of the Commission to bring forward legislative proposals that have no chance of being approved by the Council and/or the EP. It therefore anticipates Council and EP reactions, which may lead to it adjusting preferred positions when drafting legislation. More 'open' compromise is seen when legislative processes formally begin, with the Commission, Council and EP searching constantly for accommodations that will enable legislative proposals to become EU law. In most cases, this proves possible, even if the process is sometimes long and difficult. Within EU legislative processes there is what may be termed 'a culture of negotiating leading to compromise' between the three institutions. The legislative wheels are oiled by an array of informal contacts and exchanges between the three– including trilogues and conciliation meetings that have as their precise

purpose the identification and negotiation of compromise deals. The outcome of all this inter-institutional activity within legislative processes is that very few proposals completely fail in the sense that the institutions cannot agree on a text.

The 2006 Services Directive, which has a good claim to be the most contested directive in the EU's history, illustrates, albeit in a particularly sharp way, the many sorts of compromises that may be required for policy processes to be concluded with a positive outcome. As shown in Chapter 8, when the Directive was launched by the Commission in 2004 it was based on the mutual recognition principle (which essentially means that the regulations to be applied to products traded in the internal market are based on home country standards) and was wide-ranging in its coverage of service areas. By the time the Directive was eventually adopted in 2006, varying sorts of opposition from member state governments, MEPs, and policy interests to core aspects of the perceived distributional consequences of the Commission's draft proposal had resulted in all policy actors having to make concessions. The adopted Directive was radically changed from the Commission's proposal, with home country standards having been largely replaced by those of the host country (though this was not stated formally), and with a number of very important service areas – including health services, public transport and utilities – having been placed outside of the scope of the Directive (on the 'story' of the Services Directive, see Schmidt, 2008).

Consensus and the compromises between key actors that consensus requires are thus core features of EU policy processes. Compromises are vital in unblocking processes when stalemate is the alternative, while consensus serves to promote confidence in the system, both in that nothing too distasteful is imposed on a reluctant minority and in that there is usually 'something for everybody'. But, inevitably, consensus also comes with a price, or rather a number of prices. One is that, where policy differences between key policy actors on an issue are deep, no general agreement may be possible, with the consequence that either no decision is made or it is so only on a differentiated basis. A second is that disproportionate power may be placed in the hands of small dissenting minorities. And a third is, as Wurzel and Hayward (2012) have put it, that giving priority to reaching consensual agreements is usually 'at the cost of policy expedition and effectiveness'. In consequence, decisional outcomes may be neither as strong nor as clear as is ideally desirable. The former may result in unsatisfactory policy content, while the latter may result in it falling to the CJEU to clarify just what the law is. (A strong policy role for central courts as a 'clarifier' is a persistent feature of federal systems, with a particularly important consequence of court decisions usually being to protect and strengthen internal markets.)

The Role of Ideology

Ideology is generally seen as being less salient at the EU level in shaping policy-making than it is at the national level. The main reason for this is the fundamentally different natures of the political systems at the two levels. At the national level, the main policy leads are expected to be provided by governments that have been elected to office on the basis of party political manifestos. At the EU level, there is no such equivalent political actor.

In addition to this lack of an ideologically-guided political body at the centre of policy processes, other factors are also seen as giving EU processes a somewhat non-ideological character. There is, for example, the way in which national interests rather than ideological beliefs can be the most important factor in guiding the behaviour of national representatives on certain policy issues; there is the dispersal of power within and between the policy-process institutions, which results in contestation over policies not normally assuming conventional majority/minority and left/right forms; there is the supposedly technical nature of many EU policies, with the most obvious left/right issues – such as welfare, health, education and direct taxation policies – largely being national responsibilities and with much of the EU's policy time taken up with such matters as market regulation and environmental protection; and there is the highly consensual nature of EU policy processes, which is no more clearly demonstrated than in the way the two major political groups in the EP – the centre-right European People's Party and the centre-left Progressive Alliance of Socialists and Democrats – frequently vote together on important issues

But the case that ideology does not feature much in EU policy processes should not be overstated. Indeed,

from a critical political economy viewpoint, ideology is absolutely central. This is because policy processes are viewed as being largely concerned with consolidating and extending liberal market principles across the policy spectrum. (See, for example, Apeldoorn, 2002; Bieler and Morton, 2001; Cafruny and Ryner, 2003.) This importance of economic liberal ideas in driving the EU's socio-economic policy agenda is seen – and not just by critical political economists – to be no more clearly demonstrated than in the near abandonment of Keynesian principles by member state governments in response to the post-2008 economic crisis. The response has involved most governments slashing public spending and enacting such long-term cost-saving policies as reforming pensions systems and reducing the sizes of civil services. In the same vein, another important policy area where critical political economists see the role of ideology shining through is enlargement policy. So, for example, Cafruny and Ryder (2009, p. 235) argue, with respect to the accessions of Central and Eastern European countries:

> Enlargement has resulted in nominal equality but has also served to reproduce the power of transnational European capital over the new member states. Full Union membership played an important role in facilitating market discipline and the penetration of western capital on a scale that otherwise might not have been possible.

But even if a critical political economy position is not taken, ideology can still be seen as featuring strongly in EU policy processes. One reason for this is that many EU policy issues are undeniably highly ideological in nature: social policy, for example, and labour market policy. A second and related reason is that there is no clear demarcation between technical and political issues. A market-related issue concerning, for example, the requirements that must be met by financial institutions wishing to conduct business in EU states beyond the state of origin may be seen as being essentially technical by some but as highly political by others if it is thought to have potential implications for such matters as employment levels, availability of mortgages for first-home buyers, or working conditions. When policy actors take steps on such issues during policy processes – from the Commission drafting proposals to ministers and MEPs taking final decisions – choices between alternative courses of action have to be made. And a third reason is that ideology as measured by the significance of political affiliation *is* important. This importance is seen, for example, in the leaders of Europe's major centre-right and centre-left political parties (including those in domestic opposition) often holding separate meetings before European summits to try and agree on joint positions. An example of such a meeting was that held by the EU's centre-right leaders two weeks before the March 2011 summit, which was scheduled to be focused mainly on measures designed to create greater economic stability. At their meeting, held in Helsinki, the leaders agreed on a five-point economic reform plan (Willis, 2011). The importance of political affiliation is seen also in the EP, where political group membership is the single most important factor in shaping the voting behaviour of MEPs (see Hix and Noury, 2009; Hix *et al.*, 2007; Scully *et al.*, 2012).

The potential importance of ideology to the conduct of EU policy processes may be said to have been put to the test since October 2004, when the first Barroso College assumed office. There had been a centre-right majority in the EP since the 1999 elections, and a majority of the heads of government in the European Council and of ministers in the Council of Ministers had been from centre-right governments since the early 2000s. The new College, therefore, was naturally also centre-right in orientation, because Commissioners are nominated by the national governments – formally in agreement with the College President-designate – and so the political composition of the first Barroso College naturally reflected the political orientations of the member state governments at the time the Commissioners-designate were nominated. So, from 2004, and as it has turned out up to the time of writing, the majority of the membership of all three of the EU's main policy-making institutions has been of a similar centre-right political orientation. Have there been policy consequences of this existence of an ideological majority across the principal policy-making institutions? Undoubtedly so in that there has been a greater emphasis in policy circles on the need to advance economic liberalization, as has been demonstrated by, for example, a renewed emphasis on the breaking-open of still protected markets – such as energy and telecoms – and the reduced attention that has been given to the social dimensions of the Lisbon Strategy (despite the prominence given in the Europe 2020 programme to human resource training). However, this picture of an ideologically-driven policy agenda must not be over-stated, not least because those who might have been expected to be in the economic liberalization majority have sometimes opposed liberalizing policy initiatives, while those who might have been expected to oppose liberalizing initiatives have sometimes supported them. This changing of camps is no more clearly illustrated than with the conservative French governments of Jacques Chirac and Nicolas Sarkozy, which resisted many economically liberal policy initiatives dealing with such topics as competition, company takeovers and mergers, and social protection measures. They opposed these because the initiatives were seen either to be damaging to French interests, as in the case of a number of attempted takeovers of French companies, or at variance with long-standing French policies, as in the case of EU challenges to various types of governmental support for business activities. This French attitude highlights how historical statecraft can sometimes be more important than economic ideology in determining national policy in EU policy forums. As Vivien Schmidt (2006) has argued in a broader context: 'Europeanization of national policy-making has been more disruptive to member states with statist processes than to those with corporatist processes.'

The Production of Policy Outputs

This chapter has emphasized, both directly and indirectly, the seemingly unsatisfactory nature of many aspects of EU policy processes. It has shown that not only are there a great many processes, but also that they are very diverse and often highly complex in nature, with leadership within them being dispersed, shifting and often contested. In terms of their outputs, the processes can be seen as producing too many policies that are permeated not by strong and clear decisions but rather by compromises in which there is something for everyone.

EU policy processes can also be criticized for not producing sufficiently holistic policies. Too often there is what Scharpf (2002) has called a 'problem solving gap', in which EU solutions are precluded by the heterogeneity and political saliency of national interests and preferences, while national solutions are impeded by an array of EU laws and constraints. Scharpf sees social welfare policies as a case in point, with EU policies on liberalization and competition restricting what member states can do on the one hand, but with the diversity of national welfare traditions and systems preventing the adoption of strong EU social welfare policies on the other.

Lack of robustness and clarity in policy outputs is often cited as a fundamental weakness in federal systems, especially ones that are similar to the EU, with divided governmental systems (or some pattern of disconnectedness of the executive from the legislature) and a strong pluralistic element. The weakness is further exacerbated when, as can be the case in federal systems, and is certainly the case in the EU, federal identity is weak. So, the absence of a clear European (federal) identity among the European citizenry adds to the difficulties that have just been noted in developing strong EU social welfare policies, because incorporating strong redistributive elements into the policy portfolio would damage the EU's legitimacy among the European public. The outrage expressed by Europeans from many EU states – particularly Germany – when the EU, and more particularly the eurozone, led the first financial 'bail-out' of Greece in 2010, indicates the lack of solidarity among wide swaths of the European electorate.

In key respects, EU policy processes can thus be seen as being less than satisfactory, not least in that they produce too many policies that are less than optimal. However, the criticism should not be overdone, for there clearly have been very considerable EU-level policy achievements and advances over the years. To cite just a few of the EU's most important policy advances since the mid-1990s: EMU and the single currency have been established; the internal market has continued to deepen on many fronts, with significant legislation passed in such key areas as the liberalization of network industries, the opening-up of services, and protection for consumers; justice and home affairs policy has almost rushed forward, with many measures being adopted – on matters including immigration, visas, management of external borders, and police and judicial co-operation – in pursuit of the goal of creating an 'area of freedom, security and justice'; enlargement policy has continued apace, with the 2004 and 2007 accessions, and with (at the time of writing) the scheduled

anticipated accession of Croatia in 2013 and the anticipated continuation of negotiations with Iceland and Turkey; and the CFSP and CSDP have both greatly advanced, to the point that the EU has now undertaken many civilian/police/military operations – something that was almost unimaginable until relatively recently.

This success of EU policy processes can be judged not only in qualitative terms but also quantitatively, with the EU producing a very considerable volume of a wide range of policy outputs each year. A useful way of distinguishing between these outputs is via the classificatory system suggested by Peterson (1995) and Peterson and Bomberg (1999), in which three types of decision are identified: history-making decisions, which are decisions that shape the very nature of the EU, such as those taken on enlargement, financial frameworks and major new policy initiatives; policy-setting decisions, which are decisions that determine the direction of policy in particular policy sectors, such as permitting the principle of government subsidies to be given to industrial enterprises in areas of high unemployment; and policy-shaping (possibly better called policy application) decisions, which cover policy details, such as what levels of government subsidies can be given, to what sorts of enterprises, and for how long. Naturally, history-making decisions are only for occasional use, but policy-setting, and even more so, policy-shaping, decisions are part of everyday EU policy-making. (On these three types of decisions, see also Lelieveldt and Princen, 2011, pp. 229–51.)

Most policy-setting and policy-shaping decisions take the form of EU legislation. As Hix (2008), König et al (2006), and others have shown, the volume of legislation is lower than it was in the late 1980s and the first half of the 1990s. Whereas approximately the same number of directives (which deal with policy principles and frameworks) are passed per year – usually between 100 and 120 – the number of regulations and decisions (both of which deal mainly with detailed and technical matters) has fallen from about 4,000 and 2,000, respectively, to around 1,200–1,400 and 800–900, respectively.

There are a number of reasons why, despite the policy portfolio being broader than ever, the number of directives being passed has not increased. One is that the particular circumstances of the late 1980s and early 1990s, when a very high volume of legislation was required as the EU sought to meet its deadline of completing the internal market by December 1992, no longer apply. A second reason, and one that is closely linked to the first, is that, as Hix (2008, ch. 3) has emphasized, the nature of the policy agenda has shifted in the direction of more contested and divisive issues. There was a broad consensus among policy actors about the principle of creating the internal market, but once the essential foundations of the market were largely in place and the political debate moved on to the extent to which, and the ways in which, the market should be social or economically liberal in character, consensus became less easy to find and decisions harder to make. (This is hardly surprising, given that the extent to which governments should intervene in the private market to level out incomes continues to be the principal basis for party competition in Western democracies.) A third reason is that since the early 1990s it has become logistically more difficult for the Commission to bring forward legislative proposals. It must now produce impact assessments for any new legislation of significance and must be able to justify new legislative proposals in terms of the principles of subsidiarity (EU actions must be more likely to advance policy goals than national actions) and proportionality (EU actions must not exceed what is necessary to achieve the objectives of the treaties). The working assumption has thus become that new EU-level legislative activity must be seen to be fully justified. Inevitably, this has made the Commission more cautious than it used to be about bringing forward legislative proposals. A fourth reason is that, as the EU has moved into more difficult and sensitive policy areas – both of a socio-economic nature, such as Lisbon Strategy/Europe 2020-related policies, and of a non-economic nature, such as security-related policies – then so has much of its policy-making activity become focused on using non-legislative policy instruments. In such policy areas, the member states accept that there is a need for EU policy activity but are not necessarily persuaded that this need always take the form of enacting binding legislation. (This trend in the direction of making increasing use of non-legislative policy instruments is examined in detail in Chapter 7.)

Despite some expectations to the contrary, a development that has not weakened the EU's decision-making capacity significantly is the 2004/7 enlargement, as a number of studies have shown (see, for example, Best and Settembri, 2008a; Hagemann and De Clerck-Sachsse, 2007). Certainly there has been no significant quantitative reduction in the total number of acts being adopted post-enlargement. To take, for example, figures compiled by Best and Settembri (2008b) comparing two 12-month periods before and after the 2004 enlargement, a total of 479 acts were adopted under the Greek and Italian Presidencies in 2003, while 455 were adopted under the British and Austrian presidencies in the second half of 2005 and the first half of 2006. Of these acts, just under half were 'Community legislation', around a quarter were 'other Community acts' (which are similar to legislation 'except for the fact that they are not adopted directly on the basis of a treaty article'), and around a quarter were 'intergovernmental acts' (which are not based on a Commission proposal and mainly cover CFSP matters).

But, confirming the trend noted above of the decline in EU legislative activity, while Best and Settembri's figures indicate no significant decline in the total volume of EU acts, they do show a decline in the proportion of them that are legislative acts: from 56 per cent to 49 per cent, thus confirming the more widely-observed feature of EU policies and policy-making of a decline in the use of the Community method to make legislation, and an increase in the use of other methods to produce non-legislative outputs.

Variations in the Speed of Policy Processes

EU policy processes are subject to great variations in terms of how quickly they proceed. Whereas at the national level a government with a working majority in the legislature can normally be confident of making reasonably rapid progress with a policy initiative, at the EU level no such assumption can be made – especially if the policy issue in question is controversial and/or is strongly contested.

There are two, in practice interrelated and overlapping, main reasons why policy progress can be very slow. The first is that, unlike the situation at national levels, policy proposals do not emanate from a government – be it a single or a multi-party government – elected to office on the basis of policy promises and which can expect political support for its policy initiatives by the legislature. So the EU is unlike the Westminster model of governance but rather shares features of the Madisonian compound republic model with multiple centres of power (Ostrom, 1987). The second reason is that the EU's main decision-making bodies – the Council and the EP – contain a wide range of significantly different perspectives and views on most policy issues.

Examples of very slow and in some cases *no* policy progress in seemingly important policy areas are not difficult to find. Corporate taxation policy is an example of the latter, with the Commission having first made the case for some harmonization of corporate tax rates, and shifting responsibility for corporate taxes from the national to European level, as long ago as the early 1960s. But nothing much beyond the 1997 voluntary Tax Code and the European Corporate Statute has been achieved. In consequence, the Commission's attention has turned increasingly to the need for a common corporate tax base, but this idea has also met with stiff resistance from some member states.

An example of very slow policy-making is provided by the EP and Council regulation on the Registration, Evaluation, Authorisation and Restriction of Chemicals (REACH). Proposed by the Commission in October 2003 – with the aim of reducing health risks and protecting the environment through the required registration and authorization over an eleven-year period of some 30,000 substances – the regulation was not passed until December 2006, by which time the contents of the regulation had been much diluted. The protraction of the policy process was caused by the complexity of the legislation (it was some 1,000 pages in length) and by fierce disagreements in the Council and EP – which were partly fuelled by intense lobbying from environmental and business interests – about where the balance should lie between environmental protection on the one hand and competitiveness on the other.

But slow though EU policy processes can be, they are not necessarily so. Several factors can make for a relatively speedy legislative process. The extent to which a proposal is or is not controversial is, of course, one factor. Another is the legislative process applying, with measures that are subject to the single-stage

consultation procedure naturally tending to proceed more quickly than those that are subject to the potentially three-stage ordinary procedure. But within the ordinary procedure around 90 per cent of proposals are decided at the first or second reading – some 60 per cent at first reading and 30 per cent at second reading – which makes for much faster processes than when the third conciliation stage has to be used. And another factor that can help to inject speed is the availability of QMV in the Council. As was explained in Chapter 3 and earlier in this chapter, when QMV is available, member state governments usually prefer to find a consensus and do not rush to vote, but nevertheless votes are increasingly held or 'threatened' to enable progress to be made.

It was noted above that the 2004–7 enlargement has not diminished the volume of policy outputs. The evidence with regard to whether it has reduced decision-making speeds is not wholly consistent. Two major research studies show that decision-making speeds have slowed, albeit only marginally, as a result of the enlargement (Hertz and Leuffen, 2011; König, 2007). But two other studies detect no such decrease in decision-making speed as a result of the enlargement (Best and Settembri, 2008a, 2008b; Golub, 2007). The explanation for the contrasting findings in the studies lies in a mixture of differences in the methodology used as well as some differences in the decisions being studied.

Yet however one evaluates the empirical evidence, it is clear that, regardless of the increased transaction costs involved, the 2004–7 enlargement round has not slowed the speed of EU decision-making significantly. There appear to be three main reasons for this. The first is that policy actors from the 2004–7 member states have adapted quickly to the EU's prevailing decision-making norms and mores, and in particular to coalition dynamics. So representatives from the new member states have come to recognize the importance of coalition formation and of not being isolated in the Council, as representatives from EU-15 states have long done. The second reason is that, within legislative processes, the pre-2004 trends of increasingly using explicit and implicit QMV and settling matters as early as possible (such as by reaching agreement at first reading under the ordinary legislative procedure), both of which speed up decision-making, have continued. And the third reason is that the enlargement round has further stimulated the already developing movement away from the use of tight legislation and towards the use of policy instruments that give more room for adjustments to suit local circumstances. This is most obviously the case with the increasing use of non-legislative instruments, but even where legislative instruments are used they are often now looser and more flexible in form than formerly. As such, they are more likely to be politically acceptable.

What, then, are decision-making speeds? Taking legislative proposals that are subject to the ordinary procedure, the average length of time from the Commission issuing a proposal to it being finally adopted is around 20 months. Since 20 months is an average, much legislation is naturally passed at a much faster speed. Best and Settembri (2008b) calculate that what they categorize as 'major' legislative acts take, on average, almost 900 days from the initial reference from the Commission to the Council and EP to adoption; 'ordinary' acts take almost 400 days; and 'minor' acts just over 200 days. These time-scales are longer than is common in national legislatures, but given the enormous diversity of interests and the large number of actors involved in EU decision-making processes they are not as protracted as perhaps might be anticipated. That said, the figures given here do not, of course, allow for acts that the Commission would like to have proposed but did not do so because it knew that they had no chance of commanding the required support.

The Impact of Differentiation

As shown in Chapter 1, differentiation of various kinds – that is, policy activity without all member states participating fully – has become increasingly important in the EU.

Where differentiation exists – and it does so in such key policy areas as EMU, AFSJ and defence – member states that are not full participants are often excluded from, or at least are confined to the fringes of, policy processes. Even where they formally have policy process rights, full participants have often been reluctant to allow non- or partial participants to have all the policy process privileges. In the policy area where differentiation is most advanced – EMU – new policy and decision-making forums have been developed from which non-euro member states are excluded.

A related impact of differentiation on policy processes is that it sometimes creates uncertainties as to precisely who should be participating in a process. This is seen, for example, with the CSDP, where Denmark has opted out of EU military activities since a declaration to this effect was included in the Conclusions of the 1992 Edinburgh European Council meeting: 'Denmark does not participate in the elaboration and the implementation of decisions and actions of the Union which have defence implications' (Council of the European Union, 1992, p. 58). However, the civilian and military aspects of the CSDP overlap and intermesh, which can create considerable difficulties – not least for Danish ministers and representatives – regarding which meetings, and which parts of meetings, they should attend. A further complication to this Danish position is that Denmark is a member of NATO, and a Danish national, Anders Fogh Rasmussen, became NATO's Secretary General in 2009!

Conclusions

An underlying theme of this chapter has been that, in important ways, EU policy processes are both similar to and different from policy processes in the member states.

The similarities stem from the core fact that the EU is a political system which, like all open political systems, translates needs and demands for policies into policy outputs. This translation is effected through policy-making mechanisms. These mechanisms are more numerous and complex than their counterparts in member states, but they serve much the same purpose: sorting out policy priorities, requirements and preferences; and moving policy ideas from conception and formulation through to adoption and implementation.

The differences between EU and national policy processes are not restricted to their greater number and complexity but also cover many other matters. EU processes are, for example, characterized more by compromise, by dispersal of leadership, and often by being less explicitly ideological in nature. These traits contribute to producing a policy process system in which, as Vivien Schmidt (2009) has put it, there is not much *real* politics in the sense that politics is understood at national level. In particular, there is little open competition between actors over policy options, with citizens making choices as to which they prefer of the sets of options on offer. Of course, in the policy-making systems of the EU's member states it is also the case that the active policy-makers are relatively few in number and work largely behind closed doors. But, unlike the EU's policy-makers, national policy-makers work within a more clearly politically partisan framework and are ultimately directly responsible to citizens.

Chapter 6
The Policy Cycle

This chapter applies the policy cycle approach to EU policy processes. In so doing, it shows that even though the EU is a highly distinctive political system, the policy cycle is as much a feature of its policy processes as it is of 'normal' political systems. A theme running through the chapter is that what happens within the policy cycle in the EU varies considerably across policy areas, both within and between policy stages. The variations occur in response to such differences as the number and nature of the policy actors, the powers of the policy actors, and the policy procedures – both formal and informal – that apply.

The first section introduces the concept of the policy cycle, and the following five sections – on agenda-setting, policy-shaping, decision-making, policy implementation, and evaluation – detail the stages of the cycle. The final section offers concluding comments.

The Concept of the Policy Cycle

Many policy analysts believe that a useful way of examining the processes that result in the emergence and creation of public policies is through the concept of the policy cycle (see, for example, Hogwood and Gunn, 1984; Howlett *et al.*, 2009; Parsons, 1995). For an application of the policy cycle approach to EU policy processes, see Versluis *et al.* (2011).

The concept of the policy cycle is based on the notion that policy processes can be seen as being located within a 'a set of interrelated stages through which policy issues and deliberations flow in a more or less sequential fashion from "inputs" (problems) to "outputs" (policies)' (Howlett *et al.*, 2009, p. 10). To put this another way, a policy cycle is made up of policy stages that have an inbuilt sequential order to them.

What are the stages in the policy cycle? Analysts provide different answers to this question, with some identifying more stages than others. Broadly speaking, however, the main stages that are identified by most analysts are agenda-setting, policy-shaping (sometimes broken down into policy proposing and policy formulating), decision-making, implementation, and evaluation.

As with most analytical devices and tools, there are problems associated with the policy cycle approach. One problem is that, in practice, the stages are far from being rigidly compartmentalized. Indeed, with the numerous comings and goings that characterize EU policy processes – with all sorts of formal and

Figure 6.1 A linear conception of the policy cycle

Agenda setting › Policy shaping › Decision-making › Policy implementation › Policy evaluation

informal meetings and the circulation of many types of formal and informal papers – the stages not only overlap and intertwine but often appear to merge into one another. So, to take the decision-making stage as an example, it is very difficult to say when precisely it begins, and even after a decision has been formally taken it may need to be followed up with 'sub-decisions' of various sorts – with, for example, EP and Council directives often requiring subsequent 'administrative' legislation to deal with detailed and technical matters, and with implementation arrangements.

Another problem with the policy cycle approach is that there is generally no rigid linear development of the stages from one to the next. Figure 6.1 presents an

'idealized' linear policy cycle, but other versions of it, such as that set out in Figure 6.2, are often closer to reality. One reason why there is frequently a lack of linearity is that in the EU the same policy actors – drawn from, for example, the Commission and the member state Permanent Representations – are often involved at more than one policy stage. Another reason is that the highly consensual nature of so much EU policy-making – with attempts constantly being made to develop policies that are both effective and command as much support as possible – means there is a considerable backwards and forwards movement between stages.

But despite there undoubtedly being analytical problems with the notion of policy cycles, and recognizing that policy cycles do not provide a perfect match for what happens in the real world, the policy cycle approach is none the less still of considerable use in helping to throw light on how policy processes operate. It enables highly complex processes to be broken down, it facilitates the identification of different types of policy activity, and it helps to bring out how policy-making does have – for the most part – an ongoing and forward momentum.

Figure 6.2 A circular (and more dynamic) conception of the policy cycle

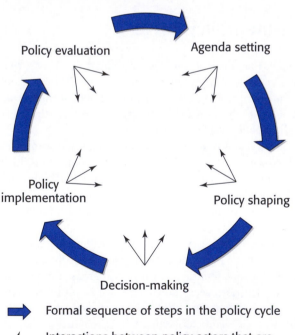

Policy evaluation

Agenda setting

Policy implementation

Policy shaping

Decision-making

→ Formal sequence of steps in the policy cycle

↗ Interactions between policy actors that are not part of the formal policy cycle (but which may none the less be frequent and very important).

Agenda-setting

The first stage of policy development is that an issue begins to attract attention on the policy agenda. So, agenda-setting is about policy-makers coming to give an issue consideration. As Princen (2009, p. 1) has put it: 'Agenda-setting is not concerned with the actual decisions that are taken, but with the issues that decision-makers devote attention to: the issues they talk about, think about, write about and take into consideration'.

The manner by which an issue enters the political agenda is often crucial in determining the terms in which it is considered, who are to be the lead policy actors, and what sort of policy actions are considered to be possible.

Who are the agenda-setters?

Kingdon (1995) makes a useful distinction between the 'governmental agenda' and the 'decision agenda'. The former consists of issues that are being discussed by policy-makers but on which specific proposals are not yet being considered. The latter consists of proposals on which decisions are to be taken.

There are a myriad of actors in the EU who are capable of influencing the governmental agenda. This is especially so in respect of what are sometimes called low politics issues – that is, issues that are not perceived as affecting national sovereignty or security concerns – because these are issues where there is often considerable room for agenda-setting to start 'from below'. In this context, among the many different forms that 'from below' can take are lobbying by non-governmental interests, the floating of ideas by national governments, suggestions from the many expert and advisory committees that are clustered around the Commission, and own initiative reports from EP committees.

On almost any low politics issue – be it annual fishing quotas, standards applying to the disposal of toxic substances, or health and safety rules in mines – there are almost invariably significant differences between those who promote particular policy positions. With respect to annual fishing quotas, for example, organizations representing fishermen and governments from member states where sea fishing is an important industry always press for much higher quotas than are favoured by environmentalists and most scientists specializing in fish stocks. Sometimes, there are even significant policy differences articulated by different arms of the same organization – as with the frequent differences that exist over aspects of industrial policy between 'market-focused' Commission DGs, such as Competition and Internal Market, and 'intervention-ist' DGs, such as Environment and Regional Policy.

The number of actors who are capable of influencing, and more especially of setting, the decision agenda is narrower, with the main actors being those who are in a position to formally table policy proposals. For most policy areas other than the CFSP/CSDP, the Commission is the main actor in this regard, largely because of its monopolistic power – apart from in a few AFSJ areas – to table legislative proposals. In the CFSP/CSDP area, the High Representative assumes much of the policy initiating responsibility that the Commission undertakes in other areas.

How, and in what ways, do issues come to be established on the policy agenda?

There are, partly in consequence of the large number of policy actors that 'want something', always many issues that have the potential to become part of the EU policy agenda. What determines which issues make it through?

An initial point to be made here is that most of the issues on the EU's policy agenda – both the governmental and the decision agendas – are ongoing issues in one way or another. That is, the policy agenda is taken up mainly with developing, refining and updating existing policies. The reasons for this are clear enough: the initial political resistance that usually accompanies new policy development has been weakened; new policy development is often cautious and very partial, and consequently is soon seen to need extending and strengthening if it is to be effective; and once a policy has been created the policy cycle is set up, with monitoring and reviews leading to ideas as to how it can be improved.

But how do new policies make their way on to the agenda? A conceptual device that helps to explain this is Kingdon's (1995) multiple stream model. In essence, Kingdon suggests that policy processes consist of three separate streams: a problem stream in which policy-makers identify issues that need to be tackled; a solution stream that consists of proposals for official public action; and a politics stream consisting of the political context that is shaped by such factors as changes in government and the offering of political leadership. According to Kingdon, these streams normally operate fairly independently of one other but at times two, or even all three, of them can converge in a favourable way for a time, and when they do a 'window of opportunity', or a 'policy window', opens that facilitates policy action.

An example of such a policy window opening is seen with defence policy in the late 1990s and early

2000s. Defence policy was given treaty recognition in the Maastricht Treaty, with the provision that the newly established CFSP 'shall include all questions related to the security of the Union, including the eventual framing of a common defence policy, which might in time lead to a common defence'. This provision thus laid the foundations for a solution stream, which began tentatively to be developed after the Maastricht Treaty came into force with, for example, the launching in 1994 of what was called the European Security and Defence Identity (ESDI), and with some upgrading of the treaty language on defence policy in the Amsterdam Treaty. However, progress was very slow and cautious, mainly because of disagreements between France and the UK over how European defence policy should be organized and orientated. But, in the late 1990s a policy window began to open for defence policy to be given greater attention and more urgency. This occurred because of changes in the problem and political streams. The main change in the problem stream occurred as a consequence of the very limited role the EU was able to play in the 1990s in the warring Balkans. The US led virtually all the initiatives to stop the fighting and 'ethnic cleansing', with the EU member states being left largely on the sidelines. This was a situation that many EU governments recognized was wholly unsatisfactory and needed to be addressed. The political stream thus began to change, with a greater interest being seen among EU governments towards advancing EU defence policy. These changing attitudes were then given a major boost with the emergence of a greater willingness of French and UK leaders to conciliate their national positions on European defence policy: a willingness that in the UK's case was partly explained by the election to power in 1997 of a much less Eurosceptic government. At a meeting in St Malo in 1998, UK Prime Minister Tony Bair and French President Jacques Chirac called for the creation of a European Security and Defence Policy, which opened the way to the very considerable advances that have since occurred in building what is now called the Common Security and Defence Policy (CSDP).

Another example of a policy area benefiting from the opening of a policy window is given by Princen (2010), who has written extensively on agenda-setting in the EU (see also Princen, 2009, on this subject). The example Princen gives is the circumstances that led to the adoption of the European arrest warrant in 2002. The idea of European action to ease extradition for wanted persons between member states had been discussed since at least the mid-1990s (and hence had been on the governmental agenda – though not highly placed), but the events of 9/11 served to bring the urgency of the matter to the fore and to place it prominently on the decision agenda. The problem stream (the perceived need to adopt as a matter of urgency measures dealing with the tackling of terrorism and the movement of criminals across national borders), the solution stream (the putting in place of a European arrest warrant allowing suspected criminals to be moved much more easily than hitherto to the jurisdictions of other member states), and the politics stream (wide political support for such action) all fell into alignment.

Sometimes, the nature of the policy agenda can be influenced by a 'policy entrepreneur', especially if this involves taking advantage of a policy window. The most cited, but still arguably the most important and successful, example of such a policy entrepreneur in the EU is Jacques Delors, President of the Commission for the period 1985–95. He assumed office at a time when: European business was being seen increasingly as too uncompetitive in the progressively more globalized market (the problem stream); the European Court of Justice had, by establishing the principle of mutual recognition, shown a way in which the internal market could be opened up (the solution stream); and there was wide support in the business community and among member state governments for the liberalization of the internal market to be prioritized (the political stream). Delors took advantage of this policy window to champion the Commission's programme of 'completing' the internal market by 1992.

* * *

Agenda-setting in the EU thus takes place in a number of ways, and with many different types of actors involved. However, a distinctive feature of all EU agenda-setting, compared with national agenda-setting, is that, as Lelieveldt and Princen (2011, pp. 205–27) have noted, it is heavily based on inside access. That is, the public agenda (what citizens regard as being important) and the media agenda (what is being focused on by the print and electronic media) tend not to 'intrude' as much on the EU political agenda as they do on national political agendas. This is because of the nature of the EU's system of governance, which to a marked degree isolates EU policy processes from 'the outside'. EU agenda-setting tends to arise within and be sustained by active EU policy players.

Policy-shaping

Once an issue has come to be recognized as needing to be addressed – that is, once it has become established on the policy agenda – it then needs to be taken forward with the identification of policy goals and the formulation of specific policy proposals. These processes constitute policy-shaping. Policy-shaping does not decide EU policy, but it does identify options, determines which options are possible and which are not, and filters and narrows-down the number of realistic policy alternatives.

Of course, much of what happens at the agenda-setting stage can involve attempts at policy-shaping, since actors who voice views that an issue needs attention do not usually confine themselves to saying 'something needs to be done'. Rather, they usually give some indication, albeit often in only rather general terms, of *what* needs to be done. So, for example, in the wake of the international financial crisis that set in during 2007/8 many interested EU policy actors were quick to say that the EU had been over-lax in its monitoring and regulation of EU-based financial institutions, and proceeded from this position to say that the EU should now adopt a more interventionist and tighter regulatory approach. Attempted agenda-setting thus shaded into attempted policy-shaping.

As with agenda-setting, there are thus many policy actors who try to become involved in policy-shaping. However, nothing very much is likely to happen unless ideas for policy action are taken up and advanced by core policy actors. Outside the special area of CFSP/CSDP – where, as is shown in Chapter 13, intergovernmentalism remains the dominant policy mode and member states, the European Council President and the High Representative all have potentially significant policy-shaping capacities – the Commission is by far the most important of the core policy actors in respect of policy-shaping. This is seen no more clearly than in the fact that, in any average year, it issues several Green Papers (which usually outline initial thoughts on policy actions), over 300 communica-

tions and reports, and well over 100 significant legislative proposals. The Commission's central policy-shaping position stems from the fact that, as was shown in Chapter 3, it has a number of institutional resources that give it clear advantages over other policy actors. Prominent among these resources are its access to key information (about both the nature of EU policies and of what is politically possible), the wide perception of it as the place from which policy initiatives should most naturally stem, and the monopolistic power it is given by the TFEU over the drafting of most EU legislation. Of course, in exercising its policy-shaping role, the Commission works closely with other policy actors, as other chapters of this book show. One reason for this is that most EU policies cover specialized ground, and so the Commission needs outside technical expertise and advice if its proposals are to be credible on such matters as the public safety implications of authorizing the use of genetically modified organisms (GMOs) or the financial implications for businesses of strengthening waste disposal legislation. Another reason why the Commission must work closely with other policy actors when making policy and legislative proposals is that it is not in its institutional interest to advance proposals that will meet with stiff resistance at the decision-making stage and will have little chance of being approved: the Commission must attempt to anticipate the likely reactions of policy-makers to its proposals.

So, before issuing policy or legislative proposals the Commission usually consults widely. This consultation can take many different forms, including: issuing consultation calls, such as the one set out in Box 6.1, accompanied by consultation papers that outline the existing situation and set out policy options; producing Green Papers that set out initial ideas and invite interested parties to submit their views; listening to the opinions of subject experts – many of which are channelled via the hundreds of advisory and expert committees linked to the Commission; exchanging ideas with national governmental representatives in a variety of formal and informal settings; and talking to members of relevant EP committees.

This general need for extensive consultation with non-Commission actors in the period that proposals are being devised is often paralleled by a need for extensive intra-Commission consultations. A proposal 'starts life' in a particular part of the Commission – say DG Enterprise and Industry, or DG Environment –

Box 6.1

Example of a consultation call

Title
Consultation on a New European Regime for Venture Capital

Policy field
Internal Market, Asset Management

Target group
All citizens and organizations are welcome to contribute to this consultation. Contributions are particularly sought from investors, asset managers, small and medium-sized enterprises (SMEs), and public authorities.

Period of consultation
From 15/06/2011 to 10/08/2011

Objective of the consultation
The objective of the consultation is to find the best possible approach in order to achieve a real internal market for venture capital funds in the EU.

How to submit your contribution
We welcome contributions from citizens, organisations and public authorities.

Consultation document
- A New European Regime for Venture Capital [This is a 17-page document that summarizes the existing situation and sets out policy options.]

Reference documents
- Press release (15/06/2011)
- Investment Funds

Contact details
Responsible services:
Directorate General Internal Market and Services/Unit G4 – Asset Management

work of DG Agriculture and Rural Development, and perhaps also for DG Internal Market and Services and DG Environment. Where there are such potential overlaps, the lead DG, and more particularly the *chef de dossier* (the Commission official in the lead DG who carries the main responsibility for the proposal) must ensure that all potentially interested and affected parts of the Commission are given the opportunity to make an input. Such inputs can be made in various ways, but usually involve the convening of inter-service (that is, inter-departmental) meetings. Not until inter-service deliberations have resulted in an agreement is a proposal moved up the Commission system for eventual formal adoption by the College as a Commission proposal. (If agreements cannot be reached at the inter-service level, Commissioners – working largely via their *cabinets* – may have to settle issues.)

This need for extensive internal and external deliberations in the Commission before proposals are finalized inevitably means that the policy-shaping stage can often last for many months, and sometimes even years. Quite what form such deliberations take depends on an array of contextual circumstances, but several quasi-formal steps may have to be taken before a specific policy proposal is formally issued: inclusion in a relevant multi-annual work programme that has been approved by the Council and EP (such programmes exist in several policy areas, including environment, R&TD and public health); discussion in a relevant Commission advisory and/or expert group; mention in a Commission Communication on a policy area or in a Green and/or a White Paper; and tabling in the Commission's annual work programme.

Decision-making

At this stage of the policy cycle, proposals formulated at the policy-shaping stage are considered by the appropriate decision-makers with a view to decisions being taken, or not.

How and by whom decisions are taken in the EU is discussed extensively elsewhere in this book. Only a few key points will therefore be made here.

One of these points is that this is the most politicized policy process stage. It is so because it involves

but it may overlap with and have potential implications for the policy responsibilities of other parts of the Commission. So, for example, a food safety proposal is likely to originate in DG Health and Consumers, but it may well have implications for the final choices being made on matters that are often of considerable public importance. Whereas earlier and later policy stages do not involve such choices, and indeed are often quite technical in the matters they cover, this stage involves policy actors entering into hard commitments. As a result, this is the stage where national politicians – in (depending on the status and nature of the decision concerned) the European Council, the Council of Ministers and the EP – are most involved.

Another key point about the decision-making stage is that it takes many different forms, with the line-up of participating actors and the nature of procedures being used varying considerably both between policy areas and the types of decisions being taken. As shown in Chapter 7, just what determines what type or types of process apply in particular circumstances depends essentially on what member states perceive to be necessary and are prepared to accept. But because the member states take different views on what is necessary and what is acceptable, a very 'messy', complicated and pluralistic system of decision-making processes has emerged.

It might, for example, be anticipated that highly sensitive policy matters touching directly on national sovereignties would be based mainly on intergovernmental decision-making processes, with decisions being taken at the highest political level, while policy matters having a direct effect on the internal market – which has long been the EU's core policy concern – would be more supranational in character and more subject to lower-level decision-making. But while there is something in this generalization, it is very far from capturing the whole truth. This is largely because the extent to which policies are sensitive varies between member states, as does the extent to which sovereignty issues are seen to be a concern. Twenty and more years ago the governments of virtually all member states would have regarded such policy areas as currency control, internal security, criminal justice, and defence as being both highly sensitive and at the heart of the retention of national sovereignty, but attitudes in most states have since softened considerably as interdependency has given these policy areas an increasingly cross-national character. It has also become increasingly apparent that there are advantages to be gained from working closely in these areas with other member states. Accordingly, there have been increases in and a strengthening of supranational-based policy processes in these areas, with greater decision-making capacities being given to EU-level institutions. But:

- the increases and strengthening have not been applied consistently across the policy board, as the still predominantly intergovernmental nature of foreign and defence policy processes show;
- where they have occurred, the increases and strengthening have taken different forms, as the very different character of the supranational processes that apply in the EMU and AFSJ policy areas demonstrate; and
- there have been variations in the extent to which member states have been prepared to associate themselves with and participate in the more supranational processes that have been created over the years, which has resulted in a great increase in the number of policy processes that do not involve, or do not fully involve, all member states.

As a result of the many differences that have existed, and still exist, between the member states regarding which decision-making procedures should apply in which policy areas, the EU has, as was shown in Chapter 5, a large number of significantly different decision-making procedures. These can, however, as shown in Chapter 7, be grouped into four broad modes: the Community method; intensive transgovernmentalism; supranational centralization; and new modes of governance. Each of these modes involves different sets of EU political actors exercising different powers in differing ways. The European Council, for example, is generally only directly involved in transgovernmental decision-making, and then just in respect of major directional and highly politicized decisions. The Commission, by contrast, is involved directly in almost all aspects of EU decision-making, whether it is: in an advisory capacity – as often in Council working parties; in a brokerage capacity – as in conciliation procedure processes; or in a decision-taking capacity – as with respect to many competition policy matters and much secondary (implementation) legislation.

The reference that has just been made to the Commission exercising a brokerage function draws attention to what is the most prominent and important of all the general features of EU decision-making: irrespective of which decision-making modes or rules are being employed, compromise and consensus are almost invariably necessary. The reasons for this were set out in Chapter 5.

The preference for compromise and consensus does not, however, mean that EU decision-making is necessarily slow. As was shown in Chapter 5, average 'transmission rates' of legislative proposals, from the issuing of drafts to final adoption, are, for the most part, quite respectable. Nor does the preference for compromise and consensus mean that decisions are necessarily over-fudged and over-diluted. Indeed, much of the EU's legislative content – be it dealing with the regulation of the internal market, the management of the environment, or the inter-operability of communications systems – is highly detailed and specific in character.

But when there are very significant divisions between key actors – especially member state governments – and when policy issues are seen as being particularly important and sensitive, decision-making processes can be slow, and decisional outcomes much diluted. The Services Directive, discussed in Chapter 5, illustrates this: resistance from various quarters, especially to the mutual recognition principle that was at the heart of the Commission's proposal, resulted in the decision-making process being spread over three years and the final adopted version of the Directive being a much weaker policy instrument than had originally been envisaged by the Commission. The Registration, Evaluation, Authorisation and Restrictions of Chemicals (REACH) Regulation, which was also discussed in Chapter 5, further illustrates how decision-making processes can sometimes be slow and result in diluted outcomes. Originally issued by the Commission in October 2003 as an essentially environmental protection measure, the Regulation became the subject of intense lobbying from industry, which was successful in moving much of the debate on the Regulation onto industrial competitive issues. When the Regulation was eventually adopted, in December 2006, it was much weaker than the Commission's original proposal.

A quite different example of slow and less than satisfactory decision-making was seen from the first half of 2010, when the eurozone states struggled to find a quick and strong response to the crisis of confidence in the euro that arose following an escalating public debt crisis in Greece and, less dramatically, also in Ireland, Portugal, Italy and Spain. Calls from the Commission, the European Central Bank, and several eurozone states, including France, for the creation of new financial arrangements and funds to better enable the eurozone to assist members in financial difficulties were viewed with suspicion by the German Chancellor, Angela Merkel, who knew that Germany would have to be the main contributor to new financial loan and guarantee arrangements. As a result, new arrangements were put in place only slowly, in stages, and in a setting in which German reluctance to bail out perceived profligate states was clear for all to see. The consequence of this less than wholehearted and convincing policy response to the crisis resulted in pressures on the euro from 2010 being much greater than they otherwise might have been.

Policy Implementation

Policy implementation involves the putting into effect of policy decisions.

In the EU, the many very different sorts of decisions that are taken, coupled with the complex and multi-layered nature of the EU system, means that, correspondingly, there are both many different sorts of policy implementation and many policy implementation actors. So, regarding different sorts of policy implementation, there are huge differences between the implementation of EU legislation, of the semi-voluntaristic agreements aimed at meeting identified policy targets that are characteristic of much of the new modes of governance, and of decisions that involve the assembly and putting into action of missions of various types under the CFSP/CSDP. Regarding different sorts of policy implementation actors, the Commission is the pre-eminent EU-level actor, but it is far from being the only one. Among other important policy implementation actors at the EU level are: the Council, the High Representative and the European External Action Service, all of which have key implementing responsibilities with respect to the CFSP/CSDP; the ECB, which implements eurozone monetary policy; European agencies, some of which have implementing responsibilities in particular policy areas; and the CJEU, which is the final decision-maker on whether EU law is being properly applied in the member states. As for the sub-EU level actors – where most front-line EU policy implementation actually occurs – a vast array of national, regional and local bodies of different types act, in effect, as EU implementing agencies on matters as varied as ensuring consumer protection, monitoring the quality of sea-bathing water, and paying out grants to farmers.

The full range of this multifaceted policy implementation system cannot be covered here. But, in any event, it is not necessary since several of the specialized forms of policy implementation that exist in the EU are dealt with in other parts of the book: in Chapter 4, for example, the role of European agencies was outlined; in Chapter 7, the open method of co-ordination is examined; and in Chapter 13, the nature of CFSP/CSDP missions is explained.

Attention in what follows is focused on what might be thought of as 'the core' of the EU's policy implementation system: the implementation of EU law. It is an immense task with, in recent years, the accumulated body of EU law – the *acquis* – including almost 2,000 directives, about 8,400 regulations, plus primary law in the form of the treaties (European Commission, 2011u, p. 3).

The implementation system is highly complex and needs to be broken down into three different aspects: the transposition into national law of EU directives; the issuing of administrative legislation that fills in the technical details that are often necessary to give effect to the policy principles set out in the treaties and directives; and the 'front-line' application and enforcement of EU law. Difficulties of various kinds can arise with respect to all these aspects of implementation, and when they do EU law is not fully or properly applied if the difficulties have not been overcome.

Transposition

There are three main forms of EU legislation: first, legislative acts setting out the broad principles and frameworks of law are almost invariably issued as *directives*; second, technical and specific adjustments to existing EU law are usually issued as *regulations*; third, *decisions* are like regulations in that they also are mainly for the purpose of making administrative rather than political legislation, but unlike regulations (and directives) they are normally not generally applicable but apply only to whom they are addressed.

Directives may thus be said generally to deal with 'policy', while regulations and decisions normally deal

with 'administration' –though, of course, in practice the two greatly overlap. Under Article 288, TFEU directives 'shall be binding, as to the result to be achieved, upon each Member State ... but shall leave to the national authorities the choice of form and methods'. What this means in practice is that, unlike regulation and decisions, directives are not applicable directly in the member states but must be transposed – that is, incorporated – into national legal systems by appropriate national procedures. Directives do not normally become legally binding until they have been transposed. However, transposition does not enable member states to postpone indefinitely the incorporation of unwanted EU laws into national law, since directives always include a date by which they must be transposed: a date that may be just a few weeks after the formal adoption of a directive or, as with highly complex directives or directives that may involve major capital outlays (such as with much environmental legislation), could be several years away. Non- or incorrect transposition is a breach of EU law and can lead to the Commission taking action against member states – ultimately in the CJEU. This, in turn, can result in Court rulings that directives are directly applicable in member states where they have not been incorporated or where they have been incorporated incorrectly.

Transposition problems commonly occur in member states which: opposed or expressed strong reservation in the Council about a directive; have existing legislation that is very different from the contents of a directive; and have a weak legislative and/or administrative capacity. Problems also commonly occur in connection with directives that allow particularly wide margins of flexibility to member states to adjust aspects of directives to fit national circumstances, for while some manoeuvrability is often permitted the main principles and purposes of directives cannot be changed during transposition.

So as to try and minimize transposition problems, the Commission, to which the details of all transpositions must be notified, keeps a close watch – via a battery of lawyers distributed around its services – to ensure that national incorporation does not involve the main provisions of directives being avoided or misunderstood. (See Falkner *et al.*, 2004, for a review of the main reasons that result in non- or incorrect transposition.)

But while transposition problems certainly exist, the extent of them should not be overstated. For the most part, transposition processes work reasonably smoothly, with Commission reports and academic analyses showing that most directives are transposed on time by member states (see Thomson, 2010). With respect to internal market legislation, for example, in December 2010 the transposition deficit – that is, the percentage of internal market directives that had not been implemented into national law in time – was just 0.9 per cent, with only seven states not meeting the 1 per cent target (European Commission, 2011p, p. 5).

The passing of administrative legislation

As explained above, the main principles of EU policies that are given a legislative base are set out in directives. But, for policy to be applied uniformly and consistently across the EU, many policy areas require directives to be supported by what is commonly called administrative (or secondary) legislation, which is usually issued via regulations and decisions. That is, there is a need for legislation that translates policy principles into detailed, and often highly technical, rules on such matters as product standards, health and safety conditions, inspection rules, authorizations for marketed products and practices, and import duties. During the Barroso 1 Commission, no fewer than 14,522 administrative acts were passed, compared with 454 legislative acts (Hardacre and Kaeding, 2011, p. 29). In 2011, 2,290 administrative acts were passed, of which 1,389 were regulations and 901 decisions.

Since the passing of administrative legislation involves the making of decisions, it is, as Versluis *et al.* (2011) note, open to debate whether it is best regarded as the final part of the decision-making stage in the policy cycle or an early part of the implementation stage. In fact, it contains elements of both, and in so doing serves to highlight why the policy cycle approach should not be used in too rigid a manner. On balance, it seems best to view it as being part of policy implementation, but this is admittedly a marginal judgement.

Because administrative legislation normally covers specialized and essentially technical matters and does not usually raise politically-charged issues, it is not subject to a full legislative process. That is, it is not subject to the ordinary or one of the special legislative

procedures. Rather, it is much more in the hands of the Commission, as is evidenced by the fact that, unlike directives, it is not issued as EP and Council or Council legislation but usually as Commission legislation. Since the Lisbon Treaty came into force this distinction between 'political' and 'non-political' legislation has been recognized formally in Articles 289–91 of the TFEU, with the former being labelled 'legislative acts' and the latter being sub-divided into 'delegated acts' and 'implementing acts'. Delegated acts are for the purpose of adopting 'non-legislative acts of general application to supplement or amend certain non-essential elements of the legislative act' (Article 290, TFEU), while implementing acts are used '(w)here uniform conditions for implementing legally binding Union acts are needed' (Article 291, TFEU). What this means is that delegated acts are usually the more broadly-based of the two types of acts.

Prior to the Lisbon Treaty there were frequent tensions and disagreements between the Commission, the Council and the EP over the issuing of administrative legislation. At the heart of the tensions and disagreements was the functioning of the so-called comitology system, under which the Commission's use of its secondary legislation powers was monitored, and to some extent controlled, by more than 250 committees of various kinds composed of member state governmental representatives. The Council's main complaint was that Commission legislation was sometimes inappropriately channelled via a type of comitology committee that gave the member states insufficient powers, whilst the EP habitually complained – though less so after 2006 reforms that strengthened its position – that it had insufficient powers to examine and object to comitology decisions. The Lisbon Treaty reforms sought to defuse these problems (Brandsma and Blom-Hansen, 2011) by providing for clearer specifications to be laid down in advance regarding the nature of the delegated and implementing powers to be assigned to the Commission:

- In respect of delegated acts, the parent act should lay down explicitly the conditions to which the delegation is subject. The conditions may be as follows: 'a) the European Parliament or the Council may decide to revoke the delegation; b) the delegated act may enter into force only if no objection has been expressed by the European Parliament or the Council within a period set by the legislative act' (Article 290, TFEU). The EP must act via an absolute majority and the Council may act via QMV.

- With respect to implementing acts, the EP and Council 'shall lay down in advance the rules and general principles concerning mechanisms for control by Member States of the Commission's implementing powers' (Article 291, TFEU).

So, for delegated acts, which are regarded as being quasi-legislative, no comitology system is used. Control over their content is exercised directly by the EP and the Council. Implementing acts, which are more limited in scope, are controlled by the member states acting via comitology committees. (On the post-Lisbon Treaty comitology system, see Blom-Hansen, 2011, pp. 18–22; Brandsma and Blom-Hansen, 2011; Hardacre and Kaeding, 2011.)

The application and enforcement of EU policies

Variations between member states

The front-line, day-to-day, application of most EU policies is undertaken not by the EU itself but by an array of authorities in the member states. It is left to the member states to determine who these authorities are and how they are organized. The EU, acting through the Commission, has to be satisfied that appropriate policy application and enforcement arrangements are in place in all member states, but it does not attempt to dictate what the precise nature of the arrangements should be. As a result, a wide variety of arrangements exist, which in large part reflect existing national arrangements for dealing with domestic policies. So, for example, in federalist and regionalist member states such as Belgium, Germany and Spain, administering authorities that in other states are organized and managed from the central level are in their cases often dealt with at the regional level. This results in differences in administrative arrangements existing not only between member states but also, in some cases, within them.

To give just a few examples of the sorts of authorities that are involved in EU policy application and enforcement: import tariffs under the common commercial policy are collected by national customs and excise officers; the checking of whether products being sold in the EU's marketplaces are in conformity with EU specifications is undertaken by national, regional and local inspection agencies of many different kinds; the monitoring of fish landings at ports to see whether they are in conformity with Common Fisheries Policy rules on such matters as size and allocated allowable catches is the responsibility of national fisheries officers; and the operation and management and surveillance of landfill sites to ensure that substances and materials that under EU rules must not be dumped but must be disposed of in some other way is the job of environmental health authorities at various levels.

This reliance of the EU on national and subnational authorities to undertake most of its policy application does, of course, create potential difficulties with respect to trying to ensure that EU policies are applied in a uniform and consistent manner in all member states. One difficulty is that there are very great differences in the resources, capacities and experiences of national implementing authorities. With many EU policies being multifaceted in nature, and with the wording of many EU laws being less than precise, it is thus inevitable that, even with the best will in the world, some national implementing bodies – especially those that are under-resourced and under-trained – struggle to apply EU policies and laws fully and 'properly'. Versluis (2003) and Versluis et al. (2011, pp. 190–1) provide a good example of such a variation in national implementation, with the Seveso II Directive, which requires chemical companies that stock amounts of dangerous chemicals above specified levels to produce safety reports showing how they contain any danger and how they respond to emergencies. Comparing the Netherlands and Spain, Versluis and Versluis et al. show chemical companies in the Netherlands putting more resources into the preparation of the reports and inspectors in the Netherlands taking more time in examining the reports than their counterparts in Spain. A combination of factors are seen as explaining the differences, among which are a lack of clarity in the Directive as to precisely what the reports should contain, more detailed guidance from the Dutch government to national chemical companies regarding their obligations under the Directive, and greater prior experience and expertise in the Netherlands in regulating the policy area.

Differing national legal traditions and practices can also result in variations in and difficulties with policy application. Caranta (2011, p. 54), for example, observes of the key EU directive 2007/66/EC on improving the effectiveness of review procedures concerning the award of public contracts:

> Member States have approached the implementation of Directive 2007/66/EC differently. At times, rules on remedies in public procurement have been rewritten almost from scrap. Other times, the new remedies have been grafted onto existing legislation ... In both cases, the peculiar legal traditions of each Member State are deemed to influence the way remedies are not just implemented *but applied* [emphasis added]. Harmonization by EU law is partial at best here.

Another difficulty arising from the reliance of the EU on national authorities and agencies to undertake most of its policy application is that they do not all wish to apply EU policies and laws fully and properly. A desire to protect national, regional and local interests may be one reason why this may be so with, for example, national bodies sometimes tempted to circumvent EU law on public contracting (which, for tenders above specified amounts, must be open) so that they can favour – for often quite understandable reasons (especially the protection of jobs) – the contract bids of national and local firms. With public procurement accounting for around 15 per cent of total EU GDP, any evasion of EU law in this area clearly constitutes a very significant problem.

Sometimes a policy is applied unevenly or incorrectly because public authorities do not have complete faith in its implementation in other EU member states. The Common Fisheries Policy is a policy area where such problems are believed to exist. The passport-free Schengen travel regime has also experienced such problems, with some Schengen-member zone states making use of emergency provisions (for example, to combat a temporary increase in crime or to control football hooliganism) to reinstate internal border checks. Occasionally, smooth Schengen policy implementation has been upset by a new national government or a shifting coalition resisting implementation in order to gain domestic political advan-

tage (see, for example, Maloney and Pop, 2011, with respect to Denmark's moves to reintroduce border controls with Germany and Sweden).

Public sector corruption can also account for an unwillingness or inability to apply EU policies and laws fully and properly. This is a significant problem in a few member states, especially in south-east Europe.

* * *

The delegation of most EU policy application responsibilities to national and sub-national levels thus paves the way to considerable variations between member states regarding the extent to which policies are fully applied. It does so because national enforcement systems differ in so many ways, not least in their political willingness and their administrative capacity to apply particular policies: a willingness and capacity that can vary between member states, and that within member states can vary between policy areas (see Hartlapp and Leiber, 2010). Generally speaking, both successful and unsuccessful national policy application are not consequences of one factor but rather of several. So, for example, Di Lucia and Kronsell (2010) show in a study of the application of the 2003 Biofuels Directive (which requires member states to support the consumption of minimum levels of biofuels) that the prospects of application are enhanced when there is a match between policy ideas at the EU and national levels, when key national actors are given an opportunity to voice their views to their government in a consensual context, and when the positions and interests of nationally-based potential veto players – that is, actors whose co-operation is required (such as oil companies and car manufacturers in the biofuels case) – are reflected in the national policy.

Minimizing national variations

Despite it creating policy application difficulties, the delegation of most EU policy implementation to national and sub-national levels is necessary. The only alternative to this delegation is for the EU to have its own administrative apparatus spread throughout all member states. Such an administration would have to be very large given the great width and depth of the EU's policy portfolio, would be very expensive to fund, and would be impossible to organize in such a way that it operated with maximum effectiveness and efficiency given the many ways in which EU and national policies overlap and intertwine with one another.

However, in spite of the problems with delegation to national and sub-national agencies, the EU clearly needs effective monitoring and sanctioning mechanisms to try to minimize the difficulties and ensure that there is as much consistency in implementation as possible. The principal mechanisms for this are in the hands of the Commission, which, acting in a legal guardian role, monitors and exercises surveillance over national policy implementation, and when appropriate uses sanctions it has available to deal with transgressors.

Most of the monitoring and surveillance is undertaken through regular reports that national implementing authorities must submit to the Commission, but the Commission also undertakes a limited number of on-the-spot investigations that are conducted by specialist teams. These investigations can even include dawn raids, such as one carried out in late May 2011 on companies that make and distribute piston engines that were suspected of engaging in anti-competitive practices. However, the Commission's relatively limited resources mean that there is only so much it can itself do directly with regard to investigating and taking action against suspected transgressors – be they member states or private companies.

The procedures that apply when a member state is suspected of not applying, or only partially applying, an EU law are outlined in Box 6.2. An important feature of the procedures is that they are designed with a view to resolving matters before they become too confrontational, because there is usually no advantage to either the Commission or to member states to be in open conflict with one other over an implementation matter. The Commission's prime aim is for policies to be fully implemented, while member states – though sometimes prepared to seek an advantage by delaying the application of policies (which may, for example, result in trading advantages or the saving of public expenditure) – do not usually want to build a reputation as laggardly implementers and therefore as unhelpful and untrustworthy member states. Accordingly, as proceedings unfold, both 'sides' search increasingly for an accommodation – in the form, for example, of the Commission granting an extension to a deadline or a member state agreeing to tighten its inspection practices. In consequence, at each of the stages in the procedure, the number of actions taken by the Commission drops progressively.

But while the Commission prefers to persuade suspected transgressors to 'fall into line' voluntarily, if they do not do so it is willing to use the CJEU. This can result in the imposition of financial penalties, and can sometimes also result in judgments that usefully strengthen implementation powers. In the public procurement area, for example, the Court has 'interpreted the law in a very dynamic manner in a number of landmark cases leading to fundamental improvements of the enforcement system both at national and supranational level' (Treumer, 2011, pp. 17–18). For example, in *Commission v. Germany* (case C-503/04) the Court ruled in July 2007 that a breach of the procurement rules can result in a duty to terminate the public contract in question.

Direct implementation by the Commission

There are a few policies, of which competition is by far the most important, where the Commission exercises direct implementation powers. Compared with its dealings with member states in respect of policy application, where fines are rarely issued, a striking feature of the application of competition policy is the frequency with which the Commission issues fines against private companies for breaches of competition law. Fines are issued most regularly for breaches of EU rules on restrictive practices and abuse of dominant trading positions. So, for example, in 2006, the Commission imposed a fine of €219.1 million on Arkema, a French chemicals company, for its part in a cartel in the acrylic glass sector. It also fined Arkema's two parent companies – Total (€140.4 million) and Elf Aquitaine (€181.35 million). Appeals were then made by the companies to the ECJ, and in 2011 the General Court upheld the Total and Elf Aquitaine fines but reduced the Arkema fine to €113.3 million.

The Commission's most publicized anti-competitive cases have involved two US firms: Microsoft and Intel. In 2004, Microsoft was fined €497 million (the largest fine ordered by the Commission at that time) for abusing its position in the group server operating systems and media player markets, and then in 2006 it was fined a further €280.5 million and in 2008 an additional €899 million (again, then the largest fine in the EU's history) for not having complied with conditions in the 2004 decision that were designed to open markets. The Commission and Microsoft eventually

---

Box 6.2

Procedures that apply when a member state is suspected of being non-compliant

- The starting point is when the Commission becomes aware that there may be a problem with the application of a policy in a member state. This awareness usually comes from one of three sources: self-notification from the member state, with relevant national officials seeking clearance for certain policy application practices; information provided by the member state in a monitoring report; and – the most common source – whistle-blowing, often by people, organizations or companies who feel they are being disadvantaged by the way in which policy is being applied, or not being applied, in a part of the EU.
- Before any formal action is taken, the Commission almost invariably initiates informal contacts with the member state – usually via the state's Permanent Representation – to try to resolve matters. Around three-quarters of suspected infringements are resolved at this stage.
- The first formal stage involves the issuing by the Commission of a 'letter of formal notice', informing the member state that it is in possible breach of its obligations. More than 1,000 letters of formal notice are issued each year (including letters covering non- or incorrect transposition). These letters, and subsequent exchanges with member states in infringement cases, are channelled via the Permanent Representations – with it then being up to the member states themselves as to who is involved and how cases are managed at the national level. Member states are usually given about two months to respond to letters of formal notice and where, as is often the case, responses provide enough evidence that the state is now complying, then the Commission closes proceedings.
- If the problem remains unresolved, the Commission is likely to carry out an investigation.
- If, after the investigation, a breach is confirmed and continues, a formal procedure under Article 258 TFEU comes into play, under which the Commission 'shall deliver a reasoned opinion on the matter after giving the State concerned the opportunity to submit its observations'. Reasoned opinions usually include deadlines by which the member state must comply fully with EU law. More than 500 reasoned opinions are issued in an average year.
- If the state concerned fails to comply with the reasoned opinion, the Commission may, again under Article 258 TFEU, 'bring the matter before the Court of Justice of the European Union'. There are around 150 references to the Court each year.
- If the member state concerned does not comply with the judgment of the Court, the Commission may, under Article 260 TFEU, bring the case back to the Court, but this time may specify a lump sum or penalty payment which the member state must pay. The Court may reduce, increase or uphold the recommended lump sum or penalty payment (though it cannot instruct an increase in transposition cases). Only a handful of cases lead to fines on member states.

---

settled the case in late 2009, when Microsoft agreed to bundle nearly a dozen additional browsers with Microsoft Explorer. The Commission, however, did not waive the 2008 €899 fine, which resulted in Microsoft appealing (filed in May 2011) and the General Court (June 2012) upholding €860 of the fine issued, bringing the three fines levied against Microsoft to a total of €1.64 billion (Arthur, 2012). Intel was fined a record €1.03 billion fine in 2009 (a record that still stands at the time of writing) for

having engaged in illegal anti-competitive practices by giving rebates to major computer manufacturers provided they bought the computers' central processing units from Intel.

A different sphere of competition policy where the Commission also exercises direct and very important implementing powers is proposed company mergers. Under the 1989 Merger Regulation, which was amended in 2004, intended concentrations between companies that have an EU-wide dimension are subject to Commission vetting to ensure that competition will not be harmed. Normally, Commission approval is given, though often only following long negotiations during which the firms concerned agree to conditions – usually covering the divesting of some of their activities – being attached to the authorization. A typical example of a Commission investigation into a proposed merger was one the Commission approved in October 2011 for American-based Seagate Technology to buy a part of the South Korean company, Samsung. This merger did not involve a European company, but it was deemed to be justified because of the volume of business being conducted by the companies in the European market (European Commission, 2011s).

The best-known example of a proposed merger not being authorized occurred in 2001, when the Commission decided that the proposed €42 billion merger between the US companies General Electric and Honeywell would severely reduce competition in the aerospace industry. Significantly, in terms of how the Commission undertakes this implementing role, in announcing the 2001 decision the Competition Commissioner stated that the companies had been too rigid during the negotiations and had made too few concessions. While at the time of the Commission's rejection some observers thought GE's reluctance to be flexible in the negotiations with the Commission was because the merger had already been approved by the US competition authority, subsequent research has uncovered a purposeful strategy on the part of GE's CEO, Jack Welch. According to Büthe (2011), Welch submitted the merger request to the US authorities well in advance of the European application so as to be able to use an almost certain US approval to pressurize DG Competition, and particularly its head, Mario Monti. In a classic case study of strategic miscalculation, Welch assumed that the European authorities would not overrule the Americans

The impact of enlargement

A concern in EU-15 quarters prior to the 2004/7 enlargements was that the new member states were not fully ready to apply EU policies. This concern did, perhaps, contain something of a hypocritical element, given that there was no shortage of implementation problems among the existing member states, but none the less the concern was certainly felt and was a key

reason why some EU-15 policy practitioners believed the enlargement was too rushed. In practice, some of the concern has proved to be justified because, as a number of studies have shown, while new member states generally have a good formal compliance record in terms of transposing legislation and dealing with infringement proceedings against them, the record in respect of practical implementation (which is often unseen and even more often is unrecorded) is, for the most part, less satisfactory (see, for example, Falkner *et al.*, 2008; Schimmelfennig and Trauner, 2009; Sedelmeier, 2008). A number of factors have been identified in studies to explain the relatively poor application performances of new member states, most of which are rather more intense versions of the factors that are normally cited to explain unsatisfactory application in EU-15 states. The most prominent of the factors are: insufficient administrative capacity; high domestic adjustment costs; the incongruence of some EU policies with domestic norms; political salience; and the orientations of important domestic policy actors. These factors, which apply also to most prospective EU members, are not, it should be stressed, necessarily mutually reinforcing. Indeed, as Schimmelfennig and Trauner (2009, p. 6) observe, even if administrative structures are supportive and capable of compliance, there are likely to be implementation delays and failures when 'adjustment costs and political salience are high and governments as well as strong domestic interest groups do not agree with EU rules'.

Evaluation

Policy evaluation involves assessing the effectiveness (have objectives been achieved?) and efficiency (how do results achieved compare with the costs incurred?) of policies.

All EU policies, from the most general – such as the overall operation of the CAP – to the highly specific – such as energy research programmes – should in theory be subject to full evaluations. In practice, whether they are conducted, the extent to which they are conducted, and with what vigour and effect they are conducted, varies considerably. There are several reasons for this. One is that some policy areas cannot be evaluated systematically using 'rational' tools such as cost–benefit analysis or performance-based metrics because they are driven in no small part by political considerations. The overall nature of the CAP is an obvious such example, with much of the rationale behind it being based on political considerations related to pressures from member state governments and from agri-interests. In such cases, it is difficult to set measurable goals and objectives on which rational evaluation is based. Another reason why some policy areas are difficult to evaluate is that features of the policy activity make evaluation intrinsically difficult in terms of measured outcomes. CFSP/CSDP missions and how they contribute to overall CFSP/CSDP goals are of this type. And a third reason why policy evaluation can be difficult to conduct is the multi-layered nature of policy responsibilities in such policy areas as the environment, employment promotion and equal opportunities.

However, despite such barriers in the way of policy evaluation, it certainly has been given a higher priority over the years. This increased priority reflects the greater attention that has been given in the EU since the 1990s to best practices in policy management, particularly in achieving accountability, transparency and encouraging results-oriented decision-making based on quantitative and qualitative evidence.

Normally, broad and overarching policy areas are only – and arguably can only be – evaluated in rather general terms. The periodic assessments the Commission issues of the impact of the internal market programme and its impact on such indicators of success as economic growth and employment fall into this category of general evaluations. More detailed and scientific evaluations tend to be directed towards narrower policy areas and activities. As Versluis *et al.* (2011, p. 207) observe, evaluations usually focus 'on a single piece of legislation, operational programme, or individual project, given that these are bite-sized initiatives through which policy budgets are normally channelled with the explicit aim of achieving certain policy goals. That is to say, policies are translated into workable "courses of action" often for a fixed duration and with an estimated cost'.

The discussion of policy evaluation that now follows is organized around the three stages or points in time at which policy evaluation takes place: during policy development (known as *ex-ante* evaluation); while policy is being implemented; and after a policy programme has been completed (*ex-post* evaluation). Typically, what are known as formative evaluations,

which are aimed at improving existing programmes, are conducted at the *ex-ante* and mid-term stages, while summative evaluations, which are aimed at assessing outcomes, take place at the *ex-post* stage.

Evaluation thus occurs throughout policy processes, which reinforces the need not to view the policy cycle model in too strict or too linear a manner.

Ex ante evaluation

In developing policies and policy programmes the EU must, if their effectiveness and efficiency are to be maximized, seek to satisfy itself on a number of key questions, prominent among which are: are the policy goals clear; have all possible ways of achieving the goals been fully analysed; what are the benefits and what are the costs; do the benefits exceed the costs; and are sufficient resources available?

Quite how the EU goes about engaging in such *ex ante* evaluation, or appraisal as it is perhaps more accurately described, varies according to the policy type. Where, however, legislation is envisaged, a procedure has emerged that is now standard across the policy spectrum. Its main features are set out in Box 6.3.

The procedure outlined in Box 6.3 gives the impression of a wholly rational, neutral and technically-driven process. In most respects it is just that, but sometimes the Commission may have a preference for a particular course of action and may indeed even have started informal work on drafting the legislative proposal in question before the impact assessment (IA) has been completed (which, strictly speaking, should not happen). In such circumstances, IAs cannot be 'fixed', but they can lean in preferred directions. Moreover, when legislative instruments are drafted it is possible for unwanted contents of IAs to be discounted: an IA is, after all, not a scientific exercise but rather an informed judgement on the best possible way of dealing with a policy problem.

Mid-term evaluation

Evaluating policies while they are being implemented involves following-up on the policy goals and policy mechanisms that were identified in the policy development and decision-making stages, and checking whether they are being translated into practice.

Procedures within the Commission for evaluating new legislative proposals

- Impact assessments (IAs) are obligatory for all legislative instruments that are likely to have a significant impact. The DG that is in the lead on a legislative instrument makes the judgement as to whether an IA is necessary, but if it decides that no assessment is necessary it can be overruled by the Secretariat General.
- IAs are drawn up by the DG unit and desk officers who are responsible for writing the proposal, usually with logistical and tactical assistance from a planning or evaluation unit in the same DG (the precise organizational arrangements vary between DGs). Other DGs that have a potential policy interest must be consulted.
- IAs: (i) identify 'the problem' that needs to be addressed;(ii) identify the policy objectives to deal with the problem; and (iii) identify options (which must include that no action is to be taken) and their likely impacts. IAs must cover the economic, social and environmental aspects of proposals.
- When finalized, IAs are submitted to the Impact Assessment Board (IAB), which is based in the Secretariat General. Its membership consists of the Deputy Secretary General and a handful of senior Directors – including always the Directors from the Ecofin, Employment and Environment DGs. The IAB scrutinizes the IA and in about half of the cases refers them back for further information, changes or strengthening.

Specific evaluation questions asked at this stage include: is the policy being implemented as was intended; are there any management weaknesses; are sufficient resources being made available; are resources being used appropriately; are policy instruments being activated on schedule; are there any – perhaps unanticipated – implementation difficulties; are all stakeholders being consulted; and is feedback on implementation being used to improve delivery and/or redirect resources?

The extensive monitoring of EU policies and policy programmes undertaken by the Commission – with front-line administrators usually being obliged to submit regular reports 'to Brussels' (as it is frequently put by such administrators) – is a form of mid-term evaluation. But, more broadly, there is a sense in which all policies are being evaluated continuously once they come into operation. This is because policy stakeholders – that is, those with a direct interest in the policy (which can include politicians, administrators, sectional interests and the general public) – are, with degrees of interest and knowledge that vary according to how much they are affected, aware of policy activities and their consequences. So, for example, farmers hoping to benefit from a scheme designed to encourage diversification of land use will keep a close watch on the qualifying criteria for financial assistance, how the criteria are being interpreted by implementing officials, and what inspection systems have been put in place to monitor the activities of financial beneficiaries of the scheme.

Mid-term evaluations, especially if they are on a formal footing and do not consist merely of vested interests voicing complaints, can enable policy problems to be addressed on a continuous basis. Formative evaluations are especially important where innovation is involved, such as with many projects being funded by the structural funds in the CEECs.

Ex post evaluation

Strictly speaking, *ex post* evaluation occurs when a policy programme is completed. However, most specific EU policy programmes are not one-off programmes scheduled for a specified number of years and then are finished. Rather, they are generally part of broad ongoing policy activities that are subject to continual revision and renewal. As a result, what amount to *ex post* evaluations usually occur before a policy activity has strictly finished and can, in effect, virtually merge into mid-term evaluations. Questions asked in *ex post* evaluations include: were the policy goals achieved; did some aspects of the policy work better than others; was the policy implemented on time and within budget; and where could improvements be made if the policy activity is to be continued?

Ex post evaluations take a number of different forms and, in consequence, are undertaken by varying types of actors. A few are undertaken by the Commission, although usually in collaboration with outside experts. However, the relative lack of in-house evaluation experts in the Commission, the highly specialized technical ground that many policy programmes cover, and the fact that sole control by the Commission of evaluations would mean that it would often be evaluating itself, result in most *ex post* evaluations being contracted out to subject and evaluation experts.

Under Commission President Barroso, *ex post* evaluations of EU legislation have been given a much greater importance than they had in the past. Formerly, they tended to be undertaken on a rather sporadic basis and to focus often on not much more than financial instruments. Barroso has overseen a widening of both the number and scope of *ex post* evaluations. Under his presidency, much more legislation than formerly now includes an evaluation requirement, and the administrative culture of the Commission has changed – it is now generally accepted that there should not be significant changes to existing legislation without some sort of evaluation of that legislation having been undertaken.

An important role in *ex post* evaluation is also undertaken by the European Court of Auditors (ECA), which is responsible for checking EU revenue and expenditure and for providing the Council and EP with a Statement of Assurance on the reliability of the accounts, the legality of financial transactions, and whether financial management has been sound. This task is undertaken by auditing the general budget of the EU and certain non-budgetary EU financial operations (including development aid), and by conducting investigations into and issuing reports and opinions on various specific areas of expenditure. The role of the Court is not to replicate what has already been covered by internal Commission auditing, which is extensive. Rather, it is to examine the adequacy of internal auditing procedures, with a particular view to the rigour of

financial management practices and their ability to identify irregular and illegal transactions. Over the years, the ECA has continually identified weaknesses in financial administration (that is, after all, its job) – especially with respect to the CAP and cohesion funding (the two main areas of EU expenditure) – but it has also testified to a progressive lowering in the misuse of funds. Compared with the 10 per cent and more that it used to report in errors in financial payments, the Court now puts the figure for most expenditure areas at between 2 per cent and 5 per cent. So, with regard to the 2010 budget, the Court reported an estimated average error rate of 3.7 per cent (Court of Auditors of the European Union, 2011).

Conclusions

There are problems and limitations associated with taking a policy cycle approach to analysing how EU policy processes operate. The approach suggests a more rational, logical, detached and orderly approach to policy-making than usually exists in practice. Further, in itself the approach has nothing to say about the varying dynamics of EU policy-making – which are examined in Chapters 5 and 7.

None the less, the policy cycle approach does provide a very useful framework for facilitating identification of the various stages that policy-making, in the EU or elsewhere, must go through if perceived public problems or needs are to be addressed and tackled by public policies. The policy stages are, in practice, not rigidly compartmentalized, there is not necessarily a clear and smooth movement from one stage to the next, and there are huge differences between policies regarding how long each stage lasts. But, one way or another, the various stages of the policy cycle – with sometimes the exception of evaluation – always exist.

Chapter 7
Policy-making Modes

This chapter focuses on policy-making 'modes' – that is, the ways in which the EU makes decisions. The first section of the chapter introduces the four modes the EU has developed: the Community method; intensive transgovernmentalism; supranational centralization; and new modes of governance. The EU has developed multiple policy-making modes because a balance is needed between, on the one hand, policy-making efficiency and, on the other, the frequent differences of opinion among member states as to the extent to which they perceive the need for an EU-level policy (and are therefore willing to accept a policy-making mode that locates decision-making power 'in Brussels'). The next four sections explain and dissect the four policy-making modes. These sections are followed by a discussion of the relations between these modes and policy areas. While the existence of four different policy-making modes can be challenging to readers who are new to EU studies, this chapter offers guidance which should prove helpful when studying the policies themselves.

Classifying EU Policy Processes

The core features of the EU's policy processes that were described in Chapter 5 combine to produce a seemingly bewildering and impenetrable policy process system. As Tanja Börzel (2009, p. 192) has observed, the EU, like its member states (though even more so) 'features a combination of different forms of governance that covers the entire range between market and hierarchy'.

But it is incumbent on commentators on the EU to go beyond simply saying that what is being studied – the EU's policy processes in this case – is multi-featured and difficult to understand. An attempt must be made to try to see whether there are any constructs that are helpful in throwing light on the multi-dimensional and seemingly confusing nature of the policy processes: whether, in short, there are any constructs that can help to advance description and understanding.

One useful construct, which provides the organizational base for this chapter, is to view policy processes through the lens of policy-process modes. That is, to view them through broad characteristics and traits shared by particular policy processes. While such an approach necessarily involves acknowledging the existence of detailed differences between aspects of particular processes

Box 7.1

The EU's Policy-Making Modes

Policy process mode	Key features and actors	Time period came into effect	Policy areas
Community method	Commission proposes. Council and EP co-decide on over 90% of EU legislation. QMV normally available in the Council. Court adjudicates.	With the founding treaties in the 1950s.	• Applies in all policy areas with respect to the making of EU legislation.
Intensive transgovernmentalism	Decisions are taken by member state governments, usually following intense discussions and negotiations at different levels of seniority. Final decisions are taken unanimously by member state heads of government or ministers.	In the 1970s, as foreign policy was developed.	• CFSP • CSDP • Multi-annual financial frameworks • Enlargement • Can apply in other policy areas when 'history-making' decisions are taken.
Supranational centralization	Decisions are taken by the EU's 'supranational actors': notably the Commission, the CJEU and the ECB with respect to eurozone monetary policy.	In the 1960s, and more assertively in the 1970s, with respect to competition policy.	• Competition policy • EMU (via ECB) • Can apply in other policy areas when the CJEU makes 'judicial law'.
New modes of governance	Takes many different forms, but usually involves relatively non-hierarchical and open forms of government. Actors vary between policy areas, but are normally centred around the Commission and the Council, with the latter acting only by unanimity. Societal actors are often involved, as are the EU's quasi-independent agencies in some policy areas.	In the 1990s, and more especially in the 2000s.	• Used to some extent in many policy areas. Areas of particularly heavy use include such Europe 2020-related policies as cohesion, social, employment and environment.

within modes, it is none the less helpful in assisting the identification of broad patterns of EU policy-making.

There is no right or wrong way of classifying the EU's policy process modes. Everything depends on the intended purpose of the classification. If the main purpose is to identify general overall characteristics, then a classificatory system containing only a small number of broad categories is preferable. If, however, greater precision is desired, then it is better to employ a classificatory system that contains a large number of specific categories.

The position taken in this chapter leans towards the broader approach. In doing so it follows in the steps of, and portrays a general picture that overlaps with, that of some other observers of the EU, notably Wallace (2010) and Wallace and Wallace (2006) – which build on the analysis of Wallace (2005) – and Magnette (2005). In using the broader approach, considerable care is taken to try to avoid over-simplification. The main way in which this is done is by noting, as appropriate, the principal variations that exist within the categories of policy processes identified.

The classificatory system, or typology, that is used distinguishes between policy processes according to:

- the extent and nature of involvement of institutions that are independent of member state governments – and, more particularly, the degree to which the Commission, the EP and the CJEU are involved;
- the decision-making rules in the Council – and, more particularly, whether or not unanimity is required for decisions to be taken; and
- the status of decisional outcomes – and, more particularly, whether decisions taken have legal status.

These criteria lead to the identification of the four broad policy process modes introduced at the start of the chapter. Key features of the modes are set out in Box 7.1.

Before examining the modes, three points – which will be returned to in the concluding section of the chapter – need to be emphasized. First, the distinctions between the nature and effects of the modes are not always hard and fast, with the complex and multifaceted nature of EU policy processes often resulting in a considerable overlap at the edges. So, for exam-

ple, a distinguishing feature of many new modes of governance is the use of such nominally 'soft' policy instruments as 'targeting' and 'peer reviewing'. However, the effect of these instruments on member states can sometimes be almost as constraining and restrictive as EU legislation. This is because the normative pressure to be perceived as a team player is especially important in federal arrangements, where member states that 'cheat' or 'free ride' will find other member states less willing to be flexible on other policy matters which might be of great importance to the offending member state. Second, there is no clear correlation between the content of policies and the modes that are used for them. Indeed, many policy areas use a variety of policy modes. Third, the overall policy mode 'picture' is fluid and constantly evolving. When the EC was created, one mode – the Community method – was pre-eminent, but over the years new modes have been created, and all the modes have evolved.

The Community Method

The development and nature of the Community method

The founding fathers of the European Communities in the 1950s were resolved that the new organizations they created should not be hamstrung in their operational capacity by being based wholly on an intergovernmental decision-making system. That is, they did not want the Communities to be based on a system that rested wholly on decisions being made and applied only when they could command the unanimous backing of the governments of all participating member states. It was the reliance on such a system that, in their view, was primarily responsible for making the then recently created Organisation for European Economic Co-operation (OEEC) and the Council of Europe much less effective than had been hoped. The Communities must be stronger in their decision-making capacities. In particular they must be based on a system that would not make the taking of decisions dependent on the least enthusiastic member state.

The way to create a stronger decision-making capacity was seen as being to embody supranational features in decision-making arrangements. As Robert Schuman stated in 1950 of the soon-to-be-created ECSC:

> Participating states will be abandoning some degree of sovereignty in favour of a Common Authority and will be accepting a fusion of powers that are at present being exercised ... by the governments ... [The participating states] are convinced that ... the moment has come for us to attempt for the first time the experiment of a supranational authority which shall not be simply a combination or conciliation of national powers. (Quoted in O'Neill, 1996, p. 35)

In the event, the decision-making system that was eventually agreed for the ECSC in the 1951 Paris Treaty was not as supranational as some of the founding fathers would have liked. This was largely because it included a Council of Ministers that not only had considerable powers, but also powers that could usually be exercised in respect of major decisions only on the basis of unanimity. None the less, a quite new decision-making system was created, in which there was a considerable measure of supranationality. The ECSC arrangements were broadly replicated in the 1957 Treaties of Rome.

What was this decision-making system on which the EC was established? It was a system that essentially specified, in what became a much used shorthand description of the Community method as it existed for many years, that 'the Commission (High Authority in the case of the ECSC) proposes, the Parliament advises, the Council decides, and the Court adjudicates'. To develop this a little further, the system that was created was based on the following principles and arrangements:

- Proposals for Community action were to stem from an appointed institution – the Commission/High Authority – which was to have no national loyalties, was charged to be independent in its actions, and was to look to the general interest rather than the interests of just some member states when making proposals.
- The Commission's proposals were to be scrutinized, but not ultimately determined, by parliamentarians – though not until 1979 were there any directly elected parliamentarians – in the European

Parliament (or, as it was initially known, the European Assembly).

- All final decisions were to be taken by representatives of the member state governments, usually acting by unanimity, in the Council of Ministers.
- Any disputes arising in relation to Community law – the main sources of which were to be the treaties and EC legislation – were to be settled by the European Court of Justice, which was to be an appointed and neutral Court.

This earliest form of the Community method has been revised, developed and elaborated over the years. The most important changes have concerned the positions of the EP and the Council. Concerning the EP, pressures to democratize policy processes in response to the EU's ever-broadening policy responsibilities have resulted in the Parliament moving – via a staged process than can be traced through rounds of treaty reform – from its original position, which was that of a rather special sort of policy adviser, to the position it now holds of being a key actor in virtually all policy spheres, and of being a full co-decision-maker with the Council when most EU laws are being made. Concerning the Council, as well as losing its monopoly as final legislative decision-taker, its former position of generally only being able to take most legislative decisions by unanimity has also changed, with treaty reforms having gradually increased the circumstances in which decisions can be taken by a qualified majority, to the point that QMV is now available in respect of more than 90 per cent of legislative proposals. This movement away from (though not yet complete abolition of) the formal existence of national vetoes in the Council has arisen largely from concerns to ensure that the EU's broadening policy portfolio, coupled with the periodic increases in EU membership, do not result in decision-making stalemates.

A central feature of the Community method has always been, as it has been more broadly within the EU system as a whole, the striking of a balance in the national representations of the decision-making institutions between the equality of member states on the one hand and the differing population sizes of member states on the other. The nature of what this balance should be has been debated, disputed and adjusted since the Communities were first conceived in the 1950s, but it has been so particularly within the context of the Community method. This is because it is exclusively within the framework of the Community method that EU legislation can be made. The main features of the balance between and within the major institutions has remained largely unchanged over the years, with the membership of the Council of Ministers, the CJEU, and – since the Treaty of Nice – the Commission, all fully embodying the equality principle, while the membership of the EP and voting strengths in the Council of Ministers under QMV are tailored to membership size. The tailoring to membership size has, however, always been heavily muted, with larger states being greatly under-represented and smaller states greatly over-represented – which is a defining feature of federal arrangements.

Intergovernmental Conferences (IGCs) have often been much taken up, in one way or another, with these national 'representational' balance issues, both with regard to broad points of principle (should, for example, all member states have a Commissioner?) and the individual 'allocations' to states. This was particularly the case in the IGCs that produced the Treaty of Nice (where the large member states agreed to give up their second Commissioner in exchange for greater proportionate voting weight in the Council) and then the Constitutional and Lisbon Treaties (with the latter IGC deciding that from 2014/17 assigned voting weights in the Council will be replaced by voting strength based directly on population size). Significantly, the Lisbon Treaty originally provided for the 'one Commissioner per member state' principle being dropped in favour of the size of the College being reduced to two-thirds of the number of member states. However, this provision played a part in the Treaty being rejected by the Irish people after a referendum campaign in 2008 during which there was a vigorous defence of Ireland always having a Commissioner (Kubosova, 2008). The 'No' vote, which brought to light concerns of other small states over their loss of a permanent Commissioner, resulted in the pre-Lisbon Treaty configuration of the Commission being restored.

But while the composition of the Community method's institutional actors have been much debated and in almost constant evolution, some of the core features of the system itself still recognizably stem from the system that was created in the 1950s – most particularly the Commission's initiating powers, the Council's decision-making powers (albeit that most of

them are now shared with the EP), and the Court's judicial powers. However, as the evolution has taken place, so have the number of specific processes within the method increased, with the powers and roles of policy actors – especially the Council and the EP – varying according to the precise procedure applying. This is most obviously the case in respect of the EU's legislative procedures.

The Community method and the EU's legislative procedures

As noted above, all EU legislation is made via the Community method. Three basic legislative procedures now exist, each of which contains variations with respect to such matters as voting rules in the Council and the consultation rights of the EESC and the CoR. The three procedures are the consultation procedure, the ordinary legislative procedure, and consent. (The former co-operation procedure was abolished by the Lisbon Treaty.) The main features of each of the procedures are outlined below (for a fuller description of the EU's legislative procedures, see Nugent, 2010, pp. 308–19).

The consultation procedure

The consultation procedure was the only legislative procedure until others were created by the 1986 Single European Act. It involves a single reading by the Council and the EP. The Council must generally act by unanimity under the procedure, though in a handful of cases it may use QMV. The EP can vote to reject proposed legislative measures and can table amendments, but the Council is not obliged to act on the EP's opinions – the very reason why the procedure is known as consultation. If the Council acts prematurely and does not wait for Parliament to make its views known, the law will be ruled invalid by the CJEU – a point that was established in the famous 1980 isoglucose case ruling. The isoglucose case ruling did not give the EP an indefinite veto over legislation under the procedure, because it is obliged by treaty to issue opinions, and in some of its judgments the Court has referred to the duty of loyal co-operation among EU institutions, but it did give the EP a useful delaying power.

Where the EP wishes to amend a proposal that falls under the procedure, it does what it can to persuade and/or pressurize the Commission to amend its draft. Pressurizing normally takes the form of voting on amendments to proposals, but delaying voting on the resolution that formally constitutes the opinion until after the Commission has stated – as it is obliged to do – whether or not it accepts the amendments. If the Commission does accept the amendments, the EP votes for the legislative resolution and the amendments are incorporated into the Commission's proposal – on which the Council then takes a decision. If, however, the Commission does not accept the amendments, or at least not all of them, the EP may judge the Commission's position to be unsatisfactory and as a result may seek to delay the progress of the proposal by referring it back to the appropriate parliamentary committee for further consideration.

The EP's power of delay under the consultation procedure clearly falls a long way short of having full legislative power. But, it is, none the less, a very significant power, because it can be used as very useful tool to bargain and negotiate with the Commission and the Council. Indeed, Kardasheva (2009) has shown that the Parliament exercises much greater influence over the content of legislation under the procedure than has been generally recognized. Its leverage under the procedure is greatest when it gains the Commission's support and when the member states want a decision to be made quickly, because then the EP can force concessions during informal negotiations between the institutions. Kardasheva (2009, p. 404) goes so far as to suggest that these informal negotiations can virtually amount to an additional reading to what formally is a single-reading procedure.

The application of the consultation procedure has been greatly reduced over the years by treaty reforms, but among important areas to which it still applies are much of fiscal, social and citizenship policies.

The ordinary legislative procedure

Until the coming into force of the Lisbon Treaty, the ordinary legislative procedure was known as the co-decision procedure. This former name captures the essence of the procedure, because under it the Council and the EP each have full legislative powers and their joint agreement is necessary for proposals to be adopted. As can be seen in Figure 7.1, the ordinary procedure is a three-reading procedure, though if the

Council and the EP can reach agreement on proposals at either first or second reading stage they can be adopted at that stage.

If the Council and the EP are still at odds after the second reading, proposals fall if the Parliament has rejected them by an absolute majority of its members, and they are referred to a conciliation committee if the EP has amended them by an absolute majority. Conciliation committees are composed of an equal number of representatives from the Council and the Parliament. If agreement is reached in the conciliation committee, texts must be approved by the EP by a majority of the votes cast and by the Council acting by qualified majority. If no agreement is reached, proposals fall.

By contrast with the consultation procedure, the ordinary legislative procedure thus provides the EP with the power to veto legislative proposals. The significance of the Parliament's powers under the procedure is symbolized by the fact that whereas legislation made under the consultation procedure is made in the name of the Council only, legislation that is subject to the ordinary legislative procedure is made in the name of the EP and the Council. When the procedure was created initially it applied to approximately 40 per cent of EU legislation, but its remit has been so extended by the Amsterdam, Nice and Lisbon Treaties that it is now is used for most significant EU legislation, hence its change of name.

The absolute number of decisions taken under the ordinary procedure in the EP's 6th term (2004–9) was 454, a slight increase from the 403 co-decided in its 5th term (1999–2004) (Kratsa-Tsagaropolou et al., 2009, p. 6). However, there was an exponential increase in the adoption of legislation in the first and early second readings. A Commission analysis of the 6th EP term (2004–9) found that 72 per cent of legislation was adopted at the first reading, compared to a 33 per cent rate in the 5th EP term (European Commission, 2009a, p. 1). Another 23 per cent of legislation was adopted at the second reading in the 6th term, leaving just 5 per cent of legislation to be referred to conciliation – compared to 21 per cent in the 5th EP term (European Commission, 2009a, p. 5). (For an academic analysis of legislative early agreements, which reports similar figures, see Toshkov and Rasmussen, 2012.) As is shown below, a number of factors account for the increased number of early adoptions.

Figure 7.1 **The Ordinary Legislative Procedure**

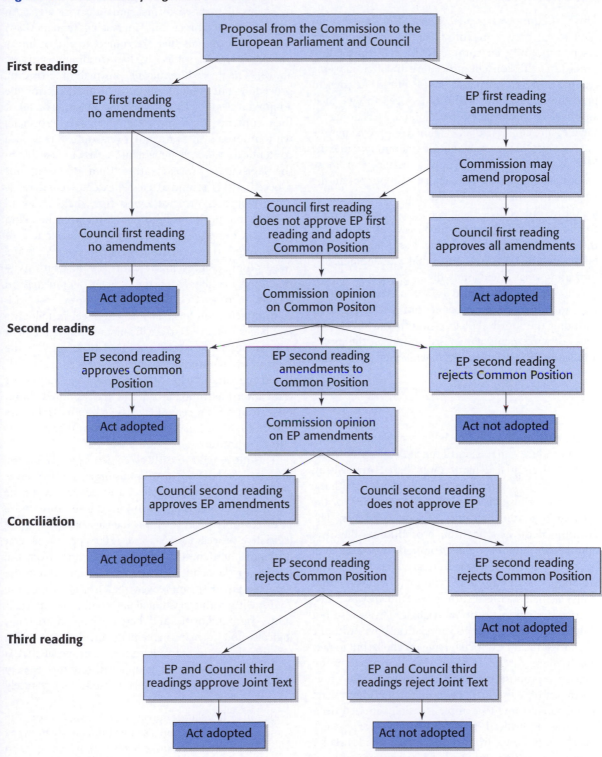

Source: UK Parliament, 2009.

The consent procedure

This procedure was created by the SEA, though until the Lisbon Treaty came into force it was known as the assent procedure. In common with the consultation procedure, the consent procedure involves just one reading in the Council and the EP, but in the consent procedure's case both institutions need to give their approval for proposals to be adopted. Depending on the measure concerned, the Council's approval may be possible by QMV or may require unanimity, while the EP's approval may need only a majority of those voting or may necessitate majority support of all the Parliament's members. Unlike the case with other legislative procedures, there is no provision for the EP to be able to table amendments. However, in practice, the procedure is not quite as rigid as it might appear, because the EP can attempt to make amendments by indicating what it will and will not approve.

The consent procedure is not used for 'normal' legislation but is reserved for certain special measures, including the approval of accessions to the EU, various types of agreements with third countries, the multi-annual financial frameworks in which the EU's annual budgets are set, and treaty reforms.

* * *

When the consultation procedure was the sole legislative procedure – that is, until the SEA came into effect in 1987 – legislative dynamics were based primarily on a Commission–Council institutional tandem, with the EP being not insignificant but being restricted for the most part to pressurizing and advisory roles. The creation of the co-operation procedure by the SEA, and then even more so the creation of the co-decision procedure by the Maastricht Treaty, transformed this situation. The EP rapidly became an absolutely central policy actor and the institutional tandem was transformed into an institutional triangle. This was so not only in terms of formal power relationships – with the Commission and Council having no choice but to take much more careful note of the EP's positions on legislative proposals – but also in terms of the whole operation of legislative procedures. The Commission and Council came to realize, especially after co-decision was introduced, that they would have to work closely with the EP from the very start of a legislative proposal to its final adoption. Close working relation-

ships between the three institutions have thus developed, in all sorts of formal and informal ways. An illustration of this is the increasing tendency for legislative proposals that are subject to the ordinary procedure to be settled at first reading (as noted above). The procedure may be a formal three-reading procedure, but because legislative proposals cannot be adopted unless the Council and the EP agree on all of their contents, there are clear advantages, especially with proposals that are not over-controversial and contentious, to reach agreement as early as possible in the legislative process rather than dragging out proceedings. First, and to a lesser extent, second, reading agreements save work and time, help to avoid institutional positions becoming too entrenched, and for the Council Presidency have the attraction of increasing the decision-making success rate. Accordingly, representatives of the institutions – involving people from the relevant Commission DG(s), from COREPER, and from the EP committee(s) responsible – usually meet in trilogues (see pages 78 and 84) to see if a first reading agreement is possible. Sometimes these early meetings take the form of what amounts to virtually first reading conciliation meetings. Such is the intensity and success of these inter-institutional contacts that, as noted above, only around 5 per cent of legislative proposals that are subject to the ordinary procedure get as far as a conciliation committee.

This movement to early agreements has, of course, impacted on how the institutions organize themselves and operate. This is no more clearly seen than with the Commission, which has been forced to become more interventionist than it was in the earlier stages of the legislative process (Kurpas et al., 2008, pp. 30–1). If it does not maintain a strongly activist stance from the outset, it risks being bypassed by the Council and the EP. This is a risk, moreover, that has grown in the 2000s, with both the Council and the EP having clear centre-right majorities and therefore being more ideologically able to reach agreements on their own. The Commission can always withdraw a proposal that is amended in a way that it opposes, but this is very much an option of last resort and one that is rarely used.

Beyond legislative procedures, aspects of the Community method can also be said to apply to many of the EU's non-legislative actions. For example, in what used to be called the EU's first pillar, the Council adopts many resolutions, declarations and agreements that do not have the status of EU law but which are certainly intended to guide policy direction. Because legislation is not being made, the EP is usually confined to an advisory role at best when such non-statutory policy instruments are being developed and considered, and, of course, there is no subsequent judicial role for the CJEU. But, none the less, the focus of deliberations in the processes that lead to the adoption of soft policy instruments such as resolutions is almost invariably a Commission document, and processes within the Council are much as they are with legislation when the unanimity principle applies, so a sort of Community method could be said to be employed.

More commonly, however, the Community method is associated with the making of EU legislation. As has just been seen, there are variants in the way that legislation is made but, regardless of the variations, the method has at its heart a set of arrangements that contains two core features. First, there is a significant distribution of power between the main political actors. The exact nature of the distribution depends on which legislative procedure is being used, but normally, for a legislative proposal to become a legislative act, the Commission, the Council and the EP must all be firmly on board, and within the Council most, if not all, member states must give their support. The Community method is thus most decidedly not a system in which political elites or narrow majorities can force decisions through against significant opposition. Second, the method contains a significant degree of supranationalism – that is, policy procedures which can result in the making of decisions that are binding on the member states without necessarily being approved by the governments of all the member states. The extent of supranationalism does, however vary, with two features *almost invariably* being present and two *mainly being* present. The two features that are *almost invariably* present are the Commission's exclusive power to propose legislative measures and the supreme authority of the CJEU to give judicial rulings on EU law. These features are not always present, because the gradual transfer of the AFSJ policy area from the former third pillar of the EU to 'the Community pillar' has been accompanied by some undermining of the Commission's and the EU's courts' former powers under this method. In particular, under Title V of the TFEU, which covers the AFSJ,

the Commission no longer enjoys monopolistic legislation proposal rights, but rather has to share them with the member states. This sharing makes it possible for an act to be adopted 'on the initiative of one quarter of the member states' (Article 76, TFEU) in the policy areas of judicial co-operation in criminal matters (Chapter 4, TFEU) and police co-operation (Chapter 5, TFEU). The two supranational features that are *mainly* present are the capacity of the Council to take decisions by QMV (which is the case in the vast majority of legislative measures since the Lisbon Treaty) and the EP fully sharing final decision-making power with the Council (which it does under both the ordinary and consent procedures).

Because it always applies when EU legislation is being made, the Community method naturally covers a very considerable range of policy areas. Foremost among these are internal market matters. Broadly defined, these matters include not only laws directly concerned with the operation of the market – such as laws on product standards, on public procurement, and on aspects of the regulation of particular sectoral areas – but also in such related areas as social policy, regional policy and consumer protection policy. Beyond internal market-related policies, EU law is also extensive – and therefore the Community method is much used – in aspects of such policy areas as the environment, AFSJ, and transport (all policy areas that have at least some internal market dimensions).

The decline of the Community method?

The main problem with the Community method from the viewpoints of the governments of member states is that they do not have full control of events when this method is used. The loss of control is not, it should be said, as great as it might appear, because underlying the method is a political culture based on a number of norms and values that give national governments a certain amount of 'protection' from being dominated by others. Features of this political culture include a reasonable – though varying – degree of trust between member state governments, an understanding that the interests and priorities of other member states will be respected and not readily overridden, and an acceptance that there will be a search for compromises when attempting to make decisions. But, despite such protective features of the method, it is still the case that the national governments are heavily dependent on the Commission for proposals, can normally be outvoted in the Council, need the EP to be co-operative, and are in the hands of the CJEU when interpretations of the law are made. Such dependence on others is not welcomed by many governments, especially in policy areas that are particularly sensitive for, or important to, them. It is a dependence that has been instrumental in the development and use of other policy process methods.

This development and use of other policy methods is, it should be stressed, not, as is sometimes misleadingly implied, of very recent vintage. Indeed, the founding treaties themselves provided for some limited departure from the Community method within the Community framework, notably by allocating strong independent powers to the Commission in respect of aspects of competition policy. Also within the Community framework, from a relatively early stage discussions, explorations and co-operation on particularly sensitive and contested policy matters occurred without the Community method necessarily being employed fully. For example, the European Monetary System (EMS) – the forerunner of European and Monetary Union (EMU) – was forged in the late 1970s largely through high-level exchanges between a few key leaders of the time – notably the German Chancellor, Helmut Schmidt, the French President, Valery Giscard D'Estaing, and the President of the Commission, Roy Jenkins. After the EMS was established, its management was largely a matter for the national economic and financial ministers, with the Commission and the EP being kept largely to the sidelines. Outside the Community framework, the building of foreign policy from the early 1970s, and of justice and home affairs policy from the mid-1980s, were both firmly based on intergovernmental – that is, non-Community method – processes.

However, while a relative decline in the use of the Community method is thus now of some years' standing, there is no doubt that the decline has increased in recent years. Giandomenico Majone (2006a, p. 614) suggests that a key reason for this has been that, since the early 1990s, some member state governments have been uneasy with the role of the Commission and have had concerns that it has been tempted to over-reach in its policy aims: 'The decline of the Community method begins when the member states become

convinced that the Commission is incapable or unwilling to exercise self-restraint'. On this point, it certainly is true that that the Commission has sought to make maximum use of the Community method, in large part because, as Kelemen (2011, p. 7) argues, the EU has very weak implementation and enforcement capabilities when policies are not based on the law. So, rather than favouring 'soft' methods of governance, such as the open method of co-ordination, the Commission is more interested in promoting 'Eurolegalism across a wide range of policy areas' (ibid., p. 9).

But Majone's explanation is not the only reason why there has been a relative decline in the use of the Community method. Other factors have also contributed. The first of these has been that as the internal market has been increasingly completed and as it has come to be believed increasingly that the market should not be over-regulated, so has there has been some decline in the volume of proposed market-related legislation. That is, there has been some decline in the expansion of the policy sphere where the use of the Community method has been most used. A second factor has been that because new legislation proposed by the Commission now has to be justified more than was previously the case – in terms, most notably, of subsidiarity and proportionality – the Commission necessarily tends to move with greater caution than previously when considering launching new legislative proposals. A third factor has been that as the EU has moved into an ever-wider range of policy areas, many of which are highly sensitive and/or sharply contested, then so have other forms of policy process – including forms that are more flexible than the Community method – often been seen to be more suitable and/or acceptable for certain policy purposes. And a fourth factor has been enlargement, which, in making the EU not only more numerous in terms of the number of its member states but also more heterogeneous in terms of the policy preferences of its member states, has resulted in other forms of policy process often being deemed to be seen as desirable and/or necessary.

The extent of the decline in use of the Community method should not, however, be over-stated. There has been a *relative decline* in that other modes are increasingly being used, but there has not been an *absolute decline* because there are just as many legislative texts being channelled by the method as there were in the mid-/late 1990s. The method continues to be a very important policy process mode, for two main reasons. First, it has evolved to adjust to changing needs and expectations – as witnessed by the growing availability of QMV, the increased powers of the EP, and the increased flexibility of some EU laws. Second, it is still *the* mode that is used for the making of EU legislation. The transfer of what remained of the EU's third pillar, covering a number of important AFSJ policy areas, to the TFEU by the Lisbon Treaty is testimony to the Community method's continuing importance: the transfer was made primarily for the very reason of allowing the method to be used. (For a fuller exploration of the nature and importance of the Community method, see Dehousse, 2011.)

Intensive Transgovernmentalism

As a way of conducting policy processes in an international organizational setting, intergovernmental co-operation implies two main operating principles. First, the governments of the member states of the organization retain control of organizational decision-making and of their national sovereignty. This is achieved by requiring that all key policy decisions are taken by the national governments acting unanimously and by giving few independent powers to those who hold appointed positions within the organizations – essentially the organization's employees, usually grouped together in a secretariat. Second, and this follows from national governmental control over decision-making, the governments of the member states are not legally obliged to engage in actions arising from organizational membership that are against their preferences or their will, and they are not legally prevented from undertaking independent actions of which they are in favour.

Intergovernmental co-operation is the dominant way of operating in international governmental organizations (IGOs), though what amounts to something closely akin to elements of supranationalism is sometimes also present with, for example, independent conflict resolution panels (as in the World Trade Organization) and (usually very limited and circumscribed) provisions for some use of majority voting. But even if a decision is taken against the wishes of a member state, it cannot be forced to fall in line by recourse to legal action on the part of the IGO. This is because IGOs cannot make laws, but rather are restricted to making organizational decisions and rules. The strongest disciplinary action that can normally be taken against a recalcitrant member state is that it can be deprived of organizational benefits, or even of membership.

The EU is, of course, much more than an IGO, not least because, as has been shown in the outline of the Community method, it makes such extensive use of supranationalism in its policy processes. However, the EU also makes considerable use of intergovernmental co-operation in some policy areas. But it does so in such an intense way that, as Wallace (2010, pp. 100-3) suggests, 'intensive transgovernmentalism' is perhaps a more accurate term to describe the nature of the processes. What, then, are the principal features of intensive transgovernmental processes in the EU? There are four, the first three of which concern the EU's main 'non-governmental' institutions holding only relatively weak powers:

- Unlike under the Community method, the right of policy initiation is not exclusive to the Commission but is held also by the governments of the member states. This is seen clearly in the foreign and defence policy spheres, where initiatives come from the national governments in a number of different ways: directly from individual governments; through *ad hoc* groupings of governments; and, post-Lisbon Treaty, from the European Council President (who is the representative of the heads of government) and the High Representative (who, despite also being a Commissioner, is in many respects an agent of the Council).
- The EP is in a generally weak consultative position, with few formal powers. In policy areas where this is the case, such as with the CFSP and EMU, the Parliament does what it can to be a significant policy player – by, for example, working through EP committees to monitor progress and produce recommendations – but ultimately it is not usually able to exert much influence other than at the margins.
- The CJEU is largely excluded from intergovernmental policy processes. It is so partly because the policy areas covered by intergovernmental processes do not, for the most part, fall within its jurisdiction as specified by the EU's treaties. It is

also partly because EU legislation is not made by intergovernmental processes.

- All key decisions are made either by the European Council or by the Council of Ministers acting by unanimity. So, no government can be outvoted and thus have a decision imposed on it with which it does not agree. However, decisions are only taken after intensive, and often long and highly detailed, discussions and negotiations by national governmental representatives at lower levels. These discussions and negotiations are conducted in many ways, but are channelled formally through the Council's elaborate and hierarchical structures, which provide for a filtering-up of views and positions from national officials, to EU ambassadors and their deputies (in COREPER), to ministerial meetings and, where appropriate, to Heads of Government.

Intensive transgovernmentalism is used mainly in highly sensitive policy areas, where at least some member states wish to retain national sovereignty and do not want to risk the loss of control that the introduction of supranational features can involve. The origins of intensive transgovernmentalism in the EU are to be found in the development of foreign policy from the early 1970s. The then member states moved tentatively towards trying to co-operate on foreign policy matters, but most wished to do so in a much looser way than the use of the Community framework would have allowed. They did not wish the Commission to be much involved, they did not want the EP to have any powers, they did not want EU laws to be made or the ECJ to adjudicate on disputed matters, and they wanted all decisions to be based on unanimous agreements between the governments of the member states. Accordingly, policy processes took the form of a Council-based intergovernmental system. While foreign policy has been much developed since it was first given attention in the 1970s – with the Common Foreign and Security Policy (CFSP) now being an extremely important policy area and it having been joined in recent years by an increasingly established Common Security and Defence Policy (CSDP) – its core inter- and transgovernmental features remain.

The AFSJ policy area was also initially developed – in its case from the mid-1980s – on an intergovernmental basis. Indeed, like foreign policy, AFSJ was given its own intergovernmental pillar by the Maastricht Treaty. But subsequent pressures for the advancement of AFSJ policy – related mainly to the ever-expanding internal market, increased international migration, and the combating of terrorism – have resulted in the policy area being gradually standardized, or 'communautarized', via the Amsterdam, Nice and Lisbon rounds of treaty reform. AFSJ thus demonstrates how it is possible for a policy to move from one process mode to another.

Beyond the CFSP and CSDP policy areas, the other most prominent use of intensive transgovernmentalism in the EU today is in respect of 'history-making' decisions (see Peterson and Bomberg, 1999, pp. 9–16): that is, decisions that have major implications for the overall integrationist direction of the EU. Examples of such decisional matters are treaty reforms, the overall size and shape of the EU's multi-annual financial frameworks, and enlargement issues. The processes used in respect of these sorts of decisional matters are different in character from CFSP and CSDP processes in that they are more for periodic rather than day-to-day use, and in that almost invariably they involve the key decisions being taken at the highest political level – in European Council meetings. But regardless of these differences, key features are shared with CFSP and CSDP decision-making processes: the main decision-takers are representatives of the member state governments; key decisions are taken by unanimity; and the formal powers of the EU's supranational institutions are limited.

Supranational Centralization

As noted above, the Community method contains important supranational features. But it is generally accepted in EU circles that there are circumstances in which it is necessary that supranational institutions are assigned particularly strong and independent powers. The most obvious and recurring of such circumstances is with regard to being able to ensure that EU law is fully and properly applied. Accordingly, though practicalities mean that the day-to-day, front-line implementation of EU law has to be the responsibility of national authorities acting on the EU's behalf, this implementation is undertaken within frameworks overseen and monitored by the Commission and which can become the subject of actions in the CJEU when there are thought to be departures from legislative intentions.

These powers of the Commission and the CJEU stem from a recognition that the application of EU law must be, and must be seen to be, efficient, effective and fair across all member states. This would not be possible if national authorities were not subject to direction and control from the EU level. Without such overseeing and monitoring, national authorities could be tempted to interpret EU laws in an over-flexible manner, or even ignore them altogether when laws were deemed to be damaging, inconvenient or discriminatory. It is judged to be best, therefore, to assign important responsibilities in respect of the interpretation and application of EU laws to neutral, independent and EU-level institutions.

But, in interpreting and applying EU laws, EU institutions sometimes are in effect making such laws. This is because the accumulated body of EU law contains gaps where the meaning of the law is less than concise. These gaps and lack of precision – which are mainly a consequence of the formal decision-makers being unable to agree on tight and comprehensive legislation or to anticipate all attempts to skirt legislative intent – need to be filled and clarified. In undertaking much of this filling and clarifying, the Commission and CJEU sometimes have a wide frame of reference within which to operate, and their judgments can have a very considerable policy effect. For example, in such policy areas as competition, taxation and social welfare, CJEU rulings have done much to assist in the opening of the internal market: by, for example, making it easier for firms to establish business premises in other member states without risking being subject to discriminatory or double taxation, and by making it easier for people to live and work in other member states while still having access to educational, health and social insurance schemes and facilities. This policy impact of the Court, which was considered in Chapter 3, reflects the experience of other federal systems, where constitutional courts customarily adjudicate 'on the side of' internal markets.

However, in addition to this recognition of the need for the existence of strong supranational powers concerning policy implementation, it is also generally accepted in the EU that in a small number of policy areas there is a need for supranational institutions to have strong and independent decision-making powers. These are policy areas where there is a perceived need to de-politicize decision-making and/or to protect decision-makers from political pressures.

The best known of these policy areas is competition policy, where the Commission has very considerable independent powers – independent in the sense that its decisions do not require approval or legitimation by any other EU body. In one sense these powers constitute a form of policy implementation in that they do not involve making new rules but rather involve applying existing rules. But the wide scope within which the Commission operates when applying competition rules, the great discretion it has in determining judgments, and the often very considerable economic and social impacts of its decisions, mean that if this is policy implementation it is of a very special sort. The main reason the Commission has such strong decision-making powers in the sphere of competition is that the issue area is regarded as being too sensitive and potentially too subject to political interference to be left either to the Council or to national authorities. Evidence that these concerns have a solid foundation is seen in the fact that it is not unknown for supposedly independent Commissioners to favour the position of their member state when highly charged and disputed competition cases have been referred to the College of Commissioners.

From the early 1990s it increasingly came to be thought that the concentration of competition decision-making powers in the hands of DG Competition was leading to policy inefficiencies. In particular, it was clear that the DG was overloaded in its work commitments and that this was resulting in many competition matters not being fully addressed and/or being subject to excessive delays in being handled. As a result, after extensive deliberations it was decided to decentralize much of the responsibility for enforcing restrictive practices and abuse of dominant trading position policies to the national level. This was done via the 2003 so-called Modernization Regulation (Council of the European Union, 2003a), which came into effect in May 2004 and which paved the way for some aspects of competition policy to be implemented by national competition authorities (NCAs) operating within the framework of a Commission-managed European Competition Network (ECN). (On this modernization of aspects of competition policy, see: Cini and McGowan, 2008, especially Chapters 4 and 9; Wilks, 2005.) However, major aspects of competition policy were not made subject to the new arrangements, and so they remain based on the traditional, Commission-controlled, system. These aspects include: restrictive practices and the abuse of dominant trading cases that involve trade between three or more states, plus any other such cases the Commission decides it should deal with; whether or not proposed company mergers between companies should be permitted, and if so whether they should be made subject to conditions; and whether state aid has been, or proposed state aid should be, permissible. (See also Chapters 6 and 8 on the Commission's competition policy powers.)

Another prominent example of an EU institution with important and independent decision-making powers is the European Central Bank (ECB), which is responsible for the monetary policy of the eurozone. It was given its powers because of a recognition that, given the likely differing economic performances and needs of eurozone states, there would be enormous political friction between the states if decisions over, most crucially, interest and exchange rate policies were to be given to a body composed of national representatives – be they politicians or bankers. What was required, it was decided, was to de-politicize and de-nationalize decision-making processes on these issues by assigning them to high-level and EU-level bankers charged to take their decisions in the interests of the eurozone as a whole.

New Modes of Governance

What are the new modes of governance?

The EU has long employed a wide variety of policy instruments for the purpose of promoting policy convergence. Box 7.2 sets out the main types of these policy instruments along a hard-to-soft spectrum. The fact that it is possible to place them on a spectrum implies the important point that the distinction between hard and soft instruments is more a matter of degree than of a fundamental difference.

Hard (sometimes also described as strong) instruments are composed mainly of EU laws and are bind-

ing in that they must be applied in the member states. Soft (sometimes also described as weak) instruments do not have full legal status and are usually more exhortive than obligatory in nature. The purpose of softer policy instruments is normally to promote dialogue and co-operation in policy areas where legislation is seen as being premature, or inappropriate, or politically unfeasible. In recent years, soft policy has increased in importance in the EU, in large part as a result of the increasing use of 'new modes of governance' (NMG) approaches.

New governance influences began to impact on public policy and administration in the EU member states from around the mid-1980s, and from the early 1990s they began to impact on the EU itself. Made up of a variety of specific policy forms, in essence new governance involves basing the making and administering of public policy less on hierarchical and legislation-based forms of operation and moving them in the direction of more flexible, open and participatory forms of policy development and practice. New governance is less controlling in spirit than traditional forms of governance, and often indeed is semi-voluntaristic in nature. In the EU, new governance approaches are seen as being especially useful and applicable in policy areas where there is a need for new thinking and innovative ways of operating outside established bureaucratic channels, in newly emerging policy areas where key policy actors have yet to be convinced of the need for binding regulation and policy conformity, in policy areas where there has been some sort of legislative breakdown, in policy areas where there are advantages to be had from involving private actors in policy development and implementation, and in policy areas where EU policy activity is recognized as being desirable and/or necessary but where the preservation of national diversities is also seen as being important. New governance thus has many potential advantages and possibilities where, on the one hand, tight and hierarchical forms of policy-making are not seen as being desirable and/or possible and, on the other hand, where loose intergovernmental cooperation is seen as being too weak. In short, new governance can be used to extend and improve governing capacity in a variety of situations. (Useful readings on the development and use of new governance approaches in the EU include Caporaso and Wittenbrinck, 2006; Citi and Rhodes, 2007; Eberlein and Kerwer, 2004; Héritier, 2003; Kohler-Koch and

Box 7.2

Policy instruments and policy convergence

Hard ←――――――――――――――――――――――――――――→ Soft

| Legally binding and detailed law (mainly in the form of regulations) | Legally binding objectives (mainly in the form of directives and treaty provisions) | Agreed objectives supported by strong peer review, benchmarking and structured co-operation | Agreed objectives, but with some optionality regarding active participation – as with CFSP and CSDP operations | Agreed objectives supported by weak peer review and benchmarking | Recommendations, but with little or no follow-up |

Rittberger, 2006; Linsenmann, Meyer, and Wessels, 2007; Scott and Trubek, 2002.)

New governance approaches in the EU take many different forms, including:

- the issuing of non-binding texts that are designed to further policy advancement through such means as the issuing of recommendations, guidelines and targets;
- the creation of decision-making mechanisms that give opportunities for the participation of non-EU institutional and non-state actors;
- the compilation of evaluation and monitoring reports that have the effect of putting peer pressure on poor performers to address their policy weaknesses; and
- the establishment of specialized and quasi-independent agencies – such as the European Food Safety Authority and the Monitoring Centre for Drugs and Drug Addiction – to carry out mainly non-executive tasks that otherwise would have been assigned to the Commission.

Examples of the 'policy reach' of different forms of NMG are given in Box 7.3.

While new modes of governance can provide policy opportunities for the EU, they do not always offer a way out of difficulties when other policy process modes are unavailable or unsuitable. Because, as Kohler-Koch and Rittberger (2006, p. 37) have noted,

'The effectiveness and problem-solving capacity of NMGs vary according to the type of policy and actor preference constellations at hand.' In this context, Héritier (2003, p. 124) has suggested that NMGs are of limited use in policy areas dealing with redistributive matters and with 'deeply entrenched problems'.

In their study of the – slow and still uncompleted – liberalization of utilities across the EU since the late 1980s, Bulmer et al. (2007) provide evidence to show that NMGs – and more particularly the open method of co-ordination (OMC), on which they mainly focus – also have limited operational effectiveness when member states are not fully in accord regarding the end goals of policy. NMGs supposedly facilitate policy transfer between member states in policy areas where obligatory or forced policy standardization via the Community method is not deemed to be desirable or possible, but Bulmer and his colleagues show that if NMGs are not used alongside more hierarchical forms of governance then those member states that have doubts about the suitability or impact of an EU policy are likely to hover somewhere between being foot-draggers and complete non-implementers. This is in line with similar findings in developed federal systems, such as the US, where mechanisms of horizontal federalism are found to be less effective than vertical mechanisms (Zimmerman, 2002).

NMGs also appear to be of limited capacity in member states that have, until relatively recently, been based on command and control regimes and that are

---

Box 7.3

Policy examples of the use of new modes of governance in the EU

Environmental policy. A particular feature of new modes of governance in the environmental policy area – and it is a statutory requirement in many cases – is the involvement of private actors and stakeholders in local planning and in policy implementation processes (see Lenschow, 2002).

Telecommunications policy. While much of the EU's package of measures to regulate telecommunications is based on hard law, NMG has come to be used increasingly for refining the package and for eradicating operational deficiencies. As Simpson (2011, p. 1115) notes, 'voluntarism, opinion giving, advice taking and the pursuit of best practice are key features of the revised regulatory system'. Other key features include the promoting of networking and policy learning between national regulatory authorities (NRAs).

Cohesion policies. A variety of non-state actors are involved at sub-national levels in the making of funding decisions, and in project management and monitoring tasks (Bache, 2008; Marks, 1996; Piattoni, 2010).

AFSJ policies. A distinctive feature of AFSJ NMG is the use of a wide range of non-legislative policy instruments, including target-setting texts of various sorts – often in the form of action plans, programmes and strategies. Specific policy areas covered by NMG approaches include the combating of terrorism, the prevention of the trafficking of people, and controlling violence associated with football matches (see Monar, 2011a).

Corporate taxation policy. Under the 1997 voluntary Tax Code, member states have agreed not to engage in harmful corporate tax competition that might have an effect on business location. The Tax Code is an early example of what has become, since the late 1990s, the most commonly used and most important form of NMG, namely the open method of co-ordination.

---

now in transition to becoming fully functioning liberal democracies with market economies. Starting with the Mediterranean enlargement round of the 1980s, most states that have become members of the EC/EU have been – with the exception of those that joined in 1995 (Austria, Finland and Sweden) – of this transitional type. As Börzel (2009) has shown, the operationalization of new forms of governance has been very slow to develop in the three Mediterranean accession states, and in the Central and Eastern European countries (CEECs) that joined the EU in 2004/7. This has been because of a mismatch between the nature of their state apparatuses and societies and NMG requirements.

Regarding the mismatch with state apparatuses, state traditions that have involved hostility to non-state actors participating in policy-making have been slow to change, with public officials in CEECs being reluctant to open up to private actors. Even when there has been some such willingness, state actors that are themselves relatively weak – usually because of some mixture of operating inexperience, being under-resourced, and being politically and administratively fragmented – do not have the capacity or skills to bring non-state actors into policy-making and policy management other than on a consultative basis. Furthermore, weak state actors are usually cautious about engaging in real co-operation with non-state actors for fear of being over-influenced, or even captured, by them.

Regarding the mismatch with the nature of societies, not only do state actors tend to be relatively weak in transition states but so too does social organization. Accordingly, non-state actors have only a limited capacity to engage with state actors on the basis of being fully informed, reliable and deliverable negotiating partners, and so have little to offer state actors in return for being included in policy processes. Moreover, even when they do have something to offer, they can often be hesitant about risking

Box 7.4

The key operational principles of OMC, as set out by the 2000 Lisbon European Council meeting

Implementation of the strategic goal [of the Lisbon Strategy] will be facilitated by applying a new open method of co-ordination as the means of spreading best practice and achieving greater convergence towards the main EU goals. This method, which is designed to help member states to develop their own policies progressively, involves:

- fixing guidelines for the Union combined with specific timetables for achieving the goals which they set in the short, medium and long terms;
- establishing, where appropriate, quantitative and qualitative indicators and benchmarks against the best in the world and tailored to the needs of different member states and sectors as a means of comparing best practice;
- translating these European guidelines into national and regional policies by setting specific targets and adopting measures, taking into account national and regional differences;
- periodic monitoring, evaluation and peer review organised as mutual learning processes.

A fully decentralized approach will be applied in line with the principle of subsidiarity in which the Union, the member states, the regional and local levels, as well as the social partners and civil society, will be actively involved, using variable forms of partnership. A method of benchmarking best practices on managing change will be devised by the European Commission networking with different providers and users, namely the social partners, companies and NGOs.

Source: Council of the European Union, 2000.

their autonomy by becoming too close to policy-makers. The EU has done much to try to address these two problems by promoting – both pre- and post-accession – the strengthening of both governance capacities and of civil society in CEECs, but this is a long-term process. As the experiences of the three Mediterranean states show, deeply-entrenched hierarchical forms of governance tend to adapt only very slowly.

The open method

The nature of the open method

The best-known and most important use of a new governance approach in the EU is the open method, or the open method of coordination (OMC) to give it its full name. OMC began to be used as a means of making and applying EU policies in the 1990s, most notably in connection with the Broad Economic Policy Guidelines (BEPGs), which were designed to promote the coordination of national economic policies, and the employment guidelines of the European Employment Strategy (EES), which were aimed at creating a policy framework focused on the creation of jobs. However, it has come to be associated mainly with the Lisbon Strategy (now Europe 2020 programme), which arose from the March 2000 European Council meeting in Lisbon when the Union set itself a new ten-year strategic goal 'to become the most competitive and dynamic knowledge-based economy in the world, capable of sustainable economic growth with more and better jobs and greater social cohesion' (Council of the European Union, 2000, p. 1). The March 2000 summit identified OMC as a key policy process to be used in the pursuance of the Lisbon aims, and set out OMC's core operational principles, which are reproduced in Box 7.4.

Building on the Lisbon-specified operational principles, in practice OMC involves a decision-making and decision-implementing system in which: the Council (generally working largely on the basis of papers and proposals prepared for it by the Commission) identifies policy goals and ways in which they are to be pursued; considerable discretion is left to the member states as to how the goals are to be interpreted and implemented; and the Commission, working closely with the member states on an individual basis as well as via the Council, undertakes overseeing and monitoring responsibilities. Overall, the approach is gentle and relatively loose rather than compulsive and rigid. It involves the member states working with one another in a mid-position between policy co-operation and policy integration. Whereas the former usually involves governments not doing much more than liaising with one another and using only very weak policy instruments, and the latter involves governments making binding laws to achieve policy purposes, OMC involves the setting of policy goals but using non-legally-binding instruments to achieve them. OMC is thus a semi-voluntaristic process designed to try to deal in some policy areas with one of the EU's core organizational challenges: finding a balance between respecting the diversities of member states on the one hand and engaging in collective EU action on the other. As such, OMC places stronger pressures on member states to fall into line than exist under pure intergovernmental arrangements, but does not legally oblige them to act against their will on policy matters. As part of this balancing act, the Commission is given only limited licence to interfere in what ultimately remain national responsibilities. The softness of OMC is perhaps demonstrated no more clearly than in the fact that one of its principal benefits is hailed as being policy learning, with desirable policy results seen as following from the exchange of knowledge between participating partners and mutual learning leading to the wide adoption of 'best practice'.

Key OMC instruments that are used in an attempt to give effect to the policy goals include information exchange, the encouragement of best practice, benchmarking, peer review (usually channelled via the relevant formation of the Council of Ministers), and – though this has come to be downgraded – the publication of 'league tables' showing the progress member states have and have not made in achieving the specified policy goals. However, as with the policy goals themselves, these policy instruments do not have a legal base and so ultimately are not enforceable. Member states may be embarrassed if they are shown to be in breach of their OMC 'obligations', but no formal action can be taken against them. OMC goals are thus likely to be fully effective only if they are internalized at national levels.

The applicability and the uses and limitations of the open method

The OMC has grown in importance as an EU policy process because it offers a possible way forward in policy areas where at least some member state governments wish to see policy advances made, but where other governments are hesitant about, or are even resistant to, the passing of EU laws. As Borrás and Jacobsson (2004, pp. 191–2) have shown, policy areas where OMC is used fall broadly into three groups. The first group consists of policy areas where previous attempts to develop stronger policy forms have failed because of national political sensitivities. Included here are a number of social policies – including pensions, social inclusion and family law – where EU-level legislation is often precluded on both practical and political grounds. Research and Technological Development (R&TD) policy also falls into this group, with the EU's own long-standing R&TD policy having had only limited success in co-ordinating the very diverse national systems of innovation (Kaiser and Prange, 2002). The second group is composed of policy areas where the need for EU level policy activity has come to be recognized only relatively recently but where traditional regulatory or distributive policy approaches do not seem likely to be efficient. Included here are employment policy and information society policy. The third group is made up of policy areas 'showing very strong functional interdependencies with the EU level' (Borrás and Jacobsson, 2004, p. 192). The most important and obvious of these policies are national macroeconomic policies, especially of the eurozone member states, with economic stability and success seemingly requiring that macroeconomic policies are 'in tune' with one another.

OMC is thus potentially useful in these policy areas because it offers a middle way when intergovernmental co-operation is thought to be too weak to meet policy needs but where sensitivities associated with the preservation of national independence remain strong. The increasing importance of OMC is thus to be explained in functional terms: it focuses on policy outputs rather than inputs and by doing so offers possible policy benefits without being too threatening to the governments of those member states that are concerned to maintain control in the policy areas being covered. As to the possible benefits, there are differing views about this among both policy practitioners and academic commentators, but broadly speaking they are seen as being of two kinds: general benefits such as policy learning and the diffusion of best practice arising from the intrinsic nature of OMC operations; and specific policy benefits arising from the identification of policy goals and priorities – such as increased investment in research and training, and raising the employment rates of women and young people. (On the reasons for the increasing use of OMC in the EU from the late 1990s, see Borrás and Jacobsson, 2004; Heidenreich and Bischoff, 2008; Schäfer, 2005.)

Within the broad OMC framework, there are variations in how OMC functions and applies in particular sectoral areas. Indeed, there can be said to be different OMCs with respect to such matters as the precision with which policy goals are identified, the implementing techniques used, and the precise roles exercised by EU and national institutions and agencies. So to take, for example, the roles exercised by EU institutions, the fact that OMC does not involve the making of legislation would lead to an expectation that the positions and influence of both the Commission and the EP would be generally much weaker than when laws are being made under the Community method. However, though this is true of the EP, it is much less so of the Commission because, while it certainly is the case that OMC involves many more horizontal policy processes than the more hierarchical Community method, there is still a great deal of vertical steering led by the Commission, much of which is channelled via its representation on, and its servicing of, Council committees that have been established to deal with OMC-based policy activities. Included among these are the Economic and Financial Committee, the Employment Committee and the Social Protection Committee. Working often in close liaison with, and through, such committees, the nature and extent of the steering undertaken by the Commission – in terms, for example, of issuing guid-

ance documentation and collecting information on the performance of member states – is considerable. Indeed, Heidenreich and Bischoff (2008, pp. 515–16) suggest that, in the employment and social policy fields, the extensive liaison, information exchange and bargaining processes the OMC requires have contributed to 'a considerable intensification of the supranational regulatory structures'.

Two very different OMC policy areas may be examined briefly to further illustrate how OMCs can vary in character. As noted above, the BEPGs were one of the first forms of OMC. Under the post-2005 Lisbon Strategy (commonly known as Lisbon II) they were linked to the European Employment Guidelines (EEGs) to provide what were called the Integrated Guidelines of the Lisbon Strategy. The Integrated Guidelines – of which there were initially 24 under Lisbon II, but this number has been reduced under Europe 2020 (European Commission, 2010f, p. 26) – have provided the overall policy framework for the Lisbon Strategy/Europe 2020 as a whole. Included among the Guidelines are that member states should safeguard economic and fiscal sustainability, should promote an efficient and a growth- and employment-orientated allocation of resources, and should ensure that wage developments contribute to economic stability. The Integrated Guidelines are also a relatively hard form of OMC, with the Commission having issued extensive policy guidance to the member states in its annual reports on Lisbon Strategy/Europe 2020, and with it also both making and publicizing what are often relatively sharp comments on implementation performance by member states.

By contrast, gender mainstreaming is a more specific and somewhat softer form of OMC. The Commission issues guidance documentation, but follow-up at the EU level is spottier and weaker than is the case with the Integrated Guidelines. Like all OMC policies, gender mainstreaming is reliant on the co-operation of national authorities to be effective, but being a somewhat controversial and contested policy area – in some member states at least – it is particularly vulnerable to the whims of national decision-makers. That this is so is seen in the differences that exist in the provisions for gender mainstreaming contained in the three-year National Reform Programmes (NRPs) that all member states are required to produce, in the practical follow-ups to the NRPs, and in the ability of governments that are not over-sympathetic to gender mainstreaming to be less than zealous in ensuring fair consideration of gender in policy implementation.

The 'softness' of OMC has led to suggestions that it is somewhat ineffective. Certainly there is no doubt that case studies of the use of OMC in different policy areas have generally reported rather poor results (see, for example, the studies in Copeland and Papadimitriou, 2012). This is, however, not altogether surprising given that a central reason that OMC is used is because member states, or at least some of them, wish to avoid the binding commitments that use of the Community method involves. As Tsoukalis (2007, p. 59) has observed, there are inevitably limitations to an exercise in which 'the final responsibility lies with member states, while the role of the EU is limited to "soft" coordination at best'. In the view of its critics, OMC just does not put enough pressure on member states to 'fall into line', with the consequence that OMC-based policy provisions can ultimately be avoided by member states. As Bulmer *et al.* (2007, p. 191) say of the use of OMC to give effect to the Lisbon Strategy, 'unless they are committed to the Lisbon Agenda, member states may simply pay lip-service to the objectives while continuing along pre-existing policy trajectories'.

Moreover, the effectiveness of OMC, like the effectiveness of all soft policy instruments, can be difficult to measure in a precise way, emphasizing as it does flexibility, discretion and the merits of policy learning almost as much as policy actions. But to criticize the OMC as being weak and soft because its policy approaches are not based on EU law is arguably not very helpful, since the alternative to using OMC is not usually the Community method but rather is no policy of any sort. The policy areas covered by OMC are covered in this way precisely because hard law either has not been possible in these areas or has not been seen as being appropriate. As Caporaso and Wittenbrinck (2006, p. 476) point out, OMC, like other new modes of governance, appears to make policy agreement between the member states easier to reach precisely because the agreements are not binding and can be broken more easily. In sensitive policy areas such as labour market standards, welfare provision, and interventionist measures to assist underemployed sections of the population, if policy agreements were to require the making of EU laws – that would be subject to Commission infringement

proceedings and to CJEU jurisdiction – it is likely that few agreements would be made at all.

This likelihood does, of course, lie at the heart of one of OMC's weaknesses: namely that it tends to be used not so much because it is seen as being the ideal way to develop and manage a policy, but rather because harder policy methods are not available. As a number of commentators have observed (see, for example, Héritier and Lehmkuhl, 2008; Héritier and Rhodes, 2011), new forms of governance, including OMC, tend to work best when they are in 'the shadow of hierarchy': that is, when public and private actors have a strong incentive to co-operate because the alternative is the hierarchical imposition of policies by policy-makers. Such imposition is possible, however, only when policy-makers have the capacity to adopt and enforce decisions, and in the areas covered by OMC in the EU this is generally not the case: the shadow is absent. This lack of enforcement capacity is a persistent problem in coping with the voluntarism that characterizes most forms of horizontal federalism (see, for example, Zimmerman, 2002).

Another OMC weakness, at least in the view of some commentators, is that while, like other forms of new governance, it appears to encourage policy participation by non-state actors, in practice the big EU OMC decisions – on policy priorities, goals and instruments – have been largely the outcome of negotiations conducted by the governments of the member states (Armstrong, 2003 ; Borrás and Jacobsson, 2004; Büchs, 2008). This has been partly for logistical reasons, but often also because governments do not wish to encourage, and do not welcome, private actor involvement in many of the sensitive policy areas that OMC covers.

However, notwithstanding its weaknesses, OMC does allow some policy development in areas where hard policy development is not possible for political reasons. This has been seen no more clearly than in the area of corporate taxation policy, where a combination of policy resistance from some member states coupled with a treaty provision that all Council decisions on tax be taken by unanimous vote has resulted in proposed laws that are designed to harmonize tax rates and bases being resisted successfully in the Council. But by using what in effect was a form of OMC, the governments of the member states agreed in 1997 – as part of a broader 'tax package' – on a Code of Conduct under which they would refrain from harmful tax competition that might impact significantly on business location. (The tax package was originally in the form of a working framework, and was upgraded in 2003 to a political agreement.)

As well as allowing some sort of policy development in areas where the alternative is often very little or no policy development at all, OMC also has other potential advantages. One is that responsibility for policy remains in national more than in EU hands, with the consequence that national diversities can be more easily respected and accommodated. As part of this, OMC provides national authorities with considerable room for manoeuvre in choosing appropriate national implementation mechanisms, which is potentially crucial in areas such as social and employment policy where effective implementation has been, or could be, problematic. As Knill and Lenschow (2000, p. 281) have shown in their study of the (rather poor) record of EU environmental policy implementation, the decisive factor in explaining implementation effectiveness is the 'institutional "fit" or "misfit" of national administrative traditions and European requirements'.

A second potential advantage is that, by being open and participatory in its stance, OMC offers prospects for the involvement of a wider range of actors – regional, local and non-governmental – than is normal in EU policy processes. The potential is not, of course, always realized and, as de la Porte and Pochet (2005) report, and as many policy studies have shown, the extent to which such actors are actually involved varies between member states and between policy areas. Regarding variations between member states, pre-existing variations in the involvement of sub-national, social and civil society actors in public policy-making appear largely to have been maintained. Regarding variations between policy areas, Armstrong (2006, p. 92) is among those who have suggested that inclusion policies have come to adopt a more participatory approach, but de la Porte and Nanze (2004) indicate that, in the employment and pensions areas, policy processes generally remain heavily centralized and top-down, with social partners not much involved. Heidenreich and Bischoff (2008, p. 502) confirm the de la Porte and Nanze findings in the employment policy area.

A third potential advantage of OMC is that it has resulted in the creation at both national and EU levels of co-ordinating structures and channels that have served to promote policy exchanges of many different kinds between national and EU policy-makers. These exchanges may take the form of what Jacobsson and Vifell (2007, p. 184) describe as 'a type of elite deliberation, and sometimes expert deliberation, which hardly fulfils all the requirements of deliberative democratic theory', but they can none the less produce such desirable policy consequences as increased knowledge and understanding by policy-makers of possible policy options, of what works, and of how policy collaboration can be beneficial.

A fourth potential advantage is that OMC can be a sort of transitional policy process by opening doors to more advanced policy. This is because cautious and tentative policy development in 'difficult' policy areas can help to break down suspicions, can – within the network framework on which OMC is often based – create foundations for the building-up of trust, and can help to create an acceptance that soft policy approaches are always ultimately limited in what they can achieve, and need eventually to be strengthened. An example of OMC leading the way to hard policy can be found in the eurozone, where much of the Fiscal Compact replaced OMC (see Box 10.9 on p. 220).

Looking at the overall impact of OMC, have its possible uses and potential advantages been realized in practice? There is no consensus among observers and commentators on this. Some take the view that OMC is never likely to have much effect, because its non-hierarchical and essentially voluntary nature is not suitable for inducing effective policy development in an organizational setting with so large and diverse a membership (see, for example, Lodge, 2007). Some think that there is not much empirical evidence of it having had a significant impact on policy outcomes (see, for example, Moravcsik, 2005, p. 366). And some, who probably articulate the majority view, suggest that while OMC achievements have for the most part been modest – especially with respect to bringing about policy change directly and leading the way to the use of harder and bolder EU policy instruments – it has none the less had a generally positive effect on policy building (Copeland and Papadimitriou, 2012; see also, for example, Heidenreich and Zeitlen, 2009; and Zeitlen, 2011). This positive effect is seen as taking different forms across policy areas and between member states, but generally includes raising the salience in member states of many policy issues (especially social and employment policy-related issues), promoting mutual learning, and contributing to changes in national policy thinking and national policy agendas. These effects are, in turn, seen as assisting EU policy momentum in areas where alternative policy approaches have been either not appropriate or politically impossible.

Relations between Policy Process Modes and Policy Areas

The policy processes applying in particular EU policy areas are not usually of a pure policy process mode type. They are not normally completely open *or* closed, top-down *or* bottom up, supranational *or* intergovernmental, rigid *or* flexible, or producing binding *or* non-binding policy instruments. Rather, they generally display aspects of more than one mode. They may, for example:

- be primarily hierarchically-based, but also display features of network-based and/or open systems of governance. So, as Sabel and Zeitlen (2009) and Zeitlen (2011) have shown, in such policy areas as telecommunications, energy, environmental protection and competition, the Community method is increasingly accompanied by a variety of NMG-inspired implementing mechanisms that allow for some manoeuvrability, openness and participation by stakeholders;
- be largely intergovernmental in nature but also display hierarchical features. The CFSP is of this type in that it is essentially based on a system of intensive intergovernmental and transgovernmental negotiations, but its provisions for some use of QMV and its reliance in many circumstances on policy instruments where the Commission's position is strong (as with trade and development assistance) give it some supranational features. Indeed, CFSP is the prime example of a policy area that has, in the words of a former long-standing Belgian Permanent Representative to the EU, 'been "contaminated" by the Community factor' (de Schoutheete, 2011, p. 2).

Policy process modes thus do not necessarily have a monopoly in particular policy areas. Rather, in an increasing number of areas more than one policy process mode is used and is done so with a reasonable degree of comfort. Pochet (2011), for example, has shown that while much has been made of the growing importance of the use of NMG, and in particular of the OMC, with respect to EU social policy since the late 1990s, this has not resulted in less use of the Community method to make EU social policy laws. Monar (2011a) has made much the same observation about AFSJ policy, where an increased use of soft policy instruments, such as target-setting and peer review, has taken place in parallel with a great expansion of hard law. Similarly, competition policy has seen an increasing use of aspects of NMG since the late 1990s – mainly via the use of networked governance between EU-level and national-level policy implementers – but this has not been accompanied by a decline in the Commission's supranational powers with respect to major competition policy decisions.

In short, the EU's modes of governance are not mutually exclusive or antagonistic. Rather, they exist – sometimes separately and sometimes alongside one another – to serve the many different policy aims and organizational preferences of the EU's main policy actors. Nevertheless, as Figure 7.2 shows, these policy modes in their pure (rather than mixed) form do mirror the various relationships among the EU member states (horizontal relationships) and between the member states and the EU (vertical relationships). Intensive transgovernmentalism is characterized by tight linkages and horizontal relationships; both the Community method and supranationalism operate in the realm of tight linkages and vertical relationships; and OMC is characterized by loose linkages among actors, but it can move in a more vertical direction (when the Commission operates at the centre of a policy network) or in a decidedly horizontal direction (when industry or other stakeholders take the lead with little Commission direction/involvement – such as in the setting of many product safety standards).

Conclusions

The EU has many distinctive policy processes. This reflects the fact that the EU features combinations of

Figure 7.2   Hierarchy and linkages in the four policy modes

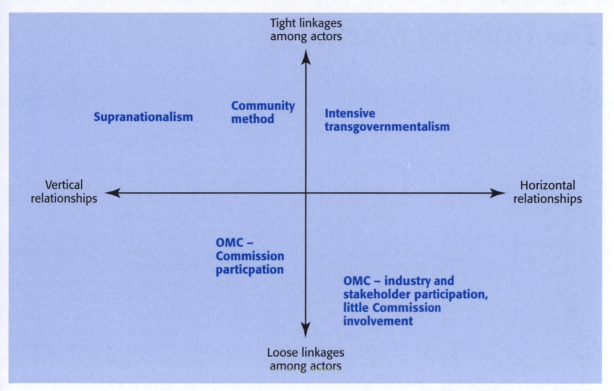

governance forms. These forms, which are not hermetically sealed from one another but which rather overlap and indeed almost merge at their edges, vary in the extent to which they are open or closed and are hierarchical or flat.

The EU has so many policy processes because, quite simply, member states have different views over what sorts of policies they want and how they want the policies to be made. The policy processes have been devised, and applied to particular types of policy activity, in response to differing perspectives on where the balance should be with respect to such considerations as policy-making efficiency versus respect for national rights, making binding laws versus not going further than structured co-operation, and permitting larger member states possibly to dominate versus protecting smaller member states.

It has been suggested in this chapter that a useful way of acquiring an overall perspective on the nature of the EU's many policy processes is to see them as being clustered into policy process modes. There is, to be sure, overlapping and intertwining between the modes, and they do contain internal variations, but they none the less are useful as broad classificatory concepts.

The increasing use of policy process modes other than the Community method signifies a very important shift in how the EU is governed and how it operates. Alongside increased differentiation (policies with not all member states participating, or at least not participating fully), the increasing use of a variety of policy process modes heralds a move towards a more flexible, often less hierarchical, but perhaps also more potentially adventurous, European Union.

Chapter 8

The Internal Market

The name of the policy project that has been at the heart of the European integration process since the early days of the European Communities in the 1950s has not remained constant. Over the years, the term 'common market' – an economic term associated with regional trading blocs – has gradually been replaced in everyday usage by Single European Market, single market, and increasingly – and, since the Lisbon Treaty, the only name that is now used in the EU's treaties – internal market.

This chapter on the internal market begins with an explanation of why, more than 50 years after the EEC Treaty set out the aim of creating a common market, market-building still occupies a central place on the EU's policy agenda and a completely integrated internal market is still not in place. The chapter then considers the market's rationale and explains why market integration is seen as being desirable. The market's historical development is then described, with a central theme of the description being the ever-broadening nature of the market's reach. The fourth section of the chapter explains the three methods the EU employs to reduce barriers to free movement. The fifth section summarizes the principal actions the EU has taken to establish the four freedoms. The sixth section describes how the EU attempts to ensure that its policies on the four freedoms are implemented. The seventh section discusses EU competition policies that deal with the types of market failure with which all advanced capitalist societies struggle, such as dominant position abuse and anti-competitive mergers. The eighth section of the chapter returns to the issue of the internal market's extensive reach by providing a short illustrative study of how the market's impact is being felt increasingly, and indeed encouraged, even in highly nationally sensitive sectoral areas. The chapter ends with concluding comments.

A Constantly Ongoing Process

Article 2 of the 1957 European Economic Community (EEC) Treaty specified:

> The Community shall have as its task, by establishing a common market and progressively approximating the economic policies of Member States, to promote throughout the Community a harmonious development of economic activities, a continuous and balanced expansion, an increase in stability, an accelerated raising of the standard of living and closer relations between the States belonging to it.

The TFEU reiterates the EEC Treaty's commitment to the creation of a common market, albeit in different terms, with Article 26 stating:

1. The Union shall adopt measures with the aim of establishing or ensuring the functioning of the internal market, in accordance with the relevant provisions of the Treaties.
2. The internal market shall comprise an area without internal frontiers in which the free movement of goods, persons, services and capital is ensured in accordance with the provisions of the Treaties.

A pertinent question to address here is why was it necessary to insert in the TFEU the phrase 'with the aim of establishing … the functioning of the internal market'? After all, did not Article 8 of the EEC Treaty require that 'The common market shall be progressively established during a transitional period of twelve years'?

The answer is, quite simply, that the internal market project has never been completed. While the internal market has been the EU's principal policy achievement, it has always been a work in progress and will continue to be so in the future.

Four reasons mainly account for this apparent slow progress in completing the internal market.

First, European governments and citizens identify primarily – politically, socially, economically and psychologically – with their member states. While member state governments generally subscribe to the rhetoric of the EU having a fully open and competitive economy, there are many circumstances in which they are prepared to accommodate, and even to press for, national market protections and variations. As in all federal and quasi-federal systems, the 'common good' often is not easily discerned, and considerable leeway is given to constituent units to deviate from central rules, and indeed to test those 'rules' to seek local advantages.

These EU level/national level tensions result in the internal market being something of a leaky bucket, with some 'holes' having proved to be very difficult to plug, and new holes always likely to appear. Accordingly, much of the policy work undertaken on the internal market requires careful vigilance, especially on the part of the Commission, often working through the CJEU.

Second, there are many differences between the governments of the member states regarding the extent to which the internal market should be based on liberal (that is, non-interventionist) principles on the one hand, and the extent to which it should have 'public responsibility' functions on the other. Should, for example, 'public services' such as health, education and social welfare be part of the internal market, and if so, to what extent and in what ways? And where should the balance lie between free market competition on the one hand and EU regulation designed to avoid 'races to the bottom' on the other? Ideologically-based differences on such questions divide not just labour from capital but also divide member states.

Third, differences have arisen from varying perceptions of what a properly functioning EU-wide market needs if it is to operate with maximum efficiency. Are there, for example, certain infrastructure industries – such as energy and transport – that are best run on protected, perhaps monopolistic, bases? And when it comes to the single currency, while the governments of most member states have long accepted the case that a single currency enhances market efficiency, this has not meant that they have all wanted to, or been able to, join.

Fourth, market forces, practices and products do not stand still but rather evolve in all sorts of ways. So, the original plans for a common market were negotiated by just six states of comparable economic development and before the intensification of globalization and competition from the newly-industrialized countries, the shift to knowledge-based industries, the acceptance in Europe of the dangers of global warming, and the admission to the EU of states with per capita GDPs significantly lower than the EU average. Such changes in the nature of markets – both the internal market itself and the external markets with which the EU's market does business – have posed constant challenges to the EU's policy-makers to 'keep pace'.

The Rationale for the Internal Market

The idea of European market integration is not a post-Second World War phenomenon. Continental Europeans have long recognized the desirability and advantages of removing cross-border barriers to trade. So, for example, in a petition for a German customs union (*Zollverein*) submitted to the independent German states in 1818 by a united German trade and tradesmen's union, the advocates wrote:

> To make a commercial shipment from Hamburg to Austria and from Berlin to Switzerland, one must cross ten states, study ten sets of customs regulations, pay six different transit duties. He who has the misfortune to reside at a frontier where three or four states touch each other, passes his entire life bickering with customs officials. (Quoted in Viner, 1950, p. 62)

The *Zollverein*, established in 1818 and expanded to eventually include most of the German states, was credited with building a vibrant German economy while protecting its members from foreign competition in a period of early industrialization.

After the Second World War, not dissimilar arguments to those that produced the *Zollverein* were increasingly heard for forging stronger relations between the markets of Western European countries. They were in the context of the generally co-operative postwar mood that existed in the Western world, and particularly in Western Europe. To the background of this co-operative mood, in the early days of developing the internal market the rationale was both political and economic. Many of the European Community's founding fathers believed that impediments to free movement had contributed greatly to Europe's troubled history and that opening up Europe through economic integration would provide a firm base for peace. Many further believed that creating a common market would help Europe, which had become squeezed between the two post-Second World War superpowers of the United States and the Soviet Union, to regain its 'rightful' place as a global economic and political power.

However, by no means all of the political leaders who participated in the building of European market integration from the 1950s were motivated by a desire to use market integration as a vehicle for the building of a more general European integration. Rather, there were many who saw market integration as being desirable in and of itself. They did so often as a consequence of looking to the large and very wealthy single market of the United States.

This perception of European market integration as having its own intrinsic advantages and merits – a

perception that has become increasingly widely-held over the years – was, and is, essentially based on a belief that open markets are more conducive to the promotion of growth and prosperity than are protected ones. This is because lowering barriers to trade creates a larger and more competitive market by allowing a freer circulation of the factors of production, which in turn:

- fosters external and internal economies of scale in production and distribution;
- lowers production costs – thanks in no small part to the establishment of common product specifications and requirements throughout the market;
- increases funding of technological advancement – through the creation of larger business enterprises;
- reduces the administrative costs of multiple customs authorities.

In response to such considerations, there is today a broad consensus at the heart of public discussions and actions that the removal of barriers to the conduct of economic activity between EU member states is, provided that appropriate safeguards are put in place, a good thing. It is deemed to be so because it is seen as assisting the pursuit of such economic desirables as increased trade, investment, employment, growth and return on capital.

The Development of the Internal Market

Early progress and difficulties

As part of its aim to create a common market, the EEC Treaty provided for the creation of a customs union (see Chapter 12). With the rapid removal of tariff and quota restrictions on trade between member states and the construction of a common external tariff, this was achieved, ahead of schedule, by 1968.

However, the common market was not to be achieved so easily. One key reason for this was, and indeed still is, that there are numerous potential restrictions on cross-border trade in addition to tariffs and quotas, and many of these are difficult to remove.

The removal of tariffs and quotas does not automatically reduce, let alone eliminate, regulatory barriers to trade. On the contrary, indeed, the creation of a free trade area, and even more so of a customs union, can tempt states to cheat by implementing non-tariff barriers (NTBs) to trade – many of which take the form of technical barriers to trade (TBTs). The EU has had to struggle with NTBs from the very beginning of its attempts to create a fully open internal market.

Until the 1980s, harmonization (in the French text of the treaty) or approximation (in the English text) of product standards was the EU's principal legislative response to overcome NTBs. Approximation, however, was fraught with difficulties, not least because the complexity and technical character of many traded products made it impossible, and in many cases simply unnecessary, to agree on the standards applying to thousands of goods (let alone services), especially in such product areas as food, electrical engineering, vehicles, precious metals and chemicals (European Commission, 1999). (See below for a detailed discussion of approximation.)

In addition to the problem of NTBs and the imperfect solution offered by approximation, another very important reason why the internal market developed only slowly in the EC's early years was that policy promoting the free movement of people, services and capital was relatively neglected, with most attention being given to creating the free movement of goods. To take, for example, free movement of people, until the 1980s EC governments were much more focused on the national social, employment and security implications (perceived usually as threats) of permitting easy and unchecked access into their national territory than they were on extending the rights of workers to move around, or the potentially dynamic effects that labour mobility might have for the European economy.

Prior to the mid-1980s, further core problems in attempts to make progress in removing barriers to the free movement of people, services and capital arose from the EC still being very much a fledgling polity: decisions in these politically sensitive areas depended on unanimity in the Council; the critical policy networks in the various policy fields that would later assist policy development were not yet much developed; the member states were still learning the art of bargaining in a quasi-federal structure; and the social construction of 'Europe' existed only for the most ardent federalists.

The White Paper 're-launch'

For the reasons outlined above, the internal market thus developed only slowly in the 1960s and 1970s. It applied in practice mainly to trading in goods, and much of that achievement was bypassed by the continuation, and indeed in some sectors the growth, of NTBs – and in particular TBTs.

In the 1970s and early 1980s, dissatisfaction with the continuing fragmentation of most of the market, and the lack of progress being made in removing barriers to trade, grew considerably. It did so because it was increasingly apparent to all those who took an interest in economic performance that Europe was becoming gradually less competitive. In the so-called 'sunrise' industries in particular – that is, the new high-tech industries – Europe was lagging behind its major competitors. Europe's difficulties in being able to compete successfully against the US and Japan (as well as against such Asian 'upstarts' as Hong Kong, Singapore, South Korea and Taiwan, all of which were pursuing export-led growth policies) created a sense of impending crisis for European business operating both at home and abroad. Prominent among those expressing concern about the situation was large-scale industry which, through the European Round Table of Industrialists (ERT) in particular, became highly active in the early 1980s in pressing EU decision-makers to launch initiatives designed to create a much more open and level internal market.

Many of the perceived necessary legislative requirements for constructing such an internal market were wrapped together in a Commission White Paper that was published in April 1985 and was strongly championed by the new Commission President, Jacques Delors, and the new Internal Market Commissioner, Lord Cockfield. Entitled *Completing the Internal Market* (European Commission, 1985), the White Paper set the end of 1992 as the target date for the adoption of nearly 300 directives and regulations which would give the four freedoms a much broader and more solid base. The directives and regulations identified in the White Paper included measures for tackling distortions to trade in goods and services, the harmonization of VAT rates and excise taxes, the opening up government procurement, and liberalizing financial markets.

The White Paper was accepted by the heads of government at their June 1985 European Council meeting. At that meeting they also recognized that the required legislative measures would be unlikely to be passed unless the EEC Treaty was amended to allow most internal market proposals to be subject to QMV in the Council. Accordingly, they convened an Intergovernmental Conference (IGC), which resulted in the 1986 SEA that included most of the necessary changes to Council voting rules among its provisions. Most of the White Paper's measures were duly approved by the 1992 deadline.

A broadening internal market agenda

The incorporation into EU law of the measures identi-fied in the White Paper did not mean that the task of building the internal market was fully realized. One reason for this was that despite the word 'completing' in the White Paper's title, there were in fact many require-ments of a truly open market for which the White Paper did not provide, especially with regard to services and the right of establishment. Many of these require-ments, such as opening up network industries, have since become important policy goals. Another reason why the passing into law of the measures contained in the White Paper did not mark the end of the road of the building of the internal market was that the Paper contained a rather narrow understanding of what a fully functioning internal market requires. There has never been a consensus among EU policy practitioners on exactly what the requirements for a fully operational and effective internal market are, but it is certainly the case that, as economic integration theory predicts, the range of the perceived requirements has grown as economic integration has advanced.

Many of the disputes over the nature of the internal market, and in particular those that continue to arise between the Commission, as guarantor of the internal market, and member states, which are inclined to protect domestic industries, can be understood in the context of federal relations. Federal arrangements can exacerbate the perennial debate of 'equalization' versus 'efficiency', because constituent units retain a great deal of independent economic power. This can lead, and in the EU has led, to considerable debate and disagreement over, for example, should it be forbidden for member states to offer incentives for companies to relocate (or remain where they are); should all compa-nies operating in the EU be able to bid on equal terms

for public contracts; and must sectors in which governments have traditionally dominated – such as postal services, telecommunications and energy – be opened up to bidding from other EU companies? In seeking to deal with such questions, the EU has moved progressively in an economically liberal direction, but many of the moves – to open up postal services, for example – have been protracted and subject usually to Commission proposals being both watered-down and introduced only in stages.

None the less, great advances have been made, largely because of the use of a number of policy devices that make market integration easier to achieve. One very important such device, which was being established in the years before the White Paper and SEA, is the principle of mutual recognition, which, as explained below, greatly reduces the need for approxi-mation legislation. Another device is QMV in the Council – which, thanks to expansions in every treaty reform round starting with the SEA – is now available for most internal market measures. A third device is the use of European standardization bodies, rather than EU legislation, to establish the essential require-ments of marketed products. And a fourth device is increased use of the specialized and regulatory agen-cies described in Chapter 4.

The building of the internal market has thus been, and remains, a continuing project, as noted above, with an increasingly wide range of activities being seen as requiring attention if the market is to be fully effec-tive. One important way in which advances in market integration have been made has been via the frame-work of strategic plans, which have been drawn up by the Commission and approved by the Council. Some of these have been multi-annual plans, such as that set out in the 1985 White Paper, while others have been annual plans, such as the Single Market Act for 2012 (European Commission, 2011v, 2012r).

Methods for Reducing Barriers to Free Movement

The EU uses three methods to achieve free movement: liberalization, approximation – which takes old and new forms – and mutual recognition (Pelkmans, 2005).

There is, in practice, some overlap between the three methods, both in terms of their nature and their usage. Regarding their nature, the greatest over-lap is between liberalization and mutual recognition, which at times almost blend together. A sharper distinction exists between liberalization and mutual recognition (which do not use EU legislation) on the one hand and approximation (which uses EU legislation) on the other. Regarding the usage of the three methods, this varies greatly between market areas – though with more than one method being used in most cases.

Liberalization

In the internal market it is assumed that goods and services have an automatic right to enter the markets of all member states, except in circumstances in which the treaty has provided for exceptions (called 'derogations') or the CJEU has interpreted the treaty in such a way that limitations to free movement are permitted (Pelkmans, 2005, p. 88). Key reasons why limitations to free movement may be judged to be necessary and permissible include that a product or service may raise concerns about human health or public safety. On this basis, the sale of, for example, chemical products, could not be subject to full liberalization, while the sale of, say, men's shoes could.

So, for those products and services that do not need to be regulated 'free movement prevails automatically' (ibid.). This means that that it can be difficult for national governments to defend barriers to free movement, especially when they do not themselves regulate the relevant products in their own markets.

Threats to free movement, therefore, are most likely to be associated with products and services that are regulated in national markets – which is where approximation and mutual recognition come into play.

'Old' and 'new' approximation

Approximation involves laying down laws that specify EU-wide common standards and requirements pertaining to free movement. It thus involves regulation.

Approximation has had a firm treaty base from the EU's inception, with Article 3 of the EEC Treaty stating:

the activities of the Community shall include…. (h) the approximation of the laws of Member States to the extent required for the proper functioning of the common market.

Internal market approximation was for a long time based on a somewhat rigid and essentially top-down process in which whatever was to be regulated – be it the materials used for sofa stuffing, the minimum depth of tread on car tyres, or the permitted additives in long-life milk – was subject to detailed legislation. In effect, approximation meant that standards had to be common throughout the member states. The main instrument for giving effect to approximation was EU directives. But this sort of approximation was very difficult to achieve, with approximation measures – concerning products as diverse as chocolate, beer and lawnmowers – almost invariably taking a long time, sometimes years, to be passed – if they were ever passed at all. Even when they were passed, the measures were often weak, because of the compromises that had to be made to enable decisions to be reached. Among the reasons for this highly inefficient approach to approximating standards were the numerous and often very different natures of national standards and laws, rapid changes that were altering the nature of both markets and marketed products, and the requirement in the Council's voting rules that market-related decisions had usually to be adopted by unanimity (a requirement that, as was noted above, the SEA changed to QMV for most market measures). Up to the mid-1980s, only very modest progress was therefore made in tackling the problem of internal market fragmentation.

In response to this problem, and in parallel with a developing new mutual recognition policy and a growing mutual recognition culture (see below), from the mid-1980s the Council began increasingly to use a 'new approach' to approximation. Drawing on the basic precepts of mutual recognition, the new approach embraced a much lighter touch than traditional approximation, being based not on trying to establish common standards but only 'essential features' which must be present in a product if it is 'designed and made in very different ways' (European Commission, 2008f, p. 7). As Pelkmans (2005, p. 92) explains, approximation thus evolved from relying solely on the 'old approach' (specific and/or vertical laws) to including a 'new approach' (broad and/or horizontal laws) in which the EU stipulates essential requirements – such as on health and safety – but the specification of technical standards is undertaken by European Standards Organizations (ESOs). The most important ESO is the European Committee for Standardization (CEN), which covers more than 18 sectors including air and space, chemicals, construction, energy and utilities, and food. The other two ESOs – the European Committee for Electrotechnical Standardization (CENELEC) and the European Telecommunications Standards Institute (ETSI) – are, as their names indicate, more narrowly focused. Unlike essential requirements, which member states must transpose into national law, additional 'common' standards agreed by the ESOs are initially voluntary.

The new approach to approximation is guided by 'action plans' that cover roughly four-year periods. So, under the 2010–13 Action Plan for European Standardisation, a number of diverse product types are identified as needing standardization, including: products in the European defence sector, and in particular in emerging technologies; products in the field of greenhouse gas emissions; a wide range of animal feed; scientific instrumentation and navigation used for space policy; and European film archives.

At the time of writing, approximately half of all goods traded within the EU are subject to approximation directives, while the remainder are 'non-harmonized' (European Commission, 2012q). As Figure 8.1 shows, approximation is used most frequently for high-risk products such as chemicals, pharmaceuticals, construction goods, automobiles and some foodstuffs. For example, the automotive sector is governed by 100 approximation and 300 implementing directives (European Commission, 2008f, pp. 2 and 7).

Mutual recognition

Mutual recognition occupies a 'middle ground' between liberalization (where there is no need for regulation) and approximation. Essentially, it involves EU member states recognizing and accepting the regulatory standards of other member states.

Mutual recognition in the single market is based on the assumption that constituent governments share broadly similar objectives. The EU had been inching towards the concept of mutual recognition since its

earliest years but, as with any federal construction, two factors prevented this principle from coming to the fore. First, levels of economic development varied enough among EU member states to cause concern among the more economically developed member states that regulations dealing with market failure were substandard in poorer member states. Second, building trust among member states would naturally take time.

The initial breakthrough was provided by the ECJ, which concluded in 1974, on the basis of the then Article 30 of the EEC Treaty – which stated that 'Quantitative restrictions on imports and all measures having equivalent effect shall ... be prohibited between Member States' – that 'trading rules enacted by Member States which are capable of hindering, directly or indirectly, actually or potentially, intra-Community trade are to be considered as measures having an effect equivalent to quantitative restrictions' (Dassonville decision, 1974). The ECJ in its Dassonville ruling had (seemingly) struck down all TBTs. The Dassonville decision thus underscored liberalization (Pelkmans, 2005, p. 90) as the primary goal of the EEC Treaty, but created a great deal of concern and uncertainty about situations where member states might be acting in good faith to protect their citizens from harmful products imported from other member states. The Court clarified Dassonville in its 1979 Cassis de Dijon ruling (case 120/78) by deciding that a product lawfully produced and marketed in one member state could not be prohibited in another unless it was authorized by a derogation provided in the 'safeguard article' – Article 30 of the EEC Treaty (now Article 36, TFEU).

Under the mutual recognition principle established by the Court, member states must mutually recognize and accept each others' standards where national regulatory objectives are similar. Where regulatory objectives differ, member states must attempt to agree on the objectives. The point of mutual recognition is that member states are obliged, without exception, to work together to find ways of ensuring free movement. Unlike the situation with approximation, mutual recognition is used most commonly for lower-risk goods, such as pasta or office equipment (European Commission, 2012q).

Mutual recognition is grounded in the principle of proportionality, whereby restrictions on trade should not be greater than they need be to achieve legislative

Figure 8.1 **Methods for opening up the internal market**

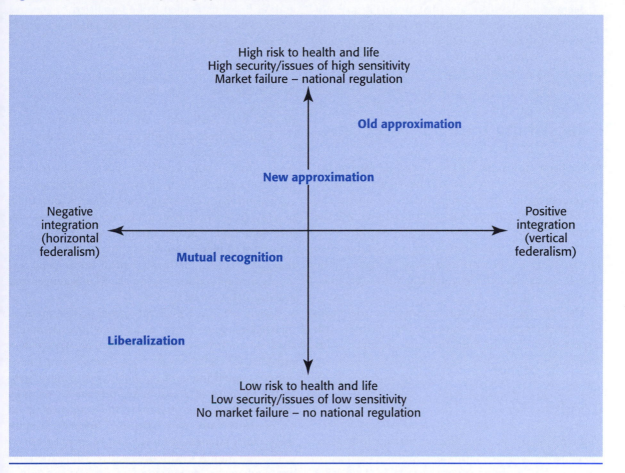

aims. So, for example, if an aim is to protect the health of citizens by reducing their consumption of salt, it should be assumed that a label will usually do the job of protecting and informing consumers, and that a ban on specified food products from other member states is unnecessary. In the same spirit, member states are required to include a mutual recognition clause in relevant national legislation (Pelkmans, 2005, p. 92).

Each of the three methods of achieving free movement – liberalization, mutual recognition, and approximation (the latter, as we have seen, having two forms) – involve disparate levels of product risk and different types of federal relationships, as depicted in Figure 8.1. Regarding the placement of the methods on this two-dimensional figure, these observations can be made:

- *Old approximation* is used mainly for 'risky' and 'sensitive' products. It involves vertical federalism

in the form of EU laws (usually directives) that specify the standards goods that must meet to be allowed market access. Thus EU rules replace national rules.

- *New approximation* is used for products that are not as risky as those deemed to require old approximation. It involves a more flexible form of vertical federalism in that it is managed through EU-agreed essential standards (usually in the form of directives) rather than detailed top-down specifications.
- *Mutual recognition* involves lower-risk products than those subject to approximation. The process constitutes horizontal federalism because there is little direct EU-level involvement (other than in an overseeing capacity). Member states may set national requirements for non-approximated products, but they must not obstruct free movement.

- *Liberalization* applies to products that are not deemed to be risky and that normally are not subject to national regulation. The process falls under horizontal federalism because EU institutions need not be involved and EU legislation is not necessary for markets to be opened up.

Establishing the Four Freedoms

As has been shown, the internal market is based on the concept of 'the four freedoms', involving freedom of movement within the European economic space. The EEC Treaty and its successors have all emphasized the commitment and obligation of the EU to enhance the free movement of goods, services, capital and people. The language used by the treaties has changed a little over the years, but the essential intent has remained constant.

The main steps taken and the progress made by the EU in facilitating cross-border economic activity with respect to each of the four freedoms are now considered.

Goods

The removal of the most obvious barriers to the free movement of goods – tariffs and quotas – was prioritized in the Community's early years, and all were abolished by 1968 as part of the establishment in that year of the customs union. However, as was noted above, other obstacles to free trade in goods – in the form of NTBs – proved to be, and many of them still continue to be, much more difficult to eliminate. This is partly because NTBs are often much less visible than tariffs and quotas, but is mainly because national standards and specifications, which are the main components of NTBs, are created for a variety of usually beneficial purposes – such as ensuring product quality and protecting product purchasers – and therefore often cannot be removed without being replaced by EU-wide standards and specifications. So, except where liberalization or mutual recognition has been deemed to be acceptable, national deregulation has usually needed to be accompanied by EU level re-regulation in the form of the establishment of either approximated or at least agreed EU standards and specifications (see discussion above). Negative integration has thus needed to be paralleled by positive integration, which has been a major challenge for EU decision-makers.

Services

Services cover a wide range of major economic activities, including transport, education, health, communications, construction, insurance, financial transactions, computer support, information, personal services (such as hair stylists and electricians), and many government activities (Lejour, 2008, p. 118). The Commission has become increasingly focused on intra-European trade in services because it is the area of highest growth among developed countries and accounts for 77 per cent of value added and 78 per cent of employment in the EU (Badinger and Maydell, 2009, p. 694).

Article 59 of the EEC Treaty stated that 'restrictions on freedom to provide services within the Community shall be progressively abolished'. The Treaty also provided for the removal of restrictions on the freedom of establishment of nationals of a member state in the territory of another member state: removals that were vital if services were to be opened up to Community-wide competition. However, despite these Treaty provisions, for the first twenty years or so of the Community's existence relatively little attention was paid to the liberalization of the services sector. One reason for this was that agriculture and manufacturing accounted for the majority of jobs. Another reason was that the barriers in the way of opening up of services were generally more complex than they were for trade in goods: for services, there was no 'equivalent' to abolishing tariffs and quotas. And a third reason was that the UK, which had a competitive advantage in a number of service sectors, especially financial services, was not yet a member state. After the UK joined in 1973 services began to receive more attention, but as they did so an increasingly protective attitude towards the national provision of services became apparent in several member states.

This protective attitude, which still remains, was, and is, partly because in the services sector member states hold and wish to retain their comparative advantages. Lejour (2008, p. 118), for example, evaluates member states using a 'trade-orientedness indicator' (value of exports by a services sector divided by value-added in that sector), and finds that the Netherlands has a very strong trade orientation towards transport and communication (70.8) compared to the UK, France and Germany with 20.2, 20.4 and 17.7, respectively. Conversely, the UK exhibits a far stronger trade orientation in 'financial intermediation and insurance' with a score of 52.6 compared to scores of 3.2 (France), 7.8 (Germany), 2.2 (Italy), 4.0 (the Netherlands) and 6.4 (Spain). Another reason for national resistance to aspects of the liberalization of services has been because services inhabit disparate competitive frameworks, which has affected their reaction (and lobbying) to market liberalization proposals. So, on the one hand: utilities, such as postal services and the gas and electricity industries, have traditionally been protected from competition by being national monopolies; computer and information industries have been advantaged by near monopolistic markets in which product distinctions have been protected by patents; and the market of major shipping lines has been characterized by oligopolistic competition. On the other hand, by contrast, retailers and purveyors of professional services operate in conditions more closely resembling perfect or atomistic competition.

The establishment of the principle of mutual recognition (see above) has not benefited trade in services as much as it has trade in goods. One reason for this is that many services are provided locally, which brings cultural, linguistic and geographical distance factors into play. Another reason is that free movement of services has greater implications for cross-border movements of people and of establishment than does free movement of goods – and so it is more politically sensitive.

None the less, over the years, restrictions on the freedom to provide services across the EU have forced themselves increasingly on to the policy agenda, with the Court being much to the fore in advancing EU law on both services and establishment. However, despite repeated calls from the Commission for a comprehensive legislative approach to establishment and services, there was little movement on this front until the early 2000s, when EU policy-makers linked competition in services to the Lisbon Strategy on growth and competitiveness (see Chapter 9). The main outcome of the intensive work that was undertaken to liberalize services was the Commission's issuing in March 2004 of a

Services Directive. At the heart of the Directive was the idea that service provision in the EU should be based on the country of origin principle; that is, 'according to which a service provider is subject only to the law of the country in which he is established and Member States may not restrict services from a provider established in another Member State' (European Commission, 2004d, p. 6). The rationale behind the use of the country of origin principle in the Directive was to address one of the main complaints of service businesses when attempting to operate outside their home states: the byzantine number of government authorities (at different levels) involved in approving business operations. The Commission's intention with the Services Directive was to remove this barrier to cross-border business activity by putting in place a 'one-stop-shop'.

For the Commission, for many centre-right politicians, and for service providers in a position to operate in other member states, a Cassis de Dijon (the ECJ case that established the mutual recognition principle in goods) for services was highly desirable, because in all likelihood it would quickly begin to break down the barriers in the way of a more open EU services market. But, for much the same reason, the prospect was not welcomed by two very important sets of actors:

- For the governments of member states, many of the thousands of national, regional and local rules regulating service industries were seen as being necessary and appropriate. The public justifications for this usually covered such reasons as the maintenance of standards and the preservation of customs and traditions, but in reality the reason was often straightforward trade protection. For those states with higher wages and high levels of social protection, application of the country of origin principle to services seemed to pose a particular threat to many national businesses and jobs.
- For centre-left politicians and trade unionists, the proposed use of the country of origin principle was seen as a potential betrayal of the European social model. For both of these sets of actors, it was one thing for national regulators to be told to accept the alcohol content of a French blackcurrant liqueur (as happened in the case of Cassis de Dijon), but quite a different matter for Swedes, for example, to have to agree to a Greek construction company building port facilities in Sweden whilst employing

Greek nationals subject to Greek wages and social protections.

It was not therefore unexpected that the Services Directive was greatly changed as it made its way through the EU's legislative stages during 2004–6. Indeed, the country of origin principle did not survive the EP's first reading, and nor did some service areas: the EP deleted broadcasting, computer and information services, postal services, audiovisual services, temporary employment agencies, social services, public transport, gambling, and healthcare from the remit of the Directive. (Financial services were already excluded because this sector is regulated via other directives.) The Directive, which was eventually adopted in December 2006, has been described as 'a neat retreat compared to the (over)-ambitious proposal of the Commission' (Hatzopoulos, 2008, p. 161). Most important, the 'free provision of services' principle – 'Member States shall respect the right of providers to provide services in a Member State other than that in which they are established' – replaced the 'country of origin' clause. Hatzopoulos (2008, p. 188) suggests that, none the less, despite the abandonment of the country of origin principle, the Services Directive represents a positive contribution by codifying the Court's case law in services, promulgating some rules to simplify procedures, providing limited approximation, and setting the conditions to adopt more far-reaching rules in the future. In total, about one-third of value-added services activities are covered, with business services representing the most important sector (Badinger and Maydell, 2009, p. 696).

The special case of financial services

The financial sector is comprised of numerous actors, the main ones being commercial banks, investment banks, brokerage firms, rating agencies, stock exchanges and insurance companies.

The sector is intensely globalized, with the behaviour of financial actors under one regulatory regime having an impact (usually negative) on actors operating in others. The EU is a major participant in this increasingly globalized system and is a firm supporter of a 'co-ordinated global approach' to financial rules through the G-20 (European Commission, 2010o, p. 4). A particularly important aspect of financial services is its strong transatlantic dimension because of

the risk of 'regulatory arbitrage' – disparate rules on each side of the Atlantic could offer loopholes for financial actors to 'play one regime off the other' (Wishart, 2011b).

There have been two main aspects to EU policy activity covering financial services – opening member states' financial sectors to competition and establishing EU regulatory rules for financial actors. Until the economic downturn that began in 2007, the EU focused its efforts on liberalizing financial services. The principal legislation in this regard is the Markets in Financial Instruments Directive (MiFID) 2004/39/EC, adopted in 2004, implemented in 2007, and covering all financial services. Its core features are the deregulation of stock markets, thereby encouraging 'alternative trading venues to emerge' (Wishart, 2011c), and the 'passport' which, by harmonizing national rules for investment services and the operation of exchanges, enables authorized investment firms, banks and exchanges to provide their services freely across borders (European Commission, 2007d).

Application of financial services policy is based on the 'Lamfalussy Process'. The Process is depicted in Figure 8.2 for the regulation of market securities. It has four levels. At level 1, the EP and Council adopt framework legislation. At the second level, implementing measures are adopted, with a key role in the drafting of measures being exercised by one of the three financial services authorities that have existed since January 2011 (see below and Figure 8.3). At the third level, the relevant authority works with national regulators to promote consistency in the application of financial services policy. And at the fourth level, the Commission – with assistance from the appropriate authority – is responsible for ensuring that EU financial services law is uniformly implemented.

The MiFID pre-dated the global financial crisis and lacks a strong regulatory component. The new MiFID II – which the Commission tabled in October 2011 and at the time of this writing is being negotiated with implementation possible as early as 2014 – focuses on tying liberalization to a stricter regulatory regime, particularly in improving transparency to protect investors and introducing additional supervisory functions.

The regulatory aspects of MiFID II reflect the fact that there has been major policy activity in recent years in the area of financial market regulation, because it is widely believed that lax regulation of

Figure 8.2 **The Lamfalussy Process**

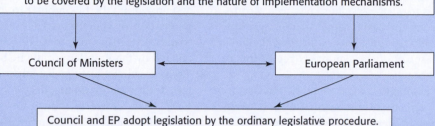

LEVEL 1

After a full consultation process with relevant policy interests and actors – including the European Securities and Markets Authority (ESMA) – the Commission makes formal proposals for directives/regulations that focus on the broad objectives of the area(s) to be covered by the legislation and the nature of implementation mechanisms.

Council of Ministers ⟷ European Parliament

Council and EP adopt legislation by the ordinary legislative procedure.

LEVEL 2

Implementing measures are adopted in the form of delegated and implementing acts. Although formally adopted in the name of the Commission, most such acts are drafted by financial and technical experts in the ESMA – with much of this drafting work being undertaken via specialised sub-committees and involving extensive liaison with other arms of the EU's financial supervisory system (see Figure 8.3).

LEVEL 3

The ESMA develops and issues to national authorities (non legislative) guidelines and recommendations designed to establish consistent, efficient and effective securities' supervision and to ensure common and consistent application of EU law.

LEVEL 4

Commission checks member state compliance with EU legislation

Commission may take action against member states suspected of being in breach of EU law, including referring cases to the CJEU.

Fast Track Procedure: the EP, Council, Commission, competent national authorities, and stakeholders (via the Securities and Markets Stakeholder Group) can request the ESMA to launch an enquiry into possible failure to apply legislation. The ESMA can issue a recommendation addressed to a national authority.

Source: European Commission, 2004a, p. 16

financial markets (in both the US and Europe) caused the financial crisis. As Wishart (2011b) has observed, in 2011 in particular barely a month would go by 'without a new proposal from the European Commission in the area of financial services'. This activist approach – which has left no financial sector untouched and has been aimed at creating a robust EU financial services regulatory regime – has been accompanied by strong protests from affected groups (particularly banks and insurers), which have argued that the EU has come to over-emphasize regulation at the expense of growth.

Finding a reasonable balance between ensuring stability in the markets and protecting investors while not fundamentally depressing growth is indeed arguably the key challenge for financial services policy over the next several years. Or, to borrow a phrase from the economist Arthur Okun (1975), the EU's dilemma is to find the magic balance between 'equality and efficiency': a balance that, ideally, satisfies EU member states, G20 partners, consumers and financial actors.

In the wake of the financial crisis, the Commission began the process of overhauling financial services policy by appointing Jacques de Larosière (former Governor of the Banque de France) to convene 'a wisemen's group' to advance recommendations (de Larosière Report, 2012). The Commission, in its follow-up to the Report, distilled problems with the financial services sector into four categories (European Commission, 2010o, p. 5):

- an unstable and inadequately supervised financial system;
- opaque financial operations and products;
- irresponsibility in some financial institutions, which pursued short-term profit, neglected risk management and paid unjustifiable bonuses; and
- a financial system that overlooked the fact that it was supposed to serve the real economy and society as a whole, contributed to the creation of bubbles (inflated prices caused by very high demand), and often disregarded consumer interests.

The de Larosière Report concluded with 31 recommendations for reform of the financial regulatory system. Among the recommendations were two far-reaching structural changes that have been put in place and are now important components of a new 'European System of Financial Supervision'. Figure 8.3 contains a schematic diagram of the European Financial Services Supervisory Architecture that has been in place since January 2011. Its core elements are:

- The newly-created European Systemic Risk Board (ESRB) is an independent EU body responsible for the 'macro-prudential oversight of the financial systems within the EU in order to contribute to the prevention of systemic risks' (European Systemic Risk Board, 2012). It is located in Frankfurt and is chaired by the President of the ECB.
- Three existing EU financial supervisory committees dealing with banking, insurance and securities have been converted into European Security Authorities (ESAs). These authorities, one of which is the ESMA described in Figure 8.2, work closely with national authorities and have real teeth – including the power both to overrule national regulators and to draft laws.

With a new regulatory infrastructure in place, the Commission then set out to build a tougher regulatory policy regime, based on parameters agreed by the G-8. While the Commission had been able to take advantage of the policy window provided by the financial crisis to overhaul the institutional structure of the financial services regulatory regime, the policies themselves now became subject to intense contestation among member states, EU institutions, consumer groups and financial sector actors. The Commission's controversial proposal for stronger regulation of short-selling (where traders bet that the price of a security will fall) and derivatives illustrates this point, with the UK government – believing such regulation would damage the interests of the City of London – insisting that decisions on the regulation of such activities should remain with the member states and not be transferred to the European Securities and Markets Authority.

* * *

The federal integration approach to explaining European integration, outlined in Chapter 2, suggests that in federal and quasi-federal systems crises often lead to more centralized decision-making. This pattern is certainly occurring in the EU's financial services regulatory regime where, after the most severe economic downturn since the Great Depression, the EU has established regulatory authorities conferred

Figure 8.3 **European financial services supervisory architecture**

Source: European Commission, 2010o, p. 15.

with very significant powers. Moreover, the policy reach of the ESAs is being extended as regulatory reforms have come to cover, or in the near future are likely to cover, such matters as: high-frequency trading (computer algorithms used to buy and sell stocks and bonds rapidly); credit-rating agencies (which are seen to require greater restrictions to curb conflicts of interest relationships with the financial institutions whose instruments they are rating); the capital requirements of banks (many banks needed to be bailed out by national governments in the aftermath of the global financial crisis); and mortgages (particularly in respect of the information that must be provided to mortgage customers).

In recent years, financial services regulation has thus become, in both institutional and policy terms, significantly more integrated.

Capital

Capital has long been potentially highly mobile and has become so increasingly in sectors that do not have high fixed costs in immobile infrastructure, such as high-tech industries. Capital may be moved for a number of reasons, prominent among which are lower labour costs, lower corporate taxes, and less generously mandated employer-provided social benefits. So the mobility of capital is of great importance to the operation and performance of the European economy and impacts directly on the viability of the European Social Model.

The full liberalization of capital movements in the EU has been in effect since 1988 (Directive 88/361/EEC). Technically, free movement of capital is concerned mainly with cross-border capital transfers, but in a practical policy sense it refers to all cross-border investment. It also covers the purchase of real estate and securities, and the portability of pensions. An example of the real-estate dimension of EU capital movements is seen in the negotiations that led to the 2004/7 enlargements, where some CEECs were concerned about being priced out of their domestic real estate market by wealthy West Europeans: the EU's response was to include temporary derogations for some CEECs in the accession provisions.

Examples of Commission actions to ensure free capital movements include dealing with member state actions that discriminate against foreign capital investment in their countries. One example is when the Republic of Cyprus tried to prevent EU citizens from purchasing a second home on the island, which the Commission ruled as a violation of free movement of capital. Another example was the Commission's request that Italy modify privatization law to remove onerous investment restrictions.

People

Council Regulation (EEC) No 1612/68 entitles all nationals of a member state to take up and engage in gainful employment in the territory of another member state in conformity with the relevant regulations applicable to national workers. Italy, with an approximate population growth rate of 13 per cent in the mid-1950s, had insisted on free movement of labour as the price of its signature to the EEC Treaty, even though France, with a population growth rate of 3 per cent, feared being overrun by job-seekers from southern Italy. In the event, a significant cross-border movement of people searching for jobs did not occur, and has never occurred. Even today, after some increase in cross-border movement following the

2004 enlargement, only about 1.5 per cent of EU citizens live and work in a member state that is different from their country of origin: a percentage that has not changed since the 1980s (European Commission, 2006).

Why is there such relatively limited movement of people, and what are the obstacles to it? It is not a lack of clear treaty authorization, because in seeking to establish the conditions for the free movement of people there has always been full provision for both the employed and the self-employed. Regarding the employed, Article 45 TFEU states that:

1. Freedom of movement for workers shall be secured within the Union.
2. Such freedom shall entail the abolition of any discrimination based on nationality between workers of the Member States as regards employment, remuneration and other conditions of work and employment.

Regarding the self-employed, the ability of people as varied as dentists, building contractors, hair stylists and accountants to obtain a licence and establish offices in another EU member state is a major litmus test of free movement of people. They are covered principally by Articles 49–55 TFEU which, subject to certain limited exceptions, prohibit restrictions on the right of establishment: that is, on the right of individuals and undertakings to establish businesses in the territory of other member states.

Over the years, especially since the mid-1980s, Court rulings and legislation have served to give these treaty articles a more practical effect than they had initially. One way in which they have done so is by providing for the mutual recognition of many educational, professional and trade qualifications. Another way is by providing legal entitlements of various sorts to EU citizens when they live and work in another member state: entitlements in the form, for example, of access to education systems, health care facilities, social welfare payments, and the purchase of property. The EU also has all sorts of mobility programmes for young people and professionals to encourage network formation.

In the negotiations that led to the 2004/7 enlargement, the governments of many EU-15 member states responded to voters' fears that the accession of poorer countries would inundate West European countries with job-seekers by instituting derogations – national restrictions on labour migration for transitional periods, most of which have now ended. But, in fact, in economic terms the EU's movement of people problem is not that there has been too much movement but rather that there has not been enough. This is because movement of people is an important condition for the maximization of economic growth – with labour needing to move to where skills are required and where jobs are available. The 'Polish plumber' problem – a phrase that came to be used in the wake of the 2004/7 enlargement to describe fears in Western Europe that skilled craftsmen from the new member states would undercut higher-paid domestic craftsmen and take their jobs – proved to be largely unfounded. Such movement as has occurred has been a result of labour moving to where there is a demand for it: but there has not been enough such movement. For EU economic policy-makers, the problem is seen as being one of too much continuing labour immobility rather than one of too much labour movement.

Why is movement of people low in the EU? One reason is that the EU is not a full federal system: moving involves not 'just' moving to another state but to another country, which has many cultural implications. A second reason is that while, as explained above, legal entitlements for most 'everyday things' are available, accessing some of these can in practice be difficult and very cumbersome. And a third reason is language: most EU states have their own national language, which most other EU citizens do not speak.

Free movement of people within the EU is, of course, closely linked to the problematic policy issue for the EU of immigration policy. It is so because illegal immigration into the EU is partly driven by the relative easy internal movement of people, especially between Schengen member states. This matter is considered in Chapter 11.

Implementation of the Four Freedoms

As shown in previous chapters, EU policies are implemented in various ways. However, in broad terms, the arrangements normally involve a sharing of responsibilities, with appropriate and designated authorities in member states being responsible for ensuring there is compliance 'on the ground' and the Commission being responsible for oversight and monitoring. This broad arrangement applies with respect to the four freedoms. In the member states a wide array of national and sub-national authorities are charged with tasks ranging from ensuring traded goods meet standards specified in EU laws to checking that employment practices do not discriminate against EU citizens who are not home country nationals. At the EU level, the Commission uses many hard and soft policy implementation instruments, including actively pursuing – if necessary up to the CJEU – infringement cases, benchmarking, and requiring extensive reporting to it by the appropriate member state authorities.

Despite, however, the extensiveness of these implementation arrangements, the EU has had – as it has with many of its policies – difficulties in ensuring that policies designed to advance the four freedoms' policies are fully implemented. Therefore it is worth explaining here the special steps that have been taken to try to ensure that implementation of the four freedoms – which are such a core part not only of the EU's internal market policy but also of its policy portfolio as a whole – is as thorough as possible.

How does the European Commission monitor the openness of the internal market? Beginning with a 1997 action plan, the Commission began to produce an annual internal market scoreboard designed in large part to publicize the laggards and put normative pressure on them. This relatively soft approach was, however, only partly successful, so, starting with its Strategies for the Internal Market: Priorities 2003–2006, the Commission added a supplementary, and tougher, approach by setting benchmarks, creating a problem-solving system (SOLVIT), a pre-infringement procedure (EU Pilot), and initiating infringement procedures on a tighter basis than had been the case in the past. These strategies and programmes were organized into an internal market 'governance cycle', which is depicted in Figure 8.4. The progress made at each stage of the cycle is reported in the 'Annual Governance Check Up' (European Commission, 2012r).

A particularly important stage of the cycle is 'Monitor', which deals with the transposition (incorporation into national law) of internal market legisla-

Figure 8.4   Single Market Act governance cycle

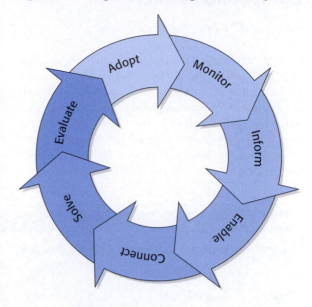

Source: European Commission, 2012r.

tion. The heart of this stage is the 'internal market scoreboard', which was published as a free-standing report between 1997 and 2010 and which has been part of the annual check-up since 2011. Three aspects of transposition are covered in the scoreboard: transposition itself; incorrect transposition into national law; and the length of time it takes a member state to transpose the law. Regarding transposition itself, the overall record on transposing internal market legislation is quite good: in 1997, the average transposition deficit – for the then EU-15 – was 6.3 per cent, but it has since steadily improved and had been meeting or even surpassing the 1 per cent annual target agreed by the European Council in 2007 until backsliding, to 1.2 per cent, in 2011 (European Commission, 2012r, p. 9). On the two other measures, the average transposition delay is 7.9 months and the rate of incorrectly transposed measures is 0.8 per cent (ibid., pp. 11–12).

This solid and generally improving record on transposition appears to be mirrored in the implementation of internal market rules as a whole. Some evidence for this is seen in the fact that the number of infringement proceedings initiated by the Commission against member states for incorrectly applying, or not applying, single market rules has fallen in recent years.

Competition Policy

What is EU competition policy?

EU competition policy is largely focused on preventing cartels, the abuse of dominant trading positions, anti-competitive mergers, and non-approved state aid in the internal market. Prior to the creation of the European Communities in the 1950s, anti-competitive practices were widespread in Western Europe. They were not, however, necessarily seen as being enemies of the people in the way in which such practices were in the US. Rather, many dominant corporate interests were seen as being virtually national champions and much business activity was protected by the state – not least because it was often tied inextricably to the power of the state. However, this situation changed with the creation of the EEC, because if member states were then to continue tolerating – let alone promoting – anti-competitive practices such as cartelization and the granting of state aid to national firms then it would not have been possible to construct an open, competitive and fair internal market.

Box 8.1

Summary of EU Competition Policy

Treaty Article or Regulation	Policy	Common company practices	Commission powers	Examples of Commission actions
101 TFEU	*Restrictive practices (cartels)* Prohibits agreements by two or more companies that restrain competition or trade – either horizontally (within the same industry) or vertically (along the supply chain).	Exclusive distribution and supply. Price fixing. Market sharing.	Can issue fines of up to 10% of the global turnover of companies.	1 January 2008–28 March 2012, fines totalling €7.5 billion were issued. In this period the highest fine was €1.38 billion, which was imposed on four vehicle glass manufacturers in 2008.
102 TFEU	*'Dominant position' article* Prohibition on actions by firms that abuse dominant trading positions.	Predatory pricing and actions of similar effect. Bundling software .	Can issue cease and desist orders. Can issue fines. Can require the break-up of the monopoly (this has never been used).	In July 2007, the Spanish telecom Telefónica was fined €152 million for abusing its dominant position in the market for access to broadband internet in Spain. (Telefónica appealed, but the fine was confirmed by the CJEU in March 2012.)
Regulation No. 139/2004	*Anti-competitive mergers* Prohibits mergers between companies that would have the effect of	Seek to create dominant market positions that could impede	Must approve before a merger can take place. (Often approval is only given on	The most famous refusal to authorize a merger was that between General Electric and Honeywell in 2001 (both US companies). In November

EU competition policy operated under basically the same system between 1962 and 2004, at which point 'modernized' competition rules took effect under Regulation 1/2003. The new system decentralized aspects of implementing EU competition policy to member states while at the same time increasing the Commission's powers of inspection (European Commission, 2004b, p. 1).

Box 8.1 summarizes key features of EU competition policy, including the TFEU articles on which it is based.

The differing aspects of competition policy will now be examined, with policy on restrictive practices and abuse of dominant trading positions taken together as the key components of antitrust policy.

Antitrust policy

Articles 101 and 102, TFEU provide the 'antitrust provisions' of EU competition policy. Article 101, which is the 'cartel' provision, prohibits agreements by companies that restrain competition or trade through such classic strategies as exclusive supply and distribution agreements, price fixing and market sharing;

Box 8.1 continued				
Treaty Article or Regulation	Policy	Common company practices	Commission powers	Examples of Commission actions
	impeding competition in the internal market or in a significant part of it.	competitive trade.	condition that the companies offload some of their holdings and/or cease some trading activities.)	2011, the Commission approved the acquisition by the US company Western Digital of Hitachi Global Storage Technology. The approval was conditional on Western Digital's divestment of some of its production assets.
107 and 108 TFEU	*Non-approved state aid* Prohibits state aid that is not authorised.	Companies may receive aid that they and the funding body (which is most likely to be the national government) choose not to interpret as being aid – for example, favourable business tax exemptions.	Can order an end to state aid. Can require companies to repay state aid.	In January 2012, the Commission announced the outcome of investigations into state aid to several national postal operators. Some aid was approved, but Germany's Deutsche Post was ordered to pay back aid of over €500 million, while Belgium's Bpost was required to pay back €417 million.

Article 102 applies to abuses of dominant positions through such behaviour as predatory pricing and tie-in agreements meant to squeeze out competition.

Until the 'modernization' of competition policy, the Commission was fully responsible for all Article 101 and 102 actions. Since May 2004, National Competition Authorities (NCAs) have been empowered to apply the Treaty's provisions. Communications and liaison between the two levels are channelled both via direct working relationships between DG Competition and member states' competition authorities, and through the European Competition Network (ECN), which is a network of member state NCAs managed by DG Competition.

In the old system, companies had to 'notify' the Commission of potentially problematic agreements or activities for clearance. In the new system, companies are expected to consult a list of prohibited behaviours, and if they are still uncertain whether they might run afoul of competition rules they are obliged to check with their national authorities, implementation power for cartels and abuse of dominant position having now been fully devolved to NCAs except in cases involving three or more member states, which remain under DG Competition's jurisdiction. The Commission also handles 'hard core cartels' (those with European or world-wide scope), regardless of how many member states are involved (European Commission, 2008e, p. 4).

Since the new system has been put in place, the majority of investigations are conducted by NCAs, as seen in the fact that whereas in 2004 one-third of the 301 cases that year were investigated by the Commission, but in 2011 only 15 per cent of that year's 163 cases were handled by the Commission (and only 6.5 per cent in 2010). The majority of the suspected infringements – 60 per cent in 2011 – stem from Article 101 complaints; 32 per cent stem from Article 102; and the remaining 8 per cent are based on both articles (European Commission, 2012n).

An important point to be emphasized is that most antitrust cases – and indeed most EU competition policy cases as a whole – involve extensive informal interactions between the parties involved. The Commission has no interest in rushing into confrontational proceedings if an investigation shows there has been no blatant breach of EU law and that an informal settlement is possible. That said, financial penalties can be considerable if breaches have been blatant and have had serious effect on the operation of the market. So, for example, in 2011, two cartel decisions related to consumer products (consumer detergents and exotic fruit) resulted in the imposition of fines totalling €614 million on fourteen undertakings (European Commission, 2012e, pp. 11–12).

Despite frequent comparisons between EU and US antitrust policy, their regulatory infrastructures greatly differ. In the US, the main regulatory body is an independent agency (the Bureau of Competition in the Federal Trade Commission), which is responsible for civil enforcement, while criminal enforcement is housed in the Justice Department. In the EU, competition regulation has remained in the Commission rather than being farmed-out to a European agency. Given this preponderant power, it is hardly a mystery as to why the Commission has resisted proposals (which began to surface in the 1990s) to establish an independent EU cartel office, despite this proposed change being voiced by such influential advocates as the German *Bundskartellamt* (BKA) – one of the most important NCAs – and the German Economics Ministry (Cini and McGowan, 1998, p. 221). The BKA's principal objective has been for European competition policy to achieve greater political independence from the Commission, but the latter has so far deflected this reform, pointedly noting that politics is naturally a factor in antitrust policy and should be given its proper due alongside economic analysis.

Rather than agree to the establishment of an independent cartel agency, the Commission proposed devolving some antitrust enforcement to the member states which, as noted above, has since duly taken place. This development, which has moved EU competition policy not only in a more decentralized direction but also a more network-based direction, was also driven by: an expected increase in an already crushing workload for the Commission because of the impending CEEC accessions (which would bring not only an increased volume of competition cases, but also some very thorny cases because of the high percentage of state-owned industries that would need to be considered in the context of competition policy); more cross-border trade mergers with the full implementation of EMU; globalization (again, likely to precipitate more cross-border mergers); and a growing need to reconsider the location of policy responsibilities in the context of the increased importance being attached to subsidiarity.

Federal theory is useful in helping to explain this changed nature of EU competition policy, because federalism facilitates intra-union sharing of policy solutions. The 'federal' entity (DG Competition) encourages and facilitates this exchange through a number of communication modes, including briefing papers, training sessions, investigations and decisions. The ECN formalizes the federal structure.

In fact, in a very real sense, EU antitrust activity is more federalized than its counterpart in the US. One reason for this is that in the US state antitrust statutes differ substantially. A second reason is that, while the network approach is also used in the US with the 'Multi-State Anti-Trust Task Force' formed by the National Association of Attorneys General (NAAG) which, like the ECN, rests on voluntary participation, the US network is a much looser network than Europe's and is organized by state authorities (attorneys general) rather than the Federal Trade Commission (DG Competition's analogue). And a third reason is that in the US states and the federal government do not always agree, an observation famously illustrated in the Microsoft antitrust case brought to the US District Court by the US Department of Justice in 1998, which Microsoft lost. On appeal to the US Court of Appeals, D.C. Circuit, the case was remanded to the US District Court (and a new judge), with an order to find a remedy that would carry less liability than originally ruled in that court. In 2001, the Department of Justice reached agreement with Microsoft, with several of the 20 states that had joined in the federal suit concluding that it was far too lenient. Rather than disallow the bundling of Microsoft's Internet Explorer browser with its Windows operating system, it was agreed that Microsoft would share its application programming interface with third-party companies under the supervision of an appointed panel. In the EU, by contrast, the Microsoft case was dealt with exclusively at the central level, by DG Competition, which pursued the case vigorously from 2001. The Commission's main concern was that Windows XP would be packaged with a plethora of applications – instant messaging, digital photography, video software – that would squeeze other software manufacturers out of the market (Birgot, 2001). In 2003, DG Competition ruled that Microsoft must share its code with rivals and must also discontinue bundling Microsoft Media Player with the Windows operating system. (See Chapter 6 for additional information on this case.)

The Microsoft case illustrates the tenacity of the Commission *vis-à-vis* the Department of Justice in dealing with the same company over an identical issue. The role of the courts was key, with the US courts insisting on renewed negotiation that took a softer line towards Microsoft, while the ECJ agreed substantially with the Commission (but rejected the Commission's demand for full access to company proprietary information). (It should be noted that the difference in outcomes may also partly have reflected the products – the US case dealt with browser bundling, while the Commission was dealing with full-blown bundling of cutting edge applications.)

Anti-competitive mergers

Some of the most highly publicized decisions of DG Competition have been in its capacity to rule on the legality of mergers. Since 1990, merger regulation in the EU has been a 'one-stop shop', with the Commission having exclusive authority to approve mergers over a certain threshold measured in terms of European and worldwide turnover (Wilks, 2005, p. 121). Proposed mergers where turnover falls below these thresholds are evaluated by national authorities.

Most referrals to the Commission for permission to merge are granted, though often the companies concerned are required to sell parts of their businesses or to license products to competitors in order to win acceptance for the merger. If a proposed merger is not accepted by the Commission, the aggrieved parties can appeal to the General Court and can, under certain circumstances, appeal a General Court decision to the Court of Justice. Up to 2002, all appeals against Commission decisions were rejected, but in 2002 the Court of First Instance (the pre-Lisbon Treaty name of the General Court) famously overturned a 1999 Commission decision that had blocked the merger of Airtours and First Choice. Other Commission defeats soon followed, which led to reforms of the Commission review process in Regulation 139/2004. The Regulation included a slightly modified guiding rule that stated:

> A concentration that would effectively impede competition, in the common market or in a substantial part of it, in particular by the creation

or strengthening of a dominant position, shall be declared incompatible with the common market.

An example of the Commission rejecting a proposed merger is that between Deutsche Börse (the owner of the Frankfurt Stock Exchange) and NYSE Euronext (the owner of the New York, Paris, Brussels, Amsterdam and Lisbon Stock Exchanges). In making their application to the Commission in June 2011 the notifying parties made much of how the merger would create efficiencies. This argument was, however, not powerful enough to persuade the Commission to authorize the merger. The Commission concluded, among other things, 'that the merger would have led to a near-monopoly in the area of exchange-traded European financial derivatives resulting in fewer possibilities for free competition and less innovation' (European Commission, 2012e, p. 9). Subsequent efforts by the parties to allay the Commission's concerns were unsuccessful, which led to Deutsche Börse appealing the Commission's decision to the CJEU.

State aid

Article 107 TFEU, states:

> Save as otherwise provided in the Treaties, any aid granted by a Member State or through State resources in any form whatsoever which distorts or threatens to distort competition by favouring certain undertakings or the production of certain goods shall, in so far as it affects trade between Member States, be incompatible with the internal market.

Sub-article 3 of Article 107 contains the following exceptions:

(a) aid to promote the economic development of areas where the standard of living is abnormally low or where there is serious underemployment...;
(b) aid to promote the execution of an important project of common European interest or to remedy a serious disturbance in the economy of a Member State;
(c) aid to facilitate the development of certain economic activities or of certain economic areas,

where such aid does not adversely affect trading conditions to an extent contrary to the common interest;
(d) aid to promote culture and heritage conservation where such aid does not affect trading conditions and competition in the Union to an extent that is contrary to the common interest;
(e) such other categories of aid as may be specified by decision of the Council acting by a qualified majority on a proposal from the Commission.

These exceptions form the basis for 'block exemptions' that do not require member states to notify DG Competition of state aid. Normally, however, member states are required to 'notify' the Commission of any plan to grant or alter state aid (unless it is exempted from notification by a legal regulation) using an electronic notification system. On being notified, the Commission investigates the application to see if it can be justified – perhaps on the grounds that the aid will assist restructuring and enable a company to regain competitiveness. Such an approval of state aid was announced by the Commission in June 2012, when the Maltese Government's five-year restructuring plan involving €130 million of state aid for Air Malta was authorized.

If state aid is granted without notification the Commission classifies it as unlawful and if subsequent investigations show the aid to have been incompatible with state aid rules then appropriate remedial action is ordered. An example of such an order was issued by the Commission in March 2012 when it required the French Government to recover the €642 million it had paid to Sernam, a firm then owned by SNCF (the French national railway), between 2001-2008. The funding was deemed to be unlawful because it had given Sernam an unfair economic advantage.

However, restrictions on state aid can be relaxed in 'hard times'. So, since the onset of the post-2008 economic crisis the Commission has been more flexible concerning state aid and has further extended the areas covered by block exemptions in response to the member states injecting large amounts of aid into the financial sector, particularly failing banks and insurance companies (European Commission, 2010n, p. 12).

It is interesting to note that the European Union is more stringent in its approach to state aid than in some other federal systems. In, for example, the US, states routinely provide state aid to lure companies to expand or relocate to their states. Most of this US state activity would be a violation of TFEU Article 107 if practiced by EU member states.

* * *

Competition policy has clearly made very considerable advances over the years, especially since the early 1990s. Many areas of activity that previously were heavily protected have been considerably opened up. As part of this, key network industries such as gas, electricity and telecommunications have been extensively liberalized, even though they are still protected in various ways.

Despite the progress that has been made, competition does, however, remain a very difficult policy area for the EU. A key reason for this is that there continue to be important areas of activity – primarily, though not wholly, of a 'public service' nature – that member state governments do not want to see subjected to the full rigours of competition. Public procurement, which accounts for about 15 per cent of EU GDP and about €1,300 billion per annum, is an example of such an area. There is legislation in place dealing with public procurement – requiring public authorities to publish invitations to tender for goods and services exceeding pre-established values (for example, €5 million for construction projects) – but it does not operate in a wholly satisfactory manner, as the relatively large number of infringement proceedings initiated by the Commission against public authorities in member states demonstrates. The fact is that, of total public procurement in the EU, only 10 per cent is cross-border procurement, which is far lower than the 20 per cent cross-border purchasing average in the private sector. Public procurement is therefore an area that the Commission continues to target for improvement.

Another problem with competition policy is that many of the areas of economic activity that have not been fully opened up are interlinked and cross over in ways that create considerable policy-making, and policy content, problems. Such overlap is seen especially in the field of energy policy, where there have been calls to increase competition through, for example, the unbundling of energy generation from its transmission. Yet, opening up energy policy to increased competition might impact on the environment in unforeseen ways, with possible implications for renewable resources and the safety of nuclear

energy. It might impact also on foreign policy, most notably because of the interconnections with the EU's dependence on Russia for natural gas and on the Middle East for oil.

An Illustrative Study of the Reach of the Internal Market: Aerospace and Defence Procurement

A theme of this chapter, and more broadly of the book as a whole, is the very wide policy and sectoral reach of the internal market. This can be illustrated by briefly outlining how the impact of the market is being felt, and indeed is being strongly encouraged, by EU policy-makers in two very sensitive, and closely related, sectoral areas: aerospace and defence procurement.

In a pattern found in many other EU policy areas, aspects of EU defence policy – and most particularly matters concerning defence expenditure, defence equipment capability and defence procurement – have become strongly linked to the internal market in terms of promoting competitiveness and growth. It has been recognized increasingly by EU policy-makers that a dynamic European defence industry will not only reduce governmental spending (defence is still an important and costly area of expenditure for most member state governments) but could also generate high profit margins, contribute greatly to R&TD (not least via patents and consumer spin-offs), and employ highly-skilled labour. But, the nettlesome reality for Europeans is the overwhelming dominance that Americans enjoy in European defence sales. One study reports that 'not only do US exports to Europe dwarf European exports to the US – somewhere between a 5:1 and 6:1 ratio – but the US market share in Europe is greater than the European market share of the US market (Bialos *et al.*, 2009, p. 27).

Attempts to tackle this problem began as long ago as the mid-1960s, when several EC member states began to co-operate in the field of space and astronomy via the European Launcher Development Organization (ELDO) and the European Space Research Organization (ESRO). The ELDO and ESRO merged in 1975 to form the European Space Agency (ESA), which is now comprised of 19 EU member states. The member states contribute on the basis of *juste retour* (which means that the amount a member state contributes in subscriptions is more or less returned to it via contract work), which has the effect of ensuring that the majority of the ESA's contracts are with European companies. ESA has served as the catalyst for a number of European space projects, including Arianespace (launching), EUMETSTAT (meteorology), EUTELSTAT and IMMAR SAT (telecommunications), Galileo (navigation), and the Global Monitoring for Environment and Security. The latter two of these are joint European Commission–ESA programmes.

Though separate entities at the time of the ESA's founding, the ESA and the EU have become increasingly intertwined. They have done so partly through agreements of various sorts, and joint policies and programmes – many of which date from a 2004 framework agreement that led in 2007 to a comprehensive EU–ESA European Space Policy – and cofinancing: the EU currently contributes approximately €700 million a year to the ESA. They have also become entwined partly through the use of a common rhetoric steeped in the language of identity (European Space Agency, 2010):

> ESA in concert with the European Union, national bodies responsible for space and international partners, manages the research and development programmes needed to maintain the position as second to none in space for the future. The results are world-class industry, outstanding scientific discoveries and a stronger, richer European identity.

Another early example of European companies partnering on capital-intensive R&TD ventures was Airbus, which was formed in 1970 and brought together major aerospace companies from France, Germany, Spain and the UK. In 2004, it became part of an even bigger European aerospace and defence consortium when the European Aeronautic Defence and Space Company (EADS) was formed. Such has been the success of Airbus that by 2003 it had surpassed Boeing in the numbers of aircraft delivered, and in 2005 it received more orders than Boeing (Airbus, 2010; Boeing Company, 2010).

The ESA and Airbus proved that European member states could co-operate in 'pioneer groups' in aerospace and defence-related projects. But the competi-

tiveness of EU defence companies was hampered by much of the defence production sector being exempted from EU competition rules. Pressure thus grew for internal market rules to apply. The Commission, always supportive of expanding the internal market, responded to the pressure by bringing forward appropriate policy (European Commission, 2007b) and legislative proposals (adopted in 2009). The legislation applies single market rules (via the Defence and Security Procurement Directive) and a more federal approach to export licensing (via the Intra-Community Transfers Directive) in order to build a more open and competitive market for European defence manufacturers (Europe Economics, 2009, p. 1). But at the same time as opening the defence industry market, the Commission has – mirroring the US treatment of its defence industry – 'shown a tolerance for concentration' that deviates significantly from its robust antitrust policies (Bialos *et al.*, 2009, pp. 197–9).

Meanwhile, since 1999 (in *Commission v Spain*), ECJ jurisprudence has required a larger burden of proof to qualify for the 'essential security' exception that member states have routinely invoked to protect their national defence industries. The 2009 Defence Package further strengthens the Court's role by bringing the defence industry firmly into the Community method of adjudication (Bialos *et al.*, 2009, pp. 31, 181, 195).

Another way in which the EU has sought to capitalize on the internal market benefits of an integrated defence industry has been through the establishment in 2004 of the European Defence Agency (EDA), which was given treaty status by the Lisbon Treaty. The EDA has three main objectives: to develop a 'comprehensive and systematic approach' for defining CSDP capability needs; to promote European defence-relevant R&TD and European co-operation on defence equipment; and to work, in close co-operation with the Commission, on steps towards an 'internationally competitive market for defence equipment in Europe'. Increasingly, the EU has been using the EDA to accomplish this latter role. So, for example, in 2006, the EU agreed a 'voluntary Code of Conduct on defence procurement', under which member states publish their contract opportunities on the Electronic Bulletin Board of the EDA's website (European Defence Agency, 2010).

* * *

The various efforts that have been made over the years to promote and strengthen the European aerospace and defence industries have, like so much of EU policy activity, been marked by partial failures and partial successes. A partial failure is seen in the difficulties that have been experienced in fully opening up national defence procurement: it remains the case that across the EU 80 per cent of defence investment is spent with national suppliers. A partial success is seen in the advances European companies have made in world markets: advances that may be said to be symbolized by the EU and US having become embroiled in years of squabbling over government subsidies to major defence contractors, and with almost a pitched battle having been fought between Boeing and Airbus over the issue (Chaffin, 2010). When the Northrup–EADS (Airbus) consortium division won their bid in 2008 to supply refuelling aircraft to the US Air Force, the US Governmental Accountability Office cancelled the tender after investigating a complaint filed by Boeing. Northrup, EADS' North American partner, then dropped out of the competition, complaining that the new tender's guidelines favoured Boeing and effectively handed the contract to it (Vogel, 2010). This case demonstrates a phenomenon widely understood by European defence manufactures and their governments: the EU needs to do more work to establish its own defence market. Doing so requires not only the co-operation that is now taking place on the supply side (with the building of a European, rather than just a nationally-based, defence industry), but also on the demand side (through CFSP/CSDP political decisions).

Conclusions

The EU's internal market constitutes by far the most integrated market system between states that the world has seen. Its spread and depth is such that not only are most 'direct' market policies affecting member states now made at EU level but a host of other policy areas – including environment, transport and social – are shaped in important ways by internal market considerations. Indeed, an indicator of the policy importance of the internal market at the EU level is seen in the fact that only a handful of the policy portfolios of the EU's Commissioners do not include important internal market responsibilities and/or

have important internal market implications.

In the wider process of European integration, the internal market has been important in advancing the integration process in both institutional and policy terms. The most obvious example of it doing so in institutional terms is the 1986 SEA which, for the purpose of enabling much-needed internal market legislation to be passed, provided for more EU supranational governing mechanisms – specifically with regard to greater provision for majority voting in the Council and a strengthening of the powers of the EP. Examples of the internal market process advancing integration in policy terms range from the development of EU consumer safety measures (relating to such matters as GMOs, tainted food and defective products) to the driving of much of justice and home affairs policy as a result of the internal market provisions for free movement of labour.

The advance – a near triumph some might say – of the liberal market spirit throughout advanced industrialized societies since the early 1980s has done much to ensure that most of the gaps between EU leaders on what sort of market they are committed to building, and what sorts of market-related measures they are prepared to see installed, have not been unbridgeable. But liberalization has not been so deep as to prevent the existence of a host of differences among policy-makers on specific market issues: differences that have often made policy development difficult, protracted, and in some cases only partial. So, while enormous progress has been made over the years in building the internal market, it is a market that is still not complete. Or, at least, it is not complete if completion is taken to mean that the four freedoms – of goods, services, labour and capital – should operate fully throughout the market. Transport is just one of many policy area where 'gaps' and 'omissions' appear: EU directives do regulate some aspects of the sector, but there cannot be complete openness without more EU legislation dealing with, for example, harmonized rules for the operation of road transport, freight trains and inland waterways.

What, then, are the main obstacles and challenges facing the EU if the internal market is to be further 'completed'? The most important is the 'ideological' differences between the member states over where the balance should lie between economic liberalism and social protectionism, and related questions concerning the relationships that should exist between market actors, financial institutions and governments. While all member states, whether governed from liberal or social democratic positions, support market integration, their degree of commitment to how liberal the market should be varies with their economic ideology. Some wish to maximize free trade while others are favourably disposed to forms of national protectionism.

But though there are considerable obstacles in the way of the further building of the internal market, the advancement of market integration continues. The central explanation as to why it does so is that the same sort of reasons that led to the proposals in the 1950s for a common market and in the mid-1980s for a Single European Market still apply: the internal market is the most effective EU policy to achieve increased employment, growth and global competitiveness.

Chapter 9

Building a Socio-economic Union: Agriculture, Cohesion, Environment and Growth Policies

In this chapter we examine a number of policies associated with the economic union stage of integration, which was defined in Chapter 2. Considering the importance of these policies in the modern democratic state, economic union could be considered the pivotal stage of European integration.

We do not attempt to cover all of the EU's 'positive' socio-economic policies in this chapter. Rather, we focus on agriculture, cohesion the environment, and the competitiveness and growth policies that have been part of the Lisbon Strategy and Europe 2020. These policies have been selected for a number of reasons. The first is their importance. All are key EU policies, as can be seen in the considerable amount of time devoted to them in EU policy-making settings, ranging from European Council summits to networking groups. Second, taken together the selected policies account for the majority of the EU's budget. Agriculture and cohesion policy are especially important in this regard, with the former accounting for just over 40 per cent of the budget and the latter for over 35 per cent. Third, the selected policies represent a broad range of policy types. So, using Lowi's typology (see Chapter 1), policies dealing with agriculture, R&D and human resource development (the latter two of which represent key elements of the EU's competitiveness and growth policy) involve *distributive* politics; cohesion policy is broadly *redistributive*; and environmental policy is largely *regulatory*. A fourth reason for the selection of the policies is that, collectively, they embrace and display the variety of policy instruments and policy processes that were introduced earlier in the book, especially in Chapters 5–7. So, for example, agriculture rests largely on EU legislation, including a substantial quantity of administrative legislation, which is made via the Community method. Environmental policy is largely based on legislative acts – mainly directives – but since 2000 it has also been advanced increasingly through a variety of soft measures, many of them adopted via the OMC. Much of competitiveness and growth policy also rests on soft policy instruments. A distinguishing feature of cohesion policy is that while the Community method is employed to set the policy, the implementation and monitoring policy stages are characterized by a three-way partnership between the Commission, the governments of the member states and sub-national levels of government.

Box 9.1 provides a summary of the key characteristics of the selected policies. As column 2 indicates, the EU became involved in most of the major policies associated with economic union during the same time period – the 1970s. This timing is not coincidental, as this is the period when the common market

---

Box 9.1

Key characteristics of selected socio-economic policies

Policy	Decade initiated	Policy type	EU competence	Key challenges
Agriculture	(early) 1960s	Distributive	Exclusive in respect of major policy decisions	Balancing direct support for farmers with other pressures on the EU budget. Dealing with external pressures to make the CAP less protectionist. The role GMOs will play in increasing European food production
Cohesion	(mid-) 1970s	Redistributive	Shared	Extension of meaningful support to the CEECs and future member states, most of which have substantially lower average per capita incomes than the EU-15
Environment	(early) 1970s	Regulatory	Shared	Balancing high environmental standards with European companies competing with goods produced in countries with lower standards. Implementation gaps at member state level
Competitiveness and growth	1970s, but relaunched in late 1990s/early 2000s, especially via the Lisbon Strategy	Distributive and redistributive	Supporting and sharing	Industrial policy – which companies are the winners and which the losers? Balancing social welfare with economic efficiency. Providing more jobs, especially for young people and women. Tackling the looming problem of an ageing workforce. Use of OMC rather than hard policy instruments.

---

was beginning to have a significant impact throughout the Community.

Policies Associated with the Economic Union Stage of Integration

Policies associated with the economic union stage of the federal integration approach are socio-economic policies, broadly defined. However, they do not include policies dealing with fiscal union and monetary union, the core policy components of economic federalism, which are dealt with separately in the next chapter.

In the federal integration model, economic union is the stage between 'common market' and 'economic federalism'. Not surprisingly, therefore, as stages in the model are sequenced, economic union includes the policy features and architecture of the first three stages – that is, of a free trade area, a customs union and a common market – while incrementally adding 'positive' policies. Most of these policies are, in one way or another, 'by-products' of the internal market. So, there are, for example, policies dealing with 'externalities' of the four freedoms (such as social, health and safety, labour, and education policies), with market failure (such as environment and energy transmission policies), and with competitiveness itself (such as R&D policy, workforce training and educational opportunities policies, and industrial policy).

Most 'positive' EU-level socio-economic policies have thus been made necessary by the existence of the internal market. Consumer protection policy illustrates this. The necessity is because if the internal market is to remain open despite suspicions by member state governments and their citizens that partner member states are not always as vigilant as they are themselves in promoting and policing consumer protection and product safety, then strong central protections must be put in place. Without such protection, member states will be tempted to ban the importing of products from other member states at the first hint of safety concerns. So, as the internal market becomes increasingly integrated, EU-level consumer standards are ever more necessary because the presumption has to be made that goods produced within one member state, or imported through and cleared by customs in one member state, can safely be sold in all the member states. The E. coli outbreak in Germany in the summer of 2011 illustrates the suspicions that can exist, and why calls come to be made for EU-level policy management. Within days of the outbreak, regional German authorities posted a notice to the EU's *Rapid Alert System for Food and Feed* identifying Spanish cucumbers as the source. The German 'rush to judgement' about Spanish produce – which proved to be incorrect (the source of the outbreak was later traced to sprouts grown from fenugreek seeds imported from Egypt in 2009 and 2010 which entered Europe through a single German importer) – cost European farmers €400 million per week during the month-long crisis as domestic sales and exports of salad products plummeted (see Neuman and Sayare, 2011; Taylor, 2011c). This situation might have been avoided if a dependable European authority had existed, because it is likely that it would have had more information available to it and would have been more cautious about blaming a member state without hard evidence.

But while the internal market is a key driver of the economic union's 'positive' policy development, it is, as shown in Chapter 2, not the only factor determin-

ing the pace and the manner in which such policies are developed. The most important additional determining factor is the differing policy preferences of the member states arising from their distinctive political, economic and social circumstances, and policy preferences. These differing circumstances and preferences mean that member states naturally do not wholly agree on all aspects of policy priorities, or on the desirable features of particular policies. In consequence, policy development does not occur in an automatic way according to the stage of economic integration that has been reached, but rather is subject to all sorts of variations – as the early, pre-common market, development of an established agricultural policy shows.

As for the socio-economic policy issues on which member states disagree, these are almost countless in number. Should, for example, the EU harmonize the length of the work week to prevent capital moving from member states with shorter work weeks to those with longer statutory work weeks, and should the EU guarantee equal pay for both men and women? In sum, should the market be underpinned by strong social protectionist policies for its workforce? Gradually, the member states have accepted that many such social policies – collectively making up what is often referred to as the European Social Model (ESM) – need to be at least co-ordinated, and in some cases agreed, on an EU-wide basis. The reason for this is that an absence of European standards for social protection, as Balassa (1962, p. 226) warned in his early study of economic integration, unfairly advantages those parts of the market with the lowest forms of protection:

> Under *ceteris paribus* assumptions, if countries on a similar level of economic development, but with differing state-financed social security schemes, participate in a common market, capital will tend to move from the country with the more inclusive social security system to countries where income-redistributional measures are applied to a lesser degree.

The EU's member states – with their shared tradition of social democracy and state intervention – do not generally question the principle of publicly controlled and publicly provided social protection. However, as Hall and Soskice (2001) explain, while all European countries agree to the general notion of the ESM, that does not make them identical in their approach to market intervention, to the role of the state in social and economic planning, or to the appropriate sources of financing of protectionist measures. So, some EU member states, especially when centre-right parties are in government, are decidedly more sympathetic than others to the argument that market-wide social protection can diminish market competitiveness. Such disparate orientations condition member state positions on a wide range of social policies, making it very difficult, and indeed undesirable, to federalize all but those social policies that impact on the four freedoms both negatively and significantly.

Accompanying disparate orientations as an obstacle in building EU-level socio-economic policies are often a host of very practical problems. Pensions – a policy area that has been extremely difficult to develop on an EU basis – illustrates this, with problems including the heterogeneity of taxpayer-supported and private pension schemes, different retirement ages, and numerous complications associated with portability (such as taxation). This has not, however, completely prevented the EU's involvement in pensions policy, because member state pensions practices can undermine social cohesion (inadequate pensions in some member states translates into poorer Europeans and regional imbalances), impacts on public finances (a state's public pension expenditure places pressure on public finances/borrowing), can promote or inhibit the free movement of labour or capital, and is tied to competitiveness – by 2060, there will be only two Europeans of working age for every person over 65, compared to a four to one ratio in 2010 (European Commission, 2010j, p. 2). Thus, pensions policy touches on a number of concerns that clearly fall under the EU's policy competences and require EU attention.

So, the EU is involved in a wide range of 'positive' socio-economic policies, but these vary considerably in their levels of development. With respect to employment-related policies, for example – which cover subjects such as gender equality, unemployment protection and collective bargaining rights – it is recognized that national variations mean there is not a completely level market playing field. This is because member states with strong protections for employees can be at a competitive disadvantage in relation to member states with weaker protections under *ceteris*

paribus conditions. But the recognition of this problem has not been able to wholly overcome the many obstacles – in the form mainly of competitiveness pressures, funding and cultural concerns – of developing strong employment policies. As a result, most EU employment policies are based on the use of soft policy instruments and the OMC policy mode. This situation of relatively weak employment policies is not, however, unusual in dualist federal systems. Taking the US as an example, workers' rights vary widely among states, with markedly different regional patterns (for example, considerably higher protection in the Northeast, Midwest and West Coast).

The federal integration approach we developed in Chapter 2 suggests that aspects of EU integration can reach 'points of no return' as policy areas become inextricably linked with one another. This has obviously been the case with the internal market, but high policy inter-linkage can also be seen to exist in many other areas, particularly those involving socio-economic harmonization. This point about the extent of EU policy inter-linkages runs through the policy studies contained in this chapter as, for example, environmental policy shows: EU agricultural policy includes many rules and incentives for the promotion of environmental protection and environmentally-friendly land management practices; EU cohesion policy requires the implementation of EU environmental laws; and EU competitiveness and growth policies include an environmental dimension – as demonstrated, for example, by the EU's 2009 Environmental Review, which emphasized the role of environmental policy in stimulating economic recovery and competitiveness (European Commission, 2009b, p. 2).

Agriculture

The development of agricultural policy

The EEC Treaty laid down the basis for the Common Agricultural Policy (CAP) under Title II, Article 38 (4): 'The operation and development of the common market for agricultural products must be accompanied by the establishment of a common agricultural policy among the Member States.' The CAP was put in place by the mid-1960s, and as part of the new policy most national support measures for agriculture were removed and replaced with a European system based on harmonized prices set above world prices.

The prominent position of the CAP in the EEC's policy portfolio is often attributed to a 'deal' between France and Germany, in which the Treaty would give German industry unlimited access to the French market and Germany would 'pay' for this privilege by guaranteeing financial protection for French farmers. In this picture, the CAP was thus the first major example in the European integration context of the use of the regionally-based trade-offs and compromises that are necessary in federal arrangements.

But while there is some truth in this interpretation of the CAP being the consequence of a 'Franco-German deal', it does not in itself tell the full story of why the CAP was created. It needs to be supplemented by a recognition that there were a number of factors which resulted in *all* the founding member states regarding agriculture as needing special treatment of some kind. First, Europe suffered from food shortages in the years after the Second World War, so there was naturally support for a policy that would have as one of its core objectives an increase in agricultural output. Second, agriculture employed a large percentage of the workforce in the founding states: for example, 31 per cent in France, 23 per cent in West Germany, and 18 per cent in the Netherlands (Rieger, 2005, p. 396). Third, there was – because of a wide acceptance by policy-makers that agriculture had 'special requirements' – already in existence a patchwork system of financial assistance from member states to farmers. For the EEC agricultural market to operate fairly and without too much sudden disruption, it would therefore need to include a replacement of existing financial support systems by some form of common system.

The importance of the food shortages and employment factors have diminished over the years (though the latter has certainly not disappeared), but that of the perceived necessity of agriculture needing special financial support remains strong. It continues to be recognized that the unique nature and particular challenges of the agricultural sector mean that it should not be as liberal as other sectoral markets. This unique nature is seen as having many dimensions, such as unpredictable events like severe weather and animal and plant diseases that can bankrupt farmers almost overnight. It is seen also in the fungibility of produce

(which makes it difficult for farmers to market a distinctive product), in the atomistic competition related to this general substitutability of produce, and the complex and varied nature of supply chains. All these factors have been crucial in explaining the continuance of agricultural support.

But the extent and nature of the support for agriculture has always varied between the member states, primarily because of wide variations in agricultural conditions and practices across the EU. Listed below are just a few examples of some of the variations that have given rise to political differences over the CAP:

- *The sizes of agricultural sectors.* States with large agricultural sectors, with France to the fore, have been strong CAP supporters, while states with small sectors, with the UK to the fore, have pressed for reductions in CAP expenditure.
- *Climatic zones.* Northern 'temperate' farmers and Mediterranean farmers have different concerns regarding the nature of market support, storage, shipment and so on.
- *Approaches to farming.* There are differing practices and views in member states on such issues as 'factory farming', the transportation of live animals, and the use of GMOs.
- *The sizes of farms.* States such as the UK, the Czech Republic, Germany, France and Sweden have larger than average-sized farms, while states such as Italy, Greece and Hungary have farms that are smaller than average.
- *The use of traditional and organic practices.* The CEECs make more use of these than do farmers in the EU-15.
- *The extent of modernization.* CEECs, particularly Bulgaria and Romania, are less mechanized than EU-15 states.

The CAP system that was established in the 1960s rested, essentially, on a dual system of internal price support for agricultural products on the one hand, and protection from external competition via high tariff rates on the other. Once this system was established, the financial support mechanisms it contained led quickly to the CAP accounting for most of EEC expenditure. When the UK became a member of the Community in 1973, the CAP's dominance of the budget inevitably resulted in fierce inter-governmental disputes, especially between France – which has always been the CAP's strongest defender – and the UK. In spite of reductions that have been made over the years in the proportion of the EU budget assigned to agriculture, these disputes resonate to the present day.

The development and continuation of the CAP as a central EU policy has also been assisted by the fact that farmers are a well-organized interest group (Nedergaard, 2006, p. 396). As Grant (2010) and others have noted, agricultural policy has always had a strong political dimension. When farmers have felt threatened, they have often turned out *en masse* to protest – as was signalled as early as 1968 when 100,000 farmers converged on Brussels in a demonstration that turned violent, to protest against the Mansholt Plan, which proposed the elimination of support for smaller farmers and consolidating holdings into larger farms to make European farms more competitive and less dependent on subsides (European NAvigator (ENA), n.d.). Another dimension of this politicization of farming is that because the livelihood of farmers is tied directly to government support, they are inveterate swing voters (Moyer, 1993, p. 18) and have wielded this power masterfully in closely-contested elections.

Cultural considerations have also influenced the development of the CAP. In parts of Europe, semi-idealized visions of the importance of rural life and the importance of the continuation of family farming have encouraged some member state governments to press for strong CAP financial support. Other culturally-based factors that have helped to shape EU agricultural policy have included food security and food preparation issues – with recent examples including the 'slow food movement', which originated in Italy in the mid-1980s, and the anti-GMO movement found in pockets throughout Europe – which have ensured that the CAP is expected to protect uniquely European practices and the accessibility of bucolic life mores in the cultivation and preparation of food.

However, regardless of the factors that explain the creation and continuation of the CAP, the CAP system has been reformed fundamentally since the early 1990s. A key reason why this is the case is that the EU has been forced to respond to strong international pressures to become less protectionist in agricultural trade policy and less financially supportive of EU farmers. These pressures have, as is shown below, been crucial in moving the CAP away from being a price support system to becoming an income support system.

The objectives and principles of the CAP

In the same language as Article 39 of the original EEC Treaty, Article 39 of the TFEU lists the CAP's objectives as being:

1. to increase productivity, by promoting technical progress and ensuring the optimum use of the factors of production, in particular labour;
2. to ensure a fair standard of living for the agricultural Community;
3. to stabilize markets;
4. to secure availability of supplies;
5. to provide consumers with food at reasonable prices.

The importance attached to these treaty objectives has not been wholly consistent over the years. Until the early 1990s, Objectives 1, 2 and 4 were given precedence, which – particularly via the provision of incentives to increase production – meant that from the mid-1970s the EU was grappling with major problems of the oversupply of farm products and associated pressure on the EU budget. Until the mid-1990s, Objective 5 tended to be crowded out by the other goals, so that prior to reforms introduced from 2003, the CAP functioned as a classical distributive policy – favouring farmers with little regard for consumers.

As for the principles of the CAP, Schucksmith *et al.* (2005, pp. 25–6) suggest that the CAP has had four main principles: market unity, community preference, common funding, and producer co-responsibility. These principles are outlined in Box 9.2.

The most contentious of the principles has been 'common funding'. Over the first thirty years or so of the CAP, many mechanisms were established to offer financial support and to protect domestic agriculture: import levies and tariffs set to a target price; import quotas; intervention prices (involving the EU buying produce to raise the market price); direct farm subsidies; production quotas; and set-aside payments. These interventions were financed via the European Agricultural Guidance and Guarantee Fund (EAGGF).

Box 9.2

Principles of the CAP

Principle	Application	Concerns
Market unity	Agricultural goods can flow freely across internal EU borders. Financial support is from, or at least must be approved at, the EU level rather than the national level – thus ensuring that no member state unduly advantages its domestic agricultural sector	• Northern products (dairy and cereals) enjoy more protection than products that only grow around the Mediterranean • Distorts EU budget receipts in that the budgetary contributions of food importing countries are not matched by CAP returns
Community preference	Import protection encourages Europeans to buy European produce and the produce of developing countries with colonial ties to member states	• Flouts the spirit of WTO trading rules • Pits the EU against agricultural exporting countries, such as the USA and the Cairns Group
Common funding	Agricultural support financed from the EU budget rather than national budgets	• At the CAP's spending peak it accounted for 80% of the EU budget. It still accounts for just over 40%
Producer co-responsibility	Funding tied to farmers accepting EU standards on such matters as biodiversity, animal welfare and land husbandry	• Implementation difficulties

---

However, from the 1970s, the strain of the subsidization of farming began to overwhelm the EU's budget and severely constrained the EU's ability to finance initiatives and actions in other policy areas. Politicians from member states that did not share in the CAP's largesse became increasingly vocal in expressing their dissatisfaction with the system, and in the UK the CAP came to symbolize a bloated, wasteful and corrupt insiders' club. Pressures for reform thus built up from the 1970s, and became increasingly intense as budgetary pressures were joined, as explained below, by other types of reform pressures. The cumulative effect of these pressures has been to bring about a CAP that in important ways is quite different in character from the CAP constructed in the 1960s and 1970s.

CAP reform

Reform pressures

As has just been intimated, since the 1970s there have been intense pressures for CAP reform. The nature and importance of these pressures has varied over time, but some of the following have always been present:

• As there has been a decline in the economic importance of agriculture, so has the validity of allocating so much of the EU's budget to it also declined: the percentage allocated was close to 80 per cent by the mid-1960s, about 70 per cent in the 1970s and

1980s, and remains over 40 per cent today. While a quarter of the EU's population still lives in rural areas, farming accounts for only 5 per cent of EU employment and between 2 per cent and 3 per cent of the EU's GDP (Schucksmith *et al.*, 2005, p. 15). The Commission – which has been unsuccessful in convincing member states to agree a new form of budgetary revenue (see Chapter 14) – has been an important advocate of freeing-up the EU's budget for new policy initiatives, especially those related to growth and competitiveness.

- Member states that are not net beneficiaries of CAP funding but which are net contributors to the EU budget naturally favour less budgetary spending on the CAP. The number of such states has grown over the years.
- Environmentalists have increasingly targeted the CAP, arguing that EU farm policy should be closely tied to environmental policy.
- As more states have joined the EU, it has become progressively more difficult for France to hold together the pro-CAP coalition on France's terms. In addition to the persistent British dissatisfaction with the CAP, the entrance of the CEECs – many of which had large and inefficient agricultural sectors at the time of their accessions – have added to pressures on an already strained EU budget.
- From the early 1990s, the CAP became a major liability in international trade negotiations, which came to a head in the GATT Uruguay Round when most of the countries with which the EU had to negotiate strongly opposed its generous farm subsidies. It became increasingly difficult for the EU to gain concessions in other areas of trade that it judged to be important – such as the removal of non-tariff barriers to trade and the liberalization of intellectual property rights and of services – without opening up its markets more fully to agricultural trade.

Reforms

In response to the increasing pressures for CAP reform that have just been noted, measures to tighten CAP spending were introduced gradually from the late 1980s. But it was not until a major reform of the CAP in 2003/4 that decoupled subsidies from production that the EU solved the problem of oversupply and its food surpluses came under control.

Reforms have been undertaken mainly through four major reform rounds – the 1980s reforms, the MacSharry reforms (1992), the Agenda 2000 reforms (1999), and the Mid-term Review reforms (sometimes also called the Fischler II reforms) (2003) – and a fifth, more modest, reform in the 2008 Health Check. The most important features of these reform rounds are outlined in Box 9.3.

Three key points about the reforms merit special comment. First, the system that was created in the 1960s of price support for agricultural products has largely been replaced by a system of direct payments to farmers. It is a system that favours large farms, which is controversial, but the practice is supported by several member states, including the Czech Republic, Germany, Romania (where farm holdings have been consolidating), and the UK (Rankin, 2011b). The Commission has also long favoured larger farms, on the grounds that they are more competitive on world markets, but strong pressures from many member states for the EU not to develop policies that would consolidate smaller holdings has resulted in European consumers paying (literally) for the luxury of having small and medium-sized farms. The second point is that the reforms have created an agricultural policy that is now highly attuned to environmental, food safety and animal welfare issues. And the final point, which emerges from the first two points, is that the CAP is now anchored in two programmes: one based on annual direct payments and market measures; and the second on multi-annual rural development plans (European Commission, 2010c, p. 3).

Future reforms

As shown above, the CAP has evolved from its original nature to become a policy system in which farmers are now financially supported directly and in which rural development, food safety and environmental protection are also prominent features.

What is the future for the CAP? Some CAP opponents call for a complete end to direct payments to farmers. However, the 'rational efficiency'/anti-CAP bloc – led by Denmark, the Netherlands, Sweden and the UK – does not go that far, but rather takes the position that unprofitable farmers should not be supported at the taxpayers' expense. This group will attempt to reduce CAP spending and continue the shift of recent years from farm support to rural development and environmental protection. Countering this group, the firmly 'pro-CAP' camp – which includes France, Greece, Ireland, Italy, Poland and Slovakia (EurActiv, 2012a; Rankin, 2011a) – will doubtless continue to favour generous levels of support for farmers.

That the CAP has continued despite the controversy surrounding it attests to the fact that liberal and social democratic ideologies are largely set aside with respect to agricultural policy, with there being a broad acceptance among most EU governments that agriculture requires a common policy rather than separate national policies. There is also a widely-shared undercurrent of opinion that agriculture should be protected from the full application of economic liberal principles. One reason for this is tied to 'food security': the EU already imports more agricultural produce than any other global region and does not want to become wholly dependent on other parts of the world for its food. Another reason is that Europeans wish to ensure the continuation of the bucolic life, with the small or medium-sized family-owned farm being valued and supported as a viable alternative to factory farming and as constituting an important part of rural protection. And a third, and increasingly important, reason is a widely-held view that farmers should not be driven out of business by such circumstances beyond their control as the costs of adopting green practices or complying with Europe's high standards for humane animal husbandry and food quality and safety.

Nevertheless, pressures for further CAP reform will continue, and probably intensify. Two recent internal EU developments are likely to be significant in this respect. The first is that CAP decision-making procedures were changed by the Lisbon Treaty, with agriculture being 'transferred' from the consultation to the ordinary legislative procedure and with also the abolition of the distinction between compulsory (in effect, agricultural) and non-compulsory expenditures in the EU budget. As a result, the EP for the first time holds full co-legislative powers with the Council on agricultural policy. If the behaviour of national parliaments teaches us anything about protectionism, calls for reduction in the EU's import protection for Europe's farmers will fall on deaf ears in the EP. The second important internal development is that the CEECs are no longer 'new' members and are seeking a more equitable distribution of CAP funding and increased financial support for the modernization of their farm sectors. CEECs are tying their arguments to the internal market, and specifically to the CAP as a policy that is producing competitive distortions.

Another reason to expect pressures for CAP reform to continue is a growing demand for food across the world, which the Food and Agriculture Organization of the United Nations (FAO) predicts will increase by 70 per cent by 2050 (European Commission, 2010c, p. 2). Europe will need to produce more food to satisfy this demand, which could intensify the somewhat stalled debate on GMOs.

In April 2010, the European Commission launched a public debate on the EU's future farm policy. It followed this with a White Paper, which set out three broad alternative policy options for CAP reform (European Commission, 2010c). Option 1 was essentially maintaining the status quo, leaving the CAP substantially in place though with some modest changes to the payment arrangements. Option 2 envisaged rebalancing the payments system to address current inequities and continuing to expand rural development. Option 3 involved the most 'far-reaching reform', with the focus shifting to environmental and climate change objectives and a gradual movement away from income support.

It is likely that the future CAP will look most like Option 2: the system of direct payments to farmers will continue, but attempts will be made to ensure payments do not unfairly advantage some farmers over others; market support will be further tightened; and rural support measures will, as has been the pattern in recent reform packages, continue to be strengthened. As for overall spending on agriculture, there will, as shown in Chapter 14, be little change in the post-2014 multi-annual financial framework (MFF).

Cohesion Policy

Cohesion policy is focused on strengthening economic, social and territorial cohesion across the EU by reducing disparities in both opportunities and wealth. While much of cohesion policy is particularly focused on the EU's poorer regions, all parts of the EU are eligible for at least some support through the various programmes and funding operations that make up cohesion policy.

Box 9.3

Major CAP reforms

Year(s)	Reasons for reform	Main reforms	Evaluation
1980s	• Surplus production of various products, especially dairy and cereals • Pressures on EU budget (CAP accounts for around 70% of expenditure)	• A range of measures – including quotas and co-responsibility levies – are adopted, aimed at cutting production levels and cutting CAP expenditure	• Most reforms are stop-gap in nature: production levels and CAP spending remain high • Unsustainable without increased EU budget revenues
1992–4 (MacSharry reforms)	• Continuing problems of over-production and CAP dominance of EU budget • Pressures in the GATT Uruguay Round from trading competitors and partners	• Movement from price support to income support begins • Payments for land set-asides, retirement and forestation	• Takes much of the guesswork out of CAP programming and budgeting, and delivers support to farmers in a more predictable and timely manner • Does not make special allowances for small and medium-sized farms: 20% of farms receive 80% of support
1999 (based on *Agenda 2000* proposals)	• Continuing problems with over-production and budgetary costs exacerbated by looming accessions of CEECs • Continuing international pressures • Growing recognition of environmental degradation involved with farming	• First steps are taken in the 'decoupling' (separating) of payments from production • A rural development policy is established • A reduction in market support prices	• Funding becomes less heavily weighted to 'factory farms' • Establishment of rural development as a core CAP objective

The development of cohesion policy

Along with the CAP, cohesion policy is one of the most prominent and important of the EU's policy responsibilities, and is so for a number of reasons.

First, cohesion has assumed over the years a greatly increased importance with respect to the budgetary expenditure of the EU. As the percentage of the budget assigned to agriculture has decreased, so has the percentage assigned to cohesion grown: from a modest 6 per cent just after the European Regional Development Fund (ERDF) was created in the 1970s to a figure that now accounts for more than 35 per cent of the budget.

Second, cohesion policy is remarkable in its broad remit, encompassing a very wide range of EU policy activities. These include infrastructure improvements, development of telecommunications, and jobs train-

Box 9.3 continued

Year(s)	Reasons for reform	Main reforms	Evaluation
	• Growing concerns for animal welfare • Concerns regarding farm practices affecting food safety		
2003 (Mid-term review)	• The 1999 reforms had not provided for a reduction in CAP spending • The 1999 reforms had not fully met international pressures for a reduction in CAP support and protection mechanisms	• Further decoupling • Single Payment System (SPS) is established, involving a payment to farmers based on specified criteria • An intensification of support for rural development and rural protection	• Continues downward pressures on CAP production and spending • Increases 'non-payment' dimensions of agricultural policy
2008 ('Health Check')	• A scheduled check on the 2003 reforms • A growing desire to tie CAP to 'healthy' policies such as combating climate change, biodiversity, renewable energy and innovation	• Further decoupling. • Member states given more flexibility in adopting and implementing the SPS. • Abolition of arable land set-aside. • Modest reductions in direct payments, with the funds saved to be transferred to rural development.	• Continues de-emphasis of the market aspects of the CAP and focuses on mainstreaming with other core EU policies

Sources: Adapted from Garzon, 2006; Moyer, 1993, p. 6; Nedergaard, 2006.

ing. Furthermore, the Commission links many of the EU's key broad policy goals – such as expanding diversity in the workplace and promoting environmental conservation and sustainable development – to cohesion policy.

Third, cohesion policy involves, in one way or another, the direct involvement in policy-making and policy-implementation of an unusually large number of policy actors. All the major EU institutions exercise a significant role in at least some aspect of the setting, funding, implementing and monitoring of cohesion policy. So, for example, the overall spending parameters of cohesion policy are set within the framework of the multi-annual financial frameworks (MFFs) that are approved by the European Council, while the annual budgetary allocations for cohesion funding are made by the Commission, the Council and the EP. The Council and the EP (with the latter's powers over cohesion policy having been considerably strengthened by the Lisbon Treaty) set broad cohesion objectives, while the Commission develops and promulgates guidelines for specific programme opportunities as well as monitoring implementation by member states. Beyond the major institutions, the Committee of the Regions acts in a consultative capacity on cohesion policy decision-making. Cohesion policy also brings together an array of governmental and non-governmental decision-makers at member state, regional and local levels: an aspect of cohesion policy that scholars using the multi-level governance (MLG) approach to analyse the EU have found particularly noteworthy.

Fourth, and finally, cohesion policy is in a very real sense a microcosm of the EU's historical deepening and widening. In terms of deepening, most of the EU's major treaties have attested to the EU's commitment to economic and social cohesion, beginning with the Paris Treaty establishing the ECSC, which created the European Social Fund (ESF) to finance the retraining of workers who would be rendered permanently redundant by the competitive reforms in coal and steel production. Cohesion policy was discussed at the Messina Conference, and a reference to it was included in the preamble of the EEC Treaty with the signatory states affirming that they were 'anxious to strengthen the unity of their economies and to ensure their harmonious development by reducing the differences existing between the various regions and the backwardness of the less favoured regions'. EU competence in cohesion policy was then given a specific treaty basis by the 1986 Single European Act – with the addition of a new title to the EEC Treaty headed 'Economic and Social Cohesion'. Later treaties have further increased EU competence in cohesion policy, with, for example, the last of the trio of structural and cohesion funds – the Cohesion Fund – being established via the Maastricht Treaty.

In terms of widening, cohesion policy has in large part been developed in consequence of, and been shaped considerably by, enlargement rounds. This process began with the establishment of the ERDF, which was a response to the 1973 enlargement where cohesion issues featured prominently in the UK/Denmark/Ireland accession negotiations. The British government pressed for a regional fund partly to aid its de-industrialized regions as compensation for the higher food prices Britons would expect to pay

on entering the EEC, but also as *juste retour* for the UK's contribution to the CAP. Importantly, the British had an ally in the Italians, who had long sought an EU-based regional redistribution scheme for the *mezzogiorno*, and had support from the Irish, who too stood to benefit from cohesion funding (Rhodes, 1974). The Mediterranean enlargement round of the 1980s – which brought Greece, Portugal, and Spain into the EU – further expanded EU cohesion policy, and more particularly increased the size of cohesion funding, with these relatively poorer countries tying cohesion policy to their co-operation on those EU policy initiatives wealthier countries supported. The accessions of Finland and Sweden as part of the 1995 enlargement led to the inclusion of sparsely populated areas as a separate component element of cohesion policy. Finally, the enlargement of 2004/7 presented a number of interrelated cohesion policy challenges, with most of the new member states displaying: per capita GNI well below the EU-15 average; inefficient industries (a legacy of communism); a lack of 'knowledge-industries'; and the movement of workers from industry to rural employment and/or unemployment as state-owned factories began to close or to privatize. The sheer magnitude of the disparity in regional income and infrastructure between the EU-15 and the EU-12 opened a window of opportunity for the broadening of cohesion policy.

Key features and core objectives of cohesion policy

In that it involves the redistribution of funds from the centre to constituent governments, cohesion policy may be said to be the most 'federal' of EU policies. Redistribution of resources on a territorial basis is a practice found in all federal systems and may be said to be virtually a federal requirement. Watts (1997, pp. 42, 45) suggests that such financial transfers from federal governments to regions is necessary to correct two types of imbalances – vertical (constitutionally-assigned revenues collected by federal and regional levels do not match constitutionally-assigned expenditures); and horizontal (revenue capacities vary among regions). He observes that 'The need for such (equalization) transfers arise in most federations from a recognition that disparities in wealth among regions within a federation are likely to have a corrosive effect on cohesion within a federation.' The Commission, in its 2010 budgetary review, made a similar federally-based justification of cohesion policy: 'Cohesion has proved one of the most successful ways for the Union to demonstrate its commitment to solidarity, while spreading growth and prosperity across the EU' (European Commission, 2010e, p. 12).

Thus, in a policy area in which redistribution of governmental revenue is earmarked primarily for territorial units rather than individuals, the EU has constructed the typical arrangement found in federal systems, with the political representatives of the territorial units bargaining for a share of resources. In the EU's case, the political bargaining is carried out mainly in the European Council (with respect to MFFs) and in the Council of Ministers and the EP (with respect to annual budgets and cohesion legislation). Implementation is shared by the Commission and agencies in the member states, with the former being responsible for administrative rule-making and overall policy monitoring, and the latter for 'front line' implementation.

Cohesion policy therefore involves federal transfers from the centre to the constituent units, binding central (EU) and regional (member states) levels in a vertical relationship. There is also a horizontal dimension, because while the implementation mechanism flows from the Commission to member state agencies, cohesion policy classifications are based on shared regional characteristics – notably low per capita gross national income, high unemployment, poor integration of transportation infrastructure with major European metropolitan centres, and sparsely populated territory – rather than being different for each member state. (For analyses of the nature of cohesion funding distribution, see Bodenstein and Kemmerling, 2012 ; Dellmuth, 2011.)

An increasingly important feature of cohesion policy is that it is linked to innovation, which is a normal feature of multiple constituency systems (see Elazar, 1973, on this point). In federal systems, cohesion policy has come to be tied increasingly to the concept of a 'laboratory of democracies', in which – especially in more loosely organized or dual federal systems – the policy focus has broadened from the purely economic logic articulated in the economic integration model. In the EU, cohesion policy has also moved in this direction, in particular by being recalibrated to competition and growth policies and by

becoming an important part of the Europe 2020 Strategy (European Commission, 2010f, pp. 8–9). EU cohesion projects are now required to be innovative, so as to serve as demonstration projects or laboratories of good practice that can then be employed in other localities. Cohesion policy is also used to underwrite specific EU priorities in poorer regions, especially with regard to the central role that environmental and transport policies play in cohesion funding.

The cohesion policy-making cycle is based on six principles, as elaborated in Box 9.4: concentration, programming, partnerships, proportionality, co-financing and additionality. These principles are applied to the three distinct categories or 'objectives' of EU cohesion policy: convergence and competitiveness; regional competitiveness and unemployment; and European territorial co-operation. The convergence and competitiveness objective – the most important objective in terms of funding, constituting 81.5 per cent of total cohesion funding – is used to redistribute funds to poorer member states. The regional competitiveness and unemployment objective, with 15.9 per cent of cohesion funding, is available to all regions in the EU other than those qualifying under the convergence and competitiveness objective. The territorial cohesion objective is grounded in economic geography (the study of agglomeration economics) and horizontal federalism – that is, it contains elements of both the economic and political aspects of the federal integration approach. Clearly seen as 'experimental' (with only 2.5 per cent of the cohesion budget allocated in the 2007–13 MFF), advocates of a leading role for the EU in territorial cohesion argue that this third cohesion objective reduces the opportunity for beggar-thy-neighbour policies, takes account of cross-border externalities, and promotes learning and dissemination of good policy (Barca, 2009, p. 55).

Financing for the three cohesion objectives derives mainly from three funds: the European Social Fund (ESF), the European Regional Development Fund (ERDF) and the Cohesion Fund, which together account for over a third of EU budgetary expenditure. The ways in which the three funds are used to finance activities designed to achieve the cohesion objectives vary. All three funds are used to finance the convergence and competiveness objective, with the Cohesion Fund reserved for the poorest of qualifying member states. The ERDF and ESF are used to fund the regional competitiveness and unemployment objec-

Box 9.4

Cohesion policy principles

Principles	Features	Parameters
Concentration	Based on three objectives: • Convergence and competitiveness • Regional competitiveness and employment • Territorial co-operation	Since the 'Lisbonization' of cohesion policy (tying cohesion funds to competitiveness and growth), grants are targeted at the factors of production on the supply side – innovativeness, entrepreneurship and training of the labour force, infrastructure, environment, and good governance.
Programming	Multi-annual (long-term) rather than annual.	To ensure that projects are sufficiently long-term in nature and will be likely to have a greater positive impact on the member state.
Partnerships	Vertical and horizontal to include the Commission, member states, regional organizations, other public bodies, and NGOs.	Multi-level governance emphasizes the partnership dimension of cohesion policy. However, the extent to which sub-national governments are involved differs among member states, particularly according to whether they are unitary, regional or federal systems.
Proportionality	The costs of projects must be kept to reasonable levels *vis-à-vis* total expenditure.	Maximum impact of cohesion funds for the approved project.
Co-financing	EU's maximum contribution is normally between 50% and 85%: the former figure applies to the competitiveness objective and the latter to the convergence objective.	This ensures that member states are committed to projects, but also that poorer member states sometimes cannot fund their matching contributions.
Additionality	Funding cannot be used by member states to replace projects that had been, or had been scheduled to be, financed without EU funds.	Can impede the ability of poorer member states to take advantage of cohesion funds.

Sources: Adapted from Bouvet and Dall'Erba, 2010; Molle, 2007, p. 150.

tive. The European territorial co-operation objective is funded solely from the ERDF.

* * *

Cohesion policy looks to be set to continue along broadly similar lines in the foreseeable future.

Certainly in terms of overall funding there is little prospect of any significant increase, not least because of the financial pressures on most of the EU budget net contributor states brought about by the economic and financial crisis and the massive transfer of funds from wealthier and stable eurozone members to bail out those eurozone members experiencing sovereign debt problems and failing banks (see Chapter 10).

Not surprisingly, member state support for maintaining the previous levels of cohesion funding in the 2014–20 MFF broke quickly into predictable camps when negotiations got under way in 2012, with the European Affairs Ministers of the 14 countries that benefit from cohesion funds opposing the cuts advocated by several net contributor states (Vogel, 2012). As shown in Chapter 14, the proportionate overall level of cohesion funding in the 2014–20 MFF is little changed.

Environmental Policy

The development of environmental policy

Since 1967, when the EU adopted its first environmental legislation (Council Directive 67/548/EEC, on the classification, packaging and labelling of dangerous substances), the EU's policy-making role has expanded to cover virtually the full range of environmental issues. Well over 300 legal acts deal with such issues as sustainable development, the disposal of waste, pollution in its many forms, nature and biodiversity, and climate change.

As with so many of the EU's 'positive' policies, a key reason why the EU is so important with respect to environmental policy is the internal market. Much of the justification for EU environmental policy is perceived as 'market failure' and a need to harmonize environmental practices that affect cost/pricing structures. States that 'free ride' on the environment by, for example, having low air and water quality standards, are deemed to be passing on costs unreasonably to other states and/or having unfair trading advantages.

However, environmental considerations have also played a part in advancing environmental policy, especially in recent years as the nature of environmental problems have increasingly been recognized and accepted. Scientific opinion has been important here, with, for example, research findings on the role of acid rain in killing aquatic life and trees being crucial to the adoption of clean air quality directives, and with research findings on biodiversity being crucial to the adoption of directives on the protection of fauna, flora and habitats.

Specific environmental incidents and mishaps have also played a part in advancing policy, by highlighting problems that cross borders and/or that cannot be tackled fully by a single member state alone. Most notable in this respect was the 1976 Seveso dioxin crisis in Italy, which led in 1982 to the Seveso Directive on industrial safety and the 'need to know' principle in EU environmental law.

So a number of factors have led to the EU facing pressures both from below (member states and interest groups) and above (the international community, especially the US) to adopt tougher environmental standards. Hildebrand (2005) identifies three phases in the history of EU environmental policy-making: 'incidental measures', between 1957 and 1971; the 'responsive period', between 1972 and1986; and the 'initiative phase', since 1986. The first period saw the adoption of nine directives and one regulation, with these measures being tied mainly to the harmonization of laws designed to reduce barriers to trade in the internal market. The watershed event of the second period was a Council agreement authorizing the Commission to draw up the first Environmental Action Programme (EAP), which came into effect from 1973. It and subsequent EAPs have served as strategic plans for EU environmental policy. The third, and current, period has been marked by an enormous broadening-out of environmental policy concerns, and by a movement away from the policy operating independently to being integrated with other policy areas. Prior to the SEA, there were around 60 pieces of environmental legislation in place, with most of them focused on reducing impediments to the internal market. After the inclusion of an environmental title in the SEA, the pace of environmental legislation quickened to such an extent that the EU adopted far more environmental legislation between 1989 and 1991 than in the previous 20 years. The explicit internal market linkage requirement prior to the SEA – lest the legislation be vulnerable to challenge in the ECJ – no longer constrained EU policy-makers, with the result that policy has come to be extended to include such diverse matters as GMOs, protection of natural habitats and animal species (with the protection of seals being especially high-profile), sewage treatment, and climate change (Jordan, 2005, p. 6).

∗   ∗   ∗

EU environmental policy has developed in a distinctly federal manner. Looking at the accumulation of EU environmental policy content and processes, it has become a more centralized policy than even exists in such federal states as Canada and the US. Simeon and Radin (2010, p. 361) explain that, because conservative governments occupied the executive at the national level in Canada and the US for many years, it 'left political space for both states and provinces to occupy, and the response in both countries has been similar. In climate change policy, for example, the lead in both has recently been taken by states and provinces – with interesting cross-border alliances between them' (such as the 2001 Climate Change Action Plan signed by the governors and premiers of the New England states and the Canadian Atlantic provinces and Quebec; see Selin and VanDeever, 2011, p. 11). Similarly, Vogel *et al.* (2010, p. 38) report that while in the EU packaging waste and climate change responsibility is shared between the EU and member states, it is a state responsibility in the US. Also, while the regulation of auto emissions is centralized in the EU it is shared between the national and state governments in the US. So, the EU has, in important respects, been more 'successful' in achieving consensus and promulgating standards throughout its constituent regional units (the member states) than have the federal governments of the US and Canada.

Policy leaders

Much has written about the differences in member states' attitudes towards the direction and pace of environmental policy. As Börzel (2005) has put it, there have been 'pace setters, foot draggers, and fence sitters', or, as Liefferink *et al.* (2009) have described it, there have been 'leaders' and 'laggards'. Six member states have been generally identified as environmental policy leaders. The 'green troika' of Denmark, Germany and the Netherlands led in the formative years of environmental policy, and they were joined, following the 1995 EFTA accessions, by Austria, Finland and Sweden. Greece, Ireland, Portugal and Spain have generally been classified as laggards, to which the CEECs are now added. The 'neutrals' list usually includes Belgium, France, Italy, Luxembourg and the UK (Liefferink and Andersen, 2005, p. 63).

Sweden is arguably the greenest of the leader sextet. This is, at least in part, because of its experience with acid rain falling on Swedish lakes, which scientists in the 1980s and 1990s increasingly suggested originated in emissions from industrial and power plants operating in the UK and Germany – a charge that these countries originally refused to accept. Sweden turned to international forums to plead its case that the high smokestacks Germany had built to improve domestic air quality were dispersing sulphur particulates over long distances (Schreurs, 2003, p. 93).

Germany's path to the green coalition was different from Sweden's, with a key factor being domestic politics. For years, German governments had resisted international pressure to reduce sulphur emissions, but in the 1980s much of the German public came to agree with the hypothesis advanced by the German scientist, Bernhard Ulrich, that German forests were dying from acid rain or, literally, 'forest death' (*Waldsterben*). As a partial consequence of this, the Green Party began to achieve electoral successes at both national and regional levels: an achievement that reached its peak when the Greens participated in coalition governments at the federal level between 1998 and 2005. The environment thus came to be placed firmly on the German political agenda and this green 'conversion' set the stage for German governments to use their political strength generally (though not invariably) to push for more stringent environmental laws at the EU level (see Schreurs, 2003, pp. 96, 100–1).

In addition to promoting higher standards, the Green sextet has also led in ensuring that EU law does not prevent them from adopting, if they so wish, higher domestic standards than those provided in EU law – the so-called 'environmental guarantee'. The guarantee is, however, not absolute but is subject to interpretation by the Commission and the Court.

'Green states' were very concerned that the CEECs, saddled with the industrial relics of communism and with scarce funds to invest in green manufacturing, would come together with less environmentally progressive member states to undermine environmental policy gains. So, in the accession negotiations, the EU required the CEECs to transpose virtually the entire *acquis* of EU environmental law before accession. Cohesion funds were also linked more closely to environmental projects, partially in the hope that this would help CEECs to implement EU environmental law.

Naturally, 'the green coalition' of member states does not always act or hold together. There are, for example, areas where one member state, as a result of domestic pressures and its own circumstances and vulnerabilities, takes the lead in a particular area. So, for example, the Netherlands, driven by its vulnerability to rising sea levels, provided early leadership in the late 1990s on climate change policy, and Germany, reacting to strict US air quality standards that had a negative impact on German vehicle manufacturers' prices, took the policy lead in the 1980s and early 1990s in requiring that cars manufactured in the EU include catalytic converters.

Liefferink and Anderson (2005, pp. 51–2) identify four distinct policy strategies that 'pioneers' have adopted in relation to environmental policy:

- *Pusher-by-example*: for example, Denmark's unilateral introduction of a CO_2 tax.
- *Constructive pusher*: for example, the Urban Waste Water Directive of 1991 (dealing with the collection, treatment and discharge of domestic waste water and from certain industrial sectors) is based on standards promulgated by Denmark, Germany and the Netherlands to mirror their national standards.
- *Defensive forerunner*: for example, the Danish bottle law and ban on aluminium cans, which the Commission challenged in the ECJ on internal market grounds. When the ECJ upheld the Danish law, the EU used Denmark's law in the 1994 Packaging Waste Directive (aimed at harmonizing national measures to prevent or reduce the impact of packaging and packaging waste on the environment).
- *Opt-outer*: for example, Germany and the Netherlands banned PCP (a wood preservative), which France challenged and won its case in a 1994 ECJ decision.

Key features of environmental policy

Objectives and principles

The TEU and TFEU address environmental policy in several places. The TEU (Article 3) covers the broad issue of sustainable development, while the TFEU covers more specific matters in Title XX: Environment, which the Lisbon Treaty brought over largely intact from the TEC. The major objectives of environment policy, set out in Article 191.1 of the TFEU, cover a wide range of environmental policy matters, including preserving the environment, protecting human health, managing natural resources, and – newly-established by the Lisbon Treaty – a commitment to 'promoting measures at the international level to deal with regional or worldwide environmental problems, and in particular combating climate change'.

EU environmental policy is based on several principles, most notably 'the polluter pays', preventative action, a focus on the pollution media (air, water, soil and so on), and the precautionary principle. While the first three of these are commonly accepted environmental policy principles among advanced industrialized democracies, the precautionary principle sets the EU apart, particularly from the USA. The general meaning of the principle is that if a policy or action has a suspected risk but scientific evidence is not clear, the burden of proof that the policy or action is not harmful falls on those proposing the policy or action. In practice, this initially engendered substantial confusion as to its effect and application, especially when the ECJ began to apply the principle to food safety cases. The Commission attempted to clear up some of this uncertainty with its 'Communication on the Precautionary Principle' (European Commission, 2000), but nevertheless, the principle remains subject to interpretation. What, however, is not subject to interpretation is that the principle informs *all* EU policies dealing with health and wellness, which contrasts with the US, where, as Applegate (2000, p. 213) notes, there is a 'precautionary preference' or 'precautionary approach' rather than the stricter management implied by the precautionary principle.

Environmental action programmes

EU environmental policy is advanced through periodic strategic plans put forward by the Commission after extensive consultation with all key actors. Action plans focus on specific priorities for the stated time period. There have been, to the time of writing, six Environmental Action Programmes (EAPs), and the seventh was expected to be released by the end of 2012 (Committee of the Regions, 2012) – it was held up, at least in part, because the Commission felt environmental issues were addressed in the Europe 2020 (see below) strategy for growth, an opinion the Environmental Council did not share (EurActiv, 2012b).

EU environmental policy is an accumulation of the EAPs that have been in place since 1973, with the key aspects of current environmental policy having been established through earlier EAPs. So, rather than over-turning previous policy, EAPs have had a cumulative effect.

Reflecting that, at the start of the new millennium, conservative governments were in power in the majority of member states, the Sixth EAP (2002–12) involved a rather 'cautious' approach focused on natural resources and waste, environment and health, nature and biodiversity, and climate change – with the latter being tied directly to renewable energy and to a special focus on the economic benefits of green technology (van Renssen, 2011). The Sixth EAP also laid a great emphasis on 'balancing' economic growth and competitiveness with environ-mental needs. The theme of the Seventh EAP (2012 – no end date determined at the time of writing) is 'Greening Europe, 2050 vision' and is influenced by a combination of Europe 2020 and the eurozone financial crisis and economic downturn. Therefore, there is a strong emphasis on taking leadership on green technology and other aspects of environmental policy that promise to combine economic growth and green practices synergistically. Its major features are as follows (Council of the European Union, 2012a):

- Promoting a green and competitive European economy.
- Protecting biodiversity.
- Promoting human health.
- Developing a comprehensive 'EU Adaptation Strategy' with respect to climate change.
- Pursuing better implementation of environmental policies.

Global leadership

The EU seeks to be a leading international environ-mental policy actor. It is fair to say that, in terms of its ambitions, if not always its achievements, in the 2000s the EU has indeed been a leading international envi-ronmental advocate and innovator (on this point, see Kelemen and Vogel, 2010; Vogel, 2005.) Thus the EU led the push for, and its member states signed, the Kyoto Protocol, but the US neither led nor signed. The EU has also pioneered the global emission trading system (carbon trading scheme), a policy that the US federal government had first championed.

However, being an environmental champion and innovator can place domestic manufacturers at a disadvantage, so the EU has pursued twin strategies of 'greening' international organizations and steering its external trade policies to focus on the nexus of competitiveness and green initiatives (Kelemen and Vogel, 2010).

Internal tensions can thus arise from trying to be an international environmental policy leader. However, it seems likely that climate change will stay firmly on the EU's agenda. Indeed, the importance that climate change is now being given was signalled by it being accorded its first treaty recognition via the Lisbon Treaty, and by the splitting of DG Environment into two DGs in 2010 – DG Environment and DG Climate Action – with the latter being tasked to propose and manage climate change policy and to represent the EU in international nego-tiations. However, with the clock ticking, it is probable that the EU will focus increasingly on adaptation (preventing damage from global warming) rather than exclusively on mitigation (combating global warming). Indeed, adaptation is vital because, as Behrens *et al.* (2010) note, many member states are likely to be negatively affected very much by climate change – with, for example higher sea levels covering vast tracts of land and causing massive flooding across Europe (Rübbelke and Aakre, 2008, p. 11).

But while the EU is trying to provide a lead on tackling climate change, not all of its member states are following. The EU will not meet its Kyoto obliga-tions, with the lack of binding national targets putting pressure on the gap between the EU's commitments and member state implementation (Gardner, 2011; Parker and Karlsson, 2010). And non-member states are certainly not following the EU's attempted policy lead, as was demonstrated clearly at the 2009 Copenhagen United Nations Climate Change Conference, when EU attempts to press ambitious targets resulted in it being pretty well marginalized in the negotiations.

However, the Copenhagen Summit experience does not mean that the EU cannot find international allies regarding some environmental issues. As Egenhofer and Georgiev (2010, p. 3) argue, 'despite EU disappointment with the outcome of Copenhagen, it is not true to say that the US has forsaken the EU in this matter'. In their analysis, the US needs the EU more than ever, because the transatlantic partnership will be essential as a counterweight to China and India in future international negotiations on all sorts of policy issues, including the environment. So, for example, if the US and the EU – the two largest markets for developing countries – agree to implement shadow carbon pricing (border taxes on products imported from countries with lax carbon standards), this will be a key lever to use in persuading China, India and other developing countries to agree international standards to reduce carbon emissions (Egenhofer and Georgiev, 2010, p. 4).

Environment policy processes

Environmental policy-making exhibits a number of distinctive policy-making features that merit comment.

Regarding environmental law-making, most EU environmental laws are enacted as directives so as to allow maximum flexibility when transposing into national law. Since the Maastricht Treaty, environmental policy has been subject to the co-decision – which has now, post-Lisbon Treaty, become 'the ordinary' – legislative procedure. Weale (2005, p. 336) writes that a consequence of this has been that the EP 'has had more influence on environmental measures than is typically true for more well-established national parliaments'. This influence has also been facilitated by the EP's committee system, which encourages MEPs to specialize in particular spheres of EU policy such as the environment, and by the longevity of many MEPs that has enabled several of them to establish solid environmental policy credentials. The EP's influence has also been aided by green political representation in the EP. The importance of this representation should not be overstated as 'Les Verts' in the Parliament have always been dwarfed in numbers by the larger political groups, and have seen their potential influence further weakened by being split into two political groups in the 2004–9 and 2009–14 Parliaments. Nevertheless, their presence is certainly felt, and is assisted by the adoption of green

platforms by many major political parties in member states, which help to ensure that the EP's main political groups pay close attention to environmental concerns.

As for the implementation of legislation, the environmental policy area is notorious for member states delaying or improperly transposing EU directives. Prominent among the reasons for implementation difficulties are cost (environmental legislation dealing with such topics as clean air and clean sea-bathing water can involve very heavy capital expenditure), cross-border liaison (many environmental problems are not confined within national borders), and cultural opposition (there are very differing attitudes within member states towards such issues as the preservation of wildlife and the disposal of waste materials). None the less, while the Commission expresses its displeasure in its annual internal market scorecard regarding aspects of environmental policy implementation, the record is not as bad as it is often portrayed. Indeed, the record of EU environmental policy implementation came out rather well in a time-series study in which researchers compared 21 European countries, Japan, Mexico, and the US on such causal variables as culture, economic development, institutional structure and EU membership. The last named of these categories exhibited the highest explanatory value for strong domestic environmental outputs as measured by 'strictest available policy option'. The study, in short, indicated the widespread adoption of EU policies (Liefferink et al., 2009).

While the Community method is, of course, used for the making of environmental legislation, the environmental policy area has in recent years seen an increasing use of soft policy instruments and of 'new approach' policy processes that emphasize voluntary co-operation based on economic incentives. The EU's emissions trading scheme (cap and trade) has become a large-scale illustration of this policy, which has provided incentives for businesses to reduce their pollution. It is also seen, for example, in the EU Ecolabel, which involves the EU permitting the affixation of this label on products meeting EU environmental standards (thereby, presumably, increasing sales among environmentally-conscious consumers).

The European Environment Agency (EEA), established in 1994, represents another example of the 'new approach' in environmental policy. The EEA is an 'information agency' tasked with managing European environment information and acting as an observation network of national officials and experts to monitor environmental issues. The EEA is also responsible for providing DG Environment with data, analytical reports, and a 'state-of-the-art environment report', the latter being produced every five years (Martens, 2010, p. 889).

Growth and Competitiveness Policies: The Lisbon Strategy and Europe 2020

Not all of the EU's policy efforts to promote economic growth and competitiveness are based on opening-up the market and exposing it to internal competition. Much policy activity involves EU-level market intervention and direction. In part this is because of the consensus among EU policy-makers that the market should not result in a race to the bottom in terms of such matters as product standards, workers' rights, and protections for consumers. In part too it is because it is recognized that the creation of an internal market based on economically liberal principles is not enough in itself to enable Europe to be as competitive on the world stage as it could be. Direct EU interventionist activity is seen as being necessary for such tasks as promoting innovation, increasing spending on research, providing vocational training, and increasing the numbers of young people and women in paid employment.

Since 2000, much of this intervention has been framed and developed within the context of the Lisbon Strategy and its successor – Europe 2020. In essence, what the Lisbon Strategy and Europe 2020 have involved is the EU developing a wide range of 'positive' policies to tackle problems of lack of competitiveness, low growth and high unemployment.

Lisbon I and II

In March 2000, EU Heads of Government convened a special European Council meeting in Lisbon to address increasing anxiety that there was an underlying malaise in the EU economy. Particular concerns were: that, regardless of the progress that was being made in deepening the internal market, the European economy was still not growing sufficiently quickly; that globalization was posing new competitive challenges, especially in innovation and knowledge-based industries; that while European workers and citizens certainly were entitled to reasonable levels of social protection, there were aspects of national social systems that were holding back economic growth in the face of 'ever fiercer global competition' (European Commission, 2010a, p. 2); and that there was a persistent problem of relatively low levels of employment in some regions and member states.

In response to these challenges, the Lisbon summit launched a ten-year programme intended to make the EU 'the most dynamic and knowledge-based economy in the world' (Council of the European Union, 2000, p. 2). In practice, as will be shown below, the process launched at Lisbon to improve growth, employment and competitiveness, entails three sets of policy frameworks: Lisbon I (2001–5); Lisbon II (2005–10); and Europe 2020 (2010–20).

An emphasis on full employment featured prominently at the Lisbon summit. This was partly because the Amsterdam Treaty had created a new Employment Title in the TEC, the purpose of which was to encourage and exhort member states to regard the promotion of employment as a matter of high priority and common concern. As a follow-up to the Title, at a special 'jobs summit' held in Luxembourg in November 1997, the Council agreed to a procedure for giving employment promotion a higher priority and a more focused approach. But there was a growing unease among many policy actors – not least in the Commission and in some national governments – that the Employment Strategy was sitting alongside, rather than being fully integrated with, other economic programmes and planning instruments – notably the Broad Economic Policy Guidelines (BEPGs), the Stability and Growth Pact (see Chapter 10), and the (still continuing) internal market programme. It was felt that these different components needed to be pulled together more within the framework of a broad and eye-catching response to the social, and more especially the economic, challenges facing the Union.

The launch of the Lisbon Strategy in 2000 was thus a response to a number of developments that had at their core the recognition that the European economy was still not sufficiently competitive in the increasingly globalized economy. At the heart of the Strategy was to be the pursuit of economic growth and socially sensitive policies that were to be based in large part on policy co-ordination mechanisms and instruments. Prominent among these mechanisms and instruments were to be: the widespread use of the open method of co-ordination (OMC); a stronger guiding and co-ordinating role for the European Council to ensure more coherent strategic direction and effective monitoring of progress; and a meeting of the European Council to be held every spring to define 'relevant mandates' and ensure they were being followed-up (Council of the European Union, 2001, p. 4).

As was explained in Chapter 7, the rather loose and semi-voluntaristic nature of OMC was seen as being useful for the Strategy because it allowed for policy development in areas where the member states would not have permitted themselves to be legally bound to specific policies or to meeting specified targets. The intention and hope was that OMC would 'work' as the core policy approach of the Strategy because it would be seen to be based on striking a balance between alternative and contested policy approaches, between EU competence and national competence, between policy convergence and variation, and between the use of legislation and of co-ordination.

However, potentially advantageous though the OMC appeared to be, questions were soon being asked as to whether its use really was helping Lisbon goals to be achieved. It quickly became clear that most of the Lisbon goals were not going to be met by 2010. What, many practitioners and observers began to ask, was the problem? Were the goals themselves too ambitious and/or vague, or was the use of OMC insufficiently robust, with some states taking advantage of its voluntarism, albeit pressurized voluntarism, to avoid implementing policies they did not like or found to be too expensive? (There is an extensive academic literature on some of these criticisms of the Lisbon Strategy OMC: see, for example, Borrás and Jacobsson, 2004; Daly, 2006.)

Such concerns about the Lisbon Strategy resulted in the March 2004 meeting of the European Council asking the former prime minister of the Netherlands, Wim Kok, to head a high-level group of experts to conduct an independent review of the operation of the Strategy. Their report concluded that the existing Lisbon Strategy was overloaded and suffered from a number of governance failings. A number of areas for urgent action were identified, including increasing 'Europe's attractiveness for researchers and scientists, making research and development a top priority, and more actively promoting the use of information and communication technologies' (Kok, 2004, p. 6).

Basing its action on the Kok report, the Spring 2005 European Council meeting agreed to a relaunch of the Lisbon Strategy as 'A Partnership for Growth and Employment' (European Council, 2005). This relaunch has generally come to be known as Lisbon II. With there now being a centre-right majority in the European Council, Lisbon II was characterized by a more neo-liberal discourse than Lisbon I, with a stronger emphasis on competitiveness, productivity and flexibility. Significantly, there was much less emphasis on social inclusion compared with Lisbon I (which had been agreed when there had been a centre-left majority in the European Council), and so the commitment to full employment was played down. As for OMC, it was retained as a core policy approach, but its limitations were recognized and attempts were made to tackle them – in particular by assigning greater 'national ownership' to national plans and implementing strategies.

The Spring 2006 European Council meeting added to the 2005 relaunch by agreeing on four priority areas as the pillars of the new Strategy: pillars that subsequent spring summits confirmed. The pillars were: the promotion of knowledge and innovation; unlocking business potential, especially of small and medium-sized enterprises (SMEs); investing in people and the modernization of labour markets; and tackling the linked problems of energy supply and climate change (European Council, 2006).

Europe 2020

With Lisbon II showing little evidence of having been more successful in achieving its goals than Lisbon I, discussions about its successor naturally engendered questions about the ability of the EU to deliver an effective industrial policy for Europe when much of the existing policy had access to only relatively weak policy instruments and when there was only a very small budget available. How could the EU foster high economic growth without the authority to enact a strong industrial policy?

The new competitiveness and growth strategy – called Europe 2020 – was introduced by the Commission in March 2010 and adopted by the European Council at its June 2010 summit (European Council, 2010). It was launched to a background of three sets of factors that shaped its nature: economic crisis and decline; disappointment with what Lisbon I and II had produced in terms of results; and an even firmer centre-right majority in the European Council.

While in most respects it is broadly similar to the Lisbon Strategy in its overarching aims and policy mechanisms, Europe 2020 is, as Copeland and Papadimitriou (2012: 236) put it, 'packaged within a different normative discourse of competitiveness'. It is based on three broad objectives of smart growth, sustainable growth and inclusive growth. Policy activities within these objectives are listed in Box 9.5, which sets out the Commission's overview of Europe 2020.

In terms of its governance, like the Lisbon Strategy, Europe 2020 relies heavily on the OMC, but is intended to be more cohesive, flexible and partnership-based. Much of it is to be carried out through three-year National Reform Programmes (NRPs), framed within Integrated Guidelines. By replacing the previously used National Action Plans (NAPs) with NRPs, the EU has consolidated in one place, and in a single programme, national policies and activities that under the NAP system had been fragmented. As under the Lisbon systems, the Commission keeps watch on national developments and issues recommendations to member states, but more emphasis is laid on it being an encourager and a support to the member states than on being a censor of unsatisfactory performance (see European Commission, 2012f, for country-specific recommendations).

An important feature of Europe 2020 is that it is located within the 'European semester', an annual cycle of macroeconomic, structural and budgetary policy co-ordination focused on promoting economic growth, launched in 2010. It involves member states collectively agreeing on headline goals and submitting approved NRPs and EMU Stability and Convergence Programmes (as required under the SGP: see Chapter 10). During the 'European semester', member states must submit their reports and the Commission offers policy guidance and makes recommendations based on the NRPs and Stability and Growth Programmes before national government budgets are finalized (European Commission, 2012k).

The impact of the Lisbon Strategy/Europe 2020

It is not clear whether the Lisbon Strategy and Europe 2020 have had much independent beneficial effect. The main points made by their defenders are: they have been useful in making policy actors in the member states much more aware of the need for far-reaching, comprehensive and co-ordinated economic reforms; R&D investment has grown; and in most member states prior to the post-2008 economic and financial crisis growth was increasing, many new jobs were being created, and unemployment was falling. The main points made by the sceptics are: it has not been demonstrated that economic improvements in the 2000s are *because* of Lisbon/Europe 2020; clear evidence of failure is seen in the abandonment in 2005 of the 2010 'headline goal' and in the failure of Lisbon II to achieve by 2010 its goals of a 70 per cent employment rate and an average R&D investment rate of 3 per cent; and the OMC has not succeeded in its aim of opening-up policy processes to national social partners. (For analyses of the impact of the Strategy, see Armstrong *et al.*, 2008; Begg, 2007; Copeland and Papadimitriou, 2012; Tilford and Whyte, 2010; and the European Commission's Annual Progress Reports on Growth and Jobs .)

However, any assessments of the impact of the Lisbon Strategy and of Europe 2020 face several difficulties. First, the performance indicators of economic reforms take time to appear in official statistics. Second, economic performance depends on many factors, some of which are not part of, and are beyond the control of, the Strategy and Europe 2020. Most prominent among these factors are global economic circumstances and economic cycles, and, within the EU itself, the success or otherwise of the euro and its associated policy mechanisms. Third, it may be that some of the economic improvements that have occurred in the 2000s would have been achieved in any event. After all, in the 1990s national governments were becoming increasingly aware of the need for structural reforms and that considerably more than the internal market programme and EMU were needed to resolve all of Europe's problems in an ever more globalized and competitive economic system. The need for further far-reaching reforms, not least on the supply-side, was progressively being recognized

Box 9.5

Europe 2020

Headline targets

- Raise the employment rate of the population aged 20–64 from the current 69% to at least 75%.
- Achieve the target of investing 3% of GDP in R&D, in particular by improving the conditions for R&D investment by the private sector and developing a new indicator to track innovation.
- Reduce greenhouse gas emissions by at least 20% compared to 1990 levels, or by 30% if the conditions are right; increase the share of renewable energy in our final energy consumption to 20%; and achieve a 20% increase in energy efficiency.
- Reduce the share of early school leavers to 10% from the current 15% and increase the share of the population aged 30–34 having completed tertiary education from 31% to at least 40%.
- Reduce the number of Europeans living below national poverty lines by 25%, lifting 20 million out of poverty.

Smart growth	Sustainable growth	Inclusive growth
Innovation EU flagship initiative 'Innovation Union', to improve framework conditions and access to finance for research and innovation to strengthen the innovation chain and boost levels of investment throughout the Union.	*Climate, energy and mobility* EU flagship initiative 'Resource Efficient Europe' to help decouple economic growth from the use of resources, by de-carbonizing the economy, increasing the use of renewable sources, modernizing the transport sector and promoting energy efficiency.	*Employment and skills* EU flagship initiative 'An Agenda for New Skills and Jobs' to modernize labour markets by facilitating labour mobility and the development of skills throughout the lifecycle with a view to increasing labour participation and better match labour supply and demand.
Education EU flagship initiative 'Youth on the Move', to enhance the performance of education systems and to reinforce the international attractiveness of Europe's higher education.	*Competitiveness* EU flagship initiative 'An Industrial Policy for the Globalization Era' to improve the business environment, especially for SMEs, and to support the development of a strong and sustainable industrial base able to compete globally.	*Fighting poverty* EU flagship initiative 'European Platform against Poverty', to ensure social and territorial cohesion such that the benefits of growth and jobs are widely shared, and people experiencing poverty and social exclusion are enabled to live in dignity and take an active part in society.
Digital society EU flagship initiative 'A Digital Agenda for Europe', to speed up the roll-out of high-speed internet and reap the benefits of a digital single market for households and firms.		

Source: European Commission, 2010f, p. 30.

and, in consequence, policy learning and policy transfer from successful states was increasing in intensity. Fourth, a very wide range of different, and different sorts of, activities, many with different types of aims, come under the Lisbon Strategy and Europe 2020 umbrellas. As Papadimitriou (2012, p. 4) puts it: 'The overwhelming diversity of targets, monitoring tools and actor constellations within each policy area provide for a government mosaic that speaks of no 'single' Lisbon but, indeed, several.' Fifth, many of the policies and activities that have been part of, or have been associated with, the Strategy and Europe 2020 are not new but rather have, in one form or another, long been under way, albeit under different headings. These assorted policies and activities, many of which have been at least partly successful, include the opening-up of the services sector, the strengthening of EU R&D policy, the promotion of energy efficiency, the employment strategy, the use of EU budgetary resources to improve competitiveness, the Bologna Process for improving the recognition of university degrees and for improving student and faculty mobility, and the rate of secondary school completions (which made progress in the Lisbon years; see Tilford and Whyte, 2010, p. 75).

* * *

European economic union can be advanced in two broad ways: through strengthened horizontal federal relations, with the EU sometimes as the co-ordinating actor and in other cases through member states working among themselves; and through more vertical federal relations, where the EU has rule-making authority and implementing powers. The latter is never the preferred option (except in crisis situations) because it is a leap into the unknown; naturally, under *ceteris paribus* conditions citizens prefer policy to be set at a local level.

Arguably, the Lisbon Strategy and Europe 2020 have helped to advance both horizontal and vertical integration. Regarding horizontal integration, there is no doubt that the Strategy and Europe 2020 have greatly extended the policy spheres in which the EU

now shares policy competence in interventionist growth and competitiveness policies with its member states. Regarding vertical integration, the Strategy and Lisbon 2020 can be viewed not so much in terms of concrete achievements as in terms of preparing the ground for deeper integration by steering the policy rhetoric in this direction. As such, Lisbon and Europe 2020 may be regarded as much as ways of 'thinking' and 'believing' about the possibilities of European integration as of 'doing'.

Conclusions

This chapter has examined a number of internal policies, which the federal integration model that was advanced in Chapter 2 suggests are necessary to achieve economic union. Unlike the internal market stage of integration, which relies heavily on the removal of artificial barriers to the circulation of goods, capital, people and services, the policies examined in this chapter have required 'positive' action at the EU level.

While the CAP is the oldest of the policies that have been examined in the chapter, it is, like the others, subject to calls for reform. Indeed, most of the policies that have been examined in the chapter are scheduled for an overhaul in the next few years. CAP reforms will bring agriculture more into line with internal market principles (especially in light of the anticipated rise in the world demand for food) while also tying financial aid increasingly to rural development, biodiversity, conservation and animal welfare. Cohesion policy will be more closely 'Lisbonized', especially as the EU looks to build budget synergies into its action plans. Environmental policy will continue the now-established pattern of being tied closely to climate change and to energy efficiency and security. Finally, Europe 2020 will be a test of the EU's ability to generate real progress in 'difficult' policy areas – such as employment, pensions, and research and innovation – which to date have generated much activity but rather unimpressive 'real' progress.

Chapter 10

Economic and Monetary Union

This chapter focuses on Economic and Monetary Union (EMU). That is, it focuses on the economic and monetary system which has its heart the single currency – the euro – that has been adopted by most of the EU's member states.

The EMU project has always been controversial. At the centre of the controversy have been different views, among both policy practitioners and observers, as to whether a stable European currency system can exist when:

- there are great economic differences – in terms of both levels of economic development and the nature of economic structures – between the states participating in the system;
- the single currency is not underpinned by extensive economic integration; and
- the EMU system is accompanied by only weak political integration, with no strong central body with the authority to move significant economic and financial resources around the system or to impose necessary policies on states within the system.

Though widely acknowledged and debated, these potential weaknesses of the single currency system were largely brushed aside when EMU was being created in the 1990s. However, in the 2000s, and more particularly since the onset of the global financial crisis in 2007/8, they have moved to the centre of policy deliberations on EMU. In these deliberations, the very continuance of the EMU system has been questioned widely.

This chapter has been structured in such a way as to offer insights into these problems with and debates surrounding EMU. Much of the chapter is concerned with providing readers with a good basis for evaluating both the current operation of EMU and its possible future direction. This necessarily requires some abstraction and coverage of economic theories of monetary and fiscal unions.

The chapter begins with an examination of the economic and political reasons that explain the existence of EMU and of a single currency. The second section provides an overview of the establishment of EMU. The third section discusses EMU's institutions. The fourth section reviews the debate over the appropriateness of fiscal and monetary union. The fifth and sixth sections explain the two key facets of EMU – monetary policy and fiscal policy. These sections also examine the eurozone sovereign debt and banking crises. The seventh section examines options that exist, and in some cases have been partially acted upon, for creating a more stable EMU.

Why a Single Currency?

European nations attempted at various times in the nineteenth and twentieth centuries to construct and operate currency unions, but these were either short-lived or confined to limited geographical areas. These failures, however, did not diminish the sense among European business leaders and policy-makers that exchange rate stability was essential for economic growth and competitiveness. Therefore, as Europe – or, at least, Western Europe – reacted in the post-Second World War period to the dangers of excessive nationalism, and as the EC internal market began to be built from the late 1950s, the ground became increasingly favourable for returning to economic, and more particularly, monetary integration.

Taking advantage of EEC Treaty provisions that had opened the door for economic policy co-operation and co-ordination (Articles 2 and 3), from the early 1960s the European Commission began to submit memoranda and reports to the Council of Ministers suggesting that the policies of member states 'would be incomplete, and therefore possibly ineffective, if no comparable action were taken in the field of monetary policy' (European Commission, 1962). By 1968, with the customs union completed ahead of schedule, the groundwork for what eventually became EMU was being laid (European Commission, 1968a, 1968b).

Why would European states relinquish their currency for membership of a multi-national single currency system in which there is a single monetary policy and national macroeconomic policies are centrally co-ordinated and monitored? There is no single answer to this question since a number of considerations have been involved, the relative importance of which has varied between European states. Some of the considerations have been economic and some political, though separating the two is difficult since they overlap in practice.

Economic factors

There were many economic factors driving the decision to develop a single currency system in the years leading up to its launch in 1999, most of which were tied to the internal market. These factors can be divided, albeit imperfectly, into three sets of concerns.

The first concern centred on unfair competition and 'fair play' in the internal market, the second focused on the ways in which multiple currencies interfered with the internal market's completion, and the third involved deepening the internal market.

Fair play

Starting with 'fair play', by the mid-1960s some economic policy interests – with German exporters taking the lead – began to argue that a single currency would eventually be needed if the emerging European market were to function fairly and efficiently. This was seen to be so because the then existing co-operative arrangements among West European states of pegging their rates against an anchor currency – the dollar – usually fell apart at the first sign of economic distress (see below). EC member states that ran up large trade deficits were able to simply engage in 'competitive devaluations' to bring their current accounts balance back into line. So when trade competitors such as France or Italy, and later Spain – major markets for German goods – devalued their currencies in order to gain an advantage in both intra-EU and international trade, German firms and firms in those countries with Deutschmark-linked currencies would raise the spectre of protectionist remedies (thus, potentially weakening the nascent internal market).

The fair play question became particularly problematic with respect to the CAP, which at the time was the EC's signature common policy. Devaluations of currencies – such as the devaluation of the French franc against the US dollar by 11.1 per cent in August 1969 – had the effect of increasing the price of imported agricultural produce. Higher prices for agricultural goods then induced French farmers to over-produce, triggering more CAP payments for France. To deal with this unanticipated problem of divergent exchange rates among European currencies and currency devaluations, the EC introduced a dual exchange rate system, with 'green rates' being used to calculate CAP payments.

Exchange rate risk

The second concern involved the problems of multiple currencies in a single market. Foremost among these problems were the vicissitudes of exchange rate instability for the EC's rapidly growing internal trade, which hurt smaller export-dependent economies in particular. Small- and medium-sized businesses were also very vulnerable to exchange rate risks because they operate on lower profit and volume margins and often cannot afford expensive forward exchange contracts and other currency hedging financial strategies.

In the early postwar years, uncertainties associated with exchange rate fluctuations were resolved by the 'Bretton Woods' system, which worked by member states pegging their currency rates to a 1 per cent fluctuation rate to the US dollar, which in turn was based on the gold standard. However, speculative pressures on the US dollar throughout the late 1960s and early 1970s (because of domestic inflationary policies that were mainly a consequence of printing dollars to finance simultaneously the Vietnam War and President Lyndon Johnson's Great Society) caused increasing exchange rate disruptions for European currencies, with many Bretton Woods' members being obliged to devalue their national currencies to prop up the US dollar's value and preserve the peg.

During this period, despite occasional revaluation, the Deutschmark was undervalued against the dollar, which, naturally, German exporters preferred (Giersch, 2002, p. 237). Those German interests that were affected negatively by higher domestic prices, however, found a formidable ally in the Bundesbank. This anti-inflationary domestic coalition was increasingly unwilling to countenance the price instability each time the dollar weakened, preferring low inflation to the security of the Bretton Woods' peg. So, too, the French president, Charles de Gaulle, chafed under what he saw as the US taking advantage of its 'exorbitant privilege', and he began to demand that some of France's dollar reserves be paid back in gold (Chang, 2009, p. 21).

In the meantime, the US balance of payments continued to deteriorate. A floating currency (in which the value is determined by markets) became increasingly attractive to American policy-makers – in marked contrast to the European preference for fixed rates (which was in no small part because of the inconvenience and costs of fluctuating rates in a common market). As a result of the weakened dollar, in 1971 US President Nixon ended dollar convertibility to gold and the next year allowed the dollar to float.

Naturally, this currency instability threatened to damage intra-EC trade. So, in 1972, European leaders devised the 'snake in the tunnel', consisting of intra-EC currency bands of 2.25 per cent. However, currency speculation made it difficult to maintain agreed bands, with the result that countries moved in and out of the snake. Eventually, the snake stabilized, but only with the Deutschmark as the anchor currency – so that by the late 1970s, shadowing the Deutschmark (and surrendering monetary authority) was the path to European exchange rate stability. But most countries did not wish to have their fiscal and monetary policy so controlled by German central bankers in the Bundesbank, and the sentiment was returned by the Germans who did not wish to assume a hegemonic role in monetary policy. Therefore, in 1979 – under Franco-German leadership – the European Monetary System (EMS), detailed below, was launched.

As the internal market deepened, capital moved more freely, culminating in the abolition of capital controls as part of the relaunch of the single market in the mid-1980s. This placed further pressures on EC member states to manage their currencies more effectively (Chang, 2009, p. 43).

Cost-savings and convenience

In addition to its perceived fair play and currency stability advantages, a single currency also promised a number of additional, more specific, benefits. One was the elimination of the transaction costs of exchanging currencies, which, it was hoped, would help to expand activity in the single market through cost-savings and convenience to European businesses and consumers alike. Another benefit was price transparency, which, it was hoped, would also benefit the internal market by encouraging trade across member state borders as a result of consumers being able to engage more easily in comparative pricing.

* * *

The key economic driving force behind EMU – both when it was being built and still today – has thus been the perceived economic benefits it offers to producers and consumers. Foremost among these perceived benefits are the elimination of exchange rate fluctuations, security of purchasing power, the removal of transaction costs, and price transparency.

Political factors

A number of scholars have explored the intersection of domestic, European and international politics in the run up to EMU (see, for example, Chang, 2009; Dyson and Featherstone, 1999; Mazzucelli, 1999; Moravcsik, 1998). A point they all make is that political considerations as well as economic considerations lay behind the creation of EMU. An important aspect of these political considerations was that, because the establishment of a monetary union is typically accompanied by the development of centralized political institutions, integrationists saw such a union as a pathway to political integration (see McNamara, 1999, p. 456; McNamara, 2004, p. 19).

However, European leaders differed in their perceptions of what they thought the political advantages of EMU would be. For smaller states, support for the single currency was in large part conditioned by the twin factors of internationalization and the internal market, which had resulted in them being able to exercise little independent monetary power and being subject to forces beyond their borders. Their central banks had little manoeuvrability and were shadowing the Deutschmark. EMU would mean that, by adopting the currency, they would share responsibility for monetary policy and exercise at least some monetary decision-making power.

The differing political perceptions of EMU by the EU's 'big four' states (France, Germany, Italy and the UK) were outlined in Chapter 4, so will not be repeated here. A few points about the two main political 'drivers' of EMU – France and Germany – do, however, merit further comment.

With its much larger economy, France was less beholden to the Deutschmark than were smaller European states, but as its economy became more integrated in the internal market it too had to accept that only Germany had the fiscal and monetary stability to manage Europe's anchor currency. Indeed, prior to the adoption of the euro, wags liked to suggest that the independence of French monetary policy consisted of the 15 or so minutes that elapsed between the Bundesbank changing German interest rates and the Bank of France following suit with French interest rates. So France also wished to use a single currency to recover – albeit on a pooled basis – monetary power.

This wish was intensified with German unification in 1990.

French motives were, however, not just based on wanting to recover monetary power and 'rein in' Germany. They were also global in ambition: France hoped to build a European monetary area on the ashes of Bretton Woods that could challenge the dominance of the dollar and the yen in capital transactions.

Germany was much less in need of a single European currency than France: it was the EU's largest economy (and the world's third largest); it enjoyed high economic growth; its central bank – the Bundesbank – was as independent as any central bank could be in the modern world; inflation was under control; and external trade was being advanced via a highly successful policy commonly referred to as 'competitive disinflation' (Chang, 2009, pp. 37 and 39). Germany's exporters broadly supported the creation of a European currency because it would protect them from competitive devaluations, but there were also powerful domestic interests, backed by the Bundesbank, which opposed giving up the Deutschmark for a single currency – primarily on the grounds such a move risked being inflationary.

With the economic case for German involvement in a single currency thus being, at best, questionable, political factors were crucial in determining its stance. Of particular importance, especially post-unification, was a strongly felt need among most German political leaders to reassure Europe that Germany wanted, as Chancellor Kohl famously put it, a Germany in Europe and not a German Europe.

French and German political reasons for supporting a single currency were thus very different. But despite the differences, the leaders of both states increasingly took the view that the political advantages of a single currency outweighed the costs. Thus was formed the close partnership between Chancellor Kohl and President Mitterrand that, in the late 1980s and first half of the 1990s, produced the political foundations and core conditions of EMU, including the irreversibility of a single currency and the requirement that applicant member states meet specified economic requirements before gaining currency admittance.

The Building of Economic and Monetary Union

The European Monetary System

As can be seen from the timeline in Box 10.1, a major step towards EMU was taken in 1969 when the leaders of the six EC states declared their intention to establish an economic and monetary union by 1980. The prime minister of Luxembourg, Pierre Werner, was asked to prepare a feasibility report, which was issued in 1970. The Werner Report envisaged a 10-year transition period that would end with the establishment of full monetary union.

Building on the Werner Report – especially its recommendation for a fluctuation band for European currencies – and on the experience of 'the snake' (see above), the European Monetary System (EMS) was launched in 1979, with all EC member states apart from the UK joining. (The UK later joined briefly, in1990–2.)

The EMS was based on three key components:

- A basket of currencies called the European Currency Unit (ECU).
- Within what was called the Exchange Rate Mechanism (ERM), currencies were pegged to each other within bands that could float by no more than 2.25 per cent (Italy negotiated a 6 per cent exception). If a currency reached within 75 per cent of the maximum fluctuation margin, the currency was considered divergent and the relevant national authorities were required to take remedial action (lower or increase interest rates and alter fiscal policy). If the maximum fluctuation margin was breeched, central banks were required to intervene by buying and selling the currency (European Commission, 2010l).
- Arrangements were put in place for member states whose currencies were under pressure to assist each other through the European Monetary Cooperation Fund (EMCF). This fund had been founded by the EC in 1973, after the breakdown of the Bretton Woods system of pegged currencies, to enable the member states to stabilize intra-EC exchange rates by purchasing or selling currencies.

There were problems with the EMS, notably in 1992–3 when devastating runs on sterling resulted in the UK pound being withdrawn from the system, as noted above. But the EMS did have some success in reducing exchange rate uncertainty and facilitating interest and inflation rate convergence (see Chang, 2009, pp. 28-31). The EMS also produced a reservoir of skilled talent, both inside and outside of government, to manage the ERM peg. So the EMS experience helped member states to develop a pan-European monetary network, the human skill to manage closer monetary co-operation, and the mutual trust that would be necessary to manage a single currency. The EMS experience thus helped policy-makers to consider seriously the establishment of EMU (Dyson, 1994).

The Maastricht Treaty's three-stage plan

Foundations for EMU were also laid by the 1996 Single European Act, which linked the success of the internal market programme to the establishment of EMU (Verdun, 1999, p. 311). Soon after the SEA came into effect, Jacques Delors, the President of the European Commission, persuaded the European Council to appoint him as chair of a committee comprised of central bank governors and other monetary experts to investigate how EMU could be created. The Delors Report, issued in 1989, formed the basis of the blueprint for EMU within the Maastricht Treaty (Verdun, 1999).

The Maastricht Treaty set out a three-stage plan and – often crucial for successful EU policy development – a timeline for creating EMU:

- Stage 1 (1990–4). This involved completing the internal market to permit free capital movement.
- Stage 2 (1994–9). This involved establishing a European Monetary Institute (EMI) and building the requisite independence of national central banks. (The EMI was to play a critical role in this phase by preparing the ground for the European System of Central Banks (ESCB), developing the governing architecture for EMU, and establishing the fiscal rules which members would need to follow.)
- Stage 3 (1999 onwards). This stage, which was adjusted after the Maastricht Treaty but before the single currency was launched, involved: fixing final

Box 10.1

EMU building: timeline

Year	Month	Activity
1944	March	Bretton Woods Agreement.
1969	December	The leaders of the six EC states announce their intention to establish an economic and monetary union by 1980.
1970	October	The Werner Report sets out an operational plan for creating EMU.
1971	August	'Nixon Shock': US ends dollar convertibility to gold, making the US dollar a 'fiat currency', meaning that is is based on full faith and credit of the US government, rather than gold convertability. This signalled that the USA would no longer intervene to maintain the Bretton Woods status of the US dollar as the anchor currency. This undermined the fixed bands EEC currencies depended on in intra-EEC trade and set in motion the quest for a European-based system of stable currencies.
1972	March	The establishment of the Snake in the Tunnel – a mechanism for managing European currency fluctuations (snake) inside narrow limits against the dollar (tunnel). Ends in 1974 – a victim of the world-wide recession induced by the oil crisis.
1979	March	The EMS, the subject of intergovernmental negotiations for over a year, comes into operation. Its central feature is the ERM, which involves fixed but adjustable exchange rate bands between participating currencies. All EC states apart from the UK join.
1985	December	Single European Act agreed by the EC Heads of Government. It contains a new chapter entitled 'Co-operation in Economic and Monetary Policy'.
1988	June	The European Council appoints a committee, with Jacques Delors as chair, to examine and propose a plan to build an EMU.
1989	April	The 'Delors Committee' presents its Report on EMU. It recommends proceeding via a three-stage strategy.
1990	October	The UK joins the ERM near the bottom of the band.
1992	September	The UK exits the ERM after a run on the pound that costs the UK Treasury billions in its attempt to stay within the band.
1991	December	The Maastricht Treaty is agreed politically by EU Heads of Government. It includes: (i) a three-stage strategy and a schedule for creating EMU, which will include a single currency, by 1 January 1999 at the latest; (ii) criteria for membership; and (iii) an opt-out for the UK (also extended later to Denmark).
1995	December	The name 'euro' is officially adopted.
1999	January	The euro comes into operation. Exchange rates are irrevocably fixed. All EU member states participate apart from Denmark, Greece, Sweden and the UK. ERM II is established.
2000	September	In a referendum, the Danish people reject eurozone membership by 53.1 to 46.9 per cent.

Box 10.1 continued

Year	Month	Activity
2001	January	Greece becomes a member of the eurozone.
2002	January	Euro coins and notes come into circulation and the national currencies of the 12 eurozone countries are phased-out.
2003	September	In a referendum, the Swedish people vote against membership of the euro by 56.1 to 41.8 per cent.
2003	November	France and Germany successfully persuade other Ecofin Council members to vote against the proposed action the Commission is to take against them for breaching the 3 per cent SGP budgetary ceiling.
2005	March	The Ecofin Council makes the terms of the SGP more flexible.
2007	January	Slovenia becomes a eurozone member.
2008	January	Cyprus and Malta become eurozone members.
2009	January	Slovakia becomes a eurozone member.
2010	May	Ecofin Council establishes two rescue funds: the European Financial Stabilisation Mechanism (EFSM) – using the EU budget as collateral (€60 billion); and the European Financial Stability Facility (EFSF), which is guaranteed directly by eurozone members according to a pre-agreed contribution table (€440 billion)
2011	January	EFSM and EFSF issue their first bonds. Estonia becomes a eurozone member.
2011	March	Euro Plus Pact is agreed by eurozone members and some non-members.
2011	March	The Eurogroup agrees to the European Stability Mechanism (ESM) to replace the EFSF and the EFSM. It is to have a lending capacity of €500 billion, which is to be augmented by the IMF. Non-euro states can participate on an *ad hoc* basis.
2011	July	Eurogroup finance ministers sign treaty establishing the ESM.
2011	December	EU member states agree on a new Fiscal Compact with binding fiscal rules, and to incorporate it within a new treaty. The UK vetoes the treaty being incorporated into the EU's treaties.
2012	March	Heads of Government of 25 member states (Czech Republic and UK decline) sign the Treaty on Stability, Coordination and Governance (incorporating the Fiscal Compact).
2012	June	'Historic' European Council summit where it is agreed that the ESM rescue fund can loan directly to banks in the eurozone; banks are to be supervised by the ECB.
2012	September	German Constitutional Court dismisses a complaint against the ESM, but limits Germany's contribution to €190 billion, with increases beyond this amount subject to approval from Germany's parliament.
2012	October	The ESM becomes operational.

exchange rates irrevocably for transition to the single currency; introducing the euro as an account currency (that is, as a unit of account capable of being used in financial transactions such as euro-denominated checking accounts and corporate bonds); conducting a single monetary policy; entry into force of the Stability and Growth Pact (which was added after the Maastricht Treaty); and the coming into effect of ERM II – whereby non-euro currencies of future single currency members are pegged to the euro.

Introduction of the euro

The single currency – the euro – was duly introduced in 1999 as a currency unit of account, while the introduction of the physical currency – euro coins and banknotes – took place on 1 January 2002.

At the time of the 1999 launch, 11 of the EU's 15 member states became eurozone members. Of the four that did not:

- *Greece* wanted to join but was judged not to have met the entry requirements set out in the Maastricht Treaty. These entry requirements – the 'Maastricht criteria', or 'convergence criteria' – which still apply to EMU applicants today, are listed in Box 10.2. Greece was eventually admitted to the eurozone in 2001.
- *The UK* was given an opt-out from the Maastricht Treaty requirement that all member states must prepare for EMU membership and must eventually become members. As shown in Chapter 4, the UK insisted on an opt-out for a mixture of political and economic reasons, most of which still exist today: concerns about loss of sovereignty; concerns that membership would be politically unpopular; a lack of conviction that EMU could work, especially given the varied nature of the national economies of the member states; and a belief that the UK economic cycle was not wholly 'in sync' with those of continental Europe.
- Like the UK, *Denmark* has always displayed a somewhat Eurosceptic leaning, but at Maastricht its government did not negotiate a UK-style opt-out. However, when in 1992 the Danish people rejected the ratification of the Treaty in a referendum, an opt-out was quickly sought and granted. It was an

---

Box 10.2

The EMU convergence criteria (eurozone entry conditions)

- **Price stability**. Inflation should not have exceeded by more than 1.5 percentage points that of the three best-performing EU member states for a period of at least one year. (Based on the consumer price inflation rate.)
- **Sustainability of the government financial position**. The budget deficit or planned deficit should be no more than 3 per cent of gross domestic product and government debt should be no more than 60 per cent of gross domestic product.
- **Exchange rate stability**. The normal fluctuation margins provided for by the exchange-rate mechanism should have been respected without severe tensions for at least two years. In particular, there must have been no devaluation against the euro. Must have participated in ERM II for at least two years.
- **Interest rate stability**. The average nominal long-term interest rate must not have exceeded by more than two percentage points that of, at most, the three best-performing Member States for a period of one year.

Source: Treaty on the Functioning of the European Union: Article 140; Protocol 12 (on the excessive deficit procedure); and Protocol 13 (on the convergence criteria).

---

opt-out the Danish government later sought to overturn by negotiating entry terms shortly after the single currency system was launched, but in a referendum in 2000 the Danish people voted to stay out.

- Unlike Denmark and the UK, *Sweden* had, and has, no legal opt-out – it did not join the EU until 1995 and therefore was subject to the Maastricht Treaty requirement that EMU membership is obligatory for all EU members. But, popular opposition made the Swedish government initially cautious about single currency membership. It was a caution that was merited because, when membership was put to the people in a referendum in 2003, it was rejected.

(Sweden has since been able to remain legally outside the eurozone by taking advantage of a technical loophole: a two-year ERM II membership is required prior to eurozone admission – so Sweden has not joined!)

Since the launch of the euro

The euro's launch generated intense interest and excitement among those who had long sought its establishment. While some of the emotion doubtless stemmed from relief that none of the dire warnings of financial collapse that had preceded the launch had come to pass, there was also a widespread feeling that Europe had now fully broken free of the historical shackles that had plagued its past.

This feeling of breaking free was linked to a widely held perception that greater economic prosperity would follow for eurozone members. While concerns were certainly expressed in some quarters about the 'unbalanced' nature of the EMU project – full monetary integration but only very limited macroeconomic co-operation (detailed below) – the assumption in most political circles was that EMU would 'work'. And until the onset of the financial and economic crisis that unfolded from 2007/8 it did work rather well in many respects, and in some important ways has continued to do so:

- The eurozone institutional mechanisms established themselves quickly and seemingly with relative ease.
- Price and monetary stability have been maintained, with low inflation and interest rates.
- The euro has become the second most important traded international currency (39 per cent of daily global transactions), of reserve (28 per cent, with the US dollar at 60 per cent), and of government and corporate debt (Bank of International Settlements, 2010; International Monetary Fund, 2011).
- A number of third countries now use the euro as an 'anchor' currency.
- The eurozone has been seen as promoting competition and acting as an agent of much-needed structural change in member state economies.

But, on the other side of the coin:

- There is not much evidence of EMU having had a positive impact on economic growth and employment levels.
- The financial and economic crisis, and in particular the sovereign debt and banking crises within the eurozone that became increasingly apparent from 2010, have shown the weaknesses arising from the unbalanced nature of the EMU system and its lack of a strong and centralized leadership (these weaknesses are discussed below).
- The forecasts made by sceptics that some eurozone states, especially less efficient ones, would have great difficulty in being competitive and meeting their EMU obligations, and could even threaten the system as whole, have come to be seen as being justified as, from 2009, Ireland, Portugal, Spain, Italy and, above all, Greece, have experienced severe economic and financial problems.

As for the eurozone's membership, all of the 12 states that acceded to the EU in 2004/7 are obliged to eventually join the single currency system. Becoming a member depends on meeting the Maastricht convergence criteria as well as satisfactory performance within the ERM II for a two-year period (see Box 10.3). The Commission and the European Central Bank are charged with assessing, at least once every two years, the progress of eurozone candidates and publishing their conclusions in 'convergence reports'. The Commission then submits a proposal to the Ecofin Council. After consulting with the EP, Ecofin submits its recommendation to the European Council, which ultimately decides if candidates may be admitted into the eurozone. To date, five of the 2004/7 entries have joined – Cyprus, Malta, Slovenia, Slovakia and Estonia – bringing the total eurozone membership to 17 (in late 2012). The economic and financial crisis, with its damaging consequences for public deficits and debts has, of course, meant that most of the CEECs that have not yet joined the eurozone have become far-distanced from meeting the entry requirements (but, then, so too have most eurozone members!).

EMU Institutions

EMU policy is made and implemented by several EU institutions. Box 10.4 lists the main institutions and

Box 10.3

ERM II membership requirements

ERM II Requirements

- A central exchange rate between the euro and the country's currency is agreed. The currency is then allowed to fluctuate by up to 15% above or below this central rate.
- When necessary, the currency is supported by intervention (buying or selling) to keep the exchange rate against the euro within the ±15% fluctuation band. Interventions are coordinated by the ECB and the central bank of the non-euro area member state.
- Non-euro area member states within ERM II can decide to maintain a narrower fluctuation band, but this decision has no impact on the official ±15% fluctuation margin, unless there is agreement on this by ERM II stakeholders.
- The General Council of the ECB monitors the operation of ERM II and ensures co-ordination of monetary and exchange-rate policies. The General Council also administers the intervention mechanisms together with the member state's central bank.

ERM II Members*

Denmark, Lithuania and Latvia.

Note: *As of September 2012.

Source: European Commission, 2012v.

their key decision-making actors and responsibilities. The following paragraphs emphasize some particularly important points about the institutions.

The best-known EMU institution is the *European Central Bank* (ECB), which sits at the heart of the European System of Central Banks (ESCB). The ECB manages the euro, and hence also the eurozone's monetary policy. In undertaking this responsibility, the primary objective of the ESCB is, in the words of Article 127 TFEU, 'to maintain price stability'. Therefore, controlling inflation is prioritized over promoting economic growth, though the growth objective has been emphasized increasingly in response to the eurozone sovereign debt and banking crises.

The ECB is required to act in a wholly independent (and hence supranational) manner. As Article 130 of the TFEU states:

> When exercising the powers and carrying out the tasks and duties conferred upon them by the Treaties and the Statute of the ESCB and of the ECB, neither the European Central Bank, nor a national central bank, nor any member of their decision-making bodies shall seek or take instructions from Union institutions, bodies, offices or agencies, from any government of a Member State or from any other body.

Governments are involved in EMU policy-making and management in a number of ways. As with other policy areas, Heads of Government are not involved directly with EMU on a day-to day basis, but they do become involved with it, via the *European Council*, when substantive decisions have had to be made. This involvement has increased with the severity and intractability of the eurozone debt crisis since 2010, with all summit meetings having had EMU issues on their agendas in some form as national leaders have had to take major decisions to address sovereign debt problems and bank failures.

The eurozone governmental leaders strengthened their EMU institutional role in 2012 by deciding that there would be *Euro Area Summits* at least twice a year to discuss eurozone governance and economic issues. They also decided that the convenor and chair of these summits would be the European Council President.

At ministerial level, governments are involved in EMU governance via:

- *The Ecofin Council.* As shown in Chapter 3, this consists of the Finance Ministers of the 27 member states. Box 10.4 summarizes the tasks undertaken by Ecofin and its working groups.
- *The Eurogroup.* Prior to the Lisbon Treaty, this consisted of 'informal' gatherings of eurozone Ecofin minsters, but the Treaty gave the Eurogroup formal status. This elevation was an important victory for France, which had originally conceived of the Eurogroup as a political counterweight to the ECB and which had persisted in attempts to elevate its importance despite German fears that a powerful Eurogroup would threaten the ECB's independence (Chang, 2009, p. 79).

Because it exists primarily to oversee the fiscal aspects of EMU, the Eurogoup's membership is limited to Finance Ministers whose countries have adopted the euro.

The Eurogroup meets almost invariably just before Ecofin meetings, and in doing so inevitably shapes much of what subsequently happens in Ecofin. While it does not have the power to take formal decisions, the Eurogroup has become a very important institution, with its influence having grown since the onset of the eurozone sovereign debt and banking crisis.

The *European Commission* was an important driving force behind the establishment of the eurozone, but since EMU has been in place it has assumed a mainly advisory capacity in monetary policy. This is not, however, the case with respect to fiscal policy, where the Commission is assigned several very important responsibilities, including:

- The surveillance of eurozone member budgets. This surveillance power has been strengthened considerably since the global financial crisis. With the 'six-pack' reforms of 2011 (see below) the Commission gained independent power to sanction violators of the eurozone's fiscal rules. (The previous system required Ecofin approval of Commission-recommended sanctions, whereas the six-pack reforms established automatic Commission sanctions unless Ecofin overturned them in a voting process called 'reverse qualified majority voting – RQMV.) The 'two-pack' of reforms (see below), expected to be in place by the end of 2012, further increased the Commission's surveillance powers with respect to draft budgets.
- The assessment of all EU member state Stability and Convergence Programmes (SCPs) – which focus on national budgetary issues.
- The preparation of the EU's annual growth survey for the coming year, which is presented to the Council and EP and endorsed at the spring European Council summit.
- The assessment of member state National Reform Programmes (NRPs) in the context of Europe 2020 reforms (see Chapter 9).
- The issuing of recommendations to the member states based on NRPs and SCPs.

The *European Parliament's* role in monetary policy used to be limited, being confined to certain consultation rights and to overseeing the ECB. Article 284 TFEU requires the ECB's President to present the ECB's annual report to the Parliament and also states that the President and other members of the ECB's Executive Board 'may be heard by the competent committees of the European Parliament' (which, in practice, usually means the Economic and Monetary Affairs Committee).

However, since the ratification of the Lisbon Treaty the EP's role has greatly increased by virtue of it now being a co-legislator with the Council in key areas of economic and financial governance. Most importantly in this regard, the global and eurozone crises have resulted in the EP becoming involved extensively in policies and legislation concerning financial services and fiscal surveillance. (See Chapter 8 for a discussion of financial services regulation.)

The *Court of Justice* determines whether a eurozone member state has abrogated fiscal rules and can assess fines for exceeding the mandated budget deficit and debt rules (see below for more detail on this).

The eurozone crisis has pushed the formerly little-known *European Investment Bank* (EIB) into the spotlight. The EIB is the 'financing arm' of the EU for long-term projects. It uses the funds it raises in capital markets to provide loan guarantees and below market rate loans for projects that further EU goals. The EU member states own the EIB and are its shareholders (subscribers), with a capital subscription in 2012 of €232 billion (European Investment Bank Group, 2012, p. 41). Because the Bank has been a careful investor, it has earned a triple-AAA credit rating, thus enabling it to borrow at the most advantageous rates.

Since 2010, the EU has relied increasingly on the EIB to help with efforts to promote growth. Importantly, in his 2012 successful bid for the French presidency, François Hollande championed the role of the EIB as a key player in promoting growth as an alternative to austerity (Wishart, 2012a). Hollande's mantra of growth was rewarded at the June 2012 European Council summit, where the Heads of Government agreed to increase the EIB's subscription by €10 billion, along with the launch of a pilot project bond scheme worth €4.5 billion (Wishart, 2012b).

The newest eurozone institution is the *European Stability Mechanism* (ESM), which began operations in October 2012 to lend funds to eurozone member states and banks experiencing working capital shortages. The ESM's purpose and functions are summarized in Box 10.7 on page 213.

Box 10.4

Eurozone institutions

Institution	Key decision-making actors	Main responsibilities
European Central Bank	Governing Council (comprised of the governors of the eurozone's national central banks plus the members of the ECB's Executive Board) Executive Board (comprised of the ECB President, Vice President and four other members. All are appointed by the European Council)	Maintain price stability Promote growth through open market operations European bank supervisor
European Council	EU Heads of Government	Involved in broad decision-making and may make important specific decisions in emergency situations such as during the eurozone crisis
Euro Area Summit	Eurozone Heads of Government	Oversees eurozone policy and developments
Ecofin Council and Council Working Committees	Ecofin is comprised of the Finance Ministers of the member states Working committees are comprised of government officials from the member states COREPER	Ecofin: Economic policy coordination Macroeconomic surveillance Monitoring member states' budgetary policy and public finances Working committees include: Economic and Finance Committee: monitors member states' financial position and provides a variety of forms of support for Ecofin and the Eurogroup Economic Policy Committee: advises on policy and conducts economic analyses Assists in the preparation of Ecofin meetings

The Debate over the Appropriateness of Fiscal and Monetary Union

There are two components of a full economic and monetary union: fiscal policy and monetary policy. The Maastricht Treaty laid down the basis for a 'mone-tary' or 'currency' union, with a single currency managed by a central bank. It did not, however, lay any such basis for a 'fiscal union', which would have needed at its core an EU Finance Ministry or similar entity with strong fiscal (that is, revenue raising and spending) powers.

Economic integration theory (see Chapter 2) assumes that fiscal union necessarily precedes mone-

Box 10.4 continued

Institution	Key decision-making actors	Main responsibilities
Eurogroup	Finance Ministers of eurozone members	Oversees EMU, including the Fiscal Compact Prepares agenda items for Euro Area Summits
European Commission	President Commissioner for Economic and Monetary Affairs DG Economic and Financial Affairs	Proposes EMU legislation Fiscal and macroeconomic assessment and surveillance
European Parliament	Committee on Economic and Monetary Affairs	Supervisory: ECB President presents annual report to EP meeting in plenary session; EP must approve the European Council's nominee for ECB President Legislative: since the Lisbon Treaty, the EP is a co-legislator with the Council in the area of economic governance
European Stability Mechanism	Board of Governors	Provides loans to eurozone countries and banks experiencing financial difficulties
CJEU	Justices	Determines if a member state has breached deficit/debt rules Imposes financial sanctions under excessive deficit procedure
European Investment Bank	Board of Governors (comprised of one minister from each EU member state) Board of Directors (comprised of one nominee from each EU member state and one nominee of the Commission)	Helps to fund long-term projects via providing loan finance at advantageous rates Increasingly used to fund economic growth

tary union. However, as EMU was being built, political interests triumphed over the suspicions voiced by many economists and central bankers that the monetary focus and foundations of the new system were too narrow.

Related to these suspicions, one of the core concerns when EMU was being created was the extent to which the planned eurozone would be an optimal currency area (OCA). When the economist Robert Mundell (1961, p. 657) introduced OCA theory, he posed the question: 'supposing that the Common Market countries proceed with their plans for economic union, should these countries allow each national currency to fluctuate, or would a single currency area be preferable?' He advanced the view that the case for the adoption of a single currency was strengthened the more a geographic region displayed a common set of attributes. A region would be more likely to maintain a stable currency union if it had labour mobility, flexible production and financial markets, a single market in goods, services, labour, and capital, diversity in economic production, healthy growth, and similar inflation rates.

While not all of these features are necessary for an OCA (the US does not wholly meet them), certain attributes seem to be essential for an OCA to function efficiently. As Krugman (2011) and others have shown, labour mobility and a central government that can undertake fiscal transfers are essential characteristics. This is especially important if the OCA covers a wide geographical area, which by definition will be more diverse in terms, for example, of disparate price levels. So, it was always questionable whether the proposed eurozone – containing economies as diverse as Germany, Italy and Greece – would meet the conditions of an OCA. In the view of many economists, a single European currency would be much better centred on those EU countries with highly interdependent and similar economies: that is, the economies of northern European states.

However, throughout the period when the foundations for the single currency were being laid (from the Werner Report through to the Maastricht Treaty) the economic monetarist view (money supply controls inflation) prevailed, in part because of the failure of fiscal policy to deal with the oil shocks (and stagflation) of the 1970s. There was during these years what amounted to a monetarist 'counter-revolution' (Tcherneva, 2008). Indeed, so strongly did monetarist thinking develop that some free market proponents argued that markets would ensure fiscal discipline (see discussion in Sims, 1999, p. 426).

In sum, given the choice between monetary and fiscal policy, it was politically more palatable to cede control of the national currency (especially given the widespread agreement that the dollar was far too dominant, and the popular notion that a single currency would strengthen Europe's global financial position) than of the nation's budget (fiscal control). Monetary policy could be tied to the smooth operation of the single market, whereas a similar case could not be made for fiscal policy.

So, in the debate as to the proper sequencing of fiscal and monetary policy in the context of EMU, those who argued that monetary policy could precede fiscal policy gained the upper hand. In effect, the debate was 'won' by a brand of monetarists who 'advocated that convergence between the economies would naturally result from monetary integration, thus there was no pressing need to coordinate and harmonise economic and monetary policies in advance of monetary union' (Chang, 2009, p. 23).

However, even before EMU was actually established, there were economists challenging the dominance of the monetarist perspective and what was seen to be an over-emphasis on the role of money in driving fiscal policy. For example, Christopher Sims (1999), the 2011 recipient of the Nobel Prize in Economics, published a paper the year EMU was launched in which he warned that the lack of fiscal authority in EMU carried with it 'great dangers' to economic stability. It would be naïve, he explained, to expect that when a government issues debt it is 'implicitly committing itself to raise additional future revenues, in order for the new debt to have value' (ibid., p. 18). He argued that the 'new debt only commits the government to raise additional revenue in *nominal* terms [emphasis in original]' (ibid., p. 418). When an economic downturn did come, he predicted that the weaker eurozone member states would experience severe hardships – with, for example, governments cutting social benefits just when they would be most needed. Monetary policy, the basis of EMU, would not be able to help lift a struggling eurozone member out of deep recession during 'liquidity traps' (ibid., p. 421). (A liquidity trap occurs where banks hold 'nearly non-interest bearing' reserves – in the form of low-risk assets such as sovereign debt – and the central bank has set very low interest rates to try to induce member bank borrowing and lending. Despite the central bank's loose lending policy, private banks are 'gun shy' and cannot be induced to increase lending.) Furthermore, Sims argued, once investors suspected there was a sovereign debt default risk, those countries seen as most vulnerable would only be able sell their debt at higher yields. (Numerous other warnings from within Europe also went unheeded – see, for example, Jacquet and Pisani-Ferry, 2001.)

The architects of EMU, however, did not establish the 'coordinated fiscal mechanism' Sims and others had argued would be necessary to provide credit or recapitalization to central banks in those countries experiencing untenable bond yield pay-outs. So, rather than building fiscal policy, the decision was made to fashion EMU around monetary policy. The ramifications of this are explored in the next two sections.

Monetary Policy

As required by the Maastricht Treaty, all EU member states apart from Denmark and the UK must adopt the euro when they have satisfied eurozone membership conditions. On becoming eurozone members, states no longer have their own national currencies but rather share a single currency, which in turn means they have a single interest rate set by the ECB and share exchange rate policies that apply throughout the eurozone area. Therefore it is the ECB, rather than the member states, that determines the money supply: it prints euro notes and determines the amount of coinage that each of the national treasuries is permitted to mint. The ECB holds and manages the official foreign reserves of eurozone member states, conducts foreign exchange operations, and promotes the smooth operation of payment systems.

This approach to monetary policy is based on 'quantity theory', which means that, over the long run, the money supply determines the price level (the rate of inflation or deflation). (In the short-run, all sorts of factors might influence the price level.) As noted above, the primary objective of the ECB is to maintain price stability – which the Bank defines as an annual rate of inflation in the Harmonised Index of Consumer Prices (HICP) for the eurozone of below 2 per cent over the medium term.

The ECB employs three standard and two non-standard instruments for managing monetary policy. The standard instruments are standing facilities (lending to member banks), open market operations (member banks put up collateral with the ECB and receive a euro cash loan), and setting reserve requirements (for ESCB member banks). The ECB's 'non-standard' measures include the purchasing of sovereign debt on the secondary market and long-term refinancing operations (LTROs) that involve lending money at low interest rates to eurozone banks, with the LTROs collateralized with sovereign debt.

The consensus is that the ECB has performed well in achieving its primary objective of maintaining price stability, with inflation having remained low in the eurozone (hovering around 2 per cent). Furthermore, despite the sovereign debt crisis that from 2010 engulfed all the eurozone's weaker economies, the euro has remained relatively strong and has never depreciated to the dollar parity that existed when the euro was introduced. (This is not, however, to say that the eurozone crisis has not had a negative impact on the euro's value.)

However, the eurozone debt crisis precipitated calls for a more activist ECB, particularly with respect to injecting liquidity into the market, acting as a bank of last resort for the purchasing of sovereign debt, and supervising the operation of banks – especially those based in eurozone member states.

The Eurozone banking crisis and initial steps towards the formation of a European banking union

Banks are very important eurozone actors. This is because the eurozone's central bank – the ECB – relies on them to keep the eurozone economy well-oiled with money. As was shown above, the ECB controls the euro money supply through a number of operations, but it is banks that deal with consumers by making loans (the bank's assets) and taking in liabilities (deposits), which are the source of the ECB's lending capacity.

Market failure is an ever-present concern with banking activities in modern capitalist systems. It is so because, for a variety of reasons – including sudden economic downturns, property value collapses and poor bank management – banks can fail, and if they do become bankrupt they can take their depositors' funds with them. To protect depositors' money, governments offer deposit insurance. The question then becomes, how can governments ensure that bankers do not gamble with government-guaranteed deposits? The answer is the same as in other cases of market failure – governments must regulate the industry. Thus, banking regulations are the order of the day in all advanced industrialized democracies. The level at which regulation occurs, however, varies between political systems. So, in unitary systems, banking regulation naturally takes place at the national level and is uniform in its application and enforcement. This is, however, not always the case in federal systems, where component units of the federation may charter banks. In the US, for example, there is both federal- and state-level regulation of banking. A consequence of this two-level regulation is that there is the ever-present problem of some states underfunding regulatory oversight and/or passing legislation with less onerous banking regulations in order to attract banks from states with stricter regulations: in short, there is the problem of there being the temptation to 'race to the bottom'.

Difficulties associated with banking regulation have been at the heart of much of the eurozone crisis. This is because the EU has differing banking systems, with a range of lending practices, regulatory legislation, and oversight. The eurozone crisis was caused in part by these national variations and has since resulted in moves to them being curbed and a fledgling banking union being created. To explain why this has occurred, some of the features of the eurozone crisis need to be explained. (The eurozone crisis has in fact consisted of two interrelated crises – a bank debt crisis and a sovereign debt crisis. The latter crisis is examined later in the chapter.)

From 2007–8, the growing international recession resulted in increasing banking problems in some EU member states, not least Ireland and Spain, where banks had greatly 'over-lent' – in large part to fund rapidly expanding, but highly inflated, housing markets. When these and other markets crashed, banks were left with huge unpaid debts. In attempting to save their failing banks and maintain the credibility of their banking systems, the Irish, Spanish and other governments took on massive debt – with Ireland, for example, reporting in 2010 a budget deficit that amounted to 31.3 per cent of GDP. But taking on such debt puts states that belong to a single currency in a very difficult situation because they cannot devalue their currency to reduce their debt obligation to foreign holders of sovereign debt. The only option available to Ireland, Spain and similarly troubled eurozone states was austerity.

The banking crisis was quickly exacerbated by the very system that had allowed the banks to grow and prosper: free capital movement resulted in weakened banks being vulnerable to capital flight. This problem appeared fairly quickly in Greece, where it has been estimated that between late 2009, when it became apparent that Greece could not pay its debts, and mid-2012, Greek banks lost 30 per cent of their deposits

(Evans-Pritchard, 2012). Ireland's austerity measures stemmed capital flight of these proportions, but in Spain suggestions that the Spanish deposit guarantee system was bankrupt resulted in capital flight accelerating: so much so that in May 2012 net outflows were €41.3 billion, compared to €9.6 billion in May 2011 (House *et al.*, 2012).

In consequence, private banks in troubled eurozone member countries were simply starved for cash from both within Europe and across the Atlantic – with, for example, the ten largest American money market funds having ceased lending to Irish, Italian, Portuguese and Spanish banks by the end of 2011 (Ewing, 2012). So, by mid-2012, the weak eurozone economies were experiencing capital flight, and some of their governments had taken on massive debt attempting to rescue private banks.

To make the situation worse, investors began to suggest that government bailouts of failed banks had undermined the security of sovereign debt. When government regulators and national central banks required private banks to carry a larger portfolio of safe investments – in the form of low return and low risk investments – sovereign debt constituted a major portion of this requirement. As a result, private banks were saddled with the sovereign debt of countries that were suspected of possibly defaulting – especially Greece, Ireland, Italy, Portugal and Spain. Taking Italian debt as an example: in June 2011, the Bank of International Settlements reported that, of the $939 billion of Italy's debt held by foreigners, approximately $400 billion was held by French banks and $150 billion by German banks. Of a total Greek debt of $485 billion, the countries with the most exposure were France with $56.7 billion, Germany with $33.9 billion, the UK with $14.7 billion, and the US with just $7.3 billion (*The New York Times*, 11 November 2011; *The Telegraph*, 11 June 2011).

This link between bank bailouts and loss of investor confidence in sovereign debt was described in June 2012 by the European Council President, Herman Van Rompuy, as constituting a 'vicious cycle between banks and sovereigns'. In this cycle, banks held bad consumer debt, governments bailed out the banks, investors required higher yields on governments running higher deficits, and government required banks to hold more government debt (Beesley *et al.*, 2012).

But breaking the cycle was extremely difficult, especially because Chancellor Merkel insisted that EU bailouts should be made to member states' governments and not directly to banks. This was problematic because, for example, the Spanish government's bailout of its banks had already created an untenable situation in Spain, where yield rates on long-term Spanish bonds were so high as to be unsustainable. Similar situations existed in other weak eurozone states. An EU approach was necessary to solve the problem.

At the June 2012 European Council meeting, policy progress was made. Germany agreed to the use of rescue funds to recapitalize banks directly rather than via governments, while at the same time it was also agreed at the summit that banks would be controlled more centrally with the establishment of a common bank supervisor, run by the ECB.

The underlying rationale for the creation of such a common bank supervisor is that banks need to be monitored properly by EU authorities to ensure they do not engage in irresponsible asset attraction (involving overly high payouts), which encourages lending to risky ventures. Supervision, however, is not in itself a guarantee of a more stable European banking system. An effective system also needs a strong EU-wide deposit insurance scheme to prevent a run on banks in those countries experiencing budgetary difficulties. (While there are in place some EU common rules covering banking – for example, Directive 94/19/EC requires all member states to have a deposit guarantee for at least 90 per cent of the deposited amount up to at least €50,000 per depositor – current rules permit considerable latitude among national deposit insurance schemes. Furthermore, as Spain showed in 2012, national-based insurance schemes can be bankrupted.) Aware of this need, in a report tabled at the June 2012 European Council meeting by the so-called quartet of European Council President, European Commission President, Eurogroup President and ECB President, the authors called for, in addition to a common banking supervision authority, an EU-wide deposit insurance scheme. The purpose of such a scheme would be to protect investors and to minimize capital flight (as happened in Greece and Spain during their bank crises). The quartet's report also envisaged a 'resolution scheme' funded by bank contributions to assist 'in the application of resolution measures to banks overseen by the European supervisor with the aim of an orderly winding-down of non-viable institutions' (European Council, The President, 2012, p. 4).

Neither the deposit nor the resolution schemes were discussed at the June 2012 European Council summit, but it was expected that they would be taken up when the details were hammered out for the eurozone banking supervision authority.

The banking crisis and sovereign debt crisis thus combined to see the laying of foundations in 2012 of a eurozone banking union. The ECB will be centrally involved in the formation and management of this union.

A wider policy role for the ECB

As was shown above, the banking crisis and the sovereign debt crisis set the stage for an ECB that in the future will be more actively involved in regulating the behaviour of banks operating in the eurozone. The crises have also paved the way for a widening of the Bank's policy roles, with its original mandate for keeping inflation low being joined by some responsibilities for promoting growth.

As the crisis worsened, the ECB faced calls to lend more euros to its member banks and to act as a primary buyer of sovereign debt in order to promote growth in a eurozone heading toward recession. The Bank's initial response to these pressures was very cautious and framed within a reluctance to depart from its prioritization of containing inflation. However, citing dire eurozone growth forecasts of 0.5 per cent and 1.3 per cent in 2012 and 2013, respectively, the Bank's position gradually softened and it injected approximately €1 trillion into eurozone banks at the close of 2011 (Castle, 2012). Further evidence of a more activist ECB were seen in July 2012 when it cut the main interest rate to 0.75 per cent, the first time it had been below 1 per cent in the euro's history. The reason for the cut was to lower the borrowing costs of troubled eurozone economies, particularly Spain.

The ECB also responded increasingly to the crisis by expanding the types of assets its member banks could use as collateral in exchange for euros. However, its room for manoeuvre was limited because it is prohibited by the TFEU from purchasing bonds from national treasuries, though it can and does buy sovereign debt on the secondary market. With less than 10 per cent of the ECB's assets accounted for by sovereign debt, however, ECB purchases can have only a marginal impact on sovereign bond yields. In this context, Mario Draghi, the Bank's Governor since 2011, has frequently reiterated that the ECB is designed to shore up commercial banks, not governments, and thus cannot engage in substantial purchasing of, say, Italian or Spanish bonds in an attempt to lower yields (Erlanger and Castle, 2011).

However, in spite of these limitations, it is clear that since the onset of the crisis the ECB has become more centrally involved in aspects of broad economic policy-making.

Fiscal Policy

As we have seen, EMU was created as a monetary union. The fiscal side of EMU was to be essentially voluntaristic in nature.

When EMU was being created, monetarists took the view that fiscal convergence would eventually follow monetary policy. In the meantime, anything more than a co-operative arrangement in which national governments submitted economic and budgetary data each year for review would violate the principle of subsidiarity and undermine support for a single currency (Issing, 2004, p. 11). Thus, fiscal discipline would need to remain at the national level: not because all economists, or even governments, thought it was the best policy, but because the transference of fiscal authority to the European level was not politically viable. The main vehicle for ensuring budgetary discipline was to be the Stability and Growth Pact (SGP).

The Stability and Growth Pact

The lack of political viability of transferring fiscal authority to the European level was despite the fact that there was general agreement among economists and policy-makers when EMU was being created that the macroeconomic policies of eurozone states needed to be at least partly aligned. Yet on the politically-sensitive question as to what extent a central authority needed to monitor, and possibly control, the budgetary decision-making of eurozone members, there was no agreement. In consequence, while foundations for a European monetary policy were developed in the

Delors Report and adopted in the Maastricht Treaty, fiscal policy was dealt with on a fairly minimalist basis and remained largely a national responsibility.

The Maastricht Treaty laid down economic qualifying criteria that states must meet to become members of the single currency area – the convergence criteria set out in Box 10.2 – but it failed to address the possibility that states might not abide by the criteria after gaining eurozone admission. To remedy this, after the Maastricht Treaty had come into force, Germany proposed the creation of a Stability Pact, to which the French insisted on adding the inclusion of 'growth' as an additional objective (Chang, 2009, p. 124). This resulted in the 1997 Stability and Growth Pact (SGP), which consisted of a 'preventative arm' (involving the co-ordination of economic policies and surveillance of budgetary positions) and a 'corrective arm' (based on the convergence criteria and centred on any exceeding of the national deficit by 3 per cent of GDP triggering an 'excessive deficit procedure' (EDP) (Chang, 2009, p. 124). A 2005 reform added the stipulation that national debt must be no more than 60 per cent of GDP.

These requirements thus obliged eurozone members to practise prudent fiscal policies and, more particularly, to maintain broadly balanced national budgets over the economic cycle. The EDP was considered to be especially important, and non-compliance with it could, in theory, lead to financial sanctions being imposed on offenders (the 'punitive arm'): initially in the form of the lodging of a non-interest-bearing deposit and later, if excessive deficits continued, in the form of a fine. In practice, no financial penalties have ever been applied, even though several eurozone states quickly breached SGP rules.

In the early 2000s, difficulties experienced by some member states in staying within SGP rules provided the first warning sign that problems might be on the horizon for EMU. Portugal risked breaching the terms of the SGP and was obliged by the Commission and the Ecofin Council to cut back public expenditure severely. However, when Germany and France breached the budgetary deficit SGP ceilings in 2003–4 they were able to use their political and economic strength to largely evade censure. Indeed, since there was the prospect of them being in breach for some time, they chose to persuade the Ecofin Council – against strong Commission opposition – to revise the terms of the SGP so as to make it more flexible. (Given that over half of the EU was in excessive deficit procedures in 2004 – see Chang, 2009, p. 126 – Council inaction was rather predictable.) This resulted in the Commission initiating a case against the Council in the ECJ, but though the Court ruled largely in favour of the Commission (case C-27/04) political realities led to disciplinary action not being imposed and to, in March 2005, the Ecofin Council easing the terms of the SGP.

The SGP revision resulted in the system becoming more flexible, so as to allow for fluctuations in the economic cycle. There would now be a formal recognition that there were exceptional and temporary circumstances in which the 3 per cent limit could be breached without the risk of a financial penalty being imposed. The circumstances were not listed, as some member states wanted (particularly Luxembourg and the Netherlands), but rather were left to the discretion of the Commission to judge. The most likely circumstance was generally recognized as being when a national economy was experiencing temporary difficulties, with low growth and high unemployment, but the underlying structure was sound. These exceptions to the SGP rules came to be cited increasingly as the global financial and economic crisis took hold. With many EU states adopting, initially at least, aggressive fiscal stimulus measures to deal with rising unemployment and low growth, the crisis inevitably resulted in budgetary deficits and public debts quickly spiralling in most member states, and the SGP deficit and debt figures being breached – in some cases by wide margins (see Box 10.5 for deficit and debt figures).

Further to these problems in applying the SGP, many governments increasingly took the view that the SGP rules, with their emphasis on governments keeping tight control on public spending, risked exacerbating the economic downturn. So, SGP decision-makers and implementers decided that, while the SGP deficit and debt figures should remain in place, states should not be penalized for exceeding them as long as they were clearly making efforts to get back on track and (re)establish firm budgetary positions.

The eurozone sovereign debt crisis

The eurozone crisis exposed the weaknesses of the fiscal management of the eurozone and demonstrated the need for reform.

There is no agreement among informed observers about the causes of the eurozone debt crisis. As shown above, banking problems were certainly, at the very least, a significant contributory factor. Some observers argue that the underlying cause was low growth in the relatively small, export-dependent economies of Greece, Ireland and Portugal. Ireland, it has been argued, was a 'beachhead' for US multi-national corporations, making Ireland especially vulnerable to the effects of the very deep US recession that began in 2007. Greece also has considerably high exposure to global downturns because of its reliance on tourism (travel is one of the first sectors to be affected negatively by recessions) and shipping (orders for goods decline in a recession, and so demand drops for shipping services). The eurozone crisis would not have been so severe for either Greece or Ireland if they had been able to grow themselves out of the debt crisis, but this was not possible.

Poor governance certainly contributed to problems in several eurozone states that came to experience economic difficulties, with governments being either unwilling or incapable of confronting such core economic problems as low GDP growth, rising wages, inflexible labour market rules, rising and excessive public debts, and too much state capitalism. In Italy, for example, the governments headed by Silvio Berlusconi that were in power from 2001–6 and 2008–11 were ineffective in enacting necessary budgetary cuts and undertaking long-term economic structural changes such as pension reform and more flexible labour rules.

Another, quite different, factor also contributed to economic weakness in some eurozone countries. Since the establishment of the single currency, Germany had undergone labour market reforms to increase its global competitiveness: reforms that included wage freezes, welfare cuts and greater labour market flexibility. The result of this wage restraint shows clearly in comparative statistics: between 2000 and 2007, real wages grew by 1 per cent in Germany, compared to 2.7 per cent in the eurozone; and from 1999 to 2007 German unit labour costs fell by 16 per cent while rising by 4 per cent in the EU (Rohan, 2012). This German wage depression translated into lower relative export prices, which was good for German competitiveness but had a negative effect on Germany's EU partners by reducing German domestic demand for its neighbours' goods and services (Scally, 2012).

Box 10.5

Debt and deficit figures from selected countries

Country	Government debt as percentage of GDP			Budget deficit as percentage of GDP		
	2000	2005	2010	2000	2005	2010
Belgium	107.8	92.0	96.2	0.0	2.7	4.1
Estonia	5.1	4.6	6.7	−0.2	1.6	0.2
France	57.3	66.4	82.3	1.5	2.9	7.1
Germany	60.2	68.6	83.2	1.1	3.3	4.3
Greece	103.4	100.0	144.9	3.7	5.2	10.6
Ireland	37.5	27.2	92.5	4.7	1.7	31.3
Italy	108.5	105.5	118.4	0.8	4.4	4.6
Portugal	48.5	62.8	93.3	2.9	5.9	9.8
Spain	59.4	43.1	61.0	0.9	2.4	9.3
Sweden	53.9	50.4	39.7	3.6	2.2	0.2
UK	41.0	42.0	79.9	3.6	3.4	10.3
Average eurozone	69.2	70.1	85.3	0.1	2.5	6.2
Average EU-27	**61.9**	**62.8**	**80.1**	**0.6**	**2.4**	**6.6**

Source: European Commission, 2011o.

In consequence of such problems as uncompetitiveness, rising unemployment, low growth, and the need that was noted above of governments having to bail out failing banks, public debts and government deficits in eurozone countries began to rise from the early 2000s, as Box 10.5 shows. Most of the rising figures were not in themselves excessive, as a comparison with Japan and the US illustrates: in 2010, government debt as a percentage of GDP stood at 233 per cent and 100 per cent, respectively, in these two countries. Japan's debt-to-GDP ratio was thus well above Greece's 166 per cent and Italy's 123 per cent. However, two factors protect Japan and the yield (interest) rates it has to pay on bonds (loans): first, a high percentage of Japanese sovereign debt is held by Japanese citizens, with the consequence being that interest pay-outs remain within Japan's economy and the debt level is not dangerous; and Japan's economy – the third-largest in the world – is highly diversified and efficient. The US, as the world's largest economy, is similarly protected from investor behaviour. In contrast, a large portion of Greek debt – a tiny nation compared to the US and Japan – is held by non-Greek institutions and citizens. While much of Italy's debt is held by Italians, the Italian economy suffers from being relatively inefficient because of generous pensions, an inflexible labour market and a bloated public service.

As skittish investors shunned the bond issues of states with troubled economies and sought shelter in those of states with sounder economies – notably, Germany, the UK, the Netherlands, Japan and the US – states such as Ireland and Spain increasingly faced unsustainable borrowing costs. Greece simply became bankrupt and was able to stay afloat only with help from what came to be called the lending 'troika' of the IMF, the European Commission and the ECB. Box 10.6 summarizes the key features of the Greek debt crisis.

Fiscal policy reforms designed to stabilize the eurozone

The eurozone enacted several reforms between 2010 and 2012 that were designed to stabilize it. The two

Box 10.6

Anatomy of the Greek debt crisis

Odious debt

Before Greece entered the eurozone, markets required the Greek government to pay a risk premium (higher yields) on sovereign debt because of its history of devaluation and default. Similarly, Greek banks had less access to money to lend to consumers and businesses. With the introduction of the euro this risk premium on Greek bonds 'melted away' (Krugman, 2011). Greeks have been particularly singled out – perhaps unfairly – as living beyond their means. They were accused of buying luxury German cars, yachts and second homes, and evading taxes in large numbers by not reporting their purchases to the taxing authority (Steivorth, 2010). Germans, who had been under wage freezes for a decade and were being asked to come to Greece's rescue, were shocked to discover through Google Earth the number of swimming pools (many unreported to the tax authorities, as it turned out) in Athenian backyards!

Reinhart and Rogoff (2009, p. 63) explain that the 'doctrine of odious debt basically states that when lenders give money to a government that is conspicuously kleptomaniacal and corrupt, subsequent governments should not be forced to honor it'. The authors also note that 'there is quite a bit of controversy about whether odious debt can be clearly delineated in practice'. Manolopoulos's (2011) account of Greece's 'odious debt' is a case study of the Reinhart–Rogoff observation because it is so difficult to assign blame.

Assigning blame

Five aspects of the Greek situation are worth emphasizing.

First, and foremost, the Greek government was dishonest with its eurozone partners. Greece's politicians governed with short time horizons – expanding the public sector with patronage jobs (clientelism), tolerating an uneven tax collection system, permitting and perpetuating corruption, and fraudulently reporting debt levels to the European Commission by using extremely complicated 'derivative swaps' to hide its enormous budget deficit of 12 per cent. Greek officials made the ill-fated assumption that low interest rates and the high growth rate would continue, and they would be able to repay the debt. In effect, they gambled and lost when financial markets collapsed in 2007/8. It took about a year, to late 2009, for creditors and investors to catch on to the market signals that Greece was unable to service its debt, but when they did Greek officials continued to disassemble to their eurozone partners regarding the truth – that they were on the edge of default.

Second, the magnitude of Greek sovereign debt was staggering at €340 billion or about €31,000 per person (from a population of 11 million) in a country with an average salary of €25,915.

Third, Greece is an undiversified economy that is heavily reliant on three sectors – agriculture, which accounts for 12 per cent of employment compared to a 3.5 per cent EU average (Manolopoulos, 2011, p. 16), shipping and tourism. Each of these is vulnerable to global downturns, which is what happened in 2009–10: world food prices dropped, shipping declined (because there were fewer goods being shipped), and tourism plummeted when Americans and Europeans lost their jobs or feared impending layoffs.

Fourth, Greece's powerful and militant trade unions were able to prevent the Greek government enacting meaningful austerity measures before the debt crisis spun out of control.

Fifth, once Greece's shaky finances became apparent, businesses and consumers began to withdraw their funds from Greek banks, speculators bet against Greek sovereign bonds, and foreign investors began to abandon Greece, thus turning a bad situation into an untenable one.

(For in-depth examinations of the Greek debt crisis, see Featherstone, 2011; Manolopoulos, 2011.)

most important were: (i) the establishment of a permanent rescue (bailout) fund that would operate along the same lines as IMF funds loaned to countries on the verge of fiscal default;(ii) the strengthening of the SGP via a range of voluntary, legislative and (non EU-wide) treaty measures.

Rescue funds

Concerns about the size of the Greek budget deficit and public debt resulted in early 2010 in the eurozone members (apart from Slovakia, which opted out) lending funds to Greece on a bilateral basis. In exchange for the bailout, Greece agreed to reform public finances by improving the tax collection system, levying new taxes, and reducing public expenditure through such measures as increasing the pension age and cutting the size of the public sector. However, investors were not convinced that the bailout funds were sufficient to stem the short-term crisis because, with negative growth, Greece was not going to be able to 'grow' itself out of the crisis while at the same time the government was not slashing spending or undertaking structural changes at the rate needed to restore investor confidence. As the Greek crisis grew, the contagion spread to the other vulnerable eurozone economies, with investors scrutinizing balance sheets and demanding higher yields on sovereign bond issues.

The spreading crisis meant that bilateral loans would not be sufficient to calm markets. As a consequence of this, the eurozone states created two temporary bailout funds: the European Financial Stabilization Mechanism (EFSM) and the European Financial Stability Facility (EFSF). Their creation was followed by plans for a permanent bailout fund to replace the temporary funds, but as this required an amendment to the TFEU (by special procedure), its establishment was delayed. The new fund – the European Stability Mechanism (ESM) – came into effect in October 2012. Box 10.7 describes its key features.

Critics of the ESM have suggested it was undercapitalized at €700 billion: the figure of €2 trillion was widely cited as a more realistic firewall. Chancellor Merkel, however, on behalf of Germany – the ESM's main contributor – insisted that this would provide adequate capitalization (Inman and Traynor, 2011). She also insisted that, combined with binding fiscal arrangements to strengthen the SGP, the ESM would prevent a repeat of the Greek meltdown.

Strengthening fiscal discipline

With the SGP largely discredited by the eurozone debt crisis, the Eurogroup sought a new approach to fiscal discipline. This section outlines the main measures that had been adopted up to the end of 2012. Box 10.8 summarizes the principal measures.

The Euro Plus Pact The Euro Plus Pact, the brainchild of Germany and France, was agreed at the Spring 2011 European Council by eurozone member states plus Bulgaria, Denmark, Latvia, Lithuania, Poland and Romania (European Council, 2011b, Annex I). It is a voluntary pact designed to guide long-term structural changes to enhance growth and competitiveness. It focuses on five issues: fostering competitiveness, increasing employment, enhancing the sustainability of public finances, reinforcing financial stability, and the initiation of structured discussions on tax policy issues. Perceived as a complement to the SGP, the focus of the Euro Plus Pact is long-term structural changes, especially with respect to fostering growth.

Progress on achieving the Pact's goals are included in National Reform Programmes and assessed as part of the 'European semester' (see below), which since 2011 has been the agreed economic governance cycle for all EU member states.

The Euro Plus Pact, however, was not what the markets had in mind when investors called for fiscal discipline. In consequence, it was virtually ignored by markets because it was not seen as addressing the immediate needs – which were thought to be binding rules with respect to deficits and debts along with a workable and well-funded rescue plan. As a result, bond yields continued to rise on the sovereign debt issued by the troubled eurozone member states. The eurozone thus clearly needed further measures to strengthen fiscal policy.

The six-pack The six-pack reforms, consisting of five regulations and one directive, came into force in December 2011. The six-pack is, in effect, a revised and strengthened SGP. Its main features are:

- The creation of a new monitoring cycle of the economic performances of all member states. This is based on the above-mentioned 'European semester', which integrates economic, budgetary and

---

Box 10.7

The European Stability Mechanism

Treaty basis: Article 136. 3 TEFU, states: 'The member states whose currency is the euro may establish a stability mechanism to be activated if indispensable to safeguard the stability of the euro area as a whole. The granting of any required financial assistance under the mechanism will be made subject to strict conditionality.'

Type of organization: International organization located and registered in Luxembourg.

Date operational: October 2012 – after 90 per cent of the total capital commitments had been ratified (see subscription percentages below).

Membership and decision-making: Led by a Board of Governors chaired by the Eurogroup President, and comprised of one representative from each eurozone member state.

Function: To mobilize funding and provide financial assistance, under strict conditionality, to the benefit of the eurozone. The ESM is a bank of last resort similar to the IMF, but junior to it. The ESM is authorized to purchase government bonds on the open market, subject to the unanimous approval of the eurozone countries, but with emergency approval by 85 per cent of member states under certain conditions (stability of the eurozone judged to be at stake and the decision must be supported by the Commission and ECB).

Capitalization: Issues bonds or other debt instruments on capital markets. The ESM is backed by guarantee commitments (subscribed capital) from the euro area member states of €620 billion and paid-in capital of €80 billion to make a total of €700 billion. It has a lending capacity of €440 billion. Its funds are supplemented temporarily by the €258 billion held by the European Financial Stability Facility (a temporary rescue fund).

Contributors by percentage (based on GDP): Germany 27.1; France 20.4; Italy 17.9; Spain 11.9; the Netherlands 5.7; Belgium 3.5; Greece 2.8; Austria 2.8; Portugal 2.5; Finland 1.8; Ireland 1.6; Slovakia 0.82; Slovenia 0.43; Luxembourg 0.25; Cyprus 0.2; Estonia 0.19; Malta 0.07.

---

structural issues as well as measures to help boost growth (see Figure 10.1).

- Member states with unsustainable public finances are required to make significant progress towards medium-term budgetary objectives (MTOs) aimed at respecting the 3 per cent budget deficit criterion.
- The creation of an MTO enforcement system managed by the Commission based on: a graduated warning system in which failure to make progress during the 'preventative' phase can trigger a Commission *warning*; and failure to respect the rules leads to a Commission *recommendation* to the member state to take corrective action (a recom-

mendation that can only be rescinded by the Council).

- Excessive deficit procedure (EDP)-based financial sanctions can be applied to eurozone states with deficits in excess of 3 per cent of GDP and debts in excess of 60 per cent of GDP. If placed in EDP, eurozone members need to deposit 0.2 per cent of GDP in a non-interest-bearing account. In cases of non-compliance with Commission recommendations, deposit accounts are converted to fines.
- The creation of a macroeconomic surveillance – called an alert mechanism report (AMR). This report consists of macroeconomic indicators designed to detect imbalances (in the form of an

Box 10.8

Comparing the SGP, the six-pack, the Fiscal Compact and the two-pack

	SGP	Six-pack	Fiscal Compact (Title III, TSCG)	Two-pack
Adopted (came into force)	June 1997 at Amsterdam Council	13 December 2011	Expected to come into force in late 2012 after a minimum of 12 eurozone states ratify.	Under consideration as of autumn 2012; delayed by significant EP amendments proposing mutualizing of eurozone debt and increasing funding for infrastructure investments.
Form	Secondary legislation	Secondary legislation – five regulations and one directive	Extra-EU treaty	Secondary legislation
Applicability	All member states, but with special rules for eurozone states.	All member states, but with financial sanctions only for eurozone states.	Fiscal Compact applies to eurozone member states only. Other states may join, but will not be subject to financial sanctions.	Eurozone members only
Deficit limits	3% of GDP	3% of GDP	0.5% of GDP (1% for member states with a debt ratio significantly below 60% of GDP).	As in Fiscal Compact
Debt limits	60% of GDP	60% of GDP	60% of GDP	As in Fiscal Compact
Fiscal surveillance	Member states' budgetary balance must converge towards the country-specific medium-term objective (MTO) ('preventative arm').	Defines quantitatively a significant deviation from the MTO.	Monitored by independent institutions (may be the Commission, unclear at time of writing given the extra-EU nature of the Fiscal Compact).	Designed to complement the 'preventative arm' of the SGP. Eurozone members submit their draft budgetary plan and an independent macro economic forecast to the

	Commission and the Eurogroup before 15 October. Establishment of independent institutions to monitor fiscal rules. Automatic 'enhanced surveillance' for countries receiving rescue funds (ESM or other rescue funds so designated by the Commission).			Country-specific medium-term objective (MTO) – corrective action required if member state deviates from its MTO. Establishment of independent institutions to monitor MTOs.
Macroeconomic surveillance	Broad Economic Policy Guidelines (BEPGs).	Introduces 'macroeconomic imbalance procedure' (MIP) based on a scoreboard of 10 indicators.	Alert mechanism report (AMR), published annually, identifies member states whose macroeconomic situation needs to be scrutinized in more depth.	
Sanctions for non-compliance	Financial penalties for breeching excessive deficit (EDP) (corrective arm). Specifics: Council could require a non-interest-bearing account, later would convert to a fine (never used).	Financial penalties for breeching either deficit or *debt* limits under the EDP. Financial penalties imposed in stages, from the preventative arm to the latest stages of EDP.	Imposed if annual deficit exceeds 3%. Sanction of 0.1% of GDP if member state does not properly limit the Pact's budget rules into national law. Sanctions funnelled to ESM for eurozone member states and to the EU budget for non-eurozone states.	As in Fiscal Compact with respect to EDP. Those countries in enhanced surveillance (receiving rescue funds) can lose these funds for non-compliance with Commission opinions.
Voting rules for sanctions	QMV for Commission to sanction a member state.	Reverse QMV for most sanctions – Commission recommendation considered adopted unless a qualified majority of member states votes against it.	Reverse QMV for most sanctions (only applicable to eurozone states).	As in Fiscal Compact.

Box 10.8 continued

	SGP	Six-pack	Fiscal Compact (Title III, TSCG)	Two-pack
Deficit and debt rules implemented into national law	Not required	Not required	Required	n.a. – inasmuch as Fiscal Compact rules must be implemented by national parliaments.
Role of the CJEU	None	None	Decides if eurozone member has breached the Compact's rules. Can levy fines on states that break the Compact's rules on deficit spending.	n.a.
Governance	Commission makes recommendations after Ecofin approves via QMV.	Commission and Ecofin adopt recommendations on MIP at an early stage. MIPs for eurozone discussed in Eurogroup; MIPs for non-eurozone discussed in Ecofin.	Commission and Council examine and recommend changes to national budgets *before* they are adopted by national parliaments. Euro Summits at least twice a year.	Commission analyses the draft budget to see if it is in line with the SGP and the recommendations made from the European semester (which would have been received in May/June) – see Figure 10.1. If the budgetary plan shows serious SGP non-compliance, the Commission can require a revised draft budgetary plan.

Source: European Commission, 2012s.

Figure 10.1 The European Semester

The European Semester: who does what and when?

	Jan	Feb	Mar	Apr	May	Jun	Jul	Throughout the year:
European Commission	Annual Growth Survey (AGS) presented				Assessment for NRPs and SCPs	Recommendations to Member States based on NRPs and SCPs		
Council of European Union		AGS debated ahead of European Council					Recommendations to Member States formally adopted	Peer review of Member States' compliance with recommendations including consideration of possible further/enforcement measures (Excessive Imbalance Procedure)
European Parliament		AGS debated ahead of European Council						
European Council			Endorsement of reform priorities for EU Member States			Debate and endorsement of recommendations to Member States		
Member States				National Reform Programmes (NRPs) and Stability/ Convergence Programmes (SCPs) sent to Commission				**Autumn:** Governments present draft budgets to national parliaments for debate in line with established national practice

Source: European Commission, 2011h.

annual scoreboard). An excessive imbalance procedure (EIP), which mirrors the EDP, can be followed-up – with fines of 0.1 per cent of GDP – for eurozone members failing to take corrective action under the EIP.

The market's initial reaction to the six-pack was positive as a result of the new surveillance mechanisms and the inclusion of debt in the EDP (previously, only annual budget deficits had been included). But as it became apparent that the six-pack was not very different from the SGP – in the sense that it was not backed by national legislation, so still carried the risk that a government could ignore a previous government's agreement to abide by the rules – high yields continued on sovereign debt in the troubled economies. Harder law in the way of binding national commitments was necessary to persuade financial investors that sufficiently robust economic reforms were being put in place. Specifically, eurozone members needed to agree to bind national budgetary decision-makers into tight budgetary policy-making. Thus, in late 2011, the European Council moved to try to reach agreement on another, further strengthened, arrangement to tackle this problem.

The Fiscal Compact At the December 2011 European Council summit, the eurozone member states and the majority of non-eurozone EU members agreed to a 'Fiscal Compact'. The UK refused to sign the Compact or to agree to it becoming part of the EU's treaties. The publicly recorded reasons for this were that the UK's requests to the other member states that the UK be given an opt-out from EU financial regulation and be given assurances that the European Banking Authority would remain headquartered in London were both refused (Taylor, 2011a). In practice, opposition within Prime Minister David Cameron's Conservative Party was also important. The Czech Republic also refused to sign the Compact – nominally, at least, for domestic constitutional reasons. These two refusals closed the (immediate) option of giving the Compact full treaty status by amending the TFEU. In late January 2012, 25 member states signed the Fiscal Compact and in March 2012 the 25 signed the Treaty on Stability, Coordination and Governance (TSCG), an extra-EU treaty based on the measures agreed in the Compact. Addressing the issue of a free-standing treaty, the TSCG's Article 16 states that the aim is to incorporate the TSCG's substance into the

EU's legal framework within five years. The 'meat' of the TSCG is the 'Fiscal Compact': a supranational system focused on the surveillance of national budgets and with binding implementation rules. Box 10.9 summarizes the key features of the TSCG.

How might the Fiscal Compact be classified? Well, it is by no means a 'fiscal union'. Rather, it is essentially the SGP with added bite. The major criticism of the Compact as it was being devised came from the centre-left and from troubled eurozone states, which argued that it was too focused on *austerity* and not enough on *solidarity*. The austerity focus was seen as being a 'capitulation' to the German view of the underlying causes of the debt crisis – too many eurozone economies being run on profligate and irresponsibly-managed bases. According to growth advocates, in focusing on austerity the Compact would not be able to solve the long-term problems of eurozone member states with respect to growth, infrastructure reforms and deep disparities in wealth.

Some of the Compact's detractors were in, or soon entered, government – most notably François Hollande, who was elected French president shortly after the TSCG was signed, and Mario Monti, the caretaker Italian prime minister. The signing of the TSCG thus did not end debate about where the balance should lie between austerity and public intervention to stimulate economic growth.

The two-pack The two-pack – so-called because it consists of two regulations – was presented by the Commission in late 2011 to operationalize key elements of the TSCG's Fiscal Compact. These regulations, which at the time of writing have not yet been passed into law, are only applicable to eurozone member states.

The regulation on 'monitoring and assessing draft budgetary plans and ensuring the correction of excessive deficits in euro area member states' operationalizes the Fiscal Compact's budgetary surveillance and the excessive deficit procedure. Specifically, it is designed to complement the 'preventive' arm of the SGP by requiring that eurozone members submit draft budgetary reports every year in October, which are then subject to revision after Commission review. It also requires that common budgetary rules at the national level are monitored by the Commission.

The second regulation, on enhanced surveillance of the eurozone member states experiencing or threatened with financial difficulties, is to be part of an enhanced monitoring programme (in addition to the European semester). If a eurozone member does not comply with the policy requirements, it could be threatened with a cut-off of disbursements from the ESM.

During the EP's reading of the two regulations, amendments were put forward aimed at building more provisions for growth and solidarity in the SGP. But the amendments went much further than many states – especially those not experiencing fiscal difficulties – were willing to accept, and encapsulated the vast range of views that have existed, and still do exist, among policy-makers as to how far fiscal integration should be taken. Among proposals contained in the amendments were the mutualization of all national debt exceeding 60 per cent of a country's GDP through a European Redemption Fund of about €2.3 trillion, to be repaid within 25 years; a roadmap towards the issuance of eurozone bonds; and a growth instrument for mobilizing 1 per cent of the EU's GDP over a 10-year period for infrastructure investment (about €100 billion).

Where is the Eurozone Headed? Three Options

The eurozone crisis has resulted in many scenarios being advanced for the future of EMU. This section summarizes and assesses what have widely been seen as the three main options.

Defaults and exits from the eurozone

In this scenario, a eurozone member experiencing severe economic difficulties defaults on its debts and leaves the eurozone. The defaulting country wipes the slate clean of sovereign debt and its new currency is immediately devalued against major currencies, thereby (it is hoped) increasing exports and employment. This option is not risk-free, for three reasons. First, it would involve exchanging a major international currency for one used only by the population of the exiting state. This would necessitate paying for many crucial imported goods either in euros or dollars (many exporters would not accept payment in the new currency). And with a devalued currency, imports would become more expensive. While it is true that

some imported goods (such as luxury German cars and American designer handbags) are not a necessity, the same cannot be said for medicines, technology, energy products, military hardware and foodstuffs. Second, the revaluation of all national assets and liabilities to the new currency would be a Herculean task, fraught with uncertainty for all affected parties. Third, it would precipitate a run on national banks and investments (which happened in Greece when the government openly discussed leaving the eurozone, thus undermining Greece's ability to recover without even more additional outside assistance and reassurances).

Eurozone institutions and member states have sought to avoid publicly entertaining the possibility of an unmanaged default as a serious option, though they departed from this posture briefly during the spring of 2012 as the Greek debt problem became progressively more serious and an (inconclusive) Greek election brought to the verge of power a party that campaigned on a platform of abrogating the previous government's debt agreements with the lending troika (the IMF, the ECB and the Commission). One reason for avoiding public discussion of defaults and exits is that banks throughout the eurozone (and, indeed, throughout the EU a whole) hold substantial sovereign debt. Another, and arguably more important reason, is the threat of contagion. A single default would undermine creditor faith in other weak eurozone states and in doing so would increase borrowing costs to unsustainable rates. Fear of such contagion was a key reason why such efforts were made in 2011–12 to 'save Greece': because if Greece defaulted and exited the eurozone, then Portugal, Spain and Italy (the seventh-largest economy in the world!) would probably have come under even more intense market pressure.

For many months – from mid-2011 until another Greek election in June 2012 – neither Greece nor Germany blinked and many thought that the eurozone would unravel. In the end, the risk was averted with the June 2012 Greek election resulting in a broad-based coalition government that pledged to keep Greece in the euro by redoubling efforts to privatize government holdings and asking the lending troika for more time to meet its deficit targets.

However, the 2011–12 Greek crisis showed quite clearly that while there are many cool heads in national capitals and EU institutions who are resolved to see the eurozone survive intact, an exit (or exits) cannot be completely ruled out.

Treaty on Stability, Coordination and Governance

Treaty Components

The Treaty on Stability, Coordination and Governance (TSCG) is an extra-EU treaty agreed to in 2012 that replaces the SGP (which itself had been strengthened by the six-pack) with a 'fiscal compact' with new binding rules. In the negotiations that produced the Treaty, Germany was successful in pressing that austerity and budgetary restraint should be given much greater weight than policies designed to promote economic growth through public investment.

Title I of the Treaty outlines its purpose and scope. Title II states that the TSCG should be applied and interpreted in conformity with EU treaties. The 'meat' of the TSCG is found in Title III – the Fiscal Compact.

Title III Fiscal Compact

- Medium-term objectives (MTOs):
  – Balanced or surplus budget at 0.5% of GDP at market prices
  – Government debt 60% of GDP
- European Commission sets time frame for meeting the MTOs for each contracting party.
- Correction mechanisms triggered automatically if a contracting party deviates from MTOs. (Must reduce debt by one twentieth per year.)
- Contracting parties in breach must submit a 'budgetary and economic partnership programme' to the Council and the Commission for endorsement and monitoring, using existing surveillance procedures under the SGP.
- Contracting parties may temporarily deviate from MTOs in exceptional circumstances ('unusual event outside the control of the contracting party or periods of severe economic downturn as set out in the revised SGPs').
- Contracting parties must report *ex-ante* public debt issuance plans to the Council and the Commission
- Contracting parties must implement MTOs into national law ('preferably constitutional') within one year of TSCG coming into force.
- If contracting parties fail to comply with the excessive-deficit rule (triggered when a country exceeds 3 per cent of GDP), another contracting party can bring the matter to the CJEU (either on the basis of a Commission report or its own finding).
- If the CJEU finds the contracting party has not complied with its judgment, it may impose a lump sum or penalty payment under the EDP (not to exceed 0.1% of GDP).
- The amounts imposed on a contracting party whose currency is the euro is payable to the European Stability Mechanism; non-eurozone contracting parties will make their payments to the general EU budget.

The current arrangements, with strengthened policy instruments

As shown in this chapter, EMU is a complex and fast-moving policy area. What has also been shown is that, in response to the crises of recent years, the EU has been able to make important reforms. Among the most important of these have been:

- The strengthening of the SGP through the six-pack, the Fiscal Compact, and the two-pack.
- The stimulation of growth through ECB operations (especially the maintenance of lower interest rates) and increased EIB lending.
- The establishment of new rescue (bailout) funds, both temporary and permanent.
- The granting of permission to the ESM to lend directly to banks.

Box 10.9 continued

Title IV Economic Policy Coordination and Convergence

- Based on provisions in the TFEU. This title is concerned with co-operation among the contracting parties to foster competitiveness, promote employment and contribute to the sustainability of public finances. Anticipates benchmarking best practices and more closely co-ordinated economic policies, the latter being managed through EU institutions.

Title V Governance of the Euro Area

- A minimum of two Euro Summits to be held per year, immediately after European Council meetings. These meetings to be comprised of the Heads of State or Government of eurozone members, plus the President of the Commission. The ECB President is invited to attend. The meetings are to focus exclusively on governance of the eurozone.
- The President of Euro Summits is appointed by the Heads of State or Government of eurozone members. The appointment is made, by simple majority, at the same time as the European Council elects its President and for the same term of office. The President is to work with the Euro Group, which is charged with the preparation and follow up to Euro Summit meetings. The President is to make a report to the EP after each Euro Summit meeting.
- Heads of State or Government of non-eurozone states that have ratified the TSCG are to participate in Euro Summit meetings concerning competitiveness, the modification of the global architecture of the eurozone, and in least once a year discussions on specific issues of TSCG implementation in the context of EMU.

Application

- Only Titles III and IV apply to non-eurozone contracting parties.
- Does not alter the economic policy conditions under which financial assistance is granted to member states involved in stabilization programmes involving the EU and/or the IMF.
- Financial assistance from the ESM is conditional on ratification of the TSCG.

Implementation Mode

To be transposed into national legislation by national parliaments. It is an extra-EU treaty, therefore signatories are technically 'contracting parties' rather than 'member states'. The TSCG comes into force on 1 January 2013, provided that 12 contracting parties whose currency is the euro have ratified. Non-participating EU states (namely, the Czech Republic and the UK) are permitted to accede to the treaty if they wish.

- The conferral of bank supervisory powers on the ECB, bringing it closer to the Bundesbank and US Federal Reserve models.

These reforms share two very important features. First, they show that despite deep differences between the EU states, and also between the eurozone states, as to how the crises should have been (and still should be) tackled, there has consistently been a broadly held view that all reasonable steps should be taken to ensure that the eurozone survives. Second, they show that the EU's preferred approach – or at least its only politically possible approach – to dealing with EMU difficulties is gradual and incremental reform.

These two features of the EU's approach seem likely to continue. Moreover, it also seems likely that further strengthening of EMU will be necessary. For while it is unclear at the time of writing as to whether the measures that have been taken to date will, in the long-term, be viewed by markets as 'going far enough', it was significant that while European stock exchanges at first (at the end of 2011) reacted positively to the Fiscal Compact and to ECB-lowered interest rates, the credit rating agencies soon resumed their pattern of lowering their ratings on the sovereign debt in several eurozone countries. Indeed, the credit rating agency Fitch issued a statement that the EU had failed to 'put into place a fully credible financial firewall' (*Guardian*, 2011).

By late 2012, it was widely believed that more policy action would be required to encourage long-run investor confidence and avoid another eurozone crisis. On the basis of the record to date, the response will be cautious, with many ideas doubtless being floated and considered (see, for example, Thomas, 2012).

Fiscal union (to be added to the existing monetary union)

The members of the eurozone have formed a 'monetary union' because they have adopted a single currency. The eurozone is not, however, a fiscal union, because that would involve the collection of taxes from all constituent units and the redistribution of tax receipts for the benefit of the entire union. A fiscal union thus needs a central taxing authority (a treasury), an independent tax source, and mechanisms for the distribution of funds from the centre to the constituent units.

Discussion of the eurozone's possible path towards fiscal union was accelerated in 2012 when the joint report of the European Council President, European Commission President, Eurogroup President and the ECB President to the June European Council meeting contained a blueprint for an EU fiscal union. Significantly, the report was entitled 'Towards a Genuine Economic and Monetary Union' (European Council, 2012).

What might a eurozone fiscal union be like? The two critical institutions of a fiscal union would be an EU Finance Ministry, which does not currently exist, and the European Central Bank with strengthened powers. The responsibilities of these two institutions in a eurozone fiscal union will now be considered.

An EU Finance Ministry

Integral to a fiscal union is an institution that generates revenues (by being a taxing authority) and distributes public goods. This is typically a Finance Ministry. So, a eurozone fiscal union would require a European Finance Minister overseeing an EU Finance Ministry. A description of the necessary powers and policies of such a Minister and Ministry follows.

An ability to make fiscal transfers Fiscal transfers are necessary in fiscal unions to assist parts of the union that are distressed by economic downturns, especially under conditions of low labour mobility such as exist in the EU. In existing federations, transfer mechanisms for stabilization and redistribution are much higher than is possible under the EU budget (see Chapter 14 for a detailed analysis of the EU's budget). The ability to tax, which enables the central authority to transfer revenues from high-growth regions to economically-distressed regions, is absolutely crucial to the success of fiscal unions.

The ameliorative effects of 'counter-cyclical' taxation measures can be shown briefly by referencing fully federalized systems. Baimbridge and Whyman (2008) report that the Canadian and American federal governments moderate between 17 per cent and 30 per cent of fiscal shocks through fiscal transfers and taxation, while in the European federations, the average is 31 per cent. Pisani-Ferry *et al.* (1993) employ a model to compare the redistribution effect of fiscal transfers and taxation in the US and Germany, reporting that the American federal government has a 17 per cent stabilization effect (transferring funds from healthy to distressed regions for redundancy payments, health care, jobs training and other safety-net programmes) and Germany 42 per cent. Indeed, US federal transfers at over US$400 billion per year have come to be the single largest revenue sources for the American states (Greve, 2011, p. 107). Thus, fully-operational federal systems are characterized by sizeable fiscal transfers. The EU, however, has a very small budget and no sizeable direct revenue source. Therefore, attention has turned to the extent to which the EU could raise revenues that would be independent of member state funding.

An ability to raise revenues through an EU-wide tax The monies paid into the EU budget are totally insufficient to enable the size of the fiscal transfers that would be required to overcome recession-induced disparities and the relative lack of economic competitiveness in particular EU states and regions. But, as is explained in Chapter 14, enacting a new EU-wide tax requires unanimity. Some states – with the UK in the lead – are adamantly opposed to the imposition of EU taxes of any kind. The tax that arguably holds most promise – a financial transaction tax (FTT) – has no hope of being approved by all the member states. However, by the end of 2012 it had attracted support from a sufficient number of member states, including France and Germany, to permit the possibility of proceeding through enhanced cooperation.

An ability to issue eurobonds Eurobonds would be bonds issued by the eurozone rather than member states. Because they would have the full faith and resources of the eurozone behind them, they would be stronger, and therefore would be subject to lower rates of interest, than most national bonds – especially the bonds of states with weak economies.

Germany, however, has been steadfastly opposed to an EU entity – be it an EU Finance Ministry or the ECB – being given the power to issue eurobonds. The central reason for this opposition has been that Germany – as the eurozone's main economic power by far – would in effect, be the main guarantor of the eurobonds. Another, closely related, reason is the problem of 'subsidiary sovereign bonds', a term coined by the economist Charles Goodhart to explain why bonds issued by members of a monetary union are inferior to debt issued centrally by authorities of the monetary union (Peston, 2011). In a nutshell, eurobonds would create a classic collective action problem: indebted countries (such as Spain and Italy in the eurozone) would be tempted to free ride to take advantage of the lower rates available through currency union membership, thereby spreading the costs of a potential default to all other eurozone members through higher borrowing costs. This is the classic 'moral hazard' problem (see Rodden, 2006, for an in-depth analysis of the moral hazard problem in fiscal federalism).

Eurobonds would thus involve risks, especially for those states with stronger economies. However, the early US experience of bond financing offers powerful empirical evidence of the likely positive impact of eurobonds on the eurozone as a whole. For, as the American economist, Thomas Sargent (2011), argued,

in his 2011 Nobel Prize acceptance speech entitled 'United States Then, Europe Now', the underlying economics of the eurozone debt crisis echo those of the US under the Confederation (1787–9). The massive debt at the end of the Revolutionary War – US$54 million (federal government) and US$25 million (states) – threatened the very viability of the nascent American republic but, as in the current situation with respect to the EU's lack of revenue-raising power, the Continental Congress had no economic power over the states. In these highly threatening circumstances, President George Washington agreed with his Treasury Secretary, Alexander Hamilton, that the new federal government would assume the debt of both the Continental Congress and the states at par values through the vehicle of the Bank of the United States, which was granted a limited 20-year charter to act as a bank of last resort. This action is seen by many historians as having 'preserved' the United States in its formative years.

An ability to supervise national budgets Fiscal unions need to build a credible policy to reduce moral hazard (defined above). If they do not establish such a policy, the constituent units with revenue raising powers will be tempted to take advantage of their membership in a larger entity by borrowing funds, expecting that if they are not able to make good on these to investors, the central government will intervene to purchase the 'bad' bonds. The danger for the eurozone since the establishment of the single currency has been that no 'credible pre-commitment' to moral hazard exists. Thus, if the EU 'bails out' member states as it has done quite substantially with Greece, there has been little in the way of binding commitments to prevent future debted governments from spending unwisely and not taxing their citizens adequately for the costs of government. When reckless eurozone borrowers are confronted by unexpected expense (as the result, for example, of an economic recession or natural disaster), they are unable to pay their bond investors.

Thomas Sargent (2011), again in his Nobel Prize speech, noted that American states confronted budgetary crises in the antebellum (pre-Civil War) period when they began to issue revenue bonds to finance costly public works projects during the boom construction years of 1820–42. When the promised toll revenues did not materialize, some states suspended payments temporarily, and a few actually defaulted. Despite fierce lobbying from the states and bonds' investors (some of whom were ruined financially by the defaults), Congress refused to bail out these states. In refusing to do so, the US government established what was to become a 'credible pre-commitment' from moral hazard (Greve, 2011, p. 109). A crucially important precedent was set for the sound financial operation of fiscal unions, because after the federal government refused to bail out the troubled states, investors became wary of buying state-issued bonds. In order to win back the confidence of investors, in the 1840s states began to pass balanced budget amendments (today, all states apart from Vermont have a constitutional requirement to balance budgets) and no state has defaulted on a general obligation bond (which are backed by state taxing power) since the time of the Civil War.

So, the EU has now tried to short-circuit the moral hazard temptation problem in fiscal unions in much the same way as did the US when faced with a near-identical situation (although it can be argued that the situation in the US was more dire). The Fiscal Compact, which is a binding treaty (see above), requires all eurozone member states to amend their constitutions to require balanced budgets. (In this respect, the eurozone solution to moral hazard is even more draconian than that adopted in the US, because in the latter states amended their constitutions without federal mandates or an amendment to the US Constitution requiring balanced budgets.) The EU has also established a budgetary supervision system that should ensure that eurozone states do not mismanage their budgets, and an accompanying system that results in states that do mismanage becoming subject to enhanced surveillance from the Commission (see Box 10.8).

The European Central Bank

In a fiscal union, the ECB would take on additional responsibilities to those described above. The most important new role would be as the primary purchaser of eurozone member state debt, thus taking on the role of 'bank of last resort'. If the EU did issue eurobonds, the ECB would engage in purchasing and selling EU eurobonds to inject euros into the financial system (to generate economic growth) or remove euros from circulation (to slow down an overheated economy). However, as was noted above, Germany, as the ECB's major financial contributor and a country fully aware of the moral hazard risk, is opposed to ECB intervention in bond markets.

With respect to the stability of European banks within the EU's integrated financial market, in a fiscal union the ECB would need to be the main supervisory authority of the European banking system. As noted earlier in the chapter, significant moves in this direction began in 2012.

Conclusions

Inspiration for the euro symbol – € – was from the Greek letter epsilon (a reference to the cradle of European civilization) and the first letter of the word Europe. The two crossed lines are meant to signify stability (European Commission, 2010k). How ironic it is, then, that the eurozone's inherent instability would first manifest itself, and in such a ferocious manner, in Greece.

As this chapter has explained, EMU has long been a core policy in the integration project. Not many students of European integration would have predicted, however, that some 40 years after the first major step towards EMU was taken, with the Heads of Government 1969 Declaration, EMU would shake the very core of the European integration project. Yet many policy practitioners and scholars *had* predicted that EMU would create an inherently unstable regime. For example, writing in 1999, and laying the problem at the feet of a lack of fiscal co-ordination, Christopher Sims (1999, p. 426) not only predicted the eurozone debt crisis but also suggested that it would happen in 'the first decade or two' after EMU's establishment.

The French economist-politician Félix Esquirou de Parieu, who served under Napoleon III, called monetary unions 'the Chassepot of peace' (quoted in Einaudi, 2000, p. 306; the Chassepot was a state-of-the-art French rifle in the mid-1860s). This link between economics and peace seems to have been lost in the panic engendered by the eurozone crisis. However, it has always been the case that the euro is more than just an economic convenience. It is part of the political construction of an integrated Europe; it is an assertion of Europe as an integrated trade bloc; it promotes free movement of people (along with the other three freedoms); and it is both a challenge and a companion to the dollar's dominance.

Time has emerged as the crucial variable in the long-run viability of the eurozone. Kenneth Rogoff, former IMF chief economist and a scholar of debt crises and panics, observed in late November 2011: 'The Europeans hoped to have 30 to 40 years to integrate more fully. Right now they don't have 30 to 40 weeks' (quoted in Erlanger, 2011b).

But the eurozone crisis also points back to the central role of the internal market. So, for example, 'good policy' to improve competitiveness (in this case, German wage restraint) had a negative effect on the competitiveness of other Eurozone members and reduced German demand for its neighbours' goods and services. So it is that sometimes domestic policy changes can be crucial to the overall health of the eurozone. And just as German's depressed wages translated into lower demand for French and Italian goods and Greek vacations, the wage increases (some above inflation rates) that German unions negotiated throughout 2012 will help to grow other eurozone economies.

Thomas Sargent (2011) has trenchantly observed 'Fiscal crises often produce political revolutions ... in the US in 1787 and in France in 1789.' While the eurozone crisis is hardly likely to produce a similarly history-defining political revolution, it is clear that its political ramifications, including those for fiscal federalism, will be felt for some considerable time to come.

Chapter 11

The Area of Freedom, Security and Justice

The area of freedom, security and justice (AFSJ) has been a rapidly expanding aspect of EU policy activity since the mid-1990s. It consists of those policies falling within what was formerly known as Justice and Home Affairs (JHA).

The AFSJ covers a wide range of policies, many of them dealing with border issues and the free movement of people. Among particular policy matters falling under AFSJ are immigration, asylum, visas, citizenship rights, and the combating of terrorism and of organized crime.

The AFSJ policy area thus clearly contains highly sensitive matters. One reason for the sensitivity is that many of the topics covered by AFSJ involve a trade-off between individual freedoms and the duty of public decision-makers to protect life and property as well as to uphold the social order. Another reason is, as Jörg Monar (2011a, p. 181), a prominent academic commentator on AFSJ, has put it, 'EU action in the [AFSJ] domain touches upon core functions of the state: providing security and justice for citizens and sovereign control over the national territory are not only central prerogatives of the modern nation-state but also essential elements of its *raison d'être* and legitimacy.'

The sensitivity of so much AFSJ policy has resulted in AFSJ being one of the EU's most contested policy areas. There are few dimensions of AFSJ that do not result in sharp disagreements between policy actors regarding whether, and to what extent, policies that have often been at the heart of – and indeed have virtually been expressions of – national independence and sovereignty, should be Europeanized in some way.

This chapter on AFSJ is divided into six sections. The first section lays out the rationale for AFSJ. AFSJ's development is chronicled in the second section. The third section outlines AFSJ's main institutional actors and policy processes. In the fourth section key AFSJ policies are examined. The fifth section examines the nature and significance of one of AFSJ's highest-profile accomplishments: the Charter of Fundamental Rights of the European Union. The final section provides conclusions and looks to future policy challenges.

The Rationale for AFSJ

How has a 'non-state' political entity come to develop policies that normally are firmly located within sovereign states? The answer to this question lies in the central driving force of AFSJ, a force that is much emphasized throughout this book: the numerous policy impacts of the EU's commitment to integrating its internal market. Providing for free movement of people, which is a key part of opening up the market, brings many benefits to member states and their citizens, but it cannot be achieved simply by removing internal passport controls and border checks. Rather, it requires a host of supporting mechanisms to be put in place. It also requires EU-level policies and actions to deal with unwanted consequences of the free movement of people.

Take, for example, the difficulties that arise for the EU's external borders from the internal free movement of people. If a traveller from, say, Brazil enters France via Paris's Charles de Gaulle airport, or enters Italy through the Port of Naples, s/he also gains entry to all other EU member states because of the free movement principle, unless checks designed to restrict the traveller's free movement remain, or are put in place. This situation has necessitated extensive EU policy development, not least to ensure that there are measures to counter such negative side-effects of thousands of miles of often un-policed borders as human trafficking, smuggling, illegal migration, increased terrorist threats and criminal flight.

Other, quite different, examples of policy areas where the principle of the internal free movement of people has required EU policy development include the resolution of civil disputes and the regularization of aspects of criminal law. With regard to civil disputes: which laws should apply when, for example, citizens of different member states file for divorce, and under which jurisdiction should a child custody dispute be decided? With regard to criminal law, there are often differences among member states concerning, for example, the application of *habeas corpus* (protection against arbitrary imprisonment) and rules of evidence.

So, internal market-related reasons have been behind much of the rapid development of the AFSJ policy area. But they have not been the only driving force. Another important factor, for example, has been changing public attitudes towards civil rights which, along with the EU's increasingly multicultural nature, does much to explain the increased legal protection given by the EU in recent years to the civil rights of many groups. A major goal of AFSJ policy has come to be that no European should suffer racial, ethnic, religious, gender, age or sexual orientation discrimination

in any EU member state where they choose to visit, live or work.

But while AFSJ policy has come to be part of the EU 'mainstream', the depth of support that has been given to the development of AFSJ has varied between member states, both at a general level and with respect to particular AFSJ policies. These variations have greatly affected the nature and pace of AFSJ policy development. Taking border control policy as an example, a number of factors have influenced the attitudes of member states, including: geographical proximity and cultural ties (for example, passport unions existed among Nordic and among Benelux states prior to the Schengen area being created, helping to make these states sympathetic to an EU-wide passport union); whether an EU member shares borders with non-EU member states (the UK's island status is usually seen as being a key reason for it not participating fully in several AFSJ policies, including border control policy); whether a member state has extensive coastlines that are easily reachable by sea from net migration areas (Mediterranean member states are most 'exposed' in this context, and consequently have pressed for increased EU financial support for external border control measures); whether drug trafficking and cross-border organized crime is a major policing problem (as it has become for most member states); and perceptions of being vulnerable to international terrorism (perceptions that are felt most keenly in Western European member states – because they have experienced the most attacks and because of the radical Islamization of some individuals in European-born Muslim populations).

The Development of AFSJ

The Treaties

There had been co-operation in many AFSJ policy areas – some quite substantial – before the Maastricht Treaty gave JHA a treaty basis in 1992. As early as 1975, the European Council, in its Rome Summit, established the 'Trevi Group' as an intergovernmental forum in which home affairs and justice ministers exchanged information and sometimes co-ordinated efforts in combating terrorism in Europe – some of which was home grown, such as the IRA and Red

Brigade, and some from outside Europe, such as the PLO's 1972 massacre of Israeli Olympic athletes at Munich. And, from the mid-1980s, most member states co-operated within the framework of what became known as the Schengen Process, which had as its aim the removal of internal EU barriers on the free movement of people.

Because of the sensitivities associated with the policy issues it contained, when the Maastricht Treaty gave JHA formal status as an EU policy area it was cordoned off from most other areas of domestic EU policy in a separate, third, intergovernmental pillar of the TEU. This meant that JHA policy-making would not be subject to the Community method or to EU law-making.

In the Amsterdam Treaty, member states agreed to transfer most areas of JHA – including asylum, immigration, and border and visa policies – to pillar one (the EC pillar), thus allowing EU laws to be made via the Community method. This transfer had as part of its purpose the enabling, within a period of five years, of measures to be adopted that would result in the progressive establishment of a 'an area of freedom, security and justice' in which there would be free movement of people behind common external policies. The UK and Ireland were given opt-outs from these free movement provisions, and Denmark was not associated fully with them. What remained of the intergovernmental JHA pillar was renamed Police and Judicial Co-operation in Criminal Matters.

By exchanging intergovernmental decision-making for the Community method for much of JHA, the Amsterdam Treaty established a more efficient and democratic decision-making process. Of course, as with all EU policies, political horse-trading and compromises were still necessary to enable significant policy advances to be made, but such bargaining strategies were previously very difficult to undertake, and could even be precluded, by the strictly intergovernmental nature of decision-making processes. Furthermore, location by the Maastricht Treaty of JHA within the Council had made even the prospect of much policy development difficult because, unlike the Commission – to which much policy responsibility was now assigned – the Council's Secretariat is not configured as a civil service unit with policy initiating and policy formulating tasks.

The Lisbon Treaty 'completed' the treaty evolution of AFSJ. It did so by abolishing the third pillar that had been established in the Maastricht Treaty and fundamentally revised by the Amsterdam Treaty. AFSJ policies are all now located in the TFEU, under Title V, which is entitled 'Area of Freedom, Security and Justice'. However, not all of the policies are subject to decision-making with the use of QMV: policy areas that remain subject to unanimity in the Council include passports and identity cards, family law, and operational police co-operation.

Action programmes

AFSJ policy is advanced through strategic five-year action programmes, or roadmaps, which are summarized in Box 11.1. The first of these, the Tampere Programme, was launched in 1999. A significant feature of these programmes is the pairing of objectives with agreed timelines for completion. Tampere was followed by the Hague Programme (2005–9) and the Stockholm Programme (2010–14).

The three programmes have not been qualitatively different in general policy goals, but each has highlighted particular aspects of AFSJ on which to focus. So, while the Stockholm Programme envisages continuing to make progress in the AFSJ areas covered in the Hague Programme – including citizenship and fundamental rights, law and justice, internal security, border management and visa control, and migration – it lays special emphasis on the 'external dimension of internal security', citizens' rights, and the social integration of migrants into the culture and society of member states (see Council of the European Union, 2009, p. 3.).

Horizontal federalism

As the AFSJ policy area has come to be seen as increasingly important, and as differences between member states have often made strong and centralized policy and decision-making very difficult, so have member states engaged extensively in 'horizontal federalism'. That is, they have engaged in policy activities among themselves, outside the EU institutional and legal structures. In previous policy chapters in this book we have dealt mainly with policies characterized by 'vertical federalism', where member states negotiate and enact legislation and policy through EU

Box 11.1

AFSJ five-year action programmes

Key features:
- Roadmaps (rather than legislation) as to where the member states are willing to go, along with deadlines for arriving at policy destinations
- The first drafts of action programmes are bold Commission proposals laying out a more federalized vision of JHA. They are then 'watered down' in the course of member state negotiations

Programmes and their policy priorities:
- Vienna Action Plan (1998) – superseded by the Tampere Programme and the concept of five-year plans
- Tampere Programme (1999–2004)
  - Focused on implementing JHA provisions of the Amsterdam Treaty
  - Establishes JHA scoreboard
- Hague Programme (2005–9)
  - Schengen
  - Police co-operation and criminal matters
  - Asylum policy
- Stockholm Programme (2010–14)
  - Protection of fundamental rights
  - Right of privacy
  - Minority rights and other groups needing special protection
  - EU citizenship
  - Building external security dimension into AFSJ
  - Individual rights with respect to privacy in criminal and civil proceedings and freedom of movement
  - Contains over 250 measures (formative and summative reports, communications, legislative proposals, recommendations, data collection, green papers, compendiums, handbooks, factsheets, web portals). Each action is accompanied by a timetable and indication of the EU institutions responsible for carrying the action forward.

Sources: European Commission, 2008c, 2010d; Monar, 2011b.

---

institutions or supranational policy-making. In horizontal federalism, by contrast, policy processes are based on understandings reached among member states with little, if any, central involvement or interference.

In federal systems, horizontal federalism is associated particularly with civil matters (including commercial law and citizens' rights) and criminal law. This is because these policy areas are, for the most part, the responsibility of the constituent units (member states in the EU's case) rather than the central government. They cannot be left wholly to the constituent units, however, given that the greater mobility of the modern world produces such cross-border problems as dissatisfied business partners,

child custody disputes, law-breaking, and flights from justice. If the national authority, or supranational authority in the case of the EU, is not to be given the responsibility of helping to tackle such problems – and this would be viewed as a wholly undesirable intrusion in most federal systems – then constituent states must accord mutual respect for one another's law enforcement and judicial proceedings. This is a challenge the EU is now facing in AFSJ – and one that will continue to assert itself, as the experience of dualist federalist systems has illustrated.

In federal systems, citizens practice a 'mutual respect' skill to cope with the different approaches found among constituent units. While residents of one constituent unit may find the generally-accepted practices of other constituent units disagreeable, they are often willing to tolerate the practices of their neighbours in exchange for the security and economic benefits of a larger union, but only up to a point. Given this pattern of accommodation in federal systems, it is clear that, as labour mobility increases among Europeans, EU member states will be required continuously to adjust, but will also be checked by others, when their practices and actions in key AFSJ areas disrupt the federal project. A major policy area in which this may become very problematic is equality, where there are quite stark differences between member states. ILGA-Europe, a Brussels-based umbrella organization that represents lesbian, gay, bisexual, transgendered and questioning (LGBTQ) organizations throughout Europe, publishes a 'rainbow map' that demonstrates some of these differences. On a scale of 30 (the most respect for LGBTQ issues) to –12 (the least), the UK, with 21, ranks the highest among EU member states, whilst the lowest are Malta (the most Roman Catholic EU member state) with 0, and Greece, Italy and Poland, all with a score of 2 (ILGA-Europe, 2012).

Because AFSJ is still relatively underdeveloped in policy terms, mutual recognition of national laws and procedures is central to the AFSJ policy area. 'United in diversity' is the guiding principle in such areas as citizenship rights, civil justice and criminal matters. But, as integration proceeds, harmonization is increasing.

Institutional Actors and Policy Processes

Much of the description and analysis of EU institutions, policy instruments and policy processes that was given in earlier chapters of this book also holds for AFSJ. This section of the chapter will not repeat what has already been covered but rather will focus on distinctive features of AFSJ arrangements.

Institutional actors

As with most policy areas, there are, as shown in Chapter 3, five main institutional actors. These are:

- *The European Council*, which defines AFSJ strategic guidelines through intensive transgovernmentalism.
- *The Council of Ministers*, which undertakes the management of governmental inputs into AFSJ via the Council hierarchical system of working groups and committees, COREPER, and ministers. The ministerial formation of the Council is still called the JHA Council.
- *The Commission*, which is responsible for policy initiation and formulation, brokerage and executive tasks. In the Amsterdam Treaty, member states were given the power to propose legislation in what was then called the 'third pillar' (mainly criminal justice and police co-operation), with the Lisbon Treaty (Article 76, TFEU) tightening this up by requiring that a quarter of all member states must make a joint proposal (thereby encouraging co-operation and consensus among member states in this area).
- *The EP*, which is at its strongest when the ordinary legislative procedure is used.
- *The CJEU*, which has seen its responsibilities increase greatly as AFSJ has been steadily 'communautarized' since the late 1990s. So, for example, the Lisbon Treaty provided that from 2014 the CJEU will be able to hear cases concerning the approximately 130 criminal and police justice matters that had been in the third pillar.

The AFSJ has posed particular institutional problems for the Commission. This has been partly because of the extremely diverse, multi-faceted and highly complicated nature of much of the policy area, which has created internal resource and co-ordination difficulties. It has also been partly because of the political sensitivities associated with many aspects of AFSJ, which has resulted in the member states making extensive use of non-legislative instruments to advance policy, the significance of this being that the Commission's institutional powers are much weaker with respect to non-legislative instruments than they are with regard to legislation. In an attempt to better manage AFSJ policies, the 2010–15 College of Commissioners was organized in such a way that two Commissioners, rather than the previous single JHA Commissioner, would oversee AFSJ policies. Viviane Reding was appointed Commissioner for Justice, Fundamental Rights and Citizenship, with specific responsibilities including the European Charter of Fundamental Rights, citizens' rights, judicial co-operation in civil matters, and anti-discrimination. Cecilia Malmström was appointed Home Affairs Commissioner, with specific responsibilities including asylum, migration, and police and judicial co-operation in criminal matters.

To a greater extent than other policy areas, AFSJ is characterized by agencification and a proliferation of working committees. Regarding agencification, there are more AFSJ agencies than in any other policy area – a total of eight in all. As can be seen from Box 11.2, some of these agencies – and in particular EUROPOL, EUROJUST and FRONTEX – are extremely important with respect to undertaking such tasks as training, facilitating joint operations, data gathering and information sharing. Regarding the proliferation of working committees, these are of various kinds. There are, for example, more than 30 Council committee and working parties associated with the JHA Council (Monar, 2011c, p. 194). An especially important Council committee is the Standing Committee on Operational Cooperation on Internal Security (COSI), which works closely with the EU Counter-Terrorism Coordinator in giving effect to the Counter-Terrorism Strategy adopted by the Council in 2005 and aimed at combating terrorism globally.

Policy instruments and policy processes

The diversity and sensitivity of the AFSJ results in the policy area employing many differing types of policy instrument and using all of the policy process modes that were described in Chapter 7.

Regarding the AFSJ policy instruments, Monar (2011c) identifies four main types:

- *Tight regulation.* This involves fully legally binding instruments, usually in the form of regulations that require rigid implementation. This type of instrument covers mainly technical matters, such as amendments to the Schengen Border Manual.
- *Framework regulation.* This also involves legally binding instruments, usually in the form of directives, but they are normally broader in their focus and give member states some flexibility in respect of implementation. This type of regulation has

been the primary means of implementing the EU's Common Asylum System.
- *Target-setting.* A wide range of (mainly) Council texts are issued that are focused on target-setting. They constitute soft law in that, while they prescribe a line of action that the EU institutions and member states are expected to follow (often involving action plans), they are not legally enforceable.
- *Convergence support.* There are a wide variety of evaluation mechanisms and reports that identify AFSJ performance and operational needs at the EU and/or national level. They often also identify where further action is required.

With regard to policy processes, these are, of course, inextricably linked to the policy instruments being employed. So regulation requires that legislative processes be used, while target setting and convergence support requires the use of new modes of governance processes. To give a specific policy example, the enforcement of external border controls is heavily dependent on information exchange and co-ordination between national border control agencies, so OMC policy processes are widely employed.

A very important aspect of the sensitivity of many AFSJ policies is the reluctance of member states to transfer sovereignty over matters such as immigration and police powers 'to Brussels'. This reluctance – which exists in both integrationist and less-integrationist member states – has had the inevitable effect of resulting in a policy rooted in 'mutual recognition and minimal(ist) harmonization' with respect to legislative action (Monar, 2011c, p. 182). Even when the need for legislative action is accepted, distinctive legislative procedures are sometimes preferred: hence the existence of several variations across the AFSJ area in the legislative procedures that must be used – such as the difference between asylum policy (where the ordinary legislative procedure with the use of QMV in the Council is possible) and operational police co-operation in criminal matters (which still requires unanimity in the Council and only EP consultation). In a further protection of national sensitivities, in the area of judicial co-operation in criminal matters there are circumstances in which a member state concerned about the implications of draft legislation for its criminal justice system may 'appeal' the matter to the European Council.

Box 11.2

AFSJ agencies

Agency	Year Est.	Location	Functions
European Police College (CEPOL)	2005	UK	Brings together senior police officers across Europe with the aim of encouraging cross-border co-operation in the fight against crime, and to ensure the maintenance of public security and law and order.
The European Union's Judicial Cooperation Unit (EUROJUST)	2002	Netherlands	To enhance the effectiveness of the competent authorities within member states when they are dealing with serious cross-border and organized crime.
European Agency for the Management of Operational Cooperation at the External Borders (FRONTEX)	2004	Poland	Co-ordinates operational co-operation between member states in the management of external borders; assists member states in the training of national border guards, including the establishment of common training standards; carries out risk analyses; assists member states in circumstances requiring increased technical and operational assistance at external borders; and provides member states with the necessary support in organizing joint return operations.
European Police Office (EUROPOL)	1992	Netherlands	Acts as a centre of expertise in key fields of law enforcement activity and as a European centre for strategic intelligence on organized crime.
European Monitoring Centre for Drugs and Drug Addiction (EMCDDA)	1993	Portugal	Focuses both on the social and health aspects of drug addiction and studies the use of illegal drugs. An information source for police co-operation in the trafficking of illegal drugs.
European Fundamental Rights Agency (FRA)	2007	Austria	Collects evidence about the situation of fundamental rights across the EU and provides evidence-based advice about how to improve the situation. Also informs people about their fundamental rights. (Previously operated as the European Monitoring Centre for Racism and Xenophobia.)
European Asylum Support Office (EASO)	2010	Malta	Facilitates member states' practical co-operation on asylum. Supports EU states whose asylum and reception systems are under particular pressure. Seeks to enhance the implementation of the Common European Asylum System.
European Institute for Gender Equality (EIGE)	2007	Lithuania	Supports the Commission in collecting and analysing data in the field of gender equality. Facilitates the sharing of best practice and raises public awareness.

AFSJ Policies

The treaty bases of the AFSJ are set out mainly in five chapters under Title V, Articles 67–89, of the TFEU:

Chapter 1   General Provisions
Chapter 2   Policies on Border Checks, Asylum and Immigration
Chapter 3   Judicial Cooperation in Civil Matters
Chapter 4   Judicial Cooperation in Criminal Matters
Chapter 5   Police Cooperation

A potentially very wide area of policy and related activity is covered by Title V. It is not possible to cover all of this activity here, but it is possible to give a strong flavour of the nature of AFSJ policies by looking at some of the principal policies and at their varied nature.

Border controls

The EU has separate policies for its internal and external borders. At the heart of the internal borders policy is the Schengen System, of which most of the EU's states are members. External borders policy is focused mainly around policing physical borders and the enforcement of entrance requirements. But the two policies are intertwined, because a Schengen member with weak border surveillance will import problems of illegal immigration, and drugs and human trafficking to other member states. While all Western countries have to battle illegal immigration, the European situation is unique because of the proximity of the Mediterranean and Eastern European EU member states to so many poor and diverse countries – in Eastern and Central Asia, the African continent and the Middle East.

Internal borders: Schengen

Until it was ended by the First World War, European travel was passport-free (Hawley, 2004). Much of the EU's policy on internal borders has been aimed at returning Europe to being a passport-free travel area.

The policy rests on the EU's free movement principle and draws on the fact that even before the passport-free policy began to be developed from the mid-1980s, there were passport-free travel areas in Europe, with the Benelux countries having eliminated border controls among themselves in 1948 and in 1952 the Nordic Passport Union having eliminated border controls between Denmark, Finland, Iceland, Norway and Sweden. So when five of the then ten EC member states – West Germany, France, Belgium, Luxembourg and the Netherlands – met at Schengen in Luxembourg in 1985 to discuss the possibility of extending passport-free travel throughout the EC, three of the parties to the talks had had almost 40 years of passport-free experience.

There was logic in these five states being the ones to take the initiative in building passport-free travel at the EC level. Not only had they, with Italy, been working closely with one another in the Communities since the 1950s but also, and crucially, they were geographically proximate. Indeed, there was a potential highly manageable configuration of their joint borders.

At Schengen, an agreement was duly contracted. This was upgraded in 1990 to a stronger extra-EU agreement in the form of a Convention, which took effect in 1995. Treaty incorporation was delayed by resistance from the UK but, following the election of the Labour Party to office in 1997, this was lifted and the Schengen System was given treaty status via the Amsterdam Treaty. A consequence of Schengen being brought into the EU legal framework and becoming part of the EU's *acquis* was that any country seeking EU membership was now required to agree to join the Schengen Area as a condition of its accession.

As can be seen from Box 11.3, all of the EU's member states, plus four non-member states, participate in the Schengen System to at least some degree. The UK and Ireland, the only formal EU non-Schengen members, are the most minimal participators in that they have chosen not to be part of the passport-free travel area. The UK's unwillingness is because of a mixture of security and sovereignty concerns, while Ireland's position stems more from pragmatic considerations – it wishes to preserve its Common Travel Area with the UK. However, while they are not part of the passport-free zone, both Ireland and the UK are involved in the policing and information-sharing aspects of Schengen – via the Schengen Information System, a state of the art EU-wide police database – but they are not given access to the border control database.

Box 11.3

European states and Schengen*

EU member states

All EU member states are full Schengen members except:

Ireland and the UK	Both have a treaty opt-out from most aspects of Schengen, including the passport-free area. They participate in the Schengen Information System.
Denmark	It has negotiated certain opt-outs and is permitted to exercise tighter border controls than other Schengen states.
Cyprus	The implementation of the passport-free zone has been delayed because of problems associated with the division of the island.
Bulgaria	Decision pending.
Romania	Decision pending.

Non-EU Schengen members

Iceland
Liechtenstein
Norway
Switzerland

* Position at the end of 2012.

As would be expected, given the sensitivity of the matter, the elimination of border controls between Schengen members does sometimes give rise to political tension. Moreover, because member states have the right to institute border checks with other Schengen members in cases of (only vaguely defined) 'emergencies', Schengen border policy is not completely 'settled'. Indeed, increasingly, some Schengen member states have sought to re-impose, or even have already re-imposed, border controls, citing various pressures and circumstances. So, for example, the influx of irregular migrants and asylum seekers fleeing Tunisia and Libya during the 2011 Arab Spring and crossing into France through Italy resulted in France putting border checks in place. The crisis led to French and Italian calls for a revision of the Schengen rules to allow more member state control once an

irregular migrant or asylum seeker has entered the Schengen Area (see Maloney and Pop, 2011; Pignal, 2011a). Similar Danish concerns about too many 'arrivals' have resulted in the periodic placement of 'random' checks at the Swedish and German borders. Broader concerns about 'too many non-nationals' have arisen from the dependence of some EU governments on the support of far-right political parties as well as from enlargement fatigue (Vogel, 2011). The Commission has reacted vigorously against such querying of, and challenges to, open borders, but there is no doubt that Schengen is 'vulnerable', especially in run-ups to national elections.

* * *

In addition to the abolition of passport controls, Schengen also maintains a common visa system for visits of up to three months. Visits for more than three months are subject to national procedures. The Schengen visa system, which resulted in 2010 in the issuing of some 11 million visas by the then 25 Schengen states, includes lists of countries from which travellers to the EU do and do not require visas. The Council can alter the lists by a unanimous vote. So, for example, in 2009 the visa requirement was lifted for citizens of most Balkan states who carry biometric passports. For citizens of countries requiring a visa – and the list includes most Asian and African countries plus, nearer to home, Kosovo (because several EU states do not recognize Kosovo's independence from Serbia), Moldova, Turkey and the Ukraine – obtaining one can be a time-consuming activity, and is by no means guaranteed.

External borders

EU member states must monitor a territory that has nearly 1800 designated external border crossing points with controls: 665 air borders, 871 sea borders and 246 land borders (European Commission, 2008d).

Member states still have absolute authority in all external border activities, including both policing and customs activities. However, in practice, this absolute authority really only applies to the UK and Ireland, since they are the only two EU member states to check passports at internal EU crossing points. Once an individual has entered a country belonging to the Schengen Area, he or she is free to enter into all other Schengen member states.

This freedom of movement means that included among the external borders of, say, Poland or Sweden are effectively the external borders of all other Schengen states. In consequence of this, Schengen states that do not want an influx of unwanted non-EU citizens – which is all of them – have to be satisfied that all EU borders and external crossing points into the EU are properly safeguarded. But border pressures on the EU are so great that such a situation is not fully possible, because much of Europe's neighbourhood consists of impoverished and politically-unstable regions from which large numbers of people wish to move in search of a better life. Accordingly, countries on the outer rim of the EU, namely the CEECs and the Mediterranean countries, face particular border pressures.

Spain, where the narrowest point to the African continent is just 14.5 kilometres (nine miles), exemplifies the problem, with it serving as a crossing point into Europe for drugs smugglers and human traffickers, and with 'almost every' coastal town having the unmarked graves of bodies washed ashore, despite heavy spending on patrol boats, helicopters, night-vision scopes and heat-seeking cameras (Simons, 2004). The Italian island of Lampedusa – at about 113 kilometres (70 miles) from Tunisia – is closer to North Africa than to Italy's mainland, while Adriatic Italy is easily reached by migrants from Eastern Europe. Greece, which is a historical crossroads between the EU and the Caucasus, the Middle East and Turkey, is inundated with asylum seekers and undocumented migrants. Indeed, in May 2012 the Commission reported that some two-thirds of the 30,000 illegal border crossings into the EU detected in the last three months of 2011 had entered via what it calls the 'eastern Mediterranean route': that is, through Turkey into Greece (European Commission, 2012c).

The problem can sometimes be at least partly tackled by the receiving country. So, for example, when in 2006 31,700 migrants entered the Canary Islands (which are a part of Spain) illegally, the Spanish government took the lead in (largely successfully) tackling the crisis by: agreeing bilateral accords with 'sending' countries that pioneered strategies for reducing illegal migration, including obtaining permission to patrol in the sending countries' 200-mile (322-kilometre) Exclusive Economic Zone (thus enabling Spain to return migrants to their point of origin); equipping 'sending' countries to patrol their coastal waters; and establishing vocational training centres in 'sending

countries' that could send migrants for the Spanish workforce on a demand basis.

However, the sort of approach taken by Spain with respect to the Canary Islands crisis is not always available. One reason for this is that 'sending' countries may not always be willing or able to be co-operative. Another reason is that EU 'receiving' countries may already be over-stretched in resource terms: all the more so given that in the EU it is national authorities that are responsible for the costs of policing their borders as well as for housing, feeding and processing undocumented migrants, many of whom apply for asylum.

One EU response to the situation has been to make increasing use of an EU agency that was established in 2004 – the European Agency for the Management of Operational Cooperation at the External Borders of the Member States of the European Union (FRONTEX). FRONTEX's task is to assist member states with their external border control responsibilities. In so doing it co-ordinates and trains member state border control personnel, performs risk analyses, directs Rapid Border Intervention teams, and conducts and co-ordinates interdiction through the European Patrols Network. FRONTEX also co-ordinates permanent maritime missions in the Atlantic (mainly around the Canary Islands), the central Mediterranean and the western Mediterranean through a European Patrols Network which uses equipment (ships, surveillance planes, helicopters) on loan from member states (see FRONTEX, 2012, for an up-to-date list of sea, land and air operations).

In June 2011 the European Council gave FRONTEX the authority to buy or lease equipment such as helicopters, planes and patrol boats. It also authorized FRONTEX to be able to call up national border teams in irrevocable commitments, meaning that member states cannot reassign them from FRONTEX before the mission has been completed (Pignal, 2011b). However, despite this expanded capability, FRONTEX is still far from being able to provide a wholly adequate solution to the pressure on the EU's borders. There are three reasons for this. First, it has only a modest budget – approximately €85 million in 2012 (down from €118 million in 2011), and the member states have shown no inclination to increase it to the levels that would be required to carry out all the necessary operations on the EU's complex land and sea borders. Second, FRONTEX has had an unintended beneficial side effect for irregular migrants in making it safer for them to attempt a landing in Europe: if they are intercepted while at sea, FRONTEX is obligated to rescue them if their craft is not seaworthy. Third, a combination of push factors from 'sending' countries and pull factors in Europe continue to outweigh the risk of interception or death.

Because more than 90 per cent of illegal border crossings take place in just four member states – Greece, Italy, Malta and Spain (Europa, 2011) – particular attention has been given to the problems these countries face in stemming illegal entry. So, in 2008, the Commission proposed a roadmap for the creation of a European Border Surveillance System (EUROSUR). This quickly inspired the establishment of national co-ordination centres for border surveillance as a single point of contact. With a projected operational date of 1 October 2013, EUROSUR will enable member states with southern and south-western maritime borders and eastern land borders to work more easily with each other and FRONTEX to: share information and improve co-operation among border guards, the police, customs agents and the coast guards; have access to sophisticated surveillance equipment; and improve surveillance techniques (European Commission, 2009c, p. 18; 2011b, pp. 3 and 7). As for the financing of EUROSUR, in its 2008 roadmap the Commission floated the idea of an 'External Borders Fund', which the Quadro group (that is, Cyprus, Greece, Italy, Malta and Spain, formed at the ministerial level in 2008 to provide a unified front to pressure the other EU member states to provide more assistance in combating irregular migration) had been urging, but other member states balked at the establishment of a dedicated fund. Therefore, the cost of EUROSUR (projected at €338 million for 2011–20) will be covered mainly by existing EU programmes (Europa, 2011).

*   *   *

A long-standing problem with EU border control has been an artificial separation between internal and external border policy, which, of course, does not exist in federal states that operate unified border systems. The burden of external border policing weighs heavily on Europe's 'underbelly'. Northern Europeans criticize Southern European countries for what they see as inadequate patrols, the 'easy' issuance of temporary permits, and inadequate facilities for housing and processing of irregular migrants. Yet some of the states that are expected to patrol their borders for their European neighbours are relatively poor and are also among the nations that, as a result of the eurozone crisis, have had to implement draconian austerity measures either to qualify for bailouts (Greece, Portugal and Cyprus) or to reduce the costs of government borrowing (Italy and Spain). So when Italy issued thousands of temporary permits to Tunisians during the Arab Spring of 2011 to transit to France (to where most Tunisians wished to go), France (which wanted the Tunisians to remain in Italy to be processed) reacted angrily. Moreover, France was not the only member state to display anger towards Italy, with Germany's interior minister, Hans-Peter Friedrich, observing 'Italy must live up to its responsibilities … Italy is a large country and the number of immigrants was not so great.' Friedrich noted that, in 2010, Germany had accepted 40,000 asylum seekers and 'Italy must negotiate with Tunisia' (Donadio, 2011). (This proposal was somewhat unrealistic, given that Tunisia did not have a well-organized or reliable government with which the Italians could negotiate: indeed, internal disorder in Tunisia was the main reason for the rapid influx of irregular migrants to Italy!) So, as this case illustrates, border policy can generate considerable political heat, especially in troubled economic times.

Migration policy

Migration policy is closely related to, but distinct from, border policy. The most important, and controversial, aspect of border policy involves illegal border crossings, while migration policy is focused on asylum and legal immigration.

Migration policy has four main goals: protection of migrants from persecution (granting political asylum); family reunification; filling gaps in the workforce; and attracting highly-skilled workers.

Immigration policy concerns the migration to Europe of both legal and 'irregular' ('illegal') people from other countries for economic, family unification or other economic and/or social reasons. It is for individual member states to decide on entry qualifications (such as privileging family unification or labour skills) and whether migrants should demonstrate satisfactory acculturation to achieve permanent residency. Many of the core principles of asylum policy are, by contrast, 'technically' decided by international conventions rather than by the EU or its member states. If a petitioner can prove that s/he deserves asylum, the EU member state *must* grant it. So, while immigration policy is decided and carried out by the member states, asylum policy is derived from international law. This is an important point, because with its member states being signatories to the Geneva Convention (see below), the EU has a working definition and guiding rules to establish a Common European Asylum System. However, no such comparable international convention exists for immigration policy.

Migration policy is controversial in all developed countries, but has become particularly salient in Europe. One reason for this is the poor countries surrounding Europe, which was mentioned in the discussion above on EU borders policy, and which makes Western Europe so attractive for migrants. The other main reason is European demographic trends. The EU's population is ageing, through a combination of low birth rates and increased life expectancy: the share of the population aged 65 and over is projected to reach 30 per cent by 2060, compared to 17 per cent in 2008 (with the very old – aged 80 and above – accounting for 12 per cent of the EU's population by 2060) (Eurostat, 2011, p. 162). By 2050, the EU's population is projected to decrease by 8.3 per cent, while the population of the African continent – an area already exerting enormous migrant pressure on Europe – is projected to increase by 103 per cent (statistics cited in Casey, 2008). Will there be enough people to fill job vacancies in the EU, and who will support the pensioners? One clue may be found in labour statistics, where between the years 2000 and 2005 third-country immigrants accounted for more than a quarter of the rise in employment and 21 per cent of average GNP in the EU-15 (European Commission, 2011d, p. 2).

Persuading the European polity of this looming population crisis has been difficult, especially when in several Western European countries, such as Ireland and the UK, many labour shortages are filled by EU citizens from the CEECs. With member states tending to be resistant to immigration-friendly policies, attention to dealing with the impending problem has focused mainly on lifting the mandatory retirement age, which is around 65 years in most EU member states, and on the Europe 2020 programme (see

Chapter 9), which includes among its priorities skills training for policy areas experiencing shortages. But the Commission insists that migration policy will also have to be seen as crucial to ensure that skilled labour is available and that the EU's social model can be financed (European Commission, 2011d, p. 2). Naturally, these discussions have lost some salience during the high unemployment following the global financial crisis, but when the EU recovers economically, demographics ensure that they will reassert themselves.

Asylum policy

EU states have been the destination for hundreds of thousands of migrants claiming asylum protection. In 2009, for example, of over 10.3 million refugees worldwide, 1.6 million (many of whom applied for permanent asylum) were in Europe (compared to 812,300 in the Americas) (United Nations High Commission on Refugees, 2010, pp. 7, 24–6). Two EU member states – Germany (4th) and the UK (10th) – rank in the top ten countries in the world for the hosting of refugee residents (593,800 and 269,400, respectively, in 2010), compared with 275,500 refugees hosted by the US. Germany, the UK and Sweden (with over 81,000 refugees) host a much larger number of asylum seekers in proportion to their population than do other member states: France, for example, hosts just under 200,000, while Italy hosts only 55,000.

The 1951 Geneva Convention Relating to the Status of Refugees, to which all EU member states are party, provides the right of 'non-refoulement' (a refugee cannot be sent back to the place where he or she is being persecuted)

> owing to [a] well founded fear of being persecuted for reasons of race, religion, nationality, membership of a particular social group or political opinion, is outside the country of her/his nationality and is unable or, owing to such fear, is unwilling to avail herself/himrself of the protection of her/his country; or who, not having a nationality and being outside the country of her/his former habitual residence as a result of such events, is unable or, owing to such fear, is unwilling to return to it.

The non-refoulement right has been interpreted to mean that a state should grant asylum to petitioners who can prove they are in danger. It bears noting that the EU, in its Charter of Fundamental Rights (Article 18), provides the right of asylum (rather than simply non-refoulement) for the first time in history (Kaunert and Léonard, 2011, p. 15).

Because so much of what determines whether a person is a refugee who will face persecution upon return to his or her homeland is determined by the Geneva Convention and its operating bodies (notably, the UN High Commission for Refugees), EU asylum policy has been much concerned with logistics on such matters as standard living conditions, time detained before hearings, and the ability of asylum seekers to work while awaiting their hearings.

However, the EU does have a Common European Asylum System (CEAS) which, at the time of writing, is being considerably strenghtened (Council of the European Union, 2011; European Commission, 2011a). The basic principle underlying the CEAS is that migrants can petition for asylum and, if they qualify, are permitted to remain in Europe and begin the process of obtaining legal residency. Dating back to the 2001 directive for Temporary Protection for Displaced Persons, the CEAS is built on directives specifying such matters as where an asylum seeker must register (Dublin Regulation, 2003), reception conditions (2003), subsidiary protection qualifications (2004), asylum procedures (2005), a refugee fund to improve reception conditions (2004), co-operation with third countries to reduce numbers of asylum seekers (2007), increased information sharing through the European Migration Network (2008), and a joint EU resettlement programme (2012).

Nevertheless, while EU asylum policy is, for most practical purposes, now a 'common' policy, this should not be taken to mean that all entry conditions and legal hearings to determine asylum eligibility are identical across the member states. Scoreboard reports indicate substantial progress in the transposition of asylum directives (European Commission, 2008a), but transposition is not the same as implementation, with some member states having neither allocated adequate funds nor properly implemented asylum legislation. Taking the Reception Conditions Directive as an example: in specifying minimum standards it is sufficiently elastic as to permit substantial differences in the length of time asylum seekers are detained, when refugees will be permitted to work, and access to education and health care (Brunsden, 2008b).

Two particular problems have arisen with the establishment of the CEAS. First, some EU member states have deepened national protection by granting 'subsidiary protection' – which covers individuals not falling within the scope of the Geneva Convention's definition of 'refugee' but who still need international protection (for example, because of a risk of torture or inhuman or degrading treatment if returned to the home country). Because EU asylum seekers are permitted to apply in just one country, naturally 'asylum shopping' results. To put this into perspective, in 2007 there was an EU average of 25 per cent of first decisions granting asylum. Some member states, however, granted protection in just a few cases, while others had a rate close to 50 per cent (European Commission, 2009c, p. 5). Second, some member states, by virtue of topography and geographical location, are the 'first stop' for asylum seekers, which has created great resource difficulties for some member states, particularly Greece. This, in turn, has led to poor standards of asylum processing. But asylum seekers arriving in Greece cannot lodge their applications in another member state because, under the Dublin II (2003) regulation, asylum seekers must be returned to the country in which they entered the EU, where they are to be detained during the processing of their applications. However, as Monar (2011b, p. 146) reports, as a result of repeated warnings about the treatment and conditions of asylum seekers in Greece from the United Nations High Commissioner for Refugees (UNHCR), the European Council on Refugees and Exiles (ECRE), and national court rulings in several member states, a number of member states have suspended return transfers to Greece. In defending Greek policy, the Greek interior minister, Procopios Pavlopoulos, wrote in 2008 that Greece 'is daily confronted with a massive influx of illegal migrants, whose destination is not just the Greek territory, but in most occasions, the countries of western Europe' (Brunsden, 2008a).

A ruling by the European Court of Human Rights (ECHR) in January 2011 condemned Belgium for a 'Dublin transfer' to Greece of an asylum seeker from Afghanistan (who had entered Greece via Turkey, but sought asylum in Belgium). The ECHR ruled that, in Greece, the Afghan refugee was subjected to inhumane or degrading treatment and denied effective remedy (risk of expulsion without an adequate examination of the petitioner's case) (Monar, 2011b, pp. 146–7). The

EU responded to the Court's ruling by providing 'emergency funds' to Greece to reform its asylum system, and required Greece to submit an action plan for reform (see European Commission, 2010i; 2011d, p. 6). To further address these problems of administering the EU's common asylum policy, the Council and the EP agreed in Regulation (EU) No 439/2010 to establish the European Asylum Support Office (EASO), which is responsible for overseeing development of the European Asylum Curriculum, a programme designed to provide core training for member states' officials responsible for determining asylum. Also, in March 2012, the EU adopted a Joint EU Resettlement Programme (on a voluntary basis), which integrates resettled refugees into local communities and carries with it financial resources for participating states.

Immigration policy

Difficulties in building an EU-wide immigration policy The EU does not yet have a common immigration policy. While in unitary political systems the national government oversees migration policy, in federal and quasi-federal systems responsibility for immigration policy can reside at the sub-federal level. In the US, for example, the states controlled immigration policy until the late 1880s, exercising 'virtually a free hand' implementing and regulating immigration (Wittke, 1949, p. 1). US Supreme Court rulings led the way to federal control, primarily via internal-market-related issues such as the 1876 ruling that state laws taxing immigrants and the owners of vessels that carried them were unconstitutional attempts to regulate foreign commerce. The national government then began to assert control through federal legislation.

While EU member states have agreed in principle to work towards a common immigration policy, their achievements to date have, as will be shown below, been relatively modest. There are several reasons for this, and for why the EU may well never achieve a fully federalized immigration policy.

First, member states have disparate historical experiences with immigration, which helps to explain why there are now some significantly different attitudes between states towards the issue. For example, some member states – particularly the CEECs, Ireland and the Mediterranean states – were very much 'sending' rather than 'receiving' states, and this historical experience has tended to create a degree of sympathy for

those seeking a better life. The differing colonial experiences of some member states, especially France and the UK, have also played a part in influencing present-day stances on immigration. Whereas the UK took a relatively '*laissez faire*' approach towards the residents of its colonies, France sought to make Frenchmen/women of everyone. This French stance is reflected in current policy, with migrants to France having to agree to learn French and integrate into French culture (Escafré-Dublet, 2007). During the 2008 French Council presidency, Nicolas Sarkozy's team injected the idea of teaching 'European values' in the assimilation efforts of all member states. (However, in the event, as with all such identity projects, it was unclear how to implement it across the EU, and whether such a project could be delivered given that assimilation typically takes years.)

Second, member states wish to retain control of much of immigration policy because the financial burden of irregular immigration falls mainly on them – particularly in respect of social services, health and education. There is also a related concern that the children of irregular migrants are at a disadvantage, especially if they themselves are 'undocumented' – because undocumented immigrants work longer hours, sometimes have multiple jobs, and are often so fearful of deportation that they do not apply for social welfare or education programmes. This situation can create a generation of outsiders in the host country. In the US, the challenge to the federal government's exclusive competence over immigration policy initiated by the state of Arizona in 2009 (with several states enacting copycat legislation soon afterwards) serves as a reminder of how highly inflammatory immigration can be with respect to the financial strains that irregular immigration places on both local and national governments (especially if the earnings of irregular immigrants go unreported and are, therefore, untaxed).

A third reason, tied to domestic politics, has become more salient in recent years. Politicians of mainstream parties have had to grapple with the far right's agility in seizing the immigration issue to engineer electoral gains in a number of member states, including Austria, Denmark, Greece, France, Italy and the Netherlands. This in turn has led to some 'mainstream' parties stiffening their stances on immigration policy.

A fourth obstacle in the way of building a common immigration policy is member state competition to attract the brightest, highest-skilled and hardest-working migrants to their respective countries. Given the nature of the EU's internal market and competition rules, and the increasingly circumscribed manoeuvrability of member states in fiscal and monetary policy-making, immigration policy is one of the few policies affecting economic growth to remain under national control. With workforce quality being the *sine qua non* of dynamic and competitive economies, member states are locked in fierce competition to attract a limited pool of the best and the brightest. (This is, it should be noted, a competition that the EU as a whole is currently losing, with North America and Australia in particular being more attractive destinations for many skilled migrants: the percentage of skilled migrants to the EU currently constitutes about 1.75 per cent of total employment, compared to 9.9 per cent in Australia, 7.3 per cent in Canada, and 3.2 per cent in the US – European Commission, 2007a.)

Policy achievements Given these obstacles in the way of building an integrated and comprehensive EU-wide immigration policy, what has been achieved?

The legislation that the Council and the Parliament have been able to agree has dealt mainly with less controversial aspects of legal migration. So, there is legislation in place covering such matters as long-term residence (2003); family reunification (2003); the treatment of permanent residents (2003); students, pupils and volunteers (2004); researchers (2005); asylum and immigration information exchange (2006); co-operation with third countries (2007); a blue card system for admitting more highly-skilled workers (2009); social security for EU citizens and third-country nationals who move within the EU (2010); and a single application procedure for a single permit for third-country nationals to reside and work in the territory of a member state and on a common set of rights for third-country workers legally residing in a member state (2011) (European Commission, 2008a, pp. 13–15; Monar, 2011a; NEMIS, 2012).

A migration policy area that is being prioritized is co-operation with third countries. This policy is part of what is referred to in an important 2011 Commission Communication as a 'global approach' to migration and mobility (European Commission, 2011d). The approach has four thematic priorities: promoting better governance of migration; preventing and reducing illegal immigration and human trafficking; supporting the implementation of international protection standards for asylum seekers and refugees in third countries; and maximizing the development impact of migration and mobility (through, for example, improving the lives of would-be migrants in their home countries).

Another increasingly emphasized aspect of migration policy is its links with other EU policy areas. The Stockholm Programme makes much of this, calling for increased 'coherence between migration policies and other policy areas such as foreign and development policy and policies for trade, employment, health and education at the European level'. The Programme also calls for the Commission 'to explore procedures that will to a greater extent link the development of migration policy to the development of the post-Lisbon Strategy' (Council of the European Union, 2009, p. 59).

One other aspect of migration policy meriting particular comment is the assimilation of migrants. In the Stockholm Programme, the Commission is directed to encourage member states' efforts to 'support the integration process, including essential elements such as introductory courses and language classes, a strong commitment to the host community and the active participant of immigrants in all aspects of collective life' (Council of the European Union, 2009, p. 65).

Judicial co-operation in civil matters

Turning to a wholly different AFSJ policy, judicial co-operation in civil matters is extremely complicated and grounded in all sorts of horizontal relationships among judicial authorities in the member states. Yet the increasing freedom of movement of goods, services and people in the EU has naturally brought a steady rise in the number and kinds of cross-border legal disputes. To try to ensure that this does not result in parties to cross-border disputes being denied justice or being dispensed differing types of justice, the EU has put in place a range of measures. These measures are based on the principle of mutual recognition and on the practice of judicial co-operation between national courts.

The EU's increasing involvement with family law illustrates why, and how, the scope of AFSJ policy integration advances. The involvement has become necessary because, as European labour mobility has increased, so has the incidence of cross-border marriages: to such an extent that there are now 16 million 'international' couples in the EU (European Commission, 2011l). Naturally, this raises a number of questions when couples who are citizens of different EU member states divorce, including which courts have jurisdiction to hear divorce cases, to enforce child visitation rights, and to enforce maintenance payments?

The many specific measures that have been adopted to deal with such problems stem mainly from two conventions, known as Brussels I and Brussels II. Brussels I – the Convention on Jurisdiction and the Enforcement of Judgments in Civil and Commercial Matters – was adopted in 1968. Brussels II – the Convention on the Jurisdiction and the Recognition and Enforcement of Judgments in Matrimonial Matters and in Matters of Parental Responsibility for Children of Both Spouses – was adopted in 2000. Both conventions have since largely been supplanted by more focused and tighter legislation, which shows how, in the EU, and not least in the AFSJ policy area, horizontal relations that are initially somewhat broad and loose can set the stage for vertical integration in which agreements on policy are put on a firm legal basis and are directly applicable in the member states as part of the EU *acquis*.

Since 2005, when the second cycle of Brussels II – commonly referred to as *new Brussels II* – came into force, a raft of legislation has addressed family law issues. However, Brussels II has not resolved all of the obstacles divorcing couples face, let alone harmonized all relevant national laws. Irish law, for example, can be problematic for divorcing couples because there is a five-year separation requirement. 'Quickie' divorces among the Irish are possible but only, under residency rules, if one spouse resides in a different member state (Crosbie, 2007a). Divorce law is also tight in Italy, with a three-year separation requirement and at least another year for the divorce to be processed (contested divorces can drag out for a decade). But because divorces that take place anywhere in the EU must be recognized by other member states, couples can circumvent national laws by obtaining residency in another EU state which has flexible residency rules and liberal divorce laws (Povoledo, 2011), thus advantaging those couples who have the financial means to travel and meet the requirements for divorce (such as residency) in more 'permissive' member states. (In the US, where the states, rather than the federal government, have jurisdiction over marriage and divorce, a similar problem existed until the liberalization of the divorce laws in the 1970s. Even today, residency requirements to file for divorce can be quite lengthy in some states, with the consequence that Nevada – which has only a six-week residency requirement – is still used if a 'quickie' divorce is sought.)

The Commission attempted to reduce some of the difficulties and uncertainties left open in Brussels II for divorcing couples with its proposed 2006 'Rome III Regulation', but it could not generate the required unanimity in the Council. Sweden was to the fore in blocking common rules because of concerns that EU legislation would be less liberal than its own family laws, while, for the opposite reason, Malta was to the fore in blocking the proposal (Goldirova, 2008). In the light of this situation, it was not wholly surprising that the first action proposed by the Commission under the enhanced co-operation procedure created by the Amsterdam Treaty (a form of horizontal federalism discussed in Chapter 5) was in the area of divorce and legal separation. Nine member states asked the Commission to present their request for enhanced co-operation to the Council by January 2009. The Commission's subsequent proposal was approved by a Council decision in July 2010, and regulation 1259/2010 dealing with aspects of divorce and separation became applicable from June 2012 in the 14 states that had agreed to it (Austria, Belgium, Bulgaria, France, Germany, Hungary, Italy, Latvia, Luxembourg, Malta, Portugal, Romania, Slovenia and Spain). Other member states may join the agreement, but in the meantime they are continuing to apply their own national law (Council of the European Union, 2010; European Commission, 2011f).

Police and judicial co-operation in criminal matters

Most matters relating to criminal activity, and to the associated powers and roles of the police and judiciary, are recognized in the EU as being essentially national responsibilities. However, as with many commercial and civil matters, free movement has brought the EU into the policy picture. It has done so through member states increasingly recognizing the necessity of having to tackle many criminal activities on an EU-wide level. This perceived necessity has resulted in the EU's policy aims with respect to dealing with criminal activity, the types of activities in which it can engage, and the sorts of measures it is able to take, being steadily expanded. Box 11.4 sets out the key policy aims and instruments in respect of what is, slightly misleadingly, usually called police and judicial co-operation in criminal matters (PJCM).

The name PJCM is somewhat misleading because it suggests that the policy area is limited to co-operation between national agencies. Such co-operation certainly is a very important aspect of PJCM, and it does have considerable implications for national police forces, national customs services and national judicial authorities, which are both obliged and enabled to work closely with each other in matters concerning cross-border crime. This encouragement is facilitated by three EU agencies: EUROPOL, CEPOL and EUROJUST (see Box 11.2). However, the policy area is far from being confined to inter-agency co-operation. Rather, it stretches well beyond co-operation to include also the mutual recognition of judicial decisions and the approximation of laws. Regarding the latter, as Box 11.4 shows, in many areas of activity laws can be adopted via the Community method, using the ordinary legislative procedure.

* * *

A few comments are merited on what has been the most high-profile PCJM achievement: the European arrest warrant (EAW), which was designed to replace what had often been lengthy and sometimes politicized extradition requests between member states. The EAW ended the ability of EU member states to refuse to surrender to another member state their citizens who were suspected of, or who have been convicted of, committing serious crimes in the requesting country.

Long before its adoption in 2002, there had been intense interest in an EAW in the policing community but it was considered by policy-makers to be too politically sensitive to tackle because it was seen as a considerable invasion of member state sovereignty. At the time of its eventual adoption, 11 of the EU's 15 member states prevented extradition of their citizens (as did many European countries that had applied for EU membership). But the terrorist attack on the

World Trade Center in New York in September 2001 (9/11) opened a policy window, with the EAW legislation passing just nine months after the attack (Council Framework Decision 2002/584/JHA of 13 June 2002), and coming into force in January 2004.

The EAW has become an important feature in EU policing, reducing the time needed to extradite a criminal from approximately a year to between 11 days and six weeks (European Commission, 2009c, p. 4). The EAW has withstood a challenge in the CJEU (litigated on the grounds that its issuance fell outside of the EU's legislative power), with the Court upholding the EAW on the basis that it does not breach EU law because the member states have developed a 'high degree of trust and solidarity' (cited in Crosbie, 2007b). Between 2005 and 2009, 55,000 EAWs were issued (Bowcott, 2011), with some high-profile suspects being included – such as the WikiLeaks founder, Julian Assange, against whom the Swedish authorities issued an EAW for extradition from the UK despite the lack of a formal charge against him.

While the EAW has become an integral feature of EU criminal policy, a number of concerns have surfaced, both with respect to its application and to the larger issue of its implications for civil rights in the member states. Citing just three of the concerns that have been widely voiced:

- There have been some cases where states have been perhaps over-zealous in issuing EAWs for minor offences. While no EAWs have been issued for crimes that do not fall under EAW-issuing guidelines, some have seemingly failed on the 'common sense' notion of proportionality and have been excessive. Accordingly, the Commission has warned that the overuse of the EAW potentially overwhelms national judicial authorities who must comply with the EAW request, and threatens long-term public support of the EAW (European Commission, 2012l).

- On being served with an EAW, suspects have experienced considerable difficulties even when the 'sending country' has refused to extradite on health reasons. Until the requesting country agrees to remove the EAW, it remains in place and the suspect cannot travel within the EU (see Casciani and Barford, 2012, for sample cases).

- The third concern is far-reaching and therefore more difficult to address: member states do not

Box 11.4

Key policy aims and instruments of police and judicial co-operation in criminal matters

The broad areas covered by this policy area are set out in Title V, Chapters 4 and 5, of the TFEU.

Judicial Co-operation (Chapter 4)

Judicial co-operation in criminal matters is based 'on the principle of mutual recognition of judgments and judicial decisions and shall include the approximation of the laws and regulations of the Member States' in relevant areas (Article 82).

The ordinary legislative procedure may be used to adopt measures to:

1. lay down rules and procedures for ensuring recognition of all forms of judgments and judicial decisions;
2. prevent and settle conflicts of jurisdiction between member states;
3. support the training of the judiciary and judicial staff;
4. facilitate co-operation between judicial or equivalent authorities of the member states in relation to proceedings in criminal matters and enforcement of decisions.

The ordinary legislative procedure may also be used to establish minimum rules in:

1. the mutual admissibility of evidence between member states;
2. the rights of individuals in criminal procedures;
3. the rights of crime victims;
4. any other specific aspects of criminal procedure which the Council has identified in advance by a decision taken unanimously and after obtaining the consent of the European Parliament.

Eurojust is assigned the task of strengthening co-ordination and co-operation between national investigating and prosecuting authorities in relation to serious crimes affecting two or more member states.

Police Co-operation (Chapter 5)

The overall policy aim is that the Union shall 'establish police co-operation involving all Member States' competent authorities … in relation to the prevention, detection and investigation of criminal offences' (Article 87).

To enable the policy aim to be achieved, the ordinary legislative procedure may be used to establish measures concerning:

1. the collection, storage, processing, analysis and exchange of relevant information;
2. support for the training of staff, and co-operation on the exchange of staff, on equipment and on research into crime-detection;
3. common investigative techniques in relation to the detection of serious forms of organized crime.

'Operational co-operation' between authorities can be undertaken when the Council acts unanimously after consulting with the EP.

Europol is given the task of supporting and strengthening action by, and co-operation between, member states' police authorities and other law enforcement services to prevent and combat serious crime affecting two or more member states, and to tackle terrorism and forms of crime which affect a common interest covered by EU policy.

Source: Summarized from TFEU.

have uniform rules on pre-detention, pre-trial and trial evidence, trial rights, or prison conditions. This has resulted in Northern European member states expressing concerns about the treatment of their nationals in the CEECs and Mediterranean countries. UK civil society organisations have been particularly active in calling attention to these problems, leading to a formal parliamentary review of UK extradition laws (Casciani and Barford, 2012). The Charter of Fundamental Rights, which is examined later in the chapter, is one long-term attempt to harmonize civil rights throughout the EU but, as in all federal systems of a dualist nature, sub-governments do differ with regard to the rights of the accused and the treatment of prisoners.

The Internal Security Strategy

Much AFSJ policy attention in recent years has been focused on the development of an 'Internal Security Strategy' (ISS). The ISS was approved by the Council of Ministers in February 2010 and by the European Council the following month. On the basis of this approval, the Commission issued a communication in November 2010 that set out the aims of the ISS in greater detail, and identified measures aimed at putting the ISS into action (European Commission, 2010g). The communication made it clear that the core overall aim was to bring EU policy co-operation to bear on a number of cross-border threats to internal security, particularly organized crime, terrorism, cybercrime, natural and man-made disasters, and hooliganism at sporting events.

The communication, which was accepted by the JHA Council, laid out five key objectives and specific actions for the years up to 2014. These are detailed in Box 11.5. Given that it has implications for such matters as border controls, the movement of people, the safety of citizens, and individual rights, internal security is naturally one of the most politically sensitive of all AFSJ policies. Accordingly, most of it is based on intergovernmental policy arrangements. A key role in these arrangements is exercised by COSI (see p. 231).

Because so much of the content of the ISS is highly sensitive, it is also very controversial. For example, pressures – especially from the US – to expand the collection and international exchange of data on airline passengers have been widely criticized on privacy grounds by European civil libertarians and many policy-makers. Indeed, the criticisms led to the approval of an agreement between the EU and the US on the Use and Transfer of Passenger Name Records (Council of the European Union, 2012) being delayed until the matter was resolved (in April 2012) when it was agreed that US requests would need to be evaluated by EUROPOL.

Another example of how sensitive and controversial – and consequently also politically difficult – ISS issues can be is seen in the long-running controversy over the transfer of financial data to the US. The 'story' began shortly after 9/11, when the US set up the Terrorist Finance Tracking Program (TFTP), which was designed to 'follow the money': that is, to identify, track and pursue terrorists and their networks by using information from the Brussels-based banking consortium, the Society for Worldwide Interbank Financial Telecommunication (SWIFT) database (US Department of Treasury, 2011). The TFTP did not come to light until five years into its operation (see Lichtblau and Risen, 2006), at which point SWIFT officials admitted to providing data to the US Treasury Department (which worked with the CIA in assembling, maintaining and mining the financial database). SWIFT's location in Belgium naturally meant it was obliged to comply with Belgian and EU financial data privacy laws, so its involvement with the TFTP clearly raised legal questions. By 2006, the Belgian government had determined – as had most EU (and also US) policy-makers – that SWIFT's participation in TFTP was a breach of both Belgian and EU laws. To enable the programme to continue, the US therefore needed to conclude a formal agreement with the EU, which it did in late 2009.

However, the agreement – the EU–US TFTP Agreement, or the 'SWIFT agreement' as it came to be called more commonly – ran into difficulties when the EP and a wide range of policy interests objected to its contents on a number of grounds. The main policy grounds included: the lack of reciprocity – the US would receive EU banking data, but not vice versa; no provision was made for oversight of the programme's operation by either the EP or national parliaments; no courts would be involved in deciding on the legitimacy of US requests for data; no limits for the storage of SWIFT data were specified; no details were given concerning the transactions that would be monitored; there were potentially grave threats to the privacy of

---

Box 11.5

The EU's Internal Security Strategy

OBJECTIVE 1: Disrupt international crime networks
Action 1: Identify and dismantle criminal networks.
Action 2: Protect the economy against criminal infiltration.
Action 3: Confiscate criminal assets.

OBJECTIVE 2: Prevent terrorism and address radicalization and recruitment
Action 1: Empower communities to prevent radicalization and recruitment.
Action 2: Cut off terrorists' access to funding and materials, and track their transactions.
Action 3: Protect transport.

OBJECTIVE 3: Raise levels of security for citizens and businesses in cyberspace
Action 1: Build capacity in law enforcement and the judiciary.
Action 2: Work with industry to empower and protect citizens.
Action 3: Improve capability for dealing with cyber attacks.

OBJECTIVE 4: Strengthen security through border management
Action 1: Exploit the full potential of EUROSUR.
Action 2: Enhance the contribution of FRONTEX at external borders.
Action 3: Common risk management for movement of goods across external borders.
Action 4: Improve inter-agency co-operation at national level.

OBJECTIVE 5: Increase Europe's resilience to crises and disasters
Action 1: Make full use of the solidarity clause.*
Action 2: Adopt an all-hazards approach to threat and risk assessment.
Action 3: Link up the different situation awareness centres.
Action 4: Develop a European Emergency Response Capacity for tackling disasters.

Note: *Article 222 of the TFEU contains a 'solidarity clause', which states that member states 'shall act jointly in a spirit of solidarity if a Member State is the object of a terrorist attack or the victim of a natural or man-made disaster'.

Source: European Commission, 2010g.

European citizens; and there was even the possibility of American industrial espionage as a result of the banking information the Americans might potentially receive from European businesses. All of these concerns could not be satisfied given the dire warnings that terrorists would continue to escape detection without the transfer of data to experts at the US Department of Treasury and the CIA and given also the lack of an EU agency that could undertake the data analysis being performed by US government agencies. But, in spite of the recognition of these special circumstances, and anxious to use its new post-Lisbon Treaty power of consent on international agreements (see Chapter 13) the EP rejected the agreement in February 2010. As a result, a revised agreement – TFTP II – had to be negotiated, with a number of safeguards being written into it. Among these safeguards, EUROPOL was given new roles to: vet data transfer requests from the US Department of Treasury; inform EU member states on intelligence leads gleaned from the data analysis; and request information from the US Treasury on behalf of the member states and EUROJUST. TFTP II was approved by the EP in July 2010 and came into force on 1 August 2010 (European Union, 2010).

As a condition of its support for the SWIFT agreement, the EP insisted that the European Commission present a proposal for a parallel European Terrorist Finance Tracking System (TFTS). The Commission tabled this proposal in 2011, but as of late 2012 it had not been enacted. Major problems with it include problems of cost (estimated at €50 million to implement, and about €11 million in annual operating costs) and the 'unprecedented co-operation' that would be required among member state security agencies (Kanter, 2011a).

So, as the case of financial data transfer and passenger data transfer illustrates, while the EU has agreed to develop an internal security strategy, it has made only limited practical progress in this area. And it is unlikely to be able to do so without transforming EUROPOL's mission or developing an EU agency that operates as an internal security agency on a par with the FBI or Britain's MI5.

The Charter of Fundamental Rights of the European Union

Why is the EU involved with fundamental rights?

Whether a widespread European identity exists (there has always been a sense of Europeanness among the upper classes) is the subject of considerable debate among academic analysts of both modern Europe and the EU (see, for example, Checkel and Katzenstein, 2009; Fligstein, 2008; Risse, 2010; Shore and Abélès, 2004.) Of the many dimensions there can be of 'identity' – which include a shared history, culture, religion, language and social values – the EU has tended to promote an identity based on 'constitutional patriotism', which is somewhat similar to the notion of identity that has long been exemplified by France and the US.

Indeed, in one of the first formal pronouncements made on EC/EU identity, the Heads of Government of the then nine members of the EC declared in 1973, in a *Declaration on European Identity*, that:

The Nine wish to ensure that the cherished values of their legal, political and moral order are respected, and to preserve the rich variety of their national cultures. Sharing as they do the same attitudes to life, based on a determination to build a society which measures up to the needs of the individual, they are determined to defend the principles of representative democracy, of the rule of law, of social justice – which is the ultimate goal of economic progress – and of respect for human rights. All of these are fundamental elements of the European Identity. (European Communities, 1973)

Europeans are, it has been argued, *Weltbürger* (world citizens) (Gottdiener, 1995, p. 233) living under *Weltbürgerrecht* (world/cosmopolitan law) (Habermas, 1999, p. xxvi). In this view, cosmopolitanism reinforces a European sense of Europe being a more 'enlightened' civilization with a judicious balance of social, economic and political rights which not only illiberal regimes but also many liberal countries (not least the US) would do well to emulate.

For those who have taken the above-outlined view of Europe as a sort of enlightened beacon on the hill, and also for many other supporters of European integration, a key ingredient of the integration process that was missing for too long was a single, legally-enforceable, and preferably treaty-based, document specifying both the rights of EU citizens and the authority of a court to rule on the application of the rights.

Towards placing the EU's commitment to fundamental rights in a charter

Despite the support in some influential quarters for a rights document of some kind for EU citizens, until well into the 1990s such a document was generally considered by the legal community, and by many advocates of European integration, not to be a pressing need. The main reason for this was that all EU states were (as they still are) members of the Council of Europe, whose cornerstone activity since its founding in 1949 has been protection of human rights. Indeed, the Council – based in Strasbourg and which (in late 2012) has 47 members – is best known for the European Convention on Human Rights, which operates under its auspices. This has been in force since 1953, and covers the most important human rights. The Convention does not have such strong legal status as EU law, but its provisions are generally applied in member states. Disputes about the application of the Convention's rights in member states are settled by the European Court of Human Rights (ECHR).

Given this situation with the Convention, for many years it seemed to most EU policy-makers unnecessary for the EU to become involved directly with human rights issues. Indeed, it was thought that to do so risked being potentially duplicative and was a recipe for public confusion. However, although direct and 'full-scale' involvement was long avoided, from the early 1990s the EU did begin to take an increasing interest in human rights issues. It did so in two main ways:

- References to the EU's commitment to human rights appeared increasingly in the treaties as they were amended, as well as in EU documents and statements. So, with regard to treaty provisions, the Maastricht Treaty introduced the concept of EU citizenship for the purpose of strengthening 'the protection of the rights and interests of the nationals of its Member States' (TEU [1993 version], Article B). The Amsterdam Treaty followed this up, albeit somewhat tentatively, by proclaiming that 'The Union is founded on the principles of liberty, democracy, respect for human rights and fundamental freedoms, and the rule of law' (TEU [1997 version], Article 6). As regards references in EU documents and statements, a very important instance of the EU's increasing public attachment to human rights was contained in the European Council's 1993 'Copenhagen Conditions', which contained the first-ever specification by the EU of the qualifying conditions for EU membership. Candidate countries, it was declared, must be able (amongst other things) to guarantee the rule of law, human rights and respect for and protection of minorities.
- EU activity and legislative authority in various policy areas involving and touching on human rights matters were increasingly developed. Anti-discrimination was a particular focus, with legislation being introduced forbidding discrimination on the basis of race or ethnic origin, age, religion or belief, gender, disability and sexual orientation.

Building on this increasing involvement with human rights, during the 1990s support began to coalesce for the embedding of rights in an EU charter or treaty. There were four main reasons for this:

- Hopes that the issue of the lack of a high-profile document setting out the EU's commitment to human rights might be dealt with, at least partly, by EU accession to the European Convention of Human Rights were ended by the ECJ's *Opinion 2/94* of 28 March 1996, which stated that the EU's treaties did not permit the EU to accede to international treaties. (The later Constitutional Treaty included a clause that would have permitted the EU to accede to the Convention, but this was removed from the Lisbon Treaty – primarily because of a growing concern that, as the Council of Europe had expanded to include some 'questionable' democracies, some ECHR judges might have an overly narrow view of human rights.)
- The ECHR was becoming increasingly overburdened and was able to hear only a fraction of petitioners' cases.
- Opinion in more integrationist circles increasingly came to the view that, with the EU's policy portfolio now very broad and still continuing to expand – not least in sensitive justice and home affairs policy areas – there was a need for a document that tied together in a constitution-like package the rights Europeans could expect. Such a document could help to 'lay the foundations for a more proper constitutional legal order' (Zetterquist, 2011, p. 7).
- It was thought by many policy practitioners that there should be some recognition of rights not included in the Convention – including the right to 'good government'.

In response to these considerations, the 1999 Cologne European Council authorized a convention to draft an EU Charter. The result, which was agreed by the Convention in October 2000, was the Charter of Fundamental Rights of the European Union.

The contents of the Charter

The Charter draws from several documents, most notably the European Convention on Human Rights and the EU's own 1989 Charter of Fundamental Social Rights of Workers. Whereas the former focused on political and civil rights, the latter was more concerned with economic and social rights (Zetterquist, 2011, p. 4).

As shown in Box 11.6, the Charter is divided into six titles: dignity, freedoms, equality, solidarity, citizens' rights, and justice.

Prior to the Charter, AFSJ had focused mainly on EU policies that promote order and security – that is, on protecting citizens from harm. The Charter attempts to provide more balance by addressing the 'freedoms' component of AFSJ. What amounts to a 'Bill of Rights' is provided for, especially in Title II (freedoms), Title V (citizens' rights), and Title VI (justice). Among numerous specific rights that are covered are the right to liberty and security of the person, to freedom of thought, to conscience and religion, to political rights such as voting, standing for election and consular protection, and to the right to a fair trial. Particularly with respect to the latter, the Charter provides the basis for EU institutions to move beyond mutual recognition to agree minimum standards for those who are accused of legal offences.

The Charter deviates from the traditional notion of a political bill of rights in Title IV (solidarity), which guarantees the basic rights of organized workers. These include the right to collective bargaining, to social security and to health care.

Of the other two titles, Title 1 (dignity) enshrines the EU's general approach to human rights, with specific provisions including prohibition of the death penalty and of the reproductive cloning of human beings. Equality is the basis of Title III, which includes respect for cultural, religious and linguistic diversity, and the prohibition of discrimination on such grounds as gender, ethnicity and sexual orientation.

It must be emphasized that most of the rights contained in the Charter are more statements of the European 'ideal' than enforceable rights of all citizens of EU member states. This is because Article 51(2) of the Charter states that it does not confer new competences on the EU: therefore, a Latvian citizen, for example, could not claim the right to a pension in another member state because the EU does not have competence to enforce pension rights.

The status of the Charter

Most member state governments wanted the Charter to be given treaty status via the Nice Treaty, but this was not possible because of opposition by five governments led by the UK. The course then taken

---

Box 11.6

Summary of the main contents of the Charter of Fundamental Rights of the European Union

I (Articles 1–5): Dignity. Rights covered under this chapter include: the right to life, including the prohibition of the death penalty; the integrity of the person, including prohibition of the reproductive cloning of human beings; and the prohibition of torture or inhumane treatment.

II (Articles 6–19): Freedoms. Included here are the right to liberty and security; respect for private and family life; protection of personal data; freedom of thought, conscience and religion; freedom of expression; freedom to conduct business; and the right to property.

III (Articles 20–26): Equality. Among the rights recognized in this chapter are equality before the law, non-discrimination, equality between men and women, and the rights of the child.

IV (Articles 27–38): Solidarity. This chapter includes workers' rights to information and consultation within undertakings, the right of collective bargaining and action, fair and just working conditions, health care rights, and consumer protection.

V (Articles 39–46): Citizens' rights. Rights listed here include the right of a citizen to vote and stand as a candidate at EP and municipal elections in the member states in which he or she resides, the right to good administration, the right of movement and residence within the Union, and the right of diplomatic or consular protection by the authorities of any member state in a third country in which the member state of which he or she is a national is not represented.

VI (Articles 47–50): Justice. This chapter includes the right to an effective remedy and to a fair trial, the presumption of innocence and right of defence, and adherence to the principles of legality and proportionality of criminal offences and penalties.

was for the Charter to be 'solemnly proclaimed' by the EP, the Commission and the Council in December 2000. Inevitably, this gave it a rather uncertain legal status, but it did quickly take on at least some independent juridical life, with ECJ advocates general and the Court of First Instance making some use of its provisions as early as 2002 (European Commission, 2008b).

Following extensive political horse-trading and delicate compromises within the Constitutional Convention, the Charter was contained in the Constitutional Treaty agreed by all member states in 2004. However, when the Treaty failed and the European Council agreed to authorize a reform treaty, the issue of the Charter's treaty status was re-opened. This was because some member states were becoming concerned that the ECJ might interpret the Charter in such a way as to undermine the sovereignty of national governments in their relationships with their citizens. Concern was expressed particularly in the UK, which had never been wholly comfortable with the Charter, where two sets of arguments were advanced. First, British civil liberties and rights were claimed to be more advanced than in most other EU states and risked being weakened by continental interpretations of the rights enumerated in the Charter. This argument thus revived the centuries-old common law view that committing rights to paper could have the unintended consequence of diminishing those rights. Second, the economic and social rights contained in the Charter could be a Trojan Horse for the importation of continental – and particularly German and Swedish – labour rights.

The renewed debate on the Charter affected its placement and status in the Lisbon Treaty in two ways. First, it was not incorporated in the EU's treaties but rather, echoing the 2000 procedure, was 'solemnly proclaimed' by the Presidents of the EP, Council and Commission in December 2007. However, the Charter is referred to in Article 6 TEU, in such a way that makes it legally binding: 'The Union recognises the rights, freedoms and principles set out in the Charter of Fundamental Rights of the European Union of 7 December 2000, as adapted at Strasbourg, on 12 December 2007, which shall have the same legal value as the Treaties.' Second, three member states – the Czech Republic, Poland and the UK – insisted, as a condition of their support for the Treaty, on a guaran-

tee that the Charter would not create new rights for citizens in their states. The guarantee is given in Protocol 30 of the Lisbon Treaty.

The long-run impact of the Charter on EU law is uncertain. On the one hand, its 'federal' reach could become important and the CJEU, as a constitutional court, could play a central role in the process. The US experience may be instructive here, with the US Supreme Court, after having in the nineteenth century played a major part in helping to build the US common market but not having involved itself much with civil liberties and rights, in the twentieth century came to 'discover' a set of 'fundamental rights' in the Bill of Rights and to make these applicable to the states. It could be argued that the EU, having built its common market successfully (a result in no small part of CJEU rulings), could be poised to enter a new era of jurisprudence in which the rights of European citizens will be protected and even advanced by the CJEU. Certainly, there is no shortage of examples of citizenship rights issues of various kinds appearing on the EU's policy agenda. One example is the Commission's quest to obtain a minimum percentage of 40 per cent of women on the boards of directors of European corporations by 2020. Another example is the greater attention being given, especially by the Commission and EP, to addressing discrimination against the Roma (an ethnic minority consisting of a subgroup of the Romani people living primarily in Central and Eastern Europe), which has become an increasingly salient issue since the 2004 and 2007 enlargements raised the Roma population in the EU from two million to 10–12 million. On the other hand, comparisons between European and American jurisprudence in terms of the potential future importance of the Charter must be made with caution. One reason for this is that relying on CJEU interpretations to build case law in fundamental rights is thought by most European jurists (trained as they are in civil rather than common law) to be inefficient and inadequate. A second reason is that the CJEU has steadily inferred 'core rights' from many sources, including national law, international conventions to which EU member states are parties, and the *acquis communautaire*, rather than just drawing on one Bill of Rights (as in the US). And a third reason is that the expansion of fundamental rights in the US depended on the willingness of individuals to challenge court convictions on constitutional grounds. This is a route not available to EU citizens, where the Commission must be willing to challenge a member state's interpretation of the Charter. While the EP will doubtless pressure the Commission to adopt an aggressive role, it is uncertain whether the Commission will be willing to challenge member states on issues that tend to produce hostile headlines in the Eurosceptic press and provide fodder to ultra-nationalist political parties. So, at least for the near future, it is likely that the (overburdened) ECHR will continue to be the primary judicial body adjudicating cases involving European civil rights and liberties.

Conclusions

Prior to 1975, when the EC took its first tentative steps towards police and judicial co-operation through the Trevi Process, member states had exclusive competence in all AFSJ matters. Since then, the policy area has grown enormously, with some AFSJ policies now being decided mainly at the EU level (such as border control for Schengen states), some firmly under the control of member states (such as immigration policy), and some characterized by intensive co-ordination and co-operation among national authorities (such as police and judicial co-operation in criminal matters).

Over the next few years, AFSJ will continue to develop. A central reason why it will do so is that, as this chapter has sought to demonstrate, AFSJ policy is a prototypical case of the interconnectivity among EU policy areas. This is seen not least in the way in which a fundamental right enshrined in the Treaties – free movement of people – has necessitated numerous AFSJ policy actions that have further federalized member state interactions.

Because of the political sensitivities associated with AFSJ, the policy development that has taken place to date has often been extremely difficult. So much so, indeed, that AFSJ is one of the EU policy areas most associated with 'variable geometry'. This difficulty of developing AFSJ policy is likely to continue, especially given the increased support that has been given in recent years to parties of the right which have strived to demonstrate they are 'tough' on such AFSJ and AFSJ-related issues as immigration, crime, and 'welfare cheats' (with the three often being linked in the mind of the public).

Beyond issues such as immigration and border control, another sensitive AFSJ policy area that is likely to continue to provide an important and difficult challenge in the coming years is internal security, with the EU having to face such questions as whether the exchange of information among member state security services is sufficient to ensure Europe's internal security and whether there is sufficient trust among member states to support a strong, EU-level, internal security organization.

Chapter 12
Trade Policy

This chapter examines the EU's trade policy. While the policy is not *completely* common, it is with its Common Commercial Policy (CCP) – the EU's term for trade policy – that the EU most resembles a state actor in external affairs, exercising an exclusive competence to negotiate accords on behalf of all EU member states in most areas of external trade. This requirement of the EU to act in a unified way in international trade negotiations, when coupled with the very considerable volume of external EU trade, makes the EU an extremely important international trade actor.

The first section of this chapter explains the rationale for the EU's common trade policy. The second section outlines the volume and nature of EU external trade. The third section explains how EU trade policy is made. The fourth section presents and analyses the main principles of EU trade policy, and the fifth section examines the EU's major types of trade relationships. The chapter closes with an assessment of the challenges for and the future direction of EU trade policy.

Why Does the EU Have a Common Trade Policy?

The most obvious reason why the EU has a common trade policy is that it is a customs union, and customs unions necessitate a common trade policy. However, though the customs union reason certainly is crucial – especially in explaining the creation of the CCP in the 1960s – two additional factors have also contributed greatly to the rationale of the CCP and to why it has, over the years, been expanded in scope. One of these factors is the usefulness of a common trade policy for opening-up markets for European investment and exports. The other is that a common trade policy assists other key Union policies, notably foreign and security policy and development policy.

This section of the chapter examines these three bases of EU trade policy.

The customs union

Article 9 of the 1957 EEC Treaty laid the basis for a customs union:

> The Community shall be based upon a customs union which shall cover all trade in goods and which shall involve the prohibition between

Member States of customs duties on imports and exports and of all charges having equivalent effect, and the adoption of a common customs tariff in their relations with third countries.

By mid-1968, the EEC had established a fully-functioning customs union: that is, a free trade area protected by common external tariffs and quotas imposed on goods entering the area. An important consequence of the creation of a customs union is that member states must act as a unified entity when negotiating the terms on which they conduct their trade with trading partners. This is because if they negotiated their terms of trade with non-member states on an individual basis they would very quickly be agreeing to diverse trading arrangements that would result in the collapse of the customs union. Accordingly, the CCP is one of the EU's most comprehensive and integrated policies, with the EU being a single actor in most international trade negotiations. Member states wishing to protect domestic industries and firms from international competition cannot change their terms of trade unilaterally with non-EU states, but rather must seek to convince other EU member states in EU trade policy forums of the necessity of putting shared border protections in place.

Given that it thus involved the taking of a huge integrationist step, why did the EEC Treaty provide for a customs union, and why and how was one created relatively easily when in the same time period European countries and the US were negotiating a multilateral free trade regime under the General Agreement on Tariffs and Trade (GATT)? There were a number of reasons.

One reason was that while Western European governments in the postwar era generally believed that the then prevailing high international trade barriers needed to be reduced, there was little confidence that truly multilateral free trade could be achieved through the GATT (which had been established in 1947). Even if the GATT was to eventually come close to achieving its free trade ideal, it was widely understood that it would take years of painstaking negotiations to reach that point. Furthermore, as a free trade area rather than a customs union, GATT would do nothing to end the costly border delays associated with customs' collections and reporting.

A second, and related, reason was that when the EEC was being created there was evidence in place

suggesting that customs unions could work in Western Europe. The Benelux Customs Union – formed in 1944 by the governments-in-exile of Belgium, the Netherlands and Luxembourg, and which became operational in 1948 – was judged widely to be an economic success. To the EEC's founders, it demonstrated that contiguous countries enjoying similar levels of economic and political development could form and constitute a successful customs union. The Benelux Customs Union thus provided a useful pilot model for larger-scale application.

A third reason why European leaders were interested in forming a customs union was that it would provide an 'invisible' revenue: 'invisible' because the consumer would be unaware of the hidden tax (the customs tariff). This European-level tax could then be used to finance some of the EEC's operations, whereas a free trade area would not have created the revenue stream needed to begin building a supranational organization. This is not a small point as federal systems such as the US were originally financed through the customs trade, laying the basis for eventual fiscal federalism.

A fourth reason was the West German championing of a Western European customs union. While it is true that West Germany saw economic and political co-operation as its ticket from pariah to partner, the shape that European co-operation would take was by no means certain. The customs union was a model that West German policy-makers understood and respected because of their own country's history with the *Zollverein* (German customs union) of the nineteenth century, which acted as a precursor of German political integration.

A fifth reason was that many of the EEC's founders saw a customs union as a very useful and practical catalyst for further integration between contiguous Western European states. The weakness of such postwar organizations as the Council of Europe and the Organisation for European Economic Co-operation (OEEC), and then the collapse in 1954 of the projected European Defence Community and associated European Political Community, had largely undermined, for a time at least, the credibility of building European integration by political means. In consequence, an almost ideological dominance of what would come to be called neo-functionalist thinking developed among many of the EEC's key founders, with an incremental and economic-led vision of the

European integration process coming to prevail. According to this logic, European countries could learn the benefits of economic co-operation through a customs union, and from there could broaden into wider integration – as had occurred at earlier periods in Europe and elsewhere. (See, for example, the work of the influential economic historian of this period, Jacob Viner (1950, p. 62), who argued that the creation of a customs union was a major contributory factor in the establishment of the Swiss Confederation, the American republic, and Germany.)

A sixth reason stemmed from the then varying customs practices and attitudes towards external trade among Western European states. Normally, higher-tariff states will not accept a free trade area because they want the trade protection provided by a customs union. For the reverse reason, lower tariff states are usually suspicious of being part of a customs union because they favour open trade. As a result, the UK – a low tariff country – opposed the EEC's proposed customs union and founded the rival European Free Trade Association (EFTA) when it failed to win support for its view among the EEC's founding members. But higher tariff European countries, including crucially France and Italy, which would not be able to compete with low tariff states, favoured a customs union because it guaranteed a level of protection that would be unavailable in a free trade area.

Opening up foreign markets to European trade and investment

The EU's member states have long been highly dependent on international trade. Being an effective international trader depends on many factors, one of which is being able to contract favourable trading terms with trading partners. A common trade policy is extremely useful in this regard for the EU because it enables the member states to use their trading strength collectively via the CCP when negotiating trading terms with other states. This collective use of the individual trading strengths of the member states – which results in the EU being the world's largest exporting entity, the second-largest importer, the leading market for over 100 countries (see European Commission, 2010h), and leader in both inward and outward foreign direct investment (FDI) – makes the EU a very powerful international trading actor.

This trading strength enables the EU to do much to ensure that its commercial interests are well-placed to compete in global markets. Ways in which this strength is used are explained below, but include: pressing for the opening-up of global markets; protecting the EU's competitive advantages where they exist – such as by vigorously defending the intellectual property rights of EU companies; and protecting European business from discrimination – by, for example, negotiating transparent regulatory regimes that expose unfair trading practices such as government subsidization of domestic industry and discriminatory taxes.

Tying trade to other EU policy goals

The common trade policy is also very useful to the EU in the pursuit of many non-trade policy goals. This usefulness has grown as the EU's policy portfolio has broadened and as there has been an increasing overlap between trade policy and other EU policies. EU external trade policy has, in short, increasingly become not just about external trade.

The overlap between trade policy and other policy areas has long been clear with respect to internal market policy, where the EU has been able to take advantage of the size and wealth of its market. The attractiveness of the EU market for foreign companies has enabled the EU to, for example, require that imported products meet its safety and environmental standards. Such requirements have sometimes resulted in the EU coming into conflict with trading partners – as in the long-running trade dispute between the US and the EU over hormones in beef, and GMOs – but the collective trading strength of the EU is such that in conflictual situations it is in a very powerful position, even when World Trade Organization (WTO) rulings are made against it. (The WTO replaced GATT in 1995.) So, too, the EU has often made the granting of preferential access to the EU market conditional on trading partners being prepared to make non-trade commitments with respect to such matters as climate change, the improvement of employment conditions in developing countries, and the advancement of human rights and democratic governance. As the EU's dependence on foreign sources for fossil fuels has increased, the web of connections between EU trade, energy and foreign policy has become increasingly entangled.

Table 12.1 Percentage share of world trade: four largest economies, 2011 (excluding intra-EU trade)

Countries	Merchandise		Commercial services	
	Imports	Exports	Imports	Exports
EU	16.2	14.9	21.1	24.8
China	12.0	13.3	7.8	5.7
Japan	5.9	5.7	5.4	4.5
US	15.5	10.3	12.9	18.2

Source: World Trade Organization, 2012.

An important point about the usefulness of trade policy as a policy tool in non-trade policy areas is that, in some respects, it is used to compensate for the EU's relative lack of global political strength. This is seen most clearly in the foreign policy area, where the EU has long employed trade policy instruments as 'carrots and sticks' (see Vandenberghie, 2008, for a discussion of 'carrots and sticks' in EU trade policy). Trade has, of course, always been used by states for foreign policy purposes, but the EU has been especially prone to do so. A reason for this is that such credible 'hard power' as the EU has must usually be exercised through the American-dominated NATO.

The Volume and (Changing) Nature of EU External Trade

There are two main reasons why the EU is a powerful international trade actor: it accounts for a large volume of international trade and in most international trading negotiations it acts as a single bloc. So, it has collective trading strength and is able to employ this strength.

This section of the chapter outlines the nature of the first of these reasons, while the next section outlines the second.

Table 12.1, based on 2011 data, puts percentages to the EU's trading strength and to those of the world's other large trading economies. As can be seen from the table, the EU accounts for over 16 per cent of the world's imports in goods and nearly 15 per cent of

exports in goods, compared to 15.5 per cent and 10.3 per cent, respectively, for the US. The EU also dominates in trade in commercial services, accounting for 24.8 per cent of world exports and 21 per cent of imports, compared to 18.2 per cent and 12.9 per cent, respectively, for the US.

Two changing aspects of the volume of EU external trade merit particular attention: its geographical scope and its product nature.

The geographical scope of external trade

At the time that the EEC Treaty laid the foundations for the CCP, by far the greatest volume of international trade was among developed countries. The geographical spread of trade was relatively modest, with the greatest volume and competition being within Western Europe and across the Atlantic: that is, within and between those countries that had established 'a zone of transatlantic peace' and strong commercial relations after the Second World War.

With the creation of the EU's internal market, intra-European trade can, of course, no longer be thought of as international or external trade in the traditional sense. As for transatlantic trade, it remains extremely important but is not as dominant as it was, with a more genuinely international trading system having been, and still rapidly being, built as part of globalization. Much of the drive behind the globalization of trade has stemmed in recent years from Brazil, Russia, India and China (countries which, along with South Africa, are commonly referred to as the 'BRICS'), which have become increasingly powerful, competitive and assertive trading powerhouses on world markets and in global economic governance forums (McGuire and Lindeque, 2010, p. 1330). Their growing importance for the EU as both trading partners and competitors is signalled by the fact that, as can be seen from Table 12.2, China and Russia are the EU's major trade partners (imports and exports combined) after the US.

This increasing globalization and competitiveness of international trade has naturally required the EU to attempt to protect, and where possible to advance, its share of world markets. In doing so, EU decision-makers are firmly and strongly placed within the complex network of relationships that form the basis of global trade policy-making.

Table 12.2 EU's leading client and suppliers in merchandise trade, 2011

Major EU import partners				Major EU export partners				Major EU trading partners			
Rank	EU imports from...	Millions of euros	%	Rank	EU exports to...	Millions of euros	%	Rank	EU trade with...	Millions of euros	%
	Extra EU27	1,685,398			Extra EU27	1,531,358			Extra EU27	3,216,756	
1	China	292,129.6	17.3	1	US	260,553.4	17.0	1	US	444,799.0	13.8
2	Russia	198,342.6	11.8	2	China	136,222.3	8.9	2	China	428,351.9	13.3
3	US	184,245.6	10.9	3	Switzerland	121,671.5	7.9	3	Russia	306,776.6	9.5
4	Norway	93,449.8	5.5	4	Russia	108,434.0	7.1	4	Switzerland	212,876.9	6.6
5	Switzerland	91,205.4	5.4	5	Turkey	72,670.9	4.7	5	Norway	139,978.8	4.4
6	Japan	67,451.7	4.0	6	Japan	48,967.5	3.2	6	Turkey	120,263.6	3.7
7	Turkey	47,592.7	2.8	7	Norway	46,529.0	3.0	7	Japan	116,419.2	3.6
8	India	39,314.7	2.3	8	India	40,425.1	2.6	8	India	79,739.8	2.5
9	Brazil	37,776.0	2.2	9	Brazil	35,728.6	2.3	9	Brazil	73,504.6	2.3
10	South Korea	36,100.7	2.1	10	U. A. Emirates	32,614.8	2.1	10	South Korea	68,517.8	2.1
11	Saudi Arabia	28,122.6	1.7	11	South Korea	32,417.2	2.1	11	Saudi Arabia	54,517.7	1.7
12	Algeria	27,678.4	1.6	12	Australia	30,805.7	2.0	12	Canada	52,471.4	1.6
13	Nigeria	24,147.4	1.4	13	Hong Kong	30,188.0	2.0	13	Singapore	46,072.8	1.4
14	Taiwan	23,946.8	1.4	14	Canada	29,609.1	1.9	14	Algeria	44,883.8	1.4
15	Canada	22,862.3	1.4	15	Singapore	27,131.3	1.8	15	South Africa	43,419.1	1.3

Source: European Commission, 2012t.

The product composition of external trade

In the early days of the EC, most domestic economic output, and consequently by far the greatest volume of EC external trade, comprised trade in goods. However, from the EC's earliest days, the Commission sought to persuade the member states to adopt an expansive approach towards trade policy and from the early 1990s campaigned vigorously for the rapidly expanding trade areas of services, intellectual property and FDI to be located within EU trade policy. As part of its campaign, the Commission sought to use the doctrine of *parallelism*, meaning that where the EU enjoyed exclusive competence in the internal market then *ipso facto* it should also have competence in those same areas in external relations. But because of the sensitivity of many of these areas, the member states refused to accept this logic, preferring to interpret narrowly the treaty provisions on trade policy and to move only slowly towards a broader approach. The ECJ mainly backed the member states and was unwilling to accept the Commission's argument that the EU's exclusive competence in respect of trade and investment policy was an implied power through parallelism (Niemann, 2005, p. 28).

However, just as international trade has become much more geographically spread since the EEC was founded, so it has also become more multi-dimensional and complex in its product nature. The EU's member states have had to accept the reality and consequences of this by gradually extending the remit of EU trade policy. This was initially done *de facto*, but then was put on a firm legal footing by the Lisbon Treaty which, in Article 207 TFEU (formerly Article 133 TEC), established that the CCP applied not only to trade in goods but also to services, to the commercial aspects of intellectual property, and to foreign direct investment.

The changing product nature of international, and of EU external, trade is no more apparent than with respect to trade in services, which have surpassed manufacturing in their importance to the economies of most EU developed states. Just over 70 per cent of EU GNP is now derived from the service sector (European Services Forum, 2011). However, a major problem for the EU in seeking to advance the trading interests of its strong services sector is that services in markets EU-based companies target are usually more heavily protected by trade barriers than are goods.

So, for example, the Commission has estimated that the tariff equivalents of service barriers in the US are as high as 73 per cent in the construction industry, 41 per cent in finance, and 29 per cent in telecommunications (European Commission, 2010b, p. 21). Developing countries maintain even higher service trade barriers. The EU has had some success in overcoming these barriers, which partially explains why, as shown in Table 12.1, it accounts for nearly a quarter of international trade in services. Lower international barriers would probably further increase the EU's share of the global services markets, hence it having pressed consistently for liberalization of the service trade in the WTO's Doha Round of trade talks (which opened in 2001, but are stalled at the time of writing).

Another growing and increasingly important area of international trade for the EU is public procurement. Having opened-up much of its own domestic public procurement to international tendering, it is an area that the EU has sought to see being more liberalized at the international level. However, like services, public procurement remains an area of trading activity that is still heavily protected. So, for example, the Commission estimates that €312 billion of the EU's public procurement market is open to other WTO bidders, but only €34 billion is open in the US and €22 billion in Japan (European Commission, 2011j, p. 26).

The changing nature of the composition of international trade has thus posed, and still does pose, many challenges for the EU. They are challenges it seeks to meet by working for a more generally liberal international trading regime through the WTO, and through bilateral agreements where the WTO fails to make progress.

Policy Actors and Policy Processes

As shown earlier, the existence of the customs union means that the EU has to have a single trade policy. The bedrock principle of the operation of EU trade policy is thus that the terms of trade on which member states conduct trade with the rest of the world is an exclusive EU competence. No member state can conduct its own trade policy with states outside the

EU though, of course, governmental representatives of the member states can and do promote externally goods and services produced in their respective countries. This exclusivity is the second main reason (the first being the EU's accounting for such a large volume of international trade) why the EU is a first-rank international actor with respect to trade. In other external policy areas where the EU also has considerable resources but is unable to act in a wholly united way – in foreign and defence policy, for example – its potential international influence is not maximized.

The demands of international competition mean that, to be effective, the EU's trade policy must be both bold and capable of being rapidly attuned to changing global trading circumstances. This is because the EU must, on the one hand, be able to create favourable conditions for its producers as they attempt to sell their products on the world market, and on the other, to be able to provide protection for its producers when that is deemed to be necessary – which, in practice, means in particular when EU producers are subject to what is perceived as being unfair competition.

Two main decision-making processes are used with respect to trade policy: one is used to make trade legislation and the other to make trade agreements.

The making of trade legislation

Trade legislation, which normally has the purpose of adopting 'the measures defining the framework for implementing the common commercial policy' (Article 207, TFEU) is made via the ordinary legislative procedure. This procedure was described in Chapter 5, so it will suffice here merely to remind readers that the procedure involves the Commission having the exclusive right to table legislative proposals and the Council and the EP sharing decision-making powers.

The making of trade agreements

The twin requirements of the treaty obligation that there must be a single trade policy and the practical necessity that the policy should be operated in such a way as to be effective, have combined to produce a distinctive policy process for making trade agreements. It is a process that allows the EU to be able to act as one in international trading settings but also

allows the member states, and increasingly also the EP, to be able to exercise ultimate control over what policies are pursued in these settings. Key features of the process are set out in Figure 12.1.

A few points about the information that is presented in Figure 12.1 regarding the positions of the three main institutional actors – the Commission, the Council and the EP – merit some comment.

* * *

The Commission is in several respects the most pivotal trade policy actor. It takes the lead in proposing what the EU's positions should be in trade negotiations, it acts on behalf of all member states when trade negotiations are conducted, and it makes recommendations to the Council and the EP regarding which negotiating outcomes are acceptable and/or possible. The Trade Commissioner and DG Trade carry the main responsibility for undertaking these tasks, but they have to liaise carefully with other Commissioners and DGs which have, or which claim that they have, overlapping, or at least affected, interests. Amongst Commissioners and DGs with such claims and interests are those responsible for the internal market, agriculture and energy.

How much room for manoeuvre the Commission has when conducting negotiations varies according to circumstances. Usually, differences of both principle and special interest between the member states result in the negotiating directives the Council gives to the Commission being fairly tightly drawn – often reflecting a compromise between those countries tending towards protectionism and those favouring a more free trade approach. During particularly difficult or important negotiations the Commission may return to the Council for clarification of the negotiating directive, or for an amended directive that might break a deadlock.

* * *

The Council authorizes negotiating directives, takes final decisions on recommended trade agreements, and legitimates and monitors Commission trade policy actions. It does so via an organizational structure, which, in descending hierarchical order, consists of:

- *The Foreign Affairs Council* (FAC). There is no separate Trade Council, but at the FAC trade matters are usually handled by Trade Ministers rather than

Figure 12.1 The 'standard proceedure' for contracting external trade agreements under Article 207 TFEU

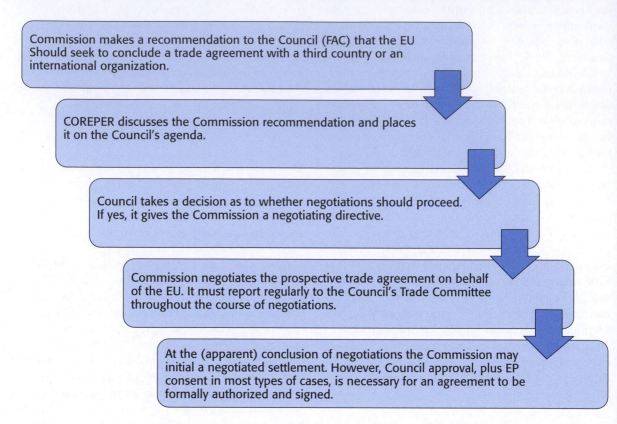

Commission makes a recommendation to the Council (FAC) that the EU Should seek to conclude a trade agreement with a third country or an international organization.

COREPER discusses the Commission recommendation and places it on the Council's agenda.

Council takes a decision as to whether negotiations should proceed. If yes, it gives the Commission a negotiating directive.

Commission negotiates the prospective trade agreement on behalf of the EU. It must report regularly to the Council's Trade Committee throughout the course of negotiations.

At the (apparent) conclusion of negotiations the Commission may initial a negotiated settlement. However, Council approval, plus EP consent in most types of cases, is necessary for an agreement to be formally authorized and signed.

Foreign Ministers. When this occurs, the Council is chaired not, as it is for CFSP/CSDP matters, by the High Representative but by the member state currently occupying the rotating Council presidency.
- *COREPER.* COREPER II (see Chapter 3) undertakes much of the preparation for Council meetings.
- *The Trade Committee.* This committee, which normally meets at least weekly, meets at two levels: full members and deputies. At full members' meetings, which are held at least once each month, national 'teams' are usually headed by senior officials from the national ministries responsible for trade. The Commission 'team' is headed by the Director General of DG Trade. At deputy members' meetings, held at least three times a month, national 'teams' are composed of officials from either relevant national ministries or the permanent representations in Brussels. The Commission is represented by officials from DG Trade.

The Committee can adjust negotiating directives during the course of negotiations, but anything that is especially political or sensitive must be referred to COREPER and, if necessary, the FAC.

The Trade Committee is supported by *specialized sub-committees* that deal with particular trade matters, including services, textiles and motor vehicles.

Policy differences between member states in the Council can be overlaid by differing general attitudes regarding the advantages of liberal free trade on the one hand and protectionism on the other, but they are invariably based also on the implications of policy recommendations for national or nationally-based industries and companies. Inevitably, therefore, discussions and negotiations in the Council – both between the member states and between the member states and the Commission – can often be very difficult and tense.

The Council normally, though not always, can take decisions by qualified majority vote. Types of decisions where unanimity is required include: cultural and audiovisual services where trade agreements 'risk prejudicing the Union's cultural and linguistic diversity' (Article 207: 4(a), TFEU); social, educational and health services where trade agreements risk 'seriously disturbing the national organisation of such services and prejudicing the responsibility of Member States to deliver them' (Article 207: 4(b), TFEU); and where unanimity is required for the adoption of internal rules. However, as in so many EU policy areas, whatever the formal voting rules may be, in practice the Council usually proceeds by consensus.

* * *

Prior to the Lisbon Treaty, the EP was largely sidelined with respect to the making and conclusion of trade deals. However, the Treaty greatly increased the Parliament's powers by stipulating that the Commission must in future report regularly to the EP on the progress of trade negotiations, and that trade agreements must be given the Parliament's consent.

Political lobbying and coalition-building

While one might think of the customs pillar as an arid and highly technical policy arena, it is in fact teeming with 'political action'. This is because external trade conditions have potentially major economic implications for the member states and trading interests. In consequence, many policy actors – in particular, member state governments, EU-level policy-makers, business interests and consumer advocates – jostle in what is often highly intensive pluralist-style bargaining. At the heart of this bargaining are both disparate attitudes towards free trade and protection, and differences arising from the goods that are exported or imported by each member state.

A maelstrom of intense political activity, involving extensive lobbying and coalition-building, thus takes place around and 'below the surface' of formal trade policy processes. While such activity is common in most EU policy areas, trade is an area where it is particularly intense. A key reason for this is that trade policy is, in effect, a prototypical distributive policy. That is, decisions on trade – and most obviously those

decisions concerning trade protection measures – financially advantage particular manufacturers, industries and member states. Unlike the situation with redistributive policies, where there are usually 'two sides' that can be clearly identified (the haves and the have-nots), distributive policies can have many 'sides' and numerous participants who shift alliances depending on the particular benefits at stake.

As a result, therefore, of the very considerable consequences of its policy decisions, trade policy is the subject of intense interest by, and often intense competition between, a wide range of EU policy actors and would-be actors. The next two sub-sections of this chapter illustrate this by focusing on two sets of key non-institutional trade policy actors – policy interests and the member states.

Policy interests

Trade policy decision-makers are subject to intense lobbying by directly-affected economic interests. As in established federal systems, this occurs at two levels, with nationally-based interests lobbying their national governments to act at the EU level in ways that protect home markets, and with these interests also often linking-up with similarly positioned interests in other member states – via either Eurogroups or the formation of coalitions of convenience – to lobby EU institutions directly (see Chapter 4 for a description of the nature of this EU-level lobbying). Circumstances favourable to the emergence of trade Eurogroups or coalitions include where geographic trade areas straddle two or more member states, when particular products and services originate in several member states, and when European companies operate in more than one member state. Such EU-level representation can lead to powerful calls by trade associations advocating and lobbying for the protection or the opening-up of particular sectoral markets. Sometimes, interests – with automobile manufacturers being a good example – lobby for both domestic (EU) protection and better access to foreign markets. Naturally there are many differences in the policy preferences of trade lobbies, which can weaken the overall impact of their activity when they are not all lobbying in the same direction. The footwear industry illustrates this, with, as is shown in Box 12.1, European manufacturers disagreeing as to whether or not import protection measures should be applied:

Box 12.1

Sectional and member state positions in a dispute on foreign footwear imports

- In the mid-2000s the European Confederation of the Footwear Industry (CEC), which makes 40 per cent of the leather footwear sold in the EU, and the European Trade Union Federation – Textiles, Clothing and Leather (ETUF:TCL), lobbied the Commission to impose anti-dumping measures on footwear imports from China and Vietnam.
- The Foreign Trade Association (European footwear makers with foreign factories) opposed the anti-dumping duties, arguing 'there is no European manufacturer of the type of low-cost shoes that are being imported from China and Vietnam' (Mallinder, 2008).
- Member states with substantial domestic footwear manufacturing (especially Italy, Portugal and Spain) supported protection being given.
- Several member states opposed protection, including those with little domestic footwear manufacturing but with substantial production based outside the EU (such as Sweden and the UK), and those that benefit substantially from the port trade in imported footwear (including the Netherlands, through the Port of Rotterdam).

In 2006, after an 'intensive bout of lobbying from domestic shoemakers' (Mallinder, 2008), the Commission imposed anti-dumping tariffs on leather shoes from China and Vietnam. However, aware of the sharply differing views on the matter, the tariffs were imposed for just two years, subject to review and renewal, rather than the longer period of five years that is sometimes applied. The anti-dumping tariffs were renewed in 2008, subject to a 15-month review. The Chinese lodged a complaint with the WTO in 2010 and the EU voluntarily lifted the anti-dumping duties in March 2011 (Pop, 2011).

---

domestic footwear manufacturers (the highest national proportion of which are based in Italy) favour protection, while manufacturers with extensive production facilities outside the EU (many of which are based in the Netherlands, the UK and Sweden) oppose protection.

Member states

As a consequence usually of some mixture of historical inheritance and policy choice, some member states are more persuaded of the merits of international free trade than are others. But, whatever their general policy position is on free trade, national interest and pragmatic calculation invariably feature prominently in explaining the stances national governments take in relation to specific trade issues, as Box 12.1 shows. No government is likely to support an external trading position – such as a reduction of tariffs or the removal of non-tariff barriers on particular products – that will threaten significant domestic industries or

producers. Nor is it likely to support a position that could be unpopular domestically. Indeed, Fiona McGillivray (2004) has pointed out the importance of regional concentration of industries to electoral promises – the greater the concentration, the more likely it is that politicians will fight for import protection.

The dual stances that can be a consequence of this is clearly demonstrated by the way in which in EU trade negotiations national governments usually support free trade with respect to those goods that are not produced domestically, but usually press for higher tariffs on products that they produce. Further to this, in his empirical analysis of common external tariff rates, Ehrlich (2009, p. 136) found that 'the more a product is produced by high-access-point countries or imported into important EU countries, the higher the tariff will be on that product; whereas, the more a product is exported by important EU countries, the lower the tariff will be on that product'. Ehrlich (2009, p. 136) also found that member states that 'want high protection and countries that want free trade can both achieve their preferences to some extent' and that countries engineer tariff rates 'in the knowledge of what goods they import and what goods they export'.

Policy implementation

There are many dimensions to trade policy implementation. Four particularly important aspects of them are noted here.

The first concerns the front-line application of import and export rules. This task is undertaken by relevant national authorities. Working within the CCP's rules and the EU's customs reporting systems, national customs authorities check imported and exported products and collect CET customs duties – which are remitted to the EU, minus a 25 per cent 'collection charge'. Naturally, geography is important here, with checking and collection burdens being much higher in member states and at points of entry that serve as important *entrepôts* for European trade.

The second aspect is what happens in the event of disputes with trading partners. The key feature of this aspect of policy implementation is that it is handled at the EU level, be it directly with the trading partner(s) concerned or via a trade organization mechanism – notably the WTO trade dispute system. The importation of rice products from China can be taken to provide a specific example of how the EU may choose to deal with a situation when trade rules are seemingly being circumvented. Most genetically modified organisms (GMOs) are banned from food use in the EU (see European Commission, 2012j, for a list of approved GMOs), but from 2006 British, French and German authorities began reporting to the Commission, under the EU's rapid alert system for food and feed, that unauthorized GMOs were being detected in Chinese rice exports (the EU has not approved any rice GMOs). The issue was quickly taken up by the European rice milling industry – via the Federation of European Rice Millers (FERM), representing over 90 per cent of Europe's milling capacity – which began to experience considerable costs as a result of disruptions to the supply chain (including the recall of products) and damage to brands. The Commission initiated what soon became repeated requests to China to ensure that unauthorized GMOs were not contained in its exports to the EU. However, these requests did

not produce a satisfactory response, so in the autumn of 2011 the EU stepped-up its internal monitoring of imported rice and its pressure on China, with the Commission requiring all member states to test all imported rice products (that is, not just those from China) and to report the results of the testing regularly to it (Taylor, 2011b, p. 2).

The third aspect of policy implementation meriting particular comment is the increasingly close relationships between the Commission, the governments of the member states and relevant trading actors in respect of trade promotion and trade protection. Trade promotion is, of course, mainly a national responsibility, but the Commission does not leave 'marketing' wholly to member states. It has taken on a similar role to that of the US Department of Commerce's International Trade Administration, with programmes such as the 'Export Helpdesk' complementing and supplementing the trade promotion efforts of the member states. Regarding trade protection, the EU's Market Access Partnership (MAP) is a programme involving the Commission, member states, and businesses in an effort to identify and report barriers to trade encountered by EU exporters. The MAP is supported by a Market Access Database, containing information about barriers to trade, which is constantly being updated.

The fourth and final aspect of trade policy implementation to be noted here is how those who are involved with it, at all levels, often need to work closely with those who are responsible for other, related, EU external policies. So, for example, in addition to their direct trade responsibilities, national customs authorities are also heavily involved in helping to apply such EU policies as those covering the health and welfare of product end users, the prevention of terrorism, and the illegal movement of people.

The Principles of EU Trade Policy

EU trade policy is guided by three main policy principles: international trade should rest on liberal foundations – meaning that international barriers to trade generally should be minimized; the liberalization of trade should not prevent the EU from being able to protect EU producers in some circumstances from the consequences of an open trading system; and preferential access to the EU market should be given to some trading partners. In practice, these policy principles intertwine, overlap and sometimes also potentially conflict.

Each of the principles will now be examined in turn.

The liberal preference

The EU is sometimes portrayed by trading partners as being protectionist and illiberal in its trading policies. In fact, with the important exception of agriculture, this is not so. For many years the EU has pursued trade policies that are, for the most part, relatively open and liberal in nature. The single tariff schedule that applies to EU imports bears witness to this liberalism: whilst at one time tariffs accounted for nearly half of the EU's revenue sources, their relative importance as a revenue contributor has gradually declined and today they constitute just over 10 per cent of the EU's budgetary revenue stream. This decrease is partly because EU tariff rates have dropped over the years – the average EU rate for industrial goods is now only about 5.4 per cent – and partly also because many countries, especially developing countries, enjoy preferential access, and often completely duty free access, to the EU market in a number of product areas.

There are several reasons why the EU has a liberal trade philosophy, of which the most important is the need for European-based companies to be able to trade globally without being subject to trading restrictions that hamper access to markets. High international trade barriers interfere with worldwide production chains and with European business – a point that is clearly demonstrated by referencing a single statistic: 66 per cent of EU imports are intermediate goods in the production process (McGuire and Lindeque, 2010, p. 1343). Accordingly, as European corporations have globalized, and as more foreign multi-nationals have located to the EU, so they have pressed both member state governments and EU-level actors to be active in opening-up foreign markets to European trade and investment.

The EU's liberal trading policy has also been reinforced by enlargement, because the range of interests affected by EU trade policy has grown. As a consequence, it is increasingly difficult to protect particular

commercial activities because this favours the member states where the activities are located.

A third reason for the EU's liberal trade policy is the internal market rules that guide competition policy. Where interests and member states seek to gain a special trading advantage via some sort of protection, they can fall foul of the EU's competition authorities.

However, the liberal trade philosophy does not mean that the member states have been, or are, always in accord with how vigorously trade liberalization with the rest of the world should be pursued. On the contrary, member states have long adopted different positions regarding where the balance is to be struck between openness and protectionism. This has been the case both as regards the general stances of states and how particular products should be treated. Regarding general stances, the UK has been the foremost advocate of free trade since it became an EC member – a legacy of British capitalism being built on openness and free competition. Germany, the Netherlands and the Nordic countries have also generally been to the fore in favouring trade liberalization. By contrast, France, Italy, Spain and Greece have been among those more disposed to protectionist measures. Regarding particular products, this very much reflects the strengths and weaknesses of national economies: the UK, for example, has a strong financial services sector and so has pressed for the EU to have a very liberal policy in this area, while France has a relatively large agricultural sector which would struggle to be able to compete on open world markets and so it has pressed for EU agriculture to be protected from cheaper imports and to be given special assistance to enable exports to be competitive.

It might have been expected that the 2004/7 enlargement would have nudged the EU slightly away from its liberal orientation. One reason for such an expectation is that, prior to their accessions, the CEECs had little experience of multilateral trade negotiations, having formerly been either satellite Soviet states or a part of the USSR. Their national leaders were thus not accustomed to the postwar international trading system created by the Americans and Western Europeans. A second reason for expecting CEECs to be relatively unsympathetic to liberal international trading rules is the nature of their economies, which are relatively inefficient and in some cases heavily dependent on the agricultural sector for revenue and employment. A third reason is that the CEECs are not home to any of Europe's Fortune 50 corporations, and their domestic corporations are not as well-positioned as their western neighbours to export significantly to emerging markets (partly because their trade flows are primarily within the EU and to Russia and other non-EU member former Soviet states).

However, despite these three reasons for expecting the CEEC accessions to result in a weakening of the EU's liberal trade policy preference, the evidence does not indicate that this has occurred. Instead, the CEECs have split on the issue, either joining the pre-existing liberal or protectionist camps among the EU-15 in such a way as to maintain the previous status quo of the EU's liberal orientation (Elsig, 2010, p. 794).

The strength of the liberal orientation seems to have withstood not only enlargement but also the post-2008 economic and financial crisis, which has been the most severe such crisis since the Great Depression of the 1930s. De Ville and Orbie (2011, p. 18) argue that the Commission has framed free trade as part of the solution to the crisis and note that it has both renewed calls to complete the Doha Round and intensified negotiations for bilateral trade agreements. The EU has not resorted, therefore, to protectionist measures in response to the crisis.

Selective protection

The EU's support of trading liberalism does not extend to it excluding all forms of protection when international competition is damaging to its member states and domestic producers. The sector that has long been the most protected from external competition is agriculture, where the CAP's combination of internal subsidies for farmers and high external tariffs has made for a very protected market. The level of protection of agriculture has been weakened over the years as international pressures have forced the EU to reduce export refunds and lower agricultural tariffs, but sharp conflicts with important agricultural exporting states – including Argentina, Australia, Brazil, New Zealand and the US – still exist over the extent of the protection the EU gives to the sector. So while, in general, the EU supports a liberal trading regime, agriculture (for the reasons elaborated in Chapter 9's discussion of the CAP) remains an important exception. The average 'bound' Most Favoured

Nation (MFN) tariff rates (the maximum tariffs agreed through the WTO) on EU agricultural imports range between 18 per cent and 28 per cent. Because the WTO permits lower rates, however, the EU's average rate is in fact closer to 10 per cent. Of course, behind these averages, EU tariffs on particular agricultural products vary substantially, with products such as cocoa, coffee and oilseeds being subject only to low tariffs, but products that compete with EU production – such as sugar, dairy products and beef – being more highly protected. Another example of selective protection is in the area of processed food (an important business for EU food manufacturers), where EU tariffs have been consistently significantly higher than the tariffs levied on raw food (Advisory Board for Irish Aid, 2010).

But agriculture is far from being the only sector that the EU has sought to protect from the full rigours of an open international market. Motor vehicles, textiles and consumer electronics are protected, among others. Measures that have been used as part of this protectionism are 'orderly marketing' agreements with more competitive states, exemptions from aspects of general trading agreements, and the imposition of special tariffs when competitors are deemed to be engaging in unfair competition.

On this last measure, the EU believes the international trading environment should be fair – in the sense that governments should not offer tax holidays and rebates, impose arbitrary safety regulations, or confer comparable advantages to domestic producers. If trading partners are believed to be in violation of WTO rules either by dumping (exporting goods at below the price at which they are sold in the home market) or by subsidizing (providing government subsidies for the purpose of making products more competitive in international markets), the Commission normally recommends that the EU imposes countervailing tariffs. An indication of the frequency with which such tariffs are imposed is seen in the fact that in 2011 the EU had no less than 55 anti-dumping measures and one anti-subsidy measure in force against China alone (Nielsen, 2012). The extensive use of such measures has led to the EU (and the US) being accused by developing countries of departing from fair competition rules and resorting to straightforward protectionism. In addition to this use of anti-dumping and anti-subsidy protections, the Commission applies safeguards if it suspects or determines that a product is unsafe (European Commission, 2009e, p. 17).

The use by the EU of such protectionist measures, and of some other measures that are designed to give advantages to its own exporters, has led to criticisms that it has sometimes misused trade policy instruments, especially in relation to emerging and developing countries. Such allegations of misuse have resulted in a number of EU trade actions being referred by aggrieved parties to the WTO's disputes settlement processes. This has led to a number of rulings against the EU and a requirement that it drop the actions in question. Among product areas where there have been WTO rulings against the EU are: bananas (the EU's banana import regime granted duty-free access to imports from African, Caribbean and Pacific [ACP]) countries, but not to Latin American countries); cotton-type bed linen (EU anti-dumping measures were declared to be in contravention of WTO rules); and sugar exports (export subsidies paid by the EU were declared to violate WTO rules because they were excessive).

The ability of the EU to deploy protectionist measures is, however, increasingly constrained by two factors. First, emerging economies now use their own defensive instruments against developed economies and are not averse to using them in retaliation for the EU's employment of defensive tactics. Second, multinational corporations (MNCs) based in emerging markets are operating increasingly in the EU and are often dependent on supplies from their home country. Import restrictions by the EU can disrupt their supply chain and hence threaten employment in EU member states (see discussion in McGuire and Lindeque, 2010).

The granting of preferential access

The EU arranges its relations with its trading partners in the framework of what McGuire and Lindeque (2010, p. 1342) call a 'pyramid of privilege': that is, within a hierarchy of preferential access to the single market. Figure 12.2 depicts this hierarchy. No preferential access is denoted at the bottom of the pyramid and the most privileged access placed at the top. Taking each of the levels of the pyramid in turn:

- At the pyramid's base are non-WTO members and countries that do not enjoy bilateral agreements with the EU.

- At the next level up, WTO countries enjoy Most Favoured Nation status, a WTO rule that compels the EU to offer the same terms of trade to all WTO members (with exceptions permitted for developing countries and countries with Preferential Trade Agreements – PTAs).

- The next level of access is enjoyed by those countries and regional associations with which the EU has negotiated PTAs – which are provided for in TFEU Articles 207 and 218. These agreements – which often contain some combination of the words 'co-operation', 'co-ordination' and 'partnership' in their titles – take various forms, but usually have preferential trading terms at their core.

- United Nations' designated 'developing' countries occupy the next level in the pyramid of privilege. Under the Generalized System of Preferences (GSP) scheme they enjoy duty free access to the EU on many items and under the Everything But Arms (EBA) system the world's very poorest states have complete free access to the EU's market for all their exports except armaments.

- At the top of the pyramid of privilege are those countries with which the EU has established 'association agreements'. The EU contracts such agreements under the authority of Article 217, TFEU, which states that 'The Union may conclude with one or more third countries or international organizations agreements establishing an association involving reciprocal rights and obligations, common action and special procedure.' There are differing types of association agreements, but all include free trade areas (FTAs) or near FTAs. The most advanced and integrated FTAs are with the member states of the European Economic Area (Iceland, Liechtenstein and Norway), Switzerland, and Turkey with which the EU has a customs union on industrial goods. The largest category of states with association agreements containing FTAs are the pre-accession states of South Eastern Europe.

An important element of this graded system of preferential access is clearly providing trading assistance to developing states, and states that are geographically close to the EU. However, the most important element of the system is that it is designed to serve EU interests. Even the assistance to developing states does not lose sight of this, with duty-free access to the EU market

Figure 12.2   **Hierarchy of EU preferential trade relationships**

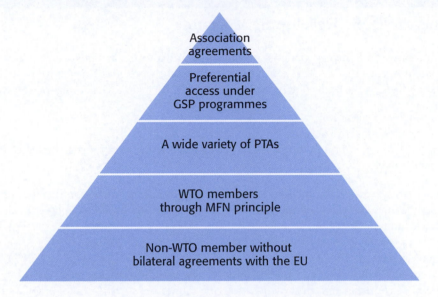

Association agreements

Preferential access under GSP programmes

A wide variety of PTAs

WTO members through MFN principle

Non-WTO member without bilateral agreements with the EU

often being of enormous benefit to European MNCs – which may locate plants in the developing world to take advantage of cheap labour, but which can then export either inputs into the production process or finished goods back to the EU.

The Main Strands of EU Trade Relations

The EU's trading relations are conducted within three broad strands – multilateral, bilateral and unilateral. Multi-lateral relations involve reciprocal trade agreements that are negotiated through the WTO. At the heart of WTO agreements are the advancement of free trade and the practice of reciprocity – the latter meaning that the same terms of trade are offered to all WTO members. Bilateral trade relations involve agreements made between both individual countries and regional trade associations. These sometimes take the form of PTAs, but they often also – as with the EU–US transatlantic agenda – cover areas that are not dealt with through WTO negotiations but are important areas of mutual interest to the EU and its trading partners. Unilateral

trade relations involve a non-reciprocal system of preferences for developing countries, with the EU opening its market without expectations of similar market access for its exports.

The breadth of the strands is such that, naturally, there are significant variations not only between the strands but also to some extent within them regarding the ways in which, and the extent to which, the principles of EU trade policy described above apply. Broadly speaking, however, it can be said that multilateralism and, for the most part, bilateralism, are driven primarily by trade liberalism, while unilateralism is heavily based on the granting of preferential access.

Multilateralism

International liberal trade policy has been long been synonymous with the GATT and the WTO. Driven in no small part by the EU and the US, the WTO has been a success in delivering lower tariffs for European manufacturers. With average import tariffs for manufactured goods traded between the US and the EU in the 2–3 per cent range, and with Japan at less than 5 per cent, European manufacturers can easily integrate such nominal rates into their production costs. Even in trade with emerging countries, important progress

Box 12.2

The EU and the Doha Development Agenda

The Doha Round of world trade negotiations was launched in Doha (Qatar) in November 2001. Named the Doha Development Agenda, the round is much broader than past global trade negotiations and is specifically targeted at addressing the needs of developing countries. The main focus of negotiations has been on:

- reforming agricultural subsidies;
- improving access to global markets; and
- ensuring that new liberalization in the global economy respects the need for sustainable economic growth in developing countries.

The EU believes that the successful conclusion of the Doha negotiations would confirm the central role of multilateral liberalization and rule-making, and would also confirm the WTO as a powerful shield against protectionist backsliding.

The EU's main objectives:

- In market access for industrial goods, the EU wants to create significant new trade flows by cutting tariffs in both developed countries and the growing emerging economies such as China, Brazil and India. The goal is to create new trade between developed countries but also between developing countries. This means lowering tariffs on industrial goods but also negotiating common rules on how to address obstacles to trade generated by an overly complex and non-transparent regulatory system.
- The EU also wants to improve and clarify the WTO rulebook on subsidies that distort the production of industrial goods. These include long-standing financial support made available to exporters on non-commercial terms as well as provision by governments of inputs to domestic producers at prices substantially more favourable than those available to foreign producers (so-called dual or discriminatory pricing).
- For the agriculture sector, the EU is committed to an agreement that reforms farm subsidy programmes throughout the rich world in line with the EU's wide-ranging 2003 reform of the Common Agricultural Policy. As part of the Doha Round, the EU has offered to cut farm tariffs by 60 per cent, reduce trade-distorting farm subsidies by 80 per cent, and eliminate farm export subsidies completely. The EU also wants to see new market access opportunities for its own processed agricultural exports.
- With respect to services, the EU wants Doha to provide for more open market opportunities. However, the EU does not seek general deregulation or the privatization of sectors where principles of public interest are at stake or where cultural diversity would be threatened.
- The EU wants the Doha Round to agree a package of development measures, including: a special agreement to address trade distortions caused by subsidies to cotton farmers in developed countries; the extension of unlimited market access to all Least Developed Countries; and a new global package of 'aid for trade' assistance to help the poorest nations build the capacity to trade.

Source: European Commission, 2011g.

has been made in lowering rates – with averages ranging between 10–20 per cent (European Commission, 2011r; McGuire and Lindeque, 2010, p. 1335).

The WTO advances its liberal programme through negotiating 'Rounds'. The first of these was dubbed the 'Dillon Round' (1960–1), which was followed by the 'Kennedy Round' (1964–7), the 'Tokyo Round' (1973–9), the 'Uruguay Round' (1986–94), and the current 'Doha Round' (which opened in 2001). Little progress has been made to date in the Doha Round and the prospects for success are dim in light of the lingering global economic recession (see Box 12.2 for a summary of the main agenda items of the Doha Round and the EU's negotiating priorities).

The stalling of the Doha Round has been disappointing, and indeed something of a setback, for the EU. One reason for this is that, as McGuire and Lindeque (2010, p. 1334) point out, the WTO is a forum in which the EU has always been 'comfortable' – not least because the intergovernmentalist decision-making processes of the WTO have partly mirrored those of the EU. In turn, the EU's comfort and familiarity with intergovernmental bargaining may have helped it to be a more effective player in the multilateral trade negotiations that have been conducted under WTO auspices. Another reason why the lack of progress in the Doha Round has disappointed the EU is that multilateral agreements are generally preferred by economic actors because their greater simplicity involves lower information and compliance costs. In other words, it is far easier to deal with one set of rules and agreements for several trade partners (multilateral) rather than one set of rules (bilateral) for every country with which the EU has made agreements. A third reason is that WTO agreements allow for substantial advances in trade liberalization at one sitting.

Bilateralism

As we have seen, the EU's general trade policy position is to favour multilateralism. However, where multilateralism has failed or stalled – which is the case with the Doha Round dragging on for a decade with little progress – or where there has simply been a wish for tighter relations (as with the EEA countries and Switzerland), the EU has turned to bilateral agreements and regional PTAs. The EU's stance towards such arrangements can be summarized by a Commission report on trade strategy: 'the bilateral is not the enemy of the multilateral. The opposite may hold truer; liberalisation fuels liberalisation' (European Commission, 2010b, p. 3).

Bilateralism is thus sometimes a consequence of unsuccessful, or what are thought to be too limited, WTO negotiations. Sometimes, however, bilateral and regional trade co-operation agreements are tied to regulatory and foreign policy goals for which WTO rounds are unsuitable and undesirable. So, taking foreign policy goals, as the European integration process has advanced the EU has sought not only to

open up markets to European trade and investment, but also to achieve its foreign policy goals by controlling access to its wealthy and sophisticated consumer market and technological know-how (Meunier and Nicolaïdis, 2006, p. 907). Or, to use the familiar language of global interdependency: the EU recognizes the value of employing soft power as a means to achieve foreign policy ends (Keohane and Nye, 1977; Nye, 2004).

Article 207 TFEU, specifies that bilateral agreements may be preferential or non-preferential in kind, but they are all subject to the international trading rules established within the framework of the WTO. These rules prohibit preferential agreements unless WTO waivers are negotiated. Regardless of this obstacle, operational PTAs account for 28 per cent of EU exports of industrial products.

The EU has negotiated bilateral trade agreements with just about every country in the world. As Table 12.3 shows, some of these are with individual countries (such as Russia and China) while others are with regional associations (such as Mercosur and ASEAN). Each agreement is unique, depending on the goals of the negotiating parties and the extent to which they are 'preferential'. The EU's priorities when negotiating the agreements reflect the increasingly multi-dimensional nature of the international trade agenda in that the agreements are by no means restricted to tariff-related issues but are focused also on such matters as product standards, licensing practices, public procurement and labour rights. With China, for example, with which the EU had a trade deficit of €155.9 billion in 2011, the EU has been very keen to remove a number of Chinese non-tariff barriers involving complex regulations and lack of transparency (European Commission, 2012a). China has also been pressed to enforce intellectual property rights. With India, the perceived unfair nature and impact of Indian domestic taxes on exports has been a problem (European Commission, 2009e, p. 13).

All bilateral agreements have to be tailor-made, because even with trading partners that may seem to be somewhat similar – such as the BRIC countries, which are grouped together because of their large land sizes, large populations, and their rapid economic growth and shared status as emerging economies – distinctive circumstances always exist. Among distinctive characteristics of the BRIC countries that give rise to different trade challenges and opportunities for the

Table 12.3 Examples of EU bilateral trade agreements

Country/Group	Agreements/Declarations/Programmes
Bilateral agreements/policies	
Brazil	EC-Brazil Framework Co-operation Agreement (1992) Agreement for Scientific and Technological Co-operation (2004)
Canada	Framework Agreement for Commercial and Economic Co-operation between the European Communities and Canada (1976)
China	Trade and Co-operation Agreement (1975) (A new Co-operation and Partnership Agreement has been under negotiation since 2007)
Japan	European Community–Japan Joint Declaration (1991) Action Plan for EU–Japan Co-operation (2001)
US	New Transatlantic Agenda (1995)
Russia	Co-operation and Partnership Agreement (1994) (A new EU–Russia agreement has been under negotiation since 2008)
Central Asia, Middle East, North Africa	European Neighbourhood Policy (2004) (Partnership programmes completed on an individual basis with 16 neighbouring states)
Regional agreements	
Andean Community	Declaration of Rome (1996) Political Dialogue and Co-operation Agreement (2003 – awaiting ratification)
Euro-Med	Union for the Mediterranean (2008)
European Free Trade Area (EFTA)	Iceland, Liechtenstein and Norway – Four freedoms enjoyed by EEA member states, but no representation in EU institutions, thus no decision-making power (1994)
Mercosur	EU–Mercosur Framework Co-operation Agreement (1995)
Norway, Iceland, Russia	Northern Dimension (1999) (focuses on north-west Russia, Kaliningrad, the Baltic and Barents seas, Arctic and Sub-Arctic areas)

Source: European Commission, 2011j.

EU are: their locations (the fact that Russia borders several EU member states naturally alters the nature of the trade relationship); energy sources (Brazil and Russia in particular have vast energy sources they are willing to trade); FDI opportunities (China, for example, uses state power to block foreign competitors); and diverse economic development models (for example, export-led economies such as Brazil act differently from the extensive state capitalist economy of China).

In the light of Doha's failures, the EU has begun to focus its efforts more intensely on bilateral trade negotiations with the countries it has identified as 'strategic partners', prominent among which are the BRIC countries, Japan and the US (European Commission, 2010p, p. 11). Of its strategic partners, the EU's most important bilateral relationship continues to be with the US. It is the EU's largest trading partner, accounting for, as can be seen in Table 12.2, nearly 14 per cent of EU merchandise trade. In total terms, the transatlantic economy generates about €3.2 trillion, and 14 million jobs. The US and the EU together account for about a third of global trade and 50 per cent of the world's GDP. In terms of investment, a third of all EU FDI flows to the US and it has more than 1 trillion euros invested in the US (more than in the next 20 countries combined) (European Commission, 2011r). In the most 'sophisticated' area of trade – commercial services – transatlantic trade dominates so completely that it makes other countries look almost like bystanders (at least for the time being...).

However, these figures provide only part of the picture of the historical and continuing importance of the transatlantic relationship. The EU and the US shaped the global trading regime as we know it, and through their significant governmental and corporate networks continue to establish shared norms in policy areas as diverse as the fair treatment of labour, product safety standards and the intellectual property regime. The New Transatlantic Agenda, which the EU and US agreed in 1995, is in many ways driven by an attempt to maintain as much of this dominance as possible: by meeting the challenges from newly-industrializing countries both in terms of the volume flows of world trade and setting the rules by which world trade is conducted.

As well as being collaborative, transatlantic trade relations are also very competitive, as has been witnessed in a number of highly-contested disputes. The best-known such dispute is the long-running US challenge and EU counter-challenge involving Boeing and Airbus civil aircraft, which has centred on governmental subsidies. The EU and US attempted in 1992 to 'cool down' what was becoming a very contentious situation by establishing ground rules regarding acceptable types of government subsidies in the 'Bilateral EU–US Agreement on Trade in Large Civil Aircraft'. However, in October 2004, the US suddenly withdrew from this agreement and filed a challenge in the WTO's Dispute Settlement Mechanism (DSM) on behalf of Boeing, accusing European governments (France, Germany, Spain and the UK) and the EU (through the European Investment Bank) of subsidizing Airbus illegally. The EU filed a counter charge that US federal, state and local authorities provided subsidies in violation of WTO rules to Boeing to the tune of

US$5–6 billion between 1989 and 2006 and an additional US$3.1 billion since then. The WTO has issued several rulings on the Airbus case (the US challenge), with the latest being in March 2011, which have largely vindicated the EU and its member states on the accusation of illegal subsidies. The 'Boeing case' (the EU challenge) was still pending in late 2012 (European Commission, 2012w).

Unilateralism

Unilateral agreements differ from multilateral and bilateral agreements in that they are 'non-reciprocal' and under WTO rules are permitted only for economically-disadvantaged countries as defined by the United Nations. The EU's non-reciprocal trade agreements have evolved within the framework of its policy – which has intensified since around the year 2000 in response to pressures from the WTO – to open its markets and give preferential access to all developing countries and not merely to focus on former colonies.

The previous trade policy with developing countries of prioritizing former colonies was originally known as the 'French policy'. The French policy may be said to have been launched formally in 1964 when the EEC negotiated the Yaoundé agreement, a trade and development programme between the EEC-6 and 18 former French colonies in Africa. The accession of the UK, with its extensive Commonwealth trade arrangements, resulted in this policy being expanded in 1975 to encompass 46 African, Caribbean and Pacific countries, when the first of what became three Lomé Conventions was agreed.

During the Cold War, when the US and its Western allies and the Soviet Union competed for the ideological allegiance of African leaders, the GATT was willing to bend its rules to accept the EU's discrimination in favour of French and British former colonies to the exclusion of other underdeveloped countries (mainly in Latin America and South East Asia). But, after the collapse of the Soviet Union, the US (taking up complaints from developing countries excluded from the EU's preferential system), pressurized the EU to end its non-reciprocal preferential arrangements with the ACP countries on the grounds that they violated the WTO's rules on reciprocity. This led to WTO decisions under which the EU is no longer permitted to

Table 12.4 EU trade agreements with developing countries

Convention or Agreement	Date of implementation	Developing countries	Main provisions
Cotonou Partnership Agreement	2003 (scheduled for 20 years, with reviews)	79 from Africa, Caribbean and the Pacific (ACP)	Most comprehensive partnership agreement between developing countries and the EU. Not just trade-based, but covers EU assistance (most of it via the European Development Fund) for such purposes as economic restructuring, sustainability, peace and civil society building.
Generalised System of Preferences (GSP)	2009 (expires 31 December 2013, with a rollover anticipated to avoid a lapse, with a reformed GSP anticipated to be in place on 1 January 2014 at the latest)	176	GSP list agreed through UN. Preferential import duties for these 176 developing countries. The preferential access to EU members states is generally not tied to other policies. 4,781 free tariff lines available.
GSP+ (Special Incentive Arrangement for Sustainable Development and Good Governance)	Expires in 2013	Variable—available to all GSP countries meeting the criteria (15 countries currently granted this status)	Unlike GSP, GSP + status is 'tied' aid. To receive GSP+ status, developing countries must ratify 16 conventions dealing with labour conditions human rights, environmental sustainability. and 11 conventions on good governance rights and rules. 9,717 free tariff lines available.
Everything But Arms, for Least Developed Countries-	2001 (no expiration date)	49	Duty- and quota-free access to the EU market for virtually all products originating in these very poor countries, apart from armaments. 11,053 free tariff lines available.

Sources: CARIS, 2010; European Commission, 2011m, 2011n; European Union, 2011; Holland, 2004, p. 276.

offer preferential trade exclusively to the ACPs and must offer its preferences to all developing countries, regardless of prior colonial status. In consequence, the successor of the Lomé Conventions, the Cotonou Agreement, centres on the concept of Economic Partnership Agreements (EPAs), which cover a wide range of development issues, including many non-trade issues, but they do not offer more advantageous market access than those offered to other developing countries.

The EU currently has four non-reciprocal trade programmes in place: the EPAs negotiated under the Cotonou Agreement, the Generalized System of Preferences (GSP), GSP+, and Everything But Arms (EBA). The main features of these programmes are summarized in Table 12.4. GSP applies to the 176 most 'developed' of the developing countries and is the least generous. GSP+, which grants broader free access than the GSP to qualifying countries, is an EU invention that ties market access to environmental sustainability, good governance and democratization. As of mid-2012, the EU had granted 15 developing countries GSP+ status. The poorest 49 'least developed countries' (LDCs) qualify for the EU's unique EBA programme, which has been in operation since 2001. A sub-set of the GSP programme, EBA status confers duty-free access to the EU market for virtually all products apart from armaments. Beyond the development potential of the EBA, David Lincoln (2008, pp. 225–6) suggests that it represents no less than 'a de-historicising of a significant colonial relationship between North and South'. This is because, unlike the Lomé and Cotonou agreements that 'denoted post-colonial European obligation (and ACP expectation), EBA has no explicit reference to the historical geography of empire'.

As noted earlier in the chapter – in the section on the granting of preferential access to the EU market – even EU trade policies that are intended to assist developing states are also designed very much with the EU's interests in mind. That this is the case is seen with reform proposals issued by the Commission in 2012 to replace the (current) GSP programme, which is scheduled to expire at the end of 2013 (European Commission, 2012d). The underlying theme of the proposals is that the reformed GSP must reflect the dramatic shift in the wealth status of countries since the EU first adopted the GSP policy in 1971. To this end, the Commission suggests that, 'the notion of "developing countries" as a group is losing relevance and trade, investment and development policies now need to be tailored to reflect this' (ibid., p. 2). As part of the GSP reforms, the Commission envisages expanding the EBA system but ending many trade concessions for states with emerging economies (in particular, states that have not responded to the EU's request for reciprocity in opening up their markets to EU trade and investment). Inevitably, the proposed reforms have generated some grumbling in the development community, with, for example, a highly critical report of the Commission's proposed strategy being issued by the Overseas Development Institute (ODI) (a British think tank). In its report, the ODI argues that the proposed GSP revisions are protectionist (by removing trade concessions); lack a clear strategy for differentiation between the newly rich and the least developed countries; and are light on the EU's commitment to 'non-trade' development (Overseas Development Institute, 2012).

Conclusions

This chapter has reviewed the complexity of the EU's trade policy. It is a policy that has been forced to adapt to the constantly changing nature and balance of international economic power. The US provided the major challenge to European competitiveness and trade at the time of the Community's establishment. By the mid-1970s, Japan and emerging South East Asian economies were posing a major threat, in particular by challenging Europe-based companies in such sectors as vehicle manufacture, shipbuilding and consumer electronics. In the 2000s, another challenge has emerged, requiring the EU to adapt to the increased competitiveness of emerging economies such as the BRIC countries, while at the same time profiting from the consumer demands of the latter's rapidly growing middle class – both in lucrative export and investment opportunities for European businesses and in attracting tourists to Europe.

With the EU's internal market not displaying as much dynamism or growth as many of its competitors, it seems likely that external trade will become increasingly important for the EU. Many European states and companies will probably come to rely less on the internal market – with its slow-growing and ageing population – for profits and will look outwards increasingly. In this context, it is significant to note that:

- A key reason why the EU is the world's biggest exporting entity is the economic power of Germany, which is the world's second-biggest exporting country (having been toppled from first place by China in 2010) and which accounts for no less than a third of the EU's exports (Ewing and Dempsey, 2011).
- While 41 per cent of German exports are sold within the EU, this internal trade fell by 2 per cent between 2008 and 2010, while the proportion of German exports to Asia rose by 4 per cent (to 16 per cent) during the same period.

- Between 2006 and 2009, German investment in manufacturing in Russia, China and Brazil increased substantially, while, during the same period, German investment decreased in the US, Italy, the UK, Spain and France (Ewing and Dempsey, 2011).

These figures for Germany reflect how EU states and EU-based companies are increasingly looking outside Europe for growth opportunities. It is symbolic of trade developments that China is now the biggest market for Volkswagen vehicles. Germany and several other EU states have become increasingly active on the trade diplomatic front in countries such as China, Russia and India (with, for example, the French government tourism agency and retailers paying heavy court to Chinese tourists; see, Erlanger, 2011a).

But, of course, traditional trading relations will continue to be important. Indeed, it is likely that the transatlantic relationship, as well as the EU's relations with Japan, will be strengthened rather than weakened by the current challenges of global competition. The EU and the US are likely to be drawn more closely together to ensure that the trading and investment regime they constructed in the years following the Second World War will evolve rather than be cast aside by the emerging economic powerhouses. For the present, the EU and the US are still the world's largest economies, and the EU's Big Four still make the top ten list of the world's largest economies. So both blocs, on either side of the Atlantic, retain considerable trading strength, which they can use to their advantage as they seek to adjust to the trading challenges from more competitive and high-growth economies. While this adjustment will involve many EU policies – particularly internal market policies, EMU and 'Europe 2020' – trade policy will also feature prominently in the EU's future role in the global economy.

Chapter 13

Foreign and External Security Policy

The EU has two interrelated policies to deal with foreign and external security matters: the Common Foreign and Security Policy (CFSP) and the Common Security and Defence Policy (CSDP). Despite the national sensitivities associated with foreign and external security policies, a number of factors have resulted in an EU policy system based on intensive transgovernmentalism coming to be established in these areas (Giegerich and Wallace, 2010).

One of these causal factors has been international and regional tensions and crises. Europe's relative lack of influence with respect to such foreign policy and external security problems as the Cold War, the Middle East and the Balkan wars of the 1990s have played an important role in encouraging EU policy-makers to develop foreign and external security policies. Related to this, there has been an increasingly felt need for European foreign and external security policy arrangements that are, to some extent at least, distinct from the American-dominated North Atlantic Treaty Organization (NATO). As with so many EU policy areas, internal market-related reasons have also contributed to foreign and external security policy development. So, for example, the common trade policy, growth policies (which require the opening-up of foreign markets to EU exports and investment while simultaneously attracting foreign investment to EU member states), and energy policy (which is dependent on the import of such products as gas from Russia and oil from the Middle East) are all partially reliant for their success on being conducted within a favourable political context.

In consequence of such factors, since the early 1970s EC/EU member states have sought increasingly to address some of the foreign policy challenges that have confronted them on a collective basis. Accordingly, the first section of this chapter reviews the development of the CSFP and CSDP in terms of the EU's quest to become a more important foreign and security player in global politics. As will be seen, the development has been slow and cautious, and has been characterized by deep differences between the member states. But despite the many problems the development has faced, the EU has evolved from having no involvement in foreign and external security in its early years to having a very extensive involvement today.

As we shall see in the course of the historical review of policy development, carrying out effective foreign and security policies has also required institutional and policy process development. Hence the second section of the chapter examines the key CFSP and CSDP institutions, while the third identifies distinctive features of CFSP and CSDP policy processes.

The chapter then moves on to policy content and policy instruments, examining these with respect to foreign policy in the fourth section and external security policy in the fifth. There is, of course, considerable overlap between the policy aims and instruments of the two policy areas, but they are sufficiently different to make the distinction useful for analytical purposes. A theme of these sections is that, despite many substantive reforms and a greatly increased ability of the EU member states to act together on foreign policy matters, the EU has continued to be dogged by accusations that it is a weak security actor. Specifically, it is often portrayed as being a 'soft power', in contrast to American 'hard power'. We indicate that while there is much in this portrayal – which is why we prefer the term 'external security policy' to 'defence policy' – since the end of the Cold War the EU has none the less stepped up efforts to increase its credibility as a global and regional security actor.

The sixth section of the chapter sets out some of the major foreign and external security policy challenges currently confronting the EU: relations with the US and with Russia; relations with NATO; and operating as a unified entity in the United Nations (UN).

The Development of CSFP and CSDP

The early postwar years

European leaders – supported by the Americans – began to lay plans for European defence and security co-operation in the closing days of the Second World War. The first postwar European defence organization – the Brussels Treaty Organisation (BTO) – was created in 1948 by five European Second World War allies (the UK, France and the Benelux countries – Belgium, the Netherlands and Luxembourg), with its centrepiece being a mutual defence clause against Germany. However, as it became apparent that the Soviet Union, not Germany, was the main threat to European security, the BTO's founders asked the US to join them in a permanent mutual defence pact. This resulted in the establishment in 1949 of NATO, which had as its aim to 'safeguard the freedom, common heritage and civilization' of the peoples of the North Atlantic area: or as

Lord Hastings Ismay, NATO's first Secretary General, put it, to keep, 'the Americans in, the Russians out, and the Germans down' (Hodge, 2005, p. 3).

When, in September 1950, the US Secretary of State, Dean Acheson, formally approached the UK and France with a plan to admit West Germany to NATO, French Prime Minister René Pleven served up a counter-proposal to be called the European Defence Community (EDC), which featured not only a mutual defence pact but also a European Defence Force (EDF) that would come very close to a European army (Judt, 2005, p. 244) and would eliminate the need for the BTO. The UK, concerned to retain national control of its defence capability and anxious that the EDC might weaken NATO, did not enter the EDC negotiations, which resulted in only the six European Coal and Steel Community (ECSC) states signing the EDC Treaty in 1952. However, the Treaty met ratification difficulties in France, with Pierre Mendes-France – the Prime Minister at the time ratification was debated (France changed its Prime Ministers frequently in the 1950s) – unwilling to stake his political career on a plan he later described as 'too much integration and too little England' (Judt, 2005, p. 245). So when, in 1954, the Foreign Minister, Robert Schuman, presented the EDC Treaty to the French Assembly, a coalition made up mainly of Socialists and Gaullists prevented its ratification, citing their opposition to placing French troops under foreign command (Smith, 2004, p. 66). With the EDC proposal having thus collapsed, the British proposed that the BTO admit Italy and West Germany. It did so in 1954, into the renamed Western European Union (WEU). The WEU subsequently proved to be little more than a 'talking shop' for European government officials, centring on security and defence issues. As part of the creation of the WEU, West Germany joined NATO.

At the same time as Western Europe was struggling with the question of defence policy, the ECSC Assembly, acting under the direction of the ECSC member states' Foreign Ministers, submitted a proposal for a European Political Community (EPC). Under the proposed EPC treaty, the European Community would: 'ensure the co-ordination of the foreign policy of Member States in questions likely to involve the existence, the security or the prosperity of the Community' (Article 2); be endowed with a legal personality (Article 4); and be empowered to conclude treaties and association agreements (Article 90). The 'catch' was that the EPC would 'constitute a single legal entity' (Article 5) with the ECSC and the EDC. The EPC's fate was thus tied to passage of the EDC Treaty – and this proved to be its downfall.

Another French-initiated attempt to forge closer European-based foreign and external security policy co-operation was made in the early 1960s. Named after the French diplomat, Christian Fouchet, who tabled the plans on behalf of President de Gaulle, the Fouchet Plans were less ambitious than the EDC and EPC. Animated by de Gaulle's desire to build an alternative to the US and USSR in the international sphere, the Plans envisaged closer European political co-operation and an intergovernmentally-based union focused on common foreign and defence policies. The Plans failed, however, in no small part because the Benelux states feared that the French intergovernmental proposals for the conduct of foreign policy would infiltrate the EC's economic and other policy spheres and thus undermine the supranational foundation on which the Community was partially being established (Hill and Smith, 2000).

European Political Cooperation

Despite the inability to achieve agreement on a treaty basis for foreign and defence co-operation, Smith (2004, p. 94) notes that a 'habit of automatic consultation on important foreign policy positions' among member state capitals developed in the early years of the EC. This habit, assisted by a number of other motivations mainly related to the EC's growing international role (Diedrichs, 2011, pp. 151–2), led to the historic 1969 Hague Summit, where the EC leaders asked their Foreign Ministers to 'study the best way of achieving progress in the matter of political unification'. This led, in 1970, to the creation of European Political Cooperation (EPC): a deliberately vague name that both masked that EPC was about foreign policy cooperation and also symbolized the political sensitivities attached to moving into a policy area so associated with national identities and sovereignties.

While EPC initially consisted just of meetings of EC foreign ministers, it quickly grew to embrace a network of working groups comprised of senior foreign ministry personnel and including the Commission in an observer capacity. This network was used to develop shared understandings and positions between the member states on many foreign policy issues, and in some instances was successful in being able to extend beyond rhetoric into agreements on practical action. Most commonly, such action took the form of using Community trade policy instruments in some way – as with the use of mild economic sanctions against South Africa in the 1980s in protest against its apartheid policies.

EPC also brought changes in the status of EC missions abroad, so that by the end of the 1980s the majority of Commission offices in third countries and international organizations were considered full diplomatic posts, with the head of delegation enjoying full ambassadorial recognition and privileges (European Commission, 2004e, p. 36).

EPC was given a treaty basis in the 1986 Single European Act, but not a Community treaty status. To preserve EPC's intergovernmental nature, and in particular to ensure that the Commission and the ECJ were kept to the margins of EPC and that there could be no question of EPC decisions becoming subject to majority voting in the Council, Title III of the SEA covering 'Treaty Provisions on European Co-operation in the Sphere of Foreign Policy' took the form of an international treaty rather than an amendment or addition to the Community treaties.

The Maastricht Treaty

For most of the period of EPC, Europe was settled into the predictability of Cold War politics, the 'safety' of mutually assured destruction (MAD), and the 'comfort' of the NATO security alliance. However, the routine of Cold War politics ended quite abruptly when the Soviet Union and the Soviet Bloc collapsed between 1989 and 1991, with the consequence that the EU found itself facing a number of extremely difficult foreign and security policy questions. Among these questions were: could the EU articulate a common foreign policy with respect to the CEECs and Russia; what structure might be devised and agreed to replace the Cold War security apparatus; would the US continue to staff its military installations and bases in Western Europe; which threats to security would an anticipated American disengagement create; and would the newly reunited Germany be tempted to move policy more towards a German Europe rather than its established policy of Germany in Europe?

The 1990–1 Intergovernmental Conference (IGC) that produced the Maastricht Treaty was negotiated against the background of these questions. It was also negotiated against the backdrop of the 1990–1 Gulf War (in which NATO forces evicted Iraqi forces from Kuwait following Iraq's 1990 invasion) and the start of the civil war in Yugoslavia. The IGC was thus held at a time when events were heralding in all sorts of ways – ranging from lack of effective policy cohesion to the non-compatibility of much European weaponry – that the EU had outgrown the EPC.

In consequence, the Maastricht Treaty greatly advanced the status and strengthened the nature of EU foreign and external security policy. One way in which it did so was by re-naming EPC the Common Foreign and Security Policy (CFSP) and establishing it under its own pillar – albeit a pillar based on intergovernmental principles – in the new three-pillar system of the EU. A second way was by establishing new foreign policy instruments, notably common positions and joint actions. And a third way was by formally, albeit tentatively, entering the external security and defence policy areas by permitting member states to begin working together in these areas and by establishing a formal connection between the EU and the WEU (see Cameron, 2000, for more detailed information on the Maastricht Treaty CFSP changes).

As well as laying foundations for significant foreign and security policy advances, the IGC negotiations also showed how, even at a time of momentous world events and great challenges for Europe, some member states were unwilling to permit too much integration in these policy areas. Two matters, which to the present day remain highly problematic in foreign and external security policy deliberations and negotiations, were especially contentious:

- *The intergovernmental/supranational balance.* Leaders of the more pro-integrationist states and of most of the smaller states (who in many cases were one and the same) opposed the pillar system: the more integrationist states because they thought it made for an awkward and almost ungovernable institutional structure; and the smaller states because a more supranational system worked to their advantage in terms of both the Council's voting system (in which they were over-represented) and in providing more opportunity for their concerns to be heard on the world stage.

However, the leaders of larger and less integrationist states (of which the UK was the most prominent) were not prepared to countenance much supranationalism in such sensitive areas as foreign and defence policy, and were certainly not willing to subsume their own national prominence in world affairs to the EU.

- *The nature and focus of defence policy.* The inclusion in the TEU of the subsequently much-quoted Article J.4, that the foreign and security policy 'shall include all questions related to the security of the Union, including the eventual framing of a common defence policy, which might in time lead to a common defence' was symbolically highly significant since it involved the use of the word 'defence' in an official treaty for the first time. The inclusion of the words at this particular historical juncture – just as the Cold War had ended and the Balkan wars were beginning – also evidenced what can now be seen as a feature of the development of EU external security and defence policy throughout: it has been driven more by external events than it has by strong internal political commitment. The vague Article J.4 phrasing is not, therefore, surprising. Indeed, it had to be vague if it was to hide the considerable divisions that existed between the member states.

The Maastricht Treaty thus marked policy advance, but it also created a great deal of uncertainty and disagreement over the role that the EU would have in future defence policy: so much so that Denmark opted out of the defence policy area as a condition of its support for the Treaty.

Since Maastricht

With Maastricht, the EU had a treaty base from which to address foreign and external security policy. But many challenges had to be overcome before anything like collective and effective policies could be put in place. Among these challenges was the building of structures to support collective policies. Part of this building has included: putting someone in charge of the policy areas; the establishment of effective policy co-ordination among the actors, and the linking up of foreign policy and defence policy; and the institutional development and acceptance of agreed policy goals.

Dealing with these and related tasks was politically difficult from the start, and has continued to be so. This has been mainly because of differences between the member states regarding what should be done and how it should be done. However, regardless of the differences, significant progress has been made, much of it in consequence of the Balkan wars and atrocities of the 1990s. At the onset of the civil war in the former Yugoslavia (when Slovenia and Croatia seceded in 1991), Luxembourg's Foreign Minister (holding the EU's presidency at that time) called it 'the hour of Europe' (Mowle, 2004, p. 118). For most of the 1990s, however, Europe largely failed in its hour, being unable as an organization to agree to intervene in response to such events as: the three-year (1992–5) siege of Sarajevo led by Serb nationalists in the Yugoslav National Army; the 1995 massacre of 8,000 Bosnians in Srebrenica (mainly men of battle age, captured by Serbians from under the protection of Dutch soldiers operating as UN peacekeepers inside the UN 'safe zone' of Srebrenica); and the Serbian war in the late 1990s against Albanians in Kosovo. Such European intervention as there was, including participation in NATO bombing, occurred within an US-led and dominated NATO context. James Baker, George H. W. Bush's Secretary of State, recalled in his memoirs that there was 'an undercurrent in Washington, often felt but seldom spoken, that it was time to make the Europeans step up to the plate and show they could act as a unified power' (Baker and DeFrank, 1995, p. 637). But, no such stepping-up occurred. (See Ginsberg, 2001, p. 57 for a more nuanced interpretation of the EU's foreign policy performance with respect to the Yugoslavian civil war as 'baptism by fire in a zone of war'.)

This lack of stepping-up created increasing unease in EU capitals and a greater resolve to strengthen the capability of the EU's foreign and external security policies. In consequence, the IGC that led to the 1997 Amsterdam Treaty produced a number of important treaty changes:

- Regarding the 'who is in charge?' problem – or, as Henry Kissinger had supposedly put it – 'who do I call if I want to call Europe?' – a new post of High Representative for the Common Foreign and Security Policy was created, with NATO's former Secretary General, Javier Solana, being selected for the post. The High Representative was to be appointed by and to report to the Council – mainly because member states hoped to remove some of the foreign policy power the Commission had slowly accumulated.
- QMV was established as the normal decision-making procedure for CFSP implementing decisions.
- Decision-making was also eased with the creation of the device of 'constructive abstentionism', which enabled a state to abstain from a CFSP vote while at the same time issuing a declaration that would result in it not being obliged to apply the decision taken.
- The nature of security policy was made much more specific with the adoption of the WEU's so-called Petersberg tasks of 'humanitarian and rescue tasks, peacekeeping tasks and tasks of combat forces in crisis management, including peacekeeping'. Security policy was thus given a focus – based on 'soft security'.

With the wars in the Balkans continuing to reveal Europe's external security weaknesses, not least in terms of its need for American approval for most forms of effective action, the Amsterdam Treaty was quickly followed by what was to be a turning point in the quest to build European security policy: a meeting at St Malo in December 1998 at which Tony Blair and Jacques Chirac, the leaders of the EU's two strongest defence powers – the UK and France, respectively – agreed to the establishment of European military co-operation within a NATO framework. This agreement, which the Americans had already signalled they would welcome (a European Security Defence Identity had been initiated within NATO in 1994) led to the launching of a European Security Defence Policy (ESDP) at the 1999 Cologne Summit.

As Box 13.1 and later discussion in this chapter show, the 1999 launch of the ESDP was just the first step of many that have been taken as the EU has moved in the direction of building an external security policy. As noted above, it has been a journey motivated more by responses to external events than by internally generated enthusiasm for a common external security policy as such.

Whatever the motivation, however, there is no doubt that the journey in building EU external security policy has been difficult, littered as it has been with numerous ideas and plans, countless discussions

---

Box 13.1

Key dates in the development of a European foreign and external security policy

1948	The Brussels Treaty Organisation (BTO) founded by the UK, France and the Benelux states
1949	The North Atlantic Treaty Organization (NATO) established
1950	France proposes a European Defence Community (EDC), which would include a European army
1952	EDC Treaty signed by France, West Germany, and the Benelux states
1954	French National Assembly rejects EDC Treaty. This paves the way to the BTO being extended to Italy and West Germany and to the enlarged organization being named the Western European Union (WEU)
1955	A remilitarized West Germany admitted to NATO
1961–4	French-promoted Fouchet Plans launched, but eventually rejected by other EC states
1966	France withdraws from NATO
1970	The Luxembourg Report launches European Political Cooperation (EPC)
1986	EPC given treaty status, but not Community status, by the SEA
1987	WEU Foreign and Defence Ministers issue a declaration that European integration is incomplete without a security and defence policy
1991	Start of the Balkan wars
1992	Signing of the TEU. In the Treaty, the CFSP is established – as the second pillar of the EU. For the first time, defence policy is given treaty recognition
1994	A European Security and Defence Identity (ESDI) is launched within NATO
1997	The Amsterdam Treaty creates the new post of High Representative for the CFSP and identifies the WEU's Petersburg tasks as constituting the focus of EU external security policy.
1998	In their St. Malo Declaration, Prime Minister Blair and President Chirac declare their support for a stronger EU security capability within the NATO framework
1999	ESDP is established at the Cologne and Helsinki European Councils
2003	Iraq war European Security Strategy adopted by the member states First ESDP missions
2009	The Lisbon Treaty seeks to strengthen foreign and external security policy, including by means of: revamping the High Representative position; changing the name ESDP to CSDP and assigning it a separate section in the TEU; broadening the potential policy scope of CFSP and CSDP
2009	France re-enters NATO's integrated command

---

in forums from the European Council downwards, and a number of false starts. Of the false starts, the most notable has been the downgrading of early proposals for a large and quickly mobilizable army – the European Rapid Reaction Force (ERRF) – and its replacement by much smaller units. These units have consisted of: standby battle groups (groups of member states rotate in the battle group roster every six months), comprised commonly of 1,500 or so military personnel from just a few member states; and ad hoc missions of various kinds consisting of military and civilian personnel as required (International Security Information Service, Europe, 2012, p. 1). In practice, ad hoc missions have been much more important, because, while 18 battle groups have been formed, none of them has been deployed at the time of writing. In contrast, as shown later in the chapter, nearly 30 ad hoc missions have been activated to date.

From the early 2000s, the existing pressures to develop an effective ESDP were further strengthened by additional external events:

- the 9/11 terrorist attacks in the US, which highlighted the changing and more uncertain nature of international threats to security;
- the NATO-led (and more specifically American-led) armed campaign against the Taliban in Afghanistan from 2001, to which EU member states reacted – in terms both of their rhetoric and their willingness to give practical help – in different ways;
- the 2003 Iraq war, which saw about half of the EU states support the US-led invasion (with the UK the most forceful supporter) and about half (including France and Germany) opposing it;
- the generally unilateralist policy stance of US foreign policy under the George W. Bush presidency, which increased feelings in much of Europe that it would be wise not to be too dependent on the US in the foreign and external security policy spheres.

Pressures to strengthen the CFSP, and more particularly the ESDP, thus increased, which led to important treaty changes being made by the Lisbon Treaty. The status of the external security policy area was upgraded, with ESDP being re-named the Common Security and Defence Policy (CSDP). Decision-making processes were eased in some circumstances, most particularly by the creation of a new mechanism of 'permanent structured co-operation' in which some states may choose to make binding CSDP commitment to one another, and by extending the reach of enhanced co-operation to include matters with military and defence implications (see the sub-section below headed 'Flexibility'). And a number of institutional changes, outlined in the next section of this chapter, tied security policy more closely to foreign policy.

The Key Policy Institutions

There are four main CFSP/CSDP institutions: the European Council; the Foreign Affairs Council; the High Representative; and the European External Action Service (EEAS). In addition, though they are not 'first division' CFSP/CSDP actors, the Commission and the EP also have significant roles to play. The key general features of most of these actors were described in Chapter 3 and so will not be repeated here. Rather, the focus in what follows is on the institutions and the CFSP/CSDP.

The European Council

As was made clear in Chapter 3, the policy role of the European Council is usually directed towards identifying broad policy goals and sometimes also to tackling particularly intractable policy problems. It does not usually get involved in handling detailed policy matters. This 'overarching' policy role is very much the role the European Council exercises with respect to the CFSP and CSDP. Indeed, it is charged by treaty to do so, with Article 26 TEU, stating: 'The European Council shall identify the Union's strategic interests, determine the objectives of and define general guidelines for the common foreign and security policy, including for matters with defence implications.' Accordingly, summits frequently discuss currently important international issues and often issue policy guidelines that are expected to be followed up by – in a combination that depends on the nature of the policy in question – the High Representative, the Foreign Affairs Council, and (particularly if economic and other 'low policy' matters are involved) the Commission. So, for example, in connection with increasing concerns about Iran's nuclear programme, the December 2011 European Council invited 'the Council [of Ministers] to proceed with its work related to extending the scope of EU restrictive measures and broadening existing sanctions by examining additional measures against Iran as matter of priority and to adopt these measures no later than by its next session' (European Council, 2011a, p. 6). Stiffer sanctions against Iran were subsequently adopted by the Foreign Affairs Ministers.

The occupant of the post of semi-permanent President of the European Council, created by the Lisbon Treaty, is also assigned CFSP and CSDP responsibilities, with Article 15.6 TEU, stating: 'The President of the European Council shall, at his level and in that capacity, ensure the external representation of the Union on issues concerning its common foreign and security policy'. This ambiguous phrasing creates the potential for turf wars between the President and the High Representative (this Lisbon-created post is explained below), but to date the first occupant of the European Council President post, Herman Van Rompuy, has adopted a low profile in the foreign and external security policy areas – partly because he has been preoccupied with the financial and economic crisis – and no clashes have as yet materialized.

The Foreign Affairs Council

Responsibility for EU foreign and external security policy decision-making lies mainly with the Foreign Ministers meeting in the Council. As is shown in other sub-sections of this chapter, there are additional important institutional actors, but the Council is, and always has been, the main institutional 'workhorse'.

As the responsibilities and workload of EU foreign, and increasingly also external security, policy increased during the 1990s and early 2000s, the General Affairs and External Relations Council (GAERC) – the formation of the Council that brought together the Foreign Affairs Ministers – was seen increasingly to be in need of reform. Two problems in particular were thought to need addressing. First, the GAERC was chaired by the Foreign Minister of the member state holding the six-month Council presidency. This arrangement suited smaller states in that each was assured a turn at the helm of the powerful GAERC, but most of the smaller member states simply did not have access to the quantity of highly-trained diplomatic corps available to the larger member states, and typically also did not have much expertise in many of the areas of foreign policy with which the EU is confronted over the course of a typical six-month period. Furthermore, the rotation system did not help with the objective of unifying, and thereby strengthening, Europe's voice in foreign affairs, since it naturally made consistency – much prized in foreign affairs – difficult to achieve. Second, the portfolio of the GAERC covered not only foreign and external security policy but also a range of general affairs, including enlargement policy and aspects of budgetary policy. While the GAERC did compartmentalize its agendas into 'General Affairs' and 'External Relations', the broad range of its work

created difficulties and further burdened the state holding the presidency.

Accordingly, the Lisbon Treaty split the GAERC by creating separate General Affairs and Foreign Affairs Councils. The General Affairs Council is now responsible for the co-ordination of all EU policies and for the preparation of EU summits. It is usually chaired by either the Foreign Minister or European Minister of the member state holding the rotating Council presidency. The Foreign Affairs Council (FAC) covers most of the EU's external policies, including trade and development co-operation. It is chaired by the High Representative for CFSP and CSDP matters and by an appropriate minister from the Council Presidency for other external policy matters.

The FAC meets regularly – at least once a month (more frequently during crises) – and takes most of its decisions under the unanimity rule. The FAC is advised and kept informed by the Political and Security Committee (PSC – or COPS [the commonly-used French acronym]), which is responsible for the daily functioning of the CFSP and CSDP and usually delivers opinions to the FAC through COREPER II (see Chapter 3). The PSC is chaired by an official from the European External Action Service (EEAS) (see below) and normally meets twice a week. Below the PSC in the Council decision-making hierarchy are numerous CFSP/CSDP committees and working groups, comprised of experts from the member states, that are organized by function and geography and that are responsible for developing policy reports for the PSC. Three particularly important committees are the European Union Military Committee (EUMC), the Committee for Civilian Aspects of Crisis Management (CIVICOM), and the European Union Institute for Security Studies (EUISS), all of which report to and receive guidance from the PSC.

The High Representative of the Union for Foreign Affairs and Security Policy

The Lisbon Treaty abolished the Amsterdam Treaty-created Council position of High Representative for the CFSP and established a new post of High Representative of the Union for Foreign Affairs and Security Policy. The European Council, acting if necessary by QMV, and with the agreement of the President of the Commission, nominates the High

Representative, who must then – in his/her capacity as a member of the Commission – be approved by the EP.

Despite the similarity of title between the pre- and post-Lisbon Treaty High Representatives, the new position involved a radical departure. It was designed with the purpose of improving EU foreign and external security policy co-ordination by merging the then existing posts of Commissioner for External Relations and the Council's High Representative into a double-hatted High Representative and Vice-President (HR/VP) of the Commission: the post-holder would be *mère de la Famille Relex* (mother of the EU's external relations bodies) (Carta, 2012, p. 145). Essentially, the change requires one person to do the jobs previously assigned to two people. The new High Representative chairs the FAC for CFSP and CSDP agenda items, leads the conduct of the CFSP and CSDP, manages the EU's external aid budget, and heads the newly-created EEAS. In all but name, the High Representative is the EU's Foreign Minister.

The first person to be appointed to the post was Baroness Catherine Ashton, from the UK, who had previously served as the EU's Trade Commissioner. Ashton had no previous direct experience of dealing with foreign policy and was therefore thought by many to be unsuitable for the post, but she did have qualities that were widely circulated at the time as being desirable: she came from a large member state, she was a centre-left politician (and thus politically balanced the appointment of Herman Van Rompuy, a centre-right politician, as European Council President) and she was a woman (Dinan, 2011, p. 111). (Though being a woman was not essential, because David Miliband, the UK's Foreign Secretary at the time of her appointment, was originally pegged for the post in the event of Tony Blair not being appointed European Council President; see Traynor, 2009.)

The High Representative post clearly involves many tasks and requires many skills. It did so especially in the period after Ashton was confirmed in office in January 2010 because, in addition to dealing with CFSP and CSDP matters, she also had to attend to a number of difficult 'bedding-in' problems. In particular, she had to oversee the creation of the EEAS as well as having to deal with and create operating arrangements for policy areas overlapping with foreign policy where the Commission retains control – such as development, energy, climate change and enlargement policies.

The early reviews of Ashton's performance were mixed. Some praised her work on the problems of the Middle East, on Iran's nuclear aspirations, on North Africa at the difficult time of the 2011 Arab Spring, and on humanitarian crises – see comments by the head of Oxfam International's EU Office, Natalia Alonso (Alonso, 2012). But, in a paper released in December 2011, the Foreign Ministers of twelve member states (including France, Germany and Italy) strongly criticized her, in particular for her poor chairing of the FAC and neglect of security affairs (Rettman, 2012). In her reply, Ashton pointed to the 'particularly challenging' political and economic context in which she had been operating – including the Arab Spring, the eurozone crisis and the budgetary exigencies in EU member states having a direct effect on their diplomatic services – all of which had occurred at the very time the EEAS was being established (Ashton, 2011). She pointed also to: a productive partnership between the EEAS and the Commission in co-ordinating the EU's 'immediate' response to the crises in Libya and Tunisia; her role in the Quartet in the Middle East Peace Process; her leadership in searching for a diplomatic solution to the Iranian nuclear issue; the EEAS-led operation in Somalia fighting piracy; 'decisive engagement' in the Western Balkans; and an upgrading of EU crisis response capabilities through the establishment of a Crisis Management Board.

The mixed reviews of Ashton's performance as High Representative arguably reflect not only on her capabilities and application but also on the sheer size of the job. She was, for example, in 2011 being criticized at one and the same time for not attending enough meetings of the College of Commissioners in Brussels and for not travelling enough to world trouble spots!

The European External Action Service

The European External Action Service was provided for by the Lisbon Treaty under Article 27 (3) TEU:

> In fulfilling his mandate, the High Representative shall be assisted by a European External Action Service. This service shall work in cooperation

with the diplomatic services of the Member States and shall comprise officials from relevant departments of the General Secretariat of the Council and of the Commission as well as staff seconded from national diplomatic services of the Member States.

After considerable inter-institutional bargaining over the precise nature of its goals, organization and staffing, the EEAS became operational in January 2011 with a staff of more than 1,600 officials. These officials were drawn from the Commission (mainly from the former DG External Relations, but some also from DG Development), the Council Secretariat and national diplomatic services.

The EEAS is responsible for developing and implementing EU foreign and external security policy and missions, and for ensuring that EU external policies as a whole are coherent and co-ordinated. These tasks – which necessarily have to be undertaken in close collaboration with the EU services (especially in the Commission) that handle such closely-related policy areas as trade, development and enlargement – involve the EEAS having an important presence both in Brussels and abroad:

- *In Brussels*, the EEAS organizational structure mirrors that of national foreign ministries in the West, with divisions organized both according to geography (including the Pacific, Africa and the Americas) and function (including multi-lateral relations and global governance, human rights and democracy, and conflict prevention and security policy) (see the EEAS website for an organization chart).
- *Abroad*, the EEAS has replaced the Commission's External Service and assumed responsibility for a network of nearly 140 delegations in third countries and international organizations. These delegations act in a similar manner to embassies in that they seek to advance EU interests and co-ordinate EU policies in the countries in which they are located. They also offer some consular support to EU citizens, although opinion differs among member states as to how far they should go in this direction.

The EEAS is clearly still in the early stages of its development, but it may at some time come to rival the diplomatic services of the member states. Certainly for the smaller member states it already serves as a very useful complement and addition to their diplomatic services, as did the Commission's External Service previously.

The Commission and the EP

The creation by the Lisbon Treaty of the re-vamped High Representative post and the EEAS has resulted in the Commission losing most of its direct influence over foreign and security policy. Certainly, the High Representative is a Commission Vice-President, but in practice she is 'much more Council than she is Commission'. However, though the direct influence has largely been lost, an indirect influence remains strong, with many foreign and external security policy actions being multi-dimensional in nature and involving the use of instruments in policy areas – such as trade and development assistance – where the Commission's powers remain strong.

The EP has always been rather on the margins of the CFSP and CSDP in that it has been confined to an advisory position. This essentially remains the case after the Lisbon Treaty, but the right to be consulted has been strengthened, with the High Representative being obliged, under Article 36 TEU, to 'regularly consult the European Parliament on the main aspects and the basic choices' of the CFSP and CSDP and to 'inform it of how these policies evolve. He shall ensure that the views of the European Parliament are duly taken into consideration'.

Policy Processes

Many voices

The CFSP and CSDP policy areas are populated by an extremely large number of significant policy actors, many of them with differing views as to what the purposes and aims of EU foreign and external security policy should be and how they should be pursued.

Some of the more important of these actors – EU institutions – were examined in the previous section of this chapter. But, of course, the institutions do not operate autonomously but rather within the context of the policy preferences of the governments of the member states. As shown elsewhere in this book, there are policy areas where 'supranational' EU institutions enjoy a measure of autonomy from national governmental preferences (such as the Commission with competition policy, for example) or where decisions can be taken without the agreement of all member state governments (most notably when QMV applies in the Council). However, such 'by-passing' of the views of member state governments is very difficult in respect of the CFSP and CSDP, because their policy processes are largely intergovernmental in nature: that is, most decisions, other than policy implementation decisions, must be approved by the governments of all the member states – or, at least, must not be actively opposed by any government.

This unanimity requirement naturally creates major difficulties since the foreign and external security policy areas are characterized by significant differences between the member states on all sorts of matters. The bases of many of these differences are set out in Box 13.2. The policy differences result in many differing views being expressed in CFSP and CSDP policy forums on all sorts of important issues. During the 2011 Arab Spring, for example, many EU institutional actors, member states, and even groups of member states (a joint statement was issued by France, Germany, Italy, Spain and the UK) publicly voiced different opinions. Other CFSP and CSDP issues that since early 2011 have openly divided the member states have included whether there should be more concerted effort at the UN to upgrade Palestine's international status, whether an EU military command centre should be established, and how the EU should respond to allegations of growing political repression in the Ukraine.

Almost inevitably, the multiplicity of voices – all with their own needs and preferences – can lead to political struggles that hinder the ability of the EU to exercise clear, strong and effective decision-making. Indeed, Christopher Bickerton (2011, pp. 118–19) goes so far as to argue that 'foreign policy cooperation is oriented as much towards the balancing of the positions of different actors within the Union as it is to securing outcomes in theatres across the world'. In the foreign policy arena (though also in other policy areas) the EU is, Bickerton argues, essentially an 'introspective power'.

Competing commitments and settings

The CFSP and CSDP operate within a context in which its core actors – the governments of the member states – must often weigh their EU commitments against other obligations. The interests and priorities of the various commitments may clash.

What are these other commitments? Some of the specific obligations were mentioned in the previous section of this chapter and in Box 13.2. Eva Gross (2009) indicates a useful, and broader, framework for thinking about the nature of the commitments by suggesting that the governments of the member states can be seen as straddling three potentially conflicting sets of obligations:

- *Domestic politics*, which includes traditionally held attitudes on foreign and defence policy issues and specific domestic political circumstances regarding, for example, the political party composition and the strength of a government.
- *Transatlantic relations*, which include both a state's involvement in and commitment to NATO and the extent and nature of its bilateral relations with the US. (Regarding the latter, the UK has long had a 'special relationship' with the US, while Ireland, Italy and Poland have also been close to the US – not least by virtue of cultural ties and the large numbers of Irish-Americans, Italian-Americans and Polish-Americans in the country.)
- *The EU*, towards and with which member states have differing stances both in respect of CFSP and CSDP policy development as a whole, and particular aspects of them.

These sets of commitments suggest how the foreign and external security policies of the member state governments, and therefore also of the CFSP and CSDP, are developed and resolved in a number of different frameworks. The CFSP and CSDP do not have an exclusive call on the governments of the member states, either in terms of the EU necessarily always being the most important framework in which a policy position is developed or in terms of any adopted EU policy always being the one that is prioritized. This latter point may seem odd given that CFSP and CSDP policy positions are taken by consensus, often after exhaustive negotiations, but these positions can be very vague and permit ample room for

---

Box 13.2

Key differences among member states that impact on their CFSP/CSDP policy positions

- Different historical experiences and traditions of member states can result in different policy orientations. For example, Germany's history makes it reluctant to support offensive military actions; France's colonial past results in it having strong interests in Africa.
- Some member states (most notably the UK) regard preservation of national sovereignty as being very important in the CFSP/CSDP policy areas and as a result often do not support EU policies that are seen to be too constraining.
- Geographical location is important in determining the interest member states have in particular foreign policy theatres. For example, CEECs give a much higher priority than do most Western European states to relations with Russia; and Malta and Cyprus are not much engaged in the EU's Arctic policy.
- Most member states are members of NATO, but six (Austria, Cyprus, Finland, Ireland, Malta and Sweden) are not.
- While no member state questions the importance of the transatlantic relationship, there are differences over the extent to which EU foreign and external security policies should be pursued independently within the relationship.
- Member states differ considerably in their willingness and capacity to assign national resources to CFSP/CSDP actions and missions.
- The extent to which secessionist/centrifugal threats exist within member states can affect whether support is given to an ethnic group's/nation's demand for the right to self-determination (as illustrated by Kosovo, which Cyprus and Spain, among others, have been unwilling to recognize officially).

---

manoeuvre – deliberately so when this is necessary to enable an agreed position to be reached.

The existence of different, and sometimes competing, commitments and policy settings does, of course, make EU policy-making difficult. But there are circumstances when it can be helpful to individual member state governments: for example, when conducting bilateral trade negotiations with undemocratic states governments sometimes play a sort of two-level game and do not press democratic and related issues, on the grounds that they are dealt with by the EU (David *et al.*, 2011, p. 184).

Intensive transgovernmentalism

A core defining feature of CFSP/CSDP policy processes is their primarily intergovernmental nature, which is seen in the strong positions of the EU's 'governmental institutions' (the European Council and the Council of Ministers), the weak positions of the 'supranational institutions' (the Commission, the EP and the CJEU),

and the ability of member states to be able to exercise a veto over most major decisions. The EU's intergovernmentalism, however, is much more intense than the intergovernmentalism that customarily characterizes decision-making processes in most international organizations (IOs). Indeed, it is so much more intense that, as suggested in Chapter 7, the policy processes are best labelled intensive transgovernmentalism.

The intensity of the policy processes is seen in the 'Brusselization' of European foreign policy that has been under way since the early to mid-1990s. This involves constant and countless policy interactions between member states' governments in Brussels in a multiplicity of formal and informal settings and, in consequence, also involves decisions on both EU and national foreign policies increasingly being hammered out in EU locales (Regelsberger, 2007, p. 3). As part of Brusselization, European foreign policy elites increasingly share a 'dense normative structure' that is far more intense than exists in such international regimes and IOs as the WTO, Mercosur and NAFTA (Puetter and Wiener, 2009, p. 8).

Brusselization has made it increasingly difficult for any member state, no matter how large and influential it might be in world affairs, to forge a coherent and effective foreign policy without notification of and consultation and co-ordination with its EU partners. Though policy disagreements exist between member states on many specific issues, as Regelsberger (2007, p. 3) points out: 'What was a novelty in the days of EPC is normalcy today: taking the views of other partners into account before defining one's own position has become "a naturally done thing" according to insiders, creating an *acquis politique* which is far more than the lowest common denominator.'

Flexibility

The combination of differing policy preferences between member states on the one hand and primarily intergovernmental structures and procedures on the other is clearly not a recipe for quick or efficient decision-making. In consequence, policy development is often very slow and CFSP/CSDP statements and actions commonly have to be 'watered down' to bring 'dissenters' on board.

However, another way of dealing with the problem of the existence of differing national policy preferences and intergovernmental decision-making procedures is to adopt a flexible policy process approach, with differing processes applying in different policy situations. Such an approach has been used increasingly for CFSP/CSDP to give some manoeuvrability and choice to member states regarding the aspects and dimensions of the policy areas in which they engage.

The first major step in the direction of institutionalizing flexibility was the Amsterdam Treaty, which established the principle of 'constructive abstentionism'. This permitted a state that abstained in a vote to declare that while it recognized that the decision committed the EU, it would not itself be obliged to apply the decision. The Treaty of Nice then extended the device of 'enhanced co-operation', which had been created for internal policy areas in the Amsterdam Treaty, to the implementation of CFSP joint actions and common positions, but not to matters with defence or military implications. This device allowed a less than full complement of member states to establish closer co-operation with one other.

The Lisbon Treaty, in Article 42 (6) TEU and TEU Protocol 10, took the possibility of flexibility even further by providing for 'permanent enhanced structured cooperation' (PESCO):

> Those Member States whose military capabilities fulfil higher criteria and which have made more binding commitments to one another in this area with a view to the most demanding missions shall establish permanent structured cooperation within the Union framework.

PESCO is a significant innovation, not least in its potential for EU states to build an effective European capability outside of the NATO architecture. The global economic crisis and the Eurozone crisis could have an impact here, with one of two possible effects on momentum towards using PESCO: budgetary cuts will make some member states more amenable to finding cost-cutting ways to enhance defence (thus advancing PESCO) while some member states may use budgetary constraints as an excuse to continue to support NATO as the only realistic and viable defence structure. (The austerity measures in fiscally-troubled EU member states precipitated steep cuts in military spending in the period 2008–11 including: Greece, 26 per cent; Spain, 18 per cent; Italy, 16 per cent; Ireland, 11 per cent; and Belgium, 12 per cent – SIPRI, 2012.)

Foreign Policy

The EU does not have a clear foreign policy strategy, nor does it have a clear set of foreign policy goals. However, as it has sought to establish itself increasingly as a significant policy player it can be seen as having pursued three broad policy aims:

- To promote a number of general principles and values to which its member states adhere. These include: good governance; democracy and the rule of law; respect for human rights and individual freedoms; the preservation of peace and the strengthening of international security; the economic, social and environmental development of developing countries; and international co-operation (see Article 12 TEU for a fuller list of the general principles and values).

- To create a zone of peace and prosperity that extends beyond the EU to neighbouring countries in Central and Eastern Europe, the Middle East and North Africa.
- To create a political climate that helps with the conduct of other EU policies with significant external dimensions. The most obvious of such policies is the CCP, but among many others are agriculture, energy and the environment.

Of course, there are potential conflicts between these aims, which results in it not always being possible for them all to be pursued with full vigour. For example, when dealing with China, too much emphasis being placed on China's perceived shortcomings with respect to human rights is unhelpful for the promotion of EU–China trade.

As regards the tools of EU foreign policy, the EU has access to most of the customary foreign policy tools except (though see the discussion below on security policy) 'hard' military power. These tools include: the traditional high art of diplomacy, now handled by the EU's diplomatic corps based in the EEAS; the issuing of policy statements – usually either by the Council or the High Representative – on just about every important foreign policy issue (though, of necessity, given the differences that exist between member states on many issues, as noted above such statements are often rather bland); and the use of 'trade and aid' economic instruments – which include the granting or withholding of preferential access to the (huge) EU market, to technological know-how, to natural resources and to financial aid.

This heavy reliance of the EU on non-military policy instruments has led many academic commentators to describe it as being a 'soft' or 'civilian' foreign policy power. Joseph Nye, the scholar who coined the term, has defined 'soft power' as 'the ability to get what you want through attraction rather than coercion or payments. It arises from the attractiveness of a country's culture, political ideals, and policies' (Nye, 2004, p. x). Well, the EU does make some use of payments – both direct and indirect – but its essentially soft power nature is none the less seen in many ways. One such way is in its accelerated use of value 'conditionality' clauses (covering the likes of greater protection of human rights and consolidation of the rule of law) in EU foreign policy declara-

tions and agreements (Regelsberger, 2007, p. 4). So when deciding which policy tools to employ, the EU frequently, especially when dealing with non-democratic states, makes access – to, for example, EU programmes and financial aid – conditional on countries liberalizing their political and legal systems.

The EU can thus be thought of as a soft power proselytiser. This adopted position can be explained partially by Europe's history of empire and continental wars. In the soft power image of Europe, the EU's foreign policy is responsible, humane, mature and sophisticated – arguably, a perfect reflection of what Europe sees when it gazes in a mirror. But this soft power picture can be disputed, both in terms of its accuracy and the effectiveness of 'soft power'. Certainly, American 'realists' aggressively question the image, dismissing beneficent cosmopolitanism as a thinly-veiled rationalization for Europe's weakness in projecting military power. As Robert Kagan (2003) famously proclaimed, 'America is from Mars, Europe is from Venus'. In this realist view, soft power is lauded only by those who lack hard power. So, it was, realists note, NATO airstrikes – not trade embargoes and not the joint condemnations issued by EU member states – that forced the Serbs to the bargaining table during the Balkan civil war.

External Security Policy

Policy goals

The early policy goals of the CSDP were mainly based on the WEU's 'soft' Petersberg tasks, which were focused on humanitarian and rescue, peacekeeping, and crisis management missions. Territorial defence was not covered in the Petersberg tasks as this was seen as being an exclusive NATO function.

In the years since the CSDP was launched, its policy goals have been progressively elaborated and broadened, both in the TEU and in policy documents. The elaboration and broadening in the TEU has resulted, since the Lisbon Treaty, in provisions involving direct military matters that that would have been politically unimaginable until very recently. They include:

- An instruction to member states on their military capability responsibilities: 'Member States shall undertake to progressively improve their military capabilities' (Article 42.3).

- A mutual defence obligation: 'If a Member State is the victim of armed aggression on its territory, the other Member States shall have towards it an obligation of aid and assistance by all means in their power, in accordance with Article 51 of the United Nations Charter' (Article 42.7). (It should be noted that this provision stops short of obliging member states to intervene militarily in such circumstances.)
- A significant broadening of the Petersburg tasks, so that they are now stated as including 'disarmament operations, humanitarian and rescue tasks, military advice and assistance tasks, conflict prevention and peace-keeping tasks, tasks of combat forces in crisis management, including peace-keeping, and post–conflict stabilisation' (Article 43.1).

Regarding the elaboration and broadening in policy documents, a long-term strategy was set out in the 2003 Council document *A Secure Europe in a Better World: European Security Strategy* (Council of the European Union, 2003b). At the heart of the 2003 European Security Strategy (ESS) was the identification of five key threats – terrorism, proliferation of Weapons of Mass Destruction (WMD), regional conflicts, state failure, and organized crime – plus the identification of measures to address these threats. Among the measures were to be: the achievement of greater capability (by, for example, the systematic use of pooled/shared assets, the sharing of intelligence, and stronger diplomatic capabilities through a combination of the resources of member states); more coherence (through, for example, common diplomatic efforts and better co-ordination between external action and JHA); direct intervention in regional conflicts, which could involve the EU deploying a combination of military and civilian expertise; and EU participation in multilateral solutions (Council of the European Union, 2003b, pp. 11–14).

These 2003 goals may have been laudable, but progress made in achieving them has been slow. In a policy paper published in the months leading up to the planned five-year review of the ESS in 2008, Nick Witney, a former director of the European Defence Agency (EDA), encapsulated core problems with 'the underachieving' ESDP when he asserted that EU policy-makers commit to over-ambitious defence

goals and deadlines, celebrate inadequate outcomes, move the goalposts, and then authorize a further round of reviews and roadmaps (Witney, 2008, p. 9).

Policy capability

Based on the cumulative expenditures and capacities of its member states, the EU should have a very powerful defence capability. It has, for example, more military personnel than the US, while two of its members – France and the UK – are formidable defence powers, with both having a nuclear capability and each accounting for 3.6 per cent of global military expenditure. While the US is by far the world's largest military spender, accounting for 41 per cent of the total, collectively EU expenditure is still very significant – accounting for nearly a quarter of the total world military expenditure of US\$1,738 billion in 2011 (SIPRI, 2012).

But while these capacities and expenditures result in a significant individual defence capability for some EU member states – especially France and the UK – they do not realize the capability that might be expected for the EU as whole. There are two main reasons and one subsidiary reason for this.

The first main reason is that there is often a lack of political will on the part of member states to work closely together on defence co-operation. Sometimes this is because of differences over policy aims – as, most notably, was the case with the US-led invasion of Iraq in 2003, which some member states supported and others opposed. Sometimes it is because the EU is not viewed by some member states as being the most suitable vehicle for an external security action – with NATO in particular being seen as being more appropriate. Sometimes it is for operational reasons, with states – especially those with limited resources and/or considerable existing defence commitments and potential commitments – often hesitating to commit too much to EU-based activities over which they will not have full control. And sometimes it is for commercial reasons, with member states – especially the major defence suppliers (France, Spain, Italy, Germany, Sweden and the UK) – often being reluctant to exchange too much information in such a high-tech field.

The second main reason, which in some respects stems from the first, is that resources are not pooled as effectively as they could be. As Witney argues (2008,

p. 5), Europe's capability problem with defence 'is not at bottom a problem of money', but rather that European defence ministries are still too wedded to 'Cold War-style militaries, rather than modern, expeditionary forces' and are too persistent 'in trying to go it alone'. There are innumerable examples of duplication and overlap in the production of European defence equipment. So, according to one European Defence Agency official, there are still four main types of battle tanks in the EU, seven different attack helicopters and 23 types of armoured fighting vehicles. In addition, 16 naval shipyards produce an assortment of frigates, submarines and other equipment, whereas only three shipyards supply the US Navy (Zandee, 2010).

The subsidiary reason explaining the inability of the EU to maximize its potential capability arises from the ways in which EU operational missions are financed. The system is extremely complex, involving three different financing sources and varying rules for the financing of different sorts of operational activities (for details of the system, see Bendiek and Steele, 2009). The three sources are: the EU budget; a special mechanism known as ATHENA, to which member states contribute on the basis of a GNI scale; and national financing by the member states that contribute to missions with defence or military implications. These complex and sometimes murky financial arrangements compromise both accountability and transparency. But, most crucially in terms of the EU's operational capability, the fact that much of the cost falls on the shoulders of the states that actively contribute to missions both encourages free riding and can discourage states from offering to contribute. Consequently, as a remedy for the problem, many experts recommend a dedicated CSDP fund to which all EU members should be obliged to contribute.

However, despite all the difficulties with capability, since its first operational mission in 2003 the EU has been able to establish and activate nearly 30 CSDP missions. They have dealt mainly with tasks related to peacekeeping and peace monitoring, and have been operational both in Europe, especially the Balkans, and beyond – most notably in Africa, the Middle East and Afghanistan (European External Action Service, 2012b). Despite the fact that they have operated under CSDP auspices, most missions have been civilian ones, consisting usually of mixtures of police, lawyers, prosecutors, civil servants and border control agents; seven have been military missions; and one has been a joint civilian–military mission. Box 13.3 gives examples of some of the 13 missions that were operational in May 2012.

It is fashionable to play down the importance of the CSDP missions that have been deployed to date, with them frequently being portrayed as dealing with only the softest of security problems and as doing so with only very soft security instruments. This view is over-harsh, but in any event it has to be put in the context of the fact that it is in many ways extraordinary that CSDP missions of any sort exist at all. Because, as Ginsberg and Penksa (2012, p. 41) argue regarding the EU becoming a security provider, 'the EU faces challenges in the field of international security unique to a group of states that is neither a military alliance nor a single sovereign state. Thus, the union as a *sui generis* international security provider is breaking new ground in global security governance.'

Key Foreign and External Security Policy Challenges

Regardless of the weaknesses of the CFSP and CSDP, the EU is in a better position than at any time in its history to confront foreign and external security policy challenges in a unified manner. This section explores four different sorts of such challenges currently facing the EU: its relations with two of the world's most powerful countries, one of which – the US – is a close ally, and the other – Russia – is the cause of considerable uncertainties; its relations with NATO; and its attempts to act in a united manner in the United Nations.

Relations with the US

The EU–US relationship, which is a central global partnership in contemporary world affairs, is conducted through and within various intergovernmental and non-governmental institutions, agencies and forums. The most important and widely known forums in which American and European policymakers work together are those focused on security (for example, in NATO – see below) and on economic co-operation (in, most notably, the WTO, the G-8, and

> ### Box 13.3
>
> # Examples of CSDP missions
>
> All these missions were in operation in May 2012.
>
> **Europe**
> - European Union Police Mission in Bosnia and Herzegovina (EUPM). Since January 2003. Mission strength: 82.
> - European Union Border Assistance Mission to Moldova and Ukraine (EUBAM). Since December 2005. This is a border assistance mission to prevent smuggling, trafficking and customs fraud. Mission strength: 200.
> - European Union Rule of Law Mission in Kosovo (EULEX Kosovo). Since December 2008. The central aim of this police and civilian mission is to assist and support the Kosovo authorities in the rule of law area, specifically in the police, judiciary and customs areas. Mission strength: 2,250.
>
> **Africa**
> - European Union Security Sector Reform Mission in the Democratic Republic of the Congo (EUSEC RD Congo). Since June 2005. The mission provides advice and assistance for security sector reform in the DRC. Mission strength: 100.
> - European Union Naval Force (EU NAVFOR), Somalia. Since December 2008. Implements Operation Atalanta, which is tasked to protect shipping and to combat piracy. Mission strength: 2,500 naval and military personnel.
>
> **Asia**
> - European Union Integrated Rule of Law Mission for Iraq (EUJUST LEX). Since July 2005. The objective is to train some 800 or so judges, investigating magistrates, and senior police and prison officers. Mission strength: 60.
> - European Union Coordinating Office for Palestinian Police Support (EUPOL COPPS). Since January 2006. The EU provides support to the Palestinian civil police, and for security sector and criminal justice reform. Mission strength: 90.
> - European Union Police Mission to Afghanistan (EUPOL Afghanistan). Since 2007. This is a police mission that aims, primarily through training, to contribute to the establishment of effective policing arrangements under Afghan control, Mission size: 550.
>
> *Source*: European External Action Service, 2012b, which gives a complete list of past and present CSDP operations.

the OECD). In these and other forums, however, the working together is very often not between US policy-makers and EU policy-makers but rather between US policy-makers and those of EU member states.

Defence policy illustrates this, with transatlantic relations continuing to be conducted mainly through traditional and bilateral US government–member state government channels – involving in particular the larger EU states, and in NATO. The nature of US–Europe relations in these areas has, however, naturally been affected both by the end of the Cold War, which

has resulted in a reduced need for a collective defence of Europe, and by the rise of such countries as China and Brazil. Europe, in short, has, in traditional foreign and defence policy terms, become less important to the US.

But, as the nature of foreign and defence policy has been changing, and particularly as the security agenda has come to include a range of security issues that cut across boundaries between external and internal security, then so have new and important EU–US relations been developed. As Wyn Rees (2011, p. 14) says: 'As it has evolved as a more capable actor, the Union has found itself interacting increasingly with the US. For Washington, the EU has become a partner in a growing number of security issues, particularly in relation to issues where NATO's competences are not relevant.'

Regarding direct EU–US relations, for there to be an 'EU–US relationship', the US needed first to recognize that a political 'Europe' existed. It did so from the early post-Second World War years, and since then has consistently called for and promoted a united Europe. While the primacy of this goal in US policy has ebbed and flowed, no US presidential administration has acted to undermine European integration and most have actively promoted it. Reflecting this, formal EU–US partnerships have been established, of which the most prominent is the New Transatlantic Agenda (NTA) which the EU and the US agreed in 1995 on the basis of four main goals: promoting peace and stability, democracy and development around the world; responding to global challenges; contributing to the expansion of world trade and closer economic relations; and building bridges across the Atlantic (see European External Action Service, 1995, to read the NTA; European External Action Service, 2012c, for a detailed description of the NTA). Within the NTA framework there are, in addition to regular high- and mid-level meetings between EU and US officials to exchange policy information and discuss best practices, over 60 specific (mainly technical) agreements in place covering a wide range of policy areas, from atomic energy to the transfer of passenger name records (European External Action Service, 2012a).

Periodically, the US looks west to the Pacific and when it does so Europe frets that it will become less important to the US. As an example of the EU's concern, it has increased its regional activity in the Asia-Pacific area (dominated by APEC – the Asia-Pacific Economic Cooperation, an economic forum for the Asia-Pacific community). This is a setting that includes China, the US, Russia and a number of other Pacific Rim countries, but from which the EU is excluded for reasons of geography.

Another example of the US 'turning away' from the EU was seen in the 2009 Copenhagen Climate Summit, which produced the 'Copenhagen Accord'. The Accord was widely seen to have been a bruising loss for the EU, both because it did not achieve its relatively advanced green aims and because Brazil, South Africa, India and China (the BASIC group) set the

terms of the debate and negotiated their position beforehand with the crucially important (and much less green than the EU) US (Team Nord, 2011, p. 17).

On balance, the current theme of the EU–US relationship – 'global partners/global responsibilities' – is a reasonably apt description of its nature, but this should not imply that the two partners do not disagree on important issues. As discussed in earlier chapters, a number of – mainly economic- and trade-based – transatlantic disputes have captured headlines over the years. These have included: the banana wars of the 1990s; the continuing debates over the use of hormones in American beef cattle, and the use of GMOs more generally; the reluctance of the US to support EU-initiated environmental aims and schemes; and, as the Americans see it, Europe's unwillingness to live up to its international security responsibilities.

Relations with Russia

The EU's relations with Russia are very different from those displayed in the strong partnership with the US. The EU and the US are almost invariably on the same side on foreign and external security policy issues, but Russia often takes a very different position – especially when it involves matters that it views as being in its environs. However, if one looks beyond the realpolitik rhetoric, the fact is that Russia shares borders with many EU member states and the EU and Russia are highly interdependent trading blocs – so much so that the EU is Russia's third-largest trade partner. Relations between the EU and Russia are naturally greatly affected by this geographical proximity and trading interdependence.

David *et al.* (2011) suggest that the EU–Russia relationship is very useful in helping to understand the 'interplay' between member states and the conduct of EU foreign policy, in ways that the EU–US partnership cannot – because EU member states usually agree with most foreign policy positions taken by America. Borrowing from David *et al.*, though with some adjustments, there are four main aspects to this usefulness of the EU–Russia relationship in furthering understanding of the varying intersections of member state foreign policy preferences and obligations with those of the CFSP.

First, there are some EU member states – including Germany, France, Greece, Bulgaria and Cyprus –

which have strong and relatively close bilateral relations with Russia. These bilateral relations, which include the holding of frequent bilateral summits and a 'dense network of meetings at political, official and civil society levels' (David *et al.*, 2011, p. 183) make such member states cautious about giving EU-level policy-makers too much independence in conducting relations with Russia. Germany stands out as the most important member state actor in building bridges with Russia – dating back to Willy Brandt's *Ostpolitik* (normalization of relations with Eastern Europe, beginning with the Soviet Union), which he developed while Foreign Minister from 1966 and continued when he became Chancellor in 1969. Indeed, the German–Russian relationship is so important that it is reasonable to classify it as a 'special relationship' (Timmins, 2011, p. 189).

The caution about 'conceding' too much power to EU policy-makers is not, it should be stressed, completely restricted to member states with good bilateral relations with Russia. They are more inclined to lean in this direction, but other member states can also incline in this way, especially when economic interests are involved. This is illustrated with a Commission legislative proposal tabled in September 2011 that sought to strengthen the EU's influence in member states' bilateral energy deals, particularly with Russia. The proposal would have required member states to seek pre-approval from the Commission before signing any energy deals with third countries. If the Commission expressed concerns, the member states would be obliged to change the terms of the agreement, and if they failed to do so the Commission could bring action in the CJEU (Kanter, 2011b). Smaller member states broadly supported the proposal, but larger states were largely opposed, citing the free market and concerns over the sharing of detailed business dealings. The compromise legislation adopted by the EP in September 2012 removes the punitive aspects of the Commission's proposal and replaces it with an information exchange mechanism between the Commission and member states on all bilateral agreements between member states and third countries affecting the EU's internal energy market and the security of energy supplies. The legislation requires that all existing agreements also be submitted to the Commission for review. Finally, the Commission, with the member state's consent, may observe negotiations and provide advice or suggest non-binding clauses for the agreement to comply with the legislation (European Parliament, 2012).

Second, and in contrast with those member states that have relatively strong bilateral relations with Russia, there are also member states that have strained, and even poor, bilateral relations. Several of the CEECs – which, prior to 1989–91, were either Soviet republics or satellite countries of the Soviet Union – are in this category, and have brought considerable 'historical baggage' to the EU–Russia relationship through such matters as border disputes, the treatment of Russian-speaking minorities, and 'divergent narratives of key historical events such as WWII' (David, *et al.*, 2011, p. 183). However, not all member states with poor bilateral relations with Russia are CEECs with, for example, the UK and Sweden being among member states that have had sharp differences of opinion with Russia in recent years. But whether states with poor bilateral relations with Russia are 'old' or 'new', a consequence is that 'bilateral disputes are sometimes uploaded onto the EU-level agenda, which complicates and sours the EU–Russia relationship as a whole' (ibid., pp. 183–4).

Third, member states often play a two-level game in their dealings with Russia: taking a harder stand with respect to human rights, democratization and liberalization in Council meetings, while adopting more pragmatic stances in bilateral relations.

Fourth, and finally, EU–Russian relations illustrate an important aspect of what is always a potential EU policy weakness, given the structural nature of the CFSP: Russia is a 'classic realist power' that prefers to divide and conquer through bilateral relations, which it expects may then serve to advance its interests within EU policy-making arenas (ibid., p. 184). However, the changing nature of EU energy markets, and Russia's need to be able to sell its energy sources to EU countries, has the potential to make Russia more willing to negotiate directly with the EU. This is because, as pipelines delivering Russian natural gas are extending into more countries, the lack of unity in the EU's energy markets increases the complexity for the Russians in negotiating gas delivery volumes and the locking-in of long-term prices. So, for example, with many of the CEECs, Russia need negotiate only with state-owned utilities, but in those countries where energy markets are now subject to a great deal of competition (which the EU is further encouraging in its Third Energy Package), Russia faces competition and is weakened in its ability to negotiate long-term contracts. Thus, Russia has an added incentive to deal directly with the EU with respect to energy policy (Dickel and Westphal, 2012, p. 4). Assuming it does so increasingly, in return for accommodating Russian concerns over the stability of EU gas markets, the EU will seek to link its energy policy not only to the openness of Russian markets to EU goods but also to promoting democratization, improving human rights and reducing corruption in Russia, and encouraging Russia to move closer to EU policies in such areas as climate change and neighbourhood stability.

Coming back to EU–Russia trade interdependence, it undoubtedly results in the EU and its member states softening their public attitude towards Russia when the latter takes foreign policy stances of which EU states disapprove – such as Russia's reluctance in 2012 to criticize the Assad regime in Syria or to support UN interventionist actions as the Syrian conflict moved to become virtually a civil war.

The trading interdependence is based primarily on the EU supplying merchandise and services to Russia, and Russia supplying energy to Europe. Regarding the supply of energy, approximately a third of EU imports of crude oil, hard coal and natural gas come from Russia (European Commission, 2012g). This energy dependence naturally varies between EU member states, with states such as France and the UK being little affected (the former has a sizeable nuclear power generation capacity, while the latter has considerable domestic oil and natural gas supplies and a more diversified energy base) and others – including Bulgaria, Estonia, Finland, Latvia and Lithuania – being highly dependent on Russian energy, particularly natural gas. Dependence on Russian energy will only increase as some countries – including Germany and Italy, which are very large energy consumers – phase out nuclear power plants. Complicating the energy relationship is that some national companies of EU member states – mainly German, French and Italian – have partnered with Gasprom – Russia's gas giant, and the world's largest single gas extracting company – to build pipelines delivering Russian natural gas to the EU. Nominally a publicly-owned corporation, in reality Gasprom is controlled by the Russian government. So, this situation naturally involves a complex web of private–public partnerships (state-owned and publicly-held energy companies in EU

member states), national and EU leaders, energy regulators, retail energy providers and energy users. Involvement in this and many other investment partnerships, coupled with the EU's high energy dependence on Russia, is widely seen as giving Russia substantial economic leverage with which to influence member state behaviour in the Council – in the classic realist strategy alluded to above.

But Russian power and behaviour on energy has fed into an EU resolve that it must develop a more diversified energy security strategy that makes it less dependent on Russia. Russia inadvertently strengthened this resolve when, in 2006, it wielded energy as a blunt weapon in a dispute with Ukraine (through whose territory 80 per cent of Russian gas was carried to EU customers). It later came to light that Ukraine was illegally redirecting (stealing) gas intended for EU customers for its own domestic use. Nevertheless, when Russia cut off the gas supplies to Ukraine, it disrupted gas flows to 18 European countries, sending shock waves throughout the EU. This then led to those member states most dependent on Russian energy – notably Poland – pressing successfully for the insertion, via the Lisbon Treaty, of a solidarity clause on energy into the TEU (Article 194). It also led to disputes, which continue, between member states over the location and control of the several pipelines that have been built, are being built, and are planned to be built to bring natural gas from Russia, and from the Caspian Sea area and the Middle East, to the EU.

Of course, EU concerns about huge Russian influence over EU member states need to be tempered by a recognition of what the EU gains from Russia, and not only in energy supplies. It has, for example, been estimated that Russia's admission to the WTO in 2012 (which the EU supported) has a value of €3,900 million to the EU (European Commission, 2011i). It must also be recognized that the EU–Russia relationship is essentially one of mutual dependence, with Russia depending on European consumers to purchase its energy, and with it needing EU investment – about 75 per cent of foreign direct investment in Russia comes from EU member states (European Commission, 2012u).

This mutual dependence gives some ground for a positive outlook on the four 'common spaces' – economic; freedom, security, and justice; external security; and research, education, and culture – that the EU and Russia have conceived as the bases for improving their relations. As part of this, it is increasingly recognized in the EU that the key to promoting democratization and human rights in Russia is through more rather than less interdependence between the EU and Russia – or, more 'liberalism' and less realpolitik.

The EU and NATO

Since the end of the Cold War, NATO has struggled to redefine itself. As it has done so, opinion among US policy-makers has evolved as whether the US should support those in Europe who have canvassed for the EU to build an independent European security apparatus. While the Clinton Administration in the 1990s had hinted that the US was beginning to re-evaluate NATO as the sole instrument of Western defence co-operation, its steps were, of necessity, tentative. So, in 1994, it supported NATO recognition of a rather nebulous 'European security and defence identity' (which eventually grew into the CSDP) within NATO structures. In 1998, at a NATO news conference, Secretary of State Madeleine Albright went further when, to the background of a perceived inadequate contribution by EU states to dealing with the atrocities occurring in the Balkans, she stated that 'I think it's very important for the Europeans to carry a fair share and have a sense of their own defense identity' (USIS Washington File, 1998).

America's ambivalence on Europe developing more independent defence structures (largely) ended with US military expansion beyond its fiscal and manpower capacity on several fronts in the aftermath of 9/11: specifically, the combating of terrorism on US soil and the military engagements in Iraq and Afghanistan. As a result, the George W. Bush Administration not only gave its blessing to European defence cooperation, but supported French President Nicolas Sarkozy's decision to make it a priority of the French EU presidency in the second half of 2008. Indeed, Sarkozy's 2009 decision to bring France back into NATO's unified command (43 years after President de Gaulle withdrew France from NATO, citing US dominance), was important not only because it now meant that French officers would be integrated into NATO command structures (France had already been participating in NATO operations), but that the US would be more tolerant of French attempts to build a European

defence policy as a complement rather than a rival to NATO.

At much the same time, the EU's role in the Western security apparatus was further articulated at a NATO Summit in April 2008, when the Heads of State and Government issued a declaration recognizing the EU's security role (NATO, 2008):

> We recognise the value that a stronger and more capable European defence brings, providing capabilities to address the common challenges both NATO and the EU face. We therefore support mutually reinforcing efforts to this end. Success in these and future cooperative endeavours calls for enhanced commitment to ensure effective methods of working together. We are therefore determined to improve the NATO–EU strategic partnership as agreed by our two organisations, to achieve closer cooperation and greater efficiency, and to avoid unnecessary duplication in a spirit of transparency, and respecting the autonomy of the two organisations. A stronger EU will further contribute to our common security.

US support for CSDP continued in the Obama Administration when, for example, Vice-President Joseph Biden stated that the US will 'support the further strengthening of European defence, an increased role for the European Union in preserving peace and security, [and] a fundamentally stronger NATO–EU partnership' (Biden, 2009).

But what could be the EU's specific role in NATO? This is by no means clear, not least because there is no agreement among EU member states on the answer to the question. Indeed, as shown in Box 13.2, six EU states are not even NATO members. Further to this, Denmark has opted-out of EU defence policy, but is a strong supporter of NATO, while Turkey – an EU candidate state and an extremely important geopolitical member of NATO – objects to EU–NATO co-operation.

So, many, as yet unanswered, questions are likely to be much debated in the years to come. What could be the future of an EU caucus in NATO when it is the member states and their military commands that are integrated in NATO, not the EU? Would the US tolerate an EU 'caucus' at NATO meetings (Hunter and Biscop, 2011)? If there was to be an 'EU caucus', how would it operate in light of the fact that some EU member states are not, and do not wish to be, NATO members? Related to this is the problem that France and the UK are the only nuclear powers in the EU, which automatically divides them from some of the other EU member states with respect to disarmament and deterrence – with the EU's 'neutrals' in particular advocating a nuclear-weapons-free world (Zwolski, 2011, p. 489).

A start in answering at least some of these questions may be found in building on the foundations of the CSDP's missions to see if NATO and the EU can devise a division of labour in which in conflict management situations the EU undertakes the civilian responsibilities and NATO the military.

The EU at the United Nations

The EU, as an international organization itself, has long advocated the importance of multilateral forums for discussing and working out global issues. The EU, however, is not a formal member of IOs – rather, member states are signatories to international treaties. The Lisbon Treaty's accomplishment of establishing a single legal personality for the EU, has, however – theoretically at least – enhanced the EU's ability to promote single positions in such forums as the UN.

The EU's lack of voice in such regional organizations as the Asian-Pacific Economic Forum has led it to redouble its already existing efforts in advocating that multilateral forums – particularly the UN General Assembly, UN specialized agencies, and the G-8 and G-20 – are the most appropriate venues for negotiating many controversial international issues, from climate change to human rights. To this end, the EU has become increasingly concerned to build a collective voice in the UN system, where it is now the major financial contributor: the EU member states account for 38 per cent of the UN's regular budget and over 40 per cent of the costs of UN peacekeeping operations (European Union, 2012). The EU has missions not only in the UN headquarters in New York, but also in all the major cities where UN specialized agencies operate – Geneva, Nairobi, Paris, Rome and Vienna.

Given member state representation in the UN, students of EU foreign policy have long asked the question: to what extent do EU member states cede their national voice to the EU at the UN? On the basis of an analysis of EU member state positions and voting behaviour in the UN, Maximilian Rasch's conclusion to this question is that 'EU member states pursue their national interests much more openly in Brussels' than in New York, though they do see the UN as 'an arena to demonstrate sovereignty and prestige' (Rasch, 2009, p. 302). Rasch further suggests that while the multilateral basis of the UN actually encourages a member state perspective, member states none the less act increasingly in a unified way. That this is so is seen in voting on UN General Assembly (GA) resolutions: unanimous voting among EU member states was below 50 per cent in the 1970s, despite there being, from 1973, just nine member states; by contrast, today, and despite the EU's greatly increased size, member states cast collective votes on UN resolutions in around 75–80 per cent of all the submitted texts (on member states voting on GA roll-call votes, see also Laatikainen and Smith, 2006; Regelsberger, 2007, p. 3).

Already the value of the establishment of the single legal personality has been shown, with UN GA Resolution A/65/276 (May 2011) granting the EU's long-standing desire to be treated as a legal entity. This gives EU representatives the ability to articulate EU common positions in the GA, to participate in GA debates, and to propose amendments agreed by EU member states. However, because the EU is not recognized as a 'state' (and is not a signatory to the UN Charter), it cannot vote in the General Assembly.

The EU's ability to be represented in the UN Security Council (UNSC) is, however, a rather different matter. It is so because, arguably, the UNSC is the unparalleled epicentre of realpolitik. There is no EU seat on the UNSC and, despite some (mild) pressure for them to do so, no one expects the French and British to relinquish their seats for one collectively held by the EU. And on the much-debated issue of whether Germany, and perhaps also Italy, merits a seat in an enlarged ring of permanent UNSC seats, this is part of a larger discussion of whether the likes of Brazil, India, Japan and South Africa have demonstrated the capacity and willingness to act as international peacemakers.

The vast majority of UNSC decisions are achieved by consensus. France, the UK, and any other EU member state that holds one of the rotating, non-permanent UNSC seats normally consult with each other on votes and may consult also with the other EU states that are not represented on the Security Council. Ultimately, however, the votes they cast are national ones, and not on behalf of the EU. Moreover, as Christopher Hill (2006, p. 54) has observed, 'there is a persistent tendency on the part of [France and the UK] to see the UNSC as a key platform for promoting their foreign policy priorities'. Occasionally, this has resulted in very high-profile disagreements being put on open display. So, for example, in 2003, France opposed and the UK supported the US-led invasion of Iraq. And in 2011, Germany, occupying a rotating UNSC seat, abstained in a vote which France and the UK supported the approval of NATO action in Libya.

Conclusions

Interest in European-wide foreign and external security defence policies has been on the European Union's agenda since its earliest manifestation as the ECSC. Nevertheless, because of the political sensitivities associated with these policy areas, it was not until the 1970s that this interest began to be given practical effect, and then it was highly tentative and cautious. However, since the Maastricht Treaty – when the CFSP was created and defence was given its first treaty recognition – the two areas have been transformed into dynamic areas of policy activity. The main driving force behind this transformation has been external events, which have forced the EU to confront and try to deal with its policy weaknesses and inadequacies.

Yet, despite the many policy advances that have been made since the Maastricht Treaty – such as the creation by the Lisbon Treaty of a European diplomatic service and what amounts in practice to an EU Foreign Minister – the EU is still far from being as cohesive or influential an actor on the world stage in respect of foreign and external security policy matters as it is in respect of trade. That said, however, the EU's foreign policy role and influence is not to be dismissed. It has developed policy goals grouped mainly around the promotion of core values and of neighbourhood co-operation. It has also developed policy instruments to pursue these goals, based on diplomacy, the use of Community (primarily economic) instruments, conditionality, and, since the mid-2000s, the deployment of CSDP missions of various sorts. These goals and policy instruments have resulted in the EU being confined essentially to 'soft' tasks, but the importance of these is not to be, as it often is, dismissed too easily.

The policy area where the EU is weakest is, of course, defence. This is a consequence of political choice, differing views on what the relationship between the EU and NATO should be, and defence costs. But, after some spectacular external security policy failures, notably in the Balkans in the 1990s, and with the US increasingly looking west to the Pacific, the EU is gradually coming to terms with its need to strengthen member state co-operation on defence policy as well as the EU's military capability.

Europeans, far more than Americans, live in troubled surroundings. More than ever, it would seem that Europe needs to speak with one voice. But Europe's ability to articulate and undertake a robust foreign policy is predicated on a robust CSDP – because, as Frederick the Great observed, 'Diplomacy without armaments is like music without instruments' (quoted in Mowle, 2004, p. 114).

Some foreign and security experts are pessimistic about the EU's potential to lead an invigorated CSDP (see, for example, Menon, 2010) and cite in support of their case such evidence as the still existing significant differences between member states on key policy and strategic matters, the modesty of the aims and sizes of EU missions to date, and the very limited resourcing of CSDP in the EU budget (see Chapter 14). Certainly, the situation is highly complex and uncertain, but a scenario of a much stronger CSDP is possible if it is based on a recognition of the fact that EU defence policy co-operation, which has been developing rapidly, and European defence capability, appear increasingly to be two sides of the same coin.

Chapter 14

The EU's Budget

The EU's budget is, in relative terms, very modest in size – accounting for only 1 per cent of EU GNI and less than 3 per cent of total public expenditure in the EU. So, while the 2011 EU budget was almost €142 billion, the sum of the national budgets in EU member states was more than €6,300 billion (European Commission, 2012i). But despite this relative modesty, the nature of the budget's revenues and expenditures and the behaviour of the budget's decision-makers reveal much about the EU's policy priorities and policy-making processes. Because, behind each revenue source is a tug-of-war between integrationists and intergovernmentalists and between 'getters' and 'givers'. And beneath each expenditure item lie an array of – often sharply clashing – policy priorities and images of the EU's purpose.

Policy-makers whose ideological preference is for an EU that is focused mainly on creating an open internal market and for other policy areas to be left largely to the member states are naturally disposed to advocate a small budget. This is because negative integration is achieved mainly through legislation that imposes no great costs at EU level. For those who take such a restrictive view of what the nature of the EU should be, the budget therefore should largely be confined to funding essential internal market operating requirements, plus a few supporting policy activities. Policy-makers from member states that are net budgetary contributors – who are by no means all minimalists in their visions of their preferred nature of the EU – also generally incline to the view that the EU budget should be modest, since the larger the budget is the more they have to contribute to it.

By contrast, policy-makers who support economic union or economic federalism, with policies capable of fiscal (macroeconomic) management and economic redistribution, and even more so political federalists who want substantial funds not only for distributive and re-distributive policies but also for such policy areas as AFSJ and foreign policy, naturally support a larger budget. So too, as a general rule, do policy-makers from member states that are net budgetary beneficiaries.

The size, composition and purposes of the EU's budget are therefore much disputed, for both pragmatic and political reasons. The pragmatic reasons are associated mainly with matters related to which member states and which sectional interests 'win' from the budget and which 'lose'. The political reasons are tied in to fundamental questions about the nature of the EU: should the EU restrict itself largely to being an internal market, with a budget that is mainly limited to operating the market and providing a few modest cushioning 'side-payments', or should the EU be a broader political community that seeks to promote equity, solidarity and commonality that therefore needs a range of substantial 'spending policies'?

The examination of the budget in this chapter is organized around analyses of the evolution of the budget, the budget's components (revenue and spending), the 2014–20 multiannual financial framework, the budget's 'winners' and 'losers', and budgetary processes.

Evolution of the Budget

The 1957 EEC Treaty provided the mechanism for a budget that would be financed from national treasuries on a weighted basis. But it also provided, in Article 201, provision for the Community eventually to develop its 'own resources' – in particular from revenue accruing from the Common Customs Tariff. So, a transitional revenue-raising system was initially established, with the target being the creation of an 'own resources' system by no later than 1970. However, a 1965 proposal from the then Commission President, Walter Hallstein, for an early timetable for financing the budget from own resources was strongly resisted by the French President, Charles de Gaulle, partly because he thought it was not sufficiently advantageous to France, and partly because he was becoming increasingly concerned at what he saw to be a supranational drift in aspects of the Community's operation. French opposition was so intense that it played a major part in producing the 'empty chair' crisis of June 1965–January 1966, during which France withdrew from most EC decision-making bodies (Begg and Grimwade, 1998, p. 40; Dinan, 2004, pp. 104–8). So, from the earliest years of the European Community, the budget proved to be a sensitive issue and one that could, and did, seriously disrupt governance.

With de Gaulle's retirement from politics, an agreement was reached at the 1969 Hague Summit to end the transitional phase of funding from national budgets and move to a system of own resources. The agreement was linked to the likelihood of future UK accession. Timing was everything to the French: the new financing scheme must be put in place prior to the UK accession, because the UK would surely complain that the system discriminated against countries, of which the UK would be the leading one, with high levels of imports on the one hand (which would make them high contributors to the budget) and relatively small agricultural sectors on the other (the creation of the CAP in the 1960s meant agricultural price support was responsible for around three-quarters of budgetary expenditure). The other member states foresaw that this would be likely to create difficulties, but they were not inclined to confront the French and hoped that the British would be willing to pay a budgetary premium for finally gaining admission. These hopes that British policy-makers would accept the budgetary situation as a reasonable 'trade-off' were, however, realized for only a very short time. Within little more than a year of the UK's accession in January 1973, the strongly pro-European Prime Minister, Edward Heath, had been removed from office and British policy-makers were complaining about a predetermined and 'unfair' budget regime. Their complaints reflected the fact that a system had been established that virtually guaranteed acrimonious budgetary disputes: disputes that persist to the present day.

The 1970s saw the laying down of new treaty bases for the Community's budgetary regime. In 1970, the *Treaty Amending Certain Budgetary Provisions of the Treaties* (commonly referred to as the Luxembourg Treaty) established an own resources revenue stream. The Treaty also established what was to become an important distinction between two categories of expenditure: compulsory (arising directly from the treaties, and in practice covering mainly CAP spending) and non-compulsory (covering virtually all non-CAP spending). In 1975, a 'follow-up' treaty, the *Treaty Amending Certain Financial Provisions of the Treaties*, revised the system of budgetary decision-making, most particularly by granting joint budgetary authority to the Council and the EP, though restricting the Parliament's ability to tamper with compulsory expenditure. This restriction on the EP's powers over compulsory expenditure was to become a considerable source of grievance on the Parliament's part over the years, and a running source of Council–EP budgetary disputes. The matter was not resolved until the distinction between the two categories of expenditure was removed by the Lisbon Treaty.

During the second half of the 1970s and into the 1980s three major budgetary problems developed. First, Community responsibilities grew more rapidly than available revenue. This was largely because of high CAP support prices, but the problem was compounded by the EP's penchant for increasing funding for existing projects and adding new budgetary lines. The Council countered Parliament by setting strict expenditure limits in enabling legislation, which, the Parliament argued, violated its power to determine non-compulsory expenditure. These Council–Parliament differences constituted the second budgetary problem: growing inter-institutional tensions, which became considerably sharper after the first use of direct elections for the EP in 1979, which resulted in MEPs being more assertive. From 1979, the annual budget became a political battleground in which the Council and EP disputed budgetary levels and allocations. Nominally, the disputes were usually focused on the EP wanting higher increases than the Council in non-compulsory expenditure, but dissatisfaction on the part of the EP with its budgetary powers and a resolve to push what powers it did have to their maximum also lay not far beneath the surface. The disputes were so intense that in five of the first nine years after the introduction of direct elections (1980, 1984–8) the budget was not approved in time to be implemented at the beginning of the financial year on 1 January. The third budgetary problem was that the British government became increasingly vocal in expressing its dissatisfaction with the amount of the UK's net budgetary contributions. Various attempts were made to pacify the UK, not least by the creation in the mid-1970s of the ERDF, which, though also to the advantage of some other member states, had as its main purpose 'side payments' to the UK. But the underlying problem of a large UK net budgetary deficit persisted. The problem came to a head in the early 1980s when the British Prime Minister, Margaret Thatcher, became increasingly hectoring on the subject: 'I want my money back' she famously declared, to the intense irritation of other Heads of Government, some of whom declared that she did not understand the own resources concept. (In fact, she doubtless understood it perfectly well: but she did not like how it was working.)

A deal that supposedly would resolve at least two of these problems – the shortage of revenue and the UK's claimed excessive budgetary contributions – was concluded in 1984. Significantly, in terms both of the changing institutional balance in the Community and how politicized budgetary issues had become, the deal was concluded not by finance or budget ministers but by heads of government, at their 1984 European Council meeting at Fontainebleau. On the budgetary revenue problem, the solution was to raise the ceiling of VAT income that could be claimed by the Community. (It had been 1 per cent and was raised to 1.4 per cent.) On the British problem, a rebate of about 50 per cent was agreed (Begg and Grimwade, 1998, p. 44).

But the budgetary revenue 'solution' was quickly shown to be inadequate, with the Community hitting the increased VAT ceiling in the first year of its application. This was at a time when customs duties and agricultural levies resources were diminishing, when the accession of Spain and Portugal was producing greater agricultural surpluses and hence greater CAP expenditure, and when world commodity prices were falling and were thereby increasing the costs of farm price support in the budget (Begg and Grimwade, 1998, p. 45). In sum, a multi-variate disaster struck, derailing the carefully negotiated Fontainebleau agreement. With Council–EP budgetary battles also continuing, a new and more radical approach to the budget had to be devised: an approach that would both put the Community's revenue on a firmer footing and would end the bitter annual rows over the composition of the budget.

On the basis largely of Commission proposals, a 'solution' was agreed at the 1988 Brussels summit. The summit deal was then given operational effect through an extra-treaty *Interinstitutional Agreement on Budgetary Discipline and Improvement of the Budgetary Procedure* between the Commission, Council and Parliament. On the shortage of revenue problem, the solution was the creation of a new budgetary resource based on the gross national product (GNP) of each member state. On the annual budgetary battles problem, a three-pronged approach was devised to minimize conflict: a phased reduction in the proportion of the budget assigned to the CAP; a phased increase in the proportion of the budget assigned to non-compulsory structural expenditure (that is, essentially to regional and social policies); and the creation of new multi-annual financial frameworks (MFFs) – referred to as 'financial perspectives' at the time – within which annual budgets would be located. MFFs would set revenue and expenditure ceilings for the specified period, both on an overall basis and, on the expenditure side, under broad policy-based headings. The Commission would be responsible for updating MFFs to reflect growth and inflation. The first MFF (often referred to as Delors 1 because of its origins in the Commission) covered the years 1988–92. Subsequent MFFs have covered 1993–9, 2000–6, and 2007–13.

Significantly, and this reflects a pattern seen in several areas of EU policy development, the creation and then consolidation of MFFs occurred without any explicit treaty base. Prior to the Lisbon Treaty, there was no treaty mention of multi-annual financial frameworks. But, following the adoption of the first MFF, a consensus quickly emerged amongst EU policy-makers that MFFs provided a helpful way of tackling budgetary difficulties and of reducing the chances of a new budget not being approved in time to take effect at the beginning of the EU's budgetary year. (And, in the event, since 1988 all new budgets have been approved in time.) Increasingly, MFFs also came to be seen as being helpful to, and indeed necessary for, proper financial planning. Consequently, even without a treaty base, MFFs came to be adopted and used. Concerns on the part of the EP that this new mechanism would reduce its budgetary influence were mollified by the device of incorporating MFFs into extra-treaty interinstitutional agreements that necessitated EP approval. In time, the reality of what was happening in practice was duly given treaty status, with the Lisbon Treaty creating a new treaty chapter on MFFs (Part 6, Title II, Chapter 2, TFEU), specifying that MFFs must be established for a period of least five years and can only be adopted after receiving the consent of the EP.

MFFs do not eliminate the need for annual budgets but they are now adopted within MFF pre-set ceilings on revenues and expenditure headings. Accordingly, much of the political edge has been taken off the annual budgetary rounds, with margins for manoeuvre now relatively tight. This is not to suggest that budgetary battles have disappeared, but rather that rows over the most divisive questions – on the overall size of the budget, the size of categories of expenditure, major new initiatives, and revenue sources – are now largely confined to the two-year or so run-ups to finalizing MFFs.

The MFF system has thus been very useful politically in that, by defusing the annual budgetary process, it has helped to reduce interinstitutional and inter-member state tensions. It has also been useful in promoting more efficient governing in that policy-makers using EU funds can plan more easily for the medium-term and, in theory at least, can consequently make more effective and efficient use of resources.

Budgetary Components

Revenue sources

It was shown in the previous section that the EEC Treaty provided for, and the Community subsequently created, a system of 'own resources'. These own resources must fully cover EU expenditure, because the EU is prohibited by treaty from adopting or running a budget deficit.

The term 'own resources' should not be taken quite at face value, because the resources in question are not an EU tax or any other revenue item that the EU specifically controls. But they are own resources in the sense that they are revenue streams the member states have agreed will be earmarked for the EU. In difficult political or economic circumstances, member states cannot unilaterally decide to 'adjust' their allocations.

As can be seen from Figure 14.1, the EU derives its revenue from four sources: duties on goods imported from non-member countries (common customs tariffs) and agricultural (mainly sugar) levies; a value added tax (VAT) component; a gross national income (GNI)-based source; and a catch-all miscellaneous category. In 2012, 73 per cent of the revenue of the EU budget was derived from the GNI-based resource; 15 per cent from customs duties and agricultural levies; 11 per cent from the VAT based resource; and the remaining 1 per cent from miscellaneous sources.

As discussed above, and elaborated upon further in this section, budgetary sources have evolved since the founding of the Community, and debates regarding budgetary revenues continue today. Like much else in the EU, the composition of budgetary revenues is both complex and unique. In some respects, the funding sources resemble the customary financing arrangements of International Governmental Organisations (IGOs) – that is, national contributions from member states tied to their size and wealth – while in other respects they share characteristics with the revenue-raising arrangements of sovereign states.

Figure 14.1 EU Budget Revenues, 2012

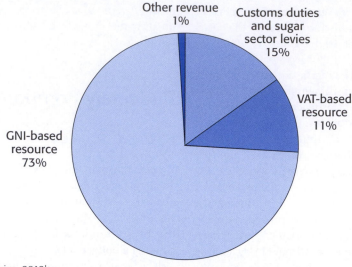

Other revenue
1%

Customs duties
and sugar
sector levies
15%

VAT-based
resource
11%

GNI-based
resource
73%

Source: European Commission, 2012h.

In 2004, in the context of helping to guide the negotiations on what became the 2007–13 MFF, the Commission issued a report evaluating the EU's resources system. In the report, eight criteria were laid down for evaluating EU budgetary resources: visibility (EU citizens should be, and should be able to see themselves to be, linked to the EU's financial arrangements); simplicity; financial autonomy; efficient allocation; sufficiency; cost-effectiveness; stability; and equity in gross contributions (European Commission, 2004c, pp. 11–12). These criteria will be used in the following review and evaluation of the EU's revenue sources.

Tariffs and agricultural levies

Tariffs The EU's Common Customs Tariff (CCT) (also often referred to as the Common External Tariff) establishes a common system of tariffs on goods entering the EU. That the tariffs should be remitted to the EU has never been in contention, as the EEC Treaty stated in Article 201 that the Community would move to a system of own resources based in particular on 'revenue accruing from the common customs tariff'. Between 1971 and 1975, CCT revenues were gradually shifted from member states to the Community, though with member states retaining 10 per cent for

administrative costs (a figure that was raised to 25 per cent in 2002). As a percentage of total budgetary resources, tariffs peaked in 1976, when they accounted for 49.7 per cent. Since then this percentage has gradually declined to its current 14 per cent. This figure is still high compared with the US, where tariffs account for only just over 1 per cent of total budgetary receipts, but it is far lower than the drafters of the EEC Treaty envisaged.

The EU's still significant reliance on tariffs as a revenue source does, in this one respect at least, make it more analogous to a developing country than to the post-industrial states that constitute its core membership. Because, in incipient political systems and/or developing countries, tariff revenues typically comprise a sizeable portion of total tax revenues. So, for example, in India they account for 24 per cent, and in Madagascar 54 per cent. But though tariff revenue remains significant for the EU, its relative decline has been inevitable. One reason for this has been the EU's increased range of spending policy commitments. As has been noted by a legion of scholars of federalism, both general and EU-focused, the negative integration that is characteristic of federal systems in their early stages – and which is necessary to level out rules between regional units that previously operated autonomously – is not particularly costly. As integration continues, however, and more positive measures are needed – in the form, for example, of social and economic harmonization, growth promotion and environmental protection – budgets must grow to finance a more activist central government. In the EU context, this has meant that the comparatively meagre and inherently limited take from customs tariffs has had to be supplemented by other budgetary sources.

Paralleling the EU's increasing demand for revenue, international trade negotiations through the GATT and later the WTO have steadily reduced tariffs in industrialized countries. By the close of the Kennedy Round in 1967, tariff levels on industrial products had been reduced by about a third among developed countries (agriculture was not covered until the later Uruguay Round). By 2006, the average EU rates for industrial and agricultural goods were just 5.4 per cent and 15.1 per cent, respectively. Thus, at the very time the EC member states began remitting the CCT (in 1971), tariff levels were beginning to fall and could not be expected to keep pace with the revenue needs required for dynamic integration. This loss of tariff revenues has subsequently been compounded by the EU entering a wide range of trading agreements that give preferential access to the EU market (see Chapter 12).

Agricultural duties and sugar levies These are imposed to bring import prices in line with EU prices; that is, to protect European farmers from foreign competition. At their peak, in 1977, agricultural duties and sugar levies represented 20.5 per cent of the total revenues collected. However, this source of revenues has diminished as the EU has become more self-sufficient in food, has opened its markets to developing countries, and has lowered agricultural protectionism as a result of world trade agreements. Today, this category contributes less than 2 per cent to total budgetary revenues.

In most respects, tariffs, agricultural duties and sugar levies – collectively known as traditional own resources – fall well short of the criteria pertaining to an effective and efficient tax. So, for example, taking the Commission's sufficiency and stability criteria, while continuing to be a useful source of income, they have, as has been shown, declined greatly as a percentage of total revenue. Indeed, the Commission now declares that duties are intended primarily to be protective measures rather than revenue-raising

instruments (European Commission, 2004c, p. 14). The cost-effectiveness criterion also barely applies, since tariffs, duties and levies carry higher collection costs than most other taxes. As for the visibility criterion, tariffs, duties and levies are visible in that they are a direct tax, but they are seen only by the relatively small number of importers who are directly involved in their payment.

Value added tax

The 1970 Luxembourg Treaty established VAT as a third resource. VAT is a form of 'consumption' tax that it is collected on each exchange rather than on total value. All EU member states are required to levy VAT on goods and services (Directive 2006/112/EC).

The VAT resource has always bedevilled the Commission because it has proved difficult to harmonize VAT bases and rates. The Council issued two directives in 1967 – 67/227/EC and 67/228/EC – mandating VAT harmonization, but it was not until 1977, with the passage of the Sixth VAT Directive (77/388/EC), that a reasonable level of harmonization was actually achieved. But that level was still far short of what the Commission had hoped for – it had originally recommended VAT as an EU resource so that it would act as an impetus to harmonize the VAT base rather than for its goodness of fit as a budgetary resource.

The VAT resource, implemented in 1979, has always been somewhat controversial. From the outset, the Community institutions disagreed as to how it should be collected. The Commission and the Parliament advocated what is known as the 'returns' method, based on the actual amount of VAT paid by individuals, with the portion allocated to the EU being specified. The Council preferred the 'revenue' method, under which the amount to be paid to the EU is calculated on a weighted basis from the total of net revenue collected (Begg and Grimwade, 1998, p. 42). The Council argued that the revenue method offered a more straightforward calculation, but the Commission and Parliament were suspicious that member state reluctance to use the returns method was rooted in their unwillingness to break the direct link between member states and budgetary contributions. The Council view prevailed, with Regulation 1552/89 settling the issue in favour of the revenue method.

In addition to this dispute about how it is best collected, VAT as a budgetary resource has also been the subject of a number of criticisms from member states. First, because it is levied on consumption, VAT is a regressive tax. As with all such taxes, a greater proportion of disposable income is spent on them by the less well-off. This is so both on an individual and a member state basis – the latter because a greater amount of disposable income is used for consumption in lower per capita GDP countries. Regressive taxes are less problematic when levied by public authorities that are able to redistribute tax receipts in programmes that benefit the less well off. But in the EU there are few redistributive polices, with the consequence that poorer member states have argued that the VAT assessment places an inequitable burden on their citizenry.

A second criticism levelled by poorer states has been that, with their less sophisticated tax administration systems, they must rely more heavily on indirect taxes such as VAT. For example, in 2004, the year that ten new states joined the EU, the percentage of total tax collected as VAT was 17.4 per cent for the EU-15, and 23.6 per cent for the CEEC-10 (European Commission, 2006b, p. 219).

A third criticism has involved disparate member state ratios of private to public ownership. Member states with smaller public sectors naturally report higher percentages of private consumption spending to gross national income (GNI). As a result, VAT can be seen as discriminating against them: a point that the UK government has long been making.

The first MFF – Delors I – sought to remedy the burden on poorer states by setting the VAT assessment basis at 55 per cent of a member state's GDP. Nevertheless, complaints continued about VAT, leading to agreement on a protocol that was attached to the Maastricht Treaty which stated that, despite capping, more action was needed regarding the EU's over-reliance on the VAT source. The protocol's sentiment was enacted in the 1993–9 MFF, with the 'call-in' rate reduced from 1.4 to 1 per cent between 1993–9, and with the capping reduced to 50 per cent for the poorer states (Spain, Portugal, Greece, Ireland) beginning in 1995 and phased-in for the remaining states between 1995 and 1999 (Laffan, 1997, p. 46). But in bringing about more equity to the VAT system, the EU inevitably lost sufficiency.

The VAT resource is also problematic in terms of visibility and simplicity. The system for calculating member state obligations from VAT is exceedingly complex because of such factors as it being calculated on a theoretically harmonized base (to ensure fairness and equity in national contributions), the capping system, differences between member states in VAT rates and the VAT base, and the fact that the UK rebate is drawn from VAT contributions rather than other budgetary resources.

In 2004, the Commission (2004c, p. 50) recommended the abolition of the VAT resource on the grounds that it is 'in practice a resource levied on member states and not on citizens that imposes an additional workload on national administrations and complicates the financing system, without providing any advantages compared to the GNI-based resource'. As these observations of the Commission imply, unlike customs duties, member states tend to regard VAT as a direct contribution (Laffan, 1997, p. 41), which rather undermines the financial autonomy criterion of what the Commission views as being a desirable tax characteristic.

From the first VAT 'pay-in' in 1979, the Commission was warning about the inability of VAT to compensate for future revenue shortfalls. These warnings were realized in 1984, when the Community faced a revenue shortfall. The Fontainebleau increase in the VAT ceiling provided a temporary solution, with VAT contributions in 1986 reaching, at 66 per cent, their peak in terms of proportion of budgetary resources. Since then, however, they have declined, to around 11 per cent of budgetary revenues by 2012.

GNI-based resource

Budgetary revenue is subject to the requirement that, as Article 311 of the TFEU specifies, 'Without prejudice to other revenue, the budget shall be financed wholly from own resources.' But the nature of the own resources has changed greatly over the years, with budgetary revenue now taking a form that is, in the words of the Commission, 'far from the original notion of EU *own resources* by the first own resources decision of 1970' (European Commission, 2004c, p.5; emphasis as in original).

The major change stems from the 1988 Brussels summit decision to establish what was initially called 'the fourth resource', which later became 'the GNP resource', and since 2002 has been the 'GNI resource'.

Put simply, the GNI resource takes the form of 'contributions' to the budget from all member states based on their size and wealth. So, it is based on ability to pay: the assessment rate for the 2007–13 MFF is 0.73 per cent of each member state's GNI.

The resource was conceived of as a 'top-up' to bridge the gap between budgetary expenditure and income, and in effect it is still treated as a budgetary balancing mechanism. But though the resource's original purpose may still be said to be in operation today, the relative importance of the resource has been totally transformed. Because, as EU expenditure has grown and the revenue from the other budgetary resources has declined, so has the relative importance of the GNI resource greatly increased. When introduced in 1988 it constituted just over 10 per cent of total revenues, but now it has far outstripped the other revenue sources – constituting 73 per cent of total budgetary revenue in 2012.

When the resource was established, the EP pressed for an uncapped system. That is, for a system that did not contain limits on the percentage of GNP that could be collected to finance the EU's budget. Not surprisingly, the national governments never seriously entertained such a notion, since such a system would have involved expenses driving revenues. To prevent spending from outpacing budgetary growth, the system that was established involves ceilings on the percentage of GNI that can be assigned to the EU's budget. In the first MFF this ceiling was set at 1.15 per cent of Community GNP, rising to 1.20 per cent in 1992. It was increased to 1.27 per cent for the second and third MFFs, but was lowered to 1.24 per cent for the 2007–13 MFF. At the time of writing, it is scheduled to be further lowered in the 2014–20 MFF. Since the establishment of ceilings in 1988, there has never been an occasion when discharge procedures have revealed that a ceiling has been reached.

As for how the GNI payments are calculated, each year all member states must submit a return to the Commission. The Commission then reviews the figures and forwards the reports to a GNI committee. On the basis of information provided to it by the committee, and after having entered into its calculations various 'corrective mechanisms' applying to particular member states, the Commission then determines the national assessments Naturally, the larger and richer member states are the main contributors; hence, in 2011, Germany, with the highest GNI, paid

€21.2 billion, while Malta paid €54.9 million Since the resource involves governments transferring funds directly to the EU, there is no problem with collection.

In terms of the criteria for evaluating revenue sources, the GNI resource offers sufficiency (because it is transferred from member state treasuries) and equity (because it is based on ability to pay) but it fails on other counts, notably visibility and financial autonomy. The financial autonomy failing, which arises from the clear intergovernmental nature of the resource, has resulted in particular criticisms of it by the Commission and EP. Many of these criticisms relate to the fact that the 'national contribution' appearance of the resource increases the tendency of member states to look for a *juste retour* in budgetary deliberations – that is, to receive funds from the budget that are at least approximately equal to the amount they contribute to the budget revenue – rather than to look more widely to the added value of all EU policies for their citizens. Such concerns about the GNI resource have been instrumental in spawning numerous proposals for alternative revenue sources: a subject that will be explored below.

Miscellaneous

In addition to the resources described above, there are also some miscellaneous sources, amounting to about 1 per cent of annual budgetary revenue. They include taxes paid by EU staff on their salaries, fines on companies in breach of EU law, bank interest, and contributions by non-member countries to EU programmes.

The debate on revenue sources

As was implied in the above account of revenue sources, the existing system is unsatisfactory in several respects. Among its defects are its complexity, its lack of transparency, and its appearance of not being an own resources system at all but rather a system based on national contributions. This latter defect has been seen by many as being especially problematic, because it highlights the lack of financial independence of the EU and encourages a *juste retour* attitude among national governments in budgetary negotiations. As the Commission stated in its mid-term review of the 2007–13 MFF: 'Budget negotiations have recently been heavily influenced by Member States' focus on the notion of net positions with the consequence of favouring instruments with geographically pre-allocated financial envelopes, rather than those with the greatest added-value' (European Commission, 2010e, p. 25).

As a result of these perceived weaknesses, many proposals have been made over the years for a fundamental revision of the revenue raising system. Most of the proposals have focused on eliminating, or at least reducing, the GNI revenue source and replacing it with an EU tax or charge of some sort. So, for example, in its mid-term review, the Commission identified the following as being among the possibilities: a financial transaction tax (FTT); revenues from auctioning under the greenhouse gas emissions trading system (ETS); a charge related to air transport; a revised VAT; an energy tax; and a corporate income tax (European Commission, 2010e, p. 27).

However, a central problem with proposals for EU taxes or charges is that they have always faced a major obstacle: that the governments of some member states – most notably the UK, but it has not been alone – have consistently opposed the idea of the EU being given a more independent financial base resting on a direct taxation system. Their opposition has been based partly on sovereignty concerns and partly on beliefs that EU budgetary processes should not become more independent.

In an attempt to accommodate these national governmental concerns with its own long-standing ambition to make budgetary sources much more 'EU in character', the Commission in 2011 proposed reform of the own resources system in its proposals for the 2014–20 MFF and suggested a FTT and new VAT resource that would replace the existing VAT regime. It estimated that, by 2020, the total of these two new revenue streams could eventually provide about 40 per cent of the EU's funding needs, and the GNI-based source could decrease by about a third (European Commission, 2011e, p. 7; European Liberal Democrats, 2011).

The idea of a FTT has dominated revenue reform discussions since the Commission tabled its proposal for such a tax, which was accompanied by a timetable for its implementation by 31 December 2014. Introduced by the President of the Commission, José Manuel Barroso, as being justified on the grounds that it was time to 'make the financial sector pay its fair share', the FTT proposal involved a 0.1 per cent tax for shares and bonds and a 0.01 per cent levy on derivatives. Pension funds would be exempt.

While a FTT is not a wholly new idea (it was proposed in 1972 by the economist James Tobin as a tax on currency exchange to discourage short-term speculation), support for this so-called 'Robin Hood tax' has steadily gathered momentum in recent years in the wake of government bailouts of financial institutions. Many EU policy-makers have become attracted to the idea that the financial services industry should pay more for the protection it has been given (European Commission, 2011c), while the idea of an FTT is also popular with EU citizens – with a 2011 Eurobarometer poll finding 65 per cent support for such a tax (European Commission, 2011k, p. 14).

Whether revenues from a FTT could be funnelled into the EU budget to replace a portion of national contributions, or would have to be channelled into another fund (such as the European Stability Mechanism) is, however, unclear. This would depend largely on whether all member states agreed to a FTT (Council unanimity is required for new tax measures), which seems unlikely given that member states vary enormously in the size and nature of their financial services industries, and that the UK – which houses Europe's most important stock exchange – is a known opponent. It is therefore likely that if a FTT does proceed it will be on the basis of not all member states participating – perhaps just the eurozone members, or an even smaller group under enhanced co-operation.

Where is the money spent?

Budgetary spending is dominated by two policy areas: agriculture and cohesion. As explained in Chapter 9, agricultural spending is directed mainly towards income support for farmers and for rural development, while cohesion policy spending mainly involves regional and social policy activities of a redistributive nature. This dominance of agricultural and cohesion spending can be seen clearly in Table 14.1, which presents the expenditure percentages for the 2012 budgetary year.

While together they have long dominated the budget, the relative proportions spent on agriculture and cohesion policies have changed greatly over the years. Initially, in the years after the CAP was created

Table 14.1 The EU budget 2012

Heading	Billions €		Percentage of total budget	Percentage change from 2011	
	CA	PA		CA	PA
1. Sustainable growth	67.5	55.3	45.9	+4.7	+3.2
1a. Competitiveness for growth and employment	14.7	11.5	10.0	+9.1	−0.2
1b. Cohesion for growth and employment	52.7	43.8	35.8	+3.5	+4.1
2. Preservation and management of natural resources	60.0	57.0	40.8	+2.2	+1.9
of which, direct aids and market related expenditure	44.0	43.9	29.9	+2.6	+2.5
of which, rural development, environment and fisheries	15.9	13.1	10.8	−1.3	−0.1
3. Citizenship, freedom, security and justice	2.1	1.5	1.4	+10.9*	−1.3*
3a. Freedom, security and justice	1.4	0.8	0.9	+15.9	−2.5
3b. Citizenship	0.7	0.6	0.5	+2.1*	0.4*
4. EU as a global player	9.4	6.9	6.4	+7.4	-4.0
5. Administration	8.3	8.3	5.6	+1.3	+1.3
of which, for the Commission	3.3	3.3	2.3	+0.2	+0.2
Total	147.2	129.1	100		
As percentage of EU-27 GNI	1.12	0.98			

Notes: CA: commitment appropriations; PA: payments appropriations.
    * excluding European Union Solidarity Fund.

Source: European Commission, 2012b.

in the 1960s, agricultural policy spending dominated – almost to the exclusion of all other policies. Its domination was such that, for much of the 1970s, CAP expenditure accounted consistently for almost 80 per cent of the budget. Since the late 1970s, however, the proportion of the budget assigned to agriculture has declined, to such an extent that in the 2007–13 MFF agriculture-related expenditure accounted for just over 40 per cent and cohesion for just over 35 per cent of total budgetary spending. The reasons for this relative decline in agriculture spending and increase in cohesion spending were explained in Chapter 9.

Under MFFs, the spending side of each annual EU budget is circumscribed by overall limits. In the 2007–13 MFF this limit was set at 1.048 per cent of total EU GNI for commitment appropriations for every year of the MFF. (EU budgetary figures distinguish between commitment appropriations and payment appropriations. The former are funds assigned to a budget line that may run longer than a budgetary year, while the latter are funds assigned to a specific year. Commitment appropriations are naturally always higher than payment appropriations.) Within the overall set limits, MFFs categorize expenditure under 'headings'. The 2007–13 MFF used the following headings: sustainable growth; preservation and management of natural resources; citizenship, freedom, security and justice; the EU as a global player; administration; and compensations. Virtually all of the headings in the 2007–13 MFF, which were devised by the Commission, were quite different from the headings used in previous MFFs. This was most notably the case with the two headings accounting for most of the expenditure: in the 2000–6 MFF, 'agriculture' was the most costly heading of expenditure, followed by 'structural operations', but in the 2007–13 MFF both of these headings had disappeared and the two headings that accounted for most expenditure were 'sustainable growth' followed by 'preservation and management of natural resources'. However, highly significant though these changes may appear to be, they were in reality largely cosmetic. The official intent behind the changes of name was to signal a shift in policy priorities, but in practice the changes did not involve dramatic shifts in the nature of the budget: 'preservation and management of natural resources' was mainly agricultural spending, and 'sustainable growth' mainly cohesion policy operations.

A few observations about the budget's areas of expenditure will now be made, using the EU's own headings:

- 'Sustainable growth' is divided into two categories: cohesion for growth and employment; and competitiveness for growth and employment. The cohesion for growth and employment category is aimed mainly at promoting the economic and social development of the EU's less developed member states and regions. Within the category, there is also funding for EU-wide programmes focused on promoting employment and competitiveness. The competitiveness for growth and employment category is taken up mainly with assisting such Europe 2020-related items as research, competitiveness and innovation, Trans-European Networks (TENs) for transport and energy, and lifelong learning.
- 'Preservation and management of natural resources' is essentially agriculture with environmental and rural development dimensions added. While 'agriculture' did not merit its own heading in the 2007–13 MFF, this should not be

taken as indicating a drastic reduction for farming. Despite the much-vaunted reforms of the CAP that have been made since the late 1980s, agricultural guarantees still loom large in the EU's budget and will continue to do so for the foreseeable future.

- 'Citizenship, freedom, security and justice' covers various AFSJ matters which, as was shown in Chapter 11, have been a expanding rapidly since the late 1990s. Most of the new policies and programmes deal, in one way or another, with fundamental rights and justice, security, liberties, solidarity, and management of migration flows. The last of these – management of migration flows and the related issue of border controls – has received particular attention and has been assigned very significant budgetary increases in the 2000s. As for the citizenship category, policies here are 'aimed at promoting a better understanding of the European Union among its people, and addressing their daily concerns' (European Commission, 2007c, p. 4).
- Previously labelled 'external actions', funds under the heading 'EU as a global player' are used for a wide range of programmes and activities, including pre-accession aid, the European Neighbourhood Policy, development co-operation, humanitarian aid, the promotion of democracy and human rights, and the CFSP.
- 'Administration' mainly covers the costs of 'running' the EU institutions, and in particular the salaries and associated costs of its employees. Enlargements and the need for additional posts have resulted periodically in this heading having to be increased by a higher amount than the overall annual budgetary increase. But, taken over time, the amount of the budget assigned to administration has been fairly steady.

Is the money being spent 'well'?

There is no difficulty in making a case that the composition of the EU's budget is distorted and not focused sufficiently on meeting the most pressing of its policy requirements. Indeed, Budget Commissioners have often made this case themselves. So, for example, in an interview in 2008, Dalia Grybauskaite commented on how

The current structure of the EU budget suggests that only two policies are important for Europe, the CAP and cohesion policy ... Is that really so? Is that the sort of budget we need today? Many aspects of these two policies are from the middle of the last century ... We spend about 80 per cent of the EU budget on these two policies. The rest is basically leftovers. Do these policies allow us to cope and to react to the challenges facing us, or do we need to radically rethink them? (Quoted in O'Connor, 2008, p. 22)

As is implied in Commissioner Grybauskaite's comments, the dominance of agriculture and cohesion in the EU budget leaves insufficient funds for other policy areas, despite the time and effort the EU has devoted over the past several years to advancing such policy priorities as Europe 2020 and external policies.

What explains this seemingly unsatisfactory situation? Well, the budget is as it is because its composition is not determined by 'dispassionate' EU-wide need considerations. Rather, the main determinant of the content of MFFs and annual budgets is inherited commitments (path dependence), which in turn are a consequence of the many differing policy preferences of the governments of the member states and the outcomes of the bargaining processes between them. In short, the nature of the EU's spending is primarily a consequence of political choices and the exercise of political power.

But, in making their political choices and exercising their political power budgetary decision-makers have had to think increasingly about the 'added value' of budgetary expenditure. That is, 'whether spending at EU level means a better deal for citizens than spending at national level' (European Commission, 2010e, p. 5). There are a number of reasons why the importance of added value has been emphasized increasingly, especially by the Commission. One reason has been additional demands on the budget caused by the expansion of the EU's policy portfolio into potentially new spending areas – such as many AFSJ matters and the increasingly interventionist CFSP/CSDP. A second reason is that, despite the increased pressures on the budget, decision-makers have been unwilling to increase the size of the budget in 'real terms' (that is, over and above allowances for inflation and for increases in size of the EU's GNI). A third reason is

that the EU, like its member states, has been much affected by the spirit of economic liberalism that has advanced so much since the 1980s and that has increased beliefs that public bodies should be seen to be providing 'value for money'. And a fourth reason is that since the early 1990s the EU has been obliged to justify policy expansion under the subsidiarity and proportionality principles. Under the former, policies should be pursued at the EU level only if they can be better achieved at this level rather than at national or lower levels; while under the latter, if policies are to be pursued at the EU level this should be in a way that does not exceed what is necessary to achieve the desired objectives.

In its budgetary planning and decision-making processes the EU has thus been forced to pay more attention to added value. But, this is not, of course, to say that political pressures that arguably have little to do with added value cannot overcome added value arguments. Indeed, the authors of the 2003 Sapir Report – an independent report on the EU budget that was commissioned by Romano Prodi, the then President of the Commission – concluded that political pressures were carrying the day far too often. There needed to be a significant shift, it was argued in the Report, from traditional spending priorities to Lisbon Strategy-related matters (Sapir, 2003, p. 162).

A particularly blatant instance of the triumph of political pressures occurred in October 2002, when a deal to maintain spending levels on agriculture in the 2007–13 MFF and to make the EU-15 states the main beneficiaries of those spending levels was 'driven through' the European Council by France and Germany. In consequence, the farming sector, and more particularly large landowners and agribusinesses in the EU-15 states, continued to be heavily protected from market forces. However, as was shown in Chapter 9, even the heavily politicized area of agricultural spending has not been wholly immune from added value pressures. This is evidenced in the way such pressures have played at least some part in helping to bring about the very considerable changes that have occurred in agricultural policy in recent years.

The increasing importance of added value is seen no more clearly than in the major budgetary review process that was launched by the Commission in September 2007. The review had its origins in the December 2005 European Council agreement on the contents of the 2007–13 MMF, which included, at

Figure 14.2   The Added Value Test

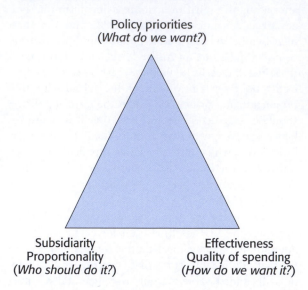

Policy priorities
(*What do we want?*)

Subsidiarity
Proportionality
(*Who should do it?*)

Effectiveness
Quality of spending
(*How do we want it?*)

the UK's insistence, that a full-scale review should be undertaken by the Commission of the budget. The mandate of the review included all aspects of EU spending, including on agriculture. From an early stage of the review process, the Commission made clear that it would be conducting a much more wide-ranging exercise than simply thinking about the next MFF, and would be paying particular attention to what sort of budgetary system would best enable the EU to meet such future challenges as the changing balance of economic power in the world, scientific and technological progress, demographic changes, and migratory pressures. At the heart of its considerations of such issues would be the extent to which EU budgetary spending would provide added value, with spending areas being expected to pass an added value test, the main principles of which are set out in Figure 14.2. According to the Commission, EU action should provide clear added value as measured by:

- Increased effectiveness: can policy goals be more completely achieved by acting at EU level?
- Increased efficiency: can policy goals be achieved at a lower cost by acting at EU level? (European Commission, 2007e, p. 30)

The findings of the Commission's budget review were issued in October 2010 (European Commission, 2010e). In addition to the importance of added value, three other key principles for determining spending priorities were identified in the review: the delivery of key policy priorities, impact and results, and the delivery of mutual benefits across the Union. Like added value, these are all – especially the delivery of policy priorities – a matter of interpretation and possible contestation.

The 2014–20 MFF

Despite the laying down of the above-listed general principles to guide policy-makers in the making of the 2014–20 MFF, the fact is that it, like all MFFs, had to be made in the context of 'the real world' of divergent member state preferences regarding spending levels and spending priorities. As such, when the Commission formally launched the MFF-making process in June 2011 it could not issue 'an ideal' MFF draft based wholly on such laudable principles as added value and the delivery of mutual benefits across the Union. Rather, it had to issue a draft MFF that incorporated the guiding principles as far as possible but that also offered a basis for eventual political acceptance

- to those who thought that, in difficult financial times, the EU's budget should, like member state budgets, be reined, in and to those who argued the budget should be used as an instrument for leading the way to economic recovery;
- to net budgetary contributors, and to net beneficiaries;
- to those who wished to see the CAP and cohesion policy continue to be prioritized, and to those who wished to see greater attention given to policy areas such as Europe 2020 and external affairs.

Not surprisingly, therefore, the Commission's proposals for 2014–20 were modest, with the main provisions being:

- Only a small increase to overall spending levels: total expenditure within the MFF would be 1.05 per cent of GNI for commitment appropriations,

Figure 14.3   Multi-annual financial frameworks, 2007–13 and 2014–20

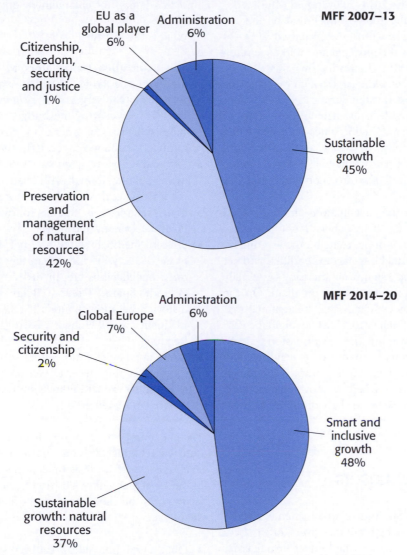

Source: European Commission, 2012m, p. 6 – Commission's draft proposal of MFF 2014–20 tabled in 2011.

though a proposed transfer of a few items outside the MFF framework would result in a 'real' figure of 1.11 per cent.

- A decline in spending on agriculture, rural support and fisheries (from 42 per cent to 37 per cent), and a very small increase in cohesion funding (up from 36 per cent to 37 per cent).
- Varying increases to certain other policy areas, including external relations (a 1 per cent increase) and such Europe 2020-related policies as research,

education and training (up from 9 per cent to 11 per cent) (European Commission, 2011e, 2012o, 2012p).

The names of most of the spending categories are slightly changed compared with the 2007–13 MFF – for example, 'Preservation and Management of Natural Resources' becomes 'Sustainable Growth: Natural Resources' – but the categories are largely unchanged in terms of their contents (see Figure 14.3

for a side-by-side comparison of the 2007–13 MFF and the Commission's 2014–20 proposed MFF).

A change from the 2007–13 MFF that resulted in much comment at the time the proposed 2014–20 MFF was issued was the movement of a few spending items outside the MFF. In reality this was of only marginal significance as the largest item by far in the 'outside the MFF' list was the European Development Fund (used to provide assistance to the group of African, Caribbean and Pacific states with which the EU has a long-established special relationship) and this has never been a part of the EU's budget. Rather, it has always been funded by direct contributions from the member states.

At the time of writing, negotiations on the 2014–20 MFF are ongoing, with the member states lining up in the customary manner of net contributors wanting no overall increase in total budgetary expenditure and net beneficiaries wanting a significant increase – especially in policy areas impacting directly on them. On the basis of past experience it can safely be assumed that the contents of the finally agreed MFF will not be very different from those of the Commission's draft. Certainly the budgetary status quo on expenditure will not be unduly disturbed. More caution is required, however, with revenues, where, as shown above, many members are sympathetic to the Commission's view that it is time for reform.

Winners and Losers

Conflicting images abound of which member states are the 'getters' and which are the 'givers' of the EU's budget – that is, which are the budget beneficiaries and which are the budget contributors. In consequence, there also are many different and conflicting images of whether the budget is 'fair'. For example, in the UK, the dominant popular image of the budget is that it is used mainly to finance the CAP, and more particularly to finance French farmers. In Germany, popular attention has been focused more on budgetary revenue than budgetary expenditure, with a widely held belief since the early to mid-1990s, when the very considerable costs of German unification began to take effect, that Germany has been the EU's main paymaster for too long. And in the CEECs it is widely felt that the budget has not benefited them as much as

had been hoped, with the EU-15 states having acted to limit the damage of enlargement on their budgetary positions.

What is the reality?

- The main gross contributors to the budget are naturally the larger member states, and more specifically the larger *and richer* member states. Over 70 per cent of the budget comes from five states, which are, in order of the size of their contributions, Germany, France, Italy, the UK and Spain.
- The main gross recipients naturally are also larger member states, though with relatively poorer larger member states this time being more to the fore. The main recipient is Spain, followed by France, Poland, Germany and Italy.
- Sixteen member states are net beneficiaries in terms of receiving more than they contribute. The main beneficiaries are, in order of most to least, Poland, Spain, Greece, Belgium (a position distorted because of funds it receives for hosting EU institutions), Hungary, Portugal and the Czech Republic.
- There are 11 net contributors in terms of paying more than they receive. Germany is the largest, followed by the UK, France, Italy, the Netherlands, Austria and Sweden.

The most important factor determining whether a state is a net budgetary contributor or beneficiary is its level of prosperity. This connection between prosperity and net budgetary position is accounted for by factors both on the revenue and expenditure sides of the budget:

- On the revenue side, wealthier states contribute 'disproportionately' to budgetary resources because: they can afford to import more goods, and therefore remit more customs duties to the EU than do poorer countries; their citizens can afford to spend a greater percentage of their disposable income on consumer goods, which results in the processing of more VAT contributions for the EU; and the GNI resource is largely calculated on the basis of population size and national wealth.
- On the expenditure side, poorer states benefit 'disproportionately' from the cohesion funds, which account for over a third of total budgetary expenditure.

Whether this situation of some member states being net budgetary contributors and others being beneficiaries is 'fair' is, of course, very much open to debate. The Commission discourages a focus on the budget in terms of contributors and beneficiaries, mainly because a straight comparison of budgetary revenues and expenses cannot measure the benefits that each member state derives from EU membership. Many of the advantages of EU membership are, of course, market-based and in this context it is significant that of the 50 largest European corporations (see CNN Money, 2010, for the full list) only two are headquartered in a member state (Spain) that is not a net contributor to the budget. It is also significant that more advanced economies have the monopolistic advantage of higher value added goods and services. Thus, despite the fact that the richer member states are net budget contributors and the poorer member states are net recipients, the former are, in most respects, the greater net beneficiaries of the internal market.

More generally on the 'fairness' issue, it all depends on what is meant by 'fair'. If a *juste retour* position is adopted, then the budget is indeed 'unfair'. Moreover, the extent of this unfairness may be said to have increased over the years because, with some states experiencing faster economic growth than others, and with the accession of a large number of poorer states in 2004–7, the number of net contributor states has grown. But 'fairness' can also be understood in other ways. One of these ways has provided part of the foundation of the French case for defending CAP funding: acceptance of the CAP, the French argument runs, was a key component of the original EEC 'deal' and has been an important element of all subsequent accession treaties; to try to dismantle it would be tantamount to not abiding by 'the rules of the game'. Another, and most policy practitioners would say much more forceful, interpretation of 'fairness' is that in any union stronger members should assist weaker members, which in the EU context means that richer member states should assist poorer ones. On this basis, the redistributive aspects of the EU's budget are perfectly fair, and in fact also in the long-term economic interests of the richer states in that they help to boost growth in the poorer states and so add to the vitality of the internal market.

But, of course, member states are less concerned about fairness than they are with their net budgetary positions. Net contributor states wish to reduce the size of their contributions while net recipient states wish to maximize the size of the contributions they receive. Pressures from the former, which began in the 1970s and 1980s when the UK pressed for a major reduction in its net contribution, have increased greatly in recent years and have resulted in 'corrective' mechanisms being established for most net contributing states. These corrective mechanisms signal that the richer states are increasingly reluctant to fund their less well-off partners via the EU budget: a reluctance that may increase, given that, as shown in Chapter 10 in the context of richer eurozone members propping up weaker members, the budget is not the only mechanism for funding some poorer member states.

Budgetary Processes

Since the establishment of MFFs in 1988 there have been two quite separate and distinct EU budgetary processes. One of these leads to MFFs and the other to annual budgets. Both processes will be described here.

Multi-annual financial frameworks

MFF-making processes are the more important of the two processes in that the contents of annual budgets must be set within the guidelines, constraints and ceilings laid down in MFFs. It is not going too far to say that, since 1988, the EU's annual budgets have been largely concerned with filling out the details of MFFs.

Key features of the making of MFFs

As noted earlier in the chapter, prior to the Lisbon Treaty there was no mention of MFFs in the treaties. They came to be used not because they were legally required but because they served a useful purpose. However, because they were developed outside the framework of the treaties, the processes by which MFFs – up to and including the 2007–13 MFF – were drafted, negotiated and contracted were highly fluid and based essentially on 'what worked' and what was politically necessary. The treaty recognition given to MFFs by the Lisbon Treaty has changed this situation a little, but overall it is not having too much impact to date because, with one exception, the new treaty provisions do not go much further than to give treaty status to existing realities. The provisions are set out in Article 312 (2) of the TFEU:

> The Council, acting in accordance with a special legislative procedure, shall adopt a regulation laying down the multiannual financial framework. The Council shall act *unanimously* after obtaining the consent of the European Parliament, which shall act by a majority of its component members. The European Council may, *unanimously*, adopt a decision authorizing the Council to act by a qualified majority when adopting the regulation referred to in the first subparagraph. (Emphasis added.)

The second of these paragraphs sets out the new provision, giving the European Council the power to authorize that a MFF be adopted by the Council via QMV. It seems most unlikely, however, that this power will ever be exercised, given the political sensitivities that exist on MFFs.

The making of each MFF is, of course, unique (see Nugent 2010, pp. 403–6 for an account of the making of the 2007–13 MFF). None the less, a number of recurring features are apparent.

First, the decision-making process is protracted. It may be said to formally begin with the issuing by the Commission of a draft MFF and end with the EP giving its consent to the MFF that has been agreed by the European Council. This process has normally taken about two years. If, however, preparation by the Commission is added to the beginning of the processes, then the time period is approximately doubled.

Second, the process is highly politicized and contentious – which, of course, is why it is also protracted. One reason why the process is so politicized and contentious is that MFFs bring different national economic needs and political preferences to the political surface, not least in the form of the many differences that exist between member states regarding the extent to which they wish to see particular policy activities supported by EU funds.

Third, key final decisions are taken at the highest political level on an intergovernmental basis. That is, they are taken by the European Council acting by unanimity.

Fourth, the overarching nature of matters covered by MFFs, coupled with the fact that final decisions are taken by the European Council, means that at Council level most of the work is handled by the General Affairs Council. This contrasts with the annual budgetary procedure, where the Ecofin Council is the main Council player.

Fifth, unlike in the annual budgetary procedure, where it has long been a co-decision-maker with the Council, until the Lisbon Treaty the EP had no formal powers in relation to MFFs. It did what it could to exercise influence, but it could not be said to have exercised anything other than a very modest influence over the final contents of MFFs. The fact that the Lisbon Treaty gave the EP a treaty-based power of consent has brought it into MFF-making at an earlier stage and made it more influential. So too will a concession extracted by the EP from the Council in the late stages of the 2011 annual budget-making process under which the incoming Council presidencies agreed, on a non-binding basis, to engage with MEPs on the 2014–20 MFF. But, the treaty change and political promise will not necessarily result in the EP becoming *very* influential. After all, it had a political power of consent on MFFs prior to the Lisbon Treaty and that had only a limited effect.

Sixth, and finally, MFFs have not brought about, and there is little foreseeable prospect of them ever bringing about, major changes in the levels or nature of budgetary expenditure. It is true that there have been some shifts, especially in the first two MFFs – those of 1988–92 and 1993–9 – which resulted in not insignificant increases in the total size of the budget and in the proportion of the budget assigned to cohesion policies. But, when placed in the wider context of overall public revenue-raising and spending throughout the EU, even these changes were relatively modest.

Explaining the only modest changes effected by MFFs and the prospects for significant budgetary changes

Given that the nature of the EU and the demands on its budget have changed so much over the years, what explains the slow pace of budgetary change? Why has the total size of the budget remained so small and so stable in relative terms when new and potentially high-spending policy issue areas – such as the CFSP and Europe 2020 – have assumed increasingly important positions in the EU's policy portfolio? A number of features of budgetary processes combine to provide the answer to this seeming puzzle, with three features that have already been described in this chapter being especially important: the unanimity requirement for MFF decisions; the desire by net contributing states that there should be a reasonable level of *juste retour*; and the opposition of net contributors to budgetary increases. These features mean that a wide range of accommodations have to be made if MFFs are to be agreed, which drives decisional outcomes in the directional of being restricted to modest changes.

Given these obstacles, what is the foreseeable prospect of MFFs being able to bring about significant budgetary changes? If there are to be future significant changes, they are likely to arise from extra-treaty factors. There are, as Schild (2008, pp. 533–5) has shown, several possible ways in which such factors could act as catalysts of change, including:

- budgetary deals being linked to a broader agenda of integrative steps (as in the 1980s and early 1990s, when the internal market and the EMU became linked to an increase in the size of the structural funds);
- changes in the policy environment (possibly brought about, for example, by the eurozone crisis);
- changes in the interests of individual member states (such as in reaction to more extreme climate change or energy dependence);
- changes in the configuration of member states (as with the admission of many poorer states in the 2004–7 enlargement – which has led to pressure to reform the CAP); and
- strong institutional leadership (the classic example of such leadership being that provided by Jacques Delors who, when President of the Commission, was pro-active in taking advantage of circumstances to help drive through the increases in the overall budget and structural fund spending of the first two MFFS).

If any of these possibilities occurs, and even more so if a number of them occur simultaneously, a 'window of opportunity' (Keeler, 1993; Kingdon, 1995) could arise for an MFF to be used to bring about substantial budgetary reform. With Europe 2020-related economic growth policies being arguably particularly under-funded, and with such policy areas as external relations and internal security arguably also in need of more EU-level funding, such a substantial reform would appear likely to make the EU budget more attuned to the EU's policy needs.

Annual budgets

Before the use of MFFs there often were, especially in the early to mid-1980s, fierce battles between the Council and the EP during the annual budgetary process. The use of MFFs has served, as was intended, to take much of the political heat out of the process. The contents of annual budgets are still contested, but the room for manoeuvre and contestation is now more constrained.

Prior to the coming into force of the Lisbon Treaty, the formal arrangements for making the EU's annual budgets involved the Council having the last word over compulsory expenditure and the EP having the last word over non-compulsory expenditure, while the budget as whole had to be approved by both the Council and the EP. As for the procedure and timetable for making the budget, a rather complex two-reading procedure existed which, if all went well, ended with EP approval of the budget at its December plenary session.

The Lisbon Treaty simplified and tightened the procedure. The main ways in which it did so was by abolishing the distinction between compulsory and non-compulsory expenditure, by giving the Council and EP equal budgetary powers, and reducing the procedure to one reading plus a conciliation stage. An outline of the post-Lisbon Treaty procedure is set out in Box 14.1, and an outline of it in operation is given in Box 14.2 where the main stages in the making of the 2011 budget are summarized.

Implementation of the budget

The implementation of the EU's budget is managed in three broad ways:

- The greater part of budgetary expenditure, covering agriculture and cohesion funds and amounting

Box 14.1

Main stages and timetable in the making of the annual budget

- The Budget Commissioner and the Budget DG carry the main responsibility within the Commission for drawing up the draft budget. In preparing the draft they are subject to many constraints and pressures. Among the constraints are that annual budgets must be set within the financial ceilings of the MFF applying, must take note of Commission and Council work programmes, and must be able to fund ongoing commitments. Among the pressures are priorities being advocated by numerous EU policy actors: for example, Commission DGs, member states, MEPs and sectional interests. During the course of preparing the draft, the Budget Commissioner and officials from the Budget DG hold many meetings to enable interested parties to explain and justify their budgetary preferences. The meetings include at least one formal trilogue meeting with representatives of the Council and EP. When the preparation of the draft budget has been completed, the Budget Commissioner presents it to the other Commissioners. All must agree on its contents and when this agreement is reached the proposals, which must be issued by no later than 1 September (but which in practice are issued much earlier), become the draft budget.
- The work of the Council and the EP on the annual budget begins long before the Commission's draft is issued formally, with both institutions seeking to influence what the Commission puts into its draft.
- The Council must adopt its position on the draft budget, if necessary by a qualified majority, by 1 October. The detailed work is undertaken by the Budget Committee, a working group of national budgetary officials that reports to COREPER, which in turn reports to the Ecofin Council.
- If within forty-two days of receiving the Council's position the EP either approves the position or has not taken a decision, the budget is deemed to have been adopted. (Given that there are always significant differences between the Council and the EP on the contents of the budget – both on the overall total [the EP always prefers a larger budget than the Council] and on specific items – neither of these eventualities is likely ever to occur.)
- If within the forty-two days the EP adopts amendments by a majority of its component members, a Conciliation Committee composed of an equal number of members of the Council and the EP must be convened. (This is always likely to happen.)
- If, within ten days of receiving the EP's amendments the Council approves all of them, the Conciliation Committee will not meet. (This is most unlikely to happen.)
- The Conciliation Committee has the task of reaching an agreement on the budget by a qualified majority of the Council representatives and a majority of the EP representatives. If no agreement is reached within twenty-one days, the Commission must submit a revised draft budget.
- The budget that is agreed in the Conciliation Committee is referred to the EP and Council for their agreement within fourteen days. If one of the institutions rejects the agreed budget, the Commission must submit a revised draft budget – though in the case of EP approval and Council rejection EP amendments can be retained by a vote of a majority of its component members and three-fifths of the votes cast. (This last provision is somewhat unrealistic, because it would involve the Council rejecting by qualified majority a text it supported by a qualified majority in conciliation.)
- If Parliament does not approve the budget by 1 January, a provisional budget comes into effect based on 'provisional twelfths'; that is, spending is limited to the monthly expenditure of the previous year. The Council and Parliament must then continue to negotiate until they reach an agreement. Such an eventuality has not occurred since the creation of MFFs.

Box 14.2

The making of the 2011 budget

27 April 2010	The Commission presents its draft budget, which calls for a 5.9% increase in payments.
12 August	The Council adopts its position on the draft budget. Seven governments had favoured a freeze in overall spending (Austria, the Czech Republic, Denmark, Finland, the Netherlands, Sweden and the UK) but a compromise is agreed on a 2.9% increase. The position is adopted by written procedure and with the seven member states voting against.
20 October	The EP adopts its position on the draft budget. It calls for a 6.0 % increase, with the general aim being to restore the cuts made by the Council to the Commission's draft.
26 October–15 November	The Conciliation Committee works to try and reconcile the different positions of the Council and the EP. Negotiations focus increasingly around attempts by the EP delegation to extract political concessions (see below) in exchange for accepting most of the Council's demands on the contents of the budget.
15 November	The Conciliation Committee fails to reach agreement on the budget. The EP accepts most of the Council's position on spending, including the overall cap of 2.9%, but insists on three political issues linked to the budget: (i) that it be given a formal role in the negotiations on the 2014–20 MFF (the Netherlands, Sweden and the UK are to the fore among a group of member states opposed to this); (ii) that a process should be launched which could lead to changes in the budget's own resources system; (iii) that a mechanism of greater flexibility be incorporated into the budget to allow for very small transfers (amounting to only 0.03% of GNI) between budget headings.
26 November	The Commission issues (several days earlier than had been expected) a revised budget that includes formulas designed to bridge the gaps between the Council and the EP.
7 December	Representatives of the Commission, the Council and the EP begin talks that result in compromises which produce an agreement.
15 December	The EP approves the budget, by 508 votes to 141. The budget provides for a 2.9% increase in expenditure and wording that is acceptable to the EP on the three disputed issues.

to around 80 per cent of total spending, is handled on a *shared management* basis. That is, the Commission and the member states are both responsible for ensuring that budgetary funds are spent in the manner for which they have been assigned. In practice, this means that, on the submission of appropriate documentation from national agencies – which includes the agencies agreeing to the Commission monitoring the substantive and financial progress of programmes – funds are transferred to member states for spending and distribution. The nature and regularity of the monitoring undertaken by the Commission varies between policy areas and programmes.

- Most other budgetary expenditure – covering virtually everything from research to educational programmes and amounting to around 18 per cent of total spending – is handled on a *direct management* basis. That is, the Commission manages the funds itself. In doing so, the Commission naturally liaises closely with fund applicants and beneficiaries in the member states, but it alone is responsible for how the money is spent.

- The third type of implementation – which involves EU activities in international forums and operations, and which accounts for only around 2 per cent of total spending – involves *management by third countries and international partners.*

Whatever management form it takes, all budgetary spending is subject to internal and external scrutiny. Internal scrutiny is the overall responsibility of the Internal Audit Service (IAS), which was created as a separate DG in 2001 as part of the reform of the Commission undertaken following the revelation in the late 1990s of unsatisfactory financial management practices. The IAS is charged with ensuring the overall quality of financial management and internal control systems. As part of this, the IAS undertakes audits of various kinds across the Commission and in European agencies and other bodies receiving funds from the budget. It also scrutinizes the annual activity reports – covering relevant information on funding programmes – which DGs, European agencies and other bodies must submit. Supporting the IAS are directorates and units of various kinds – with names such as 'budgetary control', 'management quality' and 'audit' – within the main spending DGs, European agencies and other bodies. An important task of these directorates and units is usually to carry out audit missions in member states. The number, nature and location of these audits are determined mainly by risk analyses undertaken by the DGs responsible.

External scrutiny is, as was shown in Chapter 6, undertaken by the Court of Auditors, which examines EU revenue and expenditure accounts and provides the Council and EP with an annual statement of assurance on the reliability of the accounts and the legality and reliability of the associated transactions. The Court operates, however, on the basis of only relatively limited resources and is often hampered by difficulties in gaining the information it wants from relevant agencies in the member states. It is able to examine only a small proportion of EU expenditure and its statement of assurance cannot cover the reliability of all financial transactions. None the less, the Court's annual reports provide the main basis on which the Council and EP decide whether to give the Commission discharge on the implementation of budgets, with the discharge scheduled to be given no later than 16 months after the end of the budgetary year in question.

The general theme of the Court's reports is usually along the lines that while the administrative and control systems for handling EU revenue and expenditure are broadly satisfactory, problems exist regarding the sufficiency and independence of 'front-line' inspections in the member states. Inevitably, given their dominance of budgetary expenditure, financial weaknesses and irregularities in respect of the CAP and the cohesion funds are the targets of most criticisms.

The Commission's standard responses to the Court of Auditors' criticisms almost invariably, and not unreasonably, refers to the fact that approximately 80 per cent of the EU's budget is managed on a front-line basis by agencies in the member states – over which the Commission has only limited control.

Evaluating budgetary processes

How do EU budgetary processes rate in terms of the key evaluative criteria of accountability, transparency and democracy?

With regard to them being accountable, *political* accountability to taxpayers is channelled through the policy-making roles of the European Council and, to a lesser extent, the EP, for MFFs; and through the Council of Ministers and the EP, as the joint budgetary authority, for annual budgets. Accountability through the European Council and the Council of Ministers is, of course, exercised at stages removed from the taxpayers themselves (with the number of stages removed depending on the nature of national political systems), while the accountability that operates through the EP is weak given the low levels of public understanding of the EP's budgetary powers and roles. The Council's and EP's discharge responsibilities to the Commission in respect of its implementation of annual budgets provides another dimension of political accountability. *Administrative* accountability is exercised primarily via the Court of Auditors' examinations of revenues and expenditures, and via the investigations of alleged misuses of funds that are undertaken by the European Anti-Fraud Office (OLAF).

The budget is transparent inasmuch as MFFs and annual budgets are fully and clearly laid out in the *Official Journal*. Obligations incurred by loan guarantees are also specified. Important aspects of budgetary process are, however, much less transparent, most notably the various proceedings that occur in the European Council and Council of Ministers with respect to MFFs, and in the Council of Ministers with respect to annual budgets. The latter is, however, partly offset by the Council having to share information with the EP during the conciliation processes that are necessary for annual budgets to be approved.

The most frequent complaint levelled in the context of the budget is the lack of democratic linkage between the European polity and revenue generation and expenditure. In raising this issue, one lands squarely in the debate between intergovernmentalists and supranationalists. Intergovernmentalists argue that the budget and budgetary process, like all EU policies and processes, have a reasonable democratic base, stemming primarily from the decision-making roles of the European Council and the Council of Ministers. Comprised of heads of government and ministers of democratically-elected governments, these institutions bring democratic representation to the heart of budget-making and ensure that the interests of national polities are articulated. 'Federalists' dismiss this view, suggesting that it misses the key point that the EU is not an intergovernmental organization but rather is a quasi-federal system. What is missing in the EU is the direct budgetary relationship between the European citizenry and the EU, which is a defining feature of federal systems. Federal systems tax their citizens on both the national and state/provincial level. So, too, some transfers from the federal budget are to individuals, by far most of these dealing with social welfare. But because 80 per cent of EU budgetary funds are transferred directly to national agencies, this leaves little opportunity to forge fiscal connections between the people and the EU system. Nor do Europeans see their 'tax euros' at work in Brussels, because the taxes they pay to support the EU are hidden in national budgets.

Conclusions

This chapter has addressed a range of matters concerning the nature, the shaping and the composition of the EU's budget. The budget has been shown to

be small in relative terms, and in consequence – and despite the political heat that budgetary matters can generate – the overall policy impact of the budget is relatively modest. The impact is, of course, significant with respect to agricultural and cohesion policies, where budgetary expenditure is considerable. The impact is also significant on the national economies of a few small member states that benefit significantly from budgetary funding. But, despite such examples of a significant budgetary impact, the fact is that the EU is not a fiscal federal system in which the centre raises, distributes and redistributes a large amount of funding for an array of policy purposes. This is because the policy areas that are the main consumers of public funds – such as health, social welfare and education – remain firmly located within national budgets and therefore also under national control. The EU is not in the business of running expensive policy programmes or of transferring vast amount of funds between states or individuals.

The chapter has paid a good deal of attention to budgetary revenues and expenses, both of which indicate a number of significant things about the nature of the EU. On the revenue side, all sources are 'own resources', which immediately distinguishes the EU from traditional IGOs. Of these own resources, customs duties and agricultural levies are remitted to Brussels, apart from an administrative fee. But this is not, as is sometimes thought, indicative of a fiscal union, let alone a sovereign system, because customs unions also pool collected duties and redistribute them among members according to a negotiated formula. Nevertheless, this arrangement is undeniably a measure of integration that is absent in IGOs. The VAT revenue source also indicates a measure of integration, though it is collected via the member states rather than directly by the EU. As for the GNI source, this displays features that are strongly reminiscent of the national contributions based on size and wealth that are the main feature of the funding of IGOs.

On the expenditure side, the budget is directed, in the main, towards offsetting unwanted market consequences, particularly with respect to agriculture and cohesion. Regarding agriculture, in a free and open internal market, and an internal market that has been obliged increasingly in world trade negotiations to lower its external protections, much of the EU farming industry would struggle to survive economically without subsidies. Regarding cohesion policy, less productive sectors and geographical areas are unable to protect themselves in a free and open internal market from more competitive areas because market rules prevent the construction of 'artificial' barriers to trade. In response to this, the EU has adopted and developed a range of 'non-market' measures designed to try to contain, and if possible narrow, the extent of regional – and to some extent social – disparities within its borders. But the extent of redistribution that is undertaken is held firmly in check.

The small size of the budget combined with the fact that so much of it is devoted to agriculture and cohesion does, of course, mean there is little room left for policies that are useful fiscal tools under economic union, such as educational training and workers' protection. Nor is there much funding remaining for policy areas such as foreign policy and freedom and justice policies, which are very important in sovereign states and help to make them *political* unions.

Turning to decision-making processes, there are two budgetary procedures: one that produces MFFs and the other that produces annual budgets. The first of these is the most important in that it is within financial frameworks that the annual budgetary process must work. MFFs are prepared and shaped by the Commission, but all of the more contestable aspects of them are ultimately decided – on an intergovernmental basis – in the European Council. If Commission proposals are too far out of line with what is politically acceptable, as they were with the 2007–13 MFF, they will be rejected. As for the EP, it has been kept largely to the margins of MFF-making processes and has exercised only limited influence. The extent of the Parliament's MFF roles and influence has been strengthened by being given the power of consent by the Lisbon Treaty, but its position continues to fall far short of its place in the annual budgetary process where it exercises equal budgetary powers with the Council.

Significantly in terms of the intergovernmental–supranational balance, all revenue-raising decisions are solely in the hands of the national governments. Any decision to change the revenue base requires Council, which in effect means European Council, approval by unanimity. The Commission has called repeatedly for a system of genuine own resources – based perhaps on a common European VAT, a European corporate tax, an energy tax, or a financial transactions tax – but so far to no avail. It is, however, possible (though not probable) that the policy window opened by the eurozone debt and banking crises will generate the needed support for reform.

Chapter 15
Achievements, Challenges and Prospects

We have framed much of our explanation of the evolution of EU policies and policy processes through a framework we set out in Chapter 2 based on the economics of regional integration and the politics of federalism. On the economic side, the internal market has always been at the EU's 'policy core'. However, the demands of this core have been voracious, with the aim of trying to ensure that the market is truly 'common' having resulted in a spreading out from the rather nebulous attachment to the 'four freedoms' in the EEC Treaty to a situation whereby the market in some way touches virtually every area of public policy. Many EU policies that are not typically connected to the market have been brought within the EU framework at least partly for market-related reasons. Thus, as we explained in Chapters 8 and 13, an important reason why foreign and defence policies have been developed has been to support the expanding internal market, with effective foreign relations providing opportunities for opening up foreign markets to EU goods and services. Similarly, a more integrated European defence policy helps to support economies of scale in weaponry development and production in a high-tech, dynamic industry that strengthens the EU's knowledge base and fuels demand for technicians, engineers and scientists.

But while the economic integration model goes a long way towards explaining over half a century of advancing regional economic integration in Europe, it is not equipped to explain the nature of European governance. Of the several competing politics-based models available, it is our view that a federal approach is a particularly useful framework for exploring the evolution of the policy portfolio, the many and variegated horizontal linkages among member states, the vertical policy and policy process relationship between Brussels and the member states, and the practice of experimentation (and, therefore, flexibility) that has become such a defining attribute of EU governance and policy-making. This is not to say that the EU is a fully developed and functioning federal system, but it is to suggest that it is closer to being a federal system than is often recognized and that its development does display federal dynamics.

Political geographers suggest that political territory can be organized in four main ways, along a continuum from the most centralized to the least, as follows: unitary, regional, federal, and confederal. There are examples of the first three territorial types among the EU's member states, with unitary predominating (as is the case throughout the world); Italy, Spain and the UK are regional (because of the substantial devolution to regional authorities); and Austria, Belgium and Germany are federal. The EU, however, is generally thought to be 'unclassifiable' on this continuum: it is *sui generis* or, to use the colourful phrase coined by Jacques Delors and since used by José Manuel Barroso, it is 'an unidentified political object' (Barroso, 2007). We lean towards the opinion that this notion of uniqueness is overstated. In the more than 50 years since the EEC's establishment, sufficient evidence has accumulated to rethink the 'uniqueness' hypothesis. We think that the evolution of policies and policy processes in the EU point to a federal dynamic where some policies are characterized by horizontal governance (confederal) and others by federal management – that is, with a great deal of responsibility ceded to 'Brussels'. Throughout this book we have discussed historical parallels between the EU's development and that of its closest relative on the federalism continuum – the US – in order to shed light on the evolution of the EU. Among parallels we have used from the US are the role of the federal court in shaping the internal market and the controversies in the US with respect to the federalization of immigration policy.

While there are admittedly few examples of the EU being more federal than the US, they do exist! Juenger (1998, pp. 529, 532), for example, argues that the so-called Brussels regime (derived from the Brussels Convention, which focuses on EU commercial law and civil law), 'established a system that is not merely comparable but superior to the practice of the American courts under the Full Faith and Credit Clause ... rules on jurisdiction are not only more clearly delineated; they are also better attuned to the protection of fundamental values'. Unlike in the US, where the Supreme Court 'tends to treat all litigants alike', the Brussels Convention 'bestows jurisdictional privileges upon certain weaker parties, such as support claimants, policyholders, and consumers, who are allowed to sue in their home states' (ibid., p. 532). Other legal scholars also find that 'full faith and credit' recognition is stronger in the EU than in the US (see, for example, Hay, 2007; Spamann, 2001). As noted in Chapter 2, energy and college tuition fees furnish other examples of the EU taking a more federalized approach than that practiced in the US.

We think that the two disciplines from which our federal integration approach draws – economics and political science – combine to offer not only a comprehensive explanation of the past, present and likely future direction of EU policy development and policy-making, but also a dynamic explanation. Economic integration theory offers a dynamic model because it predicts that economic integration in one area engenders unanticipated consequences in other policy areas, which can only be resolved through further integration. Federalist theory is dynamic because federalism operates through intense and constant political bargaining – and not just the bargaining based on ideology that is at the heart of politics in modern nation states, but also bargaining based on territorial affiliations and interests.

Policy Achievements

In Chapter 1 we noted that the breadth of the EU's policy portfolio has so expanded over the years that the EU now is involved in just about every possible area of public policy. Moreover, in many of these areas – from agriculture to cohesion, and from fishing to foreign policy – the EU policy responsibilities are very significant. Naturally, with so many different interests having a stake in the EU's policy responsibilities and with there being so many different views as to what the precise nature of the responsibilities should be, an array of judgements exist regarding how successful the EU has been in policy terms. But, whatever the judgements may be of the degrees of success, that there have been major policy achievements is beyond doubt. This may be illustrated by briefly taking four very important policy areas that have promoted Europeanization and that have been prominent in 'federalizing' Europe. The four areas are the internal market, environmental policy, monetary union, and the AFSJ.

The internal market

Jean Monnet, the best known of the early architects of European integration, once remarked: 'If we were beginning the European Community all over again, we should begin with culture' (quoted in Van Ham, 2000, p. 31). Jacques Delors, the European Commission President between 1985 and 1995, and arguably the principal political force behind the internal market project, also recognized that the market, by itself, does not make Europeans: 'No one will fall in love with a common market; you need something else' (quoted in Columbus, 2004, p. 105). Yet as the US experience with federalism demonstrates, and as Watts (1997, p. 5) cannily observes, the market economy is an important integrating force, so much so that 'people do not have to like each other in order to benefit from each other'.

Unquestionably, the internal market has been the EU's greatest policy achievement. It is still not completely open, with policy-makers continuing to have to be much engaged in seeking to remove resilient national protections of various sorts. But despite difficulties in some areas, the market has helped to bring the prosperity and stability to Europe that its founders predicted; enabled Europe to compete with those countries that have very large and dynamic internal markets, notably the US and Japan; and positioned Europe to adapt to competition from new market entrants, of which the BRIC countries are the most prominent.

The internal market has also been a signal success in terms of driving overall European integration and the 'federalization' of other policy areas – so much so that it can be argued that almost every policy area has an internal market dimension.

Environmental policy

The EU's policy-making role has expanded to cover virtually the full range of environmental issues, so that now more than 300 legal acts deal with such issues as sustainable development, the disposal of waste, pollution in its many forms, nature and biodiversity, and climate change.

An important aspect of EU environmental policy is the degree to which so many aspects of it are either centralized (for example, vehicle emissions) or shared with member states (for example, climate change). The *Brusselization* of EU policy is in striking contrast to the more dualist federal approach to environmental policy that exists in Canada and the US.

Perhaps more than any other policy, environmental policy has become tied closely to other policies. This is seen most obviously with policies such as agriculture, fishing, climate change, and energy efficiency and security, but it is also observed elsewhere. So, for example, cohesion funds are used in part to further environmental policy objectives, as is seen most readily in the CEECs – many of which were formerly heavy polluters – where the dispersal of cohesion funds is often closely linked to environmental projects. The 7th Environmental Action Programme (from 2013 onwards) is tied in particular to the internal market through the promotion of green technology as part of the Europe 2020 strategy.

Most EU policies dealing with market failure are focused on preventing a 'race to the bottom'. Environmental policy certainly contains this dimension, but it is also focused on 'trading up'. This is because the 'Green' member states have successfully promoted EU-wide higher standards – in some cases by tying environmental rules to competitiveness. Furthermore, Green states have been able to ensure that EU law does not prevent them from adopting higher domestic standards than those specified in EU laws – provided such national standards do not distort the operation of the market.

On the international stage, the EU has replaced the US as the leading international environmental advocate. Thus the EU led on the Kyoto Protocol and pioneered the global emissions trading system. However – as is inevitable with so many developed, developing and underdeveloped countries being reluctant to give too much priority to environmental protection over industrial expansion, and with the US increasingly reluctant to be the global environmental champion that it was in former years (as illustrated by its performance at Copenhagen) – the EU's attempted global environmental leadership has had only limited results.

Monetary union

While some of the EU's founders may privately have dreamt of a common European currency, in the early years after the Second World War politicians did not dare to entertain openly such a chimerical notion. Yet, by 1992, the leaders of the EU's member states had agreed, in the Maastricht Treaty, to establish a monetary union, and they subsequently delivered on their promise to have the single currency system in place by 1999. However, as the financial crisis that enveloped the eurozone a decade after its establishment showed, the foundations on which monetary union were built were too narrow. As many economists had warned in the 1990s when monetary union was being created, such a union – and in particular one that was planning to include economies with very different levels of competitiveness – could only work in the long-term if it was part of a broader economic, and in particular fiscal, union. In consequence, as shown in Chapter 10 and as further discussed below, as the seriousness of the global economic and financial crisis and then the eurozone crisis became ever clearer from 2010/11, EU policy-makers, and in particular eurozone policy-makers, began to edge towards some form of fiscal union and – even more tentatively – political union.

But while the political determination of some EU policy-makers that there should be a monetary union at almost any cost resulted in the union that was founded and launched being based on inadequate foundations, it is testimony to how far the policy integration process has proceeded that a monetary union was capable of being established, albeit one with not all member states involved. Moreover, it should be recognized that despite its difficulties, the monetary union can claim policy successes: it has helped to maintain low inflation and interest rates; it has promoted structural change in member state economies; and it has established itself as the second most important international currency.

The area of freedom, security and justice

Despite the internal market supposedly being based on four freedoms – of goods, services, capital and people – comparatively little attention was paid in the EU's early years to the last of these four. However, since the late 1990s free movement of people has been a rapidly developing policy area and has featured prominently in the EU's attempts to build an area of freedom, security and justice.

The AFSJ may be thought of as the EU's 'people' policy in that its concerns are focused on the security of citizens and on their ability to circulate freely throughout Europe so as to enjoy holidays, to conduct business, to marry residents of other EU member states, and to forge all the numerous personal and professional connections that citizens living in different regions enjoy unimpeded in federal systems. But, as we noted in Chapter 11, AFSJ has been one of Europe's most contested policy areas. This is because it inevitably exchanges the ability of the state to assert unilateral sovereignty over its territory and citizens to a sovereignty that is increasingly based on European prerogatives. However, in the course of federalizing AFSJ, the member states have discovered common

denominators in civil liberties, civil rights, policing, immigration, asylum and border control that have made co-operation at the European level possible.

More than in any other major EU policy area, AFSJ today illustrates the ability of the EU to adopt flexible policy processes to advance policy priorities. This is seen in the wide range of policy modes and policy instruments that are used. Hence, the AFSJ has developed through an inventive combination of co-operative federalism (for example, asylum policy, and police and judicial co-operation), dual federalism (border controls), and horizontal federalism (civil jurisprudence). Nevertheless, AFSJ faces major challenges, not least in developing a common immigration policy and an effective European internal security network.

Challenges

While remarkable in the extent to which they have developed as EU policies, the internal market, the environment, monetary union and the AFSJ have all experienced bumps, if not sometimes 'crises', along the way. So, for example, while the internal market was nominally 'completed' in 1992, EU policy-makers have since constantly had to deal with pressures for 'more' market opening as new concerns have emerged. Among these concerns have been features of the market that have been seen as either seriously impeding its full realization (as with concerns in the 1990s and 2000s about the continuing protection of many services) or as dealing inadequately with market failure (as with financial regulation today). Immigration policy also illustrates the importance of bumps and crises as, on the one hand, immigration pressures have mounted as more non-EU citizens have wanted to gain EU entry and, on the other hand, as the governments of some member states have become increasingly resistant to an external border policy they regard as being too open. The ongoing debate over a common European immigration policy and the influence on governments exerted by the opposition of electorates and far-right political parties to immigration (and cultural diversity) has served as a reminder of the nature of compromise and the limits of federal solutions among sovereign states.

The EU is thus never short of policy and policy-making challenges. Three particularly difficult challenges currently facing the EU are now considered. The first two are direct policy challenges: the need for stronger economic policy co-ordination and management; and the relative weaknesses of European foreign and defence policies. The third challenge is not a policy challenge *per se*, but speaks to the nature of public support for the European integration project.

Economic policy co-ordination and management

As shown in Chapters 9 and 10, the EU has a number of policies focused on trying to provide more co-ordinated economic policy between the member states. These polices take various forms and have different specific purposes. So, for example, the EMU-related policy that places restraints on the budgetary policies of member states – restraints that are legally enforceable in the case of eurozone members – is intended to create an economic environment that fosters economic stability and responsibility. The various policies and programmes that are located within Europe 2020 are intended to help promote economic growth and employment.

Economic policy co-ordination, however, has not been a great success. This has been the case most obviously with eurozone economic co-ordination, where the spiralling public debts of member states were a major reason behind the eurozone crisis that unfolded from 2010. As the sovereign debt and banking crises became more acute, EU, and more particularly eurozone, member states moved step-by-step (eurozone leaders met over a dozen times between 2010 and 2012) towards fiscal federalism, most notably through the creation of bailout funds to purchase sovereign debt and the signing in 2012 by 25 member states of the Treaty on Stability, Coordination and Governance – the so-called Fiscal Compact (see Chapter 10). It was, however, a very slow movement, with indebted states – notably Ireland, Portugal, Greece and Spain – pressing for loans and the pooling of eurozone debt, and creditor states – led by Germany – being very cautious about loans and the pooling of national debts, and insisting that debt assistance must be accompanied by guarantees that recipients of loans must adopt more austere public expenditure policies and restructure their national economies.

Clearly, given the intensity of the differing national interests and policy preferences associated with a fiscal union, it will take some years to be fully created and probably will not include all member states. However, constructing a banking union should be easier. The need for one arises from the fact that, as the economic integration model predicts, integration in one area puts pressure on others: free movement of capital has had unintended consequences on the stability of Europe's financial system, requiring still more integration with respect to the regulation of the financial industry, the monitoring of the behaviour of banks, and protecting citizens' savings. Regarding the last of these, nervous bank customers in states such as Ireland, Greece and Spain have worried about the safety of their deposits in those banks holding sovereign debt and questionable mortgages. At a minimum, an EU-wide, or at least eurozone-wide, deposit insurance scheme is thus needed to reduce runs on national banks by persuading depositors to keep their money in seemingly vulnerable national banks by guaranteeing deposits at the EU-level rather than through national deposit insurance schemes under threat of bankruptcy.

This building of pressures for a banking union led in June 2012 to eurozone leaders agreeing that bailout funds from the European Stability Mechanism could be used to inject capital directly to recapitalize struggling banks (rather than being funnelled through governments and thereby increasing their national debt). The price for this debt mutualization was more political union, with eurozone leaders agreeing in principle to the creation of a single banking supervisory agency run by the ECB. The remit and powers of the agency were left to be determined in the legislative process that would establish it – with the agency's strongest supporters envisaging a system operating along the lines of the US Federal Reserve System – which has the authority not only to supervise bank operations but also the power to keep afloat troubled banks, and merge or close banks.

The eurozone leaders also inched forward in 2012 towards fiscal union with respect to policies that are intended to help promote economic growth and employment. During the economic and financial crisis, citizens in EU member states suffering under government austerity measures (tax increases and spending cuts) have increasingly made it clear to their political leaders – not least via the ballot box – that they do not expect governments to set growth-based policies aside. But the problem is that the internal market's competition rules, the existence of the euro (which means eurozone members are unable to devalue to gain competitive advantage), and SGP spending rules in the form of national deficit and debt ceilings, have created a situation whereby there are restrictions on what growth policies can be pursued. Essentially, they must be grounded in productive investments, such as via R&D and human resource development. However, by mid-2012, eurozone leaders had come to accept that the EU should assume a greater role in actively promoting growth as a necessary companion to 'austerity' measures. There are therefore some hopes that Europe 2020 and related measures might produce on some of the lofty objectives that have been identified in terms of economic growth and employment creation. But, caution is warranted, not least because it is questionable whether EU-level interventionist measures, which necessarily will be only modestly funded, can substitute for the fact that labour does not – because of language and cultural barriers that do not exist to the same degree in the US – easily move about Europe from low-growth to high-growth areas.

In all probability, the next few years will see the further building of both a fiscal union and a banking union for eurozone states along the broad lines suggested in a 2012 report entitled *Towards a Genuine Economic and Monetary Union*, written by Herman Van Rompuy (European Council President) in collaboration with José Manuel Barroso (European Commission President), Jean-Claude Juncker (Eurogroup President), and Mario Draghi (ECB President) (European Council, 2012). Political and economic realities will mean that the fiscal union will need to ensure national budgetary responsibility, but also include mechanisms for assisting member states that are facing serious budgetary imbalances. Thus the fiscal union will probably need to provide for the issuance of eurobonds and for the ECB to be charged with promoting growth directly (even if doing so may pose a risk of inflation). So, too, a fiscal body (such as an EU Finance Ministry) with meaningful democratic accountability (through oversight from the EP and possibly also national parliaments) will probably need to be established in the long run to monitor the financial health of member states (as provided for in the Fiscal Compact), to co-ordinate tax policy, to support

growth measures, and to reduce the moral hazard risk inherent in fiscal federalism.

External foreign and security policies

Much has been made of where the EU and classic federal systems most obviously depart from each other in their policy competences – in their very different responsibilities for foreign and defence policy. In this context, it is relevant to note that some federalist theorists have thought the quest for external security has been the critical catalyst in federalization. For William Riker (1964, p. 11), for example, previously independent sovereign units have sought the increased tax base of a larger internal market as a means to an end – the financial means to build a stronger military capability.

However, we do not view the comparative weakness of the EU's foreign and external security policies as undermining the usefulness of federal theory in understanding EU policy and policy process development. This is because a desire for common external security is not the only driver of federalization. As economists such as Bela Balassa and James Meade have shown, for example, there are economic precursors and preconditions to political integration (see Chapter 2). And as post-Keynesians have noted, there can be a defining role for fiscal federalism in the establishment of federal systems (see Chapter 10).

Indeed, the role that foreign and external security policies have played in the EU may even be said to provide some support for the federal integration approach. European nations, in co-founding NATO with the US, established a sort of confederal security community that – though not perceived at the time – served as an important first step towards European integration and a useful arrangement to enable Europeans not to have to concentrate too much on their external security. The Atlantic Alliance's security umbrella superseded the necessity to agree a pan-European defence alliance, freeing Europeans to focus their energies on building a common market.

NATO served the security needs of West Europeans rather well until the dissolution of the Soviet Bloc and the Soviet Union in 1989–91 changed everything. Beginning with the Clinton Administration, the US began to re-evaluate NATO as the sole instrument of Western defence co-operation. The US Ambassador to NATO during the George W. Bush Administration,

Victoria Nuland (2008), articulated the US shift in a speech at the Paris Press Club in February 2008, during which she said: 'You will think this is strange, a little suspicious, to have the US Ambassador to NATO come to Paris to say that one of the most important things French leaders can do for global security is to strengthen and build the capacities of the EU.'

Pressures to develop EU foreign and external security policies thus grew in the 1990s, especially as the EU's inability to respond effectively to the Balkan wars became ever more apparent. In consequence, and as was shown in Chapter 13, considerable institutional and policy advances have been made in the 2000s, as is witnessed most obviously by the EU's ability to be able to deploy operational missions of various sorts in locations as diverse as Central Africa, Afghanistan, the Middle East and the Balkans. However, there is still much to be done if the EU is to be a significant international policy player. Because, unlike the situation with trade policy, where the EU acts as one on the international stage, it is not always able to do so under the CFSP and CSDP umbrellas. Having developed as sovereign states, it is only natural that many EU member states have distinctive historical, economic and cultural ties to particular parts of the world, and particular policy preferences that do not always align with the EU's primary goals and objectives. On most of the major foreign policy issues of the day – including the Arab Spring, Iran's nuclear proliferation, Israel and Palestine, Syria, failed and failing states in Africa – the EU has made little traction, even in those cases (such as with the Assad regime in Syria) where the member states have been able to agree and articulate a common position. There remains a sense that so long as the EU lacks a strong and unified foreign policy leadership – which probably needs to include an EU Foreign Minister who can act without a chorus of member state foreign ministers criticizing his/her work – the EU will be unable on many major foreign policy issues to translate its potential prowess into clear objectives and strong actions.

Public support for the EU's policy roles

For a federal or quasi-federal system to survive it must have a *raison d'être* that is recognized by the citizenry. Citizens need to believe that they are better off living in the system than 'going it alone'. While there will always be 'secessionist' murmurings in such systems and complaints about the powers being exercised from the centre, in the EU 'anti-integrationism' is significant and increasing. Evidence for this is seen in the response of EU citizens in November 2011 to the standard *Eurobarometer* question: 'In general, does the EU conjure up for you a very positive, fairly positive, neutral, fairly negative or very negative image?' Just over a quarter – 26 per cent – of respondents said it conjured up either a fairly or very negative image, a figure that was up by 6 per cent from *Eurobarometer*'s spring poll (European Commission, 2011t, p. 20).

In party political terms, ardent Euroscepticism is located mainly in extremist parties, usually on the far right. Given that most EU member states are parliamentary systems, some with low or no electoral thresholds, Eurosceptics can exercise a significant electoral influence: either by pushing national mainstream parties and politicians in a Eurosceptic direction, especially on sensitive issues such as Schengen and open borders; or, as in a few member states, including Austria and the Netherlands, being able to win a sufficient number of parliamentary seats to have a voice in the forming of coalition governments.

For the EU to continue to be part of the solution to the dislocations brought about by globalization, climate change and other frustrating problems, the citizenry need to believe that it is capable of delivering policy solutions. Can, for example the internal market deliver growth, jobs and prosperity? This requires a complex balance of policies, an EU leadership structure that is understandable and recognizable to Europeans, and – arguably above all – national politicians who repeatedly and publically support the European integration project and give voice to its achievements. José Manuel Barroso articulated this view in a headline-grabbing State of the Union address in autumn 2012, in which he argued that European leaders must offer citizens a 'Decisive Deal for Europe' and transform the EU into a 'federation of nation states' (European Commission, 2012x).

Prospects

Can the EU adapt to the many policy challenges it is facing? We think that the federal integration approach is a good framing tool for exploring this question. Two dynamic features of federalist arrangements are of particular use in thinking about the future direction of the EU: reaction to crises and policy flexibility.

Crises and integration

As we noted in Chapter 2, crises have often driven the big integration decisions. This is because individual member states have often been unable to tackle policy problems through national action alone. Thus the increasing lack of international competitiveness of much of European industry spawned the re-launch of the internal market in the 1980s. The EU's failure to exercise much influence over the Balkan wars of the 1990s stimulated the launch and development of the CSDP. And the eurozone debt crisis that began in 2010 has precipitated an overhaul and centralization of financial services regulation across the EU and opened the way to the eurozone moving in the direction of creating a banking union and, beyond that, a fiscal union.

Crises will doubtless continue to be important in shaping and driving EU policy development. As the economic and financial crisis and the climate change crisis both show, there are many pressing issue areas that can only be addressed effectively by member states acting together. The problems are cross-border in nature.

Of course, not all policy challenges and policy development involve crises. But a great many do. Moreover, crises do not just emerge and have to be dealt with at the 'macro' policy level but can exist also at 'lower' levels. An example of this occurred in the mid-1990s when, in response largely to the BSE (mad cow disease) crisis, the EU was forced, suddenly and totally unexpectedly, to develop a more robust food safety regulatory policy. This sudden policy switch illustrates how, while the economic integration model is based on a policy integration sequence tied to the logic of the internal market, politics often derails or postpones this 'rational' sequencing – and can bring about situations that require a federal policy approach.

Flexibility

Policy flexibility

Member states are not affected equally by policy challenges. Nor do they view the nature of challenges in similar ways. In cases where some like-minded member states wish to address a challenge by pressing ahead with deeper integration and some do not, the problem can sometimes be resolved through policy flexibility.

The EU has evolved, as have other quasi-federal and federal systems, to accept policy flexibility as a matter of course. Thus, since the Schengen system began to be created from the mid-1980s without the UK and Ireland, and even more so since the Maastricht Treaty allowed the UK, and later Denmark, to opt out of the EMU, policy differentiation has been an important feature of EU governance (see Chapters 1 and 5). However, Schengen and EMU – which remain the two most high-profile and most-cited examples of major policy areas where differentiation has occurred to date – are not *so* differentiated as they are often portrayed. Regarding Schengen, the UK and Ireland are the only members to have rejected passport-free Europe, and in Ireland's case this has not been a rejection in principle but a consequence of its special links with the UK. However, the UK and Ireland have not rejected free movement of people, and nor would they be permitted to do so. With respect to the eurozone, only Sweden has joined the UK and Denmark in opting-out. The Danish and Swedish governments tried to enter, but were prevented from doing so by their electorates in national referendums. In the UK's case there are very special circumstances accounting for its non-membership: its economy is sufficiently distinctive and dollar-connected for it not being readily apparent that adopting the euro would be advantageous; and British citizens – as many years of *Eurobarometer* polling have shown – have consistently been less enthusiastic about European integration than their continental neighbours.

Some observers think that differentiation threatens the EU's long-run viability (the logic being that once variations in policy participation are permitted, the benefits of co-operation will be traded away through a myriad of extra-EU arrangements). This 'negative' view, however, runs contrary to what we know about federal arrangements – where the ability of constituent units to work together in differing ways is a common and positive feature. So long as the participating units in policy differentiation do not co-operate in such a way as to undermine core features of the federal or quasi-federal entity – most particularly the common market – differentiation usually has the effect of strengthening rather than weakening the federal construction. This is because differentiation permits policy progress in those units of the construction where leaders and citizens are more innovative and adventurous and also in those units where similar conditions lend themselves to close co-operation. Good results from such differentiation can subsequently attract other units to the 'team'.

Differentiation in the form of enhanced co-operation exemplifies the development of horizontal federalism in the EU. Because enhanced co-operation has the advantage of being able to use EU institutions to develop, enact and implement policies, it is a much more stable form of horizontal federalism than the state compacts that are sometimes used in the US in situations where the US Congress has been unwilling to act. Up to the time of writing (autumn 2012) only one piece of legislation – involving the simplifying of divorce procedures in cross-border marriages (Council Regulation 1259/2010), which took effect in June 2012 – has been fully advanced and applied through the enhanced co-operation procedure. However, it is likely that it will come to be used increasingly. Indeed, in 2012, several governments of member states reacted to the strong opposition of other governments to the idea of a financial transactions tax (see Chapter 14) by publicly supporting the idea of asking the Commission to submit a proposal for such a tax under enhanced co-operation. It would be difficult for such a proposal to be adopted – not least because it could well be in breach of the treaty provision that enhanced co-operation measures cannot undermine the internal market or internal competition – but the very fact that the idea has been floated in such a sensitive policy area and attracted significant support indicates an increasing predisposition on the part of member states to consider using enhanced co-operation.

Enhanced co-operation – as a form of horizontal federalism – should not be seen as a substitute for vertical integration, as illustrated by the torturous path the uniform patent law has taken. Unable to agree to the languages for a uniform patent law (and which only Italy and Spain refused to support, because they were dissatisfied that patents must be translated only into English, French or German), the other member states decided to pursue a uniform patent law through enhanced co-operation. The legislative actors (the Council and the EP) agreed to a uniform patent law in 2012. When in the summer of 2012 the British, French and German heads of government, vying to host the future European patent court, struck a deal with respect to the location of the court's central office (Paris) with smaller and specialised offices in London and Munich, the UK extracted a change to the patent law that weakened CJEU jurisdiction over the patent court's rulings. An anticipated positive vote in the July 2012 EP plenary was then postponed by the EP's leadership, on the grounds that the European Council's compromise changed the legislation enough to require renewed consideration, including whether the revised legislation 'infringes EU law' (Wishart, 2012c).

Policy process flexibility

Just as policy flexibility in the EU has grown, so have policy processes taken on an increasing number of forms. And just as policy flexibility has assisted policy development, so have the increasing number of policy process forms made it possible for member states to participate in and develop policy activities that would have been precluded if other policy processes had been used. For example, the use of intergovernmental processes enabled an initially very tentative EU foreign policy to get off the ground with all member states involved, and it has since provided the base for a stronger policy that has increasingly had a fledgling defence policy attached to it. Similarly, macroeconomic policy was initially able to be developed because it was largely based on the semi-voluntaristic OMC, but as the economic and financial crises have increased pressures for more rigorous policies then so have the OMC processes been joined by more robust processes, though with some of them restricted to eurozone members.

This policy process flexibility is resulting in a situation whereby some policies have policy processes that are virtually tailored for them. It is also resulting in a situation that is witnessing an increasing tendency for key policy actors to try to take decisions, or at least to steer decisions, outside formal decision-taking arenas. A meeting held in Rome in June 2102 illustrates just how flexible the EU has become in this regard. The meeting was attended by the German Chancellor, the French President, and the Prime Ministers of Italy and Spain – the leaders of the four largest eurozone states. The meeting was significant because it was held just one week before an important European Council meeting that was scheduled to make vital decisions about the euro. The four who attended the Rome meeting were, in effect, trying (largely unsuccessfully as it turned out because of policy differences between them) to pre-set much of the European Council's outcome. Until relatively recently such a meeting would have generated howls of outrage from the capitals of member states whose leaders were not invited to the meeting, but on this occasion few protests were voiced: the meeting was generally viewed as being just one of the many ways in which the EU conducts its business.

Final Comments

A number of framing devices are available from which students of European integration can select to try to understand the development and nature of the EU (see, for example, Webber, forthcoming). We have offered, with the federal integration approach, a framing device we hope readers will find useful and that they can indeed fruitfully employ themselves in interpreting the complex subject of EU policies and policy processes.

In this book we have endeavoured to provide readers with a well-rounded examination of the past, present and future direction of EU policies and policy-making. In looking to the future, it should be remembered that federal and quasi-federal systems are above all a political bargain rather than a constitutional fact. A structure of institutions and processes is established but the evolution of policy itself is the result of negotiation and compromise among constituent units. At the same time, economics matters and we need to be mindful of the ways in which economic integration in one area triggers challenges and problems in others.

The EU has faced many challenges in the past, but none have been of the magnitude of the trials that have faced it in the wake of the post-2007/8 economic and financial crises, and ensuing sovereign debt and banking crises. These crises have brought to the fore the unforgiving logic of the economic integration model, where a monetary union cannot be sustained without a fiscal union, and arguably also a political union. Given that constructing co-operation and shared governance among the EU's member states has never been an easy task, it is not surprising that the EU's policy responses to the crises have been somewhat protracted and faltering. But they have also been, especially on the part of the eurozone states, of an increasingly integrationist – federalist one may say – nature.

In looking to the future, it seems appropriate to draw on the experience of Jean Monnet, who wrote in his memoirs (1978, p. 524):

> Some people refuse to undertake anything if they have no guarantee that things will work out as they planned. Such people condemn themselves to immobility. Today, no one can say what form Europe will assume tomorrow, for the changes born of change are unpredictable ... Day-to-day effort is needed to make one's way forward: but what matters is to have an objective clear enough always to be kept in sight.

Monnet was clearly correct to observe that prognostication is a dangerous occupation. However, it is safe to predict that the EU will continue to be confronted with very difficult policy choices in the coming years. *If* Europeans decide that their objective is to control their destinies in an unpredictable world and to continue to enjoy the fruits of democratic capitalism, the solution will most certainly involve more Europe rather than less.

References

Advisory Board for Irish Aid (2010) *Exploring Links between EU Agricultural Policy and World Poverty*. Retrieved from http://www.tcd.ie/iiis/policycoherence/eu-agricultural-policy/protection-measures.php.

Airbus (2010) *Orders and Deliveries of Airbus Aircraft: Key Documents (1989–2009 Results)*. Retrieved from http://www.airbus.com/en/corporate/orders_and_deliveries/.

Alonso, N. (2012) EU Diplomatic Service Needs Long Term Vision, eu*observer*.com, 12 January. Retrieved from http://euobserver.com/9/114837.

Andersen, S. S. and Sitter, N. (2006) Differentiated Integration: What Is It and How Much Can the EU Accommodate?, *Journal of European Integration, 28*(4), 313–30.

Apeldoorn, B. V. (2002) *Transnational Capitalism and the Struggle over European Integration*, London: Routledge.

Applegate, J. S. (2000) The Precautionary Preference: An American Perspective on the Precautionary Principle, *Human and Ecological Risk Assessment, 6*(3), 413–43.

Armstrong, K. (2003) Tackling Social Exclusion through OMC: Reshaping the Boundaries of EU Governance, in T. A. Börzel and R. Cichowki (eds), *The State of the European Union: Law, Politics and Society*, Oxford, UK: Oxford University Press, pp. 170–94.

Armstrong, K. (2006) The 'Europeanization' of Social Exclusion: British Adaptation to EU Co-ordination, *The British Journal of Politics and International Relations, 8*(1), 79–100.

Armstrong, K., Begg, I. and Zeitlin, J. (2008) JCMS Symposium: EU Governance after Lisbon, *Journal of Common Market Studies, 46*(2), 413–50.

Arregui, J. and Thomson, R. (2009) States' Bargaining Success in the European Union, *Journal of European Public Policy, 16*(5), 655–76.

Arthur, C. (2012) Microsoft Loses EU Antitrust Fine Appeal, *The Guardian*, 27 June. Retrieved from http://www.guardian.co.uk/technology/2012/jun/27/microsoft-loses-eu-antitrust-fine-appeal.

Ashton, C. (2011) *Report by the High Representative to the European Parliament, the Council and the Commission.* Retrieved from http://www.eeas.europa.eu/images/top_stories/2011_eeas_report_cor.pdf.

Aspinwall, M. (1998) Collective Attraction – the New Political Game in Brussels, in J. Greenwood and M. Aspinwall (eds), *Collective Action in the European Union: Interests and the New Policies of Accountability*, London: Routledge, pp. 196–213.

Aspinwall, M. and Greenwood, J. (1998) Conceptualizing Collective Action in The European Union: An Introduction, in J. Greenwood and M. Aspinwall (eds), *Collective Action in the European Union: Interests and the New Policies of Associability*, London: Routledge, pp. 1–30.

Aus, J. (2008) The Mechanisms of Consensus: Coming to Agreement on Community Asylum Policy, in D. Naurin and H. Wallace (eds), *Unveiling the Council of the European Union: Games Governments Play in Brussels*, Basingstoke, UK: Palgrave Macmillan, pp. 99–118.

Bache, I. (2008) *Europeanization and Multilevel Governance*, Lanham, MD: Rowman & Littlefield.

Bache, I., George, S. and Bulmer, S. (2011) *Politics in the European Union* (3rd edn), Oxford, UK: Oxford University Press.

Badinger, H. and Maydell, N. (2009) Legal and Economic Issues in Completing the EU Internal Market for Services: An Interdisciplinary Perspective, *Journal of Common Market Studies, 47*(4), 693–717.

Baimbridge, M. and Whyman, P. (2008) *Britain, the Euro and Beyond*, Abingdon, UK: Ashgate.

Baker, J. A. and DeFrank, T. M. (1995) *The Politics of Diplomacy: Revolution, War, and Peace, 1989–1992*, New York: G. P. Putnam's Sons.

Balassa, B. (1962) *The Theory of Economic Integration*, London: George Allen & Unwin.

Baldwin, R. and Cave, M. (1999) *Understanding Regulation: Theory, Strategy and Practice*, Oxford, UK: Oxford University Press.

Bank of International Settlements (2010) *Triennial Central Bank Survey of Foreign Exchange and Derivatives Market Activity in 2010 – Final Results*. Retrieved from http://www.bis.org/publ/rpfxf10t.htm.

Barca, F. (2009) *An Agenda for a Reformed Cohesion Policy: A Place-based Approach to Meeting European Union Challenges and Expectations – Independent Report prepared at the request of Danuta Hübner, Commissioner for Regional Policy*. Retrieved from http://www.europarl.europa.eu/meetdocs/2009_2014/documents/regi/dv/barca_report_/barca_report_en.pdf.

Barroso, José (2007) Comment from José Barroso at Strasbourg in response to the question at a press conference at the European Parliament: 'What will the European Union be in the Future?', 10 July. EUX.TV (Video). Retrieved from http://www.youtube.com/watch?v=-I8M1T-GgRU.

Beesley, A., Collins, S. and Schally, D. (2012). Review of Irish Bailout Likely after Merkel Climbdown, *Irish Times*, 30 June.

Begg, I. (2007) Lisbon II, Two Years On: An Assessment of the Partnership for Growth and Jobs, CEPS Special Report, Centre for Policy Studies.

Begg, I. (2011) An EU Tax: Overdue Reform or Federalist Fantasy?, *International Policy Analysis*, Friedrich-Ebert-Stiftung Foundation.

Begg, I. and Grimwade, N. (1998) *Paying for Europe*, Sheffield, UK: Sheffield Academic Press.

Behrens, A., Georgiev, A. and Carraro, M. (2010) Future Impacts of Climate Change across Europe, *CEPS Working Document*, Centre for European Policy Studies.

Bendiek, A. and Steele, H. W. (2009) *The Financing of the EU's Common Foreign and Security Policy, SWP Comments,* German Institute for International and Security Affairs. Retrieved from http://www.swp-berlin.org/en/common/get_document.php?asset_id=3085.

Benson, D. and Jordan, A. (2008) Understanding Task Allocation in the European Union: Exploring the Value of Federal Theory, *Journal of European Public Policy*, 15(1), 78–97.

Best, E. and Settembri, P. (2008a) Legislative Output After Enlargement: Similar Number, Shifting Nature, in E. Best, T. Christiansen and P. Settembri (eds), *The Institutions of the Enlarged European Union: Continuity and Change*, Cheltenham, UK: Edward Elgar, pp. 183–204.

Best, E., and Settembri, P. (2008b) Surviving Enlargement: How Has the Council Managed?, in E. Best, T. Christiansen and P. Settembri (eds), *The Institutions of the Enlarged European Union: Continuity and Change*, Cheltenham, UK: Edward Elgar, pp. 34–53.

Bialos, J., Fisher, C. and Koehl, S. (2009) *Fortresses and Icebergs: Volume 1 – Study Findings and Recommendations: The Evolution of the Transatlantic Defense Market and the Implications for U.S. National Security Policy*, Washington, DC: Brookings Institution.

Bickerton, C. (2011) *European Union Foreign Policy: From Effectiveness to Functionality*, Basingstoke, UK: Palgrave Macmillan.

Biden, J. (2009) Remarks by Vice-President Biden at 45th Munich Conference on Security Policy, 7 February. Retrieved from http://www.whitehouse.gov/the-press-office/remarks-vice-president-biden-45th-munich-conference-security-policy.

Bieler, A. and Morton, D. A. (eds) (2001) *Social Forces in the Making of the New Europe*, Basingstoke, UK: Palgrave.

Birgot, J. (2001) Brussels Poses Windows XP Question, *Financial Times*, 15 October.

Blom-Hansen, J. (2011) *The EU Comitology System in Theory and Practice: Keeping an Eye on the Commission?*, Basingstoke, UK: Palgrave Macmillan.

Bodenstein, T. and Kemmerling, A. (2012) *Ripples in a Rising Tide: Why Some EU Regions Receive More Structural Funds than Others*, European Integration online Papers (EIoP), 16.

Boeing Company (2010) *Orders and Deliveries: Recent Annual Orders*. Retrieved from http://active.boeing.com/commercial/orders/index.cfm.

Bolleyer, N. (2009) *Intergovernmental Cooperation: Rational Choices in Federal Systems and Beyond*, Oxford, UK: Oxford University Press.

Bolleyer, N. and Börzel, T. A. (2007) *Non-Hierarchical Coordination in Multilevel Settings – American, Canadian and Swiss Lessons for the European Union*, Paper presented at the American Political Science Association, Chicago, Illinois.

Borrás, S. and Jacobsson, K. (2004) The Open Method of Co-ordination and New Governance Patterns in the EU, *Journal of European Public Policy*, 11(2), 185–208.

Börzel, T. A. (2005) Pace-setting, Foot-dragging and Fence-sitting: Member State Responses to Europeanization, in A. Jordan (ed.), *Environmental Policy in the European Union: Actors, Institutions, and Processes*, London: Earthscan, pp. 162–82.

Börzel, T. A. (2009) Introduction, in T. A. Börzel (ed.), *Coping with Accession to the European Union: New Modes of Environmental Governance in Southern, Central and Eastern Europe*, Basingstoke, UK: Palgrave Macmillan.

Börzel, T. A. and Hosli, M. O. (2003) Brussels between Bern and Berlin: Comparative Federalism Meets the European Union, *Governance*, 16(2), 179–202.

Bouvet, F. and Dall'Erba, S. (2010) European Regional Structural Funds: How Large Is the Influence of Politics on the Allocation Process?, *Journal of Common Market Studies*, 48(3), 501–28.

Bowcott, O. (2011) Trivial Cases Undermining European Arrest Warrants, Warns Brussels, *The Guardian*, 10 April. Retrieved from http://www.guardian.co.uk/law/2011/apr/10/trivial-undermine-european-arrest-warrants.

Brandsma, G. J. and Blom-Hansen, J. (2011) The Post-Lisbon Battle Over Comitology: Another Round of the

Politics of Structural Choice?, *European University Institute Working Paper*, 2011(3).

Brunsden, J. (2008a) Greece to Defend its Asylum Procedures. *European Voice*, 2, 17 April. Retrieved from http://www.europeanvoice.com/article/imported/greece-to-defend-its-asylum-procedures/60332.aspx.

Brunsden, J. (2008b) Proposal Takes Shape to Harmonise Asylum Law, *European Voice*, 11 June. Retrieved from http://www.europeanvoice.com/article/imported/proposal-takes-shape-to-harmonise-asylum-law/62940.aspx

Buchan, D. (2010) Energy Policy, in H. Wallace, M. A. Pollack and A. R. Young (eds), *Policy-Making in the European Union* (6th edn), Oxford, UK: Oxford University Press, pp. 357–79.

Buchanan, J. and Tullock, G. (1969) *The Calculus of Consent*, Ann Arbor, MI: University of Michigan Press.

Büchs, M. (2008) How Legitimate Is the Open Method of Co-ordination?, *Journal of Common Market Studies*, 46(4), 765–86.

Bulmer, S., Dolowitz, D., Humphreys, P. and Padgett, S. (2007) *Policy Transfer in European Union Governance: Regulating the Utilities*, London: Routledge.

Buonanno, L. (2006) The European Food Safety Authority, in C. Ansell and D. Vogel (eds), *What's the Beef? The Contested Governance of Food Safety*, Cambridge, MA: MIT Press, pp. 259–78.

Buonanno, L. and Nugent, N. (2011) Explaining the EU's Policy Portfolio: Applying a Federal Integration Approach to EU Cohesion Policy, *Bruges Political Research Papers*, 20.

Burgess, M. (2004) Federalism, in A. Wiener and T. Diez (eds), *European Integration Theory*, Oxford, UK: Oxford University Press, pp. 24–45.

Büthe, T. (2011) *The Politics of Merger Control*, Paper presented at the European Union Studies Association, Boston, Mass.

Cafruny, A. and Ryner, M. (eds) (2003) *A Ruined Fortress? Neoliberal Hegemony and Transformation in Europe*, Lanham, MD: Rowman & Littlefield.

Cafruny, A. and Ryner, M. (2009) Critical Political Economy, in A. Wiener and T. Diez (eds), *European Integration Theory* (2nd edn), Oxford, UK: Oxford University Press, pp. 221–40.

Cameron, F. (2000) *The Foreign and Security Policy of the European Union*, Sheffield, UK: Sheffield Academic Press.

Caporaso, J. and Wittenbrinck, J. (2006) The New Modes of Governance and Political Authority in Europe, *Journal of European Public Policy*, 13(4), 471–80.

Caranta, R. (2011) Many Different Paths, but Are They All Leading to Effectiveness?, in S. Treumer and F. Lichère (eds), *Enforcement of the EU Public Procurement Rules*, Copenhagen: DJØF Publishing, pp. 53–93.

CARIS (2010) *Midterm Evaluation of the EU's Generalised System of Preferences*, Sussex University. Retrieved from http://trade.ec.europa.eu/doclib/docs/2010/may/tradoc_146196.pdf.

Carroll, W. E. (2011) The Committee of the Regions: A Functional Analysis of the CoR's Institutional Capacity, *Regional and Federal Studies*, 21(3), 341–54.

Carta, C. (2012) *The European Union Diplomatic Service: Ideas, Preferences and Identities*. New York: Routledge.

Casciani, D. and Barford, V. (2012) UK Extradition Laws: Key Cases, BBC News. Retrieved from http://www.bbc.co.uk/news/uk-15334015.

Casey, Z. (2008) Big Drop in Europe's Population Predicted, *European Voice*, 24 November. Retrieved from http://www.europeanvoice.com/article/2008/11/big-drop-in-europe-s-population-predicted/63170.aspx.

Castle, S. (2011) Some in Euro Zone Propose Further Integration for Bloc, *The New York Times*, 5 February, pp. B1, B6.

Castle, S. (2012) Spain Adjusts Deficit-Reduction Target at European Summit, *The New York Times*, 2 March. Retrieved from http://www.nytimes.com/2012/03/03/business/global/spain-unable-to-meet-goal-for-deficit-cuts-this-year.html.

Chaffin, P. C. J. (2010) Aircraft Makers Braced for Subsidy Verdict, *Financial Times*, 22 March.

Chalmers, A. W. (2011) Interests, Influence and Information: Comparing the Influence of Interest Groups in the European Union, *Journal of European Integration*, 33(4), 471–86.

Chang, M. (2009) *Monetary Integration in the European Union*. Basingstoke, UK: Palgrave Macmillan.

Charlemagne (2009) The Endless Election Round, *The Economist*, 11 June. Retrieved from http://www.economist.com/node/13825164.

Checkel, J. T. and Katzenstein, P. J. (2009) *European Identity*, Cambridge, UK: Cambridge University Press.

Cini, M. and McGowan, L. (1998) *Competition Policy in the European Union* (2nd edn), London: Macmillan.

Cini, M. and McGowan, L. (2008) *Competition Policy in the European Union*, Basingstoke, UK: Palgrave Macmillan.

Citi, M. and Rhodes, M. (2007) New Modes of Governance in the EU: Common Objectives Versus National Preferences, *European Governance Papers*, 2007(1).

CNN Money (2010) *Europe's Fortune 50 Companies*. Retrieved from http://money.cnn.com/magazines/fortune/global500/2010/europe/.

Columbus, F. (2004) *European Economic and Political Issues*, Vol. 8, Hauppauge, NY: Nova.

Committee of the Regions (2012) Towards a 7th Environmental Action Programme – Better Implementation of EU Environmental Law, 25 May. Retrieved from http://extranet.cor.europa.eu/

subsidiarity/news/Pages/Towards-a-7th-Environment-Action-Programme-(EAP)-%E2%80%93-Better-implementation-of-EU-environmental-law.aspx.

Copeland, P. and Papadimitriou, D. (eds) (2012) *The EU's Lisbon Agenda: Evaluating Success, Understanding Failure*, Basingstoke, UK: Palgrave Macmillan.

Council of the European Union (1992) *Presidency Conclusions*, Edinburgh, 11–12 December, General Secretariat of the Council.

Council of the European Union (2000) *Presidency Conclusions*, Lisbon, 23–24 March. Retrieved from http://www.consilium.europa.eu/press/press-releases/european-council?target=2002&infotarget=before&bid=76&lang=en.

Council of the European Union (2001) *Presidency Conclusions*, Stockholm, 23–24 March. Retrieved from http://www.consilium.europa.eu/press/press-releases/european-council?target=2002&infotarget=before&bid=76&lang=en.

Council of the European Union (2003a) *Council Regulation No. 1/2003 of 16 December 2002 on the Implementation of the Rules on Competition Laid Down in Articles 81 and 82 of the Treaty*. Retrieved from http://ec.europa.eu/justice_home/doc_centre/civil/doc/parental_resp_ec_vdm_en.pdf.

Council of the European Union (2003b) *A Secure Europe in a Better World: European Security Strategy*. Retrieved from http://ue.eu.int/ueDocs/cms_Data/docs/pressdata/en/reports/76255.pdf.

Council of the European Union (2008) *Report on the Implementation of the European Security Strategy-Providing Security in a Changing World*, Brussels. Retrieved from http://www.eu-un.europa.eu/documents/en/081211_EU%20Security%20Strategy.pdf.

Council of the European Union (2009) *The Stockholm Programme: An Open and Secure Europe Serving and Protecting the Citizen*, 17024/09. Retrieved from http://register.consilium.europa.eu/pdf/en/09/st14/st14449.en09.pdf.

Council of the European Union (2010) *Council Regulation (EU) No 1259/2010 of 20 December 2010 Implementing Enhanced Cooperation in the Area of the Law Applicable to Divorce and Legal Separation*. Retrieved from http://eur-lex.europa.eu/LexUriServ/LexUriServ.do?uri=OJ:L:2010:343:0010:0016:EN:PDF.

Council of the European Union (2012a) *Conclusions on Setting the Framework for a Seventh EU Environmental Programme: 3173rd Environment Council Meeting, Luxembourg*, 11 June. Retrieved from http://www.consilium.europa.eu/uedocs/cms_data/docs/pressdata/en/envir/130788.pdf.

Council of the European Union (2012b) *Justice and Home Affairs, Press Release, 25–26 October*, No 15389/12.

Retrieved from www.consilium.europa.eu/uedocs/cms_data/docs/pressdata/en/jha/133241.pdf.

Court of Auditors of the European Union (2011) *Annual Report Concerning the Financial Year 2010: Annual Report on the Implementation of the Budget*, 2011/C, 326/01.

Cram, L. (1994) The European Commission as a Multi-Organization: Social Policy and IT Policy in the EU, *Journal of European Public Policy*, 1(2), 195–217.

Crosbie, J. (2007a) Analysis: Red Lines for Double Standards?, *European Voice*, June 28, 13.

Crosbie, J. (2007b,) Arrest Warrant Still in the Dark Despite ECJ Ruling, *European Voice*, 10–15 May, 13.

Daly, M. (2006) EU Social Policy after Lisbon, *Journal of Common Market Studies*, 44(3), 461–81.

David, M., Gower, J. and Haukkala, H. (2011) Introduction: The European Union and Russia, *Journal of Contemporary European Studies*, 19(2), 183–88.

Dehousse, R. (ed.) (2011) *The Community Method: Obstinate or Obsolete?*, Basingstoke, UK: Palgrave.

de la Porte, C. and Nanze, P. (2004) The OMC – A Deliberative-Democratic Mode of Governance? The Cases of Employment and Pensions, *Journal of European Public Policy*, 11(2), 267–88.

de la Porte, C. and Pochet, P. (2005) Participation in the Open Method of Co-ordination, in J. Zeitlin and P. Pochet (eds), *The Open Method of Coordination in Action*, Brussels: Peter Lang, pp. 351–89.

de Larosière Group (2009) *The High-level Group on Financial Supervision in the EU*. Retrieved from http://ec.europa.eu/internal_market/finances/docs/de_larosiere_report_en.pdf.

Dellmuth, L. M. (2011) The Cash Divide: The Allocation of European Union Regional Grants, *Journal of European Public Policy*, 18(7), 1016–33.

Deloche-Gaudez, F. and Beaudonnet, L. (2011) *Decision-Making in the Enlarged Council of Ministers: A Softer Consensus Norm as an Explanation for its Adaptability*, Paper presented at the UACES Annual Conference College of Europe, Bruges.

de Schoutheete, P. (2011) Decision-making in the Union, *Notre Europe Policy Brief*, 24 (April).

De Ville, F. and Orbie, J. (2011) The European Union's Trade Policy Response to the Crisis: Paradigm Lost or Reinforced?, *European Integration online Papers*, 15(2).

Dickel, R. and Westphal, K. (2012) *EU–Russia Gas Relations: How to Manage New Uncertainties and Imbalances*, German Insititute for International and Security Affairs. Retrieved from http://www.swp-berlin.org/fileadmin/contents/products/comments/2012C12_Dickel_wep.pdf.

Diedrichs, U. (2011) Modes of Governance in the EU's Common Foreign and Security Policy, in U. Diedrichs, W. Reiners and W. Wessels (eds), *Dynamics of Change in*

EU Governance, Cheltenham, UK: Edward Elgar, pp. 149–79.

Di Lucia, L. and Kronsell, A. (2010) The Willing, the Unwilling, and the Unable – Explaining Implementation of the EU Biofuels Directive, *Journal of European Public Policy*, 17(4), 545–63.

Dinan, D. (2004) *Europe Recast: A History of the European Union*, Boulder, CO: Lynn Rienner.

Dinan, D. (2011) Governance and Institutions, in N. Copsey and T. Haughton (eds), *The JCMS Annual Review of the European Union in 2010*, Chicester, UK: John Wiley, pp. 103–21.

Donadio, R. (2011) Italy Lashes Out at European Union Over Immigrants, *The New York Times*, 11 April, p. A9.

Donnelly, S. (2010) *The Regimes of European Integration: Constructing Governance of the Single Market*, Oxford, UK: Oxford University Press.

Dougan, M. (2005) Legal Developments, in L. Miles (ed.), *The European Union: Annual Review 2004/2005*, Oxford, UK: Oxford University Press, pp. 89–107.

Dyson, K. (1994) *Elusive Union: The Process of Economic and Monetary Union in Europe*, New York: Longman.

Dyson, K. and Featherstone, K. (1999) *The Road To Maastricht: Negotiating Economic and Monetary Union*, Oxford, UK: Oxford University Press.

Eberlein, B. and Kerwer, D. (2004) New Governance in the European Union: A Theoretical Perspective, *Journal of Common Market Studies*, 42(1), 121–42.

Egenhofer, C. and Georgiev, A. (2010) Why the Transatlantic Climate Change Partnership Matters More Than Ever, *CEPS Commentary*.

Ehrlich, S. D. (2009) How Common Is the Common External Tariff?: Domestic Influences on European Union Trade Policy, *European Union Politics*, 10(1), 115–41.

Einaudi, L. (2000) From the Franc to the 'Europe': The Attempted Transformation of the Latin Monetary Union into a European Monetary Union, 1865–1873, *The Economic History Review*, 53(2), 284–308.

Elazar, D. (1973) Cursed by Bigness: Or Towards a Post-Technocratic Federalism, *Publius: The Journal of Federalism*, 3(Fall), 239–98.

Elazar, D. (2001) The United States and the European Union: Models for Their Epochs, in K. N. R. Howse (ed.), *The Federal Vision: Legitmacy and Levels of Governance in the United States and Europe*, Oxford, UK: Oxford University Press, pp. 31–53.

Elsig, M. (2010) European Union Trade Policy after Enlargement: Larger Crowds, Shifting Priorities and Informal Decision-making, *Journal of European Public Policy*, 17(6), 781–98.

Erlanger, S. (2011a) After a Long March, Chinese Surrender to Capitalist Shrines, *The New York Times*, 15 September.

Retrieved from http://www.nytimes.com/2011/09/15/world/europe/eager-chinese-shoppers-flock-to-paris-stores.html?pagewanted=all.

Erlanger, S. (2011b) Money Flows, but What Euro Zone Lacks Is Glue, *The New York Times*, 30 November. Retrieved from http://www.nytimes.com/2011/12/01/world/europe/new-warnings-of-euro-zone-danger-news-analysis.html?pagewanted=all.

Erlanger, S. and Castle, S. (2011) German Vision Prevails as Leaders Agree on Fiscal Pact, *The New York Times*, 9 December. Retrieved from http://www.nytimes.com/2011/12/10/business/global/european-leaders-agree-on-fiscal-treaty.html?pagewanted=2&_r=1&hp.

Escafré-Dublet, A. (2007) *France, Immigration, and the Policies of Culture: Understanding the 'French Integration Model'*, Paper presented at the European Union Studies Association, Montreal. Retrieved from http://aei.pitt.edu/7800/1/dublet-a-03i.pdf.

EurActiv (2012a) Global Food Prices and CAP Reform, *EurActiv*, 25 July. Retrieved from http://www.euractiv.com/cap/global-food-prices-cap-reform/article-184329.

EurActiv (2012b) Ministers Set out 2050 Vision for a 'Green Europe', *EurActiv.com*, 12 June. Retrieved from http://www.euractiv.com/sustainability/ministers-set-2050-vision-green-news-513241.

Europa (2011) *EUROSUR: Providing Authorities with Tools Needed to Reinforce Management of External Borders and Fight Cross-border Crime*, 12 December. Retrieved from http://europa.eu/rapid/pressReleasesAction.do?reference=MEMO/11/896&type=HTML.

European Commission (1962) *Memorandum of the Commission on the Action Programme of the Community for the Second Stage*, COM (62) 300 final, 24 October. Retrieved from http://aei.pitt.edu/1327/.

European Commission (1968a) *Outlook on the Development of the Economic Union*, Address by M. Jean Rey (President of the European Commission), Strasbourg. Retrieved from http://ec.europa.eu/economy_finance/emu_history/documentation/chapter2/19680515en024outlookeconeuro.pdf.

European Commission (1968b) *Programme en Vue de la Réalisation par Étapes d'une Monnaie Commune II-C-1/CS.sky/11.9.68*, Brussels: DG Economic Affairs and Finance.

European Commission (1985) *Completing the Internal Market, White Paper from the Commission to the European Council*, COM (85) 310 final. Retrieved from http://aei.pitt.edu/1113/.

European Commission (1999) *Communication from the Commission to the Council and the European Parliament: Mutual recognition in the Context of the Follow-up of the Action Plan for the Single Market*, COM(1999) 299 final. Retrieved from http://aei.pitt.edu/3567/.

European Commission (2000) *Communication from the Commission on the Precautionary Principle*, COM(2000) 1 final. Retrieved from http://eur-lex.europa.eu/Lex UriServ/LexUriServ.do?uri=COM:2000:0001:FIN: EN:PDF.

European Commission (2001) *European Governance, White Paper*, COM (2001) 428 final Brussels. Retrieved from http://ec.europa.eu/economy_finance/emu_history/ documentation/chapter2/19680515en024outlooke coneuro.pdf.

European Commission (2004a) *Commission Staff Working Document: The Application of the Lamfalussy Process to EU Securities Markets Legislation*, SEC (204) 1459. Retrieved from http://ec.europa.eu/internal_market/ securities/docs/lamfalussy/sec-2004-1459_en.pdf#page =16.

European Commission (2004b) *The EU Gets New Competition Powers for the 21st Century*, Competition Policy Newsletter, Special Edition.

European Commission (2004c) *Financing the European Union: Commission Report on the Operation of the Own Resources System*. Retrieved from http://eur-lex.europa. eu/LexUriServ/LexUriServ.do?uri=CELEX:52004DC0505: EN:HTML.

European Commission (2004d) *Proposal for a Directive of the European Parliament and of the Council on Services in the Internal market*, COM (2004) 2 final/3). Retrieved from http://eur-lex.europa.eu/LexUriServ/LexUriServ. do?uri=COM:2004:0002:FIN:EN:PDF.

European Commission (2004e) *The European Union's Generalised System of Preferences*. Retrieved from http:// trade.ec.europa.eu/doclib/docs/2004/march/tradoc_116 448.pdf.

European Commission (2004f) *Taking Europe to the World: 50 Years of the European Commission's External Action Service*. Retrieved from http://ue.eu.int/ueDocs/cms_ Data/docs/pressdata/en/reports/76255.pdf.

European Commission (2006a) *European Year of Workers' Mobility 2006: Facts and Figures*. Retrieved from http:// 194.185.30.69/eywmp/website/fact_figures_en.htm.

European Commission (2006b) *Structures of the Taxation Systems in the European Union: Data 1995–2004*. Retrieved from http://epp.eurostat.ec.europa.eu/cache/ ITY_OFFPUB/KS-DU-06-001/EN/KS-DU-06-001- EN.PDF.

European Commission (2007a) *Commission Staff Working Document – Accompanying Document to the Proposal for a Council Directive on the Conditions for Entry and Residence of Third Country Nationals for the Purposes of Highly-Qualified Employment. Summary of the Impact Assessment*. Retrieved from http://eur-lex.europa. eu/LexUriServ/LexUriServ.do?uri=CELEX:52007SC1382: EN:HTML.

European Commission (2007b) *Communication to the Council, the European Parliament, the European Economic and Social Committee and the Committee of the Regions: A Strategy for a Stronger and More Competitive European Defence Industry*. Retrieved from http://eur-lex.europa. eu/LexUriServ/LexUriServ.do?uri=COM:2007:0764:FIN: en:PDF.

European Commission (2007c) *General Budget of the European Union For Fiscal Year 2007: The Figures*. Retrieved from http://ec.europa.eu/budget/biblio/ documents/2007/2007_en.cfm.

European Commission (2007d) *Investment Services: Entry into Force of MiFID a Boon for Financial Markets and Investor Protection*, Europa Press Release, from http:// europa.eu/rapid/pressReleasesAction.do?reference= IP/07/1625&format=HTML&aged=0&language=EN

European Commission (2007e) *Reforming the Budget, Changing Europe*. Retrieved from http://ec.europa. eu/budget/reform/library/roadshow/roadshow_web_EN. pdf.

European Commission (2008a) *Commission Staff Working Document Annex to Communication from the Commission to the Council and the European Parliament. Report of Implementation of the Hague Programme for 2007*, COM (2008) 373 final.

European Commission (2008b) *JAI Acquis of the European Union: Title IV of the TEC, Part II of the TEC, Title VI of the TEU*, October. Retrieved from http://ec.europa.eu/ justice_home/doc_centre/intro/docs/jha_acquis_1008_ en.pdf.

European Commission (2008c) *JHA Scoreboard*. Retrieved from http://ec.europa.eu/justice_home/doc_centre/ scoreboard_en.htm.

European Commission (2008d) *New Tools for an Integrated European Border Management Strategy*, Europa Press Release. Retrieved from http://europa.eu/rapid/ pressReleasesAction.do?reference=MEMO/08/85&format =HTML&aged=1&language=EN&guiLanguage=en.

European Commission (2008e) *Report on Competition Policy 2007*. Retrieved from http://ec.europa.eu/competition/ publications/annual_report/2007/en.pdf.

European Commission (2008f) *The Single Market for Goods: Information Pack*. Retrieved from http://ec.europa.eu/ enterprise/newsroom/cf/itemdetail.cfm?&item_id=1351.

European Commission (2009a) *The Co-Decision Procedure: Analysis and Statistics of the 2004–2009 Legislature*. Retrieved from http://ec.europa.eu/codecision/statis- tics/docs/report_statistics_public_draft_en.pdf.

European Commission (2009b) *Communication from the Commission to the European Parliament and the Council: 2008 Environment Policy Review*, SEC(2009)842. Retrieved from http://eur-lex.europa.eu/LexUriServ/ LexUriServ.do?uri=COM:2009:0304:FIN:EN:PDF.

European Commission (2009c) *Communication from the Commission to the European Parliament and the Council: An Area of Freedom, Security and Justice Serving the European Citizen*, COM (2009) 262 final. Retrieved from http://eur-lex.europa.eu/LexUriServ/LexUriServ.do?uri=COM:2009:0262:FIN:en:PDF.

European Commission (2009d) *The European Union in the World – Statistics*. Retrieved from http://trade.ec.europa.eu/doclib/docs/2006/september/tradoc_122531.pdf.

European Commission (2009e) *The European Union Trade Policy*. Retrieved from http://ec.europa.eu/trade/about/introduction-to-trade/.

European Commission (2010a) *Commission Staff Working Document: Lisbon Strategy Evaluation Document*, SEC (2010) 114 final.

European Commission (2010b) *Communication from the Commission to the European Parliament, the Council, the European Economic and Social Committee and the Committee of the Regions: Trade, Growth and World Affairs: Trade Policy as a Core Component of the EU's 2020 Strategy*, SEC (2010 1268) and SEC (2010) 1269.

European Commission (2010c) *Communication from the Commission to the European Parliament, the Council, the European Economic and Social Council, and the Committee of the Regions: The CAP towards 2020: Meeting the Food, Natural Resources and Territorial Challenges of the Future*. Retrieved from http://ec.europa.eu/agriculture/cap-post-2013/communication/com2010-672_en.pdf.

European Commission (2010d) *Communication from the Commission to the European Parliament, the Council, the European Social and Economic Committee, and the Committee of the Regions: Delivering an Area of Freedom, Security and Justice for Europe's Citizens: Action Plan Implementing the Stockholm Programme*, COM (2010) 171 final. Retrieved from http://eur-lex.europa.eu/LexUriServ/LexUriServ.do?uri=COM:2010:0171:FIN:EN:PDF.

European Commission (2010e) *Communication from the Commission to the European Parliament, the Council, the European Social and Economic Committee, the Committee of the Regions, and the National Parliaments: The EU Budget Review*, Brussels. Retrieved from http://ec.europa.eu/budget/reform/library/communication/com_2010_700_en.pdf.

European Commission (2010f) *Communication from the Commission, Europe 2020 – A Strategy for Smart, Sustainable and Inclusive Growth*, COM (2010) 2020 final.

European Commission (2010g) *Communication to the European Parliament and the Council: The EU Internal Security Strategy in Action: Five Steps towards a More Secure Europe*, COM (2010) 673 final, Brussels.

Retrieved from http://register.consilium.europa.eu/pdf/en/10/st07/st07120.en10.pdf.

European Commission (2010h) *EU Trade Profile*. Retrieved from http://ec.europa.eu/trade/about/eu-trade-profile/.

European Commission (2010i) *The European Commission Provides an Additional €9.8 million and Further Technical Support to Greece on Asylum and Border Issues*, Europa Press Releases RAPID. Retrieved from http://europa.eu/rapid/pressReleasesAction.do?reference=IP/10/1719&type=HTML.

European Commission (2010j) *Green Paper: Towards Adequate, Sustainable and Safe European Pension Systems*, COM(2010)365 final. Retrieved from http://ec.europa.eu/social/main.jsp?catId=700&langId=en&consultId=3&visib=0&furtherConsult=yes.

European Commission (2010k) *How to Use the Euro Name and Symbol*. Retrieved from http://ec.europa.eu/economy_finance/euro/cash/symbol/index_en.htm.

European Commission (2010l) *Phase 2: The European Monetary System*. Retrieved from http://ec.europa.eu/economy_finance/euro/emu/road/ems_en.htm.

European Commission (2010m) Public Opinion in the EU, *Standard Eurobarometer*, 73 (Spring).

European Commission (2010n) *Report on Competition Policy*. Retrieved from http://ec.europa.eu/competition/publications/annual_report/2009/en.pdf.

European Commission (2010o) *Towards More Responsibility and Competitiveness in the European Financial Sector*. Retrieved from http://ec.europa.eu/internal_market/finances/docs/leaflet/financial_services_en.pdf.

European Commission (2010p) *Trade, Growth and World Affairs: Trade Policy as a Core Component of the EU's 2020 Strategy*. Retrieved from http://trade.ec.europa.eu/doclib/docs/2010/november/tradoc_146955.pdf.

European Commission (2011a) *Asylum – Building a Common Area of Protection and Solidarity*. Retrieved from http://ec.europa.eu/home-affairs/policies/asylum/asylum_intro_en.htm.

European Commission (2011b) *Commission Staff Working Paper: Determing the Technical and Operational Framework of the European Border Surveillance Systems (EUROSUR) and the Actions to Be Taken for Its Establishment*. Retrieved from http://ec.europa.eu/home-affairs/policies/borders/docs/20110128EUROSURCSWPSEC2011145%20final.pdf.

European Commission (2011c) *Common Rules for a Financial Transaction Tax – Frequently Asked Questions*. Retrieved from http://europa.eu/rapid/pressReleasesAction.do?reference=MEMO/11/640&format=HTML&aged=0&language=en&guiLanguage=en.

European Commission (2011d) *Communication from the Commission to the European Parliament and the Council:*

Annual Report on Immigration and Asylum, COM (2011) 291 final. Retrieved from http://eur-lex.europa.eu/LexUriServ/LexUriServ.do?uri=COM:2011:0291:FIN:EN:PDF.

European Commission (2011e) *Communication from the Commission to the European Parliament, the Council, the European Economic and Social Committee and the Committee of the Regions: A Budget for Europe 2020*, COM (2011) 500 final. Retrieved from http://ec.europa.eu/budget/library/biblio/documents/fin_fwk1420/MFF_COM-2011-500_Part_I_en.pdf.

European Commission (2011f) *Divorce and Legal Separation*. Retrieved from http://ec.europa.eu/justice/civil/family-matters/divorce/index_en.htm.

European Commission (2011g) *EU & WTO: The Doha Round*. Retrieved from http://ec.europa.eu/trade/creating-opportunities/eu-and-wto/doha/.

European Commission (2011h) *EU Economic Goverance – A Major Step Forward*. Rapid Press Release, 31 May. Retrieved from http://europa.eu/rapid/pressReleasesAction.do?reference=MEMO/11/364&format=HTML&aged=1&language=en&guiLanguage=fr.

European Commission (2011i) *EU Welcomes Conclusion of Negotiations on Russia's WTO Accession*, Rapid Press Release, 11 October. Retrieved from http://europa.eu/rapid/pressReleasesAction.do?reference=IP/11/1334.

European Commission (2011j) *The European Union Trade Policy 2011*. Retrieved from http://trade.ec.europa.eu/doclib/docs/2011/april/tradoc_147773.pdf.

European Commission (2011k) Europeans' Perceptions on the State of the Economy, *Eurobarometer*, 75 (Spring). Retrieved from http://ec.europa.eu/public_opinion/archives/eb/eb75/eb75_en.pdf.

European Commission (2011l) *Family Matters and Successions*. Retrieved from http://ec.europa.eu/justice/civil/family-matters/index_en.htm.

European Commission (2011m) *Generalised System of Preferences*, 26 October. Retrieved from http://ec.europa.eu/trade/wider-agenda/development/generalised-system-of-preferences/.

European Commission (2011n) *Generalised System of Preferences: Everything But Arms*. Retrieved from http://ec.europa.eu/trade/wider-agenda/development/generalised-system-of-preferences/everything-but-arms/.

European Commission (2011o) *Government Deficit and Debt*.Retrieved from http://epp.eurostat.ec.europa.eu/portal/page/portal/government_finance_statistics/data/main_tables.

European Commission (2011p) *Internal Market Scoreboard, No. 22*. Retrieved from http://ec.europa.eu/internal_market/score/index_en.htm.

European Commission (2011q) *Investing Today for Growth Tomorrow*, Rapid Press Release, 29 June. Retrieved from http://europa.eu/rapid/pressReleasesAction.do?reference=IP/11/799.

European Commission (2011r) *Shoulder to Shoulder: The European View of the Transatlantic Relationship and the State of the WTO*, Statement by Karel De Gucht, European Commissioner for Trade, at the NATO Parliamentary Assembly, Rapid Press Release, 22 February. Retrieved from http://europa.eu/rapid/pressReleasesAction.do?reference=SPEECH/11/114&format=HTML&aged=0&language=EN&guiLanguage=en.

European Commission (2011s) *Mergers Commission Clears Proposed Acquisition of Samsung's Hard Disk Drive Business by Seagate Technology*, Rapid Press Release, 19 October. Retrieved from http://europa.eu/rapid/pressReleasesAction.do?reference=IP/11/1213.

European Commission (2011t) Public Opinion in the European Union, *Eurobarometer*, 76 (First results).

European Commission (2011u) *Report from the Commission: 28th Annual Report on Monitoring the Application of EU Law*, (2010), COM (2010) 588 final.

European Commission (2011v) *Single Market Act: Together for New Growth*. Retrieved from http://ec.europa.eu/internal_market/smact/docs/20120206_new_growth_en.pdf.

European Commission (2012a) *Bilateral Relations – China*. Retrieved from http://ec.europa.eu/trade/creating-opportunities/bilateral-relations/countries/china/.

European Commission (2012b) *Budget 2012 in Figures*. Retrieved from http://ec.europa.eu/budget/figures/2012/2012_en.cfm.

European Commission (2012c) *Communication from the Commission to the European Parliament and the Council: Biannual Report on the Functioning of the Schengen Area – 1 November 2011–30 April 2012*, COM (2012) 230 final. Retrieved from http://eur-lex.europa.eu/LexUriServ/LexUriServ.do?uri=COM:2012:0230:FIN:EN:PDF.

European Commission (2012d) *Communication from the Commission to the European Parliament, the Council, and the European Economic and Social Committee: Trade, Growth and Development – Tailoring Trade and Investment Policy for those Countries Most in Need*, COM (2012) 22 final. Retrieved from http://trade.ec.europa.eu/doclib/docs/2012/january/tradoc_148992.EN.pdf.

European Commission (2012e) *Communication from the Commission to the European Parliament, the Council, the European Economic and Social Committee, and the Committee of the Regions: Report on Competition Policy 2011*, COM (2012) 253.

European Commission (2012f) *Country-Specific Recommendations, 2012–2013*. Retrieved from http://ec.europa.eu/europe2020/making-it-happen/country-specific-recommendations/index_en.htm.

European Commission (2012g) *Energy Production and Imports*. Retrieved from http://epp.eurostat.ec.europa.eu/statistics_explained/index.php/Energy_production_and_imports.

European Commission (2012h) *EU Budget 2012*. Retrieved from http://ec.europa.eu/budget/library/biblio/publications/2012/budget_folder/186978_2011_4429_EU_BUDGET_2012_EN_V2.pdf.

European Commission (2012i) *EU Budget: Myths and Facts*. Retrieved from http://ec.europa.eu/budget/explained/myths/myths_en.cfm#1of15.

European Commission (2012j) *EU Register of Genetically Modified Food and Feed*. Retrieved from http://ec.europa.eu/food/dyna/gm_register/index_en.cfm.

European Commission (2012k) *Europe 2020: FAQs*. Retrieved from http://ec.europa.eu/europe2020/services/faqs/index_en.htm.

European Commission (2012l) *European Arrest Warrant*. Retrieved from http://ec.europa.eu/justice/criminal/recognition-decision/european-arrest-warrant/index_en.htm.

European Commission (2012m) *European Commission Proposal for the 2014–2020 Multiannual Financial Framework*. Retrieved from http://ec.europa.eu/budget/library/biblio/publications/2011/mff2011/MFF_2011_en.pdf.

European Commission (2012n) *European Competition Network: Aggregate Figures on Antitrust Cases*. Retrieved from http://ec.europa.eu/competition/ecn/statistics.html#1.

European Commission (2012o) *Financial Framework, 2007–2013*. Retrieved from http://ec.europa.eu/budget/figures/fin_fwk0713/fwk0713_en.cfm#cf07_13.

European Commission (2012p) *The Multiannual Financial Framework, 2014–2020: A Budget for Europe 2020*. Retrieved from http://ec.europa.eu/bulgaria/documents/news/031011-ju_sofia_mff.pdf.

European Commission (2012q) *A Single Market for Goods*. Retrieved from http://ec.europa.eu/internal_market/top_layer/index_18_en.htm.

European Commission (2012r) *Single Market Governance: FAQs*. Retrieved from http://ec.europa.eu/enterprise/newsroom/cf/itemdetail.cfm?item_id=5798&lang=en.

European Commission (2012s) *Six-pack? Two-pack? Fiscal compact? A Short Guide to the New EU Fiscal Governance*. Retrieved from http://ec.europa.eu/economy_finance/articles/governance/2012-03-14_six_pack_en.htm.

European Commission (2012t) *Top Ten Trading Partners*. Retrieved from http://trade.ec.europa.eu/doclib/html/122530.htm.

European Commission (2012u) *Trade: Russia*. Retrieved from http://ec.europa.eu/trade/creating-opportunities/bilateral-relations/countries/russia/.

European Commission (2012v) *What Is ERM II?* Retrieved from http://ec.europa.eu/economy_finance/euro/adoption/erm2/index_en.htm.

European Commission (2012w) *WTO Disputes: EU/US Large Civil Aircraft*. Retrieved from http://trade.ec.europa.eu/doclib/docs/2010/september/tradoc_146486.pdf.

European Commission. (2012x) *State of the Union Address delivered by José Manuel Durão Barroso*, 12 September, Rapid Press Release. Retrieved from http://europa.eu/rapid/pressReleasesAction.do?reference=SPEECH/12/596.

European Communities (1973) *Document on the European Identity Published by the Nine Foreign Ministers*. Retrieved from http://aei.pitt.edu/4545/1/epc_identity_doc.pdf.

European Council (2005) *Presidency Conclusions*, 22–23 March. Retrieved from http://www.consilium.europa.eu/press/press-releases/european-council?target=2005&bid=76&lang=en.

European Council (2006) *Presidency Conclusions*, 23–24 March. Retrieved from http://www.consilium.europa.eu/press/press-releases/european-council?target=2006&bid=76&lang=en.

European Council (2007) *Presidency Conclusions*, 8–9 March. Retrieved from http://www.consilium.europa.eu/press/press-releases/european-council?target=2007&bid=76&lang=en.

European Council (2010) *Presidency Conclusions*, June 17. Retrieved from http://www.consilium.europa.eu/press/press-releases/european-council?target=2010&bid=76&lang=en.

European Council (2011a) *Conclusions*, 9 December. Retrieved from http://www.consilium.europa.eu/press/press-releases/european-council?target=2010&bid=76&lang=en.

European Council (2011b) *Conclusions*, March 24/25. Retrieved from http://www.consilium.europa.eu/press/press-releases/european-council?target=2010&bid=76&lang=en.

European Council (2012) *Towards a Genuine Economic and Monetary Union: Report by President of the European Council, Herman Van Rompuy*. Retrieved from http://ec.europa.eu/economy_finance/focuson/crisis/documents/131201_en.pdf.

European Defence Agency (2010) *Electronic Bulletin Board*. Retrieved from http://www.eda.europa.eu/ebbweb/.

Europe Economics (2009) *Study on the Competitiveness of Small and Medium sized Enterprises (SMEs) in the Defence Sector* (prepared for the European Commission). Retrieved from http://ec.europa.eu/enterprise/sectors/defence/files/2009-11-05_europe_economics_final_report_en.pdf.

European External Action Service (1995) *The New Transatlantic Agenda*. Retrieved from http://eeas.europa.eu/us/docs/new_transatlantic_agenda_en.pdf.

European External Action Service (2012a) *EU–US Co-operation by Sector*. Retrieved from http://eeas.europa.eu/us/sector_en.htm.

European External Action Service (2012b) *Overview of the Missions and Operations of the European Union*. Retrieved from http://www.consilium.europa.eu/eeas/security-defence/eu-operations.

European External Action Service (2012c) *United States of America*. Retrieved from http://eeas.europa.eu/us/index_en.htm.

European Food Safety Authority (2012) *European Food Safety Authority*. Retrieved from http://europa.eu/agencies/regulatory_agencies_bodies/policy_agencies/efsa/index_en.htm.

European Investment Bank Group (2012) *Activity Report 2011*. Retrieved from http://www.eib.org/attachments/general/reports/ar2011en.pdf.

European Liberal Democrats (2011) *Everything you wanted to know about where the money comes from*. Retrieved from http://www.eldrfocus2011.eu/2011/07/everything-you-wanted-to-know-about-where-the-money-comes-from/.

European NAvigator (n.d) *Reform of the CAP: The Mansholt Plan*. Retrieved from http://www.ena.lu/.

European Parliament (2012) *Better Coordinated EU External Energy Policy: Plenary Session – Energy*, 13 September. Retrieved from http://www.europarl.europa.eu/news/en/pressroom/content/20120907IPR50830/html/Better-coordinated-EU-external-energy-policy.

European Parliament and European Commission (2010) *Framework Agreement on Relations Between the European Parliament and the European Commission*. Retrieved from http://eur-lex.europa.eu/LexUriServ/LexUriServ.do?uri=OJ:L:2010:304:0047:0062:EN:PDF.

European Services Forum (2011) *Facts and Figures*. Retrieved from http://www.esf.be/new/statistics/.

European Space Agency (2010) *ESA – Space for Europe*. Retrieved from http://www.esa.int/SPECIALS/About_ESA/SEMONSEVL2F_0.html.

European Systemic Risk Board (2012) *ERSB: Mission, Objectives and Tasks*. Retrieved from http://www.esrb.europa.eu/about/tasks/html/index.en.html.

European Union (2010) *Agreement between the European Union and the United States of America on the Processing and Transfer of Financial Messaging Data from the European Union to the United States for the Purposes of the Terrorist Finance Tracking Program*. Retrieved from http://eur-lex.europa.eu/LexUriServ/LexUriServ.do?uri=OJ:L:2010:195:0005:0014:EN:PDF.

European Union (2011) *Regulation 512/2011 of the European Parliament and of the Council of 11 May 2011 amending Council Regulation (EC) No 732/2008 applying a scheme of generalised tariff preferences for the period from 1 January 2009 to 31 December 2011*. Retrieved from http://trade.ec.europa.eu/doclib/docs/2011/may/tradoc_147958.pdf.

European Union (2012) *European Union at the United Nations*. Retrieved from http://www.europa-eu-un.org/.

European Union Agency for Fundamental Rights (2012) *European Union Agency for Fundamental Rights*. Retrieved from http://europa.eu/agencies/regulatory_agencies_bodies/policy_agencies/fra/index_en.htm.

Eurostat (2011) *Europe in Figures: Eurostat Yearbook 2010*. Retrieved from http://epp.eurostat.ec.europa.eu/cache/ITY_OFFPUB/KS-CD-10-220/EN/KS-CD-10-220-EN.PDF.

Evans-Pritchard, A. (2012) Debt Crisis: Greek Euro Exit Looms Closer as Banks Crumble, *The Telegraph*, 16 May. Retrieved from http://www.telegraph.co.uk/finance/financialcrisis/9270884/Debt-crisis-Greek-euro-exit-looms-closer-as-banks-crumble.html.

Ewing, J. (2012) Report Shows Depth of Distress in Europe, *The New York Times*, 11 March. Retrieved from http://www.nytimes.com/2012/03/12/business/global/eu-bank-crisis-only-narrowly-averted-catastrophe.html?scp=1&sq=Report%20shows%20depth%20of%20distress%20in%20Europe&st=cse.

Ewing, J. and Dempsey, J. (2011) Germany and Its Exporters Look East, *The New York Times*, 19 July. Retrieved from http://www.nytimes.com/2011/07/19/business/global/Germany-Europes-Powerhouse-Drifts-East.html.

Fabbrini, S. (2007) *Compound Democracies: Why the United States and Europe Are Becoming Similar*, Oxford, UK: Oxford University Press.

Falkner, G., Leiber, S. and Treib, O. (2004) Non-Compliance with EU Directives in the Member States: Opposition Through the Backdoor?, *West European Politics*, 27(3), 452–73.

Falkner, G., Treib, O. and Holzleitner, E. (2008) *Compliance in the Enlarged European Union: Livng Rights or Dead Letters?*, Aldershot, UK: Ashgate.

Farrell, H. and Héritier, A. (2004) Interorganizational Negotiation and Intraorganizational Power in Shared Decision Making: Early Agreements Under CoDecision and Their Impact on the European Parliament and Council, *Comparative Political Studies*, 37(10), 1184–212.

Featherstone, K. (2011) The JCMS Annual Lecture: The Greek Sovereign Debt Crisis and EMU: A Failing State in a Skewed Regime, *Journal of Common Market Studies*, 49(2), 193–217.

Fligstein, N. (2008) *EuroClash: The EU, European Identity, and the Future of Europe*, Oxford, UK: Oxford University Press.

Friedrich, C. J. (1968) *Trends of Federalism in Theory and Practice*, New York: Praeger.

Frontex (2012) Home Page. Retrieved from http://www.frontex.europa.eu/.

Gardner, A. (2011) Switched on to Potential Savings?, *European Voice*, 30 June. Retrieved from http://www.europeanvoice.com/article/imported/switched-on-to-potential-savings-/71498.aspx.

Garzon, I. (2006) *Reforming the Common Agricultural Policy: History of a Paradigm Change*, Basingstoke, UK: Palgrave Macmillan.

Giegerich, B. and Wallace, W. (2010) Foreign and Security Policy: Civilian Power Europe and American Leadership, in H. Wallace, M. A. Pollack and A. R. Young (eds), *Policy-Making in the European Union* (6th edn) Oxford, UK: Oxford University Press, pp. 432–55.

Giersch, H. (2002) Germany and Europe since 1947, in H. Lim, U. K. Park and G. C. Harcourt (eds), *Editing Economics: Essays in Honour of Mark Perlman*, London: Routledge, pp. 231–49.

Ginsberg, R. H. (2001) *The European Union in International Politics: Baptism by Fire*, Oxford, UK: Rowman & Littlefield.

Ginsberg, R. H. and Penksa, S. E. (2012) *The European Union in Global Security: The Politics of Impact*, Basingstoke, UK: Palgrave Macmillan.

Goldirova, R. (2008) Two-speed Europe May Emerge over Divorce Rules, *European Voice*, July 25. Retrieved from http://euobserver.com/22/26546.

Golub, J. (2007) Survival Analysis and European Union Decision-Making, *European Union Politics*, 8(2), 155–79.

Gordon, P. and Meunier, S. (2001) *French Challenge: Adapting to Globalization*, Washington, DC: Brookings Institution.

Gottdiener, M. (1995) *Postmodern Semiotics: Material Culture and the Forms of Postmodern Life*, Oxford, UK: Blackwell.

Grant, W. (2010) *How Can Direct Payments be Justified after 2013?* Retrieved from http://commonagpolicy.blogspot.com/.

Graziano, M. (2010) *The Failure of Italian Nationhood: The Geopolitics of a Troubled Identity*, trans. B. Knowlton, New York: Macmillan.

Greenwood, J. (2011) *Interest Representation in the European Union* (3rd edn), Basingstoke, UK: Palgrave Macmillan.

Greer, S. L. (2006) Uninvited Europeanization: Neofunctionalism and the EU in Health Policy, *Journal of European Public Policy*, 13(1), 134–52.

Greve, M. S. (2011) Bailouts or Bankruptcy?, *Engage: The Journal of the Federalist Society*, 12(2), 107–10.

Gross, E. (2009) *The Europeanization of National Foreign Policy: Continuity and Change in European Crisis Management*, Basingstoke, UK: Palgrave Macmillan.

Guardian (2011) Euro Will Not Survive without Urgent Action, Says Lord Lamont, *Guardian*, 17 December. Retrieved from http://www.guardian.co.uk/business/2011/dec/17/euro-survive-urgent-action-lamont.

Haas, E. and Schmitter, P. (1964) Economics and Differential Patterns of Political Integration: Projections about Unity in Latin America, *International Organization*, 18(4), 705–737.

Haas, E. B. (1958) *The Uniting of Europe: Political, Social and Economic Forces 1950–57*, Stanford, CA: Stanford University Press.

Habermas, J. (1999) The European Nation-State: On the Post and Future of Sovereignty and Citizenship, in C. Cronin and P. D. Greiff (eds), *Inclusion of the Other: Studies in Political Theory*, Cambridge, MA: MIT Press, pp. 108–28.

Häge, F. (2008) Who Decides in the Council of the European Union?, *Journal of Common Market Studies*, 46(3), 533–58.

Häge, F. and Kaeding, M. (2007) Reconsidering the European Parliament's Legislative Power: Formal vs. Informal Procedures, *Journal of European Integration* 29(3), 341–61.

Hagemann, S. and De Clerck-Sachsse, J. (2007) Old Rules, New Game: Decision-Making in the Council of Ministers after the 2004 Enlargement, *CEPS Special Report*.

Hall, P. and Soskice, D. (2001) An Introduction to Varieties of Capitalism, in P. Hall and D. Soskice (eds), *Varieties of Capitalism: The Institutional Foundations of Comparative Capitalism*, Oxford,, UK: Oxford University Press, pp. 1–6.

Hardacre, A. and Kaeding, M. (2011) Delegated and Implementing Acts: The New Worlds of Comitology – Implications for European and National Public Administrations, *EIPA Scope*. Retrieved from publications.eipa.eu.

Hartlapp, M. and Leiber, S. (2010) The Implementation of EU Social Policy: The 'Southern Problem' Revisited, *Journal of European Public Policy*, 17(4), 468–86.

Hatzopoulos, V. (2008) Legal Aspects of the Internal Market for Services, in J. Pelkmans, D. Hanf and M. Chang (eds), *The EU Internal Market in Comparative Perspective: Economic, Political and Legal Analyses*, Brussels: Peter Lang, pp. 139–88.

Hawley, C. (2004) Hot Topic in Germany: Aggression in World War I, *The Christian Science Monitor*. Retrieved from http://www.csmonitor.com/2004/0802/p06s03-woeu.html,

Hay, P. (2007) The Development of the Public Policy Barrier to Judgment Recognition within the European Community, *The European Legal Forum*, 6, 289–94.

Hayes-Renshaw, F. and Wallace, H. (2006) *The Council of Ministers*, Basingstoke, UK: Palgrave Macmillan.

Heckathorn, D. D. and Maser, S. M. (1990) The Contractual Architecture of Public Policy: A Critical Reconstruction of Lowi's Typology, *The Journal of Politics, 52*(4), 1101–23.

Heidenreich, M. and Bischoff, G. (2008) The Open Method of Co-ordination: A Way to the Europeanization of Social and Employment Policies?, *Journal of Common Market Studies, 46*(3), 497–532.

Heidenreich, M. and Zeitlin, J. (eds) (2009) *Changing European Employment and Welfare Regimes: The Influence of the Open Method of Co-ordination on National Reforms*, Abingdon, UK: Routledge.

Heisenberg, D. (2005) The Institution of 'Consensus' in the European Union: Formal Versus Informal Decision-Making in the Council, *European Journal of Political Research, 44*, 65–90.

Heller, T. and Pelkmans, J. (1986) The Federal Economy: Law and Economic Integration and the Positive State – the USA and Europe Compared in an Economic Perspective, Book 1: A Political, Legal and Economic Overview, in M. Cappelletti, M. Seccombe and J. Weiler (eds), *Integration through Law: Europe and the American Federal Experience, Vol. 1: Methods, Tools and Institutions*, New York: Walter de Gruyter, pp. 245–411.

Héritier, A. (2003) New Modes of Governance in Europe: Increasing Political Capacity and Policy Effectiveness?, in T. A. Börzel and R. Cichowsk (eds), *The State of the European Union: Law, Politics and Society*, Oxford, UK: Oxford University Press, pp. 105–26.

Héritier, A. and Lehmkuhl, D. (2008) The Shadow of Hierarchy and New Modes of Governance, *Journal of Public Policy, 28*(1), 1–17.

Héritier, A. and Rhodes, M. (eds)) (2011) *New Modes of Governance in Europe: Governing in the Shadow of Hierarchy*, Basingstoke, UK: Palgrave Macmillan.

Hertz, R. and Leuffen, D. (2011) Too Big to Run? Analysing the Impact of Enlargement on the Speed of EU Decision-Making, *European Union Politics, 12*(2), 93–215.

Hildebrand, P. M. (2005) The European Community's Environmental Policy, 1957 to '1992': From Incidental Measures to an International Regime?, in A. Jordan (ed.), *Environmental Policy in the European Union: Actors, Institutions, and Processes*, London: Earthscan.

Hill, C. (2006) The European Powers in the Security Council: Differing Interests, Differing Arenas, in K. V. Laatikainen and K. E. Smith (eds), *The European Union at the United Nations: Intersecting Multilateralisms*, Basingstoke, UK: Palgrave Macmillan, pp. 49–69.

Hill, C. and Smith, K. E. (2000) *European Foreign Policy: Key Documents*, London: Routledge.

Hix, S. (2006) The European Union as a Polity, in K. A. Jørgensen, M. A. Pollack and B. Rosamond (eds), *Handbook of European Union Politics*, London: Sage, (pp. 141–57).

Hix, S. (2008) *What's Wrong with the European Union & How to Fix It*, Cambridge, UK: Polity Press.

Hix, S. and Noury, A. G. (2009) After Enlargement: Voting Patterns in the Sixth European Parliament, *Legislative Studies Quarterly, 34*(2), 159–74.

Hix, S., Noury, A. G. and Roland, G. (2007) *Democratic Politics in the European Parliament*, Cambridge, UK: Cambridge University Press.

Hodge, C. C. (2005) *Atlanticism for a New Century: The Rise, Triumph, and Decline of NATO*, Englewood Cliffs, NJ: Prentice-Hall.

Hoffmann, S. (1966) Obstinate or Obsolete: The Fate of the Nation State and the Case of Western Europe, *Daedelus, 95*, 862–915.

Hogwood, B. W. and Gunn, L. W. (1984) *Policy Analysis for the Real World*, Oxford, UK: Oxford University Press.

Holland, M. (2004) Development Policy: Paradigm Shifts and the 'Normalization' of a Privileged Partnership?, in D. Dinan and M. Green-Cowles (eds), *Developments in the European Union 2*, Basingstoke, UK: Palgrave Macmillan, pp. 275–95.

Hope, K. and Spiegel, P. (2011) Greece Agrees to More Austerity Cuts, *The Financial Times*, 24 June. Retrieved from http://www.ft.com/intl/cms/s/0/29203b60-9da0-11e0-9a70-00144feabdc0.html#axzz1QAKrMXkC.

House, J., Brat, I. and Roman, D. (2012) Deficit Grows in Spain as Capital Flight Accelerates, *The Wall Street Journal*, 31 July. Retrieved from http://online.wsj.com/article/SB10000872396390444860104577560860867437208.html.

Howlett, M., Ramesh, M. and Perl, A. (2009) *Studying Public Policy: Policy Cycles and Policy Subsystems* (3rd edn), Oxford, UK: Oxford University Press.

Hunter, R. and Biscop, S. (2011) *The United States, NATO and the European Union: Partnership in Balance*. Retrieved from http://www.acus.org/files/publication_pdfs/403/Partnership_SAGIssueBrief_0.pdf.

ILGA-Europe (2012) *ILGA-Europe Rainbow Map*. Retrieved from http://www.ilga-europe.org/home/publications/reports_and_other_materials/rainbow_europe_map_and_index_may_2012.

Inman, P. and Traynor, I. (2011) Stock Markets Slump as Euro Hits 11-month Low Against the Dollar, *Guardian*, December 14. Retrieved from http://www.guardian.co.uk/business/2011/dec/14/stock-markets-slump-euro-dollar.

International Monetary Fund (2011) *Currency Composition of Official Foreign Exchange Reserves*. Retrieved from http://www.imf.org/external/np/sta/cofer/eng/cofer.pdf.

International Security Information Service, Europe (2012) *The Role of EU Battlegroups in European Defence*, (56)

Brussels: ISIS Europe. Retrieved from http://www.isis-europe.eu/publication/european-security-review/esr-no-56-role-eu-battlegroups-european-defence.

Issing, O. (2004) The Stability and Growth Pact: The Appropriate Fiscal Framework for EMU, *International Economics and Economic Policy*, 1(1), 9–13.

Jacobsson, K. and Vifell, A. (2007) Deliberative Trans-nationalism? Analysing the Role of Committee Interaction, in I. Linsenmann, C. O. Meyer and W. T. Wessels (eds), *Soft Co-ordination Economic Government of the EU: A Balance Sheet of New Modes of Policy Coordination*, Basingstoke, UK: Palgrave Macmillan, pp. 163–86.

Jacquet, P. and Pisani-Ferry, J. (2001) Economic Policy Coordination in the Euro-Zone: What Has Been Achieved? What Should Be Done?, *Centre for European Reform* (January).

Jordan, A. (2005) Introduction: European Union Environmental Policy – Actors, Institutions, and Processes, in A. Jordan (ed.), *Environmental Policy in the European Union: Actors, Institutions, and Processes*, London: Earthscan, (pp. 2–15).

Judt, T. (2005) *Postwar: A History of Europe since 1945*, New York: Penguin.

Juenger, F. K. (1998) Two European Conflicts Conventions, *Wellington Law Review, 28*, 527–43. Retrieved from http://www.victoria.ac.nz/law/NZACL/PDFS/Vol_3_1997/Juenger.pdf.

Junge, K. (2007) Differentiated European Integration, in M. Cini (ed.), *European Union Politics*, Oxford, UK: Oxford University Press, pp. 391–404.

Kagan, R. (2003) *Of Paradise and Power: America vs. Europe in the New World Order*, New York: Alfred Knopf.

Kaiser, R. and Prange, H. (2002) A New Concept of Deepening European Integration? – The European Research Area and the Emerging Role of Policy Coordination in a Multi-Level Governance System, *European Integration online Papers (EIoP)*, 6(18).)

Kanter, J. (2011a) Europe Tries to Curb U.S. Role in Tracking Terrorists' Funds, *The New York Times*, July 13. Retrieved from http://www.nytimes.com/2011/07/14/world/europe/14terror.html.

Kanter, J. (2011b) European Union Seeks Power to Block Bilateral Energy Deals, *The New York Times*, 7 September. Retrieved from http://www.nytimes.com/2011/09/08/business/global/eu-seeks-power-to-bloc-bilateral-energy-deals.html?_r=1&ref=nabuccopipeline.

Kardasheva, R. (2009) The Power to Delay: The European Parliament's Influence in the Consultation Procedure, *Journal of Common Market Studies, 47*(2), 385–409.

Kassim, H. and Menon, A. (2004) European Integration since the 1990s: Member States and the European Commission, *ARENA Working Paper 6/04*.

Kaunert, C. and Leonard, S. (2011) The European Union and Refugees: Towards more Restrictive Asylum Policies in the European Union?, *GRITIM Working Paper Series, 8* (Summer).

Keeler, J. (1993) Opening the Window for Reform, *Comparative Political Studies 25*(4), 433–86.

Kelemen, R. D. (2004) *The Rules of Federalism: Institutions and Regulatory Politics in the EU and Beyond*, Cambridge, MA: Harvard University Press.

Kelemen, R. D. (2011) *Eurolegalism: The Transformation of Law and Regulation in the EU*, Cambridge, MA: Harvard University Press.

Kelemen, R. D. and Majone, G. (2012) Managing Europeanization – The European Agencies, in J. Peterson and M. Shackleton (eds), *The Institutions of the European Union* (3rd edn), Oxford, UK: Oxford University Press, pp. 219–40.

Kelemen, R. D. and Schmidt, S. K. (2012) Introduction – The European Court of Justice and Legal Integration: Perpetual Momentum?, *Journal of European Public Policy*, 19(1), 1–7.

Kelemen, R. D. and Tarrant, A. D. (2011) The Political Foundations of the Eurocracy, *West European Politics*, 34(5), 922–947.

Kelemen, R. D. and Vogel, D. (2010) Trading Places: The Role of the United States and the European Union in International Environmental Politics, *Comparative Political Studies*, 43(4), 427–56.

Keohane, R. and Nye, J. (1977) *Power and Interdependence: World Politics in Transition*, Boston, MA: Little, Brown.

Kingdon, J. (1995) *Agendas, Alternatives and Public Policies* (2nd edn), New York: Longman.

Knill, C. and Lenschow, A. (eds) (2000) *Implementing EU Environmental Policy: New Directions and Old Problems*, Manchester, UK: Manchester University Press.

Kohler-Koch, B. (2010) Civil Society and EU Democracy: 'Astroturf' Representation?, *Journal of European Public Policy*, 17(1), 100–16.

Kohler-Koch, B. and Rittberger, B. (2006) Review Article: The 'Governance Turn' in EU Studies, in U. Sedelmeier and A. R. Young (eds), *The JCMS Annual Review of the European Union in 2005*, Oxford, UK: Blackwell, (pp. 27–49).

Kok, W. (2004) *Facing the Challenge: The Lisbon Strategy for Growth and Employment (The Kok Report)*. Retrieved from http://ec.europa.eu/research/evaluations/pdf/archive/fp6-evidence-base/evaluation_studies_and_reports/evaluation_studies_and_reports_2004/the_lisbon_strategy_for_growth_and_employment_report_from_the_high_level_group.pdf.

König, T. (2007). Divergence or Convergence? From Ever-Growing to Ever-Slowing European Legislative Decision-Making, *European Journal of Political Research*, 10(4), 417–44.

König, T., Luertgert, B. and Dannwolf, T. (2006) Quantifying European Legislative Research: Using CELEX and PreLex in EU Legislative Studies, *European Union Politics*, 7(4), 555–76.

Koslowski, R. (1999) A Constructivist Approach to Understanding the European Union as a Federal Polity, *Journal of European Public Policy*, 6(4), 561–78.

Kratsa-Tsagaropolou, R., Vidal-Qudras, A. and Rothe-Behrendt, M. (2009) *Activity Report: 1 May 2004 to 13 July 2009*, Brussels: European Parliament.

Krugman, P. (2011) Can Europe Be Saved?, *The New York Times*, 11 January. Retrieved from http://www.nytimes.com/2011/01/16/magazine/16Europe-t.html?hp.

Kubosova, L. (2008) Irish No Raises Questions over EU Commission Size, *EU Observer*, 16 June. Retrieved from http://euobserver.com/9/26328.

Kurpas, S., Grøn, C. and Kaczy ski, P. M. (2008) The European Commission after Enlargement: Does More Add up to Less?, *CEPS Special Report*.

Laatikainen, K. V. and Smith, K. E. (2006) Introduction – The European Union at the United Nations: Leader, Partner or Failure?, in K. V. Laatikainen and K. E. Smith (eds), *The European Union at the United Nations: Intersecting Multilateralisms*, Basingstoke, UK: Palgrave Macmillan, pp. 1–23.

Laffan, B. (1997) *The Finances of the European Union*, London: Macmillan.

Lejour, A. (2008) Economic Aspects of the Internal Market for Services, in J. Pelkmans, D. Hanf and M. Chang (eds), *The EU Internal Market in Comparative Perspective: Economic, Political and Legal Analyses* Brussels: Peter Lang, pp. 115–37.

Lelieveldt, H. and Princen, S. (2011) *The Politics of the European Union*, Cambridge, UK: Cambridge University Press.

Lenschow, A. (2002) New Regulatory Approaches in 'Greening' EU Policies, *European Law Journal* 8(1), 19–37.

Leuffen, D., Rittberger, B. and Schimmelfennig, F. (2012) *Integration and Differentiation in the European Union*, Basingstoke, UK: Palgrave Macmillan.

Lichtblau, E. and Risen, J. (2006) Bank Data Is Sifted by U.S. in Secret to Block Terror, *The New York Times*, 26 June. Retrieved from http://www.nytimes.com/2006/06/23/washington/23intel.html?pagewanted=all.

Liefferink, D. and Andersen, M. S. (2005) Strategies of the 'Green' Member States in EU Environmental Policy-making in A. Jordan (ed.), *Environmental Policy in the European Union: Actors, Institutions, and Processes*, London: Earthscan, pp. 49–66.

Liefferink, D., Arts, B., Kamstra, J. and Ooijevaar, J. (2009) Leaders and Laggards in Environmental Policy: A Quantitative Analysis of Domestic Policy Outputs, *Journal of European Public Policy*, 16(5), 677–700.

Lincoln, D. (2008) Drawing the EBA (Everything But Arms) Map: Least Developed Country Classification and the Case of EBA Sugar, *Area 40*(2), 218–27.

Lindberg, L. (1963) *The Political Dynamic of European Economic Integration*, Oxford, UK: Oxford University Press.

Linsenmann, I., Meyer, C. O. and Wessels, W. T. (eds) (2007) *Economic Government of the EU: A Balance Sheet of New Modes of Policy Coordination*, Basingstoke, UK: Palgrave Macmillan.

Lodge, M. (2007) Comparing Non-Hierarchical Governance in Action: The Open Method of Co-ordination in Pensions and Information Society, *Journal of Common Market Studies*, 45(2), 343–65.

Lowi, T. (1964) American Business, Public Policy, Case-Studies and Political Theory, *World Politics*, 16(4), 677–715.

Lowi, T. (1972) Four Systems of Policy, Politics, and Choice, *Public Administration Review*, 32(4), 298–310.

MacMillan, C. (2009) The Application of Neofunctionalism to the Enlargement Process: The Case of Turkey, *Journal of Common Market Studies*, 47(4), 789–809.

Magnette, P. (2005) *What Is the European Union? Nature and Prospects*, Basingstoke, UK: Palgrave Macmillan.

Majone, G. (1994) The Rise of the Regulatory State in Europe, *West European Politics*, 17(3), 77–101.

Majone, G. (1996) *Regulating Europe*, New York: Routledge.

Majone, G. (2002) The European Commission: The Limits of Centralization and the Perils of Parliamentarization, *Governance*, 15(3), 375–92.

Majone, G. (2005) *Dilemmas of European Integration: The Ambiguities and Pitfalls of Integration by Stealth*, Oxford, UK: Oxford University Press.

Majone, G. (2006a) The Common Sense of European Integration, *Journal of European Public Policy*, 13(5), 607–26.

Majone, G. (2006b) Managing Europeanization: The European Agencies, in J. Peterson and M. Shackleton (eds), *The Institutions of the European Union* (2nd edn), Oxford, UK: Oxford University Press, pp. 190–209.

Mallinder, L. (2008) Shoemakers Fight Cheap Imports, *European Voice*, 24 April. Retrieved from http://www.europeanvoice.com/article/imported/shoemakers-fight-cheap-imports/60513.aspx.

Maloney, H. and Pop, V. (2011) Denmark's Border Controls 'Insufficiently Justified', Says Commission, *EUobserver.com*, 17 July. Retrieved from http://euobserver.com/news/32638.

Manolopoulos, J. (2011) *Greece's 'Odious' Debt: The Looting of the Hellenic Republic by the Euro, the Political Elite and the Investment Community*, New York: Anthem Press.

Marks, G. (1996) An Actor-centered Approach to Multi-level Governance, *Regional & Federal Studies*, 6(2), 20–40.

Martens, M. (2010) Voice or Loyalty? The Evolution of the European Environment Agency (EEA), *Journal of Common Market Studies, 48*(4), 881–901.

Mazzucelli, C. (1999) *France and Germany at Maastricht: Politics and Negotiations to Create the European Union*, London: Garland Science Publishing.

McCormick, J. (2001) *Environmental Policy in the European Union*, Basingstoke, UK: Palgrave Macmillan.

McGillivray, F. (2004) *Privileging Industry*, Princeton, NJ: Princeton University Press.

McGowan, L. (2007) Theorising European Integration: Revisiting Neofunctionalism and Testing Its Suitability for Explaining the Development of EC Competition Policy, *European Integration online Papers (EIoP), 11*(3).

McGuire, S. M. and Lindeque, J. P. (2010) The Diminishing Returns to Trade Policy in the European Union, *Journal of Common Market Studies, 48*(5), 1329–49.

McNamara, K. R. (1999) Consensus and Constraint: Ideas and Capital Mobility in European Monetary Integration, *Journal of Common Market Studies, 37*(3), 455–76.

McNamara, K. R. (2004) Making Money, Making States: Political Development, the Greenback, and the Euro, *Institute of European Studies Working Paper*.

Meade, J. E. (1953) *Problems of Economic Union*, Chicago: University of Chicago Press.

Menon, A. (2010) Foreign and Security Policy after the Lisbon Treaty, *EUSA Review, 23*(1), 2–4.

Meunier, S. and Nicolaïdis, K. (2006) The European Union as a Conflicted Trade Power, *Journal of European Public Policy, 13*(6), 906–25.

Molle, W. (2007) *European Cohesion Policy*, New York: Routledge.

Monar, J. (2010) *The European Union's Institutional Balance of Power after the Lisbon Treaty*, Paper presented at the Global Jean Monnet/ECSA-World conference, Brussels. Retrieved from www.http://ec.europa.eu/education/jean-monnet/doc/ecsa10/monarb_en.pdf.

Monar, J. (2011a) Deviations from and Alternatives to the Community Method in Justice and Home Affairs, in R. Dehousse (ed.), *The Community Method: Obstinate or Obsolete?* Basingstoke, UK: Palgrave, pp. 118–34.

Monar, J. (2011b) Justice and Home Affairs, in N. Copsey and T. Haughton (eds), *The JCMS Annual Review of the European Union in 2010*, Oxford, UK: Wiley-Blackwell, pp. 145–64.

Monar, J. (2011c) Modes of EU Governance in the Justice and Home Affairs Domain: Specific Factors, Types, Evolution Trends and Evaluation, in U. Diedrichs, W. Reiners and W. Wessels (eds), *Dynamics of Change in EU Governance*, Cheltenham, UK: Edward Elgar, pp. 180–209.

Monnet, J. (1978) *Memoirs*, London: Collins.

Moravcsik, A. (1991) Negotiating the Single European Act: National Interests and Conventional Statecraft in the European Community, *International Organization, 45*(1), 19–56.

Moravcsik, A. (1993) Preferences and Power in the European Community: A Liberal Governmentalist Approach, *Journal of Common Market Studies, 31*(4), 473–524.

Moravcsik, A. (1995) Liberal Intergovernmentalism and Integration: A Rejoinder, *Journal of Common Market Studies, 33*(4), 611–28.

Moravcsik, A. (1998) *The Choice for Europe: Social Purpose and State Power from Messina to Maastricht*, Ithaca, NY: Cornell University Press.

Moravcsik, A. (1999) A New Statecraft? Supranational Entrepreneurs and International Cooperation, *International Organization, 53*(2), 267–306.

Moravcsik, A. (2001) Federalism in the European Union: Rhetoric and Reality?, in K. Nicolaidis and R. Howse (eds), *The Federal Vision: Legitmacy and Levels of Governance in the United States and the European Union*, Oxford, UK: Oxford University Press, pp. 161–90.

Moravcsik, A. (2005) The European Constitutional Compromise and the Neofunctionalist Legacy, *Journal of European Public Policy, 12*(2), 349–86.

Moravcsik, A. (2010) *The Old Governance: Informal Institutions in the EU*, New York University Workshop: 'Rule-Making in the EU and Global Governance'.

Mowle, T. (2004) *Allies at Odds? The United States and the European Union*, Gordonsville, VA: Palgrave Macmillan.

Moyer, H. W. (1993) *EC Decisionmaking, The MacSharry Reforms of the CAP, Maastricht, and the GATT Uruguay Rounds*, Paper presented at the Third Biennial Conference of the European Community Studies Association, Omni-Shorham Hotel, Washington, DC.

Mundell, R. A. (1961) A Theory of Optimum Currency Areas, *The American Economic Review, 51*(4), 657–65.

NATO (2008) *Bucharest Summit Declaration Issued by the Heads of State and Government participating in the meeting of the North Atlantic Council in Bucharest on 3 April 2008*. Retrieved from http://www.summitbucharest.ro/en/doc_202.html.

Naurin, D. and Wallace, H. (eds) (2008) *Unveiling the Council of the European Union: Games Governments Play in Brussels*, Basingstoke, UK: Palgrave Macmillan.

Nedergaard, P. (2006) Market Failures and Government Failures: A Theoretical Model of the Common Agricultural Policy, *Public Choice, 127*(3/4), 393–413.

NEMIS (2012) *Newsletter on European Migration Issues for Judges*, 2012(2).

Neuman, W. and Sayare, S. (2011) Egyptian Seeds Are Linked to E. coli in Germany and France, *The New York Times*, 29 June. Retrieved from http://www.nytimes.com/2011/06/30/world/middleeast/30ecoli.html/.

New York Times, The (2011) The Danger of Contagion from Europe, *New York Times Interactive*, 10 November.

Retrieved from http://www.nytimes.com/interactive/2011/11/10/world/europe/the-risk-to-banks-of-europes-debt-problems.html?ref=global.

Nicholson, N. (2002) Policy Choices and the Uses of State Power: The Work of Theodore J. Lowi, *Policy Sciences*, *35*(2), 163–77.

Nielsen, N. (2012) EU–China Trade Relations 'Distorted', MEPs Say, *EUobserver*, 24 May.

Niemann, A. (2005) *Conceptualising Common Commercial Policy: Explaining Dynamics and Inertia from the Amsterdam IGC to the Constitutional Treaty*, Paper presented at the European Union Studies Association, Austin, Texas. Retrieved from http://aei.pitt.edu/3080/1/EUSA2005_paper_A.Niemann_CCP_final.pdf.

Niemann, A. (2006) Explaining Visa, Asylum and Immigration Policy Treaty Revision: Insights from a Revised Neofunctionalist Framework, *Constitutionalism Web-Paper, ERPA, 1*. Retrieved from https://www.wiso.uni-hamburg.de/fileadmin/sowi/politik/governance/ConWeb_Papers/conweb1-2006.pdf.

Nugent, N. (2010) *Government and Politics of the European Union* (7th edn), Basingstoke, UK: Palgrave Macmillan.

Nuland, V. (2008) *U.S. Ambassador to NATO, Victoria Nuland, Speech in Paris: Ambassador Discusses Strengthening Global Security for Europe*. Retrieved 13 March 2010 from http://usinfo.state.gov.

Nye, J. (2004) *Soft Power: The Means to Success in World Politics*, New York: Public Affairs.

O'Connor, S. (2008) Budgeting for Changing Times: Interview with Budget Commissioner, Dalia Grybauskaite, *E.Sharp*, November–December, 22–4.

Okun, A. (1975) *Equality and Efficiency: The Big Tradeoff*, Washington, DC: Brookings Institution.

O'Neill, M. (1996) *The Politics of European Integration: A Reader*, London: Routledge.

Ostrom, V. (1987) *The Political Theory of a Compound Republic: Designing the American Experiment* (2nd edn), Lincoln, NE: University of Nebraska.

Overseas Development Institute (2012) *The Next Decade of EU Trade Policy? Confronting Global Challenges?* Retrieved from http://www.odi.org.uk/resources/docs/7727.pdf.

Panke, D. (2010) Small States in the European Union: Structural Disadvantages in EU Policy-Making and Counter-Strategies, *Journal of European Public Policy*, *17*(6), 799–817.

Panke, D. (2012) Lobbying Institutional Key Players: How States Seek to Influence the European Commission, the Council Presidency and the European Parliament, *Journal of Common Market Studies*, *50*(1), 129–50.

Papadimitriou, D. (2012) Introduction, in P. Copeland and D. Papadimitriou (eds), *The EU's Lisbon Strategy: Evaluating Success, Understanding Failure*, Basingstoke, UK: Palgrave Macmillan, pp. 1–7.

Parker, C. and Karlsson, C. (2010) Climate Change and the European Union's Leadership Moment: An Inconvenient Truth?, *Journal of Common Market Studies*, *48*(4), 923–43.

Parsons, W. (1995) *Public Policy: An Introduction to the Theory and Practice of Public Policy*, Aldershot, UK: Edward Elgar.

Pelkmans, J. (2005) Mutual Recognition in Goods and Services: An Economic Perspective in F. Kostoris and P. Schioppa (eds), *The Principles of Mutual Recognition in the European Integration Process*, Basingstoke, UK: Palgrave Macmillan, pp. 83–128.

Peston, R. (2011) *The Eurozone's Borrowing Costs May Stay Lethally High*, BBC, 22 November. Retrieved from http://www.bbc.co.uk/news/business-15816887.

Peterson, J. (1995) Decision-Making in the European Union: Towards a Framework for Analysis, *Journal of European Public Policy*, *2*(1), 69–93.

Peterson, J. and Bomberg, E. (1999) *Decision-Making in the European Union*, Basingstoke, UK: Macmillan.

Peterson, J. and Shackleton, M. (2012) *The Institutions of the European Union* (3rd edn), Oxford, UK: Oxford University Press.

Piattoni, S. (2010) *The Theory of Multi-Level Governance*, New York: Oxford University Press.

Pignal, S. (2011a) Brussels Reveals Tighter Border-free Rules, *The Financial Times*, 21 August.

Pignal, S. (2011b) *EU Summit: A Last-minute Deal on Schengen*. Retrieved from http://blogs.ft.com/brusselsblog/2011/06/eu-summit-a-last-minute-deal-on-schengen/#axzz1X9BAfXTf.

Pinder, J. (1993) From Milan to Maastricht: Fifty Years of Federalist Struggle for the Unity of Europe, *The Federalist*, *25*(3), 152–64.

Pisani-Ferry, J., Italianer, A. and Lescure, R. (1993) Stabilisation Properties of Budgetary Systems: A Simulation Analysis, *European Economy, Reports and Studies*, *5*, 513–38.

Pochet, P. (2011) Social Europe: Why Hard Law Remains Important, in R. Dehousse (ed.), *The Community Method: Obstinate or Obsolete?*, Basingstoke, UK: Palgrave Macmillan, pp. 116–85.

Pollack, M. A. (1995) Regional Actors in an Intergovernmental Play: The Making and Implementation of EC Structural Policy, in S. Mazey and C. Rhodes (eds), *The State of the European Union, Vol 3: Building a European Polity?*, Boulder, CO: Lynne Rienner, 361–90.

Pollack, M. A. (2000) The End of Creeping Competence? EU Policy-making Since Maastricht, *Journal of Common Market Studies*, *38*(3), 519–38.

Pollack, M. A. (2003) *The Engines of European Integration*, Oxford, UK: Oxford University Press.

Pollack, M. A. and Ruhlman, M. A. (2009) The Heroic Age of European Integration Is Over: Institutional and Policy Developments, 1957–2007, in D. Phinnemore and A. Warleigh-Lack (eds), *Reflections on European Integration: 50 Years of the Treaty of Rome*, Basingstoke, UK: Palgrave Macmillan, pp. 43–73.

Pop, V. (2011) Chinese Shoes to Be Imported without Anti-dumping Tariffs, *EUobserver.com*. Retrieved from http://euobserver.com/china/32004.

Povoledo, E. (2011) Divorce Tourists Go Abroad to Quickly Dissolve Their Italian Marriages, *The New York Times*, 15 August. Retrieved from http://www.nytimes.com/2011/08/15/world/europe/15italy.html?pagewanted=all.

Princen, S. (2009) *Agenda-Setting in the European Union*, Basingstoke, UK: Palgrave Macmillan.

Princen, S. (2010) Agenda-Setting, in E. Versluis, M. van Keulen and P. Stephenson (eds), *Analyzing the EU Policy Process*, Basingstoke, UK: Palgrave Macmillan, pp. 107–31.

Puetter, U. and Wiener, A. (2009) EU Foreign Policy Elites and Fundamental Norms: Implications for Governance, *RECON Online Working Papers*. Retrieved from http://www.reconproject.eu/main.php/RECON_wp_0917.pdf?fileitem=5456591.

Rankin, J. (2011a) Clash of Visions over Agricultural Reform, *European Voice*, 10 March. Retrieved from http://www.europeanvoice.com/article/imported/clash-of-visions-over-agricultural-reform/70485.aspx.

Rankin, J. (2011b) Towards a Fairer EU Agriculture Policy?, *European Voice*, 14 April. Retrieved from http://www.europeanvoice.com/article/imported/towards-a-fairer-eu-agriculture-policy-/70836.aspx.

Rasch, M. (2009) *The European Union at the United Nations: The Functioning and Coherence of EU External Representation in a State-centric Environment*, Leiden, The Netherlands: Martinus Nijhoff.

Rees, W. (2011) *The US–EU Security Relationship*, Basingstoke, UK: Palgrave Macmillan.

Regelsberger, E. (2007) The EU as an Actor in Foreign and Security Policy: Some Key Features of CFSP in an Historical Perspective, *CFSP Forum*, 5(4), 1–8.

Reinhart, C. M. and Rogoff, K. S. (2009) *This Time Is Different: Eight Centuries of Financial Folly*, Princeton, NJ: Princeton University Press.

Rettman, A. (2012) Ministers Identify Glitches in EU Diplomatic Service, *EUobserver*, 6 January. Retrieved from http://euobserver.com/24/114783.

Rhodes, R. A. W. (1974) Regional Policy and a 'Europe of the Regions': A Critical Assessment. *Regional Studies*, 8(2), 105–14.

Rieger, E. (2005) Agricultural Policy, in H. Wallace, W. Wallace and M. A. Pollack (eds), *Policy-Making in the European Union* (5th edn), Oxford, UK: Oxford University Press, pp. 161–90.

Riker, W. H. (1964) *Federalism: Origin, Operation, Significance*, Boston, MA: Little, Brown.

Risse, T. (2010) *Community of Europeans? Transnational Identities and Public Spheres*, Ithaca, NY: Cornell University Press.

Rodden, J. A. (2006) *Hamilton's Paradox: The Promise and Peril of Fiscal Federalism*, Cambridge, UK: Cambridge University Press.

Rohan, B. (2012) German Wages to Rise but Restraint still Rules, *Reuters*, 1 February. Retrieved from http://www.reuters.com/article/2012/02/01/germany-wages-idUSL5E8CV5X420120201.

Rowe, C. (2011) *Regional Representations in the EU: Between Diplomacy and Interest Mediation*, Basingstoke, UK: Palgrave Macmillan.

Rübbelke, D. T. G. and Aakre, S. (2008) Adaptation to Climate Change in the European Union: Efficiency vs. Equity Considerations, *CEPS Report, 301*.

Sabel, C. F. and Zeitlin, J. (2009) *Experimentalist Governance in the European Union: Towards a New Architecture*, Oxford, UK: Oxford University Press.

Sandholtz, W. and Sweet, A. S. (1998a) Integration, Supranational Governance, and the Institutionalization of the European Polity, in W. Sandholtz and A. S. Sweet (eds), *European Integration and Supranational Governance*, Oxford, UK: Oxford University Press.

Sandholtz, W. and Sweet, A. S. (eds) (1998b) *European Integration and Supranational Governance*, Oxford, UK: Oxford University Press.

Sapir, A. (2003) An Agenda for a Growing Europe: Making the EU Economic System Deliver. Report of a High Level Study Group established by the President of the European Commission, Romano Prodi. Retrieved from http://www.unescap.org/tid/artnet/mtg/gmscb_growingeurope.pdf.

Sargent, T. J. (2011) United States Then, Europe Now. The Sveriges Riksbank Prize in Economic Sciences in Memory of Alfred Nobel 2011. Retrieved from http://www.nobelprize.org/nobel_prizes/economics/laureates/2011/sargent-lecture.html.

Sbragia, A. (1993) The European Community: A Balancing Act, *Publius: The Journal of Federalism*, 23(3), 23–38.

Sbragia, A. (2003) Key Policies, in E. Bomberg and A. Stubb (eds), *The European Union: How Does It Work?*, Oxford, UK: Oxford University Press.

Sbragia, A. (2006) The United States and the European Union: Overcoming Two 'Sui Generis' Systems, in A. Menon and M. Schain (eds), *Comparative Federalism: The European Union and the United States in Perspective*, Oxford, UK: Oxford University Press, pp. 15–34.

Scally, D. (2012) Germany Questions Pay Restraint Model, *Irish Times*, 20 January. Retrieved from http://www.irishtimes.com/newspaper/finance/2012/0120/1224310513431.html.

Schäfer, A. (2005) Beyond the Community Method: Why the Open Method of Coordination Was Introduced to EU Policy-Making, *European Integration online Papers (EIoP)*, 8(13).

Schalk, J., Torenvlied, R., Wessie, J. and Stokman, F. N. (2007) The Power of the Presidency in EU Council Decision-Making, *Journal of Common Market Studies*, 8(2), 229–50.

Scharpf, F. (1988) The Joint Decision Trap: Lessons from German Federalism and European Integration, *Public Administration*, 66(2), 239–78.

Scharpf, F. (2002) The European Social Model, *Journal of Common Market Studies*, 40(4), 645–70.

Schild, J. (2008) How to Shift the EU's Spending Priorities? The Multi-Annual Framework 2007–13 in Perspective, *Journal of European Public Policy*, 15(4), 531–49.

Schimmelfennig, F. and Trauner, F. (2009) Introduction: Post-Accession Compliance in the EU's New Member States, *European Integration online Papers (EIoP)*, 2(13). Retrieved from http//www.eiop.or.at/eiop/pdf/2009-SpecIssue-2_Introduction.pdf.

Schioppa, F. K. P. (ed.) (2004) *The Principle of Mutual Recognition in the European Integration Process*, Basingstoke, UK: Palgrave Macmillan.

Schmidt, S. (2000) Only an Agenda Setter? The European Commission's Power Over the Council of Ministers, *European Union Politics*, 1(1), 37–61.

Schmidt, S. (2004) The European Commission's Powers in Shaping European Policies, in D. Dimitrakopoulos (ed.), *The Changing European Commission*, Manchester, UK: Manchester University Press.

Schmidt, S. (2008) Competing in Markets, Not Rules: The Conflict Over the Single Services Market, in C. Joerges and P. F. Kjaer (eds), *Transnational Standards of Social Protection: Contrasting European and International Governance*, Oslo: Arena, pp. 31–54.

Schmidt, S. (2011) Law-Making in the Shadow of Judicial Politics, in R. Dehousse (ed.), *The Community Method: Obstinate or Obsolete?*, Basingstoke, UK: Palgrave, pp. 43–59.

Schmidt, V. (2006) Procedural Democracy in the EU: The Europeanizaton of National and Sectoral Policy-Making Processes, *Journal of European Public Policy*, 13(5), 670–91.

Schmidt, V. (2009) The EU and Its Member States: From Bottom Up to Top Down, in D. Phinnemore and A. Warleigh-Lack (eds), *Reflections on European Integration: 50 Years of the Treaty of Rome*, Basingstoke, UK: Palgrave Macmillan, pp. 194–211.

Schmitter, P. (2004) Neo-Neofunctionalism, in A. Wiener and T. Diez (eds), *European Integration Theory*, Oxford, UK: Oxford University Press, pp. 54–74.

Schreurs, M. A. (2003) *Environmental Politics in Japan, Germany, and the United States*, Cambridge, UK: Cambridge University Press.

Schucksmith, M., Thompson, K. J. and Roberts, D. (eds) (2005) *CAP and the Regions: The Territorial Impact of the Common Agricultural Policy*, Cambridge, UK: CABI Publishing.

Schütze, R. (2009) *From Dual to Cooperative Federalism: The Changing Structure of European Law*, Oxford, UK: Oxford University Press.

Scott, J. and Trubek, D. (2002) Mind the Gap: Law and New Approaches to Governance in the European Union, *European Law Journal*, 8(1), 1–18.

Scully, R., Hix, S. and Farrell, D. (2012) National or European Parliamentarians? Evidence from a New Survey of the Members of the European Parliament, *Journal of Common Market Studies*, 54(4) 670–83.

Sedelmeier, U. (2008) After Conditionality: Post-Accession Compliance with EU Law in East Central Europe, *Journal of European Public Policy*, 15(6), 806–25.

Selin, H.and VanDeever, S. (2011) *Federalism, Multilevel Governance and Climate Change Politics across the Atlantic*, Paper presented at the Twelfth Biennial European Union Studies Association, Boston, MA, USA.

Shore, C.and Abélès, M. (2004) Debating the European Union: An Interview with Cris Shore and Marc Abélès, *Anthropology Today*, 20(2), 10–14.

Siaroff, A. (2003) Comparative Presidencies: The Inadequacy of the Presidential, Semi-presidential and Parliamentary Distinction, *European Journal of Political Research*, 42(3), 287–312.

Simeon, R. and Radin, B. A. (2010) Reflections on Comparing Federalisms: Canada and the United States, *Publius*, 40(3), 357–65.

Simons, M. (2004) Under Pressure, Spain Tries to Close an Open Door, *The New York Times*, 10 October. Retrieved from http://www.nytimes.com/2004/10/10/international/europe/10spain.html.

Simpson, S. (2011) 'New' Governance in European Union Policy Making: Policy Innovation or Political Compromise in European Telecommunications?, *West European Politics*, 34(5), 1114–33.

Sims, C. A. (1999) The Precarious Fiscal Foundations of EMU, *The Economist*, 147(4), 415–36.

SIPRI (2012) Military Expenditure Data, Stockholm International Peace Research Institute, Retrieved from http://www.sipri.org/research/armaments/milex/result output/trends.

Smith, M. (2004) *Europe's Foreign and Security Policy: The Institutionalization of Cooperation*, Cambridge, UK: Cambridge University Press.

Spamann, H. (2001) *Choice of Law in a Federal System and Internal Market,* Jean Monnet Working Paper, 8(1).

Spitzer, R. (1987) Promoting Policy Theory: Revising the Arenas of Power, *Policy Studies Journal*, 15(4), 675–89.

Steivorth, D. (2010) Finding Swimming Pools with Google Earth: Greek Government Hauls in Billions in Back Taxes, *Spiegel Online International*. Retrieved from http://www.spiegel.de/international/europe/0,1518,709703,00.html.

Stresemann, G. (1929) *Compte Rendu des Débats: Actes des le Dixième Session Ordinaire de l'Assemblé*, Geneva: Société des Nations (League of Nations).

Tait, N. (2010) Brussels Backs 'Single European Patent' Plan, *Financial Times*, 14 December.

Taylor, S. (2011a) Barroso: UK Made a Compromise Deal 'Impossible', *European Voice*, 13 December. Retrieved from http://www.europeanvoice.com/article/2011/december/barroso-says-uk-compromise-was-impossible-/72934.aspx.

Taylor, S. (2011b) Rice Products to be Checked for Contamination, *European Voice*, 7 October, p. 2.

Taylor, S. (2011c) Review of EU Food Alerts to Follow E. coli Confusion, *European Voice*, 9 June. Retrieved from http://www.europeanvoice.com/article/imported/review-of-eu-food-alerts-to-follow-e-coli-confusion/71277.aspx.

Tcherneva, P. R. (2008) The Return of Fiscal Policy: Can the New Developments in the New Economic Consensus Be Reconciled with the Post-Keynesian View?, *SSRN eLibrary*. Retrieved from http://ssrn.com/paper=1159895.

Team Nord (2011) *Together Alone: BASIC Countries and the Climate Change Conundrum*, Nordic Council of Ministers. Retrieved from http://ecoadata.com/home/wp-content/upLoads/2011/10/TN2011530-web.pdf.

Telegraph, The (2011) The Countries Most Exposed to Greek Debt, 11 June. Retrieved from http://www.telegraph.co.uk/finance/economics/8578337/The-countries-most-exposed-to-Greek-debt.html.

Thatcher, M. (2010) Agency Governance in the EU and its Consequences: Summary of comments made by Mark Thatcher at the RECON workshop, Mannheim, *RECON Newsletter*, 4(3).

Thomas, L. (2012) Economic Thinkers Try to Solve the Euro Puzzle, *The New York Times*, 31 July. Retrieved from http://www.nytimes.com/2012/08/01/business/economic-thinkers-try-to-solve-the-euro-puzzle.html?pagewanted=all.

Thomson, R. (2008) The Council Presidency in the European Union: Responsibility with Power, *Journal of Common Market Studies*, 46(3), 593-617.

Thomson, R. (2010) Opposition through the Back Door in the Transposition of EU Directives. *European Union Politics*, 11(4), 577–96.

Thomson, R. (2011) *Resolving Controversy in the European Union: Legislative Decision-making Before and After Enlargement*, Cambridge, UK: Cambridge University Press.

Tilford, S. and Whyte, P. (2010) *The Lisbon Scorecard X: The Road to 2020*, Centre for European Reform.

Timmins, G. (2011) German–Russian Bilateral Relations and EU Policy on Russia: Between Normalisation and the 'Multilateral Reflex', *Journal of Contemporary European Studies*, 19(2), 189–99.

Tinbergen, J. (1954) *International Economic Integration*, Amsterdam: Elsevier.

Toshkov, D. and Rasmussen, A. (2012) Time to Decide: The Effect of Early Agreements on Legislative Duration in the EU, *European Integration online Papers (EIoP)*, 16(11).

Traynor, I. (2009) David Miliband Tipped as EU Foreign Minister: Speculation Growing that British Foreign Secretary Is in Line for High Representative Post Created by Lisbon Treaty, *Guardian*, 22 October. Retrieved from http://www.guardian.co.uk/politics/2009/oct/22/david-miliband-europe-foreign-minister.

Treib, O., Bähr, H. and Falkner, G. (2011) Social Policy and Environmental Policy: Comparing Modes of Governance, in U. Diedrichs, W. Reiners and W. Wessels (eds), *The Dynamics of Change in EU Governance*, Cheltenham, UK: Edward Elgar.

Treumer, S. (2011) Enforcement of the EU Public Procurement Rules: The State of Law and Current Issues, in S. Treumer and F. Lichère (eds), *Enforcement of the EU Public Procurement Rules*, Copenhagen: DJØF Publishing.

Tsoukalis, L. (2007) The European Model in a Globalised World, in European Commission (ed.), *Europe's Challenges in a Globalised World: Visions of Leading Policy Makers and Academics*, Brussels: European Commission Directorate-General for Education and Culture.

UK Parliament (2009) *Co-decision and National Parlimentary Scrutiny*. Retrieved from http://www.publications.parliament.uk/pa/ld200809/ldselect/ldeucom/125/12504.htm.

United Nations High Commission on Refugees (2010) 2009 Global Trends: Refugees, Asylum-seekers, Returnees, Internally Displaced and Stateless Persons. Retrieved from http://www.unhcr.org/4c11f0be9.pdf.

US Department of Treasury (2011) Resource Center: Terrorist Finance Tracking Program, 22 September. Retrieved from http://www.treasury.gov/resource-center/terrorist-illicit-finance/Terrorist-Finance-Tracking/Pages/tftp.aspx.

USIS Washington File (1998) Transcript: Albright Press Conference at NATO HDQS. Retrieved from http://www.fas.org/man/nato/news/1998/98120904_tlt.html.

Vandenberghie, J. (2008) On Carrots and Sticks: The Social Dimension of EU Trade Policy, *European Foreign Affairs Review*, 13, 561–81.

Van Ham, P. (2000) Identity Beyond the State: The Case of the European Union, COPRI Paper-George C. Marshall European Center for Security Studies.

van Renssen, S. (2011) Toxic Neighbours, *European Voice*, 19 May. Retrieved from http://www.europeanvoice.com/article/imported/toxic-neighbours/71119.aspx.

Verdun, A. (1999) The Role of the Delors Committee in the Creation of EMU: An Epistemic Community?, *Journal of European Public Policy*, 6(2), 308–28.

Versluis, E. (2003) *Enforcement Matters: Enforcement and Compliance of European Directives in Four Member States*, Delft, The Netherlands: Eburen.

Versluis, E., van Keulen, M. and Stephenson, P. (eds) (2011) *Analyzing the EU Policy Process*, Basingstoke, UK: Palgrave Macmillan.

Viner, J. (1950) *The Customs Union Issue*, New York: Carnegie Endowment for International Peace.

Vogel, D. (2005) The Hare and the Tortoise Revisited: The New Politics of Consumer and Environmental Regulation in Europe, in A. Jordan (ed.), *Environmental Policy in the European Union: Actors, Institutions, and Processes*, London: Earthscan, pp. 225–52).

Vogel, D., Toffel, M., Post, D. and Aragon, N. Z. U. (2010) Environmental Federalism in the European Union and the United States, *Harvard Business School Working Paper*, 10-085.

Vogel, T. (2010) Turf War Continues over EU's Diplomatic Corps, *European Voice*, 11 March p. 1.

Vogel, T. (2011) Commission Told to Tighten Schengen Rules, *European Voice*, 28 April. Retrieved from http://www.europeanvoice.com/article/imported/commission-told-to-tighten-schengen-rules/70943.aspx.

Vogel, T. (2012) Row over Size of EU Budget, *European Voice*, 31 May. Retrieved from http://www.europeanvoice.com/article/imported/row-over-size-of-eu-budget/74457.aspx.

Wallace, H. (2005) An Institutional Anatomy and Five Policy Modes, in H. Wallace, W. Wallace and M. A. Pollack (eds), *Policy-Making in the European Union* (5th edn), Oxford, UK: Oxford University Press, pp. 41–90.

Wallace, H. (2010) An Institutional Anatomy and Five Policy Modes, in H. Wallace, M. A. Pollack and A. R. Young (eds), *Policy-Making in the European Union* (6th edn), Oxford: Oxford University Press, pp. 69–104.

Wallace, H. and Wallace, W. (2006) Overview: The European Union, Politics and Policy-Making, in K. A. Jørgensen, M. A. Pollack and B. Rosamond (eds), *Handbook of European Union Politics*, London: Sage, pp. 339–58.

Wallace, H., Pollack, M. A. and Young, A. R. (eds) (2010) *Policy-Making in the European Union* (6th edn), Oxford, UK: Oxford University Press.

Warntjen, A. (2008) The Council Presidency: Power Broker or Burden? An Empirical Analysis, *European Union Politics*, 9(3), 315–38.

Wasserfallen, F. (2010) The Judiciary as Legislator? How the European Court of Justice Shapes Policy-Making in the European Union, *Journal of European Public Policy*, 17(8), 1128–46.

Watts, R. L. (1997) *Comparing Federal Systems in the 1990s*, Kingston, Ontario: Institute of Intergovernmental Relations, Queen's University.

Weale, A. (2005) European Environmental Policy by Stealth: The Dysfunctionality of Functionalism?, in A. Jordan (ed.), *Environmental Policy in the European Union: Actors, Institutions, and Processes*, London: Earthscan, pp. 336–54.

Webber, D. (forthcoming) How Likely Is It that the European Union Will Disintegrate? A Critical Analysis of Competing Theoretical Perspectives, *European Journal of International Relations*.

Wheare, K. C. (1953) *Federal Government* (3rd edn), Oxford, UK: Oxford University Press.

Wilks, S. (2005) Competition Policy, in H. Wallace, W. Wallace and M. A. Pollack (eds), *Policy-Making in the European Union* (5th edn), Oxford, UK: Oxford University Press, pp. 113–39.

Willis, A. (2011) Europe's Centre-Right Lays Out Pre-Summit Position, *EUobserver.com*, 8 March. Retrieved from http://euobserver.com/economic/31929.

Wincott, D. (1995) Institutional Interaction and European Integration: Towards an Everyday Critique of Liberal Intergovernmentalism, *Journal of Common Market Studies*, 33(4), 597–609.

Wincott, D. (1999) The Court of Justice and the Legal System, in L. Cram, D. Dinan and N. Nugent (eds), *Developments in the European Union*, Basingstoke, UK: Palgrave Macmillan, (pp. 84–104).

Wishart, I. (2011a) More Power, and More Problems, *European Voice*, 9 June. Retrieved from http://www.europeanvoice.com/article/imported/more-power-and-more-problems/71305.aspx.

Wishart, I. (2011b) Plotting a Course for Europe's Financial Future, *European Voice*, 9 June. Retrieved from http://www.europeanvoice.com/article/imported/plotting-a-course-for-europe-s-financial-future/71304.aspx.

Wishart, I. (2011c) The Regulation Race, *European Voice*, 9 June. Retrieved from http://www.europeanvoice.com/article/imported/the-regulation-race/71327.aspx.

Wishart, I. (2012a) EIB in the Spotlight, but not the Answer to the Eurozone's Woes, *European Voice*, 14 June. Retrieved from http://www.europeanvoice.com/article/imported/eib-in-the-spotlight-but-not-the-answer-to-the-eurozone-s-woes/74581.aspx.

Wishart, I. (2012b) Spurred into Action, *European Voice*, 5 July. Retrieved from http://www.europeanvoice.com/article/imported/spurred-into-action/74769.aspx.

Wishart, I. (2012c) Patent still Pending, *European Voice*, 12 September. Retrieved from http://www.europeanvoice.com/folder/thesinglemarket/215.aspx?artid=75130.

Witney, N. (2008) *Re-energising Europe's Security and Defence Policy*, London: European Council on Foreign Relations. Retrieved from http://ecfr.3cdn.net/c66a5b8b70f2e804a0_6xm6iywb0.pdf.

Wittke, C. (1949) U.S. Immigration Policy before World War I, *Annals of the American Academy of Political and Social Science*, *62*, 1–14.

World Trade Organization (2012) *Press Release: Trade Growth to Slow in 2012 after Strong Deceleration in 2011*, 12 April. Retrieved from http://www.wto.org/english/news_e/pres12_e/pr658_e.htm#table4.

Wurzel, R. and Hayward, J. (2012) Conclusion: European Disunion: Between Solidarity and Sovereignty, in J. Hayward and R. Wurzel (eds), *European Disunion: Between Sovereignty and Solidarity*, Basingstoke, UK: Palgrave Macmillan, pp. 314–28.

Zandee, D. (2010) How Governments Should Compensate for Defence Spending Cuts, *Europe's World*, Spring. Retrieved from http://www.europesworld.org/NewEnglish/Home_old/Article/tabid/191/ArticleType/ArticleView/ArticleID/21572/language/en-US/Default.aspx.

Zeitlen, J. (2011) Is the Open Method of Coordination an Alternative to the Community Method?, in R. Dehousse (ed.), *The Community Method: Obstinate or Obsolete?* Basingstoke, UK: Palgrave Macmillan, pp. 135–47.

Zetterquist, O. (2011) The Charter of Fundamental Rights and the European *Res Publica*, in G. Di Federico (ed.), *The EU Charter of Fundamental Rights: From Declaration to Binding Instrument*, New York: Springer, pp. 3–14.

Zimmerman, J. F. (2002) *Interstate Cooperation: Compacts and Administrative Agreements*, Westport, CT: Prager.

Zwolski, K. (2011) Unrecognized and Unwelcome? The Role of the EU in Preventing the Proliferation of CBRN Weapons, Materials and Knowledge, *Perspectives on European Politics and Society*, *12*(4), 477–92.

Index